PHILOSOPHY AND PURPOSE

This text is designed primarily for use in the introductory course in educational research that is a basic requirement for many graduate programs. Since the topic coverage of the text is relatively comprehensive, it also may be easily adapted for use in either a senior-level undergraduate course or a more advanced graduate-level course.

The philosophy that guided the development of the current and previous editions of this text was the conviction that an introductory research course should be more skill and application oriented than theory oriented. Thus the purpose of this text is to have students become familiar with research mainly at a "how to" skill and application level. The text does not mystify students with theoretical and statistical jargon. It strives to provide a down-to-earth approach that helps students acquire the skills and knowledge required of a competent consumer and producer of educational research. The emphasis is not just on what the student knows but also on what the student can do with what he or she knows. It is recognized that being a "good" researcher involves more than the acquisition of skills and knowledge; in any field, significant research is usually produced by persons who through experience have acquired insights, intuitions, and strategies related to the research process. Research of any worth, however, is rarely conducted in the absence of basic research skills and knowledge. A basic assumption of this text is that there is considerable overlap in the competencies required of a competent consumer of research and a competent producer of research, and that a person is in a much better position to evaluate the work of others after she or he has performed the major tasks involved in the research process.

ORGANIZATION AND STRATEGY

The overall strategy of the text is to promote students' attainment of a degree of expertise in research through the acquisition of knowledge and by involvement in actual research.

ORGANIZATION

Part One discusses the scientific and disciplined inquiry approach and its application in education. It describes the main steps in the research process and the purpose and methods of the various approaches to research. In Part One, each student selects and delineates a research problem of interest that has relevance to his or her professional area. Throughout the rest of the text, the student then simulates the procedures that would be followed in conducting a study designed to investigate the problem; each chapter develops a specific skill or set of skills required for the execution of such a research study. Specifically, the student reviews and analyzes related literature and formulates hypotheses (Chapter 2), develops a research plan (Chapter 3), selects and defines samples (Chapter 4), and evaluates and selects measuring instruments (Chapter 5). Part Two describes qualitative research, including the different approaches to and the collection and analysis of qualitative data. Part Three describes and discusses quantitative research, data collection and analysis, including statistics. In Part Four the student applies the skills and knowledge acquired in Parts One through Three and evaluates a research report.

STRATEGY

This text represents more than just a textbook to be incorporated into a course; it is actually a total instructional system that includes stated objectives, or competencies, instruction, and procedures for evaluating each competency. The instructional strategy of the system emphasizes demonstration of skills and individualization within structure. The format for each chapter is essentially the same. Following a brief introduction, each task to be performed is described. Tasks require students to demonstrate that they can perform particular research functions. Since each student works with a different problem, each student demonstrates the competency required by a task as it applies to his or her own problem. With the exception of Chapter 1, each chapter is directed toward the attainment of one task. Each chapter begins with a list of chapter objectives that entail knowledge and skills that facilitate students' abilities to perform a related task. In many instances objectives may be assessed either as written exercises submitted by students or by tests, whichever the instructor prefers. For some objectives the first option is clearly preferable.

Text discussion is intended to be as simple and straightforward as possible. Whenever feasible, procedures are presented as a series of steps and concepts are explained in terms of illustrative examples. In a number of cases, relatively complex topics or topics beyond the scope of the text are presented at a very elementary level, and students are directed to other sources for additional, in-depth discussion. There is also a degree of intentional repetition; a number of concepts are discussed in different contexts and from different perspectives. Also, at the risk of eliciting more than a few groans, an attempt has been made to sprinkle the text with touches of humor. Each chapter includes a detailed, often lengthy, summary with headings and subheadings directly paralleling those in the chapter. The summaries are designed to facilitate both review and location of related text discussion. Finally, each chapter concludes with suggested criteria for evaluating its task and with an example of the task produced by a former introductory educational research student.

MAJOR REVISIONS FOR THIS EDITION

Like the sixth edition, the seventh edition reflects a combination of both unsolicited and solicited input. Positive feedback suggested aspects of the text and supplementary materials that should not be changed—the writing style and the focus on ethical practice, for example. Every effort, however, was made to incorporate suggestions from users and nonusers. For example, several users requested an increased focus on qualitative research and an integration of SPSS analysis.

Content changes reflect the inclusion of new topics and the expansion or clarification of existing topics. There are many improvements in this edition, and we describe the more significant highlights here.

1. We have broadened our coverage of **qualitative research** throughout the text. Four chapters now focus on qualitative research: two new, completely revised chapters (Chapters 6 and 9) and two (Chapters 7 and 8) expanded from the sixth edition. Although the text still focuses mainly on quantitative research, this edition provides a more balanced view of qualitative and quantitative research methods.

   In Chapter 6 we describe and discuss the general characteristics and skills required to conduct qualitative research. We identify four primary research approaches—ethnography, historical research, grounded theory, and action research. The chapter then focuses on identifying research topics and reviewing the literature. An overview of mixed method research is included to reflect its increasing use.

   Chapter 7 focuses on data collection. We begin by discussing how to identify and select study participants. We then discuss collecting data using observations, interviews, and nonparticipant data collection methods.

   Chapter 8 has two topics. First, we discuss analyzing narrative research data both during and after the data collection stage of a study. Second, we focus on writing the final research report. The chapter closes with a discussion of postanalysis considerations for qualitative research.

Chapter 9 expands the sixth edition's discussion of action research. In it we discuss the benefits and nature of action research and describe in greater depth the processes specific to this type of research.

Throughout, our discussion of both qualitative and quantitative research is guided by a commitment to ethical research practice and to the competencies required to carry out the basic steps common to educational research.

2. A discussion of **mixed-method research** has been added to Chapter 6. We describe three different mixed-method approaches and present criteria for identifying and evaluating them.

3. Our discussion of qualitative research is enhanced by the presentation of two **published research reports,** new to this edition. Throughout Chapters 6, 7, and 8 we excerpt and annotate these reports, and discuss how they illustrate specific aspects of qualitative research methods.

4. **SPSS** (formerly Statistical Package for the Social Sciences) is a comprehensive, full-featured software application for analyzing quantitative research data. In Chapters 14 and 15, we illustrate our discussion of statistical data analysis by showing our calculations in two formats: a step-by-step hand analysis and a computer analysis using SPSS Student Version 10.0 for Windows.

In addition, we have added new tables and figures throughout the text. Every chapter has been edited and updated. References have been updated.

SUPPLEMENTARY MATERIALS

A number of ancillaries are available to complement the text, including a *Student Guide* and an *Instructor's Manual and Test Bank*. For each part and chapter in the text there is a corresponding part in these two ancillaries. Other supplementary materials include Prentice Hall Custom Test computerized testbank software, SPSS Student Version 10.0 statistical software, a free and expanded Companion Website with 10 modules and many opportunities to practice newly learned research skills, and a CD-ROM with interactive computer simulations of educational research concepts and scenarios, including research articles.

STUDENT GUIDE

The Student Guide has been significantly revised to coordinate with the new edition. It provides students opportunities to check their current understanding and extend their knowledge beyond definitions to application of the concepts presented in the text. For each chapter, the Student Guide contains key terms for students to explain, sample test items with answers, and a variety of examples, exercises, mini cases, and activities to support text content. Articles and portions of articles, as well as numerous examples from student research proposals, are included within the revised Student Guide. Although exercises, examples, mini cases, and activities in the Student Guide facilitate factual level content understanding, the focus of the Student Guide is to develop deeper understanding so that students can apply the concepts presented in the text. To that end, the Student Guide includes many tasks and activities that require higher-order thinking and transfer of content covered in the text. Sample responses with explanations are included. Examples that mirror the task activities in the text provide additional support for students as they apply the concepts presented in the text.

INSTRUCTOR'S MANUAL AND TEST BANK

The *Instructor's Manual and Test Bank* (ISBN 0-13-099465-0) contains suggested activities, strategies for teaching each chapter, selected resources, and hundreds of newly written and tested test items. Suggestions are based on personal experience teaching the course and research. In addition, the more than 700 test items represent a variety of levels of multiple-choice items. New test items have been added to reflect text additions and expansions—in particular, questions related to qualitative research.

PRENTICE HALL CUSTOM TEST COMPUTERIZED TEST BANK SOFTWARE

The computerized test bank software gives instructors electronic access to the test questions printed in the *Instructor's Manual and Test Bank* and allows them to create and customize exams. The computerized test bank is available in both Macintosh and PC/Windows (0-13-099467-7) versions.

SPSS STUDENT VERSION 10.0 OR 11.0

The text includes examples of SPSS calculations and screen images and output tables illustrating the calculations. To complement this new content, copies of SPSS Student Version 10.0 or 11.0 are available at a discounted price when packaged with this textbook. Contact your local Prentice Hall representative for ordering information.

STATPAK STATISTICAL SOFTWARE

STATPAK statistical software computes all of the statistics that are calculated in the text and shows students the intermediate stages as well as the final answers. The STATPAK software has been upgraded for this edition and is available in both Macintosh (ISBN 0-13-013949-1) and PC/Windows versions. For Windows users, STATPAK is available for use from the Companion Website at www.prenhall.com/gay. Mac users may obtain a disk copy from their local Prentice Hall Sales Representative.

COMPANION WEBSITE

This upgraded site, located at **http://www.prenhall.com/gay**, allows students and professors using the text free access to a wealth of newly created online resources. Here students can review chapter objectives—and more specific learning objectives within each objective—and test their knowledge by taking chapter quizzes that provide hints and automatic feedback. (Items are graded with a percentage score and correct answers.) Students can apply their newly gained knowledge in "Applying What You Know" essay questions and can browse course topics on the Internet using well-screened and evaluated Web sites related to educational research.

Other new modules on the site can expand learners' skill base. "Evaluating Articles" gives students opportunities to read, deconstruct, and critique two qualitative and two quantitative articles via questions and suggested answers and evaluative checklists; "Analyzing Quantitative Data" presents a data set and leads students through a step-by-step analysis of the data, requiring them to run SPSS and generate descriptive and inferential statistics and summarize their findings: and "Analyzing Qualitative Data" presents a narrative data set and asks students to segment, code, and categorize data. "Research Tools and Tips" is a series of read-only, printable helpful topics that can make any research project easier and less confusing. Tips include links to helpful information on the Web, handy protocol forms, and references to helpful products to aid research. In addition, the STATPAK statistical calculator tool is also available for PC/Windows users in "Calculating Statistics" on the site.

The Companion Website also contains Message Board and Live Chat areas to encourage student interaction. For professors, the Syllabus Builder™ allows easy instructional planning and convenient online access for their course.

COMPUTER SIMULATION SOFTWARE

Simulations in Educational Psychology and Research, version 2.0, features five psychological/educational interactive experiments on a CD-ROM. Exercises and readings help students explore the research concepts and procedures connected to these experiments. Qualitative and quantitative designs are included. Instructors should contact their local Prentice Hall Sales Representative to order a copy of these simulations.

ACKNOWLEDGMENTS

I sincerely thank everyone who provided input for the development of this edition. The following individuals reviewed the current edition: Chris Chiu, University of Pittsburgh; Clark J. Hickman, University of Missouri–St. Louis; Ann Mackenzie, Miami University; Geoff Mills, Southern Oregon University; Malina Monaco, Georgia State University; Ron Oliver, California State University, Fullerton, LeeAnn G. Putney, University of Nevada, Las Vegas; Rayne Sperling, Penn State University; and Paul Westmeyer, University of Texas at San Antonio. The following individuals reviewed the previous edition: James H. Banning, Colorado State University; John O. Bolvin, University of Pittsburgh; John E. Bonfadini, George Mason University; Beverly Cabello, California State University, Northridge; William T. Coombs, Oklahoma State University; Kevin D. Crehan, University of Nevada, Las Vegas; Ayres D'Costa, The Ohio State University; Thomas P. Evans, Oregon State University; David J. Flinders, Indiana University; Dale R. Fuqua, Oklahoma State University; Jo D. Gallagher, Florida International University; Andrea Guillaume, California State University, Fullerton; Gretchen Guiton, University of Southern California; Geoff Mills, Southern Oregon University; Malina Monaco, Georgia State University; Alan D. Moore, University of Wyoming; Charles L. Thomas, George Mason University; Karen L. Westberg, University of Connecticut; and Paul H. Westmeyer, University of Texas at San Antonio. These reviewers' thoughtful and detailed comments and suggestions contributed greatly to the seventh edition. Their efforts are very much appreciated.

At Prentice Hall, Julie Peters and Mary Harlan ably shepherded the manuscript through development, copyediting, and production, kept me from falling behind, and made the process almost painless. Freelance copyeditor Robert Marcum made many valuable contributions to the manuscript. They all were instrumental in the development of this edition. I sincerely thank them for their professionalism, patience, and caring.

I wish to thank my colleague Dr. Larry Ludlow for his many contributions to this text. Also, Christine M. Mills provided invaluable aid with the SPSS sections. I appreciate their help.

Peter Airasian
Boston College

BRIEF CONTENTS

CONTENTS

CHAPTER 7

QUALITATIVE RESEARCH: DATA
COLLECTION   193

CHAPTER 8

QUALITATIVE RESEARCH: DATA
ANALYSIS   227

CHAPTER 9

ACTION RESEARCH   261

PART 3   QUANTITATIVE RESEARCH 275

CHAPTER 10

SURVEY RESEARCH   277

CHAPTER 15

INFERENTIAL STATISTICS   445

CHAPTER 16

POSTANALYSIS CONSIDERATIONS   491

PART 4   PRODUCING AND CONSUMING RESEARCH   505

CHAPTER 17

PREPARING A RESEARCH REPORT   507

CHAPTER 18

EVALUATING A RESEARCH REPORT   531

TABLES AND FIGURES

TABLES

FIGURES

PART 1

INTRODUCTION

If you are taking a research course because it is required in your program of studies, raise your right hand. If you are taking a research course because it seemed like it would be a real fun elective, raise your left hand. When you have stopped laughing, read on. No, you are not the innocent victim of one or more sadists. There are several legitimate reasons why your faculty believe this research course is an essential component of your education.

First, educational research findings significantly contribute to both educational theory and educational practice. The pros and cons of practices such as grouping, testing, and ways to work with non-English speaking pupils have been studied by educational researchers. Their findings provide a guide to understanding these and many other educational practices. It is important that you, as a professional, know how to access, understand, and evaluate such findings.

Second, whether or not you seek them out, you are constantly exposed to research findings in professional publications and, increasingly, in the media. For example, research results about low student achievement scores and how to improve them, the use of statewide assessments to determine high school graduation, and the effects of whole language versus phonics on pupil learning are recurrent social and educational themes. As a professional or an informed lay person, you have a responsibility to be able to distinguish between legitimate research claims and ill-founded ones.

And third, believe it or not, research courses provide a fruitful source of future researchers. Despite a popular stereotype that depicts researchers as spectacled, stoop-shouldered women and men who endlessly hunch over computers and crunch numbers, every day thousands of men and women of all ages conduct educational research in a variety of settings. A number of the authors' students have become sufficiently intrigued by the research process that they have carried out their own research studies. Many continue to find that using the process to examine and answer their own educational questions is both engaging and intellectually rewarding. A career in research opens the door to a variety of employment opportunities in colleges and universities, research and development centers, federal and state agencies, public and private school systems, and business and industry.

We recognize that for many of you, educational research is a relatively unfamiliar discipline. To meaningfully learn about and carry out the research process, you must first develop a perspective into which you can integrate succeeding information and experiences. Therefore, the goal of Part 1 is to help you acquire a general understanding of research processes and strategies that will help you learn about specific research knowledge and skills. In succeeding parts, you will systematically study and carry out specific components of the research process.

"Despite a popular stereotype that depicts researchers as spectacled, stoop-shouldered women and men who endlessly hunch over computers and crunch numbers, every day thousands of men and women of all ages conduct educational research in a variety of settings." (p. 1)

INTRODUCTION TO EDUCATIONAL RESEARCH

OBJECTIVES

After reading Chapter 1, you should be able to do the following:

1. List and briefly describe the major steps involved in conducting a research study.
2. Given a published article, identify and state the
   a. Problem or topic chosen to study
   b. Procedures employed to conduct the study
   c. Method of analyzing collected data
   d. Description of the major conclusion of the study
3. Briefly define and state the major characteristics of a variety of research approaches.
4. For each research approach, describe briefly two appropriate research studies.

   Example:
   > Experimental—A study to determine the effect of peer tutoring on the computational skill of third graders.

After you have read Chapter 1, you should be able to perform the following tasks.

TASKS 1-A, 1-B

Given reprints of two research studies, for each study identify and briefly state:

1. the topic (purpose of the study)
2. the procedures
3. the method of analysis
4. the major conclusions

(See Performance Criteria, p. 22.)

TASK 1-C

Classify given research studies based on their characteristics and purposes. (See Performance Criteria, p. 22.)

EDUCATIONAL RESEARCH: SCIENTIFIC AND DISCIPLINED INQUIRY

Research is the formal, systematic application of the scientific and disciplined inquiry approach to the study of problems. **Educational research** is the systematic application of a family of methods employed to provide trustworthy information about educational problems, issues, and topics. Most researchers, including educational researchers, undertake inquiry to gain understanding about some problem or topic that they don't fully comprehend. Having a stake in the outcome of the research makes conducting it more interesting, useful, and satisfying for the researcher. Once research topics or problems are explained or understood, many secondary purposes of research come into play, such as helping others understand the research results, using results to improve teaching and learning, and raising new topics or questions to study. Rarely, however, does a single research study produce the certainty needed to assume that the same results will apply in all or most settings. Rather, research is usually an ongoing process, based on accumulated understandings and explanations that, when taken together, lead to generalizations about educational issues and practice, and ultimately, to the development of theories.

We humans go about understanding things in a variety of ways. At times we rely on tradition: This is the way we've always done things; why change now? At other times we rely on the opinions of people who are viewed as experts: A leading expert in the field says that this is what we should do. Our own personal experiences and our ability to generalize and make predictions based on these experiences provide us with much of our understanding. Often we use inductive and deductive reasoning to help us come to an understanding of something.

Inductive reasoning is based on developing generalizations from a limited number of related observations or experiences.

> *Example:* You examine the tables of contents of four research books, all of which contain a chapter on sampling (limited observation).
> Therefore, you conclude that all research methods books contain a chapter on sampling (generalization).

Deductive reasoning is based on developing specific predictions from general principles, observations, or experiences.

> *Example:* All research texts contain a chapter on sampling (generalization).
> This book is a research text.
> Therefore, this book contains a chapter on sampling (specific conclusion). (By the way, does it?)

Inductive and deductive approaches represent two ways to conduct research. Inductive research starts with a limited number of observations and seeks to form them into a generalization. Deductive research starts with a general statement or hypothesis and forms it into a specific conclusion. An inductive research approach is typically qualitative in nature, while a deductive research approach is typically quantitative in nature.

Although commonly used, each of these approaches to understanding has limitations. Relying on tradition inhibits change in one's perspective, thus stifling exploration and eliminating potentially new and fruitful understandings. As for depending solely on experts, even experts are not infallible. Personal experience can produce idiosyncratic interpretations and even prejudices. Moreover, most of us have relatively limited experience of many of the issues we might seek to understand.

Consider the limitations of relying on experts and personal experience illustrated by this story about Aristotle. According to the story, one day Aristotle caught a fly and carefully counted and recounted the legs. He then announced that flies have five legs. No one questioned the word of Aristotle. For years his finding was uncritically accepted. Of course, the fly that Aristotle caught just happened to be missing a leg! Whether or not you believe the story, it does illustrate the limitations of relying on personal experience and experts as sources of understanding. This story also says something about inductive reasoning. The quality of inductive reasoning (specific to general) is highly dependent on the number and representativeness of the specific observations used to make the generalization. Inductive reasoning provides no guide for this. Selecting too few or atypical examples undermines the logic of inductive reasoning. As for deductive reasoning (general to specific), it depends on the truth of the generalizations it uses as a basis for its logic. That is, if the generalization is not true, its extension to specific instances will not always be accurate. For example, if one accepts the generalization that professors are boring, extending this generalization to specific professors will not always be true for at least *some* of the professorate. Although inductive and deductive reasoning are of limited value when used individually, when combined they can be very important.

Scientific and disciplined inquiry is based on a systematic approach to examining educational issues and questions. It combines features of inductive and deductive reasoning with other characteristics to produce an approach to understanding that, though sometimes fallible, is generally more viable than relying on tradition, experts, personal experience, or inductive or deductive reasoning alone. Nonetheless, it is extremely difficult to totally remove the biases and beliefs in any research study. We can lessen but rarely eliminate errors in research studies that arise from the complexity and variability of humans and the contexts in which they act. Even the most extensive study cannot examine *all* the human and contextual factors that might influence a researcher's findings. Although the scientific and disciplined inquiry approach cannot guarantee error-free research results, it does incorporate checks and balances to help minimize the likelihood that the researcher's emotions or biases will influence research conclusions.

One very important characteristic distinguishes scientific and disciplined inquiry from other ways of understanding. The researcher is expected to describe in detail the procedures used to conduct the research study and its conclusions, thus providing a basis for examining and verifying the research results. These checks and balances permit others to examine, understand, and critique the research in ways not available by tradition, experts, personal experience, or inductive or deductive reasoning alone.

At the heart of scientific and disciplined inquiry is an orderly process that, at a minimum, involves four basic steps:

1. *Recognize and identify a topic to study.* A **topic** is a question, issue, or problem related to education that can be examined or answered through collecting and analyzing data.
2. *Describe and execute procedures to collect information about the topic being studied.* The procedures include identifying the research participants, the strategies to collect data related to the topic, and the activities describing how, when, and from whom the data will be collected. The nature of the research topic influences the research method applied, for example, the choice of a deductive or inductive approach.
3. *Analyze the collected data.* Analysis of the collected data is also related to the nature of the topic studied and to the data collected. Some research topics are best analyzed using quantitative, numerical data and a variety of statistical approaches. Other research topics are more qualitative in form and rely on data in the form of narratives, tape recordings, and field notes. Qualitative data are usually analyzed using interpretive rather than statistical analysis. Regardless of the kind of data collected, some form of analysis is necessary.
4. *State the results or implications based on analysis of the data.* Conclusions reached in the research study should relate back to the original research topic. What can be concluded about this topic based on the results of the study?

We mentioned that these are conceptually the four basic steps of research. As you begin to do research in later chapters, you will see that there are smaller steps and tasks within each of these four general groupings.

RESEARCH TOPICS: DEFINING PURPOSE AND METHODS

Consider the many questions about educational processes, activities, and topics that can be asked and systematically examined through research. Read the following research topics.

1. Do students learn more from our new social studies book than from the prior one?
2. What is the effect of positive versus negative reinforcement on elementary students' attitudes toward school?
3. How do teachers in our school district rate the quality of our teacher evaluation program?
4. What do high school principals consider to be their most pressing administrative problems?

5. Is there a relationship between middle school students' grades and their self-confidence in science and mathematics?
6. Do students' scores on an anxiety test relate to the scores they get on the Scholastic Assessment Test?
7. What factors led to the development of standardized achievement tests from 1900 to 1930?
8. What were the effects of the GI Bill on state colleges in the Midwest in the 1950s?
9. How do special needs students adapt to the culture of junior high school when transitioning from a strongly child-centered elementary school?
10. How do the first 5 weeks of school in Ms. Foley's classroom influence activities and interactions in succeeding months?

Consider the differences among these questions. For example, note the purpose of the topics posed. Questions 1 and 2 are concerned with *comparing* two things: the new versus the old social studies program and positive versus negative reinforcement. Questions 3 and 4 are concerned with *describing* teachers' ratings of their school district's teacher evaluation procedure and administrators' listing of their most pressing problems. Questions 5 and 6 are concerned with *relating* two things, grades to self-confidence and anxiety level to math and science performance. Questions 7 and 8 focus on events in the past, and are concerned with describing the *history* about each question. Questions 9 and 10 are concerned with using long-term, *in-depth observation* to obtain information about the adaptation of special needs students in a new culture (junior high school) and the impact of how one begins the school year on later classroom interactions.

Logically, if there are differences in the purposes of research topics, there also should be differences in the strategies and methods for investigating these topics. Some questions require selection of a large sample of people to provide data (e.g., question 2). Others focus in depth on the performance or activities of a small number of people to obtain data (e.g., question 9). Still others may not gather data from people at all, relying instead on artifacts, documents, pictures, and the like to provide needed data (questions 7 and 8). The way data are collected and analyzed also differs among research topics. Some methods rely heavily on formal tests and questionnaires to collect data (questions 1–6). Others rely heavily on in-depth personal observation, interviews, and tape recordings to collect data (questions 9–10). Methods that emphasize the use of tests and measurements typically are analyzed with statistical procedures (questions 1–6). These are *quantitative* research topics. Methods based on observation, interviews, and the like rarely employ statistical analysis, relying instead on the researcher's interpretive skills to analyze, integrate, and make sense of the data collected (questions 7–10). These are *qualitative* research topics.

Although there are a number of different questions, methods, and analyses related to conducting educational research, the threads that unite these differences are the four basic steps in the scientific and disciplined inquiry approach. Regardless of the nature of a research study, sections of it will be devoted to the purpose of the research, the methods used to carry out the research, the procedures used to analyze the collected data, and the interpretations or conclusions of the study.

This text focuses on a range of research methods exemplified by the questions just discussed. Research methods can be classified by the degree of direct applicability of the research to educational practice or settings (basic or applied research), or by the methods the researcher uses to conduct the study (quantitative or qualitative research). The intent of this book is to provide you with basic insights and understandings about a variety of research methods and strategies. It seeks to help you think about and critique your own and other people's research studies. To this end, it focuses on issues of finding research topics, selecting appropriate and ethical procedures for collecting data, applying meaningful methods to analyze data, and presenting research outcomes and implications. Make a list of a few research questions or topics you might wish to study and think of how you would carry out your research.

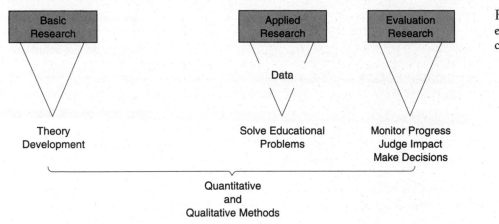

FIGURE 1.1 The education research continuum.

BASIC AND APPLIED RESEARCH

It is difficult to discuss basic and applied research separately because they are on a single continuum. Classification of a given study along the basic–applied continuum is made primarily on the degree to which the findings have direct applicability and the degree to which they generalize to other educational settings. **Basic research** involves the process of collecting and analyzing information to develop or enhance a theory. Theory development is a conceptual process that requires many research studies conducted over time. Basic researchers may not be concerned with the immediate utility of their findings, since it might be years before basic research leads to a practical educational application. The early work of Skinner on reinforcement with birds and Piaget on cognitive development with his two children were basic research efforts that subsequently led to important educational applications.

Applied research is conducted to evaluate its usefulness in solving practical educational problems. A teacher who asks, "Will the theory of multiple intelligence help improve my students' learning?" is seeking an answer to a practical classroom question. The teacher is not interested in building a new theory or even generalizing beyond her classroom, but instead is seeking specific helpful information. Letting teachers try out two methods of covering study hall and then having them decide which one results in greater student attentiveness is another example of applied research. Using portfolios in a classroom to see whether writing improves is also applied research.

Educators and researchers disagree about which end of the basic–applied research continuum should be emphasized. In its purest form, basic research is conducted solely for the purpose of theory development; it most closely resembles laboratory conditions and controls usually associated with scientific research. Applied educational research is conducted to solve current educational problems. Many educational research studies would be located on the applied end of the continuum; they are more focused on "what works best" than on finding out "why" it works as it does. Studies located in the middle of the basic–applied continuum seek to integrate both approaches. Both basic and applied research are necessary and, to a point, interdependent. Basic research provides the theory that produces the concepts for examining educational problems. Applied research provides data that can help support, guide, and revise the development of theory. Figure 1.1 illustrates the education research continuum.

EVALUATION RESEARCH

At the far end of applied research is evaluation, an important, widely used, and explicitly practical form of research. **Evaluation research** is concerned with making decisions about the quality, effectiveness, merit, or value of educational programs, products, or practices. Unlike other forms of research that seek new knowledge or understanding, evaluation focuses mainly on decision making, a highly applied and practical purpose. Although the methods of evaluation research are not different from the methods of other forms of research, evaluation is distinguished by its decision-making purpose.

Typical evaluation research questions are, "Is this special science program worth its costs?" "Is the new reading curriculum better than the old one?" "Did students reach the objectives of the diversity sensitivity program?" and "Is the new geography meeting the teachers' needs?"

Evaluations come in various forms and have different purposes.[1] Two of their main purposes are to monitor the ongoing progress of a program or product and subsequently to judge the overall impact of it. Evaluators monitor an ongoing program or product to identify weaknesses that can be remedied during implementation. This evaluation purpose is called *formative evaluation* because its function is to form and improve what is being evaluated while it is being developed. Evaluators also make decisions about the program or product at its completion in order to make a decision about the overall quality or worth of the program or product. This approach is called *summative evaluation* because its function is to make a decision that sums up the overall quality or worth of the program or product.

QUANTITATIVE AND QUALITATIVE RESEARCH

We have noted that the fundamental purpose of educational research is to increase our understanding of educational processes, practices, topics, and issues. For much of the history of educational research, there were well-defined, widely accepted procedures for stating research topics, carrying out the research process, analyzing the resulting data, and verifying the quality of the study and its conclusions. For the most part, these research procedures were based on a quantitative approach to conducting and obtaining educational understandings. **Quantitative research** methods are based on the collection and analysis of numerical data, usually obtained from questionnaires, tests, checklists, and other formal paper-and-pencil instruments. But a quantitative research approach entails more than just the use of numerical data. It also involves stating both the hypotheses to be examined and the research procedures that will be carried out in the study. The quantitative approach also calls for maintaining control over contextual factors that might interfere with the data collected, and using large samples of participants to provide statistically meaningful data. It employs data analyses that rely on statistical procedures. Quantitative researchers generally have little personal interaction with the participants they study, since most data are gathered using paper-and-pencil, noninteractive instruments.

Underlying quantitative research methods is the belief or assumption that we inhabit a relatively stable, uniform, and coherent world that we can measure, understand, and generalize about. This view, which the field of education adopted from the natural sciences, implies that the world and the laws that govern it are relatively stable and predictable, and can be understood by scientific research and examination. In this quantitative—also called *positivist*—perspective, claims about the world are not considered meaningful unless they can be verified through direct observation.

However, in recent years, other, nonquantitative approaches to educational research have emerged and attracted many advocates. Generally called *qualitative* research methods, these are based on the collection and analysis of nonnumerical data such as observations, interviews,

---

[1]Stufflebeam, D., Madaus, G., Kellaghan, T. (2000). *Evaluation models, viewpoints on educational and human services evaluation.* Norwell, MA: Kluwer Academic Publishers; Gridler, M. (1996). *Program evaluation.* Upper Saddle River, NJ: Prentice Hall; Joint committee on standards for educational evaluation. (1994). *The program evaluation standards: How to assess evaluation of educational programs,* 2nd ed., Thousand Oaks: CA, Sage.

focus groups, and videotaping. **Qualitative research** methods are based on different beliefs and purposes than quantitative research methods. For example, qualitative researchers do not accept the view of a stable, coherent, uniform world. They argue that all meaning is situated in a particular perspective or context, and, since different people and groups often have different perspectives and contexts, there are many different meanings in the world, none of which is necessarily more valid or true than another.

Some fundamental differences in how quantitative and qualitative research are conducted reflect their different perspectives on meaning and how one can approach it. For example, qualitative research tends not to state hypotheses before data are collected. However, qualitative research problems and methods tend to evolve as understanding of the research context and participants deepens, an inductive strategy. In qualitative research, context is not controlled or manipulated by the researcher as in most quantitative research studies. Additionally, in qualitative research the number of participants tends to be small, in part because of time-intensive data collection methods such as interviews and observations. Qualitative researchers analyze data interpretively by synthesizing, categorizing, and organizing data into patterns that produce a descriptive, narrative synthesis. Conversely, quantitative analysis involves statistical procedures. Finally, because of the data collection methods and the effort to understand the participants' own perspective, researchers using qualitative methods often interact extensively with participants during the study. Quantitative researchers strive to control context and rarely interact with study participants.

Despite the differences between them, you should not consider quantitative and qualitative research to be oppositional. Taken together, they represent the full range of educational research methods. The terms *quantitative* and *qualitative* are used to conveniently differentiate one approach from the other. If you see yourself as a positivist, that does not mean you cannot use or learn from qualitative research methods. The same holds true for nonpositivist quantitative researchers. Depending on the nature of the question or topic to be investigated, one of these approaches will generally be more appropriate than the other. Note, however, that this does not preclude one approach borrowing from the other when it can enhance the research finding. In fact, both may be utilized in the same studies, as when the administration of a questionnaire (quantitative) is followed up by a small number of detailed interviews (qualitative) to obtain deeper explanations for the numerical data. (See also chapters 3 and 6 for discussions of mixed-method research.) Qualitative and quantitative approaches represent complementary components of the scientific and disciplined inquiry approach; qualitative approaches involve primarily inductive reasoning, while quantitative approaches involve primarily deductive reasoning. If hypotheses are involved, a qualitative study is much more likely to generate them, whereas a quantitative study is much more likely to test them. At an operational level, qualitative approaches are more holistic and process oriented, whereas quantitative approaches are more narrowly focused and outcome oriented. Qualitative research typically studies many variables intensely over an extended time in order to capture the richness of the qualitative context and the personal perspectives of the participants. Conversely, quantitative researchers focuses on a small number of variables and tries to eliminate the influence of contextual factors (e.g., class size, teacher experience, student characteristics). Qualitative researchers might examine in depth the way two or three teachers were acclimating to the use of a new reading textbook over a 6-month period; quantitative researchers might gather evidence from 200 students to compare the self-esteem of two groups, one that was mentored and one that was not.

At this point, you should have a basic sense of the essence of the two approaches. However, to help you broadly understand the field of educational research as a whole, it is useful to make one more level of distinction among types of educational research. So, let's look now at specific types of research that fall under the broad categories of *quantitative* and *qualitative*. In succeeding chapters we will examine these and other of the procedures and underlying beliefs associated with a number of specific quantitative and qualitative research approaches.

QUANTITATIVE APPROACHES

Researchers use quantitative research approaches to describe current conditions, investigate relationships, and study cause–effect phenomena. Studies designed to describe current conditions are called *survey* or *descriptive* research. Studies designed to investigate the relationship between two or more variables are referred to as *correlational* and *causal–comparative* research. Studies that provide information about cause–effect outcomes are called *true experiments*.

Survey Research

Survey research, also called descriptive research, involves collecting data to answer questions about the current status of issues or topics. Note that qualitative research also relies on description, but qualitative description is usually in the form of verbal reports and narratives, while quantitative description is usually in the form of statistics and numbers. Qualitative researchers do use survey research, but typically with less frequency. **Surveys** are carried out to obtain information about the preferences, attitudes, practices, concerns, or interests of some group of people. A pre-election political poll or a survey about the public's perception of the quality of its local schools are examples. A substantial portion of all the quantitative research carried out is survey research.

Quantitative descriptive research (survey) data are mainly collected from tests and questionnaires that research participants self-administer and fill out. Another common (but slightly more annoying) form of survey data is the telephone interview. Increasingly we are receiving phone calls from organizations or companies that want to obtain our opinions of their organization or product. Usually they read questions and ask us to choose from a limited number of categories: "Select your answer from these choices: highly favorable, favorable, neutral, unfavorable, or highly unfavorable." Usually they seem to call in the middle of supper.

There is considerably more to conducting survey research than just asking questions and reporting answers. Because researchers are often asking questions that have not been asked before, they must develop instruments to suit each specific descriptive study. Instrument development requires clarity, consistency, and tact in constructing questions for the intended respondents. (We address instrument development in Chapter 5.) Other major problems that face survey researchers are participants' failure to return questionnaires, to agree to be surveyed over the phone, and to attend scheduled data collection sessions. Researchers depend on the chosen participants to care enough to make time to provide the sought information. If the response rate is low, researchers cannot draw valid conclusions about the issues studied. For example, suppose you were doing a study to determine attitudes of principals toward research in their schools. You send a questionnaire to 100 principals and ask the question, "Do you usually cooperate if your school is asked to participate in a research study?" Forty principals respond and they all answer "Yes." Could you then conclude that principals in general cooperate with researchers? No! Even though all those who responded said yes, 60 principals did not respond to your questionnaire. They may never cooperate with researchers. After all, they didn't cooperate with you! Without more responses it is not possible to generalize about how all principals feel about research in their schools.

The following are examples of topics investigated by quantitative survey (descriptive) research studies:

- *How do second-grade teachers spend their teaching time?* Categories of teaching time would be identified (e.g., lecture, discussion, asking and answering questions, individual student help). Second-grade teachers would be asked to fill out a questionnaire and results would probably be presented as percentages (e.g., 50% of their time is spent lecturing, 20% asking or answering questions, 20% discussion, and 10% individual student help).
- *How will citizens of Yourtown vote in the next presidential election?* A survey sample of Yourtown citizens would complete a questionnaire or interview, and results would likely be

presented as percentages (e.g., 70% indicated they will vote for Peter Pure, 20% for George Graft, and 10% are undecided).

Correlational Research

Correlational research seeks to determine whether, and to what degree, a statistical relationship exists between two or more variables. A **variable** is a concept that can assume any one of a range of values, for example, intelligence, height, test score, and the like. Correlations either establish relationships or use existing relationships to make predictions. A **correlation** is a quantitative measure of the degree of correspondence between two or more variables. For example, a college admissions director might be interested in answering the question "How does the performance of high school seniors on the SAT correspond to their first semester's college grades?" Is there a high relationship between students' SAT scores and their freshman year of college, suggesting that SAT scores might be useful in predicting how students will perform in their first year of college? Or is there a low correlation between the two variables, suggesting that SAT scores likely will not be useful? The degree of correspondence between correlational variables is measured by a **correlation coefficient,** which is a number between -1.00 and $+1.00$. Two variables that are not related will have a correlation coefficient near .00. Two variables that are highly correlated will have a correlation coefficient near -1.00 or $+1.00$. A correlation that is *positive* (near $+1.00$) means that as one variable increases, the other variable also increases. A coefficient that is *negative* (near -1.00) means that when one variable increases the other variable decreases. Since very few pairs of variables are perfectly correlated, predictions based on them are rarely perfectly positive or negative. At a minimum, correlation research requires information about at least two variables obtained from a *single group* of participants.

It is very important to note that correlational studies do not establish cause–effect relations between variables. Thus, the fact that there is a high correlation between, for example, self-concept and achievement does not imply that self-concept "causes" achievement or that achievement "causes" self-concept. The correlation only indicates that students with higher self-concepts tend to have higher levels of achievement and that students with lower self-concepts tend to have lower levels of achievement. We cannot conclude that one variable is the cause of the other. There may be a third factor, such as the amount of encouragement and support parents give their children, that underlies both variables and influences high or low achievement and self-concept.

The following are examples of correlational studies:

- *The correlation between intelligence and self-esteem.* Scores on an intelligence test and a measure of self-esteem would be acquired from each member of a given group. The two sets of scores would be correlated and the resulting coefficient would indicate the degree of relationship between intelligence and self-esteem.
- *Use of an aptitude test to predict success in an algebra course.* Scores on an algebra aptitude test would be correlated with success in algebra measured by algebra final exam scores. If the resulting correlation were high, the aptitude test might be a good predictor of participants' future grades in algebra.

Causal–Comparative Research

Causal–comparative research, also called **ex post facto research** (after the fact), explores relationships among variables that cannot meet the stringent criteria for true experimental research. In most situations, causal–comparative research fails to meet the criterion for random assignment of participants from a single pool. In a causal–comparative study (note, the word is *causal,* not *casual*), the **independent variable,** or cause, has already occurred or cannot be manipulated, so the researcher has no control over it. For this reason, causal–comparative research is also called ex post facto research. The independent variables in causal–comparative studies either cannot be manipulated (e.g., gender, height, or year in school) or should not be manipulated (e.g., smoking, prenatal care). In causal–comparative research, at least two different groups are compared on some **dependent variable** (the effect).

For example, a causal–comparative study might involve the independent or causal variable "heavy smoking," with a comparison between a group of long-time smokers and a group of nonsmokers. The dependent variable (the effect) might be the comparative frequency of lung cancer diagnoses in the two groups. In this example and in causal–comparative research in general, the researcher does not have control over the independent variable. That is, the smokers and nonsmokers had already formed themselves into groups *before* the researcher began the study. The researcher has to select research participants from two different, preexisting groups, heavy smokers and nonsmokers. This potentially creates problems. Suppose, for example, that unknown to the researcher, a large number of the long-time smokers selected had lived in a smoggy, urban environment and that only a few of the nonsmoking group did. Due to the lack of control over the selection of study participants, attempts to draw cause–effect conclusions in the study would be at best tenuous and tentative. Is it smoking that causes higher rates of lung cancer? Is it living in a smoggy, urban environment? Is it some unknown combination of smoking and environment? A clear cause–effect link cannot be obtained from this study because the researcher did not have complete control of the selection of the participants and their characteristics.

Although causal–comparative research produces limited cause–effect information, it is an important form of educational research because in many cases, seeking true cause–effect relationships would be inappropriate or unethical to research. Our smoking study is an example of the need for causal–comparative methods. To conduct the study as an experiment so that causal statements about smoking and lung cancer could be obtained would require the researcher to select a large group of participants who had never smoked and divide them into two groups, one forced to become heavy smokers and one forbidden to smoke. Obviously such a study would be unethical because of the potential harm to those forced to become heavy smokers. The only reasonable option is to conduct a causal–comparative study that approximates cause–effect results without harming the participants. Thus, like most survey and correlational studies, causal–comparative research also does not produce true experimental research outcomes, although such research sometimes leads to more rigorous experimental studies designed to either confirm or refute specific findings.

The following are examples of causal–comparative studies:

- *The effect of preschool attendance on social maturity at the end of the first grade.* The independent variable, or cause, is preschool attendance (students attending preschool and students not attending); the dependent variable, or effect, is social maturity at the end of the first grade. Two groups of first graders would be identified, one group who had attended preschool and one group who had not. The social maturity of the two groups would be compared at the end of grade one.
- *The effect of having a working mother on school absenteeism.* The independent variable is the employment status of the mother (the mother works or does not work); the dependent variable is absenteeism, or number of days absent. Two groups of students would be identified—one group who had working mothers and one group who did not. The absenteeism of the two groups would be compared.

Experimental Research

True **experimental research** allows researchers to make cause–effect statements about their research studies. Cause-and-effect research outcomes provide the strongest results of any of the quantitative research approaches. To establish that one variable causes another provides strong evidence for linking variables. To obtain cause–effect research results it is necessary to adhere to a stringent set of criteria.

The major difference between causal–comparative and experimental research is that in the experiment the researcher can control the independent variable. In fact, the experiment is the quantitative approach that provides the greatest degree of control over the research procedures. True experimental researchers control the selection of participants for the study, divide the selected participants into two or more groups that have similar characteristics at the start of the research experiment, then apply different treatments to the selected groups. They also control the condition in the research setting, such as when the treatments will be applied, by whom, for how long, and under what conditions. Finally, researchers select tests or measurements to collect data about the effects of the research groups. It is the selection of participants from a *single pool* of participants and the ability to apply different treatments or programs to participants with similar initial characteristics that permit true experimental research to provide cause–effect research results. The essence of experimentation is control, although in many education settings it is not possible or feasible to meet the stringent control conditions required by experimental research.

The following are examples of experimental studies:

- *The comparative effectiveness on computational skills of personalized instruction from a teacher versus computer instruction.* The independent variable is type of instruction (personalized teacher instruction versus computer instruction); the dependent variable is computational skills. A group of students who had never experienced either personalized teacher instruction or computer instruction would be selected and randomly divided into two groups, each taught by one of the methods. After a predetermined time, the students' computational skills would be measured and compared to determine which, if either, treatment produced higher skill levels.
- *The effect of positive reinforcement on attitude toward school.* The independent variable is type of reinforcement (e.g., positive, negative, and no reinforcement); the dependent variable is attitude toward school. In this example three groups will be studied, randomly formed from a single large group of students. One group would receive positive reinforcement, another negative reinforcement, and the third no reinforcement. After the treatments were applied for a predetermined time, student attitudes toward school would be measured and compared for each of the three groups.

QUALITATIVE APPROACHES

Qualitative research seeks to probe deeply into the research setting to obtain in-depth understandings about the way things are, *why* they are that way, and *how* the participants in the context perceive them. As with quantitative research, qualitative research encompasses many research methods. Qualitative researchers are not concerned simply with describing the way things are, they also wish to provide insights into what people believe and feel about the way things are and how they got to be the way they are. To achieve the detailed understandings they seek, qualitative researchers must undertake sustained in-depth, in-context research that allows them to uncover subtle, less overt, personal understandings. Thus, qualitative researchers typically maintain a lengthy physical presence in the chosen setting. In these settings they can assume a range of involvement, from an observer to an interviewer to a participant observer. (Only very experienced researchers should become active participants in the setting.) These levels of involvement lead to different levels of understanding.

Although the amount of time qualitative researchers spend immersed in the contexts they study varies, it is typically measured in months, not days. The researcher often strives to enter the setting with no preconceived notions about the context, participants, or data desired, letting the purpose of the study emerge as she observes and understands the setting and participants. To tell the "story" of the participants and their context requires both spending substantial time in the natural setting and collecting a great deal of data. Data are gathered from **fieldwork**, that is, from spending lengthy periods of time in the setting where participants normally spend their time. Types of data commonly collected include records of formal and informal conversations, observations, documents, audio- and videotapes, and interviews. For the most part, though not exclusively, the data collected are open ended and nonnumerical.

Data analysis is ongoing; as initial information is collected, the researcher analyzes and codes it to discover the nuances of the context and the perspectives and beliefs of the participants. As more data are collected, the researcher refines prior analyses and understandings. Thus, data collection, analysis, and interpretation occur throughout the study rather than at its end, as is common with quantitative research. Think of qualitative research as collecting waves of data; each successive wave provides information that further focuses the nature of the study until the researcher gradually zeros in on the important and recurring themes of the setting and its participants. The ongoing collection and analysis of data is important because the relationship between the researcher and participants changes as they become more familiar with each other. The final product of the study is a rich description or narrative of the essential aspects of the topic as viewed by the participants. The main focus of the qualitative study is to use language to paint a rich picture of the setting and its participants.

We describe here four qualitative research examples. Action research is used by one or more educators to work on solving their own problems, especially in classrooms. Historical methods entail collecting and interpreting information about important persons and events. Ethnography is the study of research participants' in their own natural setting or culture. Grounded theory, also called the constant comparison method, is a method for identifying patterns in quantitative research methods.

Action Research

Action research is mainly used to find and solve one or more educators' problems in their own institutions. The aims of action research are to help an educator or group of educators to change or improve a practice or to help them understand issues and problems for themselves. Thus, the focus is on solving practical issues of importance to educators. (We discuss action research in depth in Chapter 9.) In most cases, the educators themselves carry out the research, giving them a sense of "ownership" of the process and findings, unlike most other research methods. Action researchers engage in a democratic, equitable, liberating, and enabling activity; one or more teachers and/or administrators work to solve or improve a local problem or situation. Note that the insular nature of action research means that it is less rigorous than most quantitative and qualitative research methods.

As with most qualitative research, the research is carried out in a cyclical manner. Initial information is reexamined and sharpened, reexamined and sharpened again, and the process continues until there is consensus or until additional cycles fail to generate significant new information. The four basic steps of scientific and disciplined inquiry guide the process of action research: (1) identifying a problem or question; (2) group conduct meeting or *brainstorming* to gain information about the problem or question; (3) joint analysis of research data or information; and (4) taking action to rectify the problem or illuminate the question.

The following is an example of action research:

- *How can teachers deal with rude language used by students in three fifth-grade classrooms?* The problem of rude language is the "topic" and affects most students in each of the three classrooms. Acting as a group, the three teachers would brainstorm reasons why students might use rude language and how they might help the students to diminish their rudeness. The teachers would observe the times or circumstances when the rudeness is greatest, talk to colleagues about how they dealt with similar behavior, and search the literature for strategies to lessen the problem. The teachers would then meet, discuss the information they obtain, and select a remedy to attempt. In one case, three teachers attempting to solve this problem carried out a number of social competency skills with their students: practicing listening to one student without interruption; learning to be nonjudgmental listeners; and picking an interpersonal problem from a "Problem Box" and having students suggest ways to solve the problem. The teachers observed that the incidence of rude language decreased by 30 percent. (Don't be disappointed, the teachers weren't.)

Historical Research Methods

Historical research involves studying, understanding, and interpreting past events. The purpose of historical research is to reach insights or conclusions about past persons or occurrences. Historical research, like all qualitative approaches, entails more than simply compiling and presenting factual information; it also requires interpretation of the information.

Typically, histories focus on particular individuals (e.g., John Dewey, Malcolm X, Margaret Thatcher, Barbara Jordan), important social issues (e.g., school desegregation, the consequences of standardized testing), and links between the old and the new (e.g., comparing teaching methods across generations, examining and explaining reasons for textbook changes in the last six decades). Some historical research is aimed at reinterpreting prior historical work (e.g., why schools foster intolerance, how tracking diminishes incentives); this approach is often termed *revisionist history* because it attempts to revise existing understandings and replace them with new, often politically charged ones.

Historical researchers work with data that are already available, except in those instances when living reporters can provide information. Occasionally a historical researcher may collect quantitative information for a study, as when the researcher investigates a topic that includes information about the number of women graduated from medical school between 1990 and 2000. However, the main emphasis in historical research is on interpretation of documents, diaries, and the like.

Historical data are categorized into primary or secondary sources. **Primary sources** include firsthand information, such as eyewitness reports and original documents. **Secondary sources** include secondhand information, such as a description of an event by someone other than an eyewitness, or a textbook author's explanation of a researcher's theory. If you interview someone who witnessed an accident, that someone is a primary source; if you interview someone who heard about the accident from a friend, that person is a secondary source. Primary sources are admittedly harder to acquire (it would be quite a feat to find an eyewitness to the Boston Tea Party!) but are generally more accurate and preferred by historical researchers. A major problem with much historical research is excessive reliance on secondary sources.

Researchers cannot accept historical data at face value, since many diaries, memoirs, reports, and testimonies are written to enhance the writer's position, stature, or importance. Because of this possibility, historical data have to be examined for their authenticity and truthfulness. Such examination is done through external and internal criticism. **External criticism** assesses the authenticity of the data: was this diary really written by Bonnie Parker; is this her handwriting; is the diary paper and ink of the right age for her time? Questions such as these help determine the authenticity of the data. **Internal criticism** evaluates the worth or truthfulness of the content of the data. Are the writer's statements biased for some reason? Are important pieces of information omitted? Is the writer's description of the event in line with descriptions written by others? Historical researchers care about the value of the data and the degree to which they are accurate and useful.

The following is an example of historical research:

- *Trends in elementary school reading instruction, 1940–2000.* The researcher would narrow the focus of the historical study to the period 1940–2000 and to the topic "elementary school reading." The researcher would examine a number of potential sources: reading textbooks of the selected period, educational movements that affected reading methods (e.g., back to basics movement; whole language approach), students' reading achievement (quantitative data), professional development opportunities for reading teachers, and articles in major reading publications. The researcher would keep copious and detailed notes related to these sources, and apply both external and internal criticism to the data. Finally, the researcher would apply interpretive and writing skills to present a coherent, logically presented report about the nature and reasons for elementary reading trends between 1940 and 2000.

Ethnography

Ethnography is a qualitative approach that studies participants in their natural culture or setting. The focus of ethnography is on a particular site or sites that provide the researcher with a context in which to study both the setting and the participants who inhabit the setting. An ethnographic setting can be defined as anything from a bowling alley to a neighborhood, from a nomadic group's traveling range to a sixth-grade classroom. The selected context and participants are observed in their naturally occurring activities and in the setting. Because the researcher observes rather than manipulates the participants, the researcher spends much time in the context observing and interacting with the participants. Over time, a tentative research design emerges.

The ethnographic method follows those of other qualitative procedures. The researcher tries not to draw interpretations or conclusions early in the study, and strives not to observe and judge the nature of the context and its relation to the participants who inhabit it too early. The researcher must enter the setting slowly, learning to become accepted by the participants and gaining rapport with them. Then, over time, the researcher collects data in waves, making initial observations and interpretations about the context and participants, then collecting and examining more data in a second wave of refining the initial interpretation, then collecting another wave of data to further refine observations and interpretation, and so on, until the researcher has obtained a deep understanding of both the context and its participants' roles in it. Lengthy engagement in the setting is a key facet of ethnographic and qualitative research. The researcher organizes the collected data and interprets it. The result of the ethnographic study is a holistic description and interpretation that represents the participants' everyday activities, values, and events. The study is written up and presented as a narrative.

The following is an example of an ethnographic approach:

- *Study of the Hispanic student culture in an urban community college.* The study begins with a general research question and a research site in a community college with Hispanic students. The researcher must gain entry to the chosen community college and establish rapport with the participants of the study. This might be a lengthy process, depending on the characteristics of the researcher (e.g., non-Hispanic vs. Hispanic; Spanish speaking vs. non-Spanish speaking). As is common in qualitative approaches, the researcher would simultaneously collect and interpret data to help focus the general research question initially posed. Observations and interviews are common methods of data gathering, perhaps supplemented by actual participation in group activities (depending on the researcher's experience). Throughout data collection, the researcher identifies recurrent themes, integrates them into existing categories, and adds new categories as new themes or topics arise. The success of the study relies heavily on the researcher's skills in analyzing and synthesizing the qualitative data into coherent and meaningful descriptions. The research report would include a holistic description of the culture, the common understandings and beliefs shared by participants, how these relate to life in the culture, and how the findings compare to literature already published about similar groups. In a sense, the researcher seeks to provide guidelines that would enable someone not in the culture to know how to think and behave in the culture.

Grounded Theory

Grounded theory aims at deriving theory from the analysis of multiple stages of data collection and interpretation. The researcher strives to identify patterns, themes, and categories from the qualitative topic and data. However, unlike other forms of qualitative research, which focus mainly on understanding, grounded theory goes beyond to develop a theory that derives from the data.

The grounded theorist starts with a general topic or issue to study and begins gathering information about the topic and the participants. While collecting data from the participants, the researcher applies two analytic strategies: "step back and ask," and "be skeptical." The researcher steps back and asks, "What is going on in this study?" "Can I see any links among the data I'm getting from the participants?" and "Can I find common threads in the participants' responses?" Having identified some commonalities among the participants, the researcher must verify that what he sees is actually real, not wishful thinking. As we've seen in other qualitative methods, data collection and interpretation are ongoing. Using inductive methods, each research cycle narrows the focus of the topic and the key aspects of the grounded theory. Think of an upside-down megaphone that narrows as it moves up. The method of narrowing is called **constant comparison** analysis, and leads increasingly to understanding and integrating the participants' key views of the topic studied. Once the core concept or concepts are identified and integrated, the key aspect of the theory is revealed.

The following is an example of the grounded theory approach:

- *What opinion do teachers at a selected elementary school have of the teacher evaluation practices at this school?* The researcher would begin by selecting a group of teachers to respond to questions designed to elicit their feelings about the teacher evaluation process in their grade. The researcher would identify issues as they emerge, such as evaluations being seen as too time consuming, not necessary, or of little use; respondents who don't trust their administrator; and those who feel that evaluations lack clear feedback; among others. The initial teacher responses would be examined for common responses, positive or negative. Given analysis of the initial data, the researcher would use these responses to form new questions about teacher evaluation. The second analysis would add new responses, such as evaluations being poorly done and outsiders obtaining results. Additional cycles would narrow the focus or "theory" to one or a few key issues that are of concern to the participants. The constant comparison method would be used progressively to narrow the teachers' views. When the data provide little new information about teachers' views of evaluation, it is *saturated* and the researcher would then focus on two key aspects of teacher evaluation practices, such as the infrequency of being evaluated and the lack of feedback after the evaluation. These two foci serve as the basis for theorizing about opinions of teacher evaluation in the school.

GUIDELINES FOR CLASSIFICATION

We have seen that there are many types of educational research. We have noted important features of the different research approaches. Determining which type is appropriate for a given study depends on the way the research topic is defined. The same general topic area can often be investigated by several different types of research. For example, suppose you wanted to do a study in the general area of anxiety and achievement. You might conduct any one of the following different studies:

1. A survey of teachers to determine how and to what degree they believe anxiety affects achievement (descriptive)
2. A study to determine the relationship between scores on an anxiety scale and scores on an achievement measure (correlational)

3. A study to compare the achievement of a group of students classified as high-anxious and a group classified as low-anxious (causal-comparative)

4. A study to compare the achievement of two groups, one group taught in an anxiety-producing environment and one group taught in an anxiety-reducing environment (experimental)

5. A study of the research on the effect of anxiety on achievement from 1900 to 1990 (historical)

6. A study by two teachers who examined ways to lesson the anxiety on SAT scores for their students (action research)

7. A study of six parents on the cultural patterns and perspectives related to how parents view the link between anxiety and achievement (ethnography)

8. A study seeking to develop an underlying theory of the link between anxiety and achievement (grounded theory)

Note that it is the question or problem to be addressed that determines which research approach is appropriate. Method should follow, not precede, the topic or question to be studied. Note also that the general topic must often be narrowed in order to plan the conduct of the study.

Clearly, the more information about a study one has, the easier it is to categorize it. If all one has is the title of the study, words such as *survey, comparison, relationship, historical, descriptive, effect,* and *qualitative* can suggest the type of study. If one has a description of the research strategy used in the study, one can often classify based on features such as large or small samples, qualitative or quantitative data, statistical (correlational, descriptive, comparative) or nonstatistical (interpretive, participants' viewpoint) analysis. Classifying a study by type is the first step in both conducting and reviewing a study, since each type entails different specific procedures and analyses.

The following examples should further clarify the differences among the types. Can you label the type of research for each type? Can you state one characteristic that defines the type?

1. *Teachers' attitudes toward unions.* The study is determining the current attitudes of teachers. Data are probably collected through use of a questionnaire or an interview.

2. *The personal and educational interactions in a group of teachers developing social studies standards for a high school curriculum.* Teachers' interactions during the development of the standards are studied over time.

3. *The relationship of Graduate Record Examination (GRE) scores to graduate student performance.* Participants' GRE scores are compared to their graduate school academic records (e.g., GPA).

4. *Characteristics of the drama-music clique in a suburban high school.* The researcher interviews and observes participants, both members and nonmembers of the clique, to gather information about the beliefs and activities of members of the drama-music group. Participants are interviewed a number of times over the school year, and their behavior is periodically observed over the same time.

LIMITATIONS OF THE SCIENTIFIC AND DISCIPLINED INQUIRY APPROACH

The steps in the scientific and disciplined inquiry approach guide researchers in planning, conducting, and interpreting research studies. However, it is important to recognize some of the limitations of this approach. For example, it cannot provide answers to questions that seek to determine what *should* be done. Questions such as, "Should we adopt a new biology textbook or stay with the current one?" are not answerable by research studies. There is no way to solve such questions as, "Should we legalize euthanasia?" by collecting data, because issues of philosophy, values, and ethics in addition to data go into making those decisions. Simply put, *should* questions are not researchable.

No research study can capture the full richness of the individuals and sites that they study. Although some research approaches lead to deeper understanding of the research context than others, no approach provides full comprehension of a site and its inhabitants. No matter how many variables one studies or how long one is immersed in a research context, there always will be other variables and aspects of context that were not examined. Thus, all research gives us a simplified version of reality, an abstraction from the whole. Additional variables and on-site understandings could always be added to a research study.

There are limits to our research technologies. Our data collection instruments and the available theories are primitive in comparison to the instruments and theories of, say, medicine. Our measuring instruments always have some degree of error. The variables that we study are often proxies for the real behavior we seek to examine. For example, we use a multiple-choice test to assess a person's values and a 20-minute interview to decide whether to hire a teacher.

Finally, educational research is carried out with the cooperation of participants who agree to provide researchers with data. Because researchers deal with human beings, they must consider a number of ethical concerns and responsibilities to the participants. For example, they must shelter participants from real or potential harm. They must inform participants about the nature of the planned research and address the expectations of the participants.

All of these limitations will be addressed in later sections of this book. For now, bear in mind both the advantages and limitations of adopting the scientific and disciplined inquiry approach as your approach to educational research.

This chapter has provided a general introduction to fundamental aspects of scientific and disciplined inquiry. It provided examples of research methods of both quantitative and qualitative approaches. The chapter serves as an overview of educational research strategies and methods. In succeeding chapters, we will present more specific and detailed features needed to carry out, understand, and conduct useful educational research.

Now go to the Companion Website accompanying this text at www.prenhall.com/gay to check your understanding of chapter concepts in the following modules: Objectives, Practice Quiz, and Applying What You Know. Expand your research skills with Evaluating Articles, Analyzing Qualitative Data, Analyzing Quantitative Data, and Research Tools and Tips. Visit Web Links to broaden your knowledge about research.

SUMMARY

1. Knowledge of educational research methods is important because educators must be able to access, understand, and evaluate the findings of research and the claims of researchers.

Educational Research: Scientific and Disciplined Inquiry

2. Educational research is the application of scientific and disciplined inquiry to the study of educational problems. The primary goal of educational research is to explain or help understand educational issues, questions, and processes.

3. Rarely does any single study produce definitive answers to research questions. Cumulated studies are the basis for research progress and understanding.

4. Compared to other methods of knowing, such as tradition, expert advice, personal experience, and inductive or deductive logic, a scientific and disciplined inquiry approach provides the most unbiased and verifiable understandings.

5. This approach is made up of four main steps:
   - Identify a question or problem to be studied.
   - Describe and execute procedures to collect information about the problem being studied.
   - Analyze the collected information.
   - State results or implications based on the analysis.

Research Topics: Defining Purpose and Methods

6. Educational research encompasses many types of topics, procedures, methods for analyzing data, and formats for reporting conclusions, implications, and findings.

Basic and Applied Research

7. Basic research is conducted to develop or refine theory, not to solve immediate practical problems. Applied research is conducted to find solutions to current practical problems.

Evaluation Research

8. The purpose of evaluation research is to help decision making about educational programs and practices.

Quantitative and Qualitative Research

9. The purpose of quantitative research is to generalize about or control phenomena, while that of qualitative research is to provide in-depth descriptions of settings and people.
10. Because quantitative and qualitative researchers differ in their view of the world, they tend to utilize different methods to seek knowledge.
11. Quantitative and qualitative approaches should be thought of as complementary methods that, when taken together, provide broader options for investigating a range of important educational topics.
12. Quantitative methods involve collecting and analyzing numerical data from tests, questionnaires, checklists, and surveys.
13. Key features of quantitative research are hypotheses that predict the results of the research before the study begins; control of contextual factors that might influence the study; collecting data from samples of participants; and using numerical, statistical approaches to analyze the collected data.
14. The quantitative approach views the world as relatively stable, uniform, and coherent.
15. Qualitative methods involve collecting and analyzing primarily nonnumerical data obtained from observation, interviews, tape recordings, documents, and the like.
16. Key features of qualitative research include defining the problem, but not necessarily at the start of the study; studying contextual factors in the participants' settings; collecting data from a small number of purposely selected participants; and using nonnumerical, interpretive approaches to provide narrative descriptions of the participants and their contexts.
17. An important belief that underlies qualitative research is that the world is neither stable, coherent, nor uniform, and therefore, there are many "truths."

Quantitative Approaches

18. Quantitative research approaches are intended to describe current conditions, investigate relationships, and study cause–effect phenomena.
19. Survey or descriptive research collects numerical data to answer questions about the current status of the participants of the study. Most descriptive studies obtain information about the preferences, attitudes, practices, concerns, or interests of some group. Data are collected by self-administered instruments or telephone polls.
20. Important and difficult aspects of survey research are that of constructing clear and consistent descriptive instruments and failure of participants to return questionnaires.
21. Correlational research examines the degree of relationship that exists between two or more variables. A *variable* is a measure that can take on different values, such as age, IQ, or height.
22. The degree of relationship is measured by a correlation coefficient. If two variables are highly related, it does not mean that one is the cause of the other; there may be a third factor that "causes" both the related variables.
23. Causal–comparative research seeks to investigate relations between two or more different programs, methods, or groups. The activity thought to make a difference (the program, method, or group) is called the *independent variable, causal factor,* or *treatment.* The effect is called the *dependent variable.*
24. In most causal–comparative research studies the researcher does not have control over the independent variable because it already has occurred or cannot be manipulated. This means that causal–comparative research cannot produce true experimental research.
25. Causal–comparative research is useful in those circumstances when it is impossible or unethical to manipulate the independent variable.
26. True experimental research investigates causal relationships among variables.
27. The experimental researcher controls the selection of participants by choosing them from a single pool and assigning them at random to different causal treatments. The researcher also controls contextual variables that might interfere with the study.
28. Because it randomly selects and assigns participants into different treatments, experimental research permits researchers to make true cause–effect statements.

Qualitative Approaches

29. Qualitative approaches include a number of specific methods, including action research, historical research, ethnography, and grounded theory. The focus of these methods is on deep description of aspects of people's everyday perspectives and context.

30. Qualitative approaches provide field-focused, interpretive, detailed descriptions and interpretations of participants and their settings. The researcher's long-term immersion into the research setting is also a common feature of qualitative approaches because of the belief that participants and contexts are not independent.

31. Common methods of data collection include observation, interviewing, audio and video recording, examining artifacts, and participant observation.

32. Data analysis is based on categorizing and interpreting the observations; conversing with participants; and studying documents, recordings, and interviews collected to provide an explanation of the participants and their experiences.

33. The qualitative researcher writes from the perspective of the participants, not from the researcher's own perspective.

Guidelines for Classification

34. The type of research method needed for a given study depends on the problem to be studied. The same general problem can be investigated using many types of research. Knowing the type of research applied helps one identify the important aspects to examine in evaluating the study.

Limitations of the Scientific and Disciplined Inquiry Approach

35. Four main factors put limitations on the use of a scientific and disciplined inquiry approach: inability to answer "should" questions; inability to capture the full richness of the research site and participants' complexity; limitations of measuring instruments; and the need to address participants' ethical needs and responsibilities.

TASK 1   PERFORMANCE CRITERIA

On the following pages two published research reports are reprinted. Following each report, spaces are provided for listing the components required by Task 1-A and Task 1-B. Task 1-C requires classifying research topics according to the specific type of research they represent. If your responses differ greatly from the Suggested Responses in Appendix C, study the article again until you see why you were in error. Additional examples for these and subsequent tasks are included in the *Student Guide* that accompanies this text.

TASKS 1-A, 1-B

Read the articles on pages 23–26 and 28–34. Then, on pages 27 and 35, state the:

1. Topic studied
2. Procedures used to gather data
3. Method of data analysis
4. Major conclusion

One sentence should be sufficient to describe the topic. Six sentences or less will adequately describe the major procedures of most studies. For the procedures used to gather data, briefly describe the participants, instrument(s), and major steps. As with the topic, one or two sentences will usually be sufficient to state the data analysis. You are expected only to identify the analysis, not explain it. The major conclusion that you identify and state (one or two sentences should be sufficient) should directly relate to the original topic. Statements like "more research is needed in this area" do not represent major conclusions.

TASK 1-C

Seven research topic statements follow these instructions. Read each statement and decide whether it represents a survey, correlational, causal–comparative, experimental, historical, ethnography, action research, or grounded theory research approach. State the research approach for each topic statement and indicate why you selected that approach. Your reasons should be related to characteristics that are unique to the type of research you have selected.

1. This study examines changes in the public schools' legal responsibilities regarding students with disabilities during the past 50 years.
2. This study involved a group of teachers investigating ways to determine strategies to engage their students in math.
3. This study administered a questionnaire to determine how social studies teachers felt about teaching world history to fifth graders.
4. This study was conducted to determine whether the Acme Interest Test provided similar results to the Acne Interest Test.
5. This study compared the achievement in reading of fifth graders from single-parent families and those from two-parent families.
6. This study divided fifth-grade students in a school into two groups at random and compared the results of two methods of conflict resolution on students' aggressive behavior.
7. This study examined the culture of recent Armenian emigrants in their new setting.

MOTIVATIONAL EFFECTS ON TEST SCORES
OF ELEMENTARY STUDENTS

STEVEN M. BROWN
Northeastern Illinois University

HERBERT J. WALBERG
University of Illinois at Chicago

ABSTRACT A total of 406 heterogeneously grouped students in Grades 3, 4, 6, 7, and 8 in three K through 8 Chicago public schools were assigned randomly to two conditions, ordinary standardized-test instructions (control) and special instructions, to do as well as possible for themselves, their parents, and their teachers (experimental). On average, students given special instructions did significantly better ($p < .01$) than the control students did on the criterion measure, the mathematics section of the commonly used Iowa Test of Basic Skills. The three schools differed significantly in achievement ($p < .05$), but girls and boys and grade levels did not differ measurably. The motivational effect was constant across grade levels and boys and girls, but differed significantly ($p < .05$) across schools. The average effect was moderately large, .303 standard deviations, which implies that the special instructions raise the typical student's scores from the 50th to the 62nd percentile.

Parents, educators, business people, politicians, and the general public are greatly concerned about U.S. students' poor performance on international comparisons of achievement. Policy makers are planning additional international, state, district, and school comparisons to measure progress in solving the national crisis. Some members of those same groups have also grown concerned about the effects of students' high or low motivational states on how well they score on tests.

One commonly expressed apprehension is that some students worry unduly about tests and suffer debilitating anxiety (Hill, 1980). Another concern is that too much testing causes students to care little about how well they do, especially on standardized tests that have no bearing on their grades. Either case might lead to poorer scores than students would attain under ideal motivational states; such effects might explain, in part, the poor performance of U.S. students relative to those in other countries or in relation to what may be required for college and vocational success.

Experts and practicing educators have expressed a variety of conflicting opinions about motivational effects on learning and test scores (Association for Supervision and Curriculum Development, 1991, p. 7). Given the importance of testing policies, there is surprisingly little research on the topic. The purpose of the present study is to determine the effect of experimentally manipulated motivational conditions on elementary students' mathematical scores.

As conceived in this study, the term *motivation* refers to the commonsense meaning of the term, that is, students' propensity to engage in full, serious, and sustained effort on academic tests. As it has been measured in many previous studies, motivation refers to students' reported efforts to succeed or to excel on academic tasks. It is often associated with self-concept or self-regard in a successful student or test taker. A quantitative synthesis of the correlational studies of motivation and school learning showed that nearly all correlations were positive and averaged about .30 (Uguroglu & Walberg, 1979).

Previous Research

The National Assessment Governing Board (NAGB, 1990) recently characterized the National Assessment of Educational Progress (NAEP) as follows:

> . . . as a survey exam which by law cannot be reported for individual students and schools. NAEP may not be taken seriously enough by students to enlist their best efforts. Because it is given with no incentives for good performance and no opportunity for prior study, NAEP may understate achievement (NAGB, p. 17).

To investigate such questions, NAEP is adding items to ask students how hard they tried in responding to future achievement tests.

Motivation questions can be raised about nearly all standardized commercial tests, as well as state-constructed achievement tests. The content of those tests is often unrelated to specific topics that students have been recently studying; and their performance on such tests ordinarily does not affect their grades, college, or job prospects. Many students know they will not see how well they have done.

Some students admit deficient motivation, but surveys show reasonably favorable attitudes toward tests by most students. Paris, Lawton, and Turner (1991), for example, surveyed 250 students in Grades 4, 7, and 10 about the Michigan Educational Assessment Program. They found that most students reported that they tried hard, thought they did well, felt the test was not difficult or confusing, and saw little or no cheating. However, Karmos and Karmos's (1984) survey of 360 sixth- through ninth-grade student attitudes toward tests showed that 47% thought they were a waste of time, 22% saw no good reason to try to do well, and 21% did not try very hard.

Kellaghan, Madaus, and Arisian (1982) found various small fractions of a sixth-grade Irish sample disaffected by standardized tests, even though they are uncommon in Ireland. When asked

Address correspondence to Steven M. Brown, 924 South Austin, Apt. 2, Oak Park, IL 60304.

about their experience with standardized tests, 29% reported feeling nervous; 19%, unconfident; 16%, bored; and 15% uninterested. Twenty-nine percent reported that they did not care whether they took the tests, and 16% said they did not enjoy the experience.

Paris, Lawton, and Turner (1991) speculated that standardized tests may lead both bright and dull students to do poorly: Bright students may feel heightened parental, peer, or self-imposed expectations to do well on tests, which makes them anxious. Slower, disadvantaged students may do poorly, then rationalize that school and tests are unimportant and, consequently, expend less effort preparing for and completing tests. Either case might lead to a self-reinforcing spiral of decelerating achievement.

Surveys, however, cannot establish causality. Poor motivation may cause poor achievement, or vice versa, or both may be caused by other factors such as deficiencies in ability, parental support of academic work, or teaching. To show an independent effect of motivation on achievement requires an experiment, that is, a randomized assignment of students to conditions of eliciting different degrees of motivation. Such was the purpose of our study.

METHOD

Sample
The subjects for the study included students from three K through 8 public schools in Chicago. The student populations of the schools are generally lower-middle, working class, mostly Hispanic and African-American. Two normal heterogeneous classes within the schools were sampled from Grades 3, 4, 6, 7, and 8; because of exigencies, we did not sample Grade 5 classes.

Instrument
We chose Form 7 of the Mathematics Concepts subtest of the Iowa Basic Skills (ITBS) 1978 edition, Levels 9–14, because it is a commonly used, highly reliable test. An earlier-than-contemporary edition was used so it would not interfere with current testing programs. In a review of the 1978 ITBS, Nitko (1985) judged that the reliability of its subtests is generally higher than .85 and that it contains content generally representative of school curriculum in Grades 3 though 9. "The ITBS," he concluded, "is an excellent basic skills battery measuring global skills that are likely to be highly related to the long-term goals of elementary schools" (p. 723).

Procedure
Pairs of classes at each grade level from each school were randomly chosen to participate. Classes were selected for experimental and control conditions by a flip of a coin.

The first author (Brown) met with all participating teachers in each school to explain the instructions from the ITBS test manual (see Appendix A). Then, the experimental teachers were retained for the following further instructions:

> We are conducting a research study to determine the effects of telling students that the test they are going to take is very impor-

tant. It is extremely important that you read the brief script I have for you today EXACTLY as it is written to your students.

The following script was provided:

> It is really important that you do as WELL as you can on this test. The test score you receive will let others see just how well I am doing in teaching you math this year.
>
> Your scores will be compared to students in other grades here at this school, as well as to those in other schools in Chicago.
>
> That is why it is extremely important to do the VERY BEST that you can. Do it for YOURSELF, YOUR PARENTS, and ME.
>
> (Now read the instructions for the test.)

Following the administration of the test, teachers and the first author asked students for their reactions to the script that was read to them.

Analysis
An analysis of variance was run to test the effects of the experimental and normal conditions; the differences among the three schools and five grades; between boys and girls; and the interactions among the factors.

RESULTS

The analysis of variance showed a highly significant effect of experimental condition ($F = 10.59$, $p < .01$), a significant effect of school ($F = 3.35$, $p < .05$), and an interaction between condition and school ($F = 5.01$, $p < .05$). No other effects, including grade level, were significant. The means and standard deviations of selected factors are shown in Table 1.

The mean normal curve equivalent test score of the 214 students in the experimental group was 41.37 ($SD = 15.41$), and the mean of the control group was 36.25 ($SD = 16.89$). The motiva-

TABLE 1. Normal Curve Equivalent Means and Standard Deviations

GRADE	CONDITION	M	SD
3	Control	32.77	19.57
	Experimental	42.55*	16.59
4	Control	33.07	13.93
	Experimental	39.42*	13.12
6	Control	40.84	17.77
	Experimental	39.64	14.66
7	Control	43.21	16.07
	Experimental	41.21	16.48
8	Control	31.12	14.06
	Experimental	44.66**	15.94

*$p < .01$.
**$p < .001$.

tional effect is moderately large, .303 standard deviations, which implies that the special instructions raised the typical student's scores from the 50th to the 62nd percentile. The special instructions are comparable to the effects of better (though not the best) instructional practices over conventional classroom instruction (Walberg, 1986). If American students' average achievement in mathematics and science could be raised that much, it would be more comparable to that of students in other economically advanced countries.

The motivational effect was the same for boys and girls and constant across grade levels, but it differed among schools. Figure 1 shows a very large effect at School A, a large effect at School C, and the control group somewhat higher than the experimental group at School B.

Only 62 students (15% of the total sample) were tested at School B, which may account for the lack of effect in this school. At any rate, although the overall effect is moderately large and constant across grade levels and for boys and girls, the size of the effect varies from school to school. Such differences may depend on test-taking attitudes of teachers and students in the schools, motivational and cultural differences in the student populations, variations in conditions of administration, and other factors.

Several comments made by students and teachers during debriefing sessions illuminate the statistical findings. Student Comments 1, 2, and 3 illustrate students' motivation to do well to please their parents and teachers. Teacher Comments 1 and 2 also confirm the reasons for the effect. The last student and teacher comment, however, illustrate motivational states and conditions that diminish or vitiate the effect. When students are unthoughtful or when teachers keep constant pressures on for testing, special instructions may have little effect.

CONCLUSION

The results show that motivation can make a substantial difference in test scores. Students asked to try especially hard did considerably better than those who were given the usual standardized test instructions. The special conditions raised the typical student's score .303 standard deviation units, corresponding to a 12 percentile-point gain from the 50th to the 62nd percentile. Although the effect was the same for boys and girls and for students in different grade levels, it varied in magnitude among the three schools.

The results suggest that standardized commercial and state-constructed tests that have no bearing on students' grades may be underestimating U.S. students' real knowledge, understanding, skills, and other aspects of achievement. To the extent that motivation varies from school to school, moreover, achievement levels of some schools are considerably more underestimated than in others. Such motivational differences would tend to diminish the validity of comparisons of schools and districts.

We would be heartened to conclude that U.S. students' poor performance on achievement relative to students in other countries is attributable to the test-motivation effect. That conclusion is overly optimistic, however, because the effect may also operate

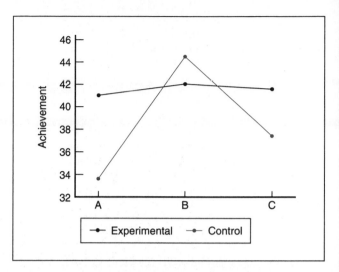

FIGURE 1. Means by condition and school

to a greater or lesser extent in other countries. Further research is obviously in order.

The motivation effect might be reduced in several ways. Highly motivating instructions could be given to all students. The content of school lessons and standardized tests could be brought into closer correspondence, making the tests more plausible to students, and perhaps justifying their use in grading. Some students, moreover, may be unmotivated because they never see the results. Providing timely, specific, and useful feedback to students, parents, and teachers on how well they have done might lead students to try harder.

APPENDIX A

Directions for Administering the Mathematics Concepts Subtest of the Iowa Test of Basic Skills (1979)

Now we are ready for the first mathematics test. Open your test booklets to page 73. (Pause) Find the section of your answer sheet for Test M-1: Mathematics Concepts. (Pause) Read the directions on page 73 silently while 1 read them aloud.

This is a test of how well you understand the number system and the terms and operations used in mathematics. Four answers are given for each exercise, but only one of the answers is right. You are to choose the one answer that you think is better than the others. Then, on the answer sheet, find the row of the answer numbered the same as the exercise. Fill in the answer space for the best answer.

Do not make any marks on the test booklet. Use your scratch paper for figuring. You will have 25 minutes for this test. If you finish early, recheck your work. Don't look at the other tests in the booklet. If you have questions, raise your hand, and I will help you after the others have begun. Now find your place to begin. (Pause)

Does everyone have the correct place? (Pause) Ready, BEGIN.

APPENDIX B

Selected Anecdotal Comments

Students

1. Third-Grade Girl: My teacher always tells us to get good scores on tests. I wanted to make her happy and my parents happy.
2. Fourth-Grade Boy: I think I did well. My teacher works hard with us. I also want my school to be the best.
3. Eighth-Grade Boy: I wanted to do really well for my teacher. She does a great job and I didn't want to let her down.
4. Seventh-Grade Girl: I just took the test, and really didn't think much about the instructions she gave.

Teachers

1. I don't know what the results will show but my gut feeling is that students in the experimental groups will do better. I think it's probably because of motivational reasons.
2. The script gives me a feeling of *family*. I think if we told students just how much we want them to do well, and that it will not only benefit themselves but the whole school, they will probably do better.
3. I think all the students (control and experimental) will probably do equally well, because we always stress how important the tests are.

REFERENCES

Association for Supervision and Curriculum Development (1991). *Update, 33*(1), 1–8.

Hill, K. T. (1980). Motivation, evaluation, and testing policy. In L. J. Fyans, Jr. (Ed.), *Achievement motivation: Recent trends in theory and research.* New York, NY: Plenum Press.

Iowa Test of Basic Skills normal curve equivalent norms (1978). Boston, MA: Houghton Mifflin.

Karmos, A. H., & Karmos, J. S. (1984, July). Attitudes toward standardized achievement tests and their relation to achievement test performance. *Measurement and Evaluation in Counseling and Development, 12,* 56–66.

Kelleghan, T., Madaus, G. F., & Arisian, P. M. (1982). *The effects of standardized testing.* Boston, MA: Kluwer-Nijhoff.

National Assessment Governing Board (1991). Issues for the 1994–1996 NAEP. Washington, DC: Author.

Nitco, A. J. (1985). Review of the Iowa Test of Basic Skills. In James V. Mitchell (Ed.), *The ninth mental measurements yearbook.* Lincoln, NE: Buros Institute.

Paris, S. G., Lawton, T. A., & Turner, J. C. (1991). Reforming achievement testing to promote students' learning. In C. Collins & Mangieri (Eds.), *Learning in and out of school.* Hillsdale, NJ: Lawrence Erlbaum Associates.

Uguroglu, M. E., & Walberg, H. J. (1979). Motivation and achievement: A quantitative synthesis. *American Educational Research Journal, 16,* 375–390.

Walberg, H. J. (1986). Synthesis of research on teaching. In M. C. Wittrock (Ed.), *Handbook of research on teaching.* New York, NY: Macmillan.

Brown, S. M., & Walberg, H. J. (1993). Motivational effects on test scores of elementary students. The Journal of Educational Research, **86**, 133–136. *Reprinted with the permission of the Helen Dwight Reid Educational Foundation. Published by Heldref Publications, 1319 Eighteenth St., N. W., Washington, DC 20036-1802. Copyright © 1993.*

MOTIVATIONAL EFFECTS ON TEST SCORES OF ELEMENTARY STUDENTS

SELF-TEST FOR TASK 1-A

The Topic

_____
_____
_____
_____
_____

The Procedures

_____
_____
_____
_____
_____
_____
_____

The Method of Analysis

_____
_____
_____
_____
_____

The Major Conclusion(s)

_____
_____
_____
_____
_____
_____
_____

A Really Good Art Teacher Would Be Like You, Mrs. C.: A Qualitative Study of a Teacher and Her Artistically Gifted Middle School Students

POLLY WOLFE
Ball State University

ABSTRACT In this paper, I examine the experiences of a teacher and her artistically gifted middle school students over the course of a school year in an attempt to add to the definition of effective teaching for that population. Identified as artistically gifted through a formal, multimethod process, the students experienced a five-phase curriculum rhythm (a construct devised to describe the chronology of the class content). The phases—image flood, reflection, art work, critique, and exhibition—enabled the veteran teacher to "translate" meaning in both the student world and the adult art world. The translation process influenced students' self-identification as artists and their abilities to reflect and to be more articulate about their art. Possible ramifications of this study include further exploration of the themes of curriculum rhythm and translation as components of art teacher effectiveness with artistically gifted and other student populations.

> A really good art teacher would be like you, Mrs. C. She would do neat projects, like this mural. And we would learn all that stuff, like mixing colors. She would be funny, too. Oh yea, she'd let us drink cokes during class, too. (Kelly, transcript; December 9, 1993)[1]

This quote by a seventh-grade participant in an artistically gifted program presents his simplified view of an area infrequently addressed in research: definitions of excellent or effective teaching relevant to the needs of artistically gifted students. Within his statement, Kelly addresses both pedagogical actions (high-interest projects, technical instruction) and personal attributes (flexibility and a sense of humor), which are mentioned in the literature as central to art teacher effectiveness (Clark & Zimmerman, 1995; Saunders, 1989).

In education literature, extensive effort has been expended to describe or define excellence and/or effectiveness (Amidon & Flanders, 1967). Long lists of qualities are proffered as characteristics of effective teachers (Langlois & Zales, 1991). In art education, studies disclose teacher traits such as artistic competence (Bradley, 1984; Hathaway, 1980; Saunders, 1989; Zimmerman, 1991, 1992), and the concomitant ability to share

that capability with students as important to art teacher effectiveness. Assuming a variety of roles, valuing art education, having organizational and evaluative skills, and being aware of student developmental and emotional needs exemplify the types of skills, knowledge, and behaviors that excellent art teachers exhibit (Capet, 1986; May, 1993; Saunders, 1989; Stokrocki, 1991; Thomas, 1992).

With the exception of two studies (Zimmerman, 1991, 1992), Clark and Zimmerman's (1984) statement that the "question of ideal teacher characteristics for students with superior abilities in the arts is virtually unexplored and unanswered at this time" (p. 94), still holds true. In learning more about effectiveness, there is a need to go beyond the "armchair lists" (Clark & Zimmerman, 1984) of teacher behaviors and characteristics. For example, what does artistic competence imply (Bradley, 1984; Hathaway, 1980; Saunders, 1989; Zimmerman, 1991)? How does a teacher use that competence with students?

Zimmerman (1991, 1992) studied painting instructors working with middle and high school artistically gifted students in a summer enrichment program. She noted one instructor who used storytelling to impart art history or technique information, allowing the reader a sense of the students' and teacher's intensity and learning atmosphere in the short-term program. However, no similar narratives of in-school artistically gifted programs and teachers exist. In this study, I explore what a group of artistically gifted students are doing, talking about, or thinking as their teacher plans and executes lessons directed toward their differentiated needs. Discerning how the teacher's and students' actions and reactions evolve as a year progresses has the potential to expand comprehension of teacher effectiveness beyond the listing of teachers' skills and characteristics.

RESEARCH FRAMEWORK

The theoretical framework of most qualitative research depends on the issues to be explored, the types of guiding questions asked by the researcher, the roles assumed by the researcher, and ways in which the study is written (Bresler, 1994; Ettinger, 1987; Jacob, 1987; Patton, 1990). Instead of generating hypotheses, as is common in quantitative research, broad-based open-ended guiding questions are developed for qualitative research. In this study such questions pertain to the teacher's role as instructional leader, the ways in which the teacher and students interact to construct meaning (or learn together), and the effects of the wider context

---

[1] Material which came directly from the collected data, such as Kelly's quote, is cited by type of data and date of data collection. The three types of data used were field notes, video notes, and transcripts. As unpublished raw data, these are not listed in the reference section.

(school, peers, family, and community) on learning. These questions reflect the broad-based focus of qualitative research. My intent in this study is to enhance the broad descriptive term *effectiveness* through the in-depth study of a teacher and her artistically gifted students.

Blumer's (1967) social interaction theory, which describes meaning-making as a social interactionary process modified through self and social interpretation, forms the theoretical basis of the study. Blumer posits that one learns through social interaction combined with internal dialogue and interpretation. In this study, I concentrated on the interactions between the teacher and students, between students and teacher and student, as well as students' internal dialogue revealed in their art work.

THE SETTING AND PARTICIPANTS

Criteria for site selection included conditions such as the presence of an ongoing artistically gifted program and a school district with administrative and community history of support for gifted and talented programming. The researcher selected the school district because it was one of the first in the state to act as a model site for gifted programs, initiating artistically gifted programs along with academic ones. The selected program began in 1987 as a pilot program for the school district.

The Community

The selected school is a largely middle-class community of 43,764 inhabitants (Department of Commerce, 1990) across the river from a university town of 25,907. With a low (3.8%) unemployment rate, the city has a varied economic base with 88% of the adults employed in manufacturing, service, government, and retail (Indiana Department of Work Force Development, 1993). The school district has one large high school (grades 9–12), two middle schools (grades 6–8), and 11 elementary schools (grades K–5). There are also 9 religion-based schools. A modest art museum, a historical museum, a performing and visual arts center, a library, a community orchestra, and the variety of offerings typical to a large university community provide opportunity for community arts involvement.

The School

Although school selection criteria were auxiliary to the teacher selection, administrative support for the artistically gifted program was central to the school site selection. The district and middle school administration supply the teacher with procedural aid in the gifted identification process, scheduling assistance, and funding for the teacher's inservice growth.

Sunnydale Middle School (a pseudonym, as are those of the teacher and students) is a typically midwestern set of brick rectangles, squatting in an "L" shape in an older section of the city. The middle school reflects the community both economically and ethnically. Of the students, 94% are Caucasian, 2% are African American, with the other 4% Hispanic, Asian, or "other." One third of all students receive the free or reduced-price lunch. Compared to students of similar economic constituency, the Sunnydale students score slightly better on the standardized tests than other middle schoolers across the state.

The Teacher

KC (or "Mrs. C." to her students) was selected because of her continuing educational pursuits, gifted and talented training (Feldhusen & Hansen, 1994), her activity in local and state art organizations, and community recognition as an active artist and teacher (Clark & Zimmerman, 1984, 1992; Zimmerman, 1991, 1992). Receiving a fellowship to attend Clark and Zimmerman's Artistically Talented Program in 1992, KC continually seeks ways to keep abreast of educational and artistic developments. She frequently mentors student- and first-year teachers. On the executive board of the state art education association, she is also active in several arts groups in the city.

The Students

All 26 students who participated in the program (called "Challenge Art") were part of the study. The sixth, seventh, and eighth graders were identified through a formal multimethod screening process based on self, teacher, and parent nomination forms, along with three drawing elements from the Clark's Drawing Abilities Test (Clark, 1989). An identification committee consisting of the teacher, the gifted-talented coordinator, and other art teachers rated the drawings and nomination forms, with the highest scoring students being invited to join the Challenge program. In 1993–1994, all of the Challenge Art students were Caucasian, although a few African-American and Asian students enrolled in prior Challenge Art classes. Fifty percent of the 1993–1994 students were also enrolled in one or more academic Challenge courses. First semester of the 1993–1994 year, the 21 students were evenly divided among grades six, seven, and eight. Five students dropped out second semester, and 5 new students were added, leaving a total of 9 seventh and eighth graders and 3 sixth graders. First semester there were 12 girls and 9 boys, while second semester there were 11 girls and 10 boys.

Researcher Role

In anthropology, the participant observer is one who attempts to become part of the target culture (Ettinger, 1987; Maitland-Gholson & Ettinger, 1994; Patton, 1990). Assuming that role, I attempted to blend with the Challenge Art class in order to experience things as they did.

Initially, I participated as a learner, sitting with different student social groups, who seemed to designate certain tables or room areas as their own. I listened, learned, drew, and painted with them, and they watched me struggle with similar decisions and problem solving. I asked their advice, and they reciprocated. As the year progressed, I shifted more into an assistant teacher role, circulating among the students, asking questions, coaching, and talking with participants. I also used that time to informally interview students, take notes, take photographs, and record class interactions on audio and video tape.

Beginning in October, the class met weekly after school for 1 to $2\frac{1}{2}$ hours. I attended 32 hours (95%) of the first semester meetings. Second semester I attended 29 hours (87%) of scheduled meetings. I met a few times with the summer school Challenge Art group, which contained many students who participated during the school year.

Data Sources and Collection

Primary data sources were field notes, taken during or shortly after class, audio or video tapes of observed classes, and interviews, along with slides and photos of student work. The video camera was placed to provide an overview of the entire classroom, while the audio recorder was placed on a table among 4 to 6 students, and moved to different tables each week. Since student social groups seemed to "claim" different areas of the room, or certain tables, moving the audio recorder allowed data collection from different social groups. Transcripts were made from both audio and video tapes, or notes taken while viewing video tapes. Multiple copies of transcripts were made, some of which were cut and placed in color-coded files to reflect analytic categories.

Slides, photos, and videos of art works became important data. These items were analyzed to reflect students' learning processes. Artifacts such as copies of student artwork, handouts, lesson plans, in-school bulletins, notes home, newspaper articles, and tapes of newscasts served as secondary data sources, augmenting the primary sources.

Data Analysis

Focusing on teacher-student, student-teacher, and student-student interactions, I began preliminary analysis within the first month of observation, using the constant comparison method of analysis, which involves combining inductive behavior coding with simultaneous comparison of all observed events (Glaser & Strauss, 1967; Strauss, 1987). The codes, which began as interaction descriptors, began to reveal patterns within the accumulation of coded transcripts. Using the coding system, 7 graduate and undergraduate art education students rated representative interaction behaviors in five video clips. Their coding reflected an inter-rater reliability of .91 with the codes I had assigned the same clips.

Linkages were sought between patterns, usually emerging from theoretical memos written as analysis progressed (Strauss, 1987). These codes, patterns, and linkages were triangulated with interview and secondary data information, and particularly scanned for disconfirming data, causing assertions to be revised to include that data.

CHALLENGE ART DESCRIPTION

The Teacher-Translator

The translation process is a construct the researcher developed to describe the complex phenomena of teacher and student behaviors, interaction patterns, and art work manifestations which reflect the intentional and unintentional classroom curricula in Challenge Art. Similar to Dillon's (1989) teacher as a cultural broker, the teacher-translator bridges the cultures/worlds of the artistically gifted middle school student and the art-world. The students' world includes school, peers, family, and community, while the artworld includes the local, regional, and international art world.

A translator is one who is fluent in more than one language. To translate efficiently, one must be able to clearly understand in one language, and almost simultaneously repeat the thought in another, retaining the same clarity, emphasis, and nuance. KC is a translator. Her "languages" are those of the artworld and the students' world. The artworld language is full of images, galleries, history, critical analyses, contact with other artists, aesthetic discussions, museums, books. The language of the students' world is full of references to the middle school culture of teachers, peers, who did what during lunch, who "likes" whom, who called whom last night, who got in trouble third period. . . .

KC is a veteran teacher. KC is an artist. She melds the two in a life-web which attracts artistically gifted middle school students around her in a bubble of giggly enthusiasm. "I have to do art," she says, and the kids begin to feel the love she has for her field. "My kids . . ." she says, and they know the beginning of trust. One cannot talk to her without hearing about one or the other—her kids, art. The synergy resulting from her dual passions of art and teaching forms the basis for KC's effectiveness as a teacher-translator.

KC's personal time is filled with the vocabulary of the artworld. Travel involves visits to galleries and museums, as she and her spouse deliver and retrieve his paintings from Chicago, or take their works to exhibitions in other Midwestern cities. She reads a number of art magazines regularly, feeling that it is important to be "on the cutting edge of our profession . . . as artists" (Transcript; December 2, 1992).

As part of the school world, KC operates successfully in both adult and student circles. With her colleagues, she serves on school and district committees, helps reading teachers by assisting on a bookmaking unit, is part of a Friday breakfast "club," and uses the Art Club to assist in school decoration and scenery construction for music and drama productions.

As part of the student world, KC interacts with the Challenge Art students as they burst through the door on Thursday afternoons, asking one how he did on an English test, another about a musical audition. Frequently snapping pictures, she tells them that "this one's for the yearbook," or "I want to show other art teachers what you're really like" (Transcript; March 3, 1994). The class milieu is full of energy and laughter. Even her disciplinary statements are humor-laced. "Tank, the Chumpette, forgot to put up his chair again," she says in mock desperation. "Poor Mrs. C." is the response (Video notes; December 9, 1993). The cheerful by-play is the background for the more serious work of artistic teaching-learning conducted through the translation process. This translation is conducted through the medium of KC's curriculum rhythm.

Curriculum Rhythm

Curriculum rhythm is a construct developed by the researcher to reflect what was observed in this classroom over time. KC's teaching has a pattern to it. Reflecting the need for differentiated instruction, the pattern used with her "regular" students is different from the one used with her Challenge Art students. KC gives her regular students a chronological overview of art history, an introduction to critical and aesthetic learning experiences combined with varied media experiences. Highly structured, her regular art classes extend 9 or 12 weeks, depending on grade level.

In Challenge Art, the thematic subject matter differs each semester, yet the pattern of learning and experience remains consistent. The thematic curriculum accommodates in-depth study and extended immersion in student-selected art projects. In Challenge Art, KC provides problem finding and problem solving. For the regular classes, KC's curriculum rhythm is staccato; for her Challenge Art class, the rhythm resembles a more sustained melody reflecting the differentiated needs of her high-interest students.

The curriculum rhythm is the medium through which KC translates the artworld to the students. Art teachers easily recognize the concept of the rhythm of an art class. If it is a production lesson, the students enter the room, put their backpacks, food, and assorted clothing aside, retrieve what they are working on, and settle down to listen to the teacher, who introduces or demonstrates the day's lesson. The students work on their projects, clean up and leave—a cycle repeated throughout the day for the teacher, throughout the term for the students.

KC employs that familiar rhythm for some Challenge Art classes, but her class rhythms fall within a larger overall pattern consisting of five phases. KC's Challenge Art classes are semester based, as is the duration of her curriculum rhythm cycle. The rhythm cycle is repeated each semester, differing in its thematic content. As the translation vehicle, each of the five phases serves to further meld the student world and the artworld. The five phases are: image flood, reflection, art work, critique, and exhibition. I observed two complete cycles and part of a third during this study. Each semester evidenced all five phases of the rhythmic cycle. Through these rhythmic cycles the translation process occurs as described here.

Phase one: The image flood. KC begins each cycle with a flood of images for her students. Assembling many books, slides, and visuals on the selected topic, she floods her students with visual images. The first semester of the study, KC selected the theme of American Western art for her Challenge Art curriculum. She showed slides and snapshots of a prior trip through the Southwest, had dozens of books and magazines (such as *Arizona Highways*) available to the students, while discussing the physical characteristics of the Southwest. She then showed slides of noted Southwestern artists' work. Some were 19th-century; some were current. She discussed various techniques used, along with color choices. Remington, T. C. Cannon, Victor Higgins, and O'Keeffe illustrate the exemplar variety. Following the slides, the students went to a museum specializing in Western art. Not one to overlook an instructional opportunity, KC distributed many of the books and magazines on Western art to the students on the bus, reiterating technique, subject matter, and style. At the museum, a capable, denim-clad docent discussed artists, painting, and historical context of the works. Finally, the students were allowed to explore. The 18 kids who attended the field trip went nose-close to works of interest, or sprawled on the floor to sketch. A museum patron commented to me about their keen absorption. When informed that they were middle schoolers, she expressed surprise. Informed that they were artistically gifted, she no longer wondered at their intensity (Field notes; October 13, 1993).

Winter semester, which centered on both public art and Victorian architecture, in preparation for painting a mural on a bridge underpass, included a similar image flood phase. Field trips included investigating community public art, visits to the city historical museum and a lovingly restored Victorian home, as well as a bus tour around the historic neighborhood. Experiences were supplemented with slides and with opportunities for students to photograph selected homes or architectural details for future reference. Student sketch books reveal gas lamps, intricate wrought iron fences, and replications of fish scale shingles. Along with visual stimulation, the students heard "stories" about the city founders who populated the neighborhood, providing a visual and verbal picture of 1800s life.

KC explained to a group of fellow art teachers the necessity of the image flood:

> As adults we have built a large store of images. We have looked at a lot of art. My students have limited experience. So it is my job to fill them with a wide variety of images to build up their imagic store. (Field notes; October 29, 1994)

As the students are bombarded with these images, they are also making critical choices in selecting images of interest and recording them either photographically or in their sketch books.

Phase two: Reflection. The second phase of the teaching-learning rhythm begins during the first, as the students select which images to sketch or photograph. This is the reflection phase wherein the students reflect upon what they have seen, and begin generating ideas for further development.

One student, intrigued with a tree seen at the Western art museum, began to sketch it at the museum. Upon returning to the classroom, Ward transferred that sketch to a masonite board as the centerpiece of his Western painting. His sketch book revealed that the texture of the tree was of greatest interest, while the form of the tree was altered and refined as he continued the painting and drawing process. That same semester, another sixth grade boy was drawn to the smooth surface of an O'Keeffe pueblo painting at the museum. Pursuing his interest in O'Keeffe, he found a black-and-white photo of a skull drawing showing an intricate antler structure. Using that as a springboard, Biker also used real bovine skulls as further reference for his drawing (Video notes; November 4, 1993).

As part of the reflective process, this combining and altering visual references occurred during the second semester as well, with a notable addition, that of written reflection. KC asked the students questions such as "Why did you choose your house or object? What style is it?" (Video notes; February 24, 1994). Sketchbook journaling included information such as chronological data about chosen buildings, architectural style, as well as stories about the object or building. Much of the resource information came from materials KC had photocopied at the historical museum. As work continued on the actual bridge murals, KC asked them to record how they felt about their work and the collaborative nature of the project. She indicated that the students should "have a record of what you did, so you can show your children someday" (Video notes; February 24, 1994). While the students laughed at the vision of their own progeny, the permanence of the project was impressed upon them.

The journals/sketchbooks were not only used in recording interesting images, developing ideas, and writing about personal and historic documentation, but were also used as references in later presentations. As the work on the mural progressed, the students were asked on numerous occasions to discuss their work with interested community groups and community media. The sketchbook material became a resource for those comments.

Phase three: Art work. As the students researched material for their art, using the abundant resources available, some generated ideas almost immediately. Others took more time, beginning with one idea, abandoning it and exploring another. KC helped them formulate ideas by referring them to the visual resources in the room (the slides, magazines, books, photos) and through technical instruction. Jack, a tall, bright, energetic seventh grader, talked about his Western art idea:

> I want it to represent all those old cowboy pictures. You know the ones where the cowboy rides off into the sunset. Only this is supposed to represent *all* the horses riding off into the sunset in *all* those movies. (Interview transcript; June 16, 1994)

Along with idea generation, two other components were central to the art-work phase, that of technical instruction and problem solving.

KC knew her students "wanted things to look real," so she gave them technique instruction which would aid them (Field notes; March 19, 1994). She used visual resources, demonstrated and repeatedly spoke of changing values to create the illusion of depth. "Those flat colors are a good start, Drake, now add some darker and some lighter right here" (Transcript; December 2, 1993). "See how this artist did that?" (Video notes; April 21, 1994). "Look at how these clouds are really flat on the bottom (referring to a photo), can you do that with yours?" (Transcript; December 9, 1993).

Formal and informal demonstrations were part of the mix. She spent two class periods in November discussing color theory and demonstrating scumbling, blending, and impressionistic paint strokes on her own painting. During the demonstration she discussed how painting was fun "because you can't make a mistake. You can let it dry and paint right over it" (Field notes; October 20 and 28, 1993).

In one-to-one situations, she would mix a bit of paint on the newspaper next to a painting, or add a little to a student's picture. The students seemed to regard this positively, as Elenie indicated: "Mrs. C. will start something on a little part of my painting, and then I get it" (Interview transcript; June 16, 1994). Most students did indeed "get it," demonstrating sophisticated layers of subtle shading in each semester's paintings.

When students encountered difficulty, they usually raised their hands or asked a friend. KC worked around the class clockwise, trying to touch base with each student as work sessions progressed. Students were confident in her help. Asked what they did when they had a problem, most responded, "I ask Mrs. C." If KC was unavailable, most indicated that they would wait until she was (Interview transcripts; June 21 and 22, 1994). Jack, however, admitted that he would "walk around and get noisy" until he figured out what to do (Interview transcript; June 21, 1994). Besides demonstrating, KC frequently referred students to the visual resources. "Why don't you look in . . ." "See if you can find the book where the picture of . . ." was a repeated song in Challenge Art. The book/visual reference table usually had two or three students thumbing through visuals to find their own help.

Informal peer instruction was common. However, it seemed limited to problems like color mixing or texture. "I mixed red and that dark blue and a little brown for this" (Video notes; March 10, 1994). They also sought affirmation from each other: "Clara, what do you think of this?" "It's great, Mildred, but you need some more of that dark stuff there. It's all the same" (Transcript, December 1, 1993). They sought this affirmation in the same tone as they asked about social things like "Do you like my new sweater?" From their friends, they expected positive answers. From KC they expected help.

While giving them tools to help them achieve realism, KC also encouraged individual styles. "Wow, that's surrealistic, Jack" (Transcript; December 21, 1993). "Your clouds have that impressionistic feel, Clara" (Transcript; December 21, 1993). The art history and stylistic references were not accidental; rather, she attempted to reinforce earlier learning along with providing affirmation.

Phase four: The critique. Two sorts of critical activities were evident in the Challenge Art class: in-process assessment and whole class critique. Documented in several studies (Stokrocki, 1991), in-process assessment occurs as a teacher helps a student decide how well he or she is progressing. Adler (1982) refers to the practice of facilitating the fine tuning of student skills as "coaching."

In the Challenge Art class it was difficult to separate the one-on-one technical instruction from in-process assessment, as the instructional and assessment comments were so interwoven. Students sought affirmation and direction at the same time. Clara said: "What do you think, Mrs. C?" KC replied: "Oh, Clara, it's beautiful. The way you have layered those colors is wonderful. Let's put it up there so you can see it from a distance" (Transcript; December 9, 1993). Balancing the painting on the chalk tray, KC and Clara discussed the contrast. Clara could see that her dark colors needed a little light to afford more clarity. Since she seemed to love thickly layered colors, she would happily continue, following KC's gentle suggestions. The chalkboard sessions would also be used to demonstrate a student's successful use of a technique to the class. Elenie's skull and cactus was used as an exemplar of skillful shading. The now familiar "dark-medium-light" exhortation was heard as KC showed how Elenie's highlighting and shading made her cactus seem real enough to prickle (Video notes; December 16, 1993).

At the end of the Western art unit, the students entered the room in a chorus of "oohs and aahs," discovering their paintings carefully balanced on drawers and counters along the north wall. As students perched on tables and chairs, KC announced that they would be "looking for things that work well, and for things that can be improved" (Transcript; December 21, 1993). Pointing out similarities and differences in technique and subject matter, KC had students point out evidences of scumbling, blending, and shading. She contrasted stylistic and color treatments of similar subject matter in discussing the several skull pastels and paintings. The effects of color on mood were tied to those who used Cannon's riotous colors and those who demonstrated "soft, velvety colors" (Transcript; December 21, 1993). Although teacher talk dominated, students were encouraged to voice opinions, make connections, and find further examples of concepts under discussion.

Phase five: Exhibition. The exhibition phase of KC's teaching/learning rhythm brings the students into the adult art-world. KC firmly believes in ensuring that her students' work is seen publicly. She takes slides of all finished work, using some slides to show her other students as exemplars, others for presentations at state and national conferences. Inevitably, she shows the students these slides before a presentation, telling them she is "showing them off to other art teachers" (Transcript; October 9,

1993; March 3, 1994). One major difference between this phase and the others is that it occurs beyond the semester framework. Thus, the work from the fall semester may be exhibited in the spring, depending on exhibition schedules. However, with the number of continuing students, and KC's consistency, each student knows his or her work will be exhibited.

KC organizes a county-wide K–8 art show, inviting friends and family to the opening. Two of the last three such exhibitions have shared space with adult artists. KC feels that this is important, as the arts community can recognize the quality of student work, while the students have the opportunity to interact with adult artists and their patrons (Interview transcript; December 2, 1992). A fall exhibition at a university gallery allowed students to explain how they had devised their sculptures to assembled friends, family, and art educators. Even the quietest students responded with alacrity to professors' questions, with answers like "I just stuffed the gloves with cotton and painted on them" (Video notes; October 30, 1993).

The second semester public art project gave students numerous opportunities to make public statements about their art. The first arose when they spoke to the local historic neighborhood association concerning their proposals for bridge murals. Using their sketch book information, students gave presentations on their drawings of buildings and events in the district, including historical information about the drawings' subjects. Mildred: "I did the circus wagon because they used to have a circus which would play in Murdock Park," followed by a bit she had written about circus day in the late 1800s. Two girls who had worked together on a drawing did a well-rehearsed presentation which included historical fact, architectural preference, and comments on their collaborative process. A blurb on the evening television news about the project was a precursor to other newscasts and newspaper features as the murals progressed. After the first newscast, KC made it a point to steer the reporters to the students, as she noted "they are the ones doing all the work" (Field notes; May 1, 1994).

The exhibitions, presentations, and news coverage had the effect of solidifying students' cognition about both art process and subject matter. The students' historical facts about local residences and events were well researched and accurately delivered. Describing their research and art process to an audience served to increase their identification as "real" artists among themselves, their peers, their families, and the community (Interview transcripts; June 16 and 21, 1994).

DISCUSSION AND IMPLICATIONS FOR FURTHER RESEARCH

Discussion
In this study, I attempted to describe how an effective art teacher and her artistically gifted students learn together over the course of a school year. Such description demonstrates how teacher and learning rhythms can impact a middle school class for artistically gifted students. The rhythm created by KC gave the students a familiarity with several art processes, both as observers and creators, as they absorbed, reflected upon, created, and interpreted art images. Through exhibition and their own explanations to various publics, the artistically gifted middle school students became

part of the art world as they helped others interpret and understand their work. Finally, the circular, rhythmic translation process cemented students' self-identification as "real" artists with peers, family, and community.

Clark and Zimmerman (1984, 1988) and Zimmerman (1991, 1992) discussed the importance to artistically gifted students of peer interaction and substantive teaching. KC and her students extend the understanding of what substantive teaching may be.

The nature of qualitative research is a collaboration between researcher and researched, as interpretations are clarified, or transcriptions revisited. The research process itself has helped KC reflect upon her own practice. Discussing and watching the growth of her students, through her own and another's eyes, has made her more aware of the choices she makes as she plans, prepares for, and teaches these students. She recognizes the rhythmic nature of her curriculum. "That's what I do, all right" (Field notes; October 29, 1994). She comprehends the translation concept, linking it with Renzulli's (1977) real products for real audiences (Field notes; October 29, 1994). Reflecting and collaborating allowed KC to perceive the effects of the publicity surrounding the bridge murals from her students' point of view. As a result, she plans to continue community-based projects for her Challenge students. Included in her future plans are a sculpture for the school and murals for a local community center.

Implications for Research
KC and teacher effectiveness definitions. This study began in a quest to understand more about teacher effectiveness in conjunction with artistically gifted students. Reflecting the nature of qualitative study, the results of this research are idiosyncratic. Yet KC does demonstrate some characteristics noted in effective art teachers such as valuing art education, organizational skills, and awareness of students' developmental and social needs (Capet, 1986; May, 1993; Saunders, 1989; Stokrocki, 1991; Thomas, 1992). She also meets some of Clark and Zimmerman's (1988, 1992, 1995) recommendations for teaching artistically gifted students: substantive teaching, providing access to professional level visual resources, and solid technical instruction. Evidenced in the discussion of each of the five phases is the way in which KC combines these qualities as she translates student-artworld languages making her teaching and the learning of her students effective.

Translation. The translation concept may be potentially significant for those responsible for developing meaningful artistically gifted/talented programming. Teachers and administrators may be able to discern the importance of bringing the outside world to the gifted/talented classroom and vice versa. Particularly at the tumultuous middle-school age, self-identification is an important issue. Clark and Zimmerman (1988) discussed the effects of positive peer interaction in artistically gifted classes. KC's students reflected that positive peer, family, school, and teacher influence. It may be meaningful to continue to monitor the students' self-identification as artists to discern any long-lasting effects.

If teachers and administrators can develop programs that allow students to see themselves as real contributors, artistically gifted students may have a better understanding of the positive ramifications of their special abilities.

Curriculum rhythm. The concept of curricular rhythm has potential as a tool for understanding more about teacher effectiveness. Although the idea developed as a way of describing the chronology of content in one class, it is a concept with resonance. Research may determine other styles of rhythms which exist in effective art teaching. Patterns of common traits may be found in particularly effective curricular rhythms, or effective rhythms may be found to be idiosyncratic to class or teacher. Rhythm types may link with specific teaching styles or unique populations in effective classrooms. Cross-case analysis, the method by which many qualitative studies are analyzed, may provide more illumination into the possibilities of the rhythm concept and its relationship to teaching effectiveness.

Eisner (1993) called for "fine grained study, description, interpretation, and evaluation of what actually goes on in art classrooms" (p. 54). This paper is an attempt to heed that call. KC is a highly effective teacher, working with her school's "best artists." She demonstrates many qualities cited in research as part of being effective. However, through her unique translation process, involving a carefully developed curriculum rhythm conducted with her gifted students' needs at the forefront, KC has forged her own brand of effectiveness from which we each may take pieces to use in our own practical or theoretical applications.

REFERENCES

Adler, M. (1982). *The paideia proposal.* New York: Collier Books, MacMillan.

Amidon, E., & Flanders, N. (1967). *The role of the teacher in the classroom.* Minneapolis, MN: Paul Amidon and Associates.

Blumer, H. (1967/1986). *Symbolic interactionism: Perspective and method.* Englewood Cliffs, NJ: Prentice Hall.

Bradley, L. (1984). Legislative impact on art teacher certification standards. *Action in Teacher Education 6*(4), 43–46.

Bresler, L. (1994). Zooming in on the qualitative paradigm in art education: Educational criticism, ethnography, and action research. *Visual Arts Research, 20*(1), 1–21.

Capet, M. (1986). An exploratory study of teaching visual arts grades one through eight: A phenomenological account of teacher cues, assumptions, intuition, and dialog during a studio experience and their implications for future research. (Doctoral dissertation, University of California, Los Angeles, 1986). *Dissertation Abstracts International.* (University Microfilms no. ADD85-00582).

Clark, G. (1989). Screening and identifying students talented in the visual arts: Clark's Drawing Abilities Test. *Gifted Child Quarterly, 33*(3), 98–105.

Clark, G., & Zimmerman, E. (1984). *Educating artistically talented students.* Syracuse, NY: Syracuse University Press.

Clark, G., & Zimmerman, E. (1988). Views of self, family background, and school: Interviews with artistically talented students. *Gifted Child Quarterly, 32*(4), 340–346.

Clark, G., & Zimmerman, E. (1992). *Issues and practices related to identification of gifted and talented students in the visual arts.* Storrs, CT: The National Research Center on the Gifted and Talented.

Clark, G., & Zimmerman, E. (1995). Programming opportunities for students gifted and talented in the visual arts. *Translations: From theory to practice, 5*(1), 1–6.

Department of Commerce. (1990). *1990 Census of population and housing: Population and housing characteristics for census tracts and block numbering areas 1990 CPH-3-199, Lafayette-West Lafayette. IN MSA.* Washington, DC: U.S. Government Printing Office.

Dillon, D. (1989). Showing them that I want them to learn and that I care about who they are: A microethnography of the social organization of a secondary low track English reading classroom. *American Educational Research Journal, 26*(2), 227–259.

Eisner, E. (1993). The emergence of new paradigms for educational research. *Art Education, 46*(6), 50–55.

Ettinger, L. (1987). Styles of on-site descriptive research: A taxonomy for art educators. *Studies in Art Education, 28*(2), 79–95.

Feldhusen, J., & Hansen, J. (1994). A comparison of trained and untrained teachers of gifted students. *Gifted Child Quarterly, 38*(3), 115–123.

Glaser, B., & Strauss, A. (1967). *The discovery of grounded theory: Strategies for qualitative research.* Chicago: Aldine.

Hathaway, J. (Ed.). (1980). *Art education: Middle/junior high school* (3rd printing). Reston, VA: National Art Education Association, 59–63.

Indiana Work Force Development (1993). *Highlights: Tippecanoe County, 1993 edition.* Lafayette, IN: Indiana Work Force Development.

Jacob, E. (1987). Qualitative research traditions: A review. *Review of Educational Research, 57*(1), 1–50.

Langlois, D., & Zales, C. (1991). Anatomy of a top teacher. *American School Board Journal, 178,* 44–46.

Maitland-Gholson, J., & Ettinger, L. (1994). Interpretative decision making in research. *Studies in Art Education, 36*(1), 18–27.

May, W. (1993). Good teachers making the best of it: Case studies of elementary art and music teaching. *Elementary Subjects' Center Series No. 100.* East Lansing, MI: Office of Educational Research and Improvement, Washington, DC, Center for Learning and Teaching of Elementary Subjects. (ERIC Documentation Reproduction Service No. ED 360 230.)

Patton, M. (1990). *Qualitative evaluation and research methods* (2nd edition). Newbury Park, CA: Sage Publications.

Renzulli, J. (1977). *The Enrichment triad model: A guide for developing defensible programming for the gifted and talented.* Mansfield Center, CT: Creative Learning Press.

Saunders, H. (1989). How to select an effective art teacher. *NASSP Bulletin,* May 1989, 4, 54–69.

Stokrocki, M. (1991). A decade of qualitative research in art education: Methodology expansions and pedagogical explorations. *Visual Arts Research, 17*(1), 42–51.

Strauss, A. (1987). *Qualitative analysis for social scientists.* New York: Cambridge University Press.

Thomas, R. (1992). Art Education: Program evaluation report. Orlando, FL: Orange County Public Schools. (ERIC Document Reproduction Service No. ED 357 057.)

Zimmerman, E. (1991). Rembrandt to Rembrandt: A case study of a memorable painting teacher of artistically talented 13–16 year old students. *Roeper Review, 13*(2), 76–80.

Zimmerman, E. (1992). A comparative study of two painting teachers of talented adolescents. *Studies in Art Education, 33*(3), 174–185.

A Really Good Art Teacher Would Be Like You, Mrs. C.: A Qualitative Study of a Teacher and Her Artistically Gifted Middle School Students

SELF-TEST FOR TASK 1-C

1. Research approach:

   _____

   _____

2. Research approach:

   _____

   _____

3. Research approach:

   _____

   _____

4. Research approach:

   _____

   _____

5. Research approach:

   _____

   _____

6. Research approach:

   _____

   _____

7. Research approach:

   _____

   _____

"Some graduate students spend many anxiety-ridden days and sleepless nights worrying about where they are going to find the problem they need for their thesis or dissertation."
(p. 40)

SELECTING AND DEFINING A RESEARCH TOPIC

OBJECTIVES

After reading Chapter 2, you should be able to do the following:

1. Make a list of at least three educational topics for which you would be interested in conducting a research study.
2. Select one of the topics and identify 10 to 15 complete references that directly relate to the selected problem. The references should include multiple sources (e.g., books, periodicals, Internet reports, etc.).
3. Distinguish between quantitative and qualitative methods of starting a research study.
4. Read and abstract the references you have listed.
5. Formulate a testable or descriptive hypothesis for your problem.

   Note: These objectives will form the basis for Task 2.

Selection and definition of a research topic is the first stage in applying the scientific and disciplined inquiry method. The *research topic* (also called the research question, problem, or purpose) focuses and provides structure for the remaining steps in the scientific and disciplined inquiry method; it is the thread that binds everything else together. The basic function of the research topic is to focus the study to a defined, manageable size. One of the common difficulties that arises among researchers seeking to develop a research topic is

selecting one that is so broad and complex that the researcher is unable to implement and complete it. Usually the first topic identified is too broad to be manageable for study, so the researcher must narrow its scope. Selecting and defining a topic is a very important component of the research process and should entail considerable thought.

The research topic that you ultimately select is the topic you will work with in succeeding stages of this text. Therefore, it is important that you select a problem relevant to your area of study and of particular interest to you. Given that you will be living with your study for a long time, it is especially important that you select a topic that will hold your interest through its completion.

The goal of Chapter 2 is for you to identify and define a meaningful topic, conduct an adequate review of related literature, and state a testable hypothesis. After you have read this chapter, you should be able to perform the following task.

TASK 2

Write an introduction for a quantitative research plan. Include a statement of the research topic, a statement concerning the importance or significance of the topic, a brief review of related literature, and a testable hypothesis regarding the outcome of your study. Include definitions of terms where appropriate (see Performance Criteria, p. 71)

IDENTIFYING A TOPIC OR QUESTION TO RESEARCH

For most of our school careers we are taught to solve problems of various kinds. Ask most people to list the 10 most important outcomes of education, and somewhere on the list will invariably be problem solving. Now, after many years of emphasis on solving problems, you face a research task that asks you not to *solve* but to *find* a problem or topic to study. If you are like most people, you have had little experience in doing this. For this reason, beginning researchers often view the selection of a research topic as the most difficult step in the whole research process. Some graduate students spend many anxiety-ridden days and sleepless nights worrying about where they are going to find the problem they need for their thesis or dissertation.

THE REALITIES OF RESEARCH AND TOPIC IDENTIFICATION

As you begin to work through the many aspects of educational research, you will be embarking on an important learning experience. We must highlight two initial realities of this experience. First, it is important for you to be clear about what educational research is and is not. Research is not haphazard data gathering. It is not a process in which the researcher knows the outcome before the study is completed. It is not the selective or biased interpretation of results. It is not verifiable by independent, nonbiased researchers. Conversely, true research is guided by an identified topic or issue. It describes a plan to carry out the research. It collects pertinent data in a systematic and unbiased manner. It analyzes the data and makes it available to other researchers for examination.

Second, it is important to understand the human face of education research. Textbooks tend to present topics in a linear form: do this and then this and then this and ultimately you'll get to where you want to be. While a linear format provides a necessary template for student learning, the reality of educational research is not solely linear. It is true that serendipity, good luck, or happenstance occasionally occurs in research, but not very often. In reality, educational research is truly a process of trial and error. As you work though your research topic, you will find things that "don't fit" as expected, or topics that are not as clear on paper as they were in your head, or topics that require considerable rethinking and writing. That is the reality of research. However, working through these realities will be an important and satisfying measure of your understanding, more important and satisfying than having everything work perfectly the first time.

SOURCES OF RESEARCH TOPICS

Where do research topics, questions, purposes, or problems come from? Where should you look to ferret out topics to study? Four main sources of research topics are theories, personal experiences, replications, and library searches.

Theories

One of the most meaningful sources of research topics is derived from theory. A **theory** is an organized body of concepts, generalizations, and principles that can be subjected to investigation. There are many educationally relevant theories and topics from which problems can be drawn, such as theories of learning and behavior. For example, Piaget posited a theory of cognitive development that had four stages of development: sensorimotor stage (birth to age 2), preoperational stage (ages 2 to 7), concrete operational stage (ages 7 to 11), and formal operational stage (ages 11 to adulthood). At each level Piaget indicated what children could or could not do. Examining whether aspects of Piaget's theory operate as suggested could be the basis for many possible topics. For example, one could study whether children who receive a great deal of attention and verbal interaction reach the concrete operational stage earlier than those who received little attention and verbal interaction. If the high attention/verbal group did reach the concrete operational stage before the low attention/verbal group, it would suggest that entry into the stage varied not just on age, but also on children's experiences. Think of two other theories that are popular in education and identify from them a few more topics

LIST SERVES

Researchers frequently use e-mail to solicit advice and feedback and conduct dialogue with peers and experts in their fields. The most common way to do so is by subscribing to an electronic mailing list, commonly known as a *listserve*. These lists are designed by organizations or special interest groups to facilitate communication among their members. Through this list, you can expect to receive announcements and bulletins related to your area of interest. In addition you can post comments or questions on the listserve. Your messages will be read by members of the listserve, who have the option of responding to you personally or to the mailing list as a whole. A well-known example is LISTSERV™, run by L-Soft International, Inc.

A listserve is a good resource to consult when you are devising a research question. You can ask listserve members what they think of a particular topic, if they know of other research pertaining to your topic, or for links (electronic or otherwise) to resources of interest. You can also bounce ideas off other listserve members at each stage of your research. You can even ask for volunteers to read your work in progress!

To subscribe to a listserve, you generally are required to send a short e-mail message to the listserve. Once subscribed, you will receive detailed information about how to post messages on the listserve, how to unsubscribe, etc. Examples of useful education listserves include the following:

American Educational Research Association List
    (aera@lists.asu.edu)
    (aera@listsx.asu.edu)
AERA-K Division Teaching and Teacher Education listserve
    (aera-k@lists.asu.edu)
    (aera-k@listsx.asu.edu)
Educational Administration Discussion List
    (edad-l@wvnvm.wvnet.edu)
Educational Resources on the Internet
    (edres-l@listserve.unb.ca)

A useful Web site to consult in your search for appropriate listserves is http://www.lsoft.com/lists/listref.html. This site, sponsored by L-Soft International, contains a catalogue of LISTSERV™ lists. At this site, you can browse over 52,599 public lists on the Internet, search for mailing lists of interest, and get information about host sites. A recent search for education lists yielded 732 LISTSERV™ mailing lists.

---

to investigate. Topics focused on aspects of a theory are not only conceptually rich, they also provide information that confirms or disconfirms some aspect of the theory. They also suggest additional studies that would further test the theory.

Personal Educational Questions

A second common way to identify research topics is to examine some of the questions we commonly ask ourselves. It is hard to imagine an educator who has never had a hunch concerning a better way to do something (e.g., to increase learning or improve student behavior) or asked questions about a program or materials whose effectiveness was untested (for example, questioning why a writing program was successful or science materials were not). We observe schools, teachers, programs, and news articles about schooling, and we ask ourselves questions usually stated in the following ways: "Why does that happen?" "What causes that?" "What would happen if . . . ?" and "How would a different group respond to this?" Normally we think briefly about such questions and get back to our everyday business. But such questions are probably the most common source of research topics because they are of interest to us. How do teachers structure their classroom cultures in the first few days of school? Would achievement go up if students were given quizzes each day on the prior day's instruction? Would I get the same results with high- and low-achieving students if I emphasized peer review in my instruction? What would happen to teacher performance if we evaluated teachers three times a year at unannounced times instead of at a single, preannounced time? Serendipity, also known as happenstance or being in the right place at the right time, is all around us and is often the source of research topics. Sensitivity to what is happening around us is an important inquiry skill to cultivate.

A veritable gold mine of research topics arises out of the questions we ask ourselves every day about education, topics that arise in class discussion, articles in local newspapers and educational journals, and similar sources. Note, first, that this approach to finding research topics is appropriate for both qualitative (How do teachers structure their classroom culture?) and quantitative (Would achievement go up with more frequent use of quizzes?) topics. Note, also, that most of the initial topics need to be refined and clarified before they become suitable research topics.

Replication

A third source of research topics is **replication,** meaning "doing it again." We noted in Chapter 1 that no single study, regardless of its focus or breadth, provides the certainty needed to assume that similar results will occur in all or most similar situations. We also noted that progress through research usually comes from accumulated understandings and explanations. Replication is a tool used to provide such accumulated information.

In most cases, a replication is not carried out identically with the original study. Rather, some feature or features of the original study are altered in an attempt to "stretch" the original findings. Thus, the researcher might select a different sample of participants for the replication in the hope of determining whether the results obtained are the same as those of the original study. Or, the replication might examine a different kind of community, a different kind of student, a different classroom climate, a different questionnaire, or a different method of data analysis. There are many interesting and useful ways to replicate studies in the many domains of education.

Library Search

Another commonly cited source of research topics is a *library search.* Many students are encouraged to immerse themselves in the library and read voraciously in their area of study until a research topic emerges. Although some research topics do emerge from library immersion, they are considerably fewer than those emerging from theory, personal experience, and replication. Trying to identify a topic amid the enormous possibilities in a library is akin to looking for a needle in a haystack; sometimes we find it, but not very often. Clearly libraries are essential sources of information in the research process. However, the library is most useful after a topic has been narrowed. Then library resources can help the researcher gather information to place the topic in perspective, find what has already been done on the topic, and suggest methods for carrying out examination of a topic.

The first step in selecting a topic is to identify a general topic or problem that is related to your area of expertise and is interesting to you. Examples of general topics are decision making in the schools, manipulatives for elementary mathematics, the effects of standardized testing, paraprofessionals in the elementary school, busing schoolchildren, and whole language reading. Note that these topic areas are broad and inclusive, containing many, many more specific potential research topics. Such general areas have to be narrowed to a more focused and manageable research topic or problem. Remember, you will be spending a great deal of time reading about, planning, and carrying out your ultimate research topic. Choosing a topic that is of interest to you will help maintain your focus during the months of conducting and writing your study.

Narrowing the Topic

For most quantitative researchers and some qualitative researchers, the next step is to narrow the general topic area to a more specific, researchable one. A topic that is too broad can lead to grief. First, a broad topic enlarges the scope of the review of related literature that one must inevitably conduct (discussed in the next section), likely resulting in many extra hours spent in the library. Second, broad topics complicate the organization of the review itself. Finally, and more importantly, a topic that is too broad tends to result in a study that is general, difficult to carry out, and difficult to interpret. Conversely, a well-defined, manageable problem results in a well-defined, manageable study.

Note the difference between a quantitative approach (based on deductive reasoning) and a qualitative approach (based on inductive reasoning). A quantitative research topic typically requires that the researcher spell out the topic studied, the hypotheses related to the topic, the strategies for conducting the research study, and the methods of collecting and analyzing the data prior to initiating the study. Thus, for quantitative research, narrowing the general topic area into a more specific and manageable research topic is essential. Without such a topic, hypotheses, instruments, strategies, and analyses cannot be specified. Conversely, for most qualitative research, it is desirable to enter the research setting with only a general topic area in mind. Based on what is observed in the research setting over a period of time, the qualitative researcher will formulate a narrowed research topic.

One way to narrow your topic is to talk to your advisors and to specialists in your area about specific suggestions for study. Another way is to read sources that provide overviews or summaries of the current status of research in your topic area. Search through handbooks that contain many chapters focused on research in a particular area (*Handbook of Research in Educational Administration, The Handbook of Educational Psychology, Handbook of Research on Curriculum, Handbook of Research on Teacher Education, Handbook of Sport Psychology, International Handbook of Early Child Education,* and many more). You could also check the *Encyclopedia of Educational Research* or journals such as the *Review of Educational Research,* which provide reviews of research in many areas. These sources often identify "next-step" studies that need to be conducted. The suggested next step might involve a logical extension of another study or a replication of the study in a different setting. For example, a study investigating the effectiveness of computer-assisted instruction in elementary arithmetic might suggest the need for similar studies in other curriculum areas. Bear in mind that at this stage in the research process you seek general research overviews that describe the nature of research in an area and that can suggest more specific topics in your chosen area.

In narrowing the problem area you should select an aspect of the general topic area that is related to your area of expertise. For example, the general problem area "the use of reviews to increase retention" could generate many specific problems, such as "the comparative effectiveness of immediate versus delayed review on the retention of geometric concepts" and "the effect of review games on the retention of vocabulary words by second graders." In your efforts to sufficiently delineate a problem, however, be careful not to get carried away; a problem that is too narrow is just as bad as a problem that is too broad. A study such as "the effectiveness of pre-class reminders in reducing instances of pencil sharpening during class time" would probably contribute little, if anything, to education knowledge.

Selecting a good topic is well worth the time and effort. As mentioned previously, there is no shortage of significant educational problems that need to be researched; there is really no excuse for selecting a trite, overly narrow problem. Besides, it is generally to your advantage to select a worthwhile problem; you will certainly get a great deal more out of it professionally and academically. If the subsequent study is well conducted and reported, not only will you earn a good grade and make a contribution to knowledge, but you might find your work published in a professional journal. The potential personal benefits to be derived from publication include increased professional status and job opportunities, not to mention tremendous self-satisfaction.

CHARACTERISTICS OF GOOD TOPICS

By definition, a research topic involves an issue in need of investigation. It follows that a fundamental characteristic of any research topic is that it is researchable or doable. A *researchable* topic is one that can be investigated through collecting and analyzing data. Problems dealing with philosophical or ethical issues are not researchable. Research can assess how people "feel" about such issues but research cannot resolve them. In education there are a number of issues that make great topics for debates (e.g., "Should prayer be allowed in the schools?" "Should students be grouped homogeneously or heterogeneously?" "Should students be held back in grade if they fail to meet defined standards of achievement?") but they are not researchable problems; there is no way to resolve these topics through collecting and analyzing data. Generally, topics or questions that contain the word *should* cannot be answered by research of any kind, because they ultimately are matters of opinion.

Note, however, that one could carry out research studies that examine the effects on teachers and students of school prayer, grouping practices, or being held back in grade. Do you see how a slight wording change creates researchable topics? Such studies, as worded, can tell us about the varied consequences of these practices, but the decision of what should be done in a school or classroom involves issues that go beyond the abilities of any research study. Issues of cost, educational philosophy, teacher and parental beliefs about the nature of schooling, and views about how students best learn are some of the other factors that would enter into the debate over what should be done. Research findings can inform decision making, but they cannot and should not be the sole or main determinant of what should or should not be done.

A second characteristic of a good research topic is that it has theoretical or practical significance. People's definitions of *significant* vary, but a general rule of thumb is that a significant study is one that contributes in some way to improve or understand education or educational practice. A third major characteristic of a good topic is that it is a good topic for you. The fact that you have chosen a topic of interest to you, in an area in which you have expertise, is not sufficient. It must be a topic that you can adequately investigate given your current level of research skill, the available needed resources, and sufficient time to carry out the study. The availability of appropriate participants and measuring instruments, for example, is an important consideration. A fourth important characteristic is that the research is ethical. That is, the research must not potentially harm the research participants. *Harm* encompasses not only physical danger, but also affective and emotional danger. Fifth, and very important, is the interest in your topic. The characteristics of a good topic are summarized in Figure 2.1. Furthermore, as a beginning researcher, you likely have access to one or more faculty advisors. They can help you to assess the feasibility of your topic.

FIGURE 2.1
Characteristics of a good research topic.

1. *The topic is interesting.* It will hold the researcher's interest through the entire research process.
2. *The topic is researchable.* It can be investigated through the collection and analysis of data and it is not stated as a topic seeking to determine what *should* be done.
3. *The topic is significant.* It contributes in some way to the improvement or understanding of education theory or practice.
4. *The topic is manageable.* It fits the researchers' level or research skill, needed resources, and time restrictions.
5. *The topic is ethical.* It does not contain practices or strategies that might embarrass or harm participants.

STATING THE RESEARCH TOPIC

Stating Quantitative Research Topics

The nature of a research topic varies in form and specificity according to the type of research undertaken and the preferences of the researcher. For a quantitative study, a well-written statement of the topic generally describes the variables of interest, the specific relationship between those variables, and, ideally, the nature of the participants involved (i.e., gifted students, learning-disabled fourth graders, teenage mothers). An example of a problem statement might be: "The topic to be investigated in this study is the effect of positive reinforcement on the quality of 10th graders' English compositions." In this statement, the variables to be examined are "positive reinforcement" and "quality of English compositions." The participants will consist of 10th graders.

Other possible topic statements:

- "The topic to be investigated in this study is secondary teachers' attitudes toward required afterschool activities."
- "The purpose of this study is to investigate the relationship between school entrance age and reading comprehension skills of primary-level students."
- "The problem to be studied is the effect of wearing required school uniforms on the self-esteem of socioeconomically disadvantaged sixth-grade students."
- "Does the effect of periodic home visits diminish the recidivism rate of middle school juvenile offenders?"

Try to identify the variable or variables in each of these examples and suggest what type of quantitative research method would likely be employed to carry out the study.

Stating Qualitative Research Topics

Qualitative research topics often are stated later in a written study and stated more generally than quantitative ones, because in many cases, the qualitative researcher needs to spend time in the research context for the focus of the study to emerge. Remember, the qualitative researcher usually is much more attuned to the specifics of the context in which the study takes place than is the quantitative researcher. Qualitative topic statements initially tend to be general, eventually becoming narrowed as the researcher learns more about the research context and its inhabitants. Qualitative research topics are typically stated as in the following examples:

- "The purpose of this study is to describe the nature of children's engagement with mathematics. The intention is to gather details about children's ways of entering into and sustaining their involvement with mathematics."
- "This qualitative study examines how members of an organization identify, evaluate, and respond to organizational change. The study examines what events members of an organization identify as significant change events and whether different events are seen as significant subgroups in the organization."
- "The purpose of this research is to study the social integration of disabled children in an integrated third-grade class."

Placement and Nature of the Topic Statement in a Study

A statement of the topic is the first component of the introductory sections of both a research plan (see Chapter 3) and the completed research report. The topic statement gives direction to the remaining aspects of the research plan and report. The statement should be accompanied by a presentation of the topic's background, a justification for the study in terms of its significance, and, often, a list of limitations of the study. The *background* includes information needed by readers to understand the nature of the topic. The topic should be justified in terms of its contribution to educational theory or practice. For example, an introduction might begin with a topic statement such as, "The purpose of this study is to compare the effectiveness of salaried paraprofessionals and nonsalaried parent volunteers with respect to the reading achievement of first-grade children." This statement might be followed by a discussion concerning (1) the role of paraprofessionals, (2) increased utilization of paraprofessionals by schools, (3) the expense involved, and (4) the search for alternatives, such as parent volunteers. The significance of the problem would be that if parent volunteers and paid paraprofessionals are equally effective, volunteers can be substituted for salaried paraprofessionals at great savings. Any educational practice that might increase achievement at no additional cost is certainly worthy of investigation! Qualitative researchers would likely wait to examine pertinent research so they may first draw their own perspectives on the topic and settings. They would want to form their own perspective before being influenced by the literature. Once a qualitative researcher has a sense of the topic and issues, she might turn to the literature for further information.

After a topic has been carefully selected, delineated, and stated, the researcher is ready to attack the review of related literature. The researcher typically has a tentative hunch or hypothesis that guides the review. In the previous example, the tentative hypothesis would be that parent volunteers are equally effective as salaried paraprofessionals. It is likely that the tentative hypothesis will be modified, even changed radically, as a result of a more extensive review of the literature related to the topic. It does, however, give direction to the literature search and narrows its scope to include only relevant topics.

REVIEW OF RELATED LITERATURE

Having happily found a suitable topic, the beginning researcher is usually "raring to go." Too often the review of related literature is seen as a necessary evil to be completed as fast as possible so that one can get on with the "real research." This perspective is due to a lack of understanding of the purpose and importance of the review, and to a feeling of uneasiness on the part of students who are not sure exactly how to go about writing the review. The lack of practice that makes finding a topic difficult for many beginning researchers is revisited when they are faced with the need to write a literature review, as they have had little or no prior experience. Nonetheless, the review of related literature is as important as any other component of the research, and it can be conducted quite painlessly if it is approached in an orderly manner. Some researchers even find the process quite enjoyable!

DEFINITION, PURPOSE, AND SCOPE

The review of related literature involves systematically identifying, locating, and analyzing documents containing information related to the research problem. These documents can include articles, abstracts, reviews, monographs, dissertations, books, other research reports, and electronic media. The literature review has several important functions that make it well worth the time and effort. Its major purpose is to determine what has already been done that relates to your topic. It provides the understandings and insights necessary to develop a logical framework into which your topic fits. The review tells you what has been done and, in so doing, also suggests what needs to be done. Studies can provide the rationale for your research hypothesis, while indications of what needs to be done often form the basis for justifying the significance of your study.

Another important function of the literature review is to point out research strategies and specific data collection approaches that have and have not been found to be productive in investigating topics such as yours. This information will help you to avoid other researchers' mistakes and to profit from their experiences. It may suggest approaches and procedures that you previously had not considered. For example, suppose your topic involved the comparative effects of a brand-new experimental method versus the traditional method on the achievement of eighth-grade science students. The review of literature might reveal 10 related studies already conducted that have found no differences in achievement between the two methods. Several of the studies, however, might suggest that the brand-new method may be more effective for certain kinds of students than for others. Thus, you might reformulate your topic to involve the comparative effectiveness of the brand-new method versus the traditional method on the achievement of low-aptitude eighth-grade science students.

Being familiar with previous research also facilitates interpretation of your study results. The results can be discussed in terms of whether and how they agree with previous findings. If the results contradict previous findings, you can describe differences between your study and the others, providing a rationale for the discrepancy. If your results are consistent with other findings, your report should include suggestions for the next step; if they are not consistent, your report should include suggestions for studies that might resolve the conflict.

Beginning researchers often have difficulty in determining how broad their literature review should be. They understand that all literature directly related to their topic should be reviewed; they just don't know when to quit! They have trouble determining which articles are "related enough" to their topic to be included. Unfortunately, there is no formula that can be applied to solve the problem; you must base your decisions on judgment and the advice of your teachers or advisor. Happily, there are some general guidelines that can assist you. First, avoid the temptation to include everything you find; bigger does not mean better. A smaller, well-organized review is definitely preferred to a review containing many studies that are peripherally related to the problem. Second, heavily researched areas usually provide enough references directly related to a specific problem to eliminate the need for relying on less related studies. For example, the role of feedback in learning has been extensively researched for both animals and human beings, for verbal learning and nonverbal learning, and for a variety of different learning tasks. If you were concerned with the relationship between frequency of feedback and chemistry achievement, you would probably not have to review feedback studies related to animal learning. Third, and conversely, new or little-researched problem areas usually require review of any study related in some meaningful way to the problem in order to develop a logical framework for the study and a sound rationale for the research hypothesis. For example, a study of the effects on GPA of an exam for non-English speaking students who are required to pass it to graduate would probably include in its literature search studies involving English as a Second Language (ESL) classes and the effects of culture-specific grading practices, and studies identifying strategies to improve the learning of ESL students. A few years from now there will probably be enough research on the academic consequences of such an exam on non-English speaking students to permit a much more narrowly focused literature review.

A common misconception is that the worth of a topic is a function of the amount of literature available on it. This is not the case. There are many new, important areas of research for which there is comparatively little available literature; the effects of high-stakes testing is one such area. The very lack of such research often increases the worth of its study. On the other hand, the fact that 1,000 studies have already been done in a given problem area does not mean there is no further need for research in that area. Such an area will generally be very well developed with additional needed research readily identifiable.

GETTING STARTED

Because it will be a second home to you, at least for a while, you should become familiar with the library before beginning your review. Most libraries, especially university libraries, provide help and education in the use of their resources. It is very important that you familiarize yourself with these many resources. Time spent initially will save more in the long run. You should find out what references are available and where they are located. You should also be familiar with services offered by the library, as well as the rules and regulations regarding the use of library materials. It also might be useful to identify three or so people who are actively conducting research in your topic area. Once identified, you could contact them to request copies of their recent articles on your topic and suggestions for useful references in the area. They might even make suggestions.

A common question asked about a literature review is, "How should I start?" Eventually you will have to examine a range of sources that are pertinent to your topic. However, to start, it is better to narrow the initial search to pertinent educational encyclopedias, handbooks, and annual reviews. These and similar resources provide broad overviews of issues in one or many subject areas, as well as initial references to examine. They allow you to get a picture of your topic in the broader context and help you understand where it fits in the field. Significant library-related technological advances have been made and libraries vary greatly in their ability to capitalize on increasingly available options. Note, however, while librarians are usually very willing to help individuals, you should learn to use the library; the librarian might not be as cheerful the ninth time you approach as he was the first time!

IDENTIFYING KEYWORDS

Having formulated your problem and acquainted yourself with the library, there is one more thing you need to do before you go marching merrily off into the book stacks—make a list of **keywords** to guide your literature search. Most of the sources you consult will have alphabetical subject indexes to help you locate specific references. You will look in these indexes under the keywords you have selected. For example, if your problem concerns the effect of interactive multimedia on the achievement of 10th-grade biology students, the logical keywords would be *interactive multimedia* and *biology*. You will also need to think of alternative words under which your topic might be listed. For example, references related to this problem might be found using the keywords *multimedia* or *interactive videodiscs* rather than just *interactive*. Usually, the keywords will be obvious; sometimes you may have to play detective.

Some years ago a student was interested in the effect of artificial turf on knee injuries in football. He looked under every keyword he could think of, such as *surface, playing surface, turf,* and *artificial turf*. He could find nothing. Since he knew that studies had been done, he kept trying. When he finally did find a reference, it was listed under, of all things, *lawns!* Identifying keywords is usually not such a big deal. In looking in initial sources you might identify additional keywords that will help you in succeeding sources. However, if you give some thought initially to possible keywords, it will facilitate an efficient beginning to a task that requires organization. After you have identified your keywords, you will finally be ready to begin to consult appropriate sources.

IDENTIFYING YOUR SOURCES

Many sources of literature may relate to a given problem. In general, however, educational researchers commonly use a number of specific major sources. Some are primary sources and some are secondary. Primary sources are definitely preferable because they describe a study written by the person who conducted it. Secondary sources are generally a much briefer, abstracted description of a study written by someone other than the original author. (An **abstract** is a summary of a study that describes its most important hypotheses, procedures, results, and conclusions.) The *Review of Educational Research,* for example, summarizes many research studies conducted on a given topic. Since secondary sources usually give complete bibliographic information on the references cited, they can direct you to relevant primary sources.

You should not be satisfied with the information contained in secondary sources; the corresponding primary sources will be considerably more detailed and will give you information "straight from the horse's mouth," as they say.

The number of individual references that you could consult for most problems is staggering. Fortunately, there are indexes, abstracts, and other retrieval mechanisms, such as computer searches, that facilitate identifying relevant references. In this section we will discuss the ones most often used in educational research; you should check your library for sources in your area of specialization. Following the discussion of the various sources, we describe computer-assisted literature searches and Internet searches.

Examples of handbooks, encyclopedias, and reviews relevant to educational research are *Encyclopedia of Educational Research, National Society for the Study of Education Yearbooks, Review of Educational Research, The Encyclopedia of Human Development and Education: Theory, Research, and Studies, The Handbook of Research on Teaching, The International Encyclopedia of Education: Research and Studies, Handbook on Social Studies Teaching and Learning, Handbook of Research in Curriculum,* and *Review of Research in Education.* These and other similar works contain summaries of important topics in education, reviews of research on various topics, and complete bibliographic information on the references cited. It is useful to photocopy the bibliographic references in the summaries that you consult, to use in your further research.

At this point, you may be asking, "How can I find such sources in my library?" If you know the title or author of the reference you are seeking, you will need to conduct a *title* or *author search.* If your reference is held in your library, you will probably be required to enter the number corresponding to the title you have selected to find out what the call number is (if your library owns it). At that point, you will need to find the call number of your book in the stacks.

If you do not know the titles of handbooks, encyclopedias, and research guides in your area of interest, you will need to conduct a *keyword search.* To do this, you will need to think of keywords or phrases that are pertinent to the type of volume you seek. For example, if you would like to find summaries of research previously conducted in an area of psychology, you might choose keywords such as *handbook* and *psychology.*

After reading a few secondary sources to get a more informed overview, you should have a clearer idea of your topic. You may want to revise your initial topic to reflect a narrower focus. After restating your topic, you should move beyond secondary sources to primary resources, including publications in which researchers report their own findings.

To sum up, you may find sources related to your topic in a variety of ways:

1. Search for books in the library.
2. Consult computer databases to locate journal articles, reports, and other publications.
3. Obtain the references listed in the bibliographies in the secondary sources you previously located.
4. Search the Internet and the World Wide Web for up-to-date information.

In the following pages we discuss these procedures in more detail.

Searching for Books on Your Topic in the Library

To locate primary sources, you need to conduct a library search much the same as those already illustrated. For example, you can conduct a title, author, or subject search on your library's computer. If you are at the beginning of your search for primary sources you should conduct a keyword search.

A keyword search may be narrow or broad; how narrow or broad depends on factors such as the purpose of the search and the amount of material available on your topic. If you need a relatively small number of references and if much has been published about your topic, a narrow search will likely be appropriate. If you need a relatively large number of references and very little has been published about your topic, a broad search will be better. If you do not have a sense of what is available, your best strategy is to start narrow and broaden as necessary. For example, if you find that there are very few references related to the effect of interactive multimedia on the achievement of 10th-grade biology students, you could broaden your search by including all sciences or all secondary students.

A useful way to narrow or broaden a keyword search is to use Boolean (wow!) operators, that involve the use of *and, or,* and *not* connectors. Put simply, using the connections *and* or *not* narrow a search, while the connector *or* broadens it. Let's say you have two keywords, *Easter* and *rabbit.* If you indicate that you are interested in obtaining references that relate to Easter *and* rabbit, you are saying that you only want references that refer to both Easter and rabbit. If you indicate that you are interested in obtaining references that relate to Easter but *not* to rabbit, your search is narrowed to references containing Easter, and references containing rabbit references will not be included in the search. If you indicate that you will take references related to Easter *or* rabbit, you are saying you will take references that relate to either or both concepts. By using various combinations of the *and* and *or* connectors, you can vary your search strategy as needed. Table 2.1 presents a summary of ways to limit keyword searches. Note that it is difficult to develop a search model that can be commonly used, since most libraries have unique search methods. Know your library.

Consulting Computer Databases to Locate Journals, Articles, Reports, and Other Publications

Computerized databases are used to conduct literature searches. Available at most university and public libraries, computer databases facilitate identifying relevant primary sources. General reference computer searches can be done online or by using a CD-ROM.

The steps involved in conducting a computer database search, be it online or CD-ROM, are similar to those involved in a book search:

1. Identify keywords related to your topic.
2. Select the databases you wish to search.
3. Specify your search strategy.

TABLE 2.1   Summary of Ways to Limit Keyword Searches

KEYWORD SEARCHES			
GENERAL	**FIELD CODES**	**BOOLEAN OPERATORS**	**FIELD QUALIFIERS**
k = assessment	k = dickonson.au	k = assessment and alternative	k = 1990.dt1,dt2. and assessment (books on assessment published in 1990)
k = book review	k = criticism.su	k = authentic or alternative	
K = automa? (retrieves automatic, automation, automating, etc.)	k = research.ti	k = assessment not standardized	k = curriculum and fre.la (Books on curriculum in French)
	Codes limit searches to specific areas or fields in the bibliographic record, such as author, title, and subject	Used to expand or limit a search	
Looks for word or phrase anywhere in a bibliographic record			
		And: retrieves records containing *both* terms	Used with Boolean operators to limit searches
Adjacency is assumed (i.e., words will be next to each other unless specified)		Or: retrieves records containing *either* term	Inquire in your library for available field qualifiers
? is used to retrieve singular, plural, or variant spellings		Not: retrieves records containing one term and *not* the other	

The most commonly used computer databases in education include the following:

ERIC.   The ERIC (Educational Resources Information Center) database contains more than 800,000 references to thousands of educational topics. It is updated monthly and includes journal articles, books, theses, conference papers, curricula, standards, and guidelines. ERIC contains entries from two sources: the RIE (Resources in Education) file of document citations and the CIJE (Current Index to Journals in Education) file of journal article citations from more than 750 professional journals. The ERIC database provides bibliographic information and abstracts of educational sources, but not full texts. Complete ERIC documents are available in libraries, either in microfiche format or in ERIC journals on the library shelves.

The first step in using ERIC resources is to become familiar with the terms that ERIC uses to index references. The *Thesaurus of ERIC Descriptors,* also available in most libraries, is a compilation of the keywords used in indexing ERIC documents. The ERIC thesaurus indicates the various terms under which a given topic is indexed.

ERIC references are labeled with the beginning codes ED or EJ. In most libraries, ED references are available on microfiche. In some libraries, you will need to ask a librarian to get the microfiche for you, while in other libraries, you are able to get it yourself. EJ references refer to literature that can be found on library shelves. To find out where an EJ reference is located at your library, do a title search on your library computer's online catalog. Enter t= and the name of the journal or book the ERIC reference is in. The resulting screen will tell you if your library owns the journal, where it is located, and whether it is available on the library shelves or on microfiche. Figure 2.2 shows the result of a sample ERIC search.

FIGURE 2.2   Results of an ERIC search.

Record 1 of 1 — ERIC 1992–12/97
AN: ED410322
AU: Schwartz, Wendy
TI: How Well Are *Charter Schools* Serving Urban and Minority Students? ERIC/CUE Digest, Number 119.
CS: ERIC Clearinghouse on Urban Education, New York, N.Y.
PY: 1996
AV: ERIC Clearinghouse on Urban Education, Institute for Urban and Minority Education, Teachers College, Box 40, Columbia University, New York, NY 10027 (free).
NT: 6 p.
PR: EDRS Price - MF01/PC01 Plus Postage.
AB: *Charter schools* are created and managed by an entity composed of parents and/or teachers, community and/or business leaders, nonprofit organizations, and for-profit businesses. Many people believe that *charter schools* can provide a high quality education without the regulatory constraints of the conventional public schools. This digest reviews many reports on the approximately 350 *charter schools* in the United States to show the various ways that charters approach funding, curriculum and instruction, assessment and accountability, parent involvement, and staffing. It focuses on the ability of *charter schools* to serve urban students. Many *charter schools* have been granted unprecedented freedom to implement their plans for a higher quality and more equitable educational system, and they have also tapped into funding sources previously unavailable to educators. Critics of *charter schools* are of the opinion that the freedom will not result in educational improvement, and that the lack of accountability may mean that a school's inaptitude will go unrecognized. It is too soon to evaluate the performance of students in charters, but it is apparent that charters are attracting urban students, in part because of their location. However, they are not attracting the most vulnerable and disadvantaged students. They are attracting dedicated and talented teachers but may not be able to offer them wages comparable to those of the public schools. Whether *charter schools* can provide a more effective public education remains to be seen, but their presence is at least serving to dramatize the need for educational improvement and increased community and business involvement and financial support. (Contains nine references.) (SLD)

Source: U.S. Department of Education.

Record 1 of 1 in Education Abstracts 6/83-6/01
TITLE: **Developing academic confidence** to build literacy: what teachers can do
AUTHOR(S): Colvin,-Carolyn; Schlosser,-Linda-Kramer
SOURCE: Journal of Adolescent and Adult Literacy v 41 Dec 1997/Jan 1998 p. 272–81
ABSTRACT: A study examined how the classroom literacy behaviors of middle school students relate to their academic success and reinforce students' evolving sense of self. The participants were at-risk students, academically successful students, and teachers from a middle school in southern California. It was found that when academically marginal students call on literacy strategies, these strategies are limited in scope and offer little help. However, more academically successful students seem well aware of the behaviors that are likely to result in a successful literacy experience. The characteristics of academically marginal and successful students are outlined, and suggestions for helping teachers create classrooms where students behave with greater efficacy are offered.
DESCRIPTORS: Attitudes-Middle-school-students; Middle-school-students-Psychology; Self-perception; Language-arts-Motivation

FIGURE 2.3   Results of an *Education Index* search.

Education Index.   The *Education Index* is an electronic index of educational periodicals with abstracts since 1983. It also includes yearbooks and monograph series, videotapes, motion pictures and computer program reviews, and citations to law cases. The *Education Index* provides bibliographic information and abstracts of sources (not the full text of articles) pertaining to the topic(s) that have been researched. A sample result of an *Education Index* search is shown in Figure 2.3.

Psychological Abstracts.   *Psychological Abstracts* presents summaries of completed psychological research studies. The sections on developmental psychology and educational psychology are generally the most useful to educational researchers. The first step in using *Psychological Abstracts* is to refer to the *Thesaurus of Psychological Index* to find the keywords used in indexing *Psychological Abstracts* documents. For example, if your research topic concerns the effect of interactive multimedia on the achievement of 10th-grade biology students, you would find that *interactive multimedia* is not a descriptor used by the *Thesaurus*. You would have to try other descriptors, such as *instructional media*. The procedure for using *Psychological Abstracts* is similar to the procedure for ERIC and the *Education Index*. In addition to the keywords, you should check the word bibliography. A bibliography related to your topic may exist and provide references. You should locate those references of interest to you in the usual way, by doing a title search on your university's computer catalog system.

Dissertation Abstracts.   *Dissertation Abstracts* contains bibliographic citations and abstracts from all subject areas for doctoral dissertations and master's theses completed at more than 1,000 accredited colleges and universities worldwide. The database dates back to 1861, with abstracts included from 1980 forward. If after reading an abstract you wish to obtain a copy of the complete dissertation, check to see if it is available in your library. If not, speak to a librarian about how to obtain a copy of the dissertation. The results of a *Dissertation Abstracts* search are shown in Figure 2.4.

Readers' Guide to Periodical Literature.   *Readers' Guide to Periodical Literature* is an index similar in format to the *Education Index*. Instead of professional publications, however, it indexes articles in nearly 200 widely read magazines. Articles located through the *Readers' Guide* will generally be nontechnical, opinion-type references. These can be useful in documenting the significance of your problem. The *Readers' Guide* lists bibliographic information for each entry. To obtain an article listed in the *Readers' Guide,* do a title search in your library of the magazine in which it appears. Then find out if your library holds that magazine.

```
┌─────────────────────────────────────────────────────────────────────────────────────────┐
│ ┌──────┐                                                                                  │
│ │ OC   │  OCLC FirstSearch: Detailed Record                                               │
│ │ LC   │  Your requested information from your library  BOSTON COL                        │
│ └──────┘                                                                                  │
│ ┌───────────────────────────────────────────────────────────────────────────────────┐   │
│ │ Dissertation  Abstracts  Online  results for:  kw:  literacy.  Record 2 of 5208    │   │
│ └───────────────────────────────────────────────────────────────────────────────────┘   │
```

Mark: ☑

Database: Dissertations

Title: **Learning community: An ethnographic study of popular education and homeless women in a shelter-based adult literacy program**

Author(s): Rivera, Lorna

Degree: Ph.D.

Year: 2001

Pages: 00264

Institution: Northeastern University; 0160

Advisor: Adviser Gordana Rabrenovic

Source: DAI, 61, no. 09A (2001): p. 3511

Standard No: ISBN: 0-599-95181-8

Abstract: This dissertation studies the impact of popular education approaches on the lives of fifty homeless and formerly homeless women who participated in the Adult Learners Program at a shelter located in one of Boston's poorest neighborhoods. Data were collected between January 1995 and June 1998. The guiding research questions are: How do poor women interpret the value of education? What poverty-related barriers interfere with their participation in popular education classes? How do the principles and practices of popular education build a sense of community and collective social action?

This ethnographic study utilizes multiple research methods to illustrate how popular education approaches make it possible for poor women to become empowered individually and collectively. Popular education is a methodology of teaching and learning through dialogue that directly links curriculum content to people's lived experience. It's roots are in critical social theory and the work of Paulo Freire. This research shows that poor women place a high value on education. They believe that a high school diploma will provide access to better economic opportunities and they struggle to complete their formal education within the context of homelessness and family violence.

It is argued that popular education's potential to build community is strengthened by the Adult Learners Program's participatory organization and the support services it offers to homeless families. Further, it is argued that popular education had a positive impact on the women's lives, as evidenced by: the women's increased levels of participation in their children's education; the women's participation in efforts to help other poor women in the community; the women's reported increase in self-confidence and group esteem; and, the women becoming stronger advocates for their basic legal rights related to welfare, housing, health, and education.

The research data suggest that the 1995 Massachusetts welfare reform legislation poses a significant barrier to adult literacy for welfare recipients. It is argued that limiting access to education through "work-first" welfare reform policies reproduces social inequalities. This dissertation about homeless women and popular education provides strong evidence in support of the social, political, and economic benefits of popular education programs for the poor.

SUBJECT(S)

Descriptor: EDUCATION, SOCIOLOGY OF
SOCIOLOGY, PUBLIC AND SOCIAL WELFARE
EDUCATION, ADULT AND CONTINUING

Accession No: AAI9988499

FIGURE 2.4 Results of a *Dissertation Abstracts* search.

Annual Review of Psychology. The *Annual Review of Psychology* includes reviews of psychological research that are often relevant to educational research. It provides bibliographic information and abstracts for specific areas such as child development, educational administration, exceptional child education, and language teaching.

Obtaining the References Listed in the Bibliographies in Your Secondary Sources

Given the prior discussion and description of library resources, you should be able to access references listed in the secondary source bibliographies you examined to start your literature review. For references that are books, do a title search in your library's computerized catalog to find out if the books are held by your library and, if so, if they are available. For references that appear to be journal articles or reports, go to ERIC or the *Education Index*. Do a title search of the article or report. This should pinpoint the article or report directly. You can then use the usual means to determine if the publication in which the article or report appears is in your library.

Searching the Internet and the World Wide Web

The Internet and the World Wide Web provide information and resources on many educational topics. The Internet links organizations and individuals all over the world. The World Wide Web is a service on the Internet that gives users access to text, graphics, and multimedia. You access the Web using a computer with a modem that is hooked up to a telephone or cable line. Your computer will also need a browser (such as Netscape® or Internet Explorer).

The resources that you can find on the Web are almost limitless. With just a few clicks, you can access electronic educational journals that provide full-text articles, bibliographic information, and abstracts. You can also obtain up-to-the-minute research reports and information about educational research activities being undertaken at various research centers, and can access education home pages that provide links to a range of education resources that other researchers have found especially valuable. At times, the sheer volume of information on the Web can be overwhelming. The best way to become adept at searching the Web efficiently is simply by surfing (browsing) it during your spare time. In this way, you will become familiar with maneuvering from site to site and implementing successful search strategies.

Here are some Web sites that are especially useful to educational researchers. Their Internet addresses are in parentheses. Search the Net to find some of your own addresses.

ERIC.   (http://www.accesseric.org/index.html) Yes, ERIC is also available on the World Wide Web, and it functions very much the same as it does on a database in your library. In addition to the Research in Education (RIE) and Current Index to Journals in Education (CIJE), which we discussed earlier, the ERIC Web site also provides extensive user assistance, including AskERIC, an electronic question-answering service for teachers working online, as well as ERIC Clearinghouses and Adjunct Clearinghouses, from which you may access ERIC Digests and other subject-specific abstracts and publications. Web page addresses and short descriptions of the contents of just some of the various clearinghouses are found in Table 2.2.

UnCoverWeb.   (http://uncweb.carl.org) UnCover is a database with brief descriptive information about articles from more than 17,000 multidisciplinary journals. If you register (for a fee) with UnCover REVEAL, an automated alerting service, you will receive monthly tables of contents from your favorite periodicals. The service also allows you to create search strategies for your research topics.

NewJour.   (http://gort.ucsd.edu/newjour/) This site provides an up-to-date list of journals and newsletters available on the Internet on any subject. Using NewJour's search option, you can do a title search to see if a specific journal is currently on the Web, or do a subject search to find out which journals in a particular subject are available on the Internet. Direct links are provided to available journals.

Education Week.   (http://www.edweek.org/) Full-text articles from *Education Week,* a periodical devoted to education reform, schools, and policy, are available at the site. In addition to current and past articles, the site provides background data to enhance current news, resources for teachers, and recommended Web sites to investigate for other information.

Journal of Statistics in Education.   (http://www.amstat.org/publications/jse/) This electronic journal provides abstracts and full-text articles that have appeared since 1993. Interesting features of the journal are "Teaching Bits: A Resource for Teachers of Statistics" and "Datasets and Stories."

TABLE 2.2   Some ERIC Clearinghouses on the World Wide Web

Clearinghouse	Web Address	Description
ERIC Clearinghouse on Assessment and Evaluation	http://ericae.net	Seeks to provide balanced information concerning educational assessment and resources to encourage responsible test use. Database contains records on more than 10,000 tests and research instruments covering a range of subjects and fields.
ERIC Clearinghouse on Counseling and Student Services	http://www.ericcass.uncg.edu	Includes information on school counseling, school social work, school psychology, mental health counseling, marriage and family counseling, career counseling, and student development, as well as parent, student, and teacher education in the human resources area.
ERIC Clearinghouse on Disabilities and Gifted Education	http://ericec.org/	Focuses on professional literature, information, and resources relating to the education and development of persons of all ages who have disabilities and/or are gifted.
ERIC Clearinghouse on Science, Math, and Environmental Education	http://www.ericse.org	Retrieves and disseminates printed materials related to science, mathematics, and environmental education.
ERIC Clearinghouse on Teaching and Teacher Education	http://www.ericsp.org/	Responds to requests for information on teaching, teacher education, and health, physical education, recreation, and dance (HPERD), and produces special publications on current research, programs, and practices.
ERIC Clearinghouse on Urban Education	http://eric-web.tc.columbia.edu/	Monitors curriculum and instruction of students of diverse racial, ethnic, social class, and linguistic populations in urban (and suburban) schools.

CSTEEP: The Center for the Study of Testing, Evaluation, and Educational Policy. (http://www.csteep.bc.edu/) This educational research organization's Web page contains information on testing, evaluation, and public policy studies on school assessment practices and international comparative research.

National Center for Education Statistics. (http://www.nces.ed.gov/) This site contains statistical reports and other information on the condition of U.S. education. It also reports on education activities internationally.

Bill Huitt's Home Page. (http://www.Chiron.valdosta.edu/whuitt) This site was created by Dr. William G. (Bill) Huitt of the Department of Psychology, Counseling & Guidance at Valdosta State University in Georgia. It contains some interesting links to general, curriculum, technology, reform, and multicultural education.

Developing Educational Standards. (http://putnamvalley.schools.org/standards.html) This site contains a wealth of up-to-date information regarding educational standards and curriculum frameworks from all sources (national, state, local, and other). The table of contents includes Governmental and General Resources, Standards and Frameworks Documents Listed by Subject Area, Standards and Frameworks Documents Listed by State, and Updates and Information. Entire standards and frameworks are available.

Internet Resources for Special Education. (http://specialed.miningco.com) This site provides links to a variety of topics, including teaching resources for regular and special education teachers; Web sites for students to visit; disability information, resources, and research; disability laws; special education laws; e-mail ideas; mailing lists and use net information; assistive technology; clearinghouses; and Internet search engines and help topics.

U.S. Department of Education.   (http://www.ed.gov/) This site contains links to the U.S. government's education databases (including ERIC). It also makes available full-text reports on current findings on education. In addition, it provides links to research offices and organizations, as well as research publications and products. The Department of Education has published a book titled *The Researcher's Guide to the Department of Education,* which helps researchers access the various resources that the department has to offer.

WWW Library Resources: Education.   (http://www.csu.edu.au/education/library.html) A section of the World Wide Web Virtual Library, this Web page contains education information on a number of different subjects.

Psych Web.   (http://www.psychology.net/) This site provides psychological information for students and teachers of psychology. Resources and links available include full-length books online, online pamphlets, discussion groups, university psychology departments on the Web, psychology journals on the Web, APA style resources, and other scholarly resources.

Using a Search Engine to Find Information Sources

It is entirely possible that you will want to access information on the World Wide Web that is not available in the Web addresses just given. The easiest, quickest way to find interesting new sites is to use a search engine to look for Web pages containing keywords that you enter. **Search engines** are sites that allow you to search large portions of the Internet for specific information. Examples of search engines include Google, Yahoo!, Lycos, Excite, and Alta Vista. Once you have entered a keyword or keywords in the appropriate place on the search engine's home page, the search engine examines a selected large portion of the Internet (or a specific domain of the Internet, if you say so) for sites that contain your keyword(s).

To facilitate your search, most search engines offer you the option of narrowing your search so that only the most relevant sites are identified. An example using Yahoo! is shown in Figure 2.5. Clicking on the subcategory "Education" in Figure 2.5a will significantly narrow your search to relevant sources in the field of education. After selecting the "Education" subcategory, a very useful page, shown in Figure 2.5b, appears. Clicking on a subtopic such as "Early Childhood Education" will then take you to another Web page that provides links to numerous sites pertaining to your topic. Clicking on any of the links shown in Figure 2.5c will access all of the information that those particular sites have to offer.

EVALUATING YOUR SOURCES

Once you have a source in hand, you will need to evaluate it. Obviously, the first thing to do is to determine if it really applies to your research topic. If it does, you then need to evaluate the quality of the information. For example, does the information come from a scholarly journal or a popular magazine? Is the information someone's personal opinion or the result of a research study? Clearly, sources of different types merit different weight in your review.

An initial appraisal of a source includes looking closely at the date of publication and where the source was found. Look at the copyright date of books that you find and the dates on which articles were published. Appropriate research in topic areas of current interest and continuing development generally require recent, up-to-date references.

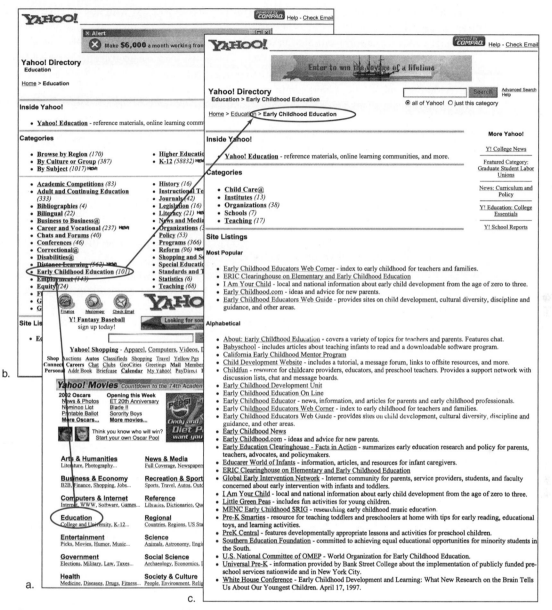

(a) Search options in opening screen; (b) search topics in Education category; (c) links in Early Childhood Education.

FIGURE 2.5 Sample search using Yahoo!

Next, identify where the source was found. For instance, did you find your source in a refereed or a nonrefereed journal? Research articles in **refereed journals** are required to comply with strict guidelines, not only in terms of format, but also in research procedures. Articles in refereed journals are reviewed by a panel of experts and thus tend to be more "trustworthy" than articles from nonrefereed or popular journals. The distinction between sources that are scholarly versus those that are popular is an important one.

It is also important to verify that the information presented in a particular source is objective and impartial. Does the author present evidence to support the interpretations made? Does the content of the article consist mainly of an individual's opinion or does it contain appropriately collected and analyzed data? Finally, does the source add to the information you have already gathered about your topic? If the source adds to your growing knowledge of your topic, it is useful and worth paying attention to.

Special care and caution must be taken when evaluating World Wide Web sources, because anyone can post information on the Web. Thus, just because an Internet search identifies a particular source does not mean that the source is accurate or credible. Sources from the World Wide Web must be closely examined for bias, subjectivity, intent, and accuracy.

Conducting effective library and Internet searches will yield an abundance of useful information about your topic. By combining the two, you will collect information that is both up to date and comprehensive. As time goes on and you become more experienced, you will be able from the beginning to conduct more efficient searches that are focused appropriately on your topic.

ABSTRACTING

After you have identified the primary references related to your topic using the appropriate resources, you are ready to move on to the next phase of a review of related literature—abstracting the references. Basically, this involves locating, reviewing, summarizing, and classifying your references. Students sometimes ask why it is necessary to read and abstract original, complete articles (or reports, or whatever) if they already have perfectly good abstracts. There are two basic reasons. First, abstracts are not necessarily "perfectly good." They may not be totally accurate interpretations or summaries of the articles' contents. And, second, there is a great deal of important information that you can only obtain by reading the complete article. (You'll see.)

Arrange the references you identified in each source in reverse chronological order (starting with the most recent). The abstracting process will be conducted in the same order. The main advantage of beginning with the latest references on a given topic is that in terms of research strategy, the most recent research is likely to have profited from previous research. Also, recent references may contain references to preceding studies you may not have identified. For each reference, we suggest the following procedure for abstracting:

1. If the article has an abstract or a summary, which most do, read it to determine the article's relevancy to your problem.
2. Skim the entire article, making mental notes of the main points of the study.
3. On an index card or in a computer database write the complete bibliographic reference, including the library call number if it is a book. This is tedious but important. You will spend much more time trying to find the full citation of a reference you failed to abstract completely than you will abstracting it in the first place. If you know that your final report must follow a particular style, put your bibliographic reference in that form. For example, a journal article using the American Psychological Association (APA) format would look like this:

Snurd, B. J. (1995). The use of white versus yellow chalk in the teaching of advanced calculus. *Journal of Useless Findings, 11,* 1–99.

In this example, 1995 refers to the date of publication, 11 to the volume, and 1–99 to the page numbers. The use of a style manual such as the APA's provides you with formats needed when citing different types of sources. If this reference is cited in the body of a paper (perhaps written by Goforth concerning the need for increased funding for useless research), its description would be followed by (Snurd, 1995). The bibliography provides the full citation. If, however, the citation is a direct quote, the appropriate page number must be included, e.g., (Snurd, 1995, p. 45). Whatever format you use, use it consistently, and be certain the reference you copy is accurate. You never know when you might have to go back and get additional information from an article.

4. Classify and code the article according to some system and add it to the database entry or place it on the index card (or a photocopy) in a conspicuous place, such as the upper right- or left-hand corner. Create a code that can be easily accessed when you want to sort your notes into the categories you devise. Any coding system that makes sense to you will facilitate your task later when you have to sort, organize, analyze, synthesize, and write your review of the literature. Coding and keeping track of articles is key for organization. Useful computer programs that simplify coding and subsequent data retrieval are HyperRESEARCH[1] and EndNote.[2]

5. Abstract, or summarize, the reference. As neatly as you can (you're going to have to read them later), write the essential points of the reference. If it is an opinion article, write the main points of the author's position—for example, "Jones believes parent volunteers should be used because . . ." and list the *becauses.* If it is a study, state the problem, the procedures (including the sample and instruments), and the major conclusions. Make special note of any particularly interesting or unique aspect of the study, such as a new measuring instrument that was utilized. Double check the reference to make sure you have not omitted any pertinent information. If the abstract provided at the beginning of the article contains all the essential information (and that is a big if), by all means use it.

6. Indicate any thoughts that come to your mind, such as points on which you disagree (mark them with an *X,* for example) or components that you do not understand (put a "?" next to them). For example, if an author stated that he or she had used a double-blind procedure, and you were unfamiliar with that technique, put a question mark in the margin next to that statement, either on your index card or on a photocopy of the page. Later, you can find out what it is.

7. Indicate any statements that are direct quotations or personal reactions: Plagiarism (intentional or not) is an *absolute* no-no, with the direst of consequences. If you do not put quotation marks around direct quotations on your card or computer, for example, you might not remember later which statements are, and which are not, direct quotations. Also, record the exact page number of the quotation in case you use the quotation later in your paper. Incidentally, direct quotations should be kept to a minimum in your research plan and report; both should be in your words, not other researchers'. Occasionally, however, a direct quotation may be quite appropriate and useful. Be sure, however, that you record all reference information required in your style manual. (You may choose to photocopy citations you plan to cite, but the main disadvantage of this is cost.)

Whatever approach you use, guard your notes with your life. Make a copy and put it somewhere in a safe place. When you have completed your reviewing task, those notes will represent many hours of work. Students have been known to be literally in tears because they left their notes "on the bus" or "on a table in the cafeteria." Beyond being sympathetic, your instructor can do little more than to tell you to start over (ouch!). Also, when the research report is completed, the cards or computer information can be filed (photocopies can be placed in notebooks), and saved for future reference and future studies (nobody can do just one!).

---

[1] ResearchWare, Inc. (2002). HyperRESEARCH 2.5. Randolph, MA.

[2] ISI ResearchSoft. (2002). EndNote 5. Berkeley, CA.

Analyzing, Organizing, and Reporting the Literature

For beginning researchers, the hardest part of writing the literature review is thinking about how hard it is going to be to write the literature review. More time is spent worrying about doing it than actually doing it. Part of the reason for this hesitancy is lack of previous experience writing a literature review and part is the fact that this is different from ordinary writing. A literature review is a technical form of writing that calls for different characteristics than most of the writing we normally do. In technical writing, facts must be documented and opinions must be substantiated. For example, if you say that the high school dropout percentage in Ohio has increased in the last 10 years, you must provide a source for this information. Technical writing is precise, requiring clarity of definitions and consistency in the use of terms. If the term *achievement* is important in your review, you must indicate what you mean by it and be consistent in using that meaning throughout the review. Figure 2.6 identifies important characteristics of technical writing used in a literature review.

If you have efficiently abstracted the literature related to your problem, and if you approach the task in an equally systematic manner, then analyzing, organizing, and reporting it will be relatively painless. First, to get warmed up, read quickly through your notes. This will refresh your memory and help you identify references that no longer seem sufficiently related to keep. Do not force references into your review that do not really "fit"; the review forms the background and rationale for your hypothesis and should contain only references that serve this purpose. The following guidelines and suggestions are based on experience acquired the hard way and should be helpful to you:

1. Make an outline. Don't groan; your eighth-grade teacher was right about the virtues of an outline. However you do it, the time and thought you put into the outline will save you time in the long run and will increase your probability of having an organized review. The outline does not have to be excessively detailed. First, identify the main topics and the order in which they should be presented. For example, the outline of the review for the problem concerned with the effectiveness of salaried paraprofessionals versus parent volunteers might begin with the headings Literature on Salaried Paraprofessionals, Literature on Parent Volunteers, and Literature Comparing the Two. Note that you can always add or remove topics in the outline as your work progresses. The next step is to differentiate each major heading into logical subheadings. In our outline for this chapter, for example, the section Review of Related Literature was subdivided into the following:

   REVIEW OF RELATED LITERATURE
   Definition, Purpose, and Scope
   Getting Started
   Identifying Keywords
   Identifying Your Sources
   Evaluating Your Sources
   Abstracting
   Analyzing, Organizing, and Reporting

   The need for further differentiation will be determined by your topic and the literature you have reviewed; the more complex these are, the more subheadings you will require. When you have completed your outline you will invariably need to rearrange, add, and delete items. It is much easier, however, to reorganize an outline than it is to reorganize a document written in paragraph form.

2. Analyze each reference in terms of your outline; in other words, determine under which subheading each fits. Recognize that some references may fit in more than one subheading. Then sort your references into appropriate piles. If you end up with references with-

1. Document facts and substantiate opinions. Cite references to support your facts and opinions. Note that facts are usually based on empirical data, while opinions are not. In the hierarchy of persuasiveness, facts are more persuasive than opinions. Differentiate between facts and opinions in the review.
2. Technical writing is precise, so clarity of definitions and consistency in the use of terms is required.
3. The review should be logically organized and aimed at a particular audience. Usually the review is aimed at a relatively naive reader, one who has some basic understanding of the topic but requires additional education to understand the topic or issue being studied. Do not assume your audience knows as much as you do about the topic and literature! They don't, so you have to write to educate them.
4. Technical writing is usually done using an accepted manual of style. The manual of style indicates the style in which chapter headings are set up, how tables must be constructed, how footnotes and bibliographies must be prepared, and the like. Follow the manual consistently. Commonly used manuals and their current editions are *Publication Manual of the American Psychological Association,* Fourth Edition, and *The Chicago Manual of Style,* Fourteenth Edition.
5. Evade affected verbiage and eschew obscuration of the obvious. In other words, limit big words; avoid jargon.
6. Start each major section of the review with an introduction that provides a brief overview of the section. "In this section, three main issues are examined. The first is . . . ." This is also useful advice for introducing chapters in the report.
7. End major sections or chapters with a summary that indicates the main ideas, findings, or points.

FIGURE 2.6
Guidelines for technical writing.

out a home, there are three logical possibilities: (1) there is something wrong with your outline; (2) they do not belong in your review and should be discarded; or (3) they do not belong in your review but do belong somewhere else in your introduction. Opinion articles or reports of descriptive research often will be useful in the introduction, whereas formal research studies will be most useful in the review of related literature section.

3. Take all the references identified for a given subheading and analyze the similarities or differences among them. If three references say essentially the same thing, there is no need to describe each one; it is much better to make one summary statement followed by three references. For example:

Several studies have found white chalk to be more effective than yellow chalk in the teaching of advanced mathematics (Snurd, 1995; Trivia, 1994; Ziggy, 1984).

Do not present your references as a series of abstracts or annotations (Jones found A, Smith found B, and Brown found C). Your task is to organize and summarize the references in a meaningful way. Do not ignore studies that are contradictory to most other studies or to your personal bias. Analyze and evaluate contradictory studies and try to determine a possible explanation. For example:

Contrary to these studies is the work of Rottenstudee (1998), who found yellow chalk to be more effective than white chalk in the teaching of trigonometry. However, the size of the treatment groups (two students per group) and the duration of the study (one class period) may have seriously affected the results.

4. The review should flow in such a way that the references least related to the problem are discussed first, and the most related references are discussed last, just prior to the statement of the hypothesis. Think in terms of a big V. At the bottom of the V is your hypothesis; directly above your hypothesis are the studies most directly related to it, and so forth. The idea is to organize and present your literature in such a way that it leads logically to a tentative, testable conclusion, namely, your hypothesis. Highlight or summarize important aspects of the review to help readers identify them. If your problem has more than one major aspect, you may have two Vs or one V hat logically leads to two tentative, testable conclusions.
5. The review should conclude with a brief summary of the literature and its implications. The length of this summary depends on the length of the review. It should be detailed

enough to clearly show the logic chain you have followed in arriving at your implications and tentative conclusions. Having systematically developed and presented your rationale, you will now be ready to state your hypothesis.

It is important to note that literature reviews are constructed in both quantitative and qualitative research, because of the obligation to place a study in the context of similar or related research. However, there often is a difference between the way the two types approach a literature review. A quantitative researcher normally follows the suggestions and steps for constructing a literature review just described.

Most qualitative researchers do not do a literature review until their study is well under way. Qualitative researchers require substantial time in the research setting (e.g., a school or classroom) and rely heavily on their observations and questioning to understand the research context. Qualitative researchers have a genuine concern about biasing their perceptions as a result of too-early immersion in the topic's related literature. In addition, most qualitative researchers enter the research setting with a broad topic or very tentative hunches about what their study will be, and only lock in a specific topic after observing, questioning, and "living" in the setting. Thus, qualitative researchers often conduct literature reviews later than do quantitative researchers, but ultimately both develop a literature review for which the suggestions just noted become pertinent.

FORMULATING AND STATING A HYPOTHESIS

To begin a research study, you have to have some idea or focus to narrow your research scope. This is true of both quantitative and qualitative research studies. Both quantitative and qualitative researchers deal with hypotheses, but the nature of each approach differs.

QUANTITATIVE DEFINITION AND PURPOSE OF HYPOTHESES

A **hypothesis** is a researcher's tentative prediction of the results of the research findings. It states the researcher's expectations about the relationship between the variables in the research topic. Many studies contain a number of variables, and it is not uncommon to have more than one hypothesis for a research topic. Note, that the researcher does not set out to prove a hypothesis, but rather, collects data that either support or do not support it. Hypotheses are essential to quantitative research studies, with the possible exception of some descriptive studies whose purpose is to answer certain specific questions.

Hypotheses are typically derived from a theory or the review of related literature. The review of the related literature often leads one to expect a certain relationship. For example, studies finding white chalk to be more effective than yellow chalk in teaching mathematics would lead a researcher to expect it to be more effective in teaching physics, if there were not other findings to the contrary. Similarly, a theory that suggested that the ability to think abstractly was quite different for 10-year-olds versus 15-year-olds might suggest a hypothesis stating that there would be a difference in the performance of 10- and 15-year-olds on a test of abstract reasoning.

Particularly with quantitative research, the hypotheses precede the conduct of the study because the nature of the study is determined by the hypothesis. Every aspect of the research is affected by the hypothesis, including participants, measuring instruments, design, procedures, data analysis, and conclusions. Although all hypotheses are based on theory or previous knowledge and are aimed at extending knowledge, they are not all of equal worth. A number of criteria are applied to construct useful hypotheses. This is especially important for quantitative researchers.

QUALITATIVE DEFINITION AND PURPOSE OF HYPOTHESES

As noted, the aims and strategies of qualitative researchers differ substantially from those of quantitative researchers. As a general rule, qualitative researchers do not state formal hypotheses prior to the study. Rather than testing a priori hypotheses, qualitative researchers are much more likely to generate new hypotheses as a result of their studies. The inductive process widely used in qualitative research is based on observing patterns and associations in the participants' natural setting without prior hunches or hypotheses of what researchers will study and observe. Qualitative researchers seek to understand the nature of their participants and contexts before stating a research focus or hypothesis. Note that qualitative researchers' reluctance to immediately start identifying variables and predictions stems from their view that contexts and participants differ and must be understood on their own terms before hypothesizing or judging. Thus qualitative researchers have more discretion in determining when and where to examine and/or narrow a topic.

Identifying patterns and associations in the setting often generates ideas and questions that lead to new hypotheses. For example, the repeated observation that early in the school year first-grade students can accurately identify who are the "smart" and who are the "not smart" students in class might suggest a hypothesis related to how teachers' actions and words communicate students' status in the classroom.

In simple terms, it is generally appropriate to say that a strength of quantitative research is in testing hypotheses, while that of qualitative research is in generating hypotheses.

CRITERIA FOR HYPOTHESES

A good hypothesis has the following characteristics:

1. It is based on sound reasoning.
2. It provides a reasonable explanation for the predicted outcome.
3. It clearly states the expected relationship between defined variables.
4. It is testable within a reasonable time frame.

By now it should be clear that *a hypothesis should be based on a sound rationale.* It derives from previous research or theory and its confirmation or disconfirming should contribute to educational theory or practice. Therefore, a major characteristic of a good hypothesis is that it is consistent with theory or previous research. The chances of your being a Christopher Columbus of educational research who is going to show that something believed to be "flat" is really "round" are slim! In areas of research where there are conflicting results, you will not be able to be consistent with all of them, but your hypothesis should follow from the rule, not from the exception.

A good hypothesis provides a reasonable explanation for the predicted outcome. If your telephone is out of order, you might hypothesize that it is because there are butterflies sitting on your telephone wires; such a hypothesis would not be a reasonable explanation. A more reasonable hypothesis might be that you forgot to pay your bill or that a repair crew is working outside. If a hypothesis suggested that schoolchildren with freckles pay attention longer than schoolchildren without freckles, it would not be a reasonable explanation for children's attention behavior. On the other hand, a hypothesis suggesting that children who have a good breakfast pay attention longer than children who have no breakfast is more reasonable.

A good hypothesis states as clearly and concisely as possible the expected relationship (or difference) between two variables and defines those variables in operational, that is, measurable, terms. A simply but clearly stated hypothesis makes it easier for readers to understand, simplifies its testing, and facilitates formulating conclusions. The relationship expressed between two variables may or may not be a causal one. For example, the variables anxiety and math achievement might be hypothesized to be significantly related (there is a significant correlation between anxiety and math achievement), or it might be hypothesized that on math problems high-anxiety students perform better than low-anxiety students. The hypothesis that on math problems high-anxiety students perform better than low-anxiety students is an example of a causal relationship.

This example also illustrates the need for operational definitions that clearly describe variables. **Operational definitions** ask questions such as, "What kind of math problems?" "What does it mean to 'perform better'?" "What observable characteristics define a high-anxiety student?" In this example, *high-anxiety student* might be defined as any student whose score on the Acme Anxiety Inventory is in the upper 30% of student scores. A *low-anxiety student* might be defined as any student who scores in the lowest 30% of students on the Acme Anxiety Inventory. Higher performance on math problems might be defined in terms of math subtest scores on the California Achievement Test. Operational variables serve to clarify the meaning of important terms in a study so that all readers will understand the precise meaning the researcher intends.

If the hypothesis variables can be operationally defined within the actual hypothesis statement without making it unwieldy, you should do so. If not, state the hypothesis statement and define the appropriate terms immediately following it. Of course, if all necessary terms have already been defined, either within or immediately following the topic statement, there is no need to repeat the definitions in the statement of the hypothesis. The general rule of thumb is to define terms the first time you use them, but it does not hurt to occasionally remind readers of these definitions.

A well-stated and defined hypothesis must be testable (and it will be if it is well formulated and stated). *It should be possible to test the hypothesis by collecting and analyzing data.* It would not be possible to test a hypothesis that indicated that some students behave better than others because some have an invisible little angel on their right shoulder and some have an invisible little devil on their left shoulder. There would be no way to collect data to support the hypothesis. In addition to being testable, *a good hypothesis should normally be testable within some reasonable period of time.* For example, the hypothesis that first-grade students who brush their teeth after lunch every day will have fewer false teeth at age 60 would obviously take a very long time to test. The researcher would very likely be long gone before the study was completed, not to mention the negligible educational significance of the hypothesis! A more manageable hypothesis with the same theme might be that first-grade children who brush their teeth after lunch every day will have fewer cavities at the end of the first grade than those who don't brush.

TYPES OF HYPOTHESES

Hypotheses can be classified in terms of how they are derived (inductive versus deductive hypotheses) or how they are stated (declarative versus null hypotheses). As noted in Chapter 1, an **inductive hypothesis** is a generalization based on specific observations. The researcher observes that certain patterns or associations among variables occur in a number of situations and uses these tentative observations to form an inductive hypothesis. For example, a researcher observes that in some eighth-grade classrooms students who are given essay tests appear to show less testing stress than those who are given multiple-choice tests. This observation could become the basis for an inductive hypothesis. **Deductive hypotheses** are generally derived from theory, based on the researcher's developing a specific prediction from general principles.

A **research hypothesis** states an expected relationship or difference between two variables. In other words, it specifies the relationship the quantitative researcher expects to verify in the research study. Research hypotheses can be nondirectional or directional. A *nondirectional hypothesis* simply states that a relationship or difference exists between variables. A *directional hypothesis* states the expected direction of the relationship or difference. For example, a nondirectional hypothesis might state the following:

> There is a significant difference in the achievement of 10th grade biology students who are instructed using interactive multimedia and those who receive regular instruction only.

The corresponding directional hypothesis might read as follows:

> Tenth-grade biology students who are instructed using interactive multimedia achieve at a higher level than those who receive regular instruction only.

The nondirectional hypothesis states that there will be a difference between the 10th-grade groups, while the directional hypothesis states that there will be a difference and that the difference will favor interactive media instruction. A directional hypothesis should only be stated if you have a basis for believing that the results will occur in the stated direction. Nondirectional and directional hypotheses involve different types of statistical tests of significance, as will be examined in Chapter 5.

Finally, a **null hypothesis** states that there is no significant relationship or difference between variables. For example, a null hypothesis might state the following:

> There is no significant difference in the achievement level of 10th-grade biology students who are instructed using interactive multimedia and those who receive regular instruction.

The null hypothesis is the hypothesis of choice when there is little research or theoretical support for a hypothesis. Also, statistical tests for the null hypothesis are more conservative than they are for directional hypotheses. The disadvantage of null hypotheses is that they rarely express the researcher's true expectations based on literature, insights, and logic. Given that few studies are really designed to verify the nonexistence of a relationship, it seems logical that most studies should be based on a nonnull hypothesis. Hypotheses are critical aspects of quantitative research approaches; they focus the study on the methods and strategies needed to collect data to test the hypotheses.

STATING THE HYPOTHESIS

A good hypothesis is stated clearly and concisely, expresses the relationship between two variables, and defines those variables in measurable terms. A general model for stating hypotheses for experimental studies is as follows:

> P who get X do better on Y than
> P who do not get X (or get some other X)

If this model appears to be an oversimplification, it is and it may not always be appropriate. However, this model should help you to understand the statement of a hypothesis. Further, this model, sometimes with variations, will be applicable in many situations. In the model,

> P = the participants
> X = the treatment, the causal or independent variable (IV)
> Y = the study outcome, the effect or dependent variable (DV)

Study the following topic statement and see if you can identify the P, X, and Y:

> The purpose of this study is to investigate the effectiveness of 12th-grade mentors on the absenteeism of low-achieving 10th graders.

In this example,

P = low-achieving 10th graders
X = presence or absence of a 12th-grade mentor (IV)
Y = absenteeism (days absent or, stated positively, days present) (DV)

A review of the literature might indicate that mentors have been found to be effective in influencing younger students. Therefore, the directional hypothesis resulting from this topic might read,

Low-achieving 10th graders (P) who have a 12th-grade mentor (X) have less absenteeism (Y) than low-achieving 10th graders who do not.

As another example, suppose your topic statement was as follows:

The purpose of the proposed research is to investigate the effectiveness of different conflict resolution techniques in reducing the aggressive behaviors of high school students in an alternative educational setting.

For this topic statement,

P = high school students in an alternative educational setting
X = type of conflict resolution (punishment or discussion) (IV)
Y = instances of aggressive behaviors (DV)

The related nondirectional hypothesis might read,

There will be a difference in the number of aggressive behaviors of high school students in an alternative educational setting who receive either punishment or discussion approaches to conflict resolution.

Got the idea? Let's try one more.
Topic Statement:

This study investigates the effectiveness of token reinforcement, in the form of free time given for the completion of practice worksheets, on the math computation skills of ninth-grade general math students.

P = ninth-grade general math students
X = token reinforcement in the form of free time for completion of practice worksheets
Y = math computation skills

Hypothesis:

Ninth-grade general math students who receive token reinforcement in the form of free time when they complete their practice worksheets have higher math computation skills than ninth-grade general math students who do not receive token reinforcement for completed worksheets.

Of course, in all of these examples there are terms that require operational definition (e.g., clearly defining *aggressive behaviors*).

For the null hypothesis for this topic statement the paradigm is as follows:

There is no difference on Y (the outcome of the study) between P_1 (treatment A) and P_2 (treatment B).

P_1 (treatment A) = free time
P_2 (treatment B) = no free time

See if you can write the null hypothesis for the following problem statement:

> The purpose of this study is to assess the impact of formal versus informal preschool reading instruction on first graders' reading comprehension at the end of the first grade.

TESTING THE HYPOTHESIS

The researcher selects the sample, measuring instruments, design, and procedures that will enable her to collect the data necessary to test the hypothesis. Collected data are analyzed in a manner that permits the researcher to determine whether the hypothesis is supported. Note that analysis of the data does not lead to a hypothesis being proven or not proven, only supported or not supported for this particular study. The results of analysis indicate whether a hypothesis was supported or not supported for the particular participants, context, and instruments involved. Many beginning researchers have the misconception that if their hypothesis is not supported by their data, then their study is a failure, and conversely, if it is supported, then their study is a success. Neither of these beliefs is true. It is just as important to know what variables are not related as it is to know what variables are related. If a hypothesis is not supported, a valuable contribution may be made in the form of a revision of some aspect of a theory; such revision will generate new or revised hypotheses. Thus, hypothesis testing contributes to education primarily by expanding, refining, or revising its knowledge base.

 Now go to the Companion Website accompanying this text at www.prenhall.com/gay to check your understanding of chapter concepts in the following modules: Objectives, Practice Quiz, and Applying What You Know. Expand your research skills with Evaluating Articles, Analyzing Qualitative Data, Analyzing Quantitative Data, and Research Tools and Tips. Visit Web Links to broaden your knowledge about research.

SUMMARY

Identifying a Topic or Question to Research

1. The first step in selecting a research topic is to identify a general area that is related to your area of expertise and is of particular interest to you.

Sources of Research Topics

2. There are four main sources of research topics: theory, personal experience, replication, and library immersion.
3. Theories are composed of organized bodies of concepts, generalizations, and principles. Research studies often study particular aspects of a theory to determine its applicability or generalizability.
4. A researcher's personal experiences and concerns often lead to useful and personally rewarding studies. Common questions, such as, "Why does that happen?" and "What would happen if . . . ?" can be rich topic sources if followed up.
5. Replication, repeating an existing study, is a common source of research topics. Replication usually involves some feature differing from the original study.
6. Library immersion in the literature in a problem area is generally not an efficient way to identify a research topic. Handbooks, encyclopedias, and yearbooks that cover many topics briefly are more useful. Of course, library resources will be invaluable once you have identified a topic to study.

Narrowing the Topic

7. Once an initial topic is identified, it often needs to be narrowed and focused into a manageable topic to study.
8. Qualitative and quantitative research often differ in the timing of narrowing their topics. Quantitative research topics are usually narrowed quickly. Qualitative research topics are not usually narrowed until the researcher has more information about the participants and their setting.

Characteristics of Good Topics

9. A basic characteristic of a research problem is that it is *researchable* using the collection and analysis of data. Topics related to philosophical, ethical, and "should" topics are not researchable.
10. A good problem has theoretical or practical significance; its solution contributes in some way to improving the educational process.

11. A good topic must be a topic that can be adequately investigated given your (1) current level of research skill, (2) available resources, and (3) time and other restrictions.
12. A good topic is one that is *ethical,* that is, a study that does not harm participants in any way.

Stating the Research Topic

13. A well-written topic statement for a quantitative study generally indicates the variables of interest to the researcher, the specific relationship between those variables that is to be investigated, and, ideally, the type of participants involved.
14. A well-written quantitative topic statement also defines all relevant variables, either directly or operationally; operational definitions define concepts in terms of measurable characteristics.
15. The statement of the problem should indicate the background of the problem, including a justification for the study in terms of its significance.
16. Qualitative research topics usually are stated later than quantitative research topics because qualitative researchers need to become attuned to the research context before narrowing their topic.
17. The topic statement is the first item in the introductory section of a research plan and provides direction for all remaining aspects of the study.

Review of Related Literature

Definition, Purpose, and Scope

18. The review of related literature involves systematically identifying, locating, and analzing documents pertaining to the research topic.
19. The major purpose of reviewing the literature is to identify information that already exists about your topic. Qualitative researchers usually review the literature later than quantitative researchers.
20. The literature review can point out research strategies, procedures, and instruments that have and have not been found to be productive in investigating your topic.
21. A smaller, well-organized review is preferred to a review containing many studies that are more or less related to the problem.
22. Heavily researched areas usually provide enough references directly related to a topic to eliminate the need for reporting less related or secondary studies. Little-researched topics usually require review of any study related in some meaningful way in order to develop a logical framework and rationale for the study.

23. A common misconception is the idea that the worth of a problem is a function of the amount of literature available on the topic. Unfortunately, there is no formula that indicates how much literature has to be reviewed for a given topic.

Getting Started

24. Find out what references are available and where they are located. Resources such as handbooks, encyclopedias, and yearbooks are useful starting places to obtain an overview of your topic and useful references to examine.
25. You should also be familiar with services offered by your library. Most libraries have tours or written materials describing the resources and their use. Reference librarians will be of most help in planning and executing your literature review.
26. Before the review, make a list of keywords related to your problem to guide your search.

Identifying Your Sources

27. A *primary source* is a study written by the person who conducted it; a *secondary source* is generally a much briefer description of a study written by someone other than the original researcher. Primary sources are preferred in the review.
28. There is a difference between the opinion of an author and the results of an empirical study. The latter is more valued in a review.

Searching for Books on Your Topic in the Library

29. A good starting point to obtain a perspective on a topic and identify literature sources is to look in your library at handbooks, encyclopedias, and reviews in your topic area.
30. Most libraries use a computer catalog system that indexes all of the sources in the library by author, title, and subject. Farmilize yourself with your library and its resources.
31. If you are at the beginning of a literature search for primary references, you might not have identified specific titles or authors to search for. A keyword search uses terms or phrases pertinent to your topic to search and identify potentially useful literature sources.
32. Keyword searches can be focused by using the Boolean operators *and, or,* and *not.* Using *and* or *not* narrows a search and the number of sources identified, while *or* broadens the search and acquired sources. It is often best to start with a narrow search.

Consulting Computer Databases

33. Computerized databases can facilitate identifying relevant primary sources. Among the most used are ERIC, *Education Index, Psychological Abstracts,* and *Dissertation Abstracts.* Most of these sources provide abstracts of literature.

Searching the Internet and the World Wide Web

34. The Internet links organizations and individuals all over the world. The World Wide Web is on the Internet.

35. To access the Internet you need a computer with a modem hooked to a telephone or cable line and a browser to get you onto the Web. Alternatively, you can access the Internet at most libraries.

36. Since the available resources on the World Wide Web are virtually limitless, the best way to become familiar with its use is to "surf around" in your spare time. Talk to other Internet users when you have a question.

37. The Web contains a variety of sites relevant to an educational researcher. Each site is reached by using its Internet address. Addresses containing *ed* or ending in *.edu* are related to educational institutions and those ending in *.com* are related to commercial enterprises.

38. Search engines allow the user to search the Internet. Most search engines list a variety of topics that can be used to focus a search. Search engines also allow keyword searches that encompass large portions of the World Wide Web.

39. It cannot be overemphasized that material on the World Wide Web is not screened for quality, honesty, bias, or authenticity. Virtually anyone can put anything on the Web. Thus, users must be careful not to assume that all material obtained from the Web is useful or accurate just because it comes from the Internet.

40. Combining a library search with a Web search will probably produce the most useful material.

Evaluating Your Sources

41. All identified sources must be evaluated for quality and applicability. Are sources up to date? Are they from refereed journals? Do they pertain directly to the research topic?

Abstracting

42. Abstracting involves locating, reviewing, summarizing, and classifying your references.

43. The main advantage of beginning with the latest references on your topic is that the most recent studies are likely to have profited from previous research. Also, references in more recent studies often contain references to other studies you had not identified.

44. For each reference, list the complete bibliographic record, including author's name, date of publication, title, journal name or book title, volume number, issue number, page numbers, and library call number. Identify main ideas. Put quotation marks around quotes taken from the reference and don't forget to get page numbers of the quote. Keep all references in the format required for research reports or dissertations.

45. Make a copy of your references and put it in a safe place.

Analyzing, Organizing, and Reporting the Literature

46. Describing and reporting research call for a different style of writing than commonly used. Technical writing requires documenting facts and substantiating opinions, clarifying definitions and using them consistently, using an accepted style manual, and starting sections with an introduction and ending them with a brief summary.

47. The following guidelines should be helpful: make an outline; sort your references into appropriate topic piles; analyze the relationships and differences between references in a given subheading; do not present your references as a series of abstracts or annotations; discuss references least related to the problem first; and conclude with a brief summary of the literature and its implications.

48. Both qualitative and quantitative researchers construct literature reviews. Qualitative researchers are more likely to construct their review after starting their study, while quantitative researchers are more likely to construct the review prior to starting their study.

Formulating and Stating a Hypothesis

49. A *hypothesis* is the researcher's tentative predictions of the research findings. Hypotheses are more common in quantitative than qualitative research.

50. Researchers do not set out to "prove" a hypothesis but rather collect data that either support or do not support it.

51. A hypothesis is formulated based on a theory or the review of related literature. The hypothesis logically follows the literature review and is based on the implications of previous research.

Criteria for Hypotheses

52. A critical characteristic of a good hypothesis is that it is based on a sound rationale. A hypothesis is a reasoned prediction, not a wild guess. It is a tentative, but rational, explanation for the predicted outcome.

53. A good hypothesis states as clearly and concisely as possible the expected relationship (or difference) between variables. Variables should be stated in measurable terms.

54. A well-stated and defined hypothesis must be testable.

Types of Hypotheses

55. An *inductive* hypothesis is a generalization made from a number of observations. A *deductive* hypothesis is derived from theory and is aimed at providing evidence that supports, expands, or contradicts aspects of a given theory. Deductive, quantitative hypotheses are more common than inductive, qualitative hypotheses.

56. A research hypothesis states the expected relationship (or difference) between two variables. It states the relationship the researcher expects to verify through the collection and analysis of data. Research hypotheses can be nondirectional, directional, or null.

57. A nondirectional hypothesis indicates that a relationship or difference exists but does not indicate the direction of the difference; a directional hypothesis indicates that a relationship or difference exists and indicates the direction of the difference. A null hypothesis states that there will be no significant relationship (or difference) between variables.

Stating the Hypothesis

58. A general paradigm, or model, for stating hypotheses for experimental studies is as follows: P who get X do better on Y than P who do not get X (or get some other X). P refers to participants, X refers to the treatment or independent variable (IV), and Y refers to the outcome or dependent variable (DV).

Testing the Hypothesis

59. Hypotheses are tested using statistical analyses of data gathered in the study.

60. It is just as important to know which variables are not related as it is to know which variables are.

PERFORMANCE CRITERIA   TASK 2

The introduction that you develop for Task 2 will be the first part of the research report required for Task 10. Therefore, it may save you some revision time later if, when appropriate, statements are expressed in the past tense (the topic investigated was or it was hypothesized, for example). Your introduction should include the following subheadings and contain the following types of information:

   Introduction (Background and significance of the problem)
   Statement of the Probem (Problem statement and necessary definitions)
   Review of the Literature (Don't forget the big V)
   Statement of the Hypothesis(es)

As a guideline, three typed pages will generally be a sufficient length for Task 2. Of course, for a real study you would review not just 10 to 15 references but all relevant references, and the introduction would be correspondingly longer.

Because of feedback from your instructor on Objective 4, and insight gained through developing your review of related literature, the hypothesis you state in Task 2 may very well be somewhat different from the one you stated for Objective 4 on page 39.

One final note: The hypothesis you formulate now will influence all further tasks—that is, who will be your participants, what they will do, and so forth. In this connection, the following is an informal observation based on the behavior of thousands of students, not a research-based finding. All beginning research students fall some place on a continuum of realism. At one extreme are the Cecil B. Demise students who want to design a study involving a cast of thousands, over an extended period of time. At the other extreme are the Mr. Magi students who will not even consider a procedure unless they know for sure they could actually execute it in their work setting, with their students or clients. Since you do not have to actually execute the study you design, feel free to operate in the manner most comfortable for you. Keep in mind, however, that there is a middle ground between Demise and Magi.

On the following pages an example is presented that illustrates the format and content of an introduction that meets the criteria just described (see the following Task 2 example). This task example (and succeeding qualitative task examples), with few modifications, represents the task as submitted by a former student in an introductory educational research course— Sara Jane Caldron, Florida International University. While an example from published research could have been used, the example given more accurately reflects the performance that is expected of you at your current level of expertise. Additional examples for this and subsequent tasks are included in the *Student Guide* that accompanies this text.

TASK 2 EXAMPLE

Effect of Interactive Multimedia on the Achievement of 10th-Grade Biology Students

Introduction

One of the major concerns of educators and parents alike is the decline in student achievement (as measured by standardized tests). An area of particular concern is science education where the high-level thinking skills and problem solving techniques so necessary for success in our technological society need to be developed (Smith & Westhoff, 1992).

Research is constantly providing new proven methods for educators to use, and technology has developed all kinds of tools ideally suited to the classroom. One such tool is interactive multimedia (IMM). IMM provides teachers with an extensive amount of data in a number of different formats including text, sound, and video, making it possible to appeal to the different learning styles of the students and to offer a variety of material for students to analyze (Howson & Davis, 1992).

When teachers use IMM, students become highly motivated, which results in improved class attendance and more completed assignments (O'Connor, 1993). Students also become actively involved in their own learning, encouraging comprehension rather than mere memorization of facts (Kneedler, 1993; Reeves, 1992).

Statement of the Problem

The purpose of this study was to investigate the effect of interactive multimedia on the achievement of 10th-grade biology students. Interactive multimedia was defined as "a computerized database that allows users to access information in multiple forms, including text, graphics, video and audio" (Reeves, 1992, p. 47).

Review of Related Literature

Due to modern technology, students receive more information from visual sources than they do from the written word, and yet in school the majority of information is still transmitted through textbooks. While textbooks cover a wide range of topics superficially, IMM provides in-depth information on essential topics in a format that students find interesting (Kneedler, 1993). Smith and Westhoff (1992) note that when student interest is sparked, curiosity levels are increased and students are motivated to ask questions. The interactive nature of multimedia allows the students to seek out their own answers and by so doing they become owners of the concept involved. Ownership translates into comprehension (Howson & Davis, 1992).

Many science concepts are learned through observation of experiments. Using multimedia, students can participate in a variety of experiments that are either too expensive, too lengthy, or too dangerous to carry out in the laboratory (Howson & Davis, 1992; Leonard, 1989; Louie, Sweat, Gresham, & Smith, 1991). While observing the experiments the students can discuss what is happening and ask questions. At the touch of a button teachers are able to replay any part of the proceedings, and they also have random access to related information that can be used to completely illustrate the answer to the question (Howson & Davis, 1992). By answering students' questions in this detailed way the content will become more relevant to the needs of the student (Smith & Westhoff, 1992). When knowledge is relevant students are able to use it to solve problems and, in so doing, develop higher-level thinking skills (Helms & Helms, 1992; Sherwood, Kinzer, Bransford, & Franks, 1987).

A major challenge of science education is to provide students with large amounts of information that will encourage them to be analytical (Howson & Davis, 1992; Sherwood et al., 1987). IMM offers electronic access to extensive information allowing students to organize, evaluate and use it in the solution of problems (Smith & Wilson, 1993). When information is introduced as an aid to problem solving, it becomes a tool with which to solve other problems, rather than a series of solitary, disconnected facts (Sherwood et al., 1987).

Although critics complain that IMM is entertainment and students do not learn from it (Corcoran, 1989), research has shown that student learning does improve when IMM is used in the classroom (Sherwood et al., 1987; Sherwood & Others, 1990). A 1987 study by Sherwood et al., for example, showed that seventh- and eighth-grade science students receiving instruction enhanced with IMM had better retention of that information, and O'Connor (1993) found that the use of IMM in high school mathematics and science increased the focus on students' problem solving and critical thinking skills.

Statement of the Hypothesis

The quality and quantity of software available for science classes has dramatically improved during the past decade. Although some research has been carried out on the effects of IMM on student achievement in science, due to promising updates in the technology involved, further study is warranted. Therefore, it was hypothesized that 10th-grade biology students whose teachers use IMM as part of their instructional technique will exhibit significantly higher achievement than 10th-grade biology students whose teachers do not use IMM.

References

Corcoran, E. (1989, July). Show and tell: Hypermedia turns information into a multisensory event. *Scientific American, 261,* 72, 74.

Helms, C. W., & Helms, D. R. (1992, June). Multimedia in education (Report No. IR-016-090). Proceedings of the 25th Summer Conference of the Association of Small Computer Users in Education. North Myrtle Beach, SC (ERIC Document Reproduction Service No. ED 357 732).

Howson, B. A., & Davis, H. (1992). Enhancing comprehension with videodiscs. *Media and Methods, 28,* 3, 12–14.

Kneedler, P. E. (1993). California adopts multimedia science program. *Technological Horizons in Education Journal, 20,* 7, 73–76.

Lehmann, I. J. (1990). Review of National Proficiency Survey Series. In J. J. Kramer & J. C. Conoley (Eds.), *The eleventh mental measurements yearbook* (pp. 595–599). Lincoln: University of Nebraska, Buros Institute of Mental Measurement.

Leonard, W. H. (1989). A comparison of student reaction to biology instruction by interactive videodisc or conventional laboratory. *Journal of Research in Science Teaching, 26,* 95–104.

Louie, R., Sweat, S., Gresham, R., & Smith, L. (1991). Interactive video: Disseminating vital science and math information. *Media and Methods, 27,* 5, 22–23.

O'Connor, J. E. (1993, April). Evaluating the effects of collaborative efforts to improve mathematics and science curricula (Report No. TM-019-862). Paper presented at the Annual Meeting of the American Educational Research Association, Atlanta, GA (ERIC Document Reproduction Service No. ED 357 083).

Reeves, T. C. (1992). Evaluating interactive multimedia. *Educational Technology, 32,* 5, 47–52.

Sherwood, R. D., Kinzer, C. K., Bransford, J. D., & Franks, J. J. (1987). Some benefits of creating macro-contexts for science instruction: Initial findings. *Journal of Research in Science Teaching, 24,* 417–435.

Sherwood, R. D., & Others (1990, April). An evaluative study of level one videodisc based chemistry program (Report No. SE-051-513). Paper presented at a Poster Session at the 63rd. Annual Meeting of the National Association for Research in Science Teaching, Atlanta, GA (ERIC Document Reproduction Service No. ED 320 772).

Smith, E. E., & Westhoff, G. M. (1992). The Taliesin project: Multidisciplinary education and multimedia. *Educational Technology, 32,* 15–23.

Smith, M. K., & Wilson, C. (1993, March). Integration of student learning strategies via technology (Report No. IR-016-035). Proceedings of the Fourth Annual Conference of Technology and Teacher Education. San Diego, CA (ERIC Document Reproduction Service No. ED 355 937).

"Part of good planning is anticipating potential problems and then doing what you can to prevent them." (p. 78)

PREPARING AND EVALUATING A RESEARCH PLAN

OBJECTIVES

After reading Chapter 3, you should be able to do the following:

1. Briefly describe three ethical considerations involved in conducting and reporting educational research.
2. Describe two major pieces of legislation affecting educational research.
3. Briefly describe each of the components of a research plan.
4. Briefly describe two major ways in which a research plan can be evaluated.

Once you have identified your topic, examined pertinent literature, and, if appropriate, stated a hypothesis or, in a qualitative approach, stated the purpose of your study and posed broad and general questions, the next step in the research process is to develop a research plan that delineates the methods and procedures you will use to carry out your study. Although research plans rarely are executed as initially stated, having a plan provides an overview of your study. Of course, we recognize that qualitative researchers will take more time with the participants and research settings before defining a topic and research strategies.

Developing a complete research plan requires expertise in a number of areas. A research plan generally describes the nature of the participants, the variables studied, the kind of data to be collected, the instruments used to collect the data, the conditions for data collection, and the techniques used to analyze the data. For example, a quantitative researcher whose topic concerns the attitude of students toward school might collect data from eighth graders using a School Attitude Survey instrument. The researcher would collect and score the data and summarize it into percentages of attitudes toward different aspects of schooling such as recess, science

class, study hall, and so on. Conversely, a qualitative researcher interested in the attitude of students toward school might collect data from 10 articulate eighth graders who vary in school performance, perhaps by a series of tape-recorded interviews. The researcher would collate any written observations and transcribe the tape recordings. The researcher would then search the transcriptions for important themes prior to writing a narrative that includes student quotes about their perceptions of school. Try to identify each of the components of the research plan in each of the studies just described. Clearly a researcher needs many competencies in order to create and carry out a viable quantitative or qualitative research plan.

The goal of Chapter 3 is to help you to understand the importance of developing a research plan and to become familiar with the components of a plan. After you have read Chapter 3, you should be able to perform the following task.

TASK 3

For the hypothesis you have formulated, develop the remaining components of a research plan for a study you would conduct to test your hypothesis. Include the following:

- Method
    Participants
    Instruments
    Design
    Procedure

- Data Analysis
- Time Schedule

Note: Include assumptions, limitations, and definitions where appropriate (see Performance Criteria, p. 97). You will have the opportunity to develop a *qualitative* research plan in Task 6.

DEFINITION AND PURPOSE OF A RESEARCH PLAN

A **research plan** is a detailed description of the procedures that you will use to investigate your topic or problem. It includes justification for hypotheses or exploration of posed research questions, and a detailed presentation of the research steps you will follow in collecting, choosing, and analyzing data. A research plan may be relatively brief and informal, such as the one that you will develop for Task 3, or it may be lengthy and formal, such as the proposals submitted to obtain governmental and private research funding.

Most colleges and universities require that students submit a proposal or prospectus for approval prior to carrying out research. Students are expected to demonstrate that they have a reasonable research plan before being allowed to begin the study. Playing it by ear is all right for the piano, but not for conducting research.

After you have completed the review of related literature and, if needed, formulated your hypothesis or research questions, you are ready to develop the rest of the research plan. In quantitative research, the hypothesis will be the basis for determining the participant group and selecting measuring instruments, as well as for the design, procedures, and statistical techniques used in your study. In qualitative research the researcher's questions will be the basis for gaining entrance to the research context, identifying research participants, spending a great deal of time in the field, determining how to gather data, and interpreting and narrating the data collected.[1] The research plan serves several important purposes. First, it forces you to think through every aspect of the study. The very process of getting it down on paper usually helps you think of something you might otherwise have overlooked. A second purpose of a written plan is that it facilitates evaluation of the study, by you and others. Problems occur and great ideas often do not look so great after they have been written down and considered. A written plan also allows others to both identify flaws and make suggestions about ways to improve the plan. This is an important aspect of the research process. A third and fundamental purpose of a research plan is to provide detailed procedures to guide conduct of the study. Also, if something unexpected occurs that alters some phase of the study, a plan allows for assessment of the impact on the rest of the study. For example, suppose you order 60 copies of a test to administer on May 1. If on April 15 you receive a letter saying that, due to a shortage of available tests, your order cannot be filled until May 15, your study might be seriously affected. At the very least it would be delayed several weeks. The deadlines in your research plan might indicate that you cannot afford to wait. You might decide to use an alternate measuring instrument. Or you might contact another vendor. The many benefits of a research plan are as viable for "old hands" as for beginning researchers.

Murphy's law states, essentially, that "if anything can go wrong, it will, and at the worst possible time." If your study is a disaster because of poor planning, you lose. If something that could have been avoided goes wrong, you might have to redo the whole study at worst, or somehow salvage the remnants of a less-than-ideal study at best. A well-thought-out plan saves time, provides structure for the study, reduces the probability of costly mistakes, and generally results in higher-quality research.

Part of good planning is anticipating potential problems and then doing what you can to prevent them. For example, you might anticipate that some principals will be less than open to your using their students as participants in your study (a common occurrence). To deal with this contingency you should work up the best, but most honest, sales pitch possible. Do not ask, "Hey, can I use your kids for my study?" Instead, tell them how the study will benefit their students or their schools. If there is still opposition, you might tell them how enthusiastic central administration is about the study. Got the idea? To avoid many

---

[1] Each of these parts of a research plan will be discussed in succeeding chapters.

problems and to obtain strategies for overcoming them, it is extremely useful to talk to more experienced researchers. Happily, you will rarely be left totally to yourself when planning and carrying out a research plan or study.

GENERAL CONSIDERATIONS IN A RESEARCH PLAN

We have already noted a number of factors you should consider in planning your research. Three additional factors are important to all research studies. First is the ethics of conducting research. As a researcher you have ethical responsibilities for your participants. For example, any potential participant in your study should have the right to refuse to participate and the right to stop involvement at any time during the study. Second, there are legal restrictions on who can obtain access to student records. Third, you should know strategies for achieving and maintaining cooperation from school personnel. Your research plan may not specifically address any of these factors, but the plan's chance of being properly and ethically executed will be increased if you are aware of them.

THE ETHICS OF RESEARCH

All researchers must be aware of and attend to the ethical considerations related to their studies. This need is important for all types and methods of research. In research, the ends do not justify the means, and researchers must not put their need to carry out their study above their responsibility to maintain the well-being of the study participants. Research studies are built on trust between the researcher and the participants; researchers have a responsibility to maintain that trust, just as they expect participants to maintain it in the data they provide.

Many professional organizations have developed codes of ethical conduct for their members. Figure 3.1 presents the general principles of the American Psychological Association for the ethical conduct of researchers. Note that additional and much more specific ethical standards are grouped into the following eight categories: (1) general standards; (2) evaluation, assessment, or intervention; (3) advertising and other public statements; (4) therapy; (5) privacy and confidentiality; (6) teaching, training, supervision, research, and publishing; (7) forensic activities; and (8) resolving ethical issues. You may read the full text online at the American Psychological Association's Web site (http://www.apa.org/ethics/code.html). Most other professional organizations, such as the American Educational Research Association and the American Sociological Society, have similar codes for ethical research.

In 1974, the U.S. Congress put the force of law behind codes of ethical research. The need for legal restrictions was graphically illustrated by a number of studies in which researchers lied to or put research participants in harm's way in order to carry out their studies. For example, in a study on the effects of group pressure (conducted some years ago) researchers lied to participants while they participated in and watched what they thought was actual electric shocking of other participants.[2] In another study, men known to be infected with syphilis were not treated for their illness because they were part of a control group in a comparative study.[3] Studies such as these prompted governmental regulations regarding research studies.

Informed Consent and Protection from Harm

Two major pieces of legislation affecting educational research are the National Research Act of 1974 and the Family Educational Rights and Privacy Act of 1974, the latter more

---

[2] Milgram, S. (1964). Group pressure and action against a person. *Journal of Abnormal and Social Psychology, 69,* 137–143.

[3] Jones, J. H. (1998). *The Tuskegee syphilis experiment.* New York: Free Press.

PRINCIPLE A: COMPETENCE

Psychologists strive to maintain high standards of competence in their work. They recognize the boundaries of their particular competencies and the limitations of their expertise. They provide only those services and use only those techniques for which they are qualified by education, training, or experience. Psychologists are cognizant of the fact that the competencies required in serving, teaching, and/or studying groups of people vary with the distinctive characteristics of those groups. In those areas in which recognized professional standards do not yet exist, psychologists exercise careful judgment and take appropriate precautions to protect the welfare of those with whom they work. They maintain knowledge of relevant scientific and professional information related to the services they render, and they recognize the need for ongoing education. Psychologists make appropriate use of scientific, professional, technical, and administrative resources.

PRINCIPLE B: INTEGRITY

Psychologists seek to promote integrity in the science, teaching, and practice of psychology. In these activities psychologists are honest, fair, and respectful of others. In describing or reporting their qualifications, services, products, fees, research, or teaching, they do not make statements that are false, misleading, or deceptive. Psychologists strive to be aware of their own belief systems, values, needs, and limitations and the effect of these on their work. To the extent feasible, they attempt to clarify for relevant parties the roles they are performing and to function appropriately in accordance with those roles. Psychologists avoid improper and potentially harmful dual relationships.

PRINCIPLE C: PROFESSIONAL AND SCIENTIFIC RESPONSIBILITY

Psychologists uphold professional standards of conduct, clarify their professional roles and obligations, accept appropriate responsibility for their behavior, and adapt their methods to the needs of different populations. Psychologists consult with, refer to, or cooperate with other professionals and institutions to the extent needed to serve the best interests of their patients, clients, or other recipients of their services. Psychologists' moral standards and conduct are personal matters to the same degree as is true for any other person, except as psychologists' conduct may compromise their professional responsibilities or reduce the public's trust in psychology and psychologists. Psychologists are concerned

about the ethical compliance of their colleagues' scientific and professional conduct. When appropriate, they consult with colleagues in order to prevent or avoid unethical conduct.

PRINCIPLE D: RESPECT FOR PEOPLE'S RIGHTS AND DIGNITY

Psychologists accord appropriate respect to the fundamental rights, dignity, and worth of all people. They respect the rights of individuals to privacy, confidentiality, self-determination, and autonomy, mindful that legal and other obligations may lead to inconsistency and conflict with the exercise of these rights. Psychologists are aware of cultural, individual, and role differences, including those due to age, gender, race, ethnicity, national origin, religion, sexual orientation, disability, language, and socioeconomic status. Psychologists try to eliminate the effect on their work of biases based on those factors, and they do not knowingly participate in or condone unfair discriminatory practices.

PRINCIPLE E: CONCERN FOR OTHERS' WELFARE

Psychologists seek to contribute to the welfare of those with whom they interact professionally. In their professional actions, psychologists weigh the welfare and rights of their patients or clients, students, supervisees, human research participants, and other affected persons, and the welfare of animal subjects of research. When conflicts occur among psychologists' obligations or concerns, they attempt to resolve these conflicts and to perform their roles in a responsible fashion that avoids or minimizes harm. Psychologists are sensitive to real and ascribed differences in power between themselves and others, and they do not exploit or mislead other people during or after professional relationships.

PRINCIPLE F: SOCIAL RESPONSIBILITY

Psychologists are aware of their professional and scientific responsibilities to the community and the society in which they work and live. They apply and make public their knowledge of psychology in order to contribute to human welfare. Psychologists are concerned about and work to mitigate the causes of human suffering. When undertaking research, they strive to advance human welfare and the science of psychology. Psychologists try to avoid misuse of their work. Psychologists comply with the law and encourage the development of law and social policy that serve the interests of their patients and clients and the public. They are encouraged to contribute a portion of their professional time for little or no personal advantage.

FIGURE 3.1   General ethical principles.

Source: From *Ethical Principles of Psychologists and Code of Conduct* by the American
Psychological Association, 1992. Copyright 1992 by the American Psychological Association.
Reprinted by permission.

commonly referred to as the Buckley Amendment. The National Research Act requires that, to ensure protection of participants, proposed research activities involving human participants be reviewed and approved by an authorized group prior to the execution of the research. Protection of participants is broadly defined and requires that they not be harmed in any way (physically or mentally) and that they participate only if they freely agree to do so (informed consent). If participants are not of age, informed consent must be given by parents or legal guardian.

Most colleges and universities have a review group, usually called the Human Subjects Review Board or the IRB (Institutional Review Board). By law, this board must consist of at least five members, not all of one gender, include one nonscientist, and include one (or more) member who is mainly concerned with the welfare of the participants. Persons who might have a conflict of interest are excluded.

Typically, the researcher submits a proposal to the chair of the board, who, in turn, distributes copies to all the members. They review the proposal in terms of proposed treatment of participants. If there is any question as to whether participants might be harmed in any way, the researcher is usually asked to meet with the review group to answer questions and clarify proposed procedures. When the review group is satisfied that the participants will not be placed at risk (or that potential risk is minimal compared to the potential benefits of the study), the committee members sign the approval forms. Members' signatures on the approval forms signify that the proposal is acceptable with respect to participant protection. Figure 3.2 shows a typical Human Subjects Review Application. Note that the research plan is placed in one of three groups, depending on how intrusive the plan is on proposed participants. The criteria for plans in Categories II and III are more extensive than those in Category I. Note, also, the many questions that have to be answered to obtain informed consent.

The Privacy Act of 1974, usually referred to as the Buckley Amendment, was designed to protect the privacy of students' educational records. Among its provisions is the specification that data that actually identify students may not usually be made available unless written permission is acquired from the students' (if of age), or a parent or legal guardian. The consent must indicate what data may be disclosed, for what purposes, and to whom. Thus, if part of your study required obtaining information from individual elementary students' record files, you would need to obtain written permission from *each* student's parent or guardian, not a blanket approval from the school principal or classroom teacher. Note that if you are interested in using only class averages (in which no individual student is identified), individual consent from the principal would likely suffice. However, if you would calculate the class average from individual student records, individual permission would be necessary because you have access to individual records.

There are some exceptions that may not require written consent provision. For example, school personnel with a "legitimate educational interest" in a student would not need written consent to examine student records. In other cases, the researcher could request that a teacher or guidance counselor either remove names from students' records completely or replace them with a coded number or letter. The researcher can then use the records without knowing the names of the individual students.

Perhaps the most basic and important ethical issues in research are concerned with participants' informed consent and freedom from harm. *Informed consent* ensures that research participants enter the research of their free will and with understanding of the nature of the study and any possible dangers that may arise. It is intended to reduce the likelihood that participants will be exploited by a researcher persuading them to participate without fully knowing what the study's requirements are. *Freedom from harm* is focused on not exposing students to risks. It involves issues of confidentiality (to protect students from embarrassment or ridicule) and issues related to personal privacy. Collecting information on participants or observing them without their knowledge or without appropriate permission is not ethical. Furthermore, any information or data that are collected, either from or about a person, should be strictly confidential, especially if it is at all personal. Access to data should be limited to persons directly involved in conducting the research. An individual participant's performance should not be reported or made public using the participant's name, even for an innocuous

**HUMAN SUBJECTS RESEARCH REVIEW
COVER SHEET**

1. Investigator(s)' Name(s) _____

2. Project Title _____

3. Email Address _____ Phone # _____

4. Campus Address _____

5. Home Address _____

6. Department or University _____

7. University Status (place initials for each investigator)

    Faculty/Staff _____

    Undergraduate Student _____

    Graduate Student _____

8. If the principal investigator is a student, list name, department and local telephone of faculty supervisor. Please note that THE FACULTY SUPERVISOR MUST INDICATE KNOWLEDGE AND APPROVAL OF THIS PROPOSAL BY SIGNING THIS FORM.

    _____

    Faculty Supervisor Name

    _____

    Local Address and Telephone _____

9. Check appropriate category of research project:

    _____ Category I (Expedited Review)
    _____ Category II (Expedited Review)
    _____ Category III (Full Review)

10. The Principal Investigator must sign this form. (If the Principal Investigator is a student, his/her faculty supervisor must also sign this form. I certify that (a) the information provided for this project is accurate, (b) no other procedures will be used in this project, and (c) any modifications in this project will be submitted for approval prior to use.

    Signature of Investigator   Date

    _____   _____

FIGURE 3.2   Human subjects review form.

APPLICATION FOR APPROVAL OF A RESEARCH PROJECT INVOLVING HUMAN SUBJECTS

ITEMS 1–10 ARE REQUIRED FOR ALL PROJECTS

1. Title of Project:

2. Principal Investigator(s):

3. Collaborators in Outside Institutions:

4. General statement of the problem and research question(s) to be tested by the proposed research.

5. Description of the overall plan and procedures and methods. (Attach any questionnaires, interview protocols, and/or testing instruments as well as cover letter or instructions to subject.)

6. Relevant characteristics and source of participants. Describe how participants will be recruited.

7. Describe how participants will be selected for participation in this project and any remuneration to be received by the subject.

8. Status and qualifications of research assistants, if any.

9. Source of funding for project.

10. Expected starting and completion dates for project.

ITEMS 11–16 ARE REQUIRED FOR CATEGORIES IN II AND III ONLY

11. Outline potential benefit of this project to the individual participant, group of participants, or society in general.

12. Outline potential risks to participants and the measures that will be taken to minimize such risks.

13. Specify procedures developed with respect to the anonymity of participants and the confidentiality of their responses. Indicate what personal identifying indicators will be kept on subjects. Specify procedures for storage and ultimate disposal of personal information.

14. Specify how subjects will be informed of the following:

    (a) the nature of their participation in the project
    (b) that their participation is voluntary and
    (c) that their responses are confidential.

    If presented orally, a copy of the presentation must be submitted to the Committee before final approval can be given. Attach a copy of the "Informed Consent" form.

15. Specify any special populations (e.g., minors, prisoners, or the mentally incompetent) involved in this project and describe the procedures for obtaining the appropriate consent.

16. If the subjects are to be drawn from an institution or organization (e.g., hospital, social service agency, prison, school, etc.) which has the responsibility for the participants, then documentation of permission from the institution must be submitted to the Committee before final approval can be given.

17. If you are working in a school or a clinic, are there some internal human subjects review procedures for those sites that you are adhering to? For example, you may need to adhere to the Boston Public Schools research guidelines at: http://www.boston.k12.ma.us/dept/supt_research1.asp

18. Researchers normally offer to provide some summary of findings to participants. Describe any plan for doing so, or a rationale for why this is not tenable.

ITEMS 19–20 ARE REQUIRED FOR CATEGORY III ONLY

19. Will the participant(s) be exposed to any psychological intervention such as deception, contrived social situations, manipulation of attitudes, opinions, or self-esteem, psychotherapeutic procedures, or other psychological influences? Describe procedures for follow-up and/or debriefing.

20. If the topic investigated involves more than normal (what is attributable to every day occurrences) risk, specify any procedures that will be designed to address any adverse effects from participating in the study.

FIGURE 3.2   Continued.

Source: Boston College, The Lynch School of Education, 2001. Used with permission.

measure such as an arithmetic test. For example, individuals identified as members of a group that performed poorly on a research instrument might be subjected to ridicule, censure by parents, or lowered teacher expectations. Lack of privacy may lead to harm.

The use of confidentiality or anonymity to avoid privacy invasion and potential harm is common. **Anonymity** means that the researcher does not know the identities of the participants in the study. It does not mean, as many think, that the researcher knows the identities of participants but promises not to release them to anyone else. This is **confidentiality.** If the researcher knows participants' identities, there can be confidentiality, but no anonymity. The preceding example of removing names or coding records is one commonly used way to maintain anonymity. When planning your study you must indicate to participants whether you will provide confidentiality (you'll know but won't tell) or anonymity (you will not know the participants' names) and be sure they know the difference. Sometimes researchers seek access to data from a prior study to examine new questions based on the old data. In such cases, the original researcher has the responsibility to maintain the confidentiality or anonymity promised the participants of the original study.

Deception

Another ethical dilemma occurs when a researcher poses a topic that, if given complete information to potential participants, would likely influence or change their responses. For example, studies concerned with participants' racial, gender, cultural, or medical orientation or attitudes are especially susceptible to such influences, so researchers often hide the true nature of the topic of study. Or a researcher might want to study how teachers interact with high- and low-achieving students. If the researcher tells the teachers what the aim of the study is, it is likely that they will change their normal behaviors more than if the researcher tells them that the study is about how high- and low-achieving students perform on oral questioning. Lying about the real focus is intended to deceive study participants. Research that plans to deceive participants must be seriously considered before being carried out. Some researchers believe that any study that requires deceitful practice should not be carried out. Others recognize that some important studies cannot be undertaken without deception. It is recommended that you not do your initial research studies using a topic that requires deception. If you do choose a topic that requires deception, your advisor and the Human Subjects Review or IRB Committee at your institution will provide suggestions about ethical ways to carry out your research plan. Note that the primary researcher (usually you) is responsible for maintaining ethical standards in the research.

Ethical Issues in Qualitative Research

The ethical issues and responsibilities discussed thus far pertain to both quantitative and qualitative research plans. However, there are features of qualitative research that raise additional issues not typically encountered in quantitative research. For the most part, quantitative research plans are specified before the researcher begins to carry out the study. The specifics of the plan and its presentation to the Human Subjects Review Committee provide a detailed examination of ethical issues. This does not mean that additional ethical issues will not arise, but because most quantitative researchers do not immerse themselves in the setting they study, the likelihood of such concerns is considerably lessened.

Qualitative research differs from quantitative in at least two major ways that produce additional ethical concerns. First, qualitative research plans typically evolve and change as the researcher's immersion in and understanding of the research setting grows. In a real sense, the research plan is "in process" and only generally formed when presented to the Human Subjects Review Committee. As the plan evolves with added understanding of the context and participants, there is increased likelihood that unanticipated and unreviewed ethical issues will arise and need to be resolved on the spot. For example, as participants become more comfortable with the researcher, they often will ask to see what has been written about them. They feel entitled to this, even though seeing what has been written may cause personal or data collection problems.

Second, qualitative researchers typically are personally involved and engaged with the research context and its participants. That is one of the defining characteristics of qualitative methods. Data collection methods such as interviews, debriefings, and the like bring the researcher and participants in close, personal contact. Qualitative researchers often refer to participants as *informants* or *collaborators* rather than as *subjects* to indicate the intended bond between qualitative researcher and participants. The closeness between participants and researcher helps to provide deep and rich data, but may also create unconscious influences that raise issues for objectivity and data interpretation.

The focus on immersion and detailed knowledge of the research context often leads the qualitative researcher to observe illegal or unprofessional behavior. Of course this can occur in quantitative research also, but generally to a lesser degree because of its limited proximity to the participants and their context. For example, the qualitative researcher might observe a janitor illegally loading school supplies into her car. Or the researcher might observe a teacher continually ridiculing a particular student for his speech impediment. In these and other similar situations, what is the researcher to do: make the school authorities aware of such activities, or keep silent on the assumption that the system will eventually identify and correct the problems? Should the researcher report the observations, knowing that it likely will end the study because participants will no longer be certain of the researcher's promise of confidentiality? Obviously if there is clear likelihood of physical or psychological danger, the researcher has a strong mandate to inform the school authorities. Unfortunately, not all situations present ethically clear actions.

There are many dimensions to the ethical conduct of research. The sources and advice noted in this chapter will help you conceive and conduct ethical studies. The suggestions provided do not cover all the ethical issues you are likely to encounter in your research. Perhaps the fundamental ethical rule is that participants should not be harmed in any way, real or possible, in the name of science. Respect and concern for your own integrity and for your participants' dignity and welfare are the bottom lines of ethical research.

GAINING ENTRY TO THE RESEARCH SITE

Very rarely is it possible to conduct educational research without the cooperation of a number of people. An initial step in acquiring needed cooperation is to identify and follow required procedures for gaining approval to conduct the study in the chosen site. In schools, research approval is usually granted by the superintendent, school board, or some other high-level administrator such as the associate superintendent for instruction. In other settings, such as hospitals or industry, there typically is someone or a committee charged with examining and approving or denying requests to do research at the site. Regardless of the site, approval will involve the researcher completing one or more forms that describe the nature of the research, the specific request being made of the site personnel, and the benefits to the site. Once approval is obtained, it will be necessary to obtain permission from the research participants themselves. For example, approval by a superintendent or school board may also require permission from the principal or principals whose schools will be involved. Even if such approval is not required, it should be sought, both as a courtesy and for the sake of a smoothly executed study. Permission, or at least acceptance, should also be obtained from the teachers who will participate in the study. If students under 18 are to be involved, written parental approval will be needed.

The potential complexity of obtaining permission to conduct your research at the chosen site or sites should indicate that you should not assume that permission will be granted easily ("we're too busy") or quickly (bureaucracies move slowly). Thus, you should prepare how you will explain your study to all those who must provide permission and approval. The key to gaining approval and cooperation is good planning, and the key to good planning is a well-designed, carefully thought-out study and research plan. Some superintendents and principals are "gun shy" about people doing research in their schools because of a previous bad experience. They don't want anyone else running around their schools, disrupting classes, administering poorly constructed questionnaires, or finding problems in the school. It is up to you to convince school personnel that what you are proposing is of value, that your study is carefully designed, and that you will work with teachers to minimize inconvenience.

Achieving full cooperation, and not just approval on paper, requires that you invest as much time as is necessary to discuss your study with the principal, the teachers, and perhaps

FIGURE 3.3
Principal's cover letter for a proposed research study.

> **THE SCHOOL BOARD OF KNOX COUNTY, MASSACHUSETTS**
>
> Oak Street Elementary School
> Gwen Gregory, Principal
> 113 Oak Street
> Clover, Massachusetts
> 555-555-5555
>
> January 23, 2002
>
> Dear Parent/Guardian:
>
> Oak Street Elementary School has been chosen to participate in a research study. Our school was selected out of the entire country as a result of our outstanding students and computer program. All third- and fifth-grade students will be able to participate. The results of this study will enable our teachers and parents to discover and understand the learning styles of our students. This knowledge will enable teachers and parents to provide special instruction and materials to improve student learning. It will also provide valuable information for the future development of effective professional computer software.
>
> This study will take place from January 29 to March 30, 2002. It will be conducted by Mrs. Joleen Levine, a recognized and experienced computer educator. She has been Director of Computer Education at Northern University for six years. During that time she has participated in many projects in Knox County, which involved teacher training, computer curriculum development, and computer assisted instruction implementation.
>
> I have reviewed this research study and feel that it is a very worthwhile endeavor for our students and school. Please review the information on the following page in order to make a decision concerning parental consent for your child to participate in this study.
>
> Sincerely,
>
> *Gwen Gregory*
>
> Gwen Gregory
> Principal

even parents. These groups have varying levels of knowledge and understanding regarding the research process. Their concerns will focus mainly on the perceived value of the study, its potential affective impact, and the actual logistics of carrying it out. The principal, for example, will probably be more concerned with whether you are collecting any data that might be viewed as objectionable by the community than with the specific design you will be using. All groups will be interested in what you might be able to do for them. Explain fully any potential benefits to be derived by the students, teachers, or principal as a result of your study. Your study, for example, might involve special instructional materials that are to be shared with the teachers and left with them after the study has ended. Even if all parties are favorably impressed, however, the spirit of cooperation will quickly dwindle if your study involves substantial extra work or inconvenience on their part. Bear in mind that principals and teachers are accommodating you, and are helping you complete your study without relief from their normal responsibilities. Thus, as much as possible, try to accommodate participants as best you can. Make any changes you can in the study to better accommodate participants' normal routine as long as you do not adversely affect your work or its results.

It is not unusual for the principal or teachers to want something in return for their participation. The request may be related to your study, as when a principal asks to review your final draft for accuracy, return to the school to brief teachers on your findings, or request that your results not be disseminated without the principal's approval. The first two requests are more easily agreed to than the third, which probably should be refused, but with an offer to discuss the principal's concerns, if any. It is common to ask the researcher to provide a session or two of professional development for teachers in the school.

Figure 3.3 presents a cover letter written by a principal in support of a doctoral student's proposed study. Note that the student secured not only the principal's permission, but also his strong support and cooperation, by sharing the potential benefits of the study with the principal's students. Figure 3.4 presents the parental consent form that accompanied the cover letter. It addresses many of the ethical and legal concerns discussed in this chapter.

Clearly, human relations is an important factor in conducting research in applied settings. That you should be your usual charming self goes without saying. But you should keep in mind that you are dealing with sincere, concerned educators who may not have your level of research expertise. Therefore, you must make a special effort to discuss your study in plain English (it is possible!) and to never give the impression that you are talking down to them. Also, your task is not over once the study begins. The feelings of involved persons must be monitored and responded to throughout the duration of the study if the initial level of cooperation is to be maintained.

COMPONENTS OF THE RESEARCH PLAN

Although they may go by other names, research plans typically include an introduction, a method section, a description of proposed data analyses, and a time schedule. Each component will be discussed in detail, but basically the format for a typical research plan is as follows:

INTRODUCTION
Statement of the Topic
Review of Related Literature
Statement of the Hypothesis (if appropriate)

METHOD
Participants
Instruments
Design
Procedure

FIGURE 3.4   Parental
consent form for a
proposed research study.

PARENTAL CONSENT FORM

The information provided on this form and the accompanying cover letter is presented to you in order to fulfill legal and ethical requirements for Northwest Eaton College (institution sponsoring this doctoral dissertation study) and the Department of Health and Human Services (HHS) regulations for the Protection of Human Research Subjects as amended on March 26, 1989. The wording used in this form is utilized for all types of studies and should not be misinterpreted for this particular study.

The dissertation committee at Northern University and the Research Review Committee of Knox County Public Schools have both given approval to conduct this study, "The Relationships Between the Modality Preferences of Elementary Students and Selected Instructional Styles of CAI as They Affect Verbal Learning of Facts." The purpose of this study is to determine the effect on achievement scores when the identified learning styles (visual, audio, tactile/kinesthetic) of elementary students in grades 3 and 5 are matched or mismatched to the instructional methods of specifically selected computer assisted instruction (CAI).

Your child will be involved in this study by way of the following:
1. Pretest on animal facts.
2. Posttest on animal facts.
3. Test on learning styles.
4. Interaction with computer-assisted instruction (CAI-software on the computer)—visual, audio, tactile CAI matching the student's own learning style.

All of these activities should not take more than two hours per student. There are no foreseeable risks to the students involved. In addition, the parent or researcher may remove the student from the study at any time with just cause. Specific information about individual students will be kept *strictly confidential* and will be obtainable from the school principal if desired. The results that are published publicly will not reference any individual students since the study will only analyze relationships among groups of data.

The purpose of this form is to allow your child to participate in the study, and to allow the researcher to use the information already available at the school or information obtained from the actual study to analyze the outcomes of the study. Parental consent for this research study is strictly voluntary without undue influence or penalty. The parent signature below also assumes that the child understands and agrees to participate cooperatively.

If you have additional questions regarding the study, the rights of subjects, or potential problems, please call the principal, Ms. Gwen Gregory, or the researcher, Ms. Joleen Levine (Director/Assistant of Computer Education, Northern University, 555-5554.

Student's Name

Signature of Parent/Guardian   Date

DATA ANALYSIS

TIME SCHEDULE

BUDGET (if appropriate)

Other headings may also be included, as needed. For example, if special materials are being developed for the study, or special equipment is being used (such as computer terminals), then headings such as Materials or Apparatus might be included under Method and before Design.

INTRODUCTION SECTION

If you have completed Task 2, you are familiar with the content of the introduction section: a statement of the topic, a review of related literature, and a statement of the hypothesis (if appropriate).

Statement of the Topic

Because the topic sets the stage for the rest of the plan, it should be stated as early as possible, given the nature of the particular research approach adopted. The statement should be accompanied by a description of the background of the topic and a rationale for its significance.

Review of Related Literature

The review of related literature should provide an overview of the topic and present references related to what is known about the topic. The literature sets a context for the topic and identifies prior research that can support the significance of your study. The literature review also can provide a basis for identifying hypotheses. The review should conclude with a brief summary of the literature and its implications. As with the statement of the topic, the timing of the review of related research may differ for quantitative and qualitative researchers.

Statement of the Hypothesis

For research plans that have one or more hypotheses, each hypothesis should have an underlying explanation for its prediction. That is, there should be some literature that supports the hypothesis. It should clearly and concisely state the expected relationship (or difference) between the variables in your study, and should define those variables in operational, measurable, or common-usage terms. The people reading your plan (and especially those reading your final report) may not be as familiar with your terminology as you are. Finally, each hypothesis should be clearly testable within a reasonable period of time.

METHOD SECTION

The specific method of research your study represents will affect the format and content of your method section. The method section for an experimental study, for example, typically includes a description of the experimental design, whereas a descriptive study may combine the design and procedure sections into one. The method section for a qualitative study may have varying forms and degrees of specificity, depending on when in the research process the method is written. In general, however, the method section includes a description of the research participants, measuring instruments, design and procedures, and data analysis.

Research Participants

The description of participants should identify the number, source, and characteristics of the sample.[4] It should also define the **population,** that is, the larger group from which the sample will be selected. What are they like? How many do you have to choose from? For example, a description of participants might include the following:

> Participants will be selected from a population of 157 students enrolled in an algebra I course at a large urban high school in Miami, Florida. The population is tricultural, being composed primarily of Caucasian non-Hispanic students, African American students, and Hispanic students from a variety of Latin American backgrounds.

---

[4] Chapter 4 describes the process of sampling participants.

The procedure for selecting the participants in the study can differ depending on whether a quantitative or qualitative study is being conducted. In general, quantitative research samples tend to be large and broadly representative, while qualitative research samples tend to be small and not necessarily broadly representative.

Instruments

This section describes the particular measures or instruments to be used in the study and how they will measure the variables stated in your hypothesis.[5] If you use instruments that are published, such as a standardized test, you should provide information about (1) the appropriateness of the chosen instruments for your study and sample; (2) the measurement properties of the instruments (especially validity[6] and reliability[7]); (3) the process of administering and scoring the instruments. If you are going to develop your own instrument, you should describe how the instrument will be developed, what it will measure, how you plan to evaluate its validity and reliability, and how it relates to your hypothesis and participants before its utilization in the actual study.

Of course, if more than one instrument is used—a common occurrence in many studies—each should be described separately and in detail. You may not yet be able to identify and describe the instrument you would use in your study. Consequently, in Task 3, you should describe the kind of instrument that would be used rather than stating a specific instrument. For example, you might say that your instrument will be a questionnaire about teacher unions that will allow teachers to express different degrees of agreement or disagreement to statements regarding teacher unions. In writing this section of a research plan, you may discover that an appropriate instrument for collecting the needed data is not available. If this occurs, you will need to decide whether to alter the hypothesis, change the selected variable, or develop your own instrument.

Qualitative research collects data using observation, note taking, and interviewing. If a formal instrument or test is used in conjunction with more qualitative data, it should be described in detail. Qualitative research should indicate the nature of evidence that will be collected and how it will be collected (e.g., observed field notes and tape recordings of teachers' perspectives on integrating special-needs students into the classroom, or photographs of dust-bowl children).

Materials/Apparatus

If special materials (such as booklets, training manuals, or computer programs) are to be developed for use in the study, they also should be described in the research plan. Also, if special apparatus (such as computer terminals) are going to be used, they should be described.

Design

A **design** is a general strategy or plan for conducting a research study. The description of the design indicates the basic structure and goals of the study. The nature of the hypothesis, the variables involved, and the constraints of the "real world" all contribute to the selection of the research design. For example, if the hypothesis involves comparing the effect of high-impact versus low-impact aerobic exercises with respect to exercise-related injuries, the study would involve comparing the number of injuries occurring in the two groups over some period of time. Thus, the design would involve two groups receiving different treatments and being

---

[5] Chapter 5 describes the nature of measures and instruments.

[6] Validity is concerned with whether the data or information being gathered are relevant to the decision to be made (see Chapter 5).

[7] Reliability is concerned with the stability or consistency of the data or information (see Chapter 5).

compared in terms of number of exercise-related injuries. Depending upon whether participants were randomly assigned to treatment or already in treatment before the study, the design would be, respectively, an experiment or a causal–comparative design. There are a number of basic research designs to select from and a number of variations within each design. Both quantitative and qualitative research rely on designs that will be discussed in more detail in later chapters.

Procedure

The procedure section describes all the steps that will be followed in conducting the study, from beginning to end, in the order in which they will occur. This section typically begins with a detailed description of the technique to be used to select the study participants. If the design includes a pretest, the procedures for its administration—when it will be administered and how—will usually be described next. Any other measure to be administered at the beginning of the study will also be discussed. For example, in addition to a pretest on current skill in reading music, a general musical achievement test might be administered in order to check for the initial equivalence of groups. For a study designed to compare two different methods of teaching reading comprehension to third graders, the procedure section might state the following:

> In September, one week following the first day of school, the Barney Test of Reading Comprehension, Form A, will be administered to both reading method groups.

In research plans that do not include a separate instrument section, relevant information concerning the instrument will be presented here.

From this point on, the procedure section will describe what is going to occur in the study. The nature of what will occur depends greatly on the kind of research study planned. The procedures for conducting an experiment are different from those for conducting a survey and different from a historical study. Further chapters will examine these differences in detail.

The procedure section should also include any identified assumptions and limitations. An **assumption** is any important "fact" presumed to be true but not actually verified. For example, in a study involving reading instruction for preschool children, it might be assumed that, given the population, none of the children had received reading instruction at home. Limitations in the study also should be noted. A **limitation** is some aspect of the study that the researcher knows may negatively affect the study but over which he or she has no control. Two common limitations are sample size and length of the study. A research plan might state, for example: "Only one class of 30 students will be available for participation" or "While ideally participants should be exposed to the experimental treatment for a longer period of time in order to more accurately assess its effectiveness, permission has been granted to the researcher to be in the school for a maximum of two weeks." Such limitations have an impact on the study and should be openly and honestly stated so readers can judge for themselves how seriously the limitations might affect the study results.

For both quantitative and qualitative research, issues such as the procedures for gaining entry to the research site, the way participants are selected, the way data are collected and scored, and study limitations belong in the procedures section. Although there may be different emphasis on these areas depending on whether the procedure section is written for quantitative or qualitative research, both should discuss all of the areas to some degree.

The procedure section should be as detailed as possible, and any new terms introduced should, of course, be defined. The key to writing this section is precision; it should be precise to the point where someone else could read your plan and conduct your study in the same way as you intended it to be conducted. The reason that a detailed description of the procedures is critical for research studies is that without detailed information of *how* a study was carried out, external readers cannot make reasonable judgments about the usefulness of the results. It is the appropriateness of the procedures that permits external readers to judge the quality of the study and its conclusions. This is true for both quantitative and qualitative research studies.

DATA ANALYSIS

The research plan must include a description of the technique or techniques that will be used to analyze study data. For certain descriptive studies, data analysis may involve little more than simple tabulation and presentation of counts and percentages. For most quantitative studies, however, one or more statistical methods will be required. Identification of appropriate analysis techniques is extremely important. Very few situations cause as much "weeping and gnashing of teeth" as collecting data only to find that there is no appropriate statistical analysis or that the analysis that is appropriate requires sophistication beyond the researcher's level of competence. Note that this caution is appropriate for both quantitative and qualitative research. Once the data are collected, it usually is too late. That is one reason you should submit a detailed research plan before beginning your study.

The hypothesis of a study determines the nature of the research design, which in turn determines the analysis. An inappropriate analysis does not permit a valid test of the research hypothesis. Which analysis technique should be selected depends on a number of factors, such as how the groups will be formed (for example, by random assignment, by matching, or by using existing groups), how many different treatment groups will be involved, how many variables will be involved, and the kind of data to be collected (e.g., counts of the number of times fifth-grade students fail to turn in their homework on time; a student's test score; or students' placement into one of five socioeconomic categories). Although you may not be familiar with a variety of specific analytic techniques, you probably can describe in your research plan the kind of analysis you would need. For example, you might say,

> An analysis will be used appropriate for comparing the achievement, on a test of reading comprehension, of two randomly formed groups of second-grade students.

By the time you get to Task 9, you will know exactly what you need (honest!).

Qualitative research sometimes combines qualitative (e.g., observation) and quantitative (e.g., test scores) data in studies, resulting in the need for statistical analysis. However, most qualitative research is heavily weighted towards interpretive, not statistical, data analysis. The researcher analyzes the qualitative data from interviews, field notes, observations, and the like by organizing and interpreting the data. Thus, qualitative research should describe the procedures for collating the various forms of data collected, the manner in which the data were categorized in terms of emergent themes in the data, and the rationale for the conclusions and interpretations made from the qualitative data. For example, you might state that you will use an analysis that allows field notes and interview data to be organized into a limited number of concepts or issues.

TIME SCHEDULE

A realistic time schedule is equally important for both beginning researchers working on a thesis or dissertation and for experienced researchers working under the deadlines of a research grant or contract. Researchers infrequently have unlimited time to complete a study. The existence of deadlines typically necessitates careful budgeting of time. Basically, a *time schedule* includes a listing of major activities or phases of the proposed study and a corresponding expected completion time for each activity. Such a schedule in a research plan enables the researcher to assess the feasibility of conducting a study within existing time limitations. It also helps the researcher to stay on schedule during the execution of the study. In developing a time frame, do not make the mistake of "cutting it too thin" by allocating a minimum amount of time for each activity. Allow yourself more time than you initially planned to account for unforeseen delays.

(Some call research a process designed to take 3 to 6 months longer than the researcher thinks it will. Be advised!) For example, your advisor might not be available when needed, your computer might malfunction and need a lengthy repair, or the teacher who agreed to let you collect data in her class might become ill and be out of school for three weeks. Plan to set the completion date for your final study sometime *before* your actual deadline. Also recognize that your schedule will not necessarily be a series of sequential steps that require one activity to be completed before another is begun. For example, while the study is being conducted, you may also be working on the first part of the research report.

BUDGET

Proposals submitted to governmental or private agencies for research support almost always require the inclusion of a tentative budget. Although researchers not seeking external funding for their research are not required to create a budget, it is useful to anticipate costs that might occur in the study. For example, costs such as computer programs, travel, printing, and mailing are common research expenses. It is not necessary to have a detailed budget for these and similar expenses, but recognize that conducting your study will include some personal expenditures.

As noted previously, there are many differences and distinctions between qualitative and quantitative research. Table 3.1 provides a contrast between the two approaches based on the discussed components of a research plan and written report. You will note that there are many differences between qualitative and quantitative research methods, but note also the similarities among the components.

REVISING AND IMPROVING A RESEARCH PLAN

Judging the adequacy of a research plan can involve both informal and formal assessment. Informally, the plan should be reviewed and critiqued by you, your advisor, and another experienced researcher. A research plan should be reviewed by at least one skilled researcher and at least one expert in the study's area of investigation. Any researcher, no matter how long she or he has been a researcher, can benefit from the insight of others. Rereading your own plan several days after having written it often identifies flaws or weaknesses.

Aspects of the research plan can be field tested in a **pilot study** in which the plan, or parts of it, are tried out on a small scale. Think of it as a dress rehearsal. In a pilot study all or part of the plan is tried out to identify unanticipated problems or issues. You can gain valuable experience from conducting a pilot study. Your research plan will almost always be modified as a result of a pilot study, and in some cases it may be substantially overhauled. One reason, aside from time, that more large-scale pilot studies are not conducted is lack of available participants. However, whenever feasible, conducting a pilot study, even a small one, should be considered a very worthwhile use of your time.

 Now go to the Companion Website accompanying this text at www.prenhall. com/gay to check your understanding of chapter concepts in the following modules: Objectives, Practice Quiz, and Applying What You Know. Expand your research skills with Evaluating Articles, Analyzing Qualitative Data, Analyzing Quantitative Data, and Research Tools and Tips. Visit Web Links to broaden your knowledge about research.

SUMMARY

Definition and Purpose of a Research Plan

1. A research plan is a detailed description of a proposed study; it includes justification for the study, a description of the steps that will be followed in the study, and information about the analysis of the collected data. The plan provides a guide for conducting the study.
2. The research plans of quantitative and qualitative researchers often differ in their construction. Quantitative researchers typically develop their research plans prior to the start of the study, while qualitative researchers typically develop their research plans as the research progresses and the researcher attains understanding of the participants and setting. Both approaches should have a research plan to guide their research activities.

TABLE 3.1   Components of a Research Plan: Comparing Quantitative and Qualitative Approaches

		QUANTITATIVE	QUALITATIVE
1.	Statement of a topic	Stated at the beginning to guide the research process	Topic not stated until the researcher has spent time in the setting and begins to understand the participants and the context in which they function
2.	Review of the literature	Conducted early in the study to identify related research, potential hypotheses, and methodological approaches	Literature typically examined after knowledge or participants and their context
3.	Hypotheses	Usually related to the review of literature; states researcher's hunches about the relations between the study variables; stated in operational terms; the hypothesis is more specific than the topic statement	Rarely states formal hypothesis; stays open to new understandings and data throughout the study; ongoing and shifting understandings
4.	Research participants	Participants chosen from a defined population, usually randomly; includes a large number of participants in the study; participants chosen at start of the study	Selects small, purposive participant group from the research context; relatively small number of participants who provide detailed data about themselves and life in their context; articulate participants' desired methods
5.	Data collection and instruments	Typically gathers data based on tests, questionnaires, and other paper and pencil instruments; little direct interaction with participants	Typically gathers data based on observations, interviews, note taking, and artifacts; deep levels of data obtained; substantial interaction between researcher and the participants
6.	Special materials or apparatus	Chosen and used as needed	Chosen and used as needed
7.	Research design	Clear, well-ordered sequence of steps to conduct the research; based on common quantitative approaches such as correlation, survey, causal–comparative, and true experiment	Variety of formats for the research; flexible and changeable during the research; based on common qualitative approaches such as ethnography, case study, action research, and grounded theory, among others.
		Note that in some cases, research designs can include *both* qualitative and quantitative methods. The two approaches are not totally independent of each other.	
8.	Research procedures	Describes what will be occurring in the research study. Although there are many different emphases in the research procedures, most of them are pertinent to both quantitative and qualitative research. Concerns such as research limits (unable to obtain needed participants or not gaining access to the research setting) and lack of research control (inability to obtain needed data or data being lost). A description of the procedures carried out in the study is critical to maintain, since without information about the researcher's processes, other researchers cannot make judgments and information about the research process and results.	
9.	Time schedule	Usually completes research in a relatively short time; data collected and analyzed relatively quickly; it is very useful to make a time schedule	Usually completes research in a lengthy time; much time to collect data in the field and interacting with participants over time; many iterations; it is very useful to make a time schedule
10.	Budget	Depends on the nature of the research study and the researcher's resources, including time; a realistic assessment of the research budget will help to decide on a reasonable research topic.	
11.	Data analysis	Includes a description of the quantitative methods used to collect primarily numerical data; data analysis is based on numerical and statistical analysis	Includes a description of the qualitative methods used to collect primarily descriptive data; data analysis is based on interpreting nonnumerical verbal data.
12.	Writing the report	Heavily focused on statistical analyses	Heavily focused on narrative description

3. Most quantitative studies test a hypothesis that influences decisions about the participation, measuring instruments, design, procedures, and statistical techniques used in the study. Researchers conducting a study with a qualitative approach rarely state and test hypotheses; they use an inductive approach instead.

4. A written research plan helps you to think through the aspects of your study, facilitates evaluation of the proposed study, and generally improves the quality of the research.

5. Part of good planning is anticipation. Try to anticipate potential problems that might arise, do what you can to prevent them, and plan your strategies for dealing with them if they do occur.

General Considerations in a Research Plan

The Ethics of Research

6. There are ethical considerations involved in all research studies, and all researchers must be aware of and attend to ethical considerations in their research.

7. Many professional organizations have developed ethical principles for their members, and the federal government has enacted laws to protect research participants from harm and invasion of privacy.

8. Most colleges and universities, as well as the U.S. government, require that proposed research activities involving human subjects be reviewed and approved by an authorized group in an institution, prior to the execution of the research, to ensure protection of the participants.

9. The two most overriding rules of ethics are that participants should not be harmed in any way (physically or mentally) and that the participants' privacy rights are maintained.

10. Probably the most definitive source of ethical guidelines for researchers is *Ethical Principles of Psychologists and Code of Conduct,* prepared for and published by the American Psychological Association (APA).

11. The Family Educational Rights and Privacy Act of 1974, referred to as the Buckley Amendment, protects the privacy of the educational records of students. It stipulates that data that identifies participants by name may not be made available to the researcher unless written permission is granted by the participants.

12. Studies involving deception of participants are sometimes unavoidable, but should be examined critically for unethical practices.

13. Both quantitative and qualitative research are subject to ethical guidelines. Qualitative researchers, because of their closeness to participants, must be aware of ethical issues.

Gaining Entry to the Research Site

14. It is rarely possible to conduct research without the cooperation of many people. The first step in acquiring needed cooperation is to follow required procedures in the setting you seek to conduct your research in.

15. A formal approval process usually involves the completion of one or more forms describing the nature of the research and the specific request being made of the school system.

16. The key to gaining approval and cooperation is good planning and a well-designed, carefully thought-out study.

17. Once formal approval for the study is granted, you should invest the time necessary to explain the study to the principal, the teachers, and perhaps even parents. If these groups do not cooperate, you likely will not be able to do your study.

18. If changes are requested and can be made to better accommodate the normal routine of the participants, these changes should be made unless the study will suffer as a consequence.

19. The feelings of participants should be monitored and responded to throughout the study if the initial level of cooperation is to be maintained. Human relations is an important aspect of conducting research in applied research settings.

Components of the Research Plan

20. Research plans typically include an introduction, a method section, a data analysis description, and a time schedule.

Introduction Section

21. The introduction includes a statement of the topic or question, a review of related literature, and a statement of the hypothesis (if appropriate) stated as an operational variable.

22. Qualitative researchers commonly withhold a statement topic, a literature review, and hypotheses until they are familiar with the participants and the research setting.

Method Section

23. The specific method of research your study represents influences the content of your method section. Particular approaches to research such as case study, causal–comparative, survey, and true experimental use different methods to carry out their unique purposes.

Research Participants

24. The description of participants should clearly define the number, source, and characteristics of the sample, as well as the population the sample was drawn from.

Instruments

25. This aspect of the method section provides a description of the particular measures, instruments, and approaches that will be used to collect data. It is necessary to provide a rationale for the specific selection of the instruments.

26. If you are going to develop your own instrument, you should describe how the instrument will be developed, what it will measure, and how you plan to determine its validity and reliability.

27. Qualitative researchers are their own data gathering instruments through observations, field notes, and interviews. The qualitative researcher describes in detail the nature and method of the data collected.

Design

28. A design is a general strategy for conducting a research study. Depending on the nature of the study's topic or question, the hypothesis (if appropriate), variables, and participants, the researcher selects an appropriate research design to carry the study. Both qualitative and quantitative researchers rely on research designs.

Procedure

29. The procedure section describes all the steps that will be followed in conducting the study, from beginning to end, in the order in which they will occur. The procedure will vary between qualitative and quantitative approaches.

30. The procedure section typically begins with a description of the strategy for selecting the sample or samples. If the study includes a pretest, the procedure and timing of it should be described next.

31. From this point on, the procedure section will describe exactly what is going to occur in the study. The nature of what will occur depends on the kind of research study planned, since the procedures for different research approaches are different.

32. The procedure section should also include any identified assumptions and limitations. An *assumption* is a "fact" presumed to be true but not actually verified, while a *limitation* is some aspect of the study that the researcher knows may alter the results.

33. The procedure section should be precise to the point that someone else could read your plan and execute your study exactly as you intended it to be conducted.

Data Analysis

34. The research plan must include a description of the techniques that will be used to analyze study data.

35. The hypothesis in a quantitative study or the question in a qualitative one determines the design, which in turn determines the data analysis.

36. Selecting an analysis technique depends on a number of factors, such as how the groups will be formed, how many there are, the number of variables that will be studied, and the kind of data to be collected.

37. Although qualitative researchers sometimes use quantitative data, their main analytical tool is their own analysis and interpretation of the qualitative data they have collected. They review their narrative data, organize it into categories and themes, and interpret it in terms of the context and participants' perspectives.

Time Schedule

38. The construction of a time schedule listing major research activities and their corresponding expected completion is a useful planning aid.

39. Allow for more time than you think you will need to complete your study. Plan for down time, and set your finishing date earlier than the final deadline for completion that you have set.

Revising and Improving a Research Plan

40. A written research plan permits careful examination by you and others regarding the quality of the plan and suggestions for how to improve it.

41. If possible, carry out a small-scale pilot study based on a few participants to help in refining or changing planned procedures. A pilot study can examine the viability of the research plan before it is fully conducted.

PERFORMANCE CRITERIA	TASK 3

The purpose of Task 3 is to have you construct a brief research plan. Your plan should state the topic or question you plan to examine and a hypothesis or research question you plan to examine. It should also provide information about the methods you will employ to carry out your study, including information about the research participants (sample), instruments, procedures, data analysis, and a time plan. While it is expected that your plan contain all the components of a research plan, it is not expected that your plan be extensive or technically accurate. Beginning with Chapter 4, you will learn ways to formulate each of a research plan's components. Feedback from your instructor concerning your research plan will also help you identify and critique aspects of a plan.

On the following pages an example is presented that illustrates the performance called for by Task 3 (see Task 3 example). This example is the task submitted by the same student whose task for Task 2 was previously presented. Thus, in this example the research plan is a continuation of the introduction. Keep in mind that the proposed activities described in this example do not necessarily represent ideal research procedure. Research plans are usually more detailed. The example given, however, does represent what you ought to be able to do at this point. Additional examples for this and subsequent tasks are included in the *Student Guide* that accompanies this text.

1

Effect of Interactive Multimedia on the Achievement of 10th-Grade Biology Students

Method

Participants

Participants for this study will be 10th-grade biology students in an upper-middle-class, all-girl Catholic high school in Miami, Florida. Forty students will be selected and divided into two groups.

Instrument

The effectiveness of interactive multimedia (IMM) will be determined by comparing the biology achievement of the two groups as measured by a standardized test, if there is an acceptable test available. Otherwise, one will be developed.

Design

There will be two groups of 20 students each. Students in both groups will be posttested in May using a test of biology achievement.

Procedure

At the beginning of the school year, 40 10th-grade biology students will be selected from a population of approximately 200. Selected students will be divided into two groups, and one group will be designated to be the experimental group. The same teacher will teach both classes.

　　During the school year, the nonexperimental group of students will be taught biology using traditional lecture and discussion methods. The students in the experimental group will be taught using IMM. Both groups will cover the same subject matter and use the same text. The groups will receive biology instruction for the same amount of time and in the same room, but not at the same time, as they will be taught by the same teacher.

2

Academic objectives will be the same for each class and all tests measuring achievement will be identical. Both classes will have the same homework reading assignments. In May, a biology achievement test will be administered to both classes at the same time.

Data Analysis

The scores of the two groups will be compared statistically.

	August	September . . . April	May	June
		Time Schedule		
Select Participants	____			
Pretest		_____		
Execute Study		_____		
Posttest			____	
Analyze Data				_____
Write Report			_____	

"[E]very individual has the same probability of being selected, and selection of one individual in no way affects selection of another individual." (p. 103)

SELECTING A SAMPLE

OBJECTIVES

After reading Chapter 4, you should be able to do the following:

1. Identify and describe four random sampling techniques.
2. Select a random sample using a table of random numbers.
3. Identify three variables that can be stratified.
4. Select stratified samples, cluster samples, and systematic samples.
5. Identify and describe three nonrandom sampling techniques.
6. Identify and briefly describe two major sources of sample bias.
7. Describe quantitative and qualitative sampling strategies.

The purpose of selecting a sample is to identify participants from whom to seek information. For example, if you were interested in the effect of daily homework assignments on the test scores of ninth-grade algebra students, it would not be possible to include all ninth-grade algebra students in the United States in your study. It would be necessary to select a smaller group that represents the characteristics of the larger group, the population. Thus, a sample is used to make an inference about the performance of the larger group. As you shall see in this chapter,

sampling strategies depend on the researcher's purpose and the selection of a research design. While all research involves the use of samples, the nature, size, and method of selecting samples vary with the research aim.

The goal of Chapter 4 is to help you to understand the importance of selecting an appropriate sample and become familiar with various sampling techniques. The first section of the chapter deals with quantitative sampling, the second with qualitative sampling. After you have read Chapter 4, you should be able to perform the following task.

TASK 4

Having selected a topic and having formulated one or more testable quantitative hypotheses, describe a sample appropriate for evaluating your hypotheses. This description will include the following:

1. A definition of the population from which the sample would be drawn
2. The procedural technique to select the sample, and if necessary, for forming it into two or more groups
3. Sample sizes
4. Possible sources of sampling bias

(See Performance Criteria, p. 119.)

QUANTITATIVE SAMPLING: DEFINITION AND PURPOSE

Sampling is the process of selecting a number of participants for a study in such a way that they represent the larger group from which they were selected. A **sample** comprises the individuals, items, or events selected from a larger group referred to as a *population*. Rarely do studies gather data from the entire population. In fact, not only is it generally not feasible to study the whole population, it is also not necessary. If the population of interest is large or geographically scattered, it's study would likely not be feasible due to prohibitive cost and/or substantive time. If a quantitative sample is well selected, the research results based on it will be generalizable to the population. If a qualitative sample is well selected, it will likely focus on a limited group of articulate participants.

As an example, suppose the superintendent of a large school system wanted to find out how the 5,000 teachers in that system felt about teacher unions, whether they would join one, and for what reasons. If interviews were selected as the best way to collect the desired data, it would take a very long time to interview each and every teacher. Even if each interview took only 15 minutes, it would take a minimum of 1,250 hours, 156 eight-hour days, or approximately 30 school weeks to collect data from all 5,000 teachers. On the other hand, if 10%, or 500, of the teachers were interviewed, it would take only 125 hours, or about 3 weeks to collect data. Assuming that the superintendent needed the information "now, not next year," the latter approach would definitely be preferable if it would yield the same information. If the sample of 500 teachers is correctly selected, the conclusions based on their interviews would in all probability be the same or very close to the conclusions based on interviews of all the teachers. Of course, selecting just any 500 teachers would not do. For example, selecting and interviewing 500 elementary teachers would not be satisfactory. In the first place, there is a highly disproportionate number of female elementary teachers, and males might feel differently about unions. In the second place, opinions of elementary teachers might not be the same as those of junior high teachers or senior high teachers. How about 500 teachers who were members of the National Education Association (NEA)? Although they would probably be more representative of all 5,000 teachers than just elementary teachers, they still would not do. Teachers who are already members of one professional organization would probably be more likely to join another organization. Nonmembers of the NEA *might* be more likely to join a different union, since it would approach certain problems differently. On the other hand, nonmembers of the NEA might hold a negative opinion of unions in general. In either case, however, it is reasonable to assume that the opinions toward unions of members and nonmembers of the NEA would be different. How, then, can we obtain an adequate representative sample?

Give up? Don't! There are several relatively simple sampling techniques that could be applied to select a representative sample of teachers. These procedures do not guarantee that a sample was perfectly representative of the population, but they would definitely increase the degree of confidence that the superintendent could have regarding the generalizability of findings based on the 500 teachers.

DEFINING A POPULATION

The first step in sampling is to define the population. The *population* is the group of interest to the researcher, the group to which the results of the study will ideally generalize. Examples of populations are all 10th-grade students in the United States, all elementary school gifted children in Utah, and all first-grade physically disabled students in Utopia County who have participated in preschool training. These examples illustrate two important points about populations. First, populations may be virtually any size and may cover almost any geographical area. Second, the entire group the researcher would really like to generalize to is rarely available. The population that the researcher would ideally like to generalize to is referred to as the **target population.** The population that the researcher can realistically select from is referred to as the **accessible,** or **available population.** In most studies, the chosen population is generally a realistic choice (e.g., accessible), not an idealistic one (i.e., target).

For example, suppose you decide to do a study of high school principals' opinions about having their students attend school 6 days a week. Suppose, also, that you wish to generalize your results to all high school principals in the United States. You quickly realize the difficulty of getting information from every high school principal in the United States, so you decide to obtain a representative sample of high school principals in the United States. But even this would be a difficult, time-consuming, and expensive effort. Faced with these obstacles, your research plan will have to be brought into line with cold, hard reality, so you decide to study only principals in your home state. By selecting from a more narrowly defined population you would be saving time and money, but you would also be losing generalizability. Your results would be directly generalizable to all high school principals in your home state, but not to all high school principals in the United States. It is important to define your population in sufficient detail so that others may determine how applicable your findings are to their situation.

Regardless of what sampling approach is used, it should describe the characteristics of the sample. This description should include the number of participants in the sample and a description of the *demographics* of the sample (e.g., average number of years teaching, percentage of each gender or racial group, level of education, achievement level). The nature of demographic data varies with the sample; the demographic information used to describe a sample of teachers would be different from that used to describe a sample of students, parents, or administrators.

SELECTING A RANDOM SAMPLE

Selecting a sample is a very important step in conducting a research study, particularly for quantitative research. The "goodness" of the sample determines the meaningfulness and generalizability of the research results. As discussed, a *good* sample is one that is representative of the population from which it was selected. As we saw with our superintendent who needed to assess teachers' attitudes, selecting a representative sample is not a haphazard process. There are several appropriate techniques for selecting a sample. Certain techniques are more appropriate for certain situations; the techniques provide different levels of assurance of sample representativeness.

Regardless of the quantitative technique, the steps in sampling are essentially the same: identify the population, determine the required sample size, and select the sample. There are four basic random sampling techniques or procedures: *simple random sampling, stratified sampling, cluster sampling,* and *systematic sampling.* They are referred to as **probability sampling** techniques because it is possible for the researcher to specify the probability, or chance, that each member of a defined population will be selected for the sample. These sampling techniques are all based on randomness in the selection of the sample.

SIMPLE RANDOM SAMPLING

Random sampling is the process of selecting a sample in such a way that all individuals in the selected population have an equal and independent chance to be selected for the sample. Randomness in sampling takes the selection of the sample completely out of the researcher's control by letting a random, or *chance,* procedure select the sample. In other words, every individual has the same probability of being selected, and selection of one individual in no way affects selection of another individual. You may recall in physical education class the teacher occasionally formed teams by having the class line up and count off by twos—one-two-one-two, and so on. With this method, you could never be on the same team as the person next to you. This selection process was *not* random, because whether you were on one team or another was determined by where you were in line and which team the person next to you was on. If selection of teams had been random, you would have had an equal (50–50) chance of being on either team, regardless of which team the person next to you played for.

Random sampling is the best single way to obtain a representative sample. Although no technique, not even random sampling, guarantees such a sample, the probability of achieving one is higher for this procedure than for any other. In most cases, the differences between the sample and the intended population are small. For example, you might not expect the exact same ratio of males and females in a sample as in a population, but random sampling assures that the ratio will be close and that the probability of having too many females is the same as the probability of having too many males. Also (and important), differences that do occur are a result of chance, not of the researcher's conscious or unconscious bias in selection.[1]

Another point in favor of random sampling is that it is required in many statistical analyses. These analyses permit the researcher to make inferences about a population based on the behavior of a sample. If samples are not randomly selected, then one of the major assumptions of many statistical analyses is violated, and inferences made from the research can be rendered suspect.

Steps in Simple Random Sampling

In general, random sampling involves defining the population, identifying each member of the population, and selecting participants for the sample on a completely chance basis. One way to do this is to write each individual's name on a separate slip of paper, place all the slips in a hat or other container, shake the container, and select slips from the container until the desired number of participants is selected. This procedure is not exactly satisfactory if a population has 1,000 or more members. One would need a very large hat—and a strong writing hand! A much more satisfactory approach is to use a *table of random numbers* (also called a table of random digits). In essence, a table of random numbers selects the sample for you, with each participant being selected on a purely random, or chance, basis. Such tables are included in the appendix of most statistics books and some educational research books; they usually consist of columns of five-digit numbers that are randomly generated by a computer to have no defined patterns or regularities (see Table A.1 in Appendix A for an example). Using a table of random numbers to select a sample involves the following specific steps:

1. Identify and define the population.
2. Determine the desired sample size.
3. List all members of the population.
4. Assign all individuals on the list a consecutive number from zero to the required number, for example, 000 to 249 or 00 to 89. Each individual must have the same number of digits as each other individual.
5. Select an arbitrary number in the table of random numbers. (Close your eyes and point!)
6. For the selected number, look at only the number of digits assigned to each population member. For example, if a population has 800 members, you only need to use the last 3 digits of the number; if a population has 90 members, you only need to use the last 2 digits.
7. If the number corresponds to a number assigned to an individual in the population, then that individual is in the sample. For example, if a population had 500 members and the number selected was 375, the individual assigned 375 would be in the sample; if a population had only 300 members, then 375 would be ignored.
8. Go to the next number in the column and repeat steps 6 and 7 until the desired number of individuals has been selected for the sample.

Once the sample has been selected, it may be used as is for a survey or correlation study or randomly subdivided into two or more subgroups for use in experimental or causal–comparative studies. If there will be only two subgroups, the full sample may be divided by flipping a coin—heads for one group, tails for the other.

---

[1] In Chapter 15 you will learn how to select and apply several commonly used inferential statistics. Don't you dare groan. You will be amazed at how easy statistics really is.

An Example of Simple Random Sampling

Actually, the random selection process is not as complicated as the step-by-step explanation might have seemed. The following example should make the procedure clear.

It is now time to help our long-suffering superintendent who wants to select a sample of teachers so that their attitudes toward unions can be determined. We will apply each of the eight random sample steps described to the superintendent's problem:

1. The population is all 5,000 teachers in the superintendent's school system.
2. The desired sample size is 10% of the 5,000 teachers, or 500 teachers.
3. The superintendent has supplied a directory that lists all teachers in the system.
4. Using the directory, the teachers are each assigned a number from 0000 to 4999.
5. A table of random numbers is entered at an arbitrarily selected number, such as the one underlined here.
   59058
   11859
   <u>53634</u>
   48708
   71710
   83942
   33278
   etc.
6. Since the population has 5,000 members, we are concerned only with the last four digits of the number, 3634.
7. There is a teacher assigned the number 3634; that teacher is therefore in the sample.
8. The next number in the column is 48708. The last four digits are 8708. Since there are only 5,000 teachers, there is no teacher assigned the number 8708. The number is therefore skipped.
9. Applying these steps to the remaining random numbers shown, teachers 1710, 3942, and 3278 are included. This procedure would be continued in succeeding columns until 500 teachers were selected.

At the completion of this process the superintendent would have, in all probability, a representative sample of all the teachers in the system. The 500 selected teachers could be expected to appropriately represent all relevant subgroups of teachers, such as elementary teachers, older teachers, male teachers, and so on. With simple random sampling, however, representation of specific subgroups is probable but not guaranteed. If you flip a quarter 100 times, the probable outcome is 50 heads and 50 tails. You might get 53 heads and 47 tails, or 45 heads and 55 tails, but most of the time you can expect to get close to a 50–50 split. (You try!) Other, more deviant outcomes are also possible, but relatively infrequent. In tossing a quarter 100 times, 85 heads and 15 tails is a possible but very low-probability outcome. Similarly, if 55% of the 5,000 teachers were female and 45% were male, we would expect roughly the same percentages in the random sample of 500. Just by chance, however, the sample might turn out to be 30% females and 70% males.

The superintendent might not be willing to leave accurate representation to chance. If there were one or more variables that the superintendent believed might be highly related to attitudes toward unions, she might adopt a different sampling approach. She might decide that teaching level (elementary, middle, high) would be a significant variable and that elementary teachers might feel differently toward unions than middle or senior high school teachers. She would want a sample that would guarantee appropriate representation of the three teaching levels. To accomplish this she would probably use stratified sampling rather than simple random sampling.

STRATIFIED SAMPLING

Stratified sampling is the process of selecting a sample in such a way that identified subgroups in the population are represented in the sample in the same proportion that they exist in the population. (A subgroup or **strata** is a variable that can be divided into groups. As examples, the variable *gender* can be divided into a male group and a female group; the variable *politicians* can be divided into groups of Democrat, Republican, Independent, and others; and the variable *level of education* can be divided into various groups—elementary, high school, college, and higher.) This method of sampling can also be used to select equal-sized samples from each of a number of subgroups if subgroup comparisons are desired. *Proportional stratified sampling,* as this method is called, would be appropriate, for example, if you were going to take a survey prior to a national election in order to predict the probable winner. You would want your sample to represent the voting population. Therefore, you would want the proportion of Democrats and Republicans in your sample to be the same as in the population. If Democrats made up 63 percent of registered voters and Republicans made up 37 percent of registered voters, you would want 63 percent of the sample to be Democrats and 37 percent to be Republicans. Other likely variables for proportional stratification might include race, gender, socioeconomic status, and level of education.

Alternatively, equal-sized or nonproportional samples would be most useful if you wanted to compare the performance of different subgroups. Suppose, for example, that you were interested in comparing the achievement of students of different ability levels (high, average, and low) being taught by two methods of mathematics instruction (teacher and computer). Simply selecting a random sample of students and assigning one half of the sample to each of the two methods would not (as you know!) guarantee equal representation of each of the ability levels in each method. In fact, just by chance, one of the methods might not have any students from one of the three ability levels. However, randomly selecting students separately for the three ability levels and then assigning half of each ability level to each of the methods would guarantee equal representation of each ability level in each method. The purpose of stratified sampling is to guarantee desired representation of relevant subgroups within the sample.

Steps for Equal-Sized Groups in Stratified Sampling

The steps in stratified sampling are similar to those in random sampling except that selection is from subgroups in the population rather than the population as a whole. In other words, random sampling is done more than once; it is done for each subgroup. Stratified sampling involves the following steps:

1. Identify and define the population.
2. Determine desired sample size.
3. Identify the variable and subgroups (strata) for which you want to guarantee appropriate, equal representation.
4. Classify all members of the population as members of one of the identified subgroups.
5. Randomly select (using a table of random numbers) an "appropriate" number of individuals from each of the subgroups. *Appropriate* in this case means an equal number of individuals.

As with simple random sampling, once the samples from each of the subgroups have been randomly selected, each may be randomly assigned to two or more treatment groups. If we were interested in the comparative effectiveness of two methods of mathematics instruction for different levels of ability, the steps in sampling might be as follows:

1. The population is all 300 eighth-grade students enrolled in general math at Central Middle School.

2. The desired sample size is 45 students in each of the two methods.
3. The variable is ability and the desired subgroups are three levels of ability—high, average, and low.
4. Classification of the 300 students indicates that there are 45 high-ability students, 215 average-ability students, and 40 low-ability students.
5. Using a table of random numbers, 30 students are randomly selected *from each of the ability subgroups,* that is, 30 high-, 30 average-, and 30 low-ability students. This gives us three samples, one for each ability group.
6. The 30 students in each sample are randomly assigned to one of the two methods; that is, 15 of each 30 are randomly assigned to one of the two methods. Therefore, each method contains 45 students—15 high-ability students, 15 average-ability students, and 15 low-ability students (Figure 4.1).

As you may have guessed, stratification can be done on more than one variable. In this example, we could have stratified on math interest or prior math grades. The following example, based on a familiar situation, should help to further clarify the process of stratified sampling.

An Example of Proportional Stratified Sampling

Let us suppose that our old friend the superintendent wanted to guarantee proportional representation of teaching level in the sample of teachers. We will apply each of the five steps previously described for selecting a stratified sample:

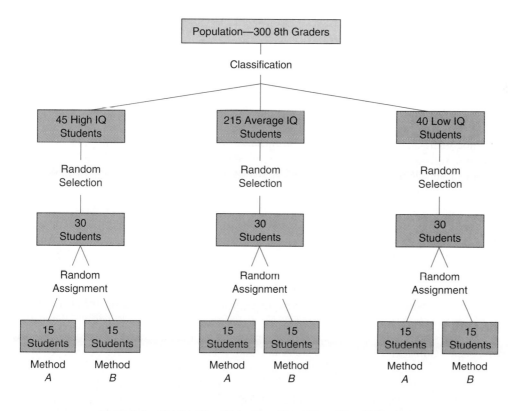

FIGURE 4.1
Procedure for selecting a stratified sample based on IQ for a study designed to compare two methods (A and B) of mathematics instruction.

Method *A* = 15 High IQ + 15 Average IQ + 15 Low IQ = 45 Students
Method *B* = 15 High IQ + 15 Average IQ + 15 Low IQ = 45 Students

1. The population is all 5,000 teachers in the superintendent's school system.
2. The desired sample size is 10% of the 5,000 teachers, or 500 teachers.
3. The variable of interest is teaching level, and there are three subgroups—elementary, middle, and high.
4. We classify the teachers into the subgroups. Of the 5,000 teachers, 65%, or 3,250, are elementary teachers; 20%, or 1,000, are middle teachers; and 15%, or 750, are senior high teachers.
5. We want 500 teachers. Since we want proportional representation, 65% of the sample (325 teachers) should be elementary teachers, 20% (100 teachers) should be junior high teachers, and 15% (75 teachers) should be senior high teachers.

Therefore, using a table of random numbers, 325 of the 3,250 elementary teachers are randomly selected (makes sense, since we want a total sample of 10%), 100 of the 1,000 junior high teachers are selected, and 75 of the 750 senior high teachers are selected.

At the completion of this process, the superintendent would have a sample of 500 teachers (325 + 100 + 75), or 10% of the 5,000, and each teaching level would be proportionally represented. Note that using proportionally sized groups requires that you have accurate information about the size of each group. Without this information, proportional group studies are not recommended.

So far we have discovered two ways in which the superintendent could get a sample of teachers, simple random sampling and stratified sampling. Both of these techniques, however, would result in a sample scattered over the entire district. The interviewer would have to visit many, many schools; some of them containing only one or two teachers. In the event that the superintendent wanted the information quickly, a more expedient method of sampling would be needed. For the sake of convenience, cluster sampling might be used.

CLUSTER SAMPLING

Cluster sampling randomly selects groups, not individuals. All the members of selected groups have similar characteristics. For example, instead of randomly selecting from all fifth-graders in a large school district, you could randomly select fifth-grade *classrooms* and use all the students in each classroom. Cluster sampling is most useful when the population is very large or spread out over a wide geographic area. Sometimes it is the only feasible method of selecting a sample because it is not always possible to obtain a list of all members of the population. Also, educational researchers frequently cannot select and assign individual participants, as they may like. For example, if your quantitative study's population were 10th-grade biology students, it is very unlikely that you would obtain administrative approval to randomly select and remove a selected few students from different classrooms for your study. You would have a much better chance of securing permission to use several intact classrooms. (Note that qualitative researchers typically work with small samples. This is one of the major differences between quantitative and qualitative sampling.)

Any location within which we find an intact group of similar characteristics (population members) is a **cluster.** Examples of clusters are classrooms, schools, city blocks, hospitals, and department stores. Cluster sampling usually involves less time and expense and is generally convenient. Consider a few examples that illustrate this point. As the prior example of 10th-grade biology students illustrated, it is easier to obtain permission to use *all* the students in several classrooms than selecting a few students in many classrooms. Similarly, in doing a survey, it is easier to use all the people in a limited number of city blocks than a few people in many city blocks. In each case you should note that cluster sampling would be easier (though not necessarily as good, as we shall see later!) than either simple random sampling or stratified sampling.

Steps in Cluster Sampling

The steps in cluster sampling are not very different from those in random sampling. The major difference, of course, is that random selection of groups (clusters) is involved, not individuals. Cluster sampling involves the following steps:

1. Identify and define the population.
2. Determine the desired sample size.
3. Identify and define a logical cluster (neighborhood, school, city block, etc.).
4. List all clusters (or obtain a list) that make up the population of clusters.
5. Estimate the average number of population members per cluster.
6. Determine the number of clusters needed by dividing the sample size by the estimated size of a cluster.
7. Randomly select the needed number of clusters (using a table of random numbers).
8. Include in your study all population members in each selected cluster.

Cluster sampling can be carried out in stages, selecting clusters within clusters. For example, a district in a state, then schools in the district, and then classrooms in the schools could be randomly selected to sample classrooms for a study. This process is called *multistage sampling.*

One common misconception about cluster sampling is that it is appropriate to randomly select only a single cluster. It is not uncommon, for example, for some researchers to define a population as all fifth graders in Knox County, to define a cluster as a school, and to randomly select only one school in the population. These same "researchers" would not dream of randomly selecting only one student! The principle is the same. Keeping in mind that a good sample is representative of the population from which it is selected, it is highly unlikely that one randomly selected student could ever be representative of an entire population. Similarly, it is unlikely that one randomly selected school could be representative of all schools in a population. Thus, one would normally have to select a number of clusters for the results of a study to be generalizable to the population. The following example makes clearer the procedures involved in cluster sampling.

An Example of Cluster Sampling

Let us see how our superintendent would get a sample of teachers if cluster sampling were used. We will follow the steps previously listed:

1. The population is all 5,000 teachers in the superintendent's school system.
2. The desired sample size is 500.
3. A logical, useful cluster is a school.
4. The superintendent has a list of all the schools in the district; there are 100 schools.
5. Although the schools vary in the number of teachers per school, there is an average of 50 teachers per school.
6. The number of clusters (schools) to be selected equals the desired sample size, 500, divided by the average size of a cluster, 50. Thus, the number of schools needed is $(500 \div 50) = 10$.
7. Therefore, 10 of the 100 schools are randomly selected by assigning a number to each school and using a table of random numbers.
8. All the teachers in each of the 10 schools are in the sample (10 schools, 50 teachers per school on average, equals the desired sample size).

Thus, the interviewer could conduct interviews at 10 schools and interview all teachers in each school instead of traveling to a possible 100 different schools. The advantages of cluster sampling are evident. As with most things, however, nothing is all good. Cluster sampling has several drawbacks. For one thing, the chances are greater of selecting a sample that is not representative of the population. The smaller the sample size, the more likely that the sample selected may not represent the population. For example, the teachers in this example are from a limited number of schools, so the possibility exists that the 10 schools selected are somehow different from the other 90 in the district, for example, in socioeconomic level of the students, teacher experience, and so forth. One way to compensate for this problem is by selecting a larger sample of clusters.

As another example, suppose our population was all fifth-graders in 10 schools (each school having an average of 120 students in four classes of 30 students each), and we wanted a sample of 120 students. There are any number of ways we might select our sample. For example, we could (1) randomly select one school and use all the fifth-graders in that school, (2) randomly select two classes from each of two schools, or (3) randomly select 120 students from the 10 schools. In any of these ways we would wind up with 120 students, but our sample would probably not be equally "good" in each case. In case 1 we would have students from only one school. It is very likely that this school would be different from the other nine in some significant way. In case 2 we would be doing a little better, but we would still only have 2 of the 10 schools represented. Only in case 3 would we have a chance of selecting a sample containing students from all or most of the schools, and the classes within those schools. If random sampling were not feasible, as is often the case, selecting two classes from each of two schools would be preferable to selecting all the students in one school. Actually, if cluster sampling were used, it would be even better to select one class each from four of the schools. One way we could attempt to compensate for the loss of representativeness associated with cluster sampling would be to select more than four classes.

Another problem is that commonly used statistical methods are not appropriate for analyzing data resulting from a study using cluster sampling. Such statistics generally require randomly formed groups, not those selected in a whole cluster. The methods that are available and appropriate for cluster samples are generally less sensitive to differences that may exist between groups. Thus, one should carefully weigh the advantages and disadvantages of cluster sampling before choosing this method of sampling.

SYSTEMATIC SAMPLING

Systematic sampling is not used very often, but it is appropriate in certain situations. In some instances it is the only feasible way to select a sample. **Systematic sampling** is sampling in which individuals are selected from a list taking every Kth name. So what's a "Kth" name? That depends on what K is. If $K = 4$, selection involves taking every 4th name; if $K = 10$, every 10th name is taken; and so forth. What K actually equals depends on the size of the list and the desired sample size. The major difference between systematic sampling and the other types of sampling discussed is that all members of the population do not have an independent chance of being selected for the sample. Once the first name is selected, all the rest of the individuals to be included in the sample are automatically determined.

Even though choices are not independent, a systematic sample can be considered a random sample if the list of the population is randomly ordered. One or the other has to be random—either the selection process or the list. Since randomly ordered lists are rarely available, systematic sampling is rarely as "good" as random sampling. While some researchers argue this point, the major objection to systematic sampling of a nonrandom list is the possibility that certain subgroups of the population can be systematically excluded from the sample. A classic example is that certain nationalities have distinctive last names that tend to group together under certain letters of the alphabet; when taking every Kth name from an alphabetized list, if K is at all large, it is possible that certain nationalities can be skipped over completely.

Steps in Systematic Sampling

Systematic sampling involves the following steps:

1. Identify and define the population.
2. Determine the desired sample size.
3. Obtain a list of the population.
4. Determine what K is equal to by dividing the size of the population by the desired sample size.
5. Start at some random place in the population list. Close your eyes and stick your finger on a name.
6. Starting at that point, take every Kth name on the list until the desired sample size is reached.
7. If the end of the list is reached before the desired sample is reached, go back to the top of the list.

Now let us see how our superintendent would use systematic sampling.

An Example of Systematic Sampling

If our superintendent used systematic sampling, the process would be as follows:

1. The population is all 5,000 teachers in the superintendent's school system.
2. The desired sample size is 500.
3. The superintendent has a directory that lists all teachers in the system in alphabetical order. The list is not randomly ordered, but it is the best available.
4. K is equal to the size of the population, 5,000, divided by the desired sample size, 500. Thus $K = (5,000 \div 500) = 10$.
5. Select one random name in the list of teachers.
6. From that point, every following 10th name is automatically in the sample. For example, if the teacher selected in step 5 were the 3rd name on the list, then the sample would include the 13th name, the 23rd, the 33rd, the 43rd, and so forth.

In this case, due to the nonrandom nature of the list, the sample might not be as representative as the samples resulting from application of the other techniques. Table 4.1 summarizes characteristics of the four quantitative random sampling approaches.

DETERMINING SAMPLE SIZE

The sampling question most frequently asked by beginning researchers is probably, "How large should my sample be?" And the answer is, "large enough!" While this answer is not very comforting—or precise—the question is a difficult one. If the sample is too small, the results of the study may not be generalizable to the population. A sample that is too small can affect the generalizability of the study regardless of how well it is selected. Suppose, for example, the population were 300 first graders. If we randomly selected only one student, clearly that student could not represent all the students. Nor could two, three, or four students, even if randomly selected, adequately represent the population. On the other hand, we would all agree that a sample of 299, 298, or 297 students would represent the population. How about 10? Too small, you say. OK, how about 30? 75? 100? At what point does the sample size stop being "too small" and become "big enough"? That is a question without an easy answer.

Knowing that the sample should be as large as possible helps some but still does not give any specific guidance as to what size sample is "big enough." In many cases, the researcher does not have access to large numbers of potential research participants. Or obtaining

TABLE 4.1   Random Sampling Strategies

Type	Process	Advantages	Disadvantages
Simple random sampling	Select desired number of sample members using a table of random numbers.	Easy to conduct; strategy requires minimum knowledge of the population to be sampled.	Need names of all population members; may over- or underrepresent sample members; there is difficulty in reaching all selected in sample.
Stratified random sampling	Divide population into separate levels or strata and randomly sample from the separate strata.	More precise sample; can be used for both proportions and stratification sampling; sample represents the desired strata.	Need names of all population members; difficulty of reaching all selected in sample; researcher must have names of all populations.
Cluster sampling	Select groups, not individuals; identify clusters and randomly select them to reach desired sample size.	Efficient; clusters are most likely to be used in school research; don't need names of all population members; reduces travel to sites.	Fewer sampling points make it less likely to have a representative sample.
Systematic sampling	Using list of population, pick a name on list at random and select each Kth person on the list to the desired sample size.	Sample selection is simple.	All members of population do not have an equal chance to be selected; Kth person may be related to a periodic order in the population list, producing unrepresentativeness in the sample.

permission from potential participants is difficult. Usually the problem is too few participants rather than too many.

The minimum sample size depends on the type of research involved. Some cite a sample size of 30 as a guideline for correlational, causal–comparative, and true experimental research. Thus, for correlational studies at least 30 participants are needed to establish the existence or nonexistence of a relationship. For causal–comparative and true experimental studies, a minimum of 30 participants *in each group* is recommended, although in some cases it might be difficult to attain this number for each group. The larger the sample, the more likely one would be to detect a difference between the different groups. We would not be very confident about the results of a single study based on small samples, but if a number of such studies obtained similar results, our confidence in the findings would generally be higher. What is important for you to understand is the consequences of a small quantitative sample size.

For descriptive research, it is common to sample 10 to 20% of the population, although this range will change with the size of the population studied. In reality, the appropriate sample size depends on a number of factors such as the specific type of descriptive research involved, the size of the population, and whether data will be analyzed for given subgroups. Based on a formula originally developed by the United States Office of Education, Krejcie and Morgan generated the numbers shown in Table 4.2. For a given population size (N), Table 4.2 indicates the sample size (S) needed for the sample to be representative, assuming one is going to survey a random sample. Although it is true that in certain respects Table 4.2 represents an oversimplified approach to determining sample size, it does suggest some

TABLE 4.2   Sample Sizes (S) Required for Given Population Sizes (N)

N	S	N	S	N	S	N	S	N	S
10	10	100	80	280	162	800	260	2800	338
15	14	110	86	290	165	850	265	3000	341
20	19	120	92	300	169	900	269	3500	346
25	24	130	97	320	175	950	274	4000	351
30	28	140	103	340	181	1000	278	4500	354
35	32	150	108	360	186	1100	285	5000	357
40	36	160	113	380	191	1200	291	6000	361
45	40	170	118	400	196	1300	297	7000	364
50	44	180	123	420	201	1400	302	8000	367
55	48	190	127	440	205	1500	306	9000	368
60	52	200	132	460	210	1600	310	10000	370
65	56	210	136	480	214	1700	313	15000	375
70	59	220	140	500	217	1800	317	20000	377
75	63	230	144	550	226	1900	320	30000	379
80	66	240	148	600	234	2000	322	40000	380
85	70	250	152	650	242	2200	327	50000	381
90	73	260	155	700	248	2400	331	75000	382
95	76	270	159	750	254	2600	335	100000	384

Source: R. V. Krejcie and D. W. Morgan (1970). Determining sample size for research activities. *Educational and Psychological Measurement, 30,* 608. Copyright © 1970 by Sage Publications. Reprinted by permission of Sage Publications, Inc.

general rules of thumb. As with other types of research, statistical techniques and related software are available for determining sample size in a more precise way, given knowledge of relevant related variables.

Table 4.2 does, however, suggest the following generalities:

1. The larger the population size, the smaller the percentage of the population required to get a representative sample.
2. For smaller populations, say, $N = 100$ or fewer, there is little point in sampling; survey the entire population.
3. If the population size is around 500 (give or take 100), 50% should be sampled.
4. If the population size is around 1,500, 20% should be sampled.
5. Beyond a certain point (about $N = 5,000$), the population size is almost irrelevant and a sample size of 400 will be adequate. Thus, the superintendent from our previous examples would be relatively safe with a sample of 400 teachers, but would be even more confident with a sample of 500.

Of course, these numbers or percentages are suggested minimums. If it is at all possible to obtain more participants, you should do so. Using samples larger than these minimums is especially important in many situations. For example, in true experimental study the difference between groups is more likely to show up if the samples are large. There are relatively precise statistical techniques and computer programs that can be used to estimate required sample sizes given knowledge of certain facts about the population.

AVOIDING SAMPLING ERROR AND BIAS

Selecting random samples does not guarantee that they will be representative of the population. **Sampling error,** which is beyond the control of the researcher, is a reality of random sampling. Of course, no sample will have a composition precisely identical to that of the population. However, if well selected and sufficiently large, the chances are that the sample will closely represent the population. Occasionally, however, just by chance (remember, *random* means out of the researcher's control and at the mercy of chance), a sample will differ significantly from the population on some important variable. If there is a variable for which the sample is greatly underrepresented, the researcher should stratify on that variable because stratification can provide proportional or equal-sized samples.

Sampling bias is quite different from sampling error. Sampling bias does not result from random differences between samples and populations. Sampling bias is nonrandom and is generally the fault of the researcher. Some aspect of the sampling creates a bias in the data. For example, suppose a researcher who wished to study the attitudes of college students toward alcohol stood outside bars and asked patrons leaving the bars to answer questions regarding their attitudes toward alcohol. This would be a biased sample. Remember, the study was to be about college students' attitudes—all types of college students. By sampling outside bars, the researcher systematically omitted college students who don't go to bars. The sampling bias in the study makes the study conclusions invalid. Similarly, when a survey researcher gets a return of only 45 percent of questionnaires sent out, the large number of nonreturns introduces a potential response bias in the results.

These examples illustrate how sample bias greatly affects the validity of the study. Researchers should be aware of sources of sampling bias and do their best to avoid it. Securing administrative approval to involve students in educational research studies is not easy, however. Of necessity, researchers often are forced to use whatever samples they can get and whatever methods that teachers and administrators will allow. Cooperating with teachers and administrators is, of course, advisable, but not at the expense of good research. If your study cannot be conducted properly under the administrators' restrictions, try hard to convince the administration to allow the study to be conducted in a way that will provide viable results. If this fails, you should look elsewhere for participants.

If it is not possible to avoid sampling bias, you must decide whether the bias is so severe that the study results will be seriously affected. If you decide to continue with the study, with full awareness of the existing bias, such bias should be completely reported in the final research report. This allows the consumers of the research to decide for themselves how serious the bias is.

SELECTING A NONRANDOM SAMPLE

Although random sampling techniques provide the best opportunity to obtain unbiased samples, it is not always possible for researchers to use random sampling. For example, teachers or administrators often select the students or classes they want researchers to study to ensure a good impression or result in the outcome, or you might not find many people willing to participate in your study. These and similar factors can introduce sampling bias. **Nonprobability sampling**—also called *nonrandom sampling*—methods do not have random sampling at any stage of sample selection.

When nonrandom samples are used, it is usually difficult, if not impossible, to describe the population from which a sample was drawn and to whom results can be generalized. Nonrandom sampling approaches include *convenience sampling, purposive sampling,* and *quota sampling.* Of these methods, convenience sampling is the most used in educational research, and is therefore the major source of sampling bias in educational research studies.

CONVENIENCE SAMPLING

Convenience sampling, also referred to as **accidental sampling** and **haphazard sampling,** includes in the sample whomever happens to be available at the time. Two examples of convenience sampling are the use of volunteers and the use of existing groups. For example, have you ever been stopped on the street or in a grocery store by someone who wants your opinion of an event or of a new kind of muffin? Those who volunteer to answer are usually different from nonvolunteers. They may be more motivated or more interested in the particular study. Since the total population is composed of both volunteers and nonvolunteers, the results of a study based solely on volunteers are not likely generalizable to the entire population. Suppose you send a questionnaire to 100 randomly selected people and ask the question, "How do you feel about questionnaires?" Suppose that 40 people respond and all 40 indicate that they love questionnaires. Should you then conclude that the group from which the sample was selected loves questionnaires? Certainly not. The 60 who did not respond may not have done so simply because they hate questionnaires!

PURPOSIVE SAMPLING

In **purposive sampling,** also referred to as **judgment sampling,** the researcher selects a sample based on his experience and knowledge of the group to be sampled. For example, if a researcher planned to study exceptional high schools, he would choose schools to study based on his knowledge of exceptional schools. Prior knowledge or experience might lead the researcher to select exceptional high schools based on criteria such as proportions of students going to four-year colleges, large numbers of AP students, extensive computer facilities, and high proportions of teachers with advanced degrees. Notice that there is an important difference between convenience samples, in which participants who happen to be available are chosen, and purposive sampling, in which the researcher uses experience and prior knowledge to identify criteria for selecting the sample. Clear criteria provide a basis for describing and defending purposive samples. Much of the sampling in qualitative research is purposive. The main weakness of purposive sampling is the potential for inaccuracy in the researcher's criteria and resulting sample selections.

QUOTA SAMPLING

Quota sampling is most often used in survey research when it is not possible to list all members of the population of interest. When quota sampling is involved, data gatherers are given exact characteristics and quotas of persons to be interviewed (e.g., 35 working women with children under the age of 16, 20 working women with no children under the age of 16). This technique of sampling is widely used in large-scale surveys. Obviously, when quota sampling is used, data are obtained from easily accessible individuals. Thus, people who are less accessible (more difficult to contact, more reluctant to participate, and so forth) are underrepresented.

QUALITATIVE SAMPLING: DEFINITION AND PURPOSE

The prior sections of this chapter focused on selecting samples for quantitative studies, those based on large samples, generalization to a population, and statistical analyses of gathered data. Qualitative research samples are generally different from those of quantitative research because the two approaches have different aims and needs. Recall that qualitative research is characterized by in-depth inquiry, immersion in a setting, emphasis on context, concern with participants' perspectives, and description of a single setting, not generalization to many settings.

These characteristics call for sampling approaches that differ from those of quantitative research. For example, the qualitative researcher's interest in participants' perspectives of both their setting and the research topic being studied requires more in-depth data collection than that typically conducted in quantitative research. While a quantitative researcher might ask, "What teacher behaviors are correlated with the amount of time students will continue on a task?" a qualitative researcher might ask, "What meanings do students and teacher create together about time on task, and how are the perspectives of different students manifested when working on tasks?" To obtain the desired depth of information required by such topics, qualitative researchers must almost always deal with small samples, normally interacting over a long period of time and in great depth.

Because qualitative samples tend to be small relative to quantitative samples, and because many potential participants are unwilling to undergo the lengthy demands of participation, sampling in qualitative research is almost always purposive. That is, the experience and insight of the researcher is used to select a sample; randomness is rarely part of the process. One reason qualitative researchers spend time in the research setting before selecting a sample is to observe and obtain information that can be generally used to select a purposive sample of participants whom they judge to be thoughtful, informative, articulate, and experienced with the research topic and setting. The primary focus is on these characteristics, not on participants who necessarily represent some larger population. Remember, one of the basic tenets of qualitative research is that each research setting is unique in its own mix of people and contextual factors. The researcher's intent is to describe a particular context in depth, not to generalize to a context or population. Representativeness is secondary to the quality of the participants' ability to provide the desired information about self and setting.

Within the domain of qualitative purposive sampling there a number of specific approaches that are used in qualitative research. Table 4.3 illustrates the range of qualitative sampling approaches, providing an example of use and a sample strategy for each of five common types.

In many qualitative studies combinations of these and other purposive sampling approaches may be used to identify and narrow a sample. For example, qualitative researchers can test the robustness of their findings by purposively selecting a few new participants and determining whether they provide similar information and perspectives as the original group of participants.

Qualitative research uses sampling strategies that produce samples that are predominantly small and nonrandom. This is in keeping with qualitative research's emphasis on in-depth description of participants' perspectives and context. The nature of data collection limits the number of research participants who can be accommodated in qualitative studies, typically leading to purposive sampling to insure that the "best" participants are included. In spite of the variety of purposive sampling techniques used by qualitative researchers, it is important to remember that purposive samples often do not provide information about the sample. This means that both qualitative and quantitative researchers who use samples must provide detailed information about purposive research participants and how they were chosen.

Now go to the Companion Website accompanying this text at www.prenhall.com/gay to check your understanding of chapter concepts in the following modules: Objectives, Practice Quiz, and Applying What You Know. Expand your research skills with Evaluating Articles, Analyzing Qualitative Data, Analyzing Quantitative Data, and Research Tools and Tips. Visit Web Links to broaden your knowledge about research.

SUMMARY

Quantitative Sampling: Definition and Purpose

1. *Sampling* is the process of selecting a number of individuals for a study in such a way that the individuals represent the larger group from which they were selected.

2. The purpose of sampling is to gain information about a larger population. A *population* is the group to which a researcher would like the results of a study to be generalizable.

TABLE 4.3   Examples of Qualitative Sampling

TYPE	EXAMPLE	SAMPLE STRATEGY
Intensity sampling	Selecting participants who permit study of different levels of the research topic; for example, the researcher might select some good and poor students, experienced and inexperienced teachers, or teachers with small and large classes.	Compare differences of two or more levels of the topic, (e.g., good versus bad students); select two groups of about 20 participants from each of the two levels.
Homogeneous sampling	Selecting participants who are very similar in experience, perspective, or outlook; this produces a narrow, homogeneous sample and makes data collection and analysis simple.	Select a small group of participants who fit a narrow, homogeneous topic; collect data from the chosen participants.
Criterion sampling	Select all cases that meet some set of criteria or have some characteristic; the researcher might pick students who have been held back in two successive years or teachers who left the profession to raise children and then returned to teaching.	Identify participants who meet the defined criterion; select a group of five or so participants to collect data from.
Snowball sampling	Select a few people who fit a researcher's needs; then use those participants to identify additional participants; and so on, until the researcher has a sufficient number of participants. (Snowballing is most useful when it is difficult to find participants of the type needed.)	Decide how many participants are needed; let initial participants recruit additional participants that fit the researcher's requirements until the desired number is reached.
Random purposive sampling	Selecting more participants than needed for the study; for example, if 25 participants were purposively selected by the researcher but only 10 participants can take part in the study, a random sample of 10 from 25 potential participants would be chosen; this strategy adds credibility to the study, although the initial sample is based on purposive selection. (This approach is typically used with small samples.)	Given a pool of participants, decide how many of them can reasonably be dealt with in the study and randomly select this number to participate. (This strategy is intended to deal with small samples.)

3. The population that the researcher would ideally like to generalize results to is referred to as the target population; the population that the researcher realistically selects from is referred to as the accessible, or available, population.

4. The degree to which the selected sample represents the population is the degree to which the research results are generalizable to the population.

Selecting a Random Sample

5. Regardless of the specific technique used, the steps in sampling include identifying the population, determining required sample size, and selecting the sample.

Simple Random Sampling

6. Simple random sampling is the process of selecting a sample in such a way that all individuals in the defined population have an equal and independent chance of being selected for the sample. It is the best single way to obtain a representative sample.

7. Random sampling involves defining the population, identifying each member of the population, and selecting individuals for the sample on a completely chance basis. Usually a table of random numbers is used to select the sample.

Stratified Sampling

8. Stratified sampling is the process of selecting a sample in such a way that identified subgroups in the population are represented in the sample in the same proportion that they exist in the population.

9. Stratified sampling can also be used to select equal-sized samples from each of a number of subgroups if subgroup comparisons are desired.

10. The steps in stratified sampling are similar to those in random sampling except that selection is from subgroups in the population rather than the population as a whole. In other words, random sampling is done for each subgroup.

Cluster Sampling

11. Cluster sampling is sampling in which groups, not individuals, are randomly selected. Clusters can be communities, states, school districts, and so on.
12. The steps in cluster sampling are similar to those in random sampling except that the random selection of groups (clusters) is involved, not individuals. Both stratified and cluster sampling often use multistage sampling.

Systematic Sampling

13. Systematic sampling is sampling in which individuals are selected from a list by taking every Kth name, where K equals the number of individuals on the list divided by the number of participants desired for the sample.

Determining Sample Size

14. Samples should be as large as possible; in general, the larger the sample, the more representative it is likely to be, and the more generalizable the results of the study will be.
15. Minimum, acceptable sample sizes depend on the type of research, but there are no universally accepted minimum sample sizes.

Avoiding Sampling Error and Bias

16. Sampling *error* is beyond the control of the researcher and occurs as part of random selection procedures.
17. Sampling *bias* is systematic and is generally the fault of the researcher. Bias can result in research findings being invalid. A major source of bias is the use of nonrandom sampling techniques.

Selecting a Nonrandom Sample

18. Researchers cannot always select random samples and occasionally must rely on nonrandom selection procedures.
19. When nonrandom sampling techniques are used, it is not possible to specify what probability each member of a population has of being selected for the sample; and it is often difficult to even describe the population from which a sample was drawn and to whom results can be generalized.
20. Three types of nonrandom sampling are convenience sampling, which involves using as the sample whoever happens to be available; purposive sampling, which involves selecting a sample the researcher believes to be representative of a given population; and quota sampling, which involves giving interviewers exact numbers, or quotas, of persons of varying characteristics who are to be interviewed.
21. Any sampling bias present in a study should be fully described in the final research report.

Qualitative Sampling: Definition and Purpose

22. Qualitative research most often deals with small, purposive samples. The researcher's insights guide the selection of participants.
23. A variety of purposive sampling approaches are used in qualitative research, including intensity sampling, homogeneous sampling, criterion sampling, snowball sampling, and random purposive sampling.
24. The use of purposive sampling requires that the researcher describe in detail the methods used to select a sample.

The definition of the quantitative population should describe its size and relevant characteristics (such as age, ability, and socioeconomic status). The description of the qualitative context should be stated.

The procedural technique for selecting study participants should be described in detail. For example, do not just say that stratified sampling will be used; indicate on what basis population members will be stratified and how they (and how many) will be selected from each subgroup. Or do not just say that snowball sampling is used; explain how and why it was chosen. In quantitative studies describe how selected participants will be placed into treatment groups, for example, by random assignment.

Include a summary statement that indicates resulting sample size for each group. For example:

> Thus there will be two groups with a sample size of 30 each; each group will include 15 participants with above-average motivation and 15 participants with below-average motivation.

Or

> There will be six participants who were chosen for their knowledge of the research context and their lengthy experience in the context studied.

Any identifiable source of sampling bias should also be discussed, for example, small sample sizes.

On the following pages we present an example that illustrates the quantitative performance called for by Task 4. (See Task 4 Example.) Again, this example represents the task submitted by the same student whose tasks for Chapters 2 and 3 were previously presented.

Additional examples for this and subsequent tasks are included in the *Student Guide* that accompanies this text.

1

Effect of Interactive Multimedia on the Achievement of 10th-Grade Biology Students

Participants in this study will be selected from the population of 10th-grade biology students at an upper-middle-class all-girl Catholic high school in Miami, Florida. The student population is multicultural, reflecting the diverse ethnic groups in Dade County. The student body is composed of approximately 90% Hispanic students from a variety of Latin American backgrounds, the major one being Cuban; 9% Caucasian non-Hispanic students; and 1% African American students. The population is anticipated to contain approximately 200 biology students.

Prior to the beginning of the school year, before students have been scheduled, 60 students will be randomly selected (using a table of random numbers) and randomly assigned to 2 classes of 30 each; 30 is the normal class size. One of the classes will be randomly chosen to receive IMM instruction and the other will not.

"Regardless of the type of research you conduct, you must collect data." (p. 123)

SELECTING MEASURING INSTRUMENTS

OBJECTIVES

After reading Chapter 5, you should be able to do the following:

1. State the links or relationships among a construct, a variable, and an operationalized variable.
2. Describe different types of variables: nominal, ordinal, interval, and ratio; categorical and quantitative; dependent and independent.
3. Explain various testing terms: standardized test, assessment, measurement, selection, supply, performance assessments, raw scores, norm- and criterion-referenced scoring.
4. Describe the purposes of various types of tests: achievement, aptitude, attitude, interest, value, personality, projective, nonprojective, and self-report.
5. Describe various scales used to collect data for cognitive and affective variables.
6. Familiarize yourself with measuring instruments and select those suited for varied research needs.
7. Describe the purposes of and ways to determine content, criterion-related, construct, and consequential validity.
8. Describe the purposes of and ways to determine stability, equivalence, equivalence and stability, internal consistency, and rater reliability.
9. Define or describe *standard error of measurement*.
10. Know useful sources for finding information about specific tests.
11. State a strategy for test selection.
12. Identify and briefly describe three sources of test information.

Whether you are testing hypotheses or seeking understanding, you must decide on a method or methods to collect your data. In many cases this is a matter of selecting the best existing instrument. Sometimes, however, you may have to develop your own instrument for data collection. At still other times you will be your own "instrument," observing, discussing, and interacting with research participants. You must consider several factors when selecting a method or instrument. The major point to remember, however, is that you should select or construct an approach that will provide pertinent data about the topic of your study.

The general goals of Chapter 5 are for you to (1) understand the link among constructs, variables, and instruments; (2) know criteria for selecting appropriate instruments; and (3) be able to select the best instrument for a given study from those available. After you have read this chapter, you should be able to perform the following task.

TASK 5

Having stated a topic to investigate, formulated one or more hypotheses or research questions, and described a sample, it is now time to describe three instruments appropriate for collecting data pertinent to your study. For each instrument selected, the description will include the following:

1. Name, publisher, and cost
2. A brief description of the purpose of the instrument
3. Validity and reliability data
4. The group for whom the instrument is intended
5. Administration requirements
6. Information regarding scoring and interpretation
7. Reviewers' overall impressions

Based on this information, indicate which instrument is most acceptable for your study, and why. (See Performance Criteria, p. 157.)

CONSTRUCTS

Regardless of the type of research you conduct, you must collect data. The scientific and disciplined inquiry approach is based on the collection, analysis, and interpretation of data.

Data are the pieces of information you collect and use to examine your topic, hypotheses, or observations. However, before you can collect data, you must determine what kind of data to collect. To do this, you must understand the relationships among constructs, variables, and instruments.

Constructs are abstractions that cannot be observed directly; they are invented to explain behavior. Examples of educational constructs are intelligence, personality, teacher effectiveness, creativity, ability, achievement, and motivation. To measure such constructs, they must be operationally defined, that is, defined in terms of processes or operations that can be observed and measured. To measure a construct, it is necessary to identify the scores or values it can assume. For example, the construct "personality" could be made measurable by defining two personality types, introverts and extroverts, as measured by scores on a 30-item questionnaire, with a high score indicating a more introverted personality and a low score indicating a more extroverted personality. Similarly, the construct "teacher effectiveness" might be operationally defined by observing a teacher in action and judging effectiveness based on four levels: unsatisfactory, marginal, adequate, and excellent. When constructs are operationally defined, they become variables.

VARIABLES

A *variable* is a construct that can take on two or more values or scores (it must have at least two). We deal with variables in all our research studies. Height, weight, hair color, test score, age, teacher experience, and performance on the WWF motivation scale are all variables; people differ on them.

There are many different approaches and instruments to measure a variable. (In educational research, an **instrument** is a tool used to collect data.) For example, to measure sixth-grade students' mathematics achievement, we can choose from a number of existing measuring instruments such as the Stanford Achievement Test or the Iowa Tests of Basic Skills. We could also use a teacher-made test to measure math achievement.

Read the following research topics and hypotheses and identify the variables in them.

1. Is there a relationship between middle students' grades and their self-confidence in science and math?
2. What do high school principals consider to be the most pressing administrative problems they face?
3. Do students learn more from our new social studies program than from the prior one?
4. What were the effects of the GI Bill on state colleges in the Midwest in the 1950s?
5. How do the first five weeks of school in Ms. Foley's classroom influence student activities and interactions in succeeding months?
6. There will be a statistically significant relationship between teachers' number of years teaching and their interest in taking new courses.
7. There will be a statistically significant difference in attitudes toward science between ninth-grade girls and boys.

The variables in these examples are as follows: (1) grades and self-confidence; (2) administrative problems; (3) learning and the new social studies program (note that the social studies program has two forms [new and old programs] and thus is also a variable); (4) effects of the GI Bill; (5) student activities and student interactions; (6) years teaching and interest in taking new courses; and (7) attitudes toward science. Variables indicate what will be examined in a research study. The researcher will select or develop an appropriate instrument for each variable. Information about the instruments should be included in the "Procedures" section of the research proposal.

Variables themselves differ in many ways. For example, variables can be represented by different kinds of measurements, they can be identified as categorical or quantitative, or they can be divided into dependent and independent variables.

MEASUREMENT SCALES AND VARIABLES

There are four types of measurement scales and associated variables: nominal, ordinal, interval, and ratio. A **measurement scale** consists of a group of several related statements that participants select to indicate their degree of agreement or lack of agreement. In other words, the scale is the instrument used to obtain the actual range of values or scores for each variable. Each type of scale may be used to express one or more of the variable types. It is important to know which type of scale is represented in your data because, as we shall see in later chapters, different scales require different methods of statistical analysis. We discuss each of the four variable types in the following subsections.

Nominal Variables

Nominal variables, also called *categorical variables,* represent the lowest level of measurement. They simply classify persons or objects into two or more categories. Nominal variables include gender (female, male); employment status (full time, part time, unemployed); marital status (married, divorced, single); and type of school (public, private, charter). For identification purposes, nominal variables are often represented by numbers. For example, the category "male" may be represented by the number 1 and "female" by the number 2. It is critically important to understand that such numbering of nominal variables does not indicate that one category is higher or better than another. That is, representing male with a 1 and female with a 2 does not indicate that males are lower or worse than females. The numbers are only labels for the groups. To avoid such confusion, it is often better to label nominal variables with letters (A, B, C, etc.), not numbers.

Ordinal Variables

Ordinal variables not only classify persons or objects, they also rank them. In other words, ordinal variables put persons or objects in order from highest to lowest or from most to least. If 50 people were ranked from 1 to 50 on the ordinal variable height, the person with rank 1 would be the tallest and the person with rank 50 would be the shortest. Rankings make it possible to say that one person is taller or shorter than another. Class rank or order of finishing a marathon are ordinal variables. Although ordinal variables permit us to describe performance as higher, lower, better, or worse, they do *not* indicate how much higher one person performed compared to another. In other words, intervals between ranks are not equal; the difference between rank 1 and rank 2 is not necessarily the same as the difference between rank 2 and rank 3. For example, consider the ranking of these three heights:

Rank	Height
1	6 ft, 5 in.
2	6 ft, 0 in.
3	5 ft, 11 in.

The difference in height between rank 1 and rank 2 is 5 inches; the difference between rank 2 and rank 3 is 1 inch. Thus, while an ordinal variable can rank persons or objects, it does not have equal scale intervals. This characteristic limits the statistical methods used to analyze ordinal variables.

Interval Variables

Interval variables have all the characteristics of nominal and ordinal variables, but also have equal intervals. Most of the tests used in educational research, such as achievement, aptitude, motivation, and attitude tests, are treated as interval variables. When variables have equal intervals it is assumed that the difference between a score of 30 and a score of 40 is essentially the same as the difference between a score of 50 and a score of 60, and the difference between 81 and 82 is about the same as the difference between 82 and 83. Interval scales, however, do not have a true zero point. Thus, if Roland's science achievement test score was 0 on a scale of 0 to 100, his score does not indicate the total absence of science knowledge. Nor does Gianna's score of 100 indicate complete mastery. Thus, we can say that a test score of 90 is 45 points higher than a score of 45, but we cannot say that a person scoring 90 knows twice as much as a person scoring 45. For most educational measurement it is sufficient to know only the score each person attained. Variables that have or are treated as having equal intervals utilize an array of statistical data analysis methods.

Ratio Variables

Ratio variables represent the highest level of measurement. A ratio variable has all the properties of the previous three types. In addition, it has a true zero point. Height, weight, time, distance, and speed are examples of ratio scales. The concept of "no weight," for example, is a meaningful one. Because of the true zero point, not only can we say that the difference between a height of 3 ft, 2 in. and a height of 4 ft, 2 in. is the same as the difference between 5 ft, 4 in. and 6 ft, 4 in., but also that a person 6 ft, 4 in. is twice as tall as one 3 ft, 2 in. Thus, with ratio variables we can say that Frankenstein is tall and Igor is short (nominal scale), Frankenstein is taller than Igor (ordinal scale), Frankenstein is 7 feet tall and Igor is 5 feet tall (interval scale), and Frankenstein is seven fifths as tall as Igor (ratio scale). Since ratio variables encompass mainly physical measures, they are not used very often in educational research. Table 5.1 contrasts types of measurement scales.

QUALITATIVE AND QUANTITATIVE VARIABLES

Nominal or categorical variables do not provide quantitative information about how people differ. They only provide information about *qualitative* differences. Nominal variables permit

TABLE 5.1   Comparing Measurement Scales

SCALE	DESCRIPTION	EXAMPLES
Nominal	Categorical	Northerners, Southerners Republicans, Democrats Eye color Male, female Public, private Gifted student, typical student
Ordinal	Rank order; unequal units	Scores of 5, 6, 10 are equal to scores of 1, 2, 3
Interval	Rank order and interval units but no zero point	A score of 10 and a score of 30 have the same degree of difference as a score of 60 and a score of 90
Ratio	All of the above and a defined zero point	A person is 5 feet tall and her friend is two-thirds as tall as she

persons or things that represent different qualities (e.g., eye color, religion, gender, political party) but not different quantities.

Quantitative variables are ones that exist on a continuum that ranges from low to high, or less to more. Ordinal, interval, and ratio variables are all quantitative variables, because they describe performance in quantitative terms. Examples are test scores, heights, speed, age, and class size.

DEPENDENT AND INDEPENDENT VARIABLES

We discussed dependent and independent variables in Chapter 1. A *dependent* variable is the variable hypothesized to depend on or be caused by another variable, the *independent* variable. Recall this research topic from that chapter:

> What is the effect of positive versus negative reinforcement on elementary students' attitudes toward school?

Based on your knowledge, identify the variables in this topic.

You probably had little trouble identifying *attitudes toward school* as a variable—and as a dependent variable—but did you also identify *type of reinforcement* as a variable? This variable contains two levels or methods of reinforcement, positive and negative. Notice that "attitudes toward school" is a quantitative variable because it is measured in terms of more or less attitude. Notice, also, that "type of reinforcement" is a categorical variable because it represents categories, not numbers (positive reinforcement versus negative reinforcement). Independent and dependent variables are primarily used in causal–comparative and experimental research studies. The independent variable (also called the treatment, causal, or manipulated variable) is the intended cause of the dependent variable (also called the effect, outcome, or criterion variable). The independent or treatment variable is manipulated by the researcher, while the dependent variable is not. For example, in this case, the researcher "manipulated" the two treatments by selecting them and then assigning participants to them. The dependent or outcome variable, attitudes toward school, is dependent on how well the two types of reinforcement function. The independent variable is the cause and the dependent variable is the effect. It is important to remember that the independent variable must have at least two levels or treatments. Two or more levels make up a variable. Thus, neither positive nor negative reinforcement is a variable by itself. It is only when both are included in the general variable (type of reinforcement) that we have two levels or treatments that vary and thus make up a variable.

Try to identify the independent and dependent variables in this research topic:

> Older teachers are less likely to express approval of new teaching strategies than younger teachers.

CHARACTERISTICS OF MEASURING INSTRUMENTS

In this section we examine the range of measuring instruments used to collect data in qualitative and quantitative research studies. There are three major ways to collect research data:

1. Administer a standardized instrument.
2. Administer a self-developed instrument.
3. Record naturally occurring or already available data (such as observations in a classroom or existing grade-point averages).

This chapter is concerned with published, standardized tests and teacher-prepared tests, the first two listed items. Although using naturally occurring or existing data requires a minimum of effort and sounds very attractive, there are not many quantitative studies for which existing data are appropriate. (Qualitative studies, especially historical and ethnographic studies, often are built around the idea that the researcher will work with naturally occurring or existing data.) Even when appropriate, there can be other problems. For example, the same grade given by two different teachers does not necessarily represent the same level of achievement. On the other hand, developing a "good" instrument has inherent drawbacks, not the least of which is that it requires considerable time, effort, and skill. Developing your own instrument greatly increases the total time needed to conduct the study. Also, at a minimum you need a course in measurement to have the skills needed for good instrument development. However, there are times when constructing your own instrument is necessary, especially if the research topic and concepts are original or relatively unresearched.

On the positive side, the time it takes to select an appropriate standardized or other instrument is invariably less than the time it takes to develop an instrument yourself. Standardized instruments tend to be developed by experts, who possess needed test construction skills. From a research point of view, an additional advantage of using a standardized instrument is that results from different studies using the same instrument can be compared.

There are thousands of published and standardized instruments available that yield a variety of data for a variety of variables. Major areas for which numerous measuring instruments have been developed include achievement, personality, attitude, interest, and aptitude. Each of these can, in turn, be further divided into many subcategories. Personality instruments, for example, can be classified as nonprojective or projective. *Nonprojective instruments* include measures of attitude and interest. A *projective instrument* provides respondents with an unstructured stimulus to respond to, like an ink blot test. Choosing an instrument for a particular research purpose involves identifying and selecting the most appropriate instrument from among alternatives. In order to do this intelligently, researchers must be familiar with a variety of instruments and know the criteria they should apply in selecting the best alternatives.

INSTRUMENT TERMINOLOGY

Given the array of instruments in educational research, it is important to know some of the basic terminology used to describe them. We start with the terms *test, assessment,* and *measurement.* A **test** is a formal, systematic, usually paper-and-pencil procedure for gathering information about peoples' **cognitive** (e.g., achievement, ability, reading) and **affective** (e.g., attitudes, emotions, interests, values) characteristics. Tests and instruments typically produce numerical scores. A **standardized test** is one that is administered, scored, and interpreted the same no matter where or when it is administered. They are typically developed by experts. For example, the SAT, ACT, Iowa Test of Basic Skills, Stanford Achievement Test, and other nationally used tests are standardized to ensure that all test takers experience the same conditions when taking them. Standardization allows comparisons among test takers from across the nation. You may remember taking a national standardized achievement test in school. They were the ones that every few pages had a stop sign that warned you to "Stop! Do not turn the page until instructed." These "stops" were used to ensure that all test takers had the same time for each part of the test. **Assessment** is a broader term than *test* or *instrument,* and encompasses the general process of collecting, synthesizing, and interpreting information, whether formal or informal, numerical or textual. Tests are a subset of assessment, as are observations and interviews. **Measurement** is the process of quantifying or scoring persons' performance on assessments. Measurement occurs after data are collected.

TYPES OF DATA COLLECTION INSTRUMENTS

There are three main methods of collecting data for a study: paper-and-pencil techniques, observations, and interviews. Paper-and-pencil methods are divided into two general categories:

selection and supply. *Selection methods* include multiple choice, true-false, and matching (one has to select from among the given answers). *Supply methods* include fill in the blank, short answer, and essay (one has to supply one's own answer). Current emphasis on supply methods in schools has spawned the rise of so-called **performance assessments,** also known as *authentic* or *alternative* assessments. These assessments emphasize student processes (lab demonstration, debate, oral speech, or dramatic performances) or products (write an essay, construct a science fair project, write a research report)—what students can, respectively, do or create. They typically are aimed at helping students perform more complex tasks than memorization. Paper-and-pencil instruments are the predominant form used in quantitative research. Observation and interviewing are important qualitative data collection approaches and will be described in detail in Chapter 7.

INTERPRETING INSTRUMENT DATA

There are four different ways of interpreting the instruments used in research. *Raw scores* are the number of items a person scored on a test or assessment. If Leron got 78 of 100 points on a test, his raw score is 78. In most quantitative research, raw scores are the basic data analyzed. However, using the bell-shaped curve, raw scores can be transformed into a variety of derived scores such as **percentile ranks, stanines,** and **standard scores** commonly used in many standardized tests. These will be discussed in more detail in Chapter 14, "Descriptive Statistics."

Norm-referenced, criterion-referenced, and self-referenced scoring approaches represent three ways of interpreting performance on tests and measures. **Norm-referenced** scoring indicates how one student did compared to other students who took a test. For example, if we ask how well Rita did in science compared to other students in her grade from across the nation, we are asking for norm-referenced information. The interpretation of Rita's score will be based on how she performed compared to her class or a national group of students in her grade. Norm-referenced scoring is also called *grading on the curve,* where the curve is the percentages of students who can receive each grade. Standardized tests and assessments frequently report norm-referenced scores in the form of derived scores such as percentile rank or stanines. **Criterion-referenced** scores also involve a comparison, but against predetermined levels of performance, i.e., criteria, not against the performance of other students. For example, if a teacher sets performance levels for grading test scores of 90 to 100 is an A, 80 to 89 is a B, 70 to 79 is a C, and so on, the teacher is using criterion-referenced grading. Students' test scores will be compared to the preestablished performance levels to determine the grade. Anyone who scores between 90 and 100 will get an A. If no one scores between 90 and 100, no one will get an A. If all students get between 90 and 100, they all will get As. This could not happen in norm-referenced grading, which requires that different scores, even very close ones, must get different grades. **Self-referenced** scoring approaches involve measuring how an individual student's performance changes over time. Student performances at different times are compared to determine improvement or regression.

TYPES OF MEASURING INSTRUMENTS

There are many different kinds of tests available and many different ways to classify them. The Mental Measurements Yearbooks (MMYs), published by the Buros Institute of Mental Measurements, are a major source of test information for educational researchers. The yearbooks, which can be found in most large libraries, provide information and reviews of published tests in various school subject areas such as English, mathematics, and reading, as well as personality, intelligence, aptitude, speech and hearing, and vocational tests. The Web addresses for the Buros Institute and its catalogues are http://www.unl.edu/buros/ and http://www.unl.edu/buros/catalog.html.

COGNITIVE TESTS

Cognitive tests measure intellectual process such as thinking, memorizing, problem solving, analyzing, reasoning, and applying information. Most of the tests school pupils take are cognitive achievement tests.

Achievement Tests

Achievement tests are designed to provide information about how well test takers have learned what they have been taught in school, and are typically applied in school settings. An individual's level of achievement on a standardized achievement test is usually determined by comparing it to the norm, the performance of a national group of students in the individual's grade or age level who took the same test. Thus, these tests can provide comparisons of a given student to similar students nationally. Standardized achievement tests typically test a number of different curriculum areas such as reading, vocabulary, language, and mathematics. A standardized test that measures achievement in a number of different curriculum areas is called a *test battery,* and each test is called a *subtest.* The California Achievement Test, Stanford Achievement Tests, TerraNova, and the Iowa Tests of Basic Skills are examples of cognitive tests commonly used in American classrooms. Depending on factors such as the number of different achievement areas tested, standardized achievement batteries can take from 1 to 5 hours to complete.

Some achievement tests, such as the Gates-McGinitie Reading Test, focus on achievement in a single subject area. Sometimes diagnostic achievement tests are used to investigate specific weaknesses in a subject area that need remedial instruction. A **diagnostic test** is a type of achievement test that yields multiple scores to facilitate identification of a student's weak and strong areas. The Stanford Diagnostic Reading Test and the Key Math Diagnostic Inventory of Essential Mathematics Test are examples of widely used diagnostic achievement instruments.

Aptitude Tests

Aptitude tests include cognitive measures, but ones that are not normally part of classroom tests. They are commonly used to predict how well an individual is likely to perform in the future. Tests of general aptitude are also referred to as *scholastic aptitude tests* and *tests of general mental ability.* Aptitude tests are standardized and are often administered as part of a school testing program. They also are used extensively in job hiring.

General aptitude tests require a participant to respond to a variety of verbal and nonverbal tasks intended to measure the individual's ability to apply knowledge and solve problems. Such tests often yield three scores: an overall score, a verbal score, and a quantitative score. A commonly used group-administered battery is the Columbia Mental Maturity Scale (CMMS). The CMMS has six versions and can be administered to schoolage children, college students, and adults. It includes 12 subtests representing five aptitude factors: logical reasoning, spatial relations, numerical reasoning, verbal concepts, and memory. Another frequently administered group aptitude test is the Otis-Lennon School Ability Test, which has versions designed for schoolage children in grades K–12. The Otis-Lennon School Ability Test measures four factors: verbal comprehension, verbal reasoning, figurative reasoning, and quantitative reasoning. The Differential Aptitude Tests (DAT), on the other hand, include tests on space relations, mechanical reasoning, and clerical speed and accuracy, among others, and are designed to predict success in various job areas.

If there is a reason to question the appropriateness of a group of tests for particular test takers (e.g., very young children or students with disabilities) an individual test should be used. Probably the most well known of the individually administered tests are the Stanford-Binet Intelligence Scale and the Wechsler scales. The Stanford-Binet is appropriate for young children and adults. Wechsler scales are available to measure the intelligence of persons from the age of 4 to adulthood: the Wechsler Preschool and Primary Scale of Intelligence (WPPSI)—ages 4 to 7; the Wechsler Intelligence Scale for Children–Revised (WISC-R)—ages 6 to 17; and the Wechsler Adult Intelligence Scale–Revised (WAIS-R)—older adolescents and adults. As an example, the WISC is a scholastic aptitude test that includes verbal tests (e.g., general information, vocabulary) and performance tests (e.g., picture completion, object assembly). Other commonly used individually administered aptitude tests are McCarthy Scales of Children's Abilities and the Kaufman-Assessment Battery for Children (ABC) Test.

AFFECTIVE TESTS

Affective tests are designed to assess individual feelings, values, and attitudes toward self, others, activities, institutions, and situations. They are often used in educational research and exist in many different formats. Most affective tests are nonprojective; that is, they are self-report measures—the test taker responds to a series of questions or statements about herself. For example, a question that asked, "Which would you prefer, reading a book or playing basketball? Circle your answer." requires the test taker to report her preference. Self-report tests are frequently used in survey or descriptive studies (e.g., to describe the personality structure of various groups such as high school dropouts), correlational studies (e.g., to determine relationships between various personality traits and other variables such as achievement), and experimental studies (e.g., to investigate the comparative effectiveness of different instructional methods for different personality types).

Instruments that examine attitudes, interests, values, and personalities tap affective, emotive feelings, and perceptions. *Values* are deeply held beliefs about ideas, persons, or objects. For example, we may value our free time, our special friendships, or a vase given by our great-grandmother. *Attitudes* indicate what things we feel favorable or unfavorable about; our tendency to accept or reject groups, ideas, or objects. For example, Greg's attitude toward brussel sprouts is much more favorable than his attitude toward green beans (which puts Greg in a distinct minority). *Interests* indicate the degree to which we seek out or participate in particular activities, objects, and ideas. For example, I have very little interest in having my nose pierced (nor do I value or have a positive attitude toward nose piercing). *Personality,* also called *temperament,* is made up of a number of characteristics that represent a person's typical behaviors; it describes what we do in our natural life circumstances.

Attitude Scales

Attitude scales determine what an individual believes, perceives, or feels about self, others, activities, institutions, or situations. There are five basic types of scales used to measure attitudes—Likert scales, semantic differential scales, rating scales, Thurstone scales, and Guttman scales. The first three are the most often used.

Likert Scale.   A **Likert scale** asks participants to respond to a series of statements by indicating whether they strongly agree (SA), agree (A), are undecided (U), disagree (D), or strongly disagree (SD). Each response is associated with a point value, and an individual's score is determined by summing the point values of each statement. For example, the following point values are typically assigned to positive statements: SA = 5, A = 4, U = 3, D = 2, SD = 1. An example of a positive statement is "Short people are entitled to the same job opportunities as tall people." A score of 5 or 4 on this item would indicate a positive attitude toward equal opportunity for short people. A high total score across all items on the test would be indicative of an overall positive attitude. For negative statements, the point values would be reversed—that is, SA = 1, A = 2, U = 3, D = 4, and SD = 5. An example of a negative statement is "Short people are not entitled to the same job opportunities as tall people." On this item scores should be reversed; "disagree" or "strongly disagree" would indicate a positive attitude toward opportunities for short people.

Semantic Differential Scale.   A **semantic differential scale** asks an individual to give a quantitative rating to a topic such as attitude toward school or attitude toward smoking. Scales of bipolar adjectives such as good–bad, friendly–unfriendly, and positive–negative are presented, and the respondent indicates the point on the continuum that represents her or his attitude. For example, a scale concerning attitudes toward property taxes might include the following items:

Necessary	____ ____ ____ ____ ____ ____ ____	Unnecessary
Fair	____ ____ ____ ____ ____ ____ ____	Unfair
Better	____ ____ ____ ____ ____ ____ ____	Worse

Each position on the continuum has an associated score value; by totaling score values for all items, it can be determined whether the respondent's attitude is positive or negative. Semantic differential scales usually have 5 to 7 intervals with a neutral attitude assigned a score value of 0. For the above items, the score values would be as follows:

Necessary	____ ____ ____ ____ ____ ____ ____	Unnecessary
	3 2 1 0 -1 -2 -3	
Fair	____ ____ ____ ____ ____ ____ ____	Unfair
	3 2 1 0 -1 -2 -3	
Better	____ ____ ____ ____ ____ ____ ____	Worse
	3 2 1 0 -1 -2 -3	

A person who checked the first interval (i.e., a score of 3) on each of these items is indicating a very positive attitude toward property taxes (fat chance!). Scores can be summed over all items to get an overall score. Usually summed scores (interval data) are used in statistical data analysis.

Rating Scales.   **Rating scales** are also used to measure attitudes toward others. Such scales ask an individual to rate another individual on a number of behavioral dimensions. One form of rating scale provides descriptions of performance or preference and asks the individual to check the most appropriate description.

> Select the choice that best describes your actions in the first five minutes of the classes you teach.
>
> _____ State lesson objectives and overview at start of the lesson
> _____ State lesson objectives but no overview at start of the lesson
> _____ Don't state objectives or give overview at start of the lesson

A second type of rating scale asks the individual to rate performance or preference using a numerical scale similar to a Likert scale.

> Circle the number that best describes the degree to which you state lesson objectives and give an overview before teaching a lesson. 5 = always, 4 = almost always, 3 = about half the time, 2 = rarely, 1 = never.
>
> 1   2   3   4   5

Note that Likert, semantic differential, and rating scales are similar, requiring the respondent to self-report along a continuum of choices. Note, also, that in certain situations, such as observing performance or judging teaching competence, Likert, semantic differential, and rating scales can be used by others (a researcher, a principal, a colleague) to collect information about study participants. For example, in some studies it might be best to have the principal, rather than the teacher, use a Likert, semantic differential, or rating scale to collect data about that teacher.

Thurstone and Guttman Scales.   A Thurstone scale asks participants to select from a list of statements that represent different points of view on a topic. Each item has an associated point value between 1 and 11; point values for each item are determined by averaging the values of the items assigned by a number of judges. An individual's attitude score is the average point value of all the statements checked by that individual. A Guttman scale also asks respondents to agree or disagree with a number of statements. A Guttman scale, however, attempts to determine whether an attitude is unidimensional. It is *unidimensional* if it produces a cumulative scale in which an individual who agrees with a given statement also agrees with all related preceding statements. For example, if you agree with statement 3, you also agree with statements 2 and 1.

Interest Inventories

An *interest inventory* asks participants to indicate personal likes and dislikes, such as the kinds of activities they prefer. The respondent's pattern of interest is compared to the interest patterns typical of successful persons in various occupational fields. Interest inventories are widely used to suggest the fields in which respondents might be most happy and successful.

Two frequently used inventories are the Strong-Campbell Interest Inventory and the Kuder Preference Record–Vocational. The Strong-Campbell Interest Inventory examines areas of interest in occupations, school subjects, activities, leisure activities, and day-to-day interactions with various types of people. Test takers are presented with many topics related to these five parts and are asked to indicate whether they like (L), dislike (D), or are indifferent (I) to each topic. A second part of the Strong-Campbell inventory consists of a choice between two options such as "dealing with people" or "dealing with things" and a number of self-descriptive statements that the individual responds to by choosing Yes (like me), No (not like me), or ? (not sure).

The Kuder Occupational Interest Survey addresses 10 broad categories of interest: outdoor, mechanical, computational, scientific, persuasive, artistic, literary, musical, social service, and clerical. Individuals are presented with three choices and must select the one they most like and the one they least like. For example, an individual would be presented with many items such as, "Would you rather: dig a hole, read a book, or draw a picture? Choose the one that you most would like to do and the one that you least would like to do."

The Strong-Campbell and the Kuder are both self-report instruments that provide information about persons' interests. Scoring the instruments requires sending data to the testing companies who produce them for computer analysis. *You cannot score them yourself.* The Strong-Campbell, the Kuder, and other attitudinal, value, and personality instruments may be found in the Mental Measurements Yearbooks.

Values Tests

The Study of Values instrument is old, but is still used. It measures the relative strength of an individual's valuing of six different areas: theoretical (discovery of truth, empirical approach); economic (practical values); aesthetic (symmetry, form, and harmony); social (altruism, philanthropic); political (personal power, influence); and religious (unity of experience, cosmic coherence). Individuals are presented with items consisting of either two or four choices and are asked to allocate points to the alternatives according to how much they value them. For example, a two-alternative item might be, "Suppose you had the choice of reading one of two books first. If the books were titled *Making Money in the Stock Market* and *The Politics of*

Political Power, which would you read first?" Respondents allocate points to the two choices indicating degree of preference. By counting up the points given to each of the six areas, an indication of an individual's preference among the six categories can be obtained. A second form of scoring provides four choices that the respondent must rank from 4 to 1 in order of preference. The Study of Values is used primarily in research studies to categorize individuals or measure the value orientation of different groups such as scientists and newspaper writers.

Personality Inventories

Personality inventories list questions or statements that describe behaviors characteristic of certain personality traits. Respondents indicate whether each statement describes them. Some inventories are presented as checklists; respondents simply check items they feel characterize them. An individual's score is based on the number of responses characteristic of the trait being measured. An introvert, for example, would be expected to respond yes to the statement, "Reading is one of my favorite pastimes," and no to the statement, "I love large parties." Personality instruments may measure only one trait or many.

General inventories frequently used in educational research studies include the Personality Adjective Checklist, California Psychological Inventory, Minnesota Multiphasic Personality Inventory, Mooney Problem Checklist, Myers-Briggs Type Indicator, and the Sixteen Personality Factor Questionnaire. The Minnesota Multiphasic Personality Inventory (MMPI) alone has been utilized in hundreds of educational research studies. Its items were originally selected on the basis of response differences between psychiatric and "normal" patients. The MMPI measures many personality traits, such as depression, paranoia, schizophrenia, and social introversion. It contains more than 370 items to which a test-taker responds True (of me), False (of me), or Cannot Say. It also has nearly 200 items that form additional scales for anxiety, ego strength, repression, and alcoholism.

Self-report general personality instruments such as the MMPI are complex and require a substantial amount of knowledge of both measurement and psychology to score. It is recommended that beginning researchers avoid their use unless they have more than a passing knowledge of these areas.

Because they are generally self-report instruments, attitude, interest, values, and personality scales suffer from some problems. The researcher can never be sure that individuals are expressing their true attitude, interest, values, or personality, as opposed to a "socially acceptable" response. Every effort should be made, therefore, to increase honesty of response by giving appropriate directions to those completing the affective instruments.

Another problem when forced-choice items are used is that of accurate responses. Scores are meaningful only to the degree that respondents are honest and select choices that truly characterize them. A common problem is the existence of a **response set,** the tendency of an individual to continually respond in a particular way. One common response set occurs when an individual selects responses that he believes are the most socially acceptable, even if they are not necessarily characteristic of him. Another form of a response set is when a test taker continually responds "yes," "agree," or "true" to items because she believes that is what the researcher desires. Thus, in studies utilizing affective tests, every effort should be made to increase the likelihood that valid test results are obtained. One strategy to overcome the problem of response sets is to allow participants to respond anonymously.

Both affective and cognitive instruments are subject to biases that distort the data obtained. **Bias** is present when respondents' ethnicity, race, gender, language, or religious orientation distort their performance or responses. For example, low scores on reading tests by students who speak little English or nonstandard forms of English are probably due in large part to language disadvantages, not reading difficulties. If one's culture discourages competition, or making eye contact, or speaking out, the responses on self-report instruments can differ according to cultural background, not personality, values, attitudes, or interests. For these students, test performance means something different than that of English-fluent students who also took the test. These issues need to be recognized in selecting and interpreting the results of both cognitive and affective instruments.

PROJECTIVE TESTS

Projective tests were developed in part to eliminate some of the problems inherent in the use of self-report and forced-choice measures. Projective tests are ambiguous and not obvious to respondents. Since the purpose of the test is not clear, conscious dishonesty of response is reduced. Such tests are called projective because respondents *project* their true feelings or thoughts onto the ambiguous stimulus. The classic example of a projective test is the inkblot or Rorschach test. Respondents are shown a picture of an inkblot and are asked to describe what they see in it. The inkblot is really just that, an inkblot made by putting a dab of ink on a paper and folding it in half to produce the blot. There are no right or wrong answers to the question, "What do you see in the inkblot?" (It's only an inkblot—honest.) The test taker's descriptions of such blots are a "projection" of his feelings and personality, which the administer interprets.

The most commonly used projective technique is the method of association. Participants react to a stimulus such as a picture, inkblot, or word on which they project their interpretation. Word-association tests are probably the most well known of the association techniques (How many movies dealing with a psychiatrist include the line, "I'll say a word and you tell me the first thing that comes to your mind"?). Similarly, the Thematic Apperception Test presents the individual with a series of pictures; the respondent is then asked to tell a story about what is happening in each picture.

Until recently, all projective tests were required to be administered individually. There have been some recent efforts, however, to develop group projective tests. One such test is the Holtzman Inkblot Technique, which is intended to measure the same variables as the Rorschach Inkblot Test.

From the preceding comments, it should not be a surprise that projective tests are utilized mainly by clinical psychologists and very infrequently by educational researchers. This is due to the fact that administering, scoring, and interpreting projective tests require lengthy and specialized training. One needs to be specially educated to use projective testing, and it is not recommended that beginning researchers utilize them.

There are other types and formats of measuring instruments beyond those discussed here. The intent of this section is to provide an overview of different types of tests, different formats for gathering data, different scoring methods, different interpretation strategies, and different limitations. To find more information about the specific tests described in this chapter and many other tests we have not described, refer to the Mental Measurement Yearbooks.

CRITERIA FOR GOOD MEASURING INSTRUMENTS

VALIDITY OF MEASURING INSTRUMENTS

Validity is the most important characteristic a test or measuring instrument can possess. **Validity** is concerned with the appropriateness of the interpretations made from test scores. When we test, we test for a purpose. For example, a researcher may administer a questionnaire to find out about participants' opinions of increasing funding for education. Or an experimental research study may give a general science test to compare learning for science students taught by method A and method B. A key question for these and other such test users is, "Does this test or instrument permit me to make the interpretation I wish to make?" That is, will responses to the opinion questionnaire or the science test allow the researchers to make appropriate interpretations about the respondents' attitudes or learning?

Validity is important in all forms of research and all types of tests and measures. In some situations a test or instrument is used to make a number of different interpretations. For example, a high school chemistry achievement test may be used to assess students' end-of-year chemistry learning. It may also be used to predict students' future performance in science courses or to select students for advanced placement chemistry. Each of these uses calls for a different interpretation of the chemistry test scores: learning in the chemistry class, predicting future science achievement, and admission into advanced placement chemistry. Each intended interpretation requires its own validation. Further, the same test given to different groups of respondents (e.g., one group who had studied the test material and one who had not) may have different validities for each group. Thus, validity is specific to the interpretation being made and to the group being tested. Given this reality, it should be clear that validity does not refer to the test or instrument itself. That is, we do not say, "This test is valid." Rather, we say, "This test is valid for this particular interpretation and this particular group." It is important to understand that validation is a matter of degree; it does not exist on an all-or-nothing basis. Validity is best thought of in terms of degree: highly valid, moderately valid, and generally invalid. Validation begins with an understanding of the interpretation(s) to be made from the selected tests or instruments. It then requires the collection of evidence to support the desired interpretation.

There are four types of test validity: content validity, criterion-related validity, construct validity, and consequential validity. They focus on, respectively, (1) the extent to which the test items or questions reflect the content or teaching area being measured; (2) the extent to which the test predicts future performance or is correlated with other measures; (3) the extent to which a construct such as anxiety, personality, or intelligence is actually being measured; and (4) the extent to which consequences arise from the testing activity. For example, test results used to place students in special education classrooms and to determine whether students will receive a high school diploma have consequences to test takers. Obviously, high test validity and beneficial test consequences are most desired. More specific information about testing in general and validity and reliability in particular can be found in the *Standards for Educational and Psychological Testing*.[1]

Content Validity

Content validity is the degree to which a test measures an intended content area. Content validity requires both item validity and sampling validity. **Item validity** is concerned with whether the test items are relevant to measurement of the intended content area. **Sampling validity** is concerned with how well the test samples the total content area being tested. A test designed to measure knowledge of biology facts might have good item validity because all the items are relevant to biology, but poor sampling validity, if, for example, all the test items were about vertebrates. On the other hand, if the test adequately samples the full content of biology, it would be said to have good content validity. This is important because we cannot possibly measure each and every test item in a content area and yet we do wish to make inferences about test takers' performance on the entire content area. Such inferences are possible only if the test items adequately sample the domain of possible items. It is recommended that you clearly identify and examine for completeness the bounds of the content area to be tested before constructing or selecting a test or measuring instrument.

Content validity is of particular importance for achievement tests. A test score cannot accurately reflect a student's achievement if it does not measure what the student was taught and

[1]*Standards for Educational and Psychological Testing*. American Education Research Association, American Psychological Association, and National Council on Measurement in Education (1999). Washington, DC: American Psychological Association.

is supposed to learn. While this seems obvious, content validity can be compromised if the test covers topics not taught, or if it does *not* cover topics that have been taught. If so, one no longer has a valid achievement test. Issues with achievement tests have been a problem in a number of research studies. A classic case is the early studies that compared the effectiveness of "new" math with the "old" math. These studies invariably found no achievement differences between students learning under the two approaches. The problem was that the "new" math was emphasizing concepts and principles, while the achievement tests were emphasizing computational skills. When tests were developed that contained an adequate sampling of items measuring concepts and principles, studies began to find that the two approaches to teaching math resulted in essentially equal computational ability, but that the "new" math resulted in better conceptual understanding. The moral of the story is, take care that your test measures what the students were expected to learn in the treatments. That is, be sure that the test is content valid for your study and for your research participants.

Content validity is determined by expert judgment. There is no formula or statistic by which it can be computed and there is no way to express it quantitatively. Usually experts in the topic covered by the test are asked to assess its content validity. These experts carefully review the process used to develop the test as well as the test itself, and then make a judgment about how well items represent the intended content area. In other words, they compare what was taught and what is being tested. When the two coincide, the content validity is strong.

The term **face validity** is sometimes used in conjunction with content validity of tests. Although its meaning is somewhat ambiguous, basically face validity refers to the degree to which a test *appears* to measure what it claims to measure. While determining face validity is not a psychometrically sound way of estimating validity, the process is sometimes used as an initial screening procedure in test selection. It should be followed up by content validation.

Criterion-Related Validity

Criterion-related validity has two forms, concurrent and predictive. The method of determining validity is the same for each form, but the time relations between them differ. *Concurrent validity* is the degree to which the scores on two tests taken at about the same time are correlated, and *predictive validity* is the degree to which the scores on two tests taken at different times are correlated. We deal with the two forms separately for clarity, but emphasize that both fit into the general category of criterion-related validity. The name *criterion-related* refers to the fact that this approach to validity involves correlating a test with a second test or measure. The second test is the criterion against which the validity of the initial test is judged.

Concurrent Validity.   **Concurrent validity** is the degree to which scores on one test correlate to scores on another test when both tests are administered in the same time frame. Often, for example, a test is developed that claims to do the same job as some other tests, except easier or faster. One way to determine whether the claim is true is to administer the new and the old test (the criterion) to a group and compare the scores. If there is a high correlation between the two tests, the concurrent validity of the new test is established and, in most cases, the new test will be utilized instead of the other test.

Concurrent validity is determined by establishing a relationship or discrimination. The relationship method involves determining the correlation between scores on the test and scores on some other established test or criterion (e.g., grade-point average). In this case, the steps involved in determining concurrent validity are as follows:

1. Administer the new test to a defined group of individuals.
2. Administer a previously established, valid criterion test (the criterion) to the same group, at the same time, or shortly thereafter.

3. Correlate the two sets of scores.
4. Evaluate the results.

The resulting correlation, or *validity coefficient,* indicates the degree of concurrent validity of the new test; if the coefficient is high (near 1.0), the test has good concurrent validity. For example, suppose Professor Jeenyus developed a 5-minute group test of children's interest in school. If scores on this test correlated highly with scores on the Almost Never Ending School Interest Test (which must be administered to one child at a time and takes at least an hour), then Professor Jeenyus's test would definitely be preferable in a great many situations.

The discrimination method of establishing concurrent validity involves determining whether test scores can be used to discriminate between persons who possess a certain characteristic and those who do not, or those who possess it to a greater degree. For example, a test of personality disorder would have concurrent validity if scores resulting from it could be used to correctly classify institutionalized and noninstitutionalized persons.

Predictive Validity.   **Predictive validity** is the degree to which a test can predict how well individuals will do in a future situation. If an algebra aptitude test administered at the start of school can fairly accurately predict which students will perform well or poorly in algebra at the end of the school year (the criterion), the aptitude test has high predictive validity. Predictive validity is extremely important for tests that are used to classify or select individuals. An example many of you are all too familiar with is the use of Graduate Record Examination (GRE) scores to select students for admission to graduate school. Many graduate schools require a minimum score for admission, often 1,000, in the belief that students who achieve that score have a higher probability of succeeding in graduate school than those scoring lower than 1,000. The predictive validity of the GRE has been the subject of many research studies. Results seem to indicate that the GRE has higher predictive validity for certain areas of graduate study than for others. For example, while the GRE appears to have satisfactory predictive validity for success in graduate studies in English, its validity in predicting success in an art education program appears to be questionable. Another example that illustrates the importance of predictive validity is the use of tests to determine which students should be assigned to special education classes. In this situation it is imperative that the decision be based on the results of predictively valid measures. Note that in such situations both predictive and consequential validity should be considered.

The predictive validity of a given instrument varies with a number of factors. The predictive validity of an instrument may vary depending on such factors as the curriculum involved, textbooks used, and geographic location. The Mindboggling Algebra Aptitude Test, for example, may predict achievement better in courses using the *Brainscrambling Algebra I* text than in courses using other texts. Thus, if a test is to be used for prediction, it is important to compare the description of its validation with the situation in which it is to be used.

No test, of course, will have perfect predictive validity. Therefore, predictions based on the scores of any test will be imperfect. However, predictions based on a combination of several test scores will invariably be more accurate than predictions based on the scores of any single test. Therefore, when important classification or selection decisions are to be made, they should be based on data from more than one indicator. In establishing the predictive validity of a test (referred to as the **predictor**), the first step is to identify and carefully define the **criterion**, which must be a valid measure of the performance to be predicted. For example, if we wished to establish the predictive validity of an algebra aptitude test, final examination scores at the completion of a course in algebra might be considered a valid criterion. As another example, if we were interested in establishing the predictive validity of a given test for predicting success in college, grade-point average at the end of the first year would probably be considered a valid criterion, but number of extracurricular activities in which the student participated probably would not.

Once the criterion has been identified and defined, the procedure for determining predictive validity is as follows:

1. Administer the predictor variable to a group.
2. Wait until the behavior to be predicted, the criterion variable, occurs.
3. Obtain measures of the criterion for the same group.
4. Correlate the two sets of scores.
5. Evaluate the results.

The resulting correlation, or validity coefficient, indicates the predictive validity of the test; if the coefficient is high, the test has good predictive validity. You may have noticed that the procedures for determining concurrent validity and predictive validity are very similar. The major difference is in terms of when the criterion measure is administered. In establishing concurrent validity, it is administered at about the same time as the predictor, while in establishing predictive validity, one usually has to wait for a longer period of time to pass before criterion data can be collected. In the discussion of both concurrent and predictive validity there was a statement to the effect that if the resulting coefficient is high, the test has good validity. You may have wondered, "How high is high?" The question of how high the coefficient must be in order to be considered "good" is not easy to answer. There is no magic number that a coefficient should reach, except the higher the better.

Construct Validity

Construct validity is the most important form of validity because it asks the fundamental validity question: What is this test really measuring? We have seen that all variables derive from constructs and that constructs are nonobservable traits, such as intelligence, anxiety, and honesty, "invented" to explain behavior. Constructs underlie the variables that researchers measure. You cannot see a construct; you can only observe its effect. Constructs, however, do an amazingly good job of explaining certain differences among individuals. For example, it was always observed that some students learn faster than others, learn more, and retain information longer. To explain these differences, a theory of intelligence was developed, and it was hypothesized that there is a construct called intelligence that is related to learning and that everyone possesses to a greater or lesser degree. Tests were developed to measure how much of it a person has. As it happens, students whose scores indicate that they have a "lot" of it— that is, they have high intelligence scores—tend to do better in school and other learning environments than those who have less of it.

Research studies involving a construct are valid only to the extent that the instrument used actually measures the intended construct and not some unanticipated, intervening variable. Determining construct validity is by no means easy. It usually involves gathering a number of pieces of evidence to demonstrate validity. If we wished, for example, to determine whether the Big Bob Intelligence Test was construct valid, we could carry out all or most of the following validation studies. First, we could see whether students who scored high on the Big Bob test learned faster, more, and with greater retention than low scorers. We could correlate scores on the Big Bob test taken at the beginning of the school year with students' grades at the end of the school year. We could also correlate performance on the Big Bob test with other, well-established intelligence tests to see whether the correlations were high. We could have scholars in the field of intelligence examine the Big Bob test items to judge whether they represented typical topics in the field of intelligence. In addition to confirmatory evidence such as this, we could seek disconfirmatory validity information. For example, we would not expect scores on an intelligence test to correlate highly with self-esteem or height. If we correlated the Big Bob Intelligence Test with self-esteem and height and found low or moderate correlations, we could conclude that the Big Bob test is measuring something different from self-esteem or height. Thus, we would have evidence that the Big Bob test correlates highly with other intelligence tests (confirmatory validation) and does not correlate highly with self-esteem and height (disconfirmatory validation). Notice how content and criterion-related forms of validity are used in studies to determine a test's construct validity. No single validation study can establish the construct validity of a test.

Consequential Validity

Consequential validity, as the name suggests, is concerned with the consequences that occur from tests. As more and more tests are being administered to more and more individuals, and as the consequences of testing are becoming more important, concern over the potential consequences of testing have increased. All tests have intended purposes (I mean, really, who would create these things for FUN?) and, in general, the intended purposes are valid and appropriate. There are, however, some testing instances that produce (usually unintended) negative or harmful consequences to the test takers. The function of consequence validity is to ferret out and identify tests that may be harmful to students, teachers, and other test users, whether the problem is intended or not.

The key issue in consequential validity is the question, "What are the effects on teachers or students from various forms of testing?" For example, how does testing students solely with multiple-choice items affect students' learning as compared with assessing them with other, more open-ended items? Should non-English speakers be tested in the same way as English speakers? Can people who see the test results of non-English speakers, but do not know about their lack of English, make harmful interpretations for such students? While most tests serve their intended purpose in nonharmful ways, consequential validity reminds us that testing can and sometimes does have negative consequences for test takers or users. Table 5.2 summarizes the four forms of validity.

A number of factors can diminish the validity of tests and instruments used in research, including the following:

- Unclear test directions
- Confusing and ambiguous test items
- Using vocabulary too difficult for test takers
- Overly difficult and complex sentence structures
- Inconsistent and subjective scoring methods
- Untaught items included on achievement tests
- Failure to follow standardized test administration procedures
- Cheating, either by participants or by someone teaching the correct answers to the specific test items

TABLE 5.2   Forms of Validity

FORM	METHOD	PURPOSE
Content validity	Compare content of the test to the domain being measured.	To what extent does this test represent the general domain of interest?
Criterion-related validity	Correlate scores from one instrument to scores on a criterion measure, either at the same (concurrent) or different (predictive) time.	To what extent does this test correlate highly with another test?
Construct validity	Amass convergent, divergent, and content-related evidence to determine that the presumed construct is what is being measured.	To what extent does this test reflect the construct it is intended to measure?
Consequential validity	Observe and determine whether the test has adverse consequences for test takers or users.	To what extent does the test create harmful consequences for the test taker?

All of these factors diminish the validity of tests because they distort or produce atypical test performance, which in turn distorts the desired interpretation of the test scores.

Validity is the most important characteristic a test or measure can have. Without validity, the desired interpretations of the variables measured have inappropriate meaning. There are multiple ways to establish the various forms of test validity. In the end, the test user makes the final decision about the validity and usefulness of a test or measure. The bases for that decision should be described in the "Procedures" section of your research plan.

RELIABILITY OF MEASURING INSTRUMENTS

In everyday English, reliability means dependability or trustworthiness. The term means the same thing with respect to measurements. **Reliability** is the degree to which a test consistently measures whatever it is measuring. The more reliable a test is, the more confidence we can have that the scores obtained from the test are essentially the same scores that would be obtained if the test were readministered to the same test takers. If a test is unreliable (i.e., if it provides inconsistent information about performance), then scores would be expected to be quite different every time the test was administered. For example, if an attitude test is unreliable, then a student getting a total score of 75 today might score 45 tomorrow and 95 the day after tomorrow. If the test is reliable, and if the student's total score is 75, then we would not expect the student's score to vary much on retesting. Of course, we also should not expect the student's score to be exactly the same on other retestings. The reliability of test scores is similar to the reliability of one's golf, bowling, or shot-putting scores. Golf, bowling, or shot-putting rarely produce the identical scores time after time after time. There is measurement error in all these activities. An individual's health, motivation, anxiety, guessing luck, attitude, and attention change from time to time and influence performance, as they do test scores. All test scores have some degree of measurement error, and the smaller the amount of error, the more reliable the scores and the more confidence we have in the consistency and stability of test takers' performances.

Reliability is expressed numerically, usually as a *reliability coefficient,* which is obtained by using correlation. A high reliability coefficient indicates high reliability. If a test were perfectly reliable, the reliability coefficient would be 1.00, meaning that students' scores perfectly reflected their true status with respect to the variable being measured. However, alas and alack, as noted, no test is perfectly reliable. High reliability indicates minimum error; the effect of errors of measurement is small.

Validity tells test users about the appropriateness of a test, and reliability tells about the consistency of the scores produced. Both are important for judging the suitability of a test or measuring instrument. However, *a valid test is always reliable but a reliable test is not always valid.* In other words, if a test is measuring what it is supposed to be measuring, it will be reliable, but a reliable test can consistently measure the wrong thing and be invalid! Suppose an instrument that intended to measure social studies concepts actually measured only social studies facts. It would not be a valid measure of concepts, but it could certainly measure the facts very consistently. For example, suppose the reported reliability coefficient for a test was .24, which is definitely quite low. Would this tell you anything about the test's validity? Yes, it would. It would tell you that the validity was not high because if it were, the reliability would be higher. What if the reported reliability coefficient were .92, which is definitely good. Would this tell you anything about the validity? H-m-m-m. The answer is—not really. It would only tell you that the validity might be good, because the reliability is good, but not necessarily; the test could be consistently measuring the wrong thing. To review, reliability is necessary but not sufficient for establishing validity. Got it?

Like validity, there are different types of reliability, each of which deals with a different kind of test consistency. Each is established in a different manner. We discuss here five general types of reliability: stability, equivalence, equivalence and stability, internal consistency, and rater agreement.

Stability

Stability, also called **test–retest reliability,** is the degree to which scores on the same test are consistent over time. It provides evidence that scores obtained on a test at one time (test) are the same or close to the same when the test is readministered some other time (retest). The more similar the scores on the test over time, the more stable or consistent are the test scores. Test stability is especially important for tests used as predictors, since these predictors are based heavily on the assumption that the scores will be stable over time.

The procedure for determining test–retest reliability is basically quite simple:

1. Administer the test to an appropriate group.
2. After some time has passed, say two weeks, administer the same test to the same group.
3. Correlate the two sets of scores.
4. Evaluate the results.

If the resulting coefficient, referred to as the *coefficient of stability,* is high, the test has good test–retest reliability. A major problem with this type of reliability is the difficulty of knowing how much time should elapse between the two testing sessions. If the interval is too short, the chances of students' remembering responses made on the test the first time are increased, and the estimate of reliability tends to be artificially high. If the interval is too long, students' test performance may increase due to intervening learning or maturation, and the estimate of reliability tends to be artificially low. Generally, though not universally, a period of from two to six weeks is used to determine a test's stability. When stability information about a test is given, the stability coefficient and the time interval between testings also should be given.

Equivalence

Equivalent or alternative forms of a test are identical in every way except for the actual items on each. **Equivalence** exists when the two forms measure the same variable, have the same number of items, the same structure, the same difficulty level, and the same directions for administration, scoring, and interpretation. Only the specific items are not the same, although they do measure the same topics or objectives. The equivalent forms are constructed by randomly sampling two sets of items from the same, well-described population. If there is equivalence, the two tests can be used interchangeably. It is reassuring to know that a person's score will not be greatly affected by the particular form administered. In some research studies two forms of a test are administered to the same group, one as a pretest and the other as a posttest.

The procedure for determining **equivalent-forms reliability** is similar to that for determining test–retest reliability:

1. Administer one form of the test to an appropriate group.
2. At the same session, or shortly thereafter, administer the second form of the test to the same group.
3. Correlate the two sets of scores.
4. Evaluate the results.

If the resulting coefficient of equivalence is high, the test has good equivalent-forms reliability. Equivalent-forms reliability is the most commonly used estimate of reliability for most tests used in research. The major problem involved with this method of estimating reliability is the difficulty of constructing two forms that are essentially equivalent. Even though equivalent-forms reliability is considered to be a very good estimate of reliability, it is not always feasible to administer two different forms of the same test. Imagine telling your students that they had to take two final examinations!

Equivalence and Stability

This form of reliability combines equivalence and stability. If the two forms of the test are administered at two different times (the best of all possible worlds!) the resulting coefficient is referred to as the *coefficient of stability and equivalence*. In essence, this approach assesses stability of scores over time as well as the equivalence of the two sets of items. Since more sources of measurement error are possible than with either method alone, the resulting coefficient is likely to be somewhat lower. Thus, the coefficient of stability and equivalence represents a conservative estimate of reliability.

The procedure for determining equivalence and stability reliability is as follows:

1. Administer one form of the test to an appropriate group.
2. After a period of time, administer the other form of the test to the same group.
3. Correlate the two sets of scores.
4. Evaluate the results.

Internal Consistency Reliability

Internal consistency is a commonly used form of reliability that deals with one test at one time. It is obtained through three different approaches: split-half, Kuder-Richardson, or Cronbach's alpha. Each provides information about the consistency among the items in a single test. Because internal consistency approaches require only one test administration, sources of measurement errors, such as differences in testing conditions, are eliminated.

Split-Half Reliability.   **Split-half reliability** involves breaking a single test into two halves. It is especially appropriate when a test is very long or when it would be difficult to administer either the same test at two different times or two different forms to a group. The procedure for determining split-half reliability is as follows:

1. Administer the total test to a group.
2. Divide the test into two comparable halves, or subtests, most commonly by dividing the test into odd and even numbered subtests.
3. Compute each participant's score on the two halves—each participant will have a score for the odd items and a score for the even items.
4. Correlate the two sets of scores.
5. Apply the Spearman-Brown correction formula.
6. Evaluate the results.

Most commonly, an odd–even strategy is used. This approach works out rather well regardless of how a test is organized. Suppose, for example, we have a 20-item test in which the items get progressively more difficult. Items 1, 3, 5, 7, 9, 11, 13, 15, 17, and 19 as a group should be approximately as difficult as items 2, 4, 6, 8, 10, 12, 14, 16, 18, and 20. In effect, we are artificially creating two equivalent forms of a test and computing their equivalent-forms reliability. In split-half reliability, the two equivalent forms just happen to be in the same test— thus the label *internal consistency reliability*.

Because longer tests tend to be more reliable, and since split-half reliability represents the reliability of a test only half as long as the actual test, a correction formula must be applied to determine the reliability of the whole test. The correction formula used is the Spearman-Brown prophecy formula. For example, suppose the split-half reliability coefficient for a 50-item test were .80. The .80 would be based on the correlation between scores on 25 even items and 25 odd items and would therefore be an estimate of the reliability of a 25-item test, not a 50-item test. The Spearman-Brown formula provides an estimate of the full 50-item test. The formula is very simple and is applied to our example in the following way:

$$r_{\text{total test}} = \frac{2r_{\text{split half}}}{1 + r_{\text{split half}}}$$

$$r_{\text{total test}} = \frac{2(.80)}{1 + .80} = \frac{1.60}{1.80} = .89$$

Kuder-Richardson and Cronbach's Alpha Reliabilities.   Kuder-Richardson (KR) and Cronbach's alpha estimate internal consistency reliability by determining how all items on a test relate to all other test items and to the total test. When its items or tasks are measuring similar things, they are internally consistent. Both KR-20 and Cronbach's alpha provide reliability estimates that are equivalent to the average of the split-half reliabilities computed for all possible halves. KR-20 is a highly regarded method of assessing reliability, but is useful only for dichotomously scored items such as in multiple-choice items. If items have more than two scores, (e.g., 0, 1, 2, 3), then Cronbach's alpha (α) should be used. **Cronbach's alpha** is the general formula of which the KR-20 formula is a special case. Many affective instruments and performance tests are scored using more than two choices. For example, Likert scales are commonly used in many affective instruments. If numbers are used to represent the response choices, analysis for internal consistency can be accomplished using Cronbach's alpha.

Kuder and Richardson provided an alternative, more easily computed from of their formaula, called Kuder-Richardson 21, or KR-21. It requires less time than any other method of estimating reliability, although its results are a more conservative estimate of reliability. The KR-21 formula is as follows:

$$r_{\text{total test}} = \frac{(K)(SD^2) - \overline{X}(K - \overline{X})}{(SD^2)(K - 1)}$$

where
   K = the number of items in the test
  SD = the standard deviation of the scores
   $\overline{X}$ = the mean of the scores

In a later chapter you will learn how to compute the mean and standard deviation of a set of scores. For the moment, let it suffice to say that the mean ($\overline{X}$) is the average score on the test for the group that took it, and the standard deviation (SD) is an indication of the amount of score variability, or how spread out the scores are. For example, assume that you have administered a 50-item test and have calculated the mean to be 40 ($\overline{X}$ = 40) and the standard deviation to be 4 (SD = 4). The reliability of the test (which in this example turns out to be not too hot) would be calculated as follows:

$$r_{\text{total test}} = \frac{(50)(4^2) - 40(50 - 40)}{(4^2)(50 - 1)}$$

$$= \frac{(50)(16) - 40(10)}{(16)(49)} = \frac{800 - 400}{784} = \frac{400}{784} = .51$$

Figure 5.1 summarizes the previously discussed methods of estimating reliabilities.

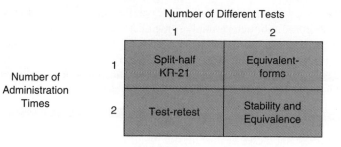

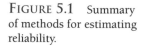

FIGURE 5.1 Summary of methods for estimating reliability.

Scorer/Rater Reliability

Reliability also must be investigated when scoring tests. Subjectivity occurs when different scorers or a single scorer over time do not agree on the scores of a single test. Essay tests, short-answer tests, performance and product tests, projective tests, and observations—almost any test that calls for more than a one-word response—raise concerns about the reliability of scoring. In such situations we are concerned with interscorer, interrater, or interobserver reliability and/or intrajudge reliability. **Interjudge reliability** refers to the scoring reliability of two or more independent scorers; **intrajudge reliability** refers to the consistency of the scoring of a single judge over time (a kind of test–retest reliability).

Subjective scoring is a major source of errors of measurement, so it is important to determine the reliability of those who score open-ended tests. It is especially important to determine scorer/rater reliability when the results of the tests are consequential for test takers, such as the awarding of a high school diploma or promotion to the next grade on the basis of a test. The more open ended test items are, the more important it is to seek consensus in scoring among judges. Subjective scoring reduces reliability and, in turn, diminishes the validity of the interpretations one wished to make from the scores. Table 5.3 summarizes the five types of reliability.

Reliability Coefficients

What constitutes an acceptable level of reliability is to some degree determined by the type of test, although very high reliability coefficients would be acceptable for any test. The question really is concerned with what constitutes the minimum level of acceptability. This will differ among test types. For example, standardized achievement and aptitude tests should have high

TABLE 5.3   Methods of Determining Reliability

Name	What Is Measured	Description
Stability (test–retest)	Stability of scores over time	Give one group the same test at two different times and correlate the two scores.
Equivalance (alternative forms)	Relationship between two versions of a test intended to be equivalent	Give alternative test forms to a single group and correlate the two scores.
Equivalance and stability	Relationship between equivalent versions of a test given at two different times	Give two alternative tests to a group at two different times and correlate the scores.
Internal consistency	The extent to which the items in a test are similar to one another in content	Give tests to one group and apply split-half, Kuder-Richardson, or Cronbach's alpha to estimate the internal consistency of the test items.
Scorer/rater	The extent to which independent scorers or a single scorer over time agree on the scoring of an open-ended test	Give copies of a set of tests to independent scorers or a single scorer at different times and correlate or compute the percentage of scorer agreement.

reliability, often higher than .90. On the other hand, personality measures do not typically report such high reliabilities (although certainly some do), and one would therefore be satisfied with a reliability somewhat lower than expected from an achievement test. Moreover, when tests are developed in new areas, reliability is often low initially. If you are using a fairly new test or using an established test with a group that is somewhat different than the test norm group, you should report reliability figures for your group. It is good practice to always report reliability information in your research plan.

If a test is composed of several subtests that will be used individually in a study, then the reliability of each subtest should be evaluated, not just the reliability of the total test. Since reliability is a function of test length, the reliability of any particular subtest is typically lower than the reliability of the total test. It is extremely difficult to state appropriate reliability coefficients for different types of tests. Obviously, the higher the reliability the better, but what's a "high" or "low" reliability for an achievement, attitude, interest, personality, or curiosity test? One way to answer this question is to get information about the typical reliabilities for particular types of tests. For example, if you find that three curiosity tests had reliabilities between .60 and .75, you have an idea of what level of reliability to expect in other curiosity tests.

It is also difficult to state appropriate reliability coefficients because reliability, like validity, is dependent on the group being tested. For example, the more heterogeneous the test scores of a group, the higher the reliability will be. Thus, if group A and group B both took the same test, but group A was made up of valedictorians and group B was made up of students ranging from low to high performers, group B will have a higher reliability than group A. Also, the more items on a test and the more the scores range from high to low, the higher the reliability. That is why it is important for researchers to report reliability for their own research participants.

Standard Error of Measurement

Reliability can also be expressed in terms of the standard error of measurement. You should be familiar with this concept, since such data are often reported for a test. Basically, the **standard error of measurement** is an estimate of how often you can expect test errors of a given size. Thus, a small standard error of measurement indicates high reliability, and a large standard error of measurement indicates low reliability.

If a test were perfectly reliable (which no test is), a person's test score would be his or her true score—that is, the score the person got would be perfectly reliable. However, we know that if you administered the same test over and over to the same group, the score of each individual would vary, like the golf, bowling, and shot-put examples discussed previously. The amount of variability in the individual scores would be a function of the test's reliability. The variability would be small for a highly reliable test and large for a test with low reliability. If we could administer the test many times to the same group, we could see how much variation actually occurred. Of course, realistically we can't do this, but it is possible to estimate this degree of variation (the standard error of measurement) using the data from the administration of a single test. In other words, the standard error of measurement allows us to estimate how much difference there is between a person's obtained score and her or his true score. The size of this difference is a function of the reliability of the test. We can estimate the standard error of measurement using the following simple formula:

$$SEm = SD\sqrt{1-r}$$

where

SEm = standard error of measurement
SD = the standard deviation of the test scores
r = the reliability coefficient

For example, for a 25-item test we might calculate the standard deviation of a set of scores to be 5 ($SD = 5$) and the reliability coefficient to be .84 ($r = .84$). In this case the standard error of measurement would be calculated as follows:

$$SEm = SD\sqrt{1-r} = 5\sqrt{1-.84} = 5\sqrt{.16} = 5(.4) = 2.0$$

As this example illustrates, the size of the SEm is a function of both the SD and the reliability coefficient. Higher reliability is associated with a smaller SEm and a smaller SD is associated with a smaller SEm. If in the previous example $r = .64$, would you expect SEm, to be larger or smaller? Right, larger, and in fact, it would be 3.0. Also, if in that example $SD = 10$, what would you expect to happen to SEm? Right, it would be larger—4.0, to be exact. While we prefer the SEm to be small, indicating less error, it is impossible to say how small is "good." This is because SEm is expressed in the same units as the test, and how small is "small" is relative to the size of the test. Thus, $SEm = 5$ would be large for a 20-item test but small for a 200-item test. In our example, $SEm = 2.0$ would be considered moderate. To facilitate better interpretation of scores, some test publishers do not just present the SEm for the total group but also give a separate SEm for each of a number of identified subgroups.

SELECTING A TEST

A very important guideline for selecting a test is: Do not, repeat, do not stop with the first test you find that appears to measure what you want, say "Eureka, I have found it!" and blithely use it in your study! Instead, identify a group of tests that are appropriate for your study, compare them on relevant factors, and select the best one. If you become knowledgeable concerning the qualities a test should possess, and familiar with the various types of tests that are available, then selecting an instrument will be a very orderly process. Given that you have defined the purpose of your study and the research participants, the first step in choosing a test is to determine precisely what type of test you need. The next step is to identify and locate appropriate tests. Finally, you must do a comparative analysis of the tests and select the best one for your needs.

SOURCES OF TEST INFORMATION

Mental Measurements Yearbooks

Once you have determined the type of test you need (e.g., a test of reading comprehension for second graders or an attitude measure for high schoolers), a logical place to start looking for specific tests to meet your needs is the Mental Measurements Yearbooks (MMYs). Currently produced by the Buros Institute of Mental Measurements at the University of Nebraska—Lincoln, the MMYs have been published periodically since 1938, and they represent the most comprehensive source of test information available to educational researchers. (As noted earlier in this chapter, you can access them on the Web at http://www.unl.edu/buros/). The *Fourteenth Mental Measurements Yearbook* is the latest publication in a series that includes the MMYs, *Tests in Print,* and many other related works such as *Vocational Tests and Reviews.* An MMY is published every few years, and a *Supplement* is published between major revisions. Most university libraries contain the MMYs. The MMYs are expressly designed to assist users in making informed test selection decisions. The stated purposes are to provide (1) factual information on all known new or revised tests in the English-speaking world, (2) objective test reviews written specifically for the MMYs, and (3) comprehensive bibliographies, for specific tests, of related references from published literature.

Getting maximum benefit from the MMYs requires, at the very least, that you familiarize yourself with the organization and the indexes provided. Perhaps the most important thing to know in using the MMYs is that the numbers given in the indexes are test numbers, not page numbers. For example, in the Classified Subject Index, under Achievement, you will find the following entry (among others): Iowa Tests of Basic Skills, Form J, grades K.1–1.5, K.8–1.9, 1.7–2.6, 2.5–3.5, 3, 4, 5, 6, 7, 8–9, see 184. The *184* means that the description of the Iowa Tests of Basic Skills is entry 184 in the main body of the volume; it does not mean that it is on page 184.

The MMY provides six indexes to help you find information about tests: Index of Titles, Index of Acronyms, Classified Subject Index (lists tests alphabetically), Publishers Directory and Index (names and addresses of publishers), and Index of Names (names of test developers and test reviewers). So, for example, if you heard that Professor Jeenyus had developed a new interest test, but you did not know its name, you would look under Jeenyus; there you would be given test numbers for all tests developed by Professor Jeenyus that were included in the volume. Finally, the Score Index directs you to information concerning the types of scores obtained from tests in the MMY.

If you are looking for information on a particular test, you can find it easily by using the alphabetical organization of the most recent MMYs. If you are not sure of the title of the test you are seeking or have no specific test in mind, but know generally what kind of test you need, you may use the following procedure:

1. If you are not sure of the title of the test you are looking for or can't find it in the alphabetical list of tests, look through the Index of Titles for possible variants of the title or consult the appropriate subject area in the Classified Subject Index for that particular test or related ones.
2. If you know the test publisher, look up that publisher in the Publishers Directory and Index and look for the test you seek.
3. If you are looking for a test that yields a particular type of score, search for that type in the Score Index to find tests that include that type of score.
4. Using the entry numbers listed in all of the sections described previously, locate the test descriptions in the Tests and Reviews section (the main body of the volume).

An example of an MMY entry is shown in Figure 5.2. Note some of the characteristics in an MMY entry—the suggested ages of the participants, the author and publisher, a review by a researcher in the subject area, information about the validity and reliability, and other useful information about the test.

Tests in Print

A very useful supplemental source of test information is *Tests in Print (TIP)*. *TIP* is a comprehensive bibliography of all known commercially available tests that are currently in print. It also serves as a master index of tests that directs the reader to all original reviews that have appeared in the MMYs to date. It is most often used to determine a test's availability. Once you know that a test is available, you can look it up in the MMY to find out if it is appropriate for your purpose. The main body of the latest *TIP* edition is organized alphabetically.

Thus, *TIP* provides information on many more tests than the MMYs, but is less comprehensive in terms of information given for each test.

PRO-ED Publications

Another source of test information is published by PRO-ED. Information on more than 3,000 tests in a number of areas such as psychology, education, and business are cited. Although no reviews are included, complete information about test publishers is provided to enable users to call or write for additional information. In addition, tests appropriate for individuals with physical, visual, and hearing impairments are listed, as well as tests that are available in a variety of languages. Visit http://www.proedinc.com/index.html on the World Wide Web to

[183]
The Hundred Pictures Naming Test.
Purpose: "A confrontation naming test designed to evaluate rapid naming ability."
Population: Ages 4-6 to 11-11.
Publication Date: 1992.
Acronym: HPNT.
Scores, 3: Error, Accuracy, Time.
Administration: Individual.
Price Data, 1992: $195 per complete kit including manual (84 pages), test book, and 25 response forms; $10 per 25 response forms.
Time: (6) minutes.
Authors: John P. Fisher and Jennifer M. Glenister.
Publisher: Australian Council for Educational Research Ltd. [Australia]

Review of The Hundred Pictures Naming Test by JEFFREY A. ATLAS, Deputy Chief Psychologist and Assistant Clinical Professor, Bronx Children's Psychiatric Center, Albert Einstein College of Medicine, Bronx, NY:
The Hundred Pictures Naming Test (HPNT) is introduced in its test manual as "a confrontation naming test designed to evaluate rapid naming ability across age groups" (manual, p. 1). Given this stated purpose, the HPNT seems to qualify as a "test," and a valuable one, for "preparatory" (preschooler) boys and girls aged 5 to 6½, a grouping that constituted roughly 66% of the test reference group of 275 children. The remaining group cells have too few children to provide truly normative data, but may be suggestive in screening subjects who may have language disability or in evaluating recovery of function after brain injury.

The manual and test plates are attractively packaged and sturdy (except for the cardboard test container which will likely be discarded after several uses), but a bit overpriced at $195 for a test with restricted norms and limited generalizability. My sample package contained repeats of the manual pages 1–6 and test plate 18. These are minor distractors that I hope do not reflect overall quality control.

The reference group has nearly equal sex distribution, satisfactory city-suburban-country stratification (64%, 25%, and 11%), but scant socioeconomic information. The fact the test was developed in Australia seems not to have resulted in much content sampling bias. Preliminary inspection for test items that might prompt minor concern suggest "unicorn" and "rake" are words that may be absent from the linguistic environment of preschoolers living in cinder-block projects in New York City, and "koala" and "crown" reflect Australian versus other English-speaking nationality locales.

The mean "accuracy" score for the reference group was 74.34 (*sd* = 15.67), with a range of 23 to 98. These numbers comprise expectable figures for a 100-item examination and the linearity of increased test scores by age was impressive, permitting some normative evaluation, especially for preschoolers. Useful indicators for evaluating poor test performance, with some error categories indicating the need for speech therapy, some response categories indicating psychological intervention (e.g., for Selective Mutism), and overall poor lexicon indicating language remediation. The inclusion of 31 speech-language problem youngsters in the reference group provides suggestive screening norms but the low sample number and uneven linearity of scores limits the usefulness of the HPNT as a test for this group. Similarly, the division of the reference group into English First, English Main(ly), and English Only is helpful in qualitative assessment of performance but inadequate in providing test norms.

A useful aspect of the HPNT may be as a monitor of recovery of function after brain injury. Test-retest data (*r* = .98, after about 1 month for a bit over a fifth of the reference pool) and interrater reliability (*r* = .97 using a little over a tenth of the pool) furnish adequate criteria for retest using the HPNT. A sample protocol in the manual illustrates 6-year-old Warren's notable improvements in accuracy and significant error reduction, reflecting good recovery of function approximately 7 months following brain injury suffered in a car accident.

In summary, The Hundred Pictures Naming Test offers a useful test of English-only preschoolers' expressive speech accuracy, of recovery of speech function in some aphasias, and a screening device for psychological, environmental, and second-language interferences. As such it represents itself as a useful addition to the armamentarium of speech-language pathologists, early childhood educators, and in a more limited way, English-as-Second-Language instructors.

Source: Conoley, J. C., and Impara, J. C. (Eds.), *The Twelfth Mental Measurements Yearbook*, pp. 380–81, Lincoln, NE: Buros Institute of Mental Measurements.

FIGURE 5.2 Sample entry from the *Twelfth Mental Measurements Yearbook*.

order a PRO-ED catalog or to order their most popular tests. PRO-ED's *Test Critiques* contains reviews for more than 800 tests widely used in psychology, education, and business. The reviews are quite extensive.

ETS Test Collection Database

The ETS (Educational Testing Service) Test Collection Database is an extremely useful online resource. A joint project of the Educational Testing Service and the ERIC Clearinghouse on Assessment and Evaluation, the ETS Test Collection is a searchable database. The ETS Collection Database contains records for more than 9,500 tests and research instruments in virtually all fields. In contrast to the MMYs, it includes unpublished as well as published tests, but provides much less information per test. To access the ETS Test Collection Database, go to http://ericae.net/testcol.htm on the Web. There you will be able to search through the ETS Test File for names, descriptions, and availability information on more than 10,000 tests and research instruments. For each test included in the database, the following information is given: title, author, publication date, target population, publisher or source, and an annotation describing the purpose of the instrument.

The ETS Test Collection also provides more than 200 annotated bibliographies representing eight major categories: achievement, aptitude, attitudes and interests, personality, sensory-motor, special populations, vocational/occupational, and miscellaneous. *News on Tests* is produced 10 times a year and includes announcements of new tests, citations of test reviews, new reference materials, and other related items.

ERIC/AE Test Locator

Two additional search features are available online in the ERIC/AE Test Locator at http://ericae.net/testcol.htm. (This is the same Web address as that of the ETS Test Collection Database.) The *Test Review Locator* allows you to search for citations about a particular testing instrument in MMY and PRO-ED directories. The *Buros/ERIC Test Publisher Directory* permits you to search for the names and addresses of more than 900 major commercial test publishers.

Professional Journals

A number of journals regularly publish information of interest to test users, many of which are American Psychological Association publications. For example, *Psychological Abstracts* is a potential source of test information. Using the monthly or annual index, you can quickly determine if *Psychological Abstracts* contains information on a given test. Other journals of interest to test users include *Journal of Applied Measurement, Journal of Consulting Psychology, Journal of Educational Measurement,* and *Educational and Psychological Measurement.*

Test Publishers and Distributors

After narrowing your search to a few acceptable tests, a good source of additional information on tests is publishers' test manuals. Manuals typically include detailed technical information, a description of the population for whom the test is intended to be appropriate, a detailed description of norming procedures, conditions of administration, detailed scoring instructions, and requirements for score interpretation. Final selection of a test usually requires examining the actual test. A test that appears from all descriptions to be exactly what you need may have one or more problems. For example, it may contain many items measuring content not covered, or its language level may be too high or low for your participants. Above all, remember that in selecting tests you must be a good consumer, one who finds an instrument that fits your needs.

SELECTING FROM ALTERNATIVES

Eventually you must reach a decision. Once you have narrowed the number of test candidates and acquired relevant information, you must make a comparative analysis of the tests. Although there are a number of factors to be considered in choosing a test, these factors are not of equal importance. For example, the least expensive test is not necessarily the best test! As you undoubtedly know by now, the most important factor to be considered in test selection is validity. Is one of the tests more appropriate for your sample? If you are interested in prediction, does one of the tests have a significantly higher validity coefficient? If content validity is of prime importance, are the items of one test more relevant to the topic of your study than other tests? These are typical questions to ask. If, after the validity comparisons, there are still several tests that seem appropriate, the next factor to consider is reliability.

You would presumably select the test with the highest reliability, but there are other considerations. For example, a test that can be administered during one class period would be considerably more convenient than a 2-hour test. Shorter tests generally are also preferable in terms of test takers' fatigue and motivation. However, since longer tests have higher reliability, a shorter test will tend to be less reliable. If one test takes half as long to administer as another and is only slightly less reliable, the shorter test is probably better. By the time you get to this point, you have probably made a decision. It probably will be a group-administered test rather than an individually administered one. Most of the time, individually administered tests will not be necessary except for certain intelligence and personality tests, and situations in which some persons with disabilities are tested. Of course, if the nature of your research study requires it, by all means use an individually administered test, but be certain you have the qualifications needed to administer, score, and interpret the results. If you do not, can you afford to acquire the necessary personnel? If, after all this soul searching, by some miracle you still have more than one test in the running, by all means pick the cheapest one!

Two additional considerations in test selection have nothing to do with their psychometric qualities. Both are related to the use of tests in schools. If you are planning to use schoolchildren in your study, you should check to see what tests they have already taken. You would not want to administer a test with which test takers are already familiar. Second, you should be sensitive to the fact that some parents or administrators might object to a test that contains "touchy" items. Certain attitude, values, and personality tests, for example, contain questions related to the personal beliefs and behaviors of the respondents. If there is any possibility that the test contains potentially objectionable items, either choose another test or acquire appropriate permissions before administering the test.

CONSTRUCTING TESTS

On rare occasions you may not be able to locate a suitable test. One logical solution is to construct your own test. Good test construction requires a variety of skills. If you don't have them, get some help. As mentioned previously, experience at least equivalent to a course in measurement is needed. If you do develop your own test, you must collect validity and reliability data. A self-developed test should not be utilized in a research study unless it has been first pretested by a group of 5 to 10 persons similar to the group you will be collecting data from in the actual study. The following discussion gives you an overview of some guidelines to follow if you need to construct a test for your study that you will administer to schoolchildren.

Writing Your Own Paper-and-Pencil Test Items

The following suggestions provide elementary strategies for constructing your own paper-and-pencil test items.[2] You should buy and read one of the many useful classroom assessment test books. We begin by noting the variety of test items that you have at your disposal. There are two general categories for paper-and-pencil testing—selection items and supply items. Selection items include multiple choice, true-false, and matching. Supply items include short-answer or completion items and essays. Note that scoring or judging responses is much more difficult for essays than the other types of test items. Get help if needed.

General rules for writing paper-and-pencil test items follow. Figure 5.3 presents further suggestions for preparing items.

---

[2] Test items on these pages are taken from Airasian, Peter W., *Classroom Assessment: Concepts and Applications,* 4th ed. New York: McGraw-Hill (2001), pp. 182–190.

FIGURE 5.3
Suggestions for preparing test items.

Multiple-Choice Items
- Set pupils' task in the item stem.
- Include repeated words in the stem.
- Avoid grammatical clues.
- Use positive wording if possible.
- Include only plausible options.
- Avoid using "all of the above" or "none of the above."

Matching Items
- Use a homogeneous topic.
- Put longer options in left column.
- Provide clear direction.
- Use unequal numbers of entries in the two columns.

Essay Items
- Use several short-essay questions rather than one long one.
- Provide a clear focus in questions.
- Indicate scoring criteria to pupils.

True-False Items
- Make statements clearly true or false.
- Avoid specific determiners.
- Do not arrange responses in a pattern.
- Do not select textbook sentences.

Completion and Short-Answer Items
- Provide a clear focus for the desired answer.
- Avoid grammatical clues.
- Put blanks at the end of the item.
- Do not select textbook sentences.

Source: Airasian, Peter W. (2001). *Classroom Assessment: Concepts and Applications,* 4th ed. New York: McGraw-Hill, p. 192. Reprinted by permission.

1. Avoid wording and sentence structure that is ambiguous and confusing.
   Poor: All but one of the following items are not elements. Which one is not?
   Better: Which one of the following is an element?
2. Use appropriate vocabulary.
   Poor: The thesis of capillary execution serves to illuminate how fluids are elevated in small tubes.   True   False
   Better: The principle of capillary action helps explain how liquids rise in small passages.   True   False
3. Write items that have one correct answer.
   Poor: Ernest Hemingway wrote _____.
   Better: The author of *The Old Man of the Sea* is _____.
4. Give information about the nature of the desired answer.
   Poor: Compare and contrast the North and South in the Civil War. Support your views.
   Better: What forces led to the outbreak of the Civil War? Indicate in your discussion the economic, foreign, and social conditions. You will be judged in terms of these three topics. Your essay should be five paragraphs in length, and spelling and grammar will count in your grade.
5. Do not provide clues to the correct answer.
   Poor: A figure that has eight sides is called an
   A. pentagon
   B. quadrilateral
   C. octagon
   D. ogive
   Better: Figures that have eight sides are called
   A. pentagons
   B. quadrilaterals
   C. octagons
   D. ogives

Be sure to align instruction and assessment when testing to ensure valid results. We strongly suggest that you try out any test you construct yourself in a research setting. Monitor test takers carefully to minimize cheating. It is not necessary to have a large number of persons to find out if your test is valid and clear. Ask four or five insightful teachers or individuals experienced in test-item writing to critique your test for clarity and logic. Based on their suggestions, you can improve your test.

TEST ADMINISTRATION

You should be aware of several general guidelines for test administration. First, if testing is to be conducted in a school setting, arrangements should be made beforehand with the appropriate persons. Consultation with the principal should result in agreement as to when the testing will take place, under what conditions, and with what assistance from school personnel. The principal can be very helpful in supplying such information as dates for which testing is inadvisable (e.g., assembly days and days immediately preceding or following holidays). Second, whether you are testing in the schools or elsewhere, you should do everything you can to ensure ideal testing conditions; a comfortable, quiet environment is more conducive to participant cooperation. Also, if testing is to take place in more than one session, the conditions of the sessions should be as identical as possible. Third, follow the Boy Scout motto and be prepared. Be thoroughly familiar with the administration procedures presented in the test manual and follow the directions precisely. If they are at all complicated, practice beforehand. Administer the test to some group or stand in front of a mirror and give it to yourself!

As with everything in life, good planning and preparation usually pay off. If you have made all necessary arrangements, secured all necessary cooperation, and are very familiar and comfortable with the administration procedures, the actual testing situation should go well. If some unforeseen catastrophe occurs during testing, such as an earthquake or a power failure, make careful note of the incident. If it is serious enough to invalidate the testing, you may have to try again another day with another group. At minimum, note its occurrence in your final research report. Despite the possibility of unforeseen tragedies, it is certain that the probability of all going well will be greatly increased if you adequately plan and prepare for the big day.

 Now go to the Companion Website accompanying this text at www.prenhall.com/gay to check your understanding of chapter concepts in the following modules: Objectives, Practice Quiz, and Applying What You Know. Expand your research skills with Evaluating Articles, Analyzing Qualitative Data, Analyzing Quantitative Data, and Research Tools and Tips. Visit Web Links to broaden your knowledge about research.

SUMMARY

Constructs

1. All types of research require collecting data; the scientific and disciplined inquiry approach depends on the collection, analysis, and interpretation of data. Data are pieces of evidence used to examine a research topic or hypothesis.

2. Constructs are mental abstractions such as personality, creativity, and intelligence that cannot be observed or measured directly. Constructs become variables when they are stated in terms of operational definitions.

Variables

3. Measurement scales describe four different levels of variable: nominal, ordinal rank, interval and ratio.

4. Categorical variables are nonnumerical (nominal); quantitative variables are numerical (ordinal, interval, and ratio).

5. An independent variable is the treatment or cause, and the dependent variable is the outcome or effect of the independent variable.

Characteristics of Measuring Instruments

6. There are three main ways to collect data for research studies: administer an existing instrument, construct one's own instrument, and record naturally occurring events (observation) or collect existing data.

7. The time and skill it takes to select an appropriate instrument are invariably less than the time and skill it takes to develop one's own instrument.

8. There are thousands of standardized and nonstandardized instruments available for researchers. A standardized test is one that is administered, scored, and interpreted in the same way no matter when and where it is administered.

9. Most quantitative tests are paper-and-pencil ones, while most qualitative research collects data by observation and oral questioning.

10. Raw scores indicate the number of items or points a person got correct. They can be transformed into derived scores such as percentile ranks, stanines, and standard scores. Derived scores are most often used with standardized tests.

11. Norm-referenced scoring compares a student's test performance to the performance of other test takers; criterion-referenced scoring compares a student's test performance to predetermined standards of performance.

Types of Measuring Instruments

Cognitive Tests

Achievement Tests

12. Achievement tests measure the current status of individuals on school-taught subjects.

13. Most standardized achievement tests are scored using norm-referencing approaches.

Aptitude Tests

14. Aptitude tests are used to predict how well a test taker is likely to perform in the future. They are standardized and used extensively in job hiring. General aptitude tests typically ask the test taker to perform a variety of verbal and nonverbal tasks.

15. Readiness tests are administered prior to instruction to determine whether and to what degree a student is ready for a given level of instruction.

Affective Tests

16. Affective tests measure characteristics such as interest, values, attitude, and personality.

17. Most affective tests are nonprojective; that is, they are self-report measures in which the individual responds to a series of questions about him- or herself.

18. There are five basic types of scales used to measure attitudes: Likert scales, semantic differential scales, rating scales, Thurstone scales, and Guttman scales. The first three are the most used.

19. Attitude scales ask respondents to state their feeling about various objects, persons, and activities. Likert scales are responded to by indicating strongly agree, agree, undecided, disagree, and strongly disagree; semantic differential scales present a continuum of attitudes on which the respondent selects a position to indicate the strength of attitude; and rating scales present statements that respondents must rate on a continuum from high to low. These are all self-report measures.

20. Interest inventories ask individuals to indicate personal likes and dislikes. Responses are generally compared to existing interest patterns.

21. Values are deeply held beliefs about ideas, persons, and objects.

22. Personality, also called temperament, describes characteristics that represent a person's typical behavior. Personality inventories present respondents with lists of statements describing human behaviors, and they must indicate whether each statement pertains to them.

23. Personality inventories may be specific to a single trait (introversion–extroversion) or may be general and measure a number of traits.

24. Use of self-report measures create the concern about whether an individual is expressing his or her true attitude, values, interests, or personality.

25. Test bias in both cognitive and affective measures can distort the data obtained. Bias is present when one's ethnicity, race, gender, language, or religious orientation influences test performance.

Projective Tests

26. Projective tests present an ambiguous situation to the test taker that requires her or him to "project" her or his true feelings on the ambiguous situation.

27. Association is the most commonly used projective technique, and is exemplified by the inkblot test. Only the specially trained can administer and interpret projective tests.

Criteria for Good Measuring Instruments

Validity of Measuring Instruments

28. Validity is the degree to which a test measures what it is supposed to measure, thus permitting appropriate interpretations of test scores.

29. A test is not valid per se; it is valid for a particular interpretation and for a particular group. Each intended test use requires its own validation. Tests are not simply valid or invalid; they are highly valid, moderately valid, or generally invalid.

30. The four main forms of validity are content, criterion-related, construct, and consequential. They are viewed as interrelated, not independent aspects of validity.

Content Validity

31. Content validity assesses the degree to which a test measures an intended content area. It requires both item validity and sampling validity. Item validity is concerned with whether the test items are relevant to the intended content area; sampling validity is concerned with how well the test sample represents the total content area. Content validity is of prime importance for achievement tests.

32. Content validity is determined by expert judgment of item and sample validity, not statistical means.

Criterion-Related Validity

33. Criterion-related validity has two forms, concurrent and predictive. Concurrent validity is the degree to which the scores on a test are related to scores on another test administered at the same time. Predictive validity is the degree to which scores on a test are related to scores on another test administered in the future. In both cases, a single group must take both tests.

34. Concurrent and predictive validity are determined by correlating one test with another, either at the same time or in the future.

Construct Validity

35. Constructs underlie research variables, and construct validity seeks to determine whether the construct underlying a variable is actually being measured.

36. Construct validity is determined by a series of validation studies that can include content and criterion-related approaches. Both confirmatory and disconfirmatory evidence are used to determine construct validation.

37. The validity of any test or measure can be diminished by factors such as unclear test directions, inappropriate teaching, subjective scoring, and failing to follow administration procedures.

Consequential Validity

38. Consequential validity is concerned with the potential of tests being harmful for test takers. This is a new but important form of validity.

Reliability of Measuring Instruments

39. Reliability is the degree to which a test consistently measures whatever it measures. Reliability is expressed numerically, usually as a coefficient ranging from 0.0 to 1.0; a high coefficient indicates high reliability.

40. Reliability provides information about the inevitable fluctuations in scores due to person and test factors. No test is perfectly reliable, but the smaller the measurement error, the more reliable the test.

41. There are five different general approaches to reliability: stability, equivalence, equivalence and stability, internal consistency, and scorer/rater.

42. Stability, also called test–retest, determines the degree to which test scores are consistent over time. It is determined by correlating scores.

43. Equivalence, also called equivalent forms, determines the degree to which two similar forms of a test produce similar scores from a single group of test takers.

44. Equivalence and stability determine the degree to which two forms of a test given at two different times produce similar scores as measured by correlations.

45. Internal consistency deals with the reliability of a single test taken at one time. It measures the extent to which the items in the test are consistent among themselves and with the test as a whole. Split-half, Kuder-Richardson 20 and 21, and Cronbach's alpha are four main forms of internal consistency reliability.

46. Split-half reliability is determined by dividing a test into two equivalent halves (odd-even), correlating the two halves, and using the Spearman-Brown formula to determine the reliability of the whole test.

47. Kuder-Richardson reliability deals with the internal consistency of tests that are scored dichotomously (right, wrong), while Cronbach's alpha deals with the internal consistency of tests that are scored with more than two choices (agree, neutral, disagree or 0, 1, 2, 3).

48. Scorer/rater reliability is important when scoring tests that are potentially subjective. Interjudge reliability refers to the reliability of two or more independent scorers, while intrajudge reliability refers to the reliability of a single scorer/rater on two or more scorings.

49. Estimates of interjudge or intrajudge reliability are obtained from correlations or indicating percent agreement.

Reliability Coefficients

50. What constitutes an acceptable level of reliability differs among test types, with standardized achievement tests having very high reliabilities and projective tests having considerably lower reliabilities.

51. If a test is composed of several subtests that will be used individually in a study, the reliability of each subtest should be determined and reported.

Standard Error of Measurement

52. The standard error of measurement is an estimate of how often one can expect test score errors of a

given size. A small standard error of measurement indicates high reliability; a large standard error of measurement, low reliability.

53. The standard error of measurement allows us to estimate how much difference there is between a person's obtained and "true" score. Big differences indicate low reliability.

Selecting a Test

54. Do not choose the first test you find that appears to meet your needs. Identify a few appropriate tests and compare them on relevant factors. The three most important factors, in order of importance, are validity, reliability, and ease of test use (administration, scoring, and interpretation).

55. Self-constructed tests should be pretested before use to determine validity, reliability, and feasibility. Pretesting is important for researcher constructed tests.

Sources of Test Information

56. The Mental Measurement Yearbooks (MMYs) are the most comprehensive sources of test information available. They provide (1) factual information on all known or revised tests, (2) test reviews, and (3) comprehensive bibliographies and indexes. The numbers given in the indexes are test numbers, not page numbers.

57. *Tests in Print* (*TIP*) is a comprehensive bibliography of all tests that have appeared in preceding MMYs. PRO-ED publications provide information on more than 3,000 tests in education, psychology, and business.

58. The ETS Test Collection is an extensive, growing library containing more than 10,000 tests, published and unpublished.

59. Other sources of test information are professional journals and test publishers or distributors.

Constructing Tests

60. Be certain to align instruction and assessment to ensure valid test results.

61. Monitor test takers to minimize cheating.

Test Administration

62. Every effort should be made to ensure ideal test administration conditions. Failing to administer procedures precisely, or altering the administration procedures, especially on standardized tests, lowers the validity of the test.

PERFORMANCE CRITERIA   TASK 5

All the information required for each test will be found in the Mental Measurements Year-books. Following the description of the three tests, you should present a comparative analysis of the tests that forms a rationale for your selection of the "most acceptable" test for your study. As an example, you might indicate that all three tests have similar reliability coefficients reported but that one of the tests is more appropriate for your participants.

On the following pages, an example is presented to illustrate the performance called for by Task 5. (See Task 5 example.) This example represents the task submitted by the same student whose tasks for Chapters 2, 3, and 4 were previously presented.

Additional examples for this and subsequent tasks are included in the *Student Guide* that accompanies this text.

1

Effect of Interactive Multimedia on the Achievement of 10th-Grade Biology Students

Test One (from an MMY, test #160)

a) High-School Subject Tests, Biology—1980–1990

American Testronics

$33.85 per 35 tests with administration directions; $13.25 per 35 machine-scorable answer sheets; $19.45 per Teacher's Manual ('90, 110 pages).

b) The Biology test of the High-School Subject Tests is a group-administered achievement test that yields 10 scores (Cell Structure and Function, Cellular Chemistry, Viruses/Monerans/Protists/Fungi, Plants, Animals, Human Body Systems and Physiology, Genetics, Ecology, Biological Analysis and Experimentation).

c) Reviewers state that reliability values (KR-20s) for the various subject tests ranged from .85 to .93, with a median of .88. Content validity should be examined using the classification tables and objective lists provided in the teacher's manual so that stated test objectives and research objectives can be matched.

d) Grades 9–12.

e) Administration time is approximately 40 minutes.

f) Scoring services are available from the publisher.

g) Reviewers recommend the test as a useful tool in the evaluation of instructional programs, recognizing that the test fairly represents the content for biology in the high school curriculum. However, they do caution that a match should be established between stated test objectives and local objectives.

Test Two (from an MMY, test #256)

a) National Proficiency Survey Series: Biology (NPSS:B)—1989

The Riverside Publishing Company

$34.98 per 35 test booklets including directions for administration; $19.98 per 35 answer sheets; $9 per technical manual (26 pages) (1990 prices)

b) The NPSS:B is a group-administered achievement test with 45 items designed to measure "knowledge about the living world ranging from single-celled organisms to the human body."

c) Content validity is good; items were selected from a large item bank provided by classroom teachers and curriculum experts. The manual alerts users that validity depends in large measure upon the purpose of the test. Although the standard error of measurement is not given for the biology test, the range of KR-20s for the entire battery is from .82 to .91, with a median of .86.

d) Grades 9–12.

e) Administration time is approximately 45 minutes.

f) Tests can be machine scored or self-scored. A program is available on diskette so that machine scoring may be done on site. Both percentile rank and NCE scores are used. NCEs allow users to make group comparisons.

g) The reviewer finds the reliability scores to be low if the test is to be used to make decisions concerning individual students. However, he praises the publishers for their comments regarding content validity, which state that "information should always be interpreted in relation to the user's own purpose for testing."

Test Three (from an MMY, test #135)

a) End of Course Tests (ECT) – 1986

CTB/McGraw-Hill

$21 per complete kit including 35 test booklets (Biology 13 pages) and examiner's manual.

b) The ECT covers a wide range of subjects in secondary school. Unfortunately, detailed information is not available for individual subjects. The number of questions range from 42 to 50 and are designed to measure subject matter content most commonly taught in a first-year course.

c) No statistical validity evidence is provided for the ECT and no demographic breakdown is provided to understand the representativeness of the standardization samples. However, reliability estimates were given and ranged from .80 to .89 using the KR-20 formula.

d) Secondary school students.

e) Administration time is from 45 to 50 minutes for any one subject test.

f) Both machine scoring and hand scoring are available. A Class Record Sheet is provided in the manual to help those who hand score to summarize the test results.

g) Users must be willing to establish local norms and validation evidence for effectual use of the ECT, since no statistical validity evidence is provided.

Conclusion

All three batteries have a biology subtest; The High-School Subject Tests (HSST) and the NPSS:B are designed specifically for 10th-grade students, while the ECT is course, rather than grade, oriented. It is acknowledged that more data are needed for all three tests, but reported validity and reliability data suggest that they all would be at least adequate for the purpose of this study (i.e., to assess the effectiveness of the use of interactive multimedia in biology instruction).

Of the three tests, the least validity evidence is provided for the ECT, so it was eliminated from contention first. Both the HSST and the NPSS:B provide tables and objective lists in their manuals that may be used to establish a match between stated test objectives and research objectives. The HSST and the NPSS:B both have good content validity but the HSST does not cross-index items to objectives, as does the NPSS:B. Also, norming information indicates that Catholic school students were included in the battery norm group. Therefore, of the three tests, the NPSS:B seems to be the most valid for the study.

With respect to reliability, all three tests provide a comparable range of KR-20 values for battery subtests. While specific figures are not given for the biology subtests, the reported ranges (low eighties to low nineties) suggest that they all have adequate internal consistency reliability.

The NPSS:B appears to be the most appropriate instrument for the study. The items (which were provided by both classroom teachers and curriculum experts) appear to match the objectives of the research study quite well. The KR-20 reliability is good, both in absolute terms and as compared to that of the other available tests. Both machine- and self-scoring are options, but an added advantage is that machine scoring can be done on site using a program provided by the publisher.

Thus, the NPSS:B will be used in the current study. As a cross-check, internal consistency reliability will be computed based on the scores of the subjects in the study.

QUALITATIVE RESEARCH

In Part One we described and differentiated a number of quantitative and qualitative research characteristics as a general introduction to educational research, and offered examples of quantitative, qualitative, and mixed method research approaches. We provided an overview of the key dimensions of conducting educational research—defining research topics, dealing with the ethical aspects of research, following steps in the research process, and identifying types of samples—and introduced research instruments, tools that cut across varied research approaches.

In this part, we examine in detail qualitative research approaches and methods. Later, in Part Three, we will closely examine quantitative research approaches and methods. The goal of Part Two is for you to be able to develop a design, or plan, for a qualitative research study: develop a qualitative topic, determine the participants, identify data collection and analysis procedures, and consider other important issues for the chosen topic. Note that the general steps in qualitative and quantitative research are the same; only their applications are different. Chapter 6 focuses on identifying qualitative research topics and conducting literature reviews. Chapter 7 is concerned with selecting research participants and collecting research data. In Chapter 8 we discuss analyzing and interpreting collected data and writing narratives based on the research results. Chapter 9 focuses on action research in school settings.

"Qualitative, interpretive research is useful for describing and answering questions about participants and contexts. . . . Qualitative research is exceptionally suited for exploration, for beginning to understand a group or phenomenon." (p. 163)

CHARACTERISTICS OF QUALITATIVE RESEARCH

OBJECTIVES

After reading Chapter 6, you should be able to do the following:

1. State the purposes of qualitative research.
2. Identify the six general steps in qualitative research.
3. State the characteristics of good qualitative methods.
4. Identify strategies for finding and selecting research topics.
5. Identify strategies for reviewing literature for a qualitative study.
6. Describe issues involved in gaining entry to the research site and obtaining gatekeeper approval.
7. Describe the three models of mixed-method research.

After you have read Chapter 6, you should be able to perform the following task.

TASK 6

Apply the six steps of qualitative research to develop a plan for your own qualitative research study. (See Performance Criteria, page 256. Task 6 Example and Performance Criteria appear at the end of Chapter 8.)

THE NATURE OF QUALITATIVE RESEARCH

Qualitative, interpretive research is useful for describing and answering questions about participants and contexts. The researcher studies the perspectives of the research participants toward events, beliefs, or practices. Qualitative research also is useful for exploring complex research areas about which little is known. Qualitative research is exceptionally suited for exploration, for beginning to understand a group or phenomenon. Such explorations often result in development of new theories. Finally, qualitative research can answer questions and illuminate issues that cannot be addressed by quantitative methods.

In considering qualitative research, it is useful to know some things about its underpinnings.[1] For example, qualitative research approaches are rooted in the disciplines of sociology, anthropology, psychology, and history. These disciplines rely heavily on rich, verbal, qualitative, interpretive descriptions in their research methods, rather than on numerical, statistical, quantitative descriptions. Similarly, qualitative disciplines strive to capture the human meanings of social life as it is lived, experienced, and understood by the research participants. Capturing this social context is very important in qualitative research

---

[1]A useful and interesting description of the genesis of qualitative research can be found in Erickson, F. (1990). *Qualitative methods. Research in teaching and learning, volume* 2. New York: Macmillan; and in Bogdan, R. C., and Biklen, S. K. (1998). *Qualitative research for education.* Chapter 1. Boston: Allyn & Bacon.

because qualitative researchers view each context studied to be unique. Because qualitative researchers rely heavily on verbal description, researchers are their own main instrument of data collection, interpretation, and written narrative. It is commonly noted that in qualitative research "the researcher is the research method." Thus, the qualitative researcher is a critical source of data collection and interpretation. Further, although different from quantitative research methods, qualitative researchers also rely on disciplined inquiry in their research. Good qualitative research is investigative, inductive, and rigorous in research methods and data collection techniques, avoids bias to ensure data accuracy, and emphasizes the voices and settings of the participants in the research.[2]

SIX GENERAL STEPS IN QUALITATIVE RESEARCH

In Chapter 1, we presented four general, conceptual research steps. For practical reasons, we here expand the steps to six to help you delineate your tasks. Similar to quantitative research, qualitative researchers follow six basic steps. As we shall see in subsequent chapters, these steps characterize both qualitative and quantitative research; however, the application of the steps differs. For example, quantitative research is often more rigid than qualitative in research procedures. Similarly, while both quantitative and qualitative researchers collect data, the nature of the data collected differs. Figure 6.1 compares the six steps of qualitative and quantitative research and lists traits that characterize each approach at every step.

For the most part, the methods used to conduct varied types of qualitative research are similar. Because of these commonalities, we will focus on general methods used to identify research topics, review related literature, select participants, collect data, analyze data, and write the research results.

1. *Identify research topics:* The researcher identifies a topic or study of interest to research. Often, the initial topic is narrowed to be more manageable.
2. *Review of research:* The researcher examines existing research to identify useful information and strategies for carrying out the study.
3. *Selecting participants:* The researcher must select participants to provide data collection; qualitative participants are usually few in number relative to quantitative samples and are selectively chosen (i.e., not randomly selected).
4. *Collecting data:* The researcher collects data from participants; qualitative data tend to be gathered from interviews, observations, or artifacts.
5. *Analyzing data:* The researcher interprets the themes and results of the collected data; qualitative analysis is interpretive in nature, rather than statistical.
6. *Reporting, evaluating, and interpreting research:* The researcher summarizes and integrates the qualitative data in narrative form.

QUALITATIVE RESEARCH APPROACHES

Table 6.1 provides a brief description of some of the most commonly utilized qualitative research approaches. Examining the table shows that the primary difference among the approaches is in the particulars of the social context examined and the participants selected. For example, some qualitative researchers focus on the characteristics of a single person or phenomenon, seeking to understand a single person or entity (case study); some focus in depth on a group's cultural patterns and perspectives to understand the relation between participants' behavior and their context (ethnography); some examine multiple cultures compared to one

---

[2]For a discussion, see Creswell, J. W. (2002), *Educational research: Planning, conducting, and evaluating quantitative and qualitative research.* Upper Saddle River, NJ: Prentice Hall.

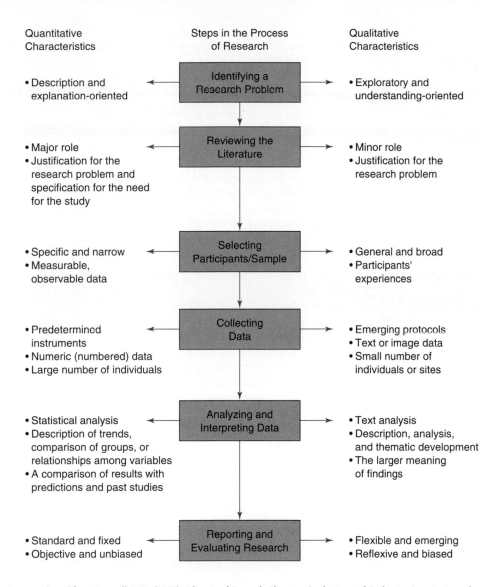

FIGURE 6.1
Characteristics of
quantitative and
qualitative research.

Quantitative Characteristics	Steps in the Process of Research	Qualitative Characteristics
• Description and explanation-oriented	Identifying a Research Problem	• Exploratory and understanding-oriented
• Major role • Justification for the research problem and specification for the need for the study	Reviewing the Literature	• Minor role • Justification for the research problem
• Specific and narrow • Measurable, observable data	Selecting Participants/Sample	• General and broad • Participants' experiences
• Predetermined instruments • Numeric (numbered) data • Large number of individuals	Collecting Data	• Emerging protocols • Text or image data • Small number of individuals or sites
• Statistical analysis • Description of trends, comparison of groups, or relationships among variables • A comparison of results with predictions and past studies	Analyzing and Interpreting Data	• Text analysis • Description, analysis, and thematic development • The larger meaning of findings
• Standard and fixed • Objective and unbiased	Reporting and Evaluating Research	• Flexible and emerging • Reflexive and biased

Source: Adapted from Creswell, J. W. (2002). *Educational Research: Planning, Conducting, and Evaluating Quantitative and Qualitative Research,* p. 51. Upper Saddle River, NJ: Prentice Hall.

another (ethology); some examine people's understanding of their daily activities (eth-nomethodology); some derive theory using multiple steps of data collection and interpretation that link actions of participants to general social science theories (grounded theory); some ask what is the meaning of this experience for these participants (phenomenology); some seek what common understandings have emerged to give meaning to participants' interactions (symbolic interaction); some seek solutions or improvement of practical, educational prob-lems (action research); and some seek to understand the past by studying documents, relics, and interviews (historical research). Overall, a common, generic name for these qualitative approaches is **interpretive research.**[3]

---

[3]For a discussion, see Patton, M. Q. (2002), *Qualitative evaluation and research methods,* 3rd ed. Thousand Oaks, CA: Sage.

TABLE 6.1   Common Qualitative Research Approaches

APPROACH	KEY QUESTION
case study	What are the characteristics of this particular entity, phenomenon, or person?
ethnography	What are the cultural patterns and perspectives of this group in its natural setting?
ethology	How do the origins, characteristics, and culture of different societies compare to one another?
ethnomethodology	How do people make sense of their everyday activities in order to behave in socially accepted ways?
grounded theory	How is an inductively derived theory about a phenomenon grounded in the data in a particular setting?
phenomenology	What is the experience of an activity or concept from these particular participants' perspective?
symbolic interaction	How do people construct meanings and shared perspectives by interacting with others?
action research	How can teachers solve or understand an identified teaching problem and improve practice based on data they have collected and analyzed?
historical research	How does one systematically collect and evaluate data to understand and interpret past events?

Source: Adapted from Michael Quinn Patton, *Qualitative Research and Evaluation Methods,* Sage Publications, 1990. Copyright 1990 by Sage Publications. Reprinted by permission of Sage Publications, Inc.

As mentioned in Chapter 1, in this text we focus on four qualitative approaches: ethnography, historical research, grounded theory, and action research.

ETHNOGRAPHY

We focus first on ethnography because it is one of the most used and established qualitative research approaches. Ethnography seeks to describe and analyze all or part of the culture of a community by identifying and describing the participants' practices and beliefs. (It is distinct from **ethnomethodology,** which studies peoples' understandings of their own culture and activities.) In qualitative research, *culture* is viewed as the things humans have learned that influence their behavior. **Context,** or background, is an important aspect of interpreting qualitative research results.

The main characteristics of ethnography are shown in Figure 6.2. The seven basic characteristics shown in Figure 6.2 substantially overlap with other types of qualitative approaches. Other qualifying terms, such as "become intimately involved with participants," "being committed to represent the views of participants," "emphases on inductive not deductive," and "interpretation of data within a defined context," are commonly used descriptions by all qualitative researchers.

HISTORICAL RESEARCH

Historical research is the systematic collection and evaluation of data related to past occurrences for the purpose of describing causes, effects, or trends of those events. It helps to explain current events and to anticipate future ones. It is a common form of qualitative research;

FIGURE 6.2

Characteristics of ethnography.

The seven characteristics that mark a study as ethnographic are as follows:
- It is carried out in a natural setting, not in a laboratory.
- It involves intimate, face-to-face interaction with participants.
- It presents an accurate reflection of participants' perspectives and behaviors.
- It uses inductive, interactive, and recursive data collection and analytic strategies to build local cultural theories.
- It uses multiple data sources, including both quantitative and qualitative data.
- It frames all human behavior and belief within a socio-political and historical context.
- It uses the concept of culture as a lens through which to interpret results.

Source: From LeCompte, M. D., and Schensul, J. J. (1999). *Designing and Conducting Ethnographic Research,* p. 9. Lanham, MD: Alta Mira/Bowman & Littlefield. Reprinted by permission.

in fact, until recently, it was the sole form recognized by many. Historical research has most of the characteristics common to other forms of qualitative research, except that it has a retrospective focus, seeking to understand and describe past characters, events, and settings. It uses data collection and interpretation procedures similar to those used in other approaches, but its main, though not sole, method tends to be literature review.

Many current educational practices, theories, and issues can be better understood in light of past experiences. Issues of grading, cooperative learning, testing, and reading methods are not new in education, nor is cooperative learning an innovation of the 1970s, and a knowledge of their history can yield insight into the evolution of the current educational system as well as into practices and approaches that have been found to be ineffective or unfeasible. In fact, studying the history of education might lead one to believe that there is little new under the educational sun, although some practices seem to appear and disappear with regularity. For example, for more than 150 years individualized instruction and group instruction have seemingly taken turns being the favored approach of the day.

The steps involved in conducting a historical research study are similar to other types of research: identify a question or issue to examine; review the literature or pertinent relics, documents, diaries, and other data sources; select participants if appropriate; collect data; analyze and interpret the data; and produce a verbal synthesis of the findings or interpretations. In conducting a historical study, the researcher can neither manipulate nor control any of the variables. There is no way the researcher can affect events of the past; what has happened has happened. The researcher can, however, describe the documents used and provide bases for her interpretations. Not everyone may agree with them, but the researcher will have provided information about the bases of her reasoning and interpretations. These will need to be confronted by anyone criticizing the work.

GROUNDED THEORY

Grounded theory is a systematic qualitative method that aims at generating a theory that explains, at a conceptual level, a process, an action, or a concept. The central focus in grounded theory is this generation of theory. The researcher begins with a research topic or situation that he seeks to understand. That is, the researcher asks, "What is happening in this situation and how can I provide a theory to explain it?" Note that the researcher initially identifies the main topic or situation to be examined, unlike many other qualitative research methods. The most common strategies used to carry out grounded theory are observation and interviews. The key to success of grounded theory is the constant comparison method (see Glaser, 1965/1967), a strategy that "constantly compares" and integrates the data the researcher collects in numerous data collection forays, and that also eliminates redundant results. The constant comparison is inductive; that is, the analysis shifts from specific information to broader, more inclusive understandings. Theory evolves during actual research, and it does this through continuous interplay between analysis and data collection.[4]

As data are continually examined and narrowed, theoretical propositions emerge that develop and link to other propositions. The literature on the topic can be examined as needed. In an emergent study, the researcher probably won't know at the beginning what literature will later turn out to be relevant. As the data are examined and related to prior data, the grounded theorist narrows the data to identify the key aspects of the theory of interest. Eventually the researcher's interviews and observations will add little or no additional data, indicating diminishing returns in subsequent data gathering. At this point, when a theory will have been developed, the grounded theorist will likely end his data collection and constant comparison.

ACTION RESEARCH

Action research is a systematic inquiry done by teachers and other educational personnel such as counselors and administrators to collect and study data that can help them to both understand and improve their practice. In action research, educators reflect on their practice, identify areas that need improvement or understanding, collect data pertinent to the issue of interest, analyze the data, and try to determine whether the obtained results do in fact improve practice or understanding. This form of teacher research has emerged relatively recently and has been adopted in many school systems and subject area departments, and by individual teachers.

Action research is based on the view that teachers, as well as counselors, principals, and other school professionals, can serve as practical researchers who can help improve practice in school. More specifically, the following results are associated with action research:[5]

- Encouraging changes in schools
- Empowering a democratic approach to education
- Empowering individuals through collaboration on projects
- Encouraging educators to reflect on their practice and have a "voice"
- Encouraging teachers to try new approaches to old problems
- Encouraging teachers to engage in professional growth
- Instilling in teachers the feeling that action research is a professional responsibility

Any teacher- or school-based question, topic, or problem is pertinent to action research and may be the start of the process. Common action research topics start with questions such as these:

How can I make this better?
Would this be better if I . . . ?
Will doing this likely improve students' . . . ?
Why does this approach not work as it should?

Although action research has gained support from educators, others do not view it as a legitimate form of research and inquiry.[6] Many researchers view action research as an informal, rather than a more rigorous, approach to educational research. The practical, limited aspect of most action research, and the fact that teachers are usually the primary action researchers, lead

---

[4]Denzin, N. K., & Lincoln, Y. S. (Eds.). (1998). *Strategies of Qualitative Inquiry.* Thousand Oaks, CA: Sage, p. 158.

[5]These results are discussed fully in Mills, G. E. (2003), *Action research: A guide for the teacher researcher,* 2nd ed. Upper Saddle River, NJ: Prentice Hall.

[6]Stringer, E. T. (1999). *Action research.* Thousand Oaks, CA: Sage, p. 19.

to distinguishing "applied" or "action" research from "true" research. While this distinction has some validity, it is also true that action research serves an important role in improving schools and schooling.

QUALITATIVE RESEARCH PROCESS

The central focus of qualitative research studies is to provide understanding of a social setting or activity as viewed from the perspective of the research participants. To achieve this goal, qualitative research is guided by five general characteristics that cut across most types of qualitative studies. First, *the sources of data for qualitative research are real-world situations,* natural, nonmanipulated settings. Researchers spend a great deal of time in the selected setting. Second, *qualitative research data are descriptive.* Data in the form of interview notes, observation records, documents, and field notes are the basis for analysis and interpretation. Numerical data are very rarely the main focus of a qualitative study. Third, *qualitative research emphasizes a holistic approach,* focusing on processes as well as final outcomes. The researcher is immersed in the details and specifics of the setting. It is the detailed recording of the processes occurring in the natural setting that provides the basis for understanding the setting, the participants, and their interactions. Without this immersion, the search for interpretation and understanding would elude the qualitative researcher. Fourth, *qualitative data are analyzed inductively;* that is, patterns and relationships are developed from collecting or observing multiple specific instances. Thus, the qualitative researcher does not impose an organizing structure or make assumptions about the relationships among the data prior to collecting evidence. As the data are analyzed, the researcher seeks specific pieces of data that can be generalized. He seeks to find patterns and common themes. The more data collected, the more likely that inductive analysis will be confirmed. Fifth, the researcher strives *to describe the meaning of the finding from the perspective of the research participants,* not of the researcher him- or herself.

Throughout this process, the focus is on the meanings that participants have identified in their own natural settings or contexts. This focus on the research context is very important in qualitative research because each research setting and its participants are viewed by the qualitative researcher as being unique, thus making the researcher's task one of describing participants' understanding of their own, unique reality.

CHARACTERISTICS OF GOOD QUALITATIVE RESEARCH

Good qualitative research displays a number of characteristics. Qualitative approaches:

1. require researchers to take a holistic stance; they look at the overall context to obtain and guide their understanding.
2. require researchers to avoid making premature decisions or assumptions about the study. They typically wait until they are in the research context before making tentative decisions based on initial data analysis.
3. focus on individual, person-to-person interactions.
4. require that the researcher spend a great deal of time in the research setting with the participants.
5. require that the researcher have the opportunity of gathering data directly from the participants.
6. require that the researcher remain open to alternative explanations.
7. include a description of the role of the researcher and her or his biases or preferences in the research topic or research processes.
8. require clear information and detailed description about the study that includes the voices of the participants.

9. are based on the researcher's responsibility to obtain informed consent from participants and to ensure their ethical treatment.
10. focus on discovery and understanding, which require flexibility in the research design.

QUALITATIVE RESEARCH QUESTIONS

At the beginning of this chapter, we mentioned that qualitative research can answer questions and illuminate participants' experiences in a way that quantitative research and its questions cannot. Rather than asking, "What percent of teachers and students in our state indicate enjoying school?" (you guessed it—a quantitative research question) the qualitative researcher asks, "What is the meaning of the way that students and teacher create a viable social setting in the classroom?"

Qualitative research questions encompass a range of topics, but most focus on participants' understanding of meanings and social life in a particular context. Note, however, that these general topics must necessarily be more focused to become useful and researchable questions. For example, the topic, "What are the cultural patterns and perspectives of this group in its natural setting?" could be narrowed by asking, "What are the cultural patterns and perspectives of teachers during lunch in the teachers' room?" Similarly, the topic, "How do people make sense of their everyday activities in order to behave in socially acceptable ways?" might be narrowed by asking, "How do rival gang members engage in socially accepted ways when interacting with each other during the school day?" The questions presented in Table 6.1 are general in nature to demonstrate the different qualitative approach. Clearly there are many ways to restate these questions to make them viable and focused research questions.

In most cases, the focus of narrowing questions is on reducing aspects of the topic, because most researchers overestimate the conduct of the study. The following strategies suggest ways to reduce the scale of a qualitative study; which one or ones the researcher chooses will depend on the nature of the planned research and the available resources.

1. Narrow the time or resource of the topic.
2. Narrow the audience to be addressed.
3. Narrow the number of participants to save time and analyses.
4. Examine the literature to determine the scale of the topic.
5. Look for potential problems during the early steps of the research.
6. Share the research work with a colleague.
7. Obtain the advice of more experienced qualitative researchers.

Erickson[7] suggests four reasons why it is important to explore qualitative topics and questions:

1. Qualitative questions have the potential to illuminate the "invisibility of everyday life," that is, to make the familiar strange and therefore more examined and understood.
2. Often, a general or generic answer to a research question is not useful; what is needed is specific, concrete details to guide understanding in a particular setting.
3. It is important to know the local meanings that activities and practices have for the groups engaged in them. Different settings or contexts may seem to carry out the same activities and practices, but may actually be quite different. How direct teaching or whole language is practiced in different classrooms might differ quite markedly, although teachers in those classrooms would indicate that they were using direct teaching or whole language.

---

[7]Erickson, F. (1970). *Qualitative methods: Research in teaching and learning,* volume 2. New York: Macmillan (pp. 83–85).

4. Groups of qualitative research studies can help the comparative understanding of different settings. That is, a study focused on a particular fifth-grade classroom can be compared to another particular fifth-grade classroom in terms of common and uncommon aspects. However, qualitative research is not well suited to answer questions about research effects.

Qualitative research topics (dissertation or otherwise) are usually more general and tentative than quantitative research topics, mainly because it is expected that a qualitative study will evolve in focus once the researcher is in the research setting and beginning to interact with the participants. This means that a proposed qualitative topic rarely provides the initial specificity of most quantitative topics or plans. However, it is important to note that the qualitative researcher does not enter the research setting with *no* idea of what the chosen study topic or research method will involve. To the contrary, all qualitative researchers have some idea or thought about their topic, even if it is sketchy and not fully developed.

Ultimately, a good research plan, as we discussed in Chapter 3, should answer the following questions, not necessarily in depth, but with some focus, rationale, and thought:

- What topics are you going to study?
- In what setting or context will you conduct the study?
- What kinds of data do you think you will collect?
- What methods do you plan to use?
- Why are you doing the study?
- What contribution might the study provide?

At the very least, the researcher must have some sense of the nature of the study to communicate information about the planned study to a doctoral advisor and/or to potential participants. As Yin notes:

> When Christopher Columbus went to Queen Isabella to ask for support for his "exploration" of the New World, he had to have some reasons for asking for three ships (why not one? why not five?), and he had some rationale for going westward (why not north? why not south?). He also had some criteria for recognizing the New World when he actually encountered it. In short, his exploration began with some rationale and direction, even if his initial assumptions might later have been proved wrong.[8]

Another way to say this is that you have ideas and assumptions about your topic before you begin your study, but you have not entirely settled on the path you will take. Qualitative proposals are not fixed contracts that cannot be altered, but neither are they so brief and general that they convey little about the proposed study.

STEP 1: SELECTING A RESEARCH TOPIC OR ISSUE

The first step in qualitative research is to select a topic or issue to study. There is an unlimited number of useful and viable educational topics worthy of study. The following are a few examples suitable for educational qualitative research: "the quality of varied classroom procedures"; "the life of students in an urban first grade"; "the development of middle school teachers' instructional practices"; "how department chairs judge the quality of their teachers' teaching"; "the effectiveness of small student mathematics learning groups"; "the methods used to develop a schoolwide policy on cheating"; "the racial attitudes of elementary children"; and "how a first-year teacher's practice changes over one school year." One recent new domain of qualitative research topics derives from the inequity and needs of lower socioeconomic-status persons, ethnically diverse groups, persons with disabilities, and other advocacy groups. Often these individuals or groups develop topics focused on their own plight.

---

[8]Yin, R. K. (1984). *Case study research: Design and methods.* Beverly Hills, CA: Sage (p. 22).

Note that topics tend to be generally stated. Each of those just listed would have to be narrowed to a manageable focus to study. This is a common practice in developing qualitative research topics. The qualitative researcher begins with an open-ended, broad research topic that will narrow and emerge as he learns more about the research participants, their thoughts, and their setting. The qualitative researcher depends heavily on information provided by participants during the research. Conversely, the quantitative researcher begins with a complete, narrowly stated research plan at the start of the research, and the study does not change throughout the entire research study. Thus, a qualitative researcher might explore the many factors included in the general research topic to understand them and then select some feature to investigate. As an exercise for yourself, select two of the general topics previously listed and for each, narrow it down until you have two more focused topics for each general topic.

To get a sense of the various ways qualitative researchers construct their research topics, examine qualitative journals such as *International Journal of Qualitative Studies in Education, Qualitative Social Work: Research and Practice, Qualitative Sociology, Educational Researcher, American Psychologists,* and *Journal of Woman's History.*

Researchers may wonder, "*When* should one expect the topic to be established in a qualitative research study?" To ask this question of a qualitative researcher is quite different from asking it of a quantitative researcher. As mentioned previously, for the most part, quantitative researchers narrowly plan their research topic, methods, variables, and strategies before they begin their study. They then implement their plan. Conversely, qualitative researchers do not narrowly predefine their research methods before the study has begun.

The nature of qualitative research is such that it is viewed holistically based on complex phenomena that must be understood before analyzing. There likely will not be a defined problem statement until the qualitative researcher has begun to become immersed in the data. Recall that most aspects of qualitative research are in flux during its conduct, and the qualitative researcher seeks to refrain from prematurely making decisions about the outcome of the research, thus making it difficult to identify a specific topic early on.

WHAT ARE THE FUNCTIONS OF A RESEARCH TOPIC?

The researcher can use her research topic in a variety of ways. It can test existing knowledge to determine its viability. It can provide a voice for groups or individuals to be heard. It can identify new directions for research. It can help identify and examine gaps in educational practice and theory. And particularly pertinent for this text, it can help students develop their research knowledge and practice. Students often ask, "Where do research topics come from?" and "How can I find good topics?" As noted in Chapter 2, the most common sources of research topics are from testing existing theories, examining questions that pique interest or curiosity, and carrying out replications, that is, conducting studies similar to existing studies. One often-cited source of research topics is a library search. However, such searches have two limitations for qualitative research topics. First, without having already identified and narrowed some form of a research topic, roaming among the stacks in search of literature is inefficient and time consuming. Second, some qualitative researchers prefer to immerse themselves into the research setting before examining the existing research. They try not to be influenced by the literature (such as the themes developed in other studies) too early in the research process.

Qualitative researchers ask open-ended, broad questions that keep the research topic open while collecting data from the study participants. Recall that qualitative researchers deal mainly with inductive reasoning, which depends on finding commonalities in the qualitative data. This is the typical approach used to develop research topics in qualitative research. Imagine a qualitative researcher who has a general topic to research. She knows that her topic needs to be narrowed so she calls on the participants to provide information that can help her understand and narrow the topic while spending time in the research setting.

Now that you have a background in topic selection, let's see what topics look like for each of the four qualitative methodologies we focus on in this text.

SELECTING A TOPIC IN ETHNOGRAPHIC RESEARCH

Ethnographic research simultaneously studies both a group of participants and the context or setting in which they interact. In selecting an ethnographic topic for study, the researcher must consider a number of issues. For example, although the topic does not have to be narrowly stated at the start of the study, some form of statement is needed to present the study to professors, colleagues, or potential gatekeepers. Also, the beginning researcher should select a research topic of strong personal interest and carry out the study itself on a small scale, with a limited number of participants and a narrow research context. Remember that the researcher needs to be able to conduct the study in the participants' natural setting. The researcher must be able to build rapport and trust; there needs to be a sense of "intimacy" between the researcher and participants. Sometimes this is difficult to obtain. Also, the researcher must be able to stay in the setting over a period of time to gather data. Because of this, the researcher "sounds out" potential gatekeepers about the feasibility of doing the study in that context with those participants. Finally, the inexperienced ethnographic researcher should, if at all possible, work with a more seasoned colleague. These issues are all factors in selecting an ethnographic research topic.

SELECTING A TOPIC IN HISTORICAL RESEARCH

The purpose of historical research is, as in all qualitative research, to help understand a person or event by providing in-depth description and interpretation of the data. Clearly, a historical research study should not be undertaken to prove the researcher's prior beliefs or to support a pet position. One can easily verify almost any point of view by consciously or unconsciously "overlooking" evidence to the contrary. There are probably data available to support almost any position; the historical researcher's task is to weigh and interpret existing evidence in arriving at a tenable description or conclusion. For example, one could cite data that would seemingly support the position that having more highly educated and trained teachers has led to increased school vandalism. One could do a historical study describing how requirements for teacher certification and rectification have increased over the years and how school vandalism has correspondingly increased. Of course such a study would indicate very poor critical analysis, since two separate, independent sets of factors are probably responsible for each of these trends rather than one being the cause or effect of the other.

To avoid this sort of biased data collection and analysis, one should probably avoid topics about which one has strong feelings. It is a lot easier to be even handed and open minded about a topic when one is not emotionally involved. Worthwhile historical research topics are identified and evaluated in much the same way as topics for other types of qualitative research. The *History of Education Quarterly* is one special resource for acquainting researchers with the range of historical research studies that have been conducted and for suggesting future studies. Given the qualitative focus of historical research, it is important to formulate a manageable, well-defined topic to study. Otherwise, it is likely that an overwhelming amount of data will be collected, making it more difficult to analyze and synthesize the data and draw properly documented interpretations. On the other hand, a concern unique to historical research is the possibility that a problem will be selected for which insufficient data are available. Historical researchers cannot "create" historical data. They are limited to whatever data are already available. Thus, if insufficient data are available, the problem will be inadequately investigated. For example, a researcher may well have difficulty studying the influence of Charles Dickens's flat feet on the themes he chose to write about. Select topics less esoteric than Dickens and his feet. There are plenty of better-documented historical topics to be studied.

Selecting a Topic in Grounded Theory

Researchers in grounded theory also plan their approaches differently than do quantitative researchers. Quantitative researchers know before the study begins what the nature of the research will be, how the study will be carried out, what the characteristics of the sample will be, how data will be collected, and how it will be analyzed. That is not the case for qualitative researchers, who carry out their studies in an interactive manner. Their qualitative research develops and grows as it becomes involved in the phenomenon, context, or group of participants being studied.

Grounded theory researchers, like other qualitative researchers, select and develop research topics that they wish to explore and understand from the participants' perspectives. The researcher selects a topic that will lead to new insights and new understanding of what aspects of the topic are most important. The initial research topic is a working model that will be altered and narrowed as the researcher applies an iterative process that seeks to help make sense of the data provided by the research participants. The grounded theory approach involves a number of iterations with participants, during which the researcher continually examines the data to identify the key emerging ideas. Examples of topics are "A study of the process of career change of jobs among 18- to 20-year-old African American males" and "How does an inductively derived theory about career development explain a theoretical model of career development among non-English speakers?" Grounded theory research topics such as these are quite broad to provide the researcher an opportunity to examine and interact with the participants over time.

Selecting a Topic in Action Research

As stated previously, action research aims to improve or better understand aspects of classroom teaching practice. Action research is intended to be carried out by teachers and other professionals who are in close contact with students and their learning, such as counselors and administrators, to improve teaching and learning. The steps in action research are similar in some respects to other types of qualitative research, but one important difference is that the topic or issue studied is identified and carried out by the teacher or administrator. Also, the action research takes place in the teacher's own classroom.

A topic or question derives from a teacher's or administrator's need to understand or correct a problem. Teachers may commonly ask questions such as: "Can I make this better?" "Would it be better if I . . . ?" "Would doing this improve student learning?" "Why does this approach not work with . . . ?" and "How do students feel about my . . . ?" Action research topics are ones that interest or concern a teacher or administrator.

When selecting an action research topic, choose a narrowly defined question to examine, especially if you are a novice qualitative researcher. The topic must be both feasible and manageable. For example, it is better to examine a narrowed research question such as, "What are the effects of positive verbal feedback on middle school students' participation in class discussions?" rather than, "How can I increase student participation in class discussions?"

The teacher-researcher commonly finds it difficult to carry on action research in depth and over very long time periods. A teacher who wishes to conduct action research usually has to make his or her own time to do so, except when the school's teacher evaluation system builds in an opportunity.

We discuss action research thoroughly in Chapter 9.

To summarize, the following suggestions can help you choose a qualitative research topic: (1) select a manageable topic and don't overestimate your time and expertise; (2) choose a topic that is interesting to you; (3) choose a topic that you think is important; (4) be flexible when narrowing your topic; (5) work with a mentor who can help you state, plan, and conduct your research.

STEP 2: REVIEWING THE LITERATURE

Unlike quantitative researchers, who spend a great deal of time examining the research on their topic at the outset of a study, some qualitative researchers will not delve deeply into their literature until their topic has emerged. As noted, a qualitative research focus emerges over time based on the data provided by the research participants. Qualitative researchers differ in their opinions on this issue. Some believe that too much emphasis on the examination of literature can bias or influence the research and prematurely narrow the focus of the intended topic prior to interaction with participants. In qualitative research, the research topic can change a number of times based on continually narrowing information. Thus, the research topic that ultimately evolves may not be identified until well into the research study. Because of this aspect of qualitative research, delving deeply into the literature is not always a fruitful undertaking, according to some researchers.

Others think that familiarity with or even immersion in the topic puts researchers in a particular frame of mind for beginning exploration.[9] Inevitably, qualitative researchers will examine existing literature if only to demonstrate that their topic is viable and credible. This approach is especially true for beginning qualitative researchers who undoubtedly will be asked by their instructor to justify their topic. Also, the research topic and some pertinent literature may be very useful or necessary when dealing with potential gatekeepers and participants.

It is important to note a subtle distinction between qualitative and quantitative research. Quantitative researchers have research plans and procedures developed before beginning their study. Because qualitative studies are open-ended in their inquiry and plans and procedures emerge during the conduct of the study, their research follows the lead of the participants, unlike that of quantitative researchers. This means that different qualitative research studies can have varied approaches. One should not be surprised to find that some qualitative researchers will deal with many literature sources and some will use very few.

Given this perspective, in a real sense, the two starting steps in qualitative research—identifying an initial topic and reviewing the research literature—are typically necessary, but flexible. They are also influenced by the information gathered from participants. Another facet of this step is that reviewing the literature in qualitative studies is an ongoing process that will continue through data collection and analysis.

While the four types of qualitative research we are discussing are similar in a number of respects, there are important distinctions that bear noting. Budding qualitative researchers should be aware of the differences when searching for literature and carrying out other research steps. For example, ethnography is the study of the cultural patterns and perspectives of a selected group. Historical research focuses mainly on events and personages from the past. Grounded theory focuses mainly on developing a theory. Action research focuses primarily on schools or classrooms to improve learning and teaching.

TYPES OF QUALITATIVE LITERATURE

As you have seen, qualitative research can be a flexible, inventive approach to research. Although specific types of research literature are linked to particular qualitative research topics, each researcher is free to consult a variety of literature sources. Ethnographic researchers seek settings in which the researcher can learn about the participants and the research setting, and may consult works by others who have worked in comparable contexts. Literature used in historical research may include artifacts, books, periodicals, diaries, videotapes, and transcripts of face-to-face discussion.

Grounded theory comes from the inductive (from the bottom up) analysis of data as the research is conducted. The theory is grounded in the data and there are no prior ideas about

---

[9]Glesne, C. (1999). *Becoming qualitative researchers: An introduction.* Reading, MA: Addison Wesley Longman, p. 20.

what that emerging theory will state. Other themes in the literature may be referred to toward the end of the study, after the theory has been developed. Action researchers, too, may use very little formal literature, relying on other teachers' experiences with the intended topic.

In a general sense, we can provide examples of particular types of literature that are frequently associated with the following qualitative approaches:

- Ethnography—sociological books and articles
- Historical—books and artifacts
- Grounded theory—themes in related literature to validate the grounded theory process used
- Action research—educational journals

EXAMPLES OF QUALITATIVE RESEARCH TOPICS AND LITERATURE REVIEW

To give you more of a sense of the nature of qualitative research, we provide here the written reports of two qualitative research studies. Understand that these two examples represent only a tiny portion of the richness of qualitative studies. We strongly suggest that you examine the wealth of research for yourself.

In this chapter and in chapters 7 and 8 we will examine these two research reports based on the six general steps in the research process. As you read them observe the use of common qualitative research terms and processes. In the first study, look for terms and processes that define qualitative research:

abstract, observation, participants, methodology, procedures, oral questioning, small number of participants, interviews, questioning—second interview, discussion, implications, describes with words not numbers

Note also that, in this study, the researcher also reported on quantitative methods in Table 1 (reprinted in Chapter 7). As we shall see subsequently, there are many research studies that rely on both qualitative and quantitative methods to obtain a richer perspective than can be obtained by either method alone.

THE EXPRESSION OF CARE IN THE ROUGH AND TUMBLE PLAY OF BOYS[10]

Tom Reed *University of South Carolina Spartanburg*
Mac Brown *University of South Carolina Columbia*

The research topic is short and fairly general. This is typical in qualitative research, since the topic evolves during the study.

Abstract

Rough and tumble play (R&T) is widely researched in relationship to social affiliation and the cognitive benefits to the participants. One less-researched aspect of R&T is the affective dimension, more specifically, the way in which boys care for one another through R&T. This qualitative study examined pre-adolescent boys participating in R&T and the ways in which they expressed care and intimacy as a result of their participation. The subjects were videotaped while engaged in their favorite R&T play in their natural surroundings, and were asked to view the videotapes and offer their personal interpretation of the R&T experience. The participants in the study were clear of

[10]Reed, T., and Brown, M. (2000). The expression of care in the rough and tumble play of boys. *Journal of Research in Childhood Education, 15*(1), 104–116. Copyright 2000 by the Association for Childhood Education. Reprinted by permission.

where and when it was appropriate to express care and intimacy for one another, which often is contrary to traditional ideas about play and recess. The need for teachers and administrators to reconsider the importance of R&T as one way boys express care, fondness, and friendships toward each other is emphasized.

The abstract of the study provides an overview. It appears at the beginning of the report, although it is written after the rest of the study is completed.

Research Topic

The expression of care in the rough and tumble play of boys.

Introduction

Play has never been universally defined in the literature. Perhaps no simple definition can be determined, as there are as many different interpretations of play as there are cultures in the world. Csikszentmihalyi (1975) suggests that play is supposed to be fun and something to be "felt," not necessarily "done." This qualitative study focuses on a specialized type of play referred to as rough and tumble play (R&T), and is rooted in pedagogical theory. Piaget and Inhelder (1969) found that R&T begins in the preoperational stage and continues into concrete operations, following a predictable developmental path. From the Piagetian perspective, R&T combines both physiological and experiential abilities, and precedes games with rules. Piagetian theory stresses that play functions to create symbols and schemas needed for an idiosyncratic view of the world. Finally, cognitive development provides the foundation for play, including exercise play, symbolic play, games with rules, and games of construction (Parten, 1932), all of which are clearly visible during R&T. For Vygotsky (Cole, John-Steiner, Scribner, & Souberman, 1978), play is more a function of culture than it is a developmental process. Vygotsky supports the notion that play is an attempt for the child to gain mastery over his or her destiny and function within the culture. From the Vygotskian perspective, play is a tool used as the child becomes a participant in his or her culture. Therefore, R&T is a function of culture and is learned behavior necessary for membership.

> Literature cited

Despite the above interpretations, the literature on R&T is somewhat limited. This may be due in part to the fact that research has focused more on the negative effects aggressive play has on behavior, rather than any potentially positive cognitive or social effects (Goldstein, 1995).

The researchers chose to place the literature review at the beginning of the report. This is characteristic of ethnography. Other qualitative approaches introduce the review later.

Rough and Tumble Play

Rough and tumble play was brought to popular notice by Harlow's (1962) research with Rhesus monkeys. Harlow described the basic tenets of R&T as running, chasing, and fleeing, wrestling, open-hand slap, falling, and play fighting. Children routinely chase one another with no intent to capture their victim. Those who engage in wrestling as part of R&T do not intend to hurt their partners. There is much slapping or pushing in R&T that remains merely playful, yet there may be feigning of injury. These socially driven and playful, yet somewhat aggressive, behaviors Harlow described also should include the "play face." Harlow described the "play face" as openedmouth, teeth-bared expression, which looks fierce but actually denotes that the intent is non-aggressive and playful. Children frequently use this same "play face," accompanied by smiles and laughter, to communicate that their rough behavior is R&T and not aggression. Conversely, aggressive behavior includes the infliction of bodily harm, and is characterized by visible signs of resentment and lasting anger. Blurton-Jones (1976) concluded that the same characteristics and strategies of R&T discussed by Harlow also applied to children playing in a nursery school. While R&T is observed equally in both genders in the Rhesus monkeys, research on humans has focused primarily on males (Blurton-Jones, 1976; Fagot, 1984; MacDonald, 1992; Pellegrini, 1988, 1995; Pellegrini & Perlmutter, 1988). During the present study, girls were observed engaging in classic R&T behaviors on a number of occasions; however, this research was limited to boys.

R&T is pervasive in Western culture and has been institutionalized or ritualized in major spectator events such as soccer, football, basketball, hockey, and stock car racing. According to Sutton-Smith (1992), R&T behaviors have become institutionalized in such time-honored games as Kickball, King of the Mountain, and Red Rover, as well as the classic "I'm Gonna Get You/You Can't Catch Me" game played by toddlers. In addition to being fun for the players, there are benefits to children who participate in R&T. Pellegrini (1994) has clearly established that engagement in R&T is positively correlated with social problem-solving ability and academic achievement

> More literature sources cited

among boys. Social competence is developed through alternating role taking, negotiating give-and-take, deciding who follows and who leads, and exploring social dominance. Furthermore, academic achievement is related to social adjustment and competence in problem solving, which are both refined during R&T (Pellegrini, 1994).

Caring in R&T

Noddings (1992) describes "to care" and "to be cared for" as basic human needs. Caring does not adhere to a prescribed formula, making it difficult for schools to assist children in learning to care for other human beings. In addition, gender- and culture-based factors must be considered when teaching children to care. It is apparent that boys and girls have different perspectives on intimate relations and different interpretations with regard to connection and expression of care (Noddings, 1992). Elementary schools are often governed by the feminine perspective that considers pushing, hitting, shoving, or games of chase and flee (factors common to R&T) as inappropriate behavior.

Aggression and R&T

All physical activity is inherently risky (Fagen, 1981). R&T has the appearance of being aggressive, which explain[s] part of its appeal to young boys. Women are more likely to view R&T as aggressive, while men are likely to see it as play (Conner, 1989). The uninformed observer of R&T may see tripping, pushing, or hitting as fighting; indeed, one definition of R&T is "play fighting" (Blurton-Jones, 1976). Play theorists have attempted to explain the difference between R&T and aggression. Donaldson (1976) theorizes that what is actually being observed is hugging, loving, compassion, embracing, mutual sharing, and concern for one another masked as aggression. He states that the R&T player is saying, "I trust you to push me, trip me, fall on me, and if I get hurt you will care for me" (Donaldson, 1976, p. 239). Research has documented that R&T is a distinct category of behavior that is separate from aggression (Blurton-Jones, 1976; Sutton-Smith, 1992). Pellegrini (1989) found that R&T breaks down into aggression in less than 3% of all cases and consumes less than 11% of all playground activity.

Friendship and R&T

The Merriam Webster's Collegiate Dictionary (1994) defines a "friend" as "one attached to another by affection or esteem." The Oxford American Dictionary (1999) further defines friendship as a relationship. Other definitions of friendship include such aspects as intimacy, mutual support, voluntary reciprocity, sacrifice, and reward (Kochenderfer & Ladd, 1996). Ginsberg, Gottman, and Parker (1986) found essential ingredients of friendships to include intimacy, affection, and ego support. Many researchers agree that the concept of friendship is a social construct that involves reaching a shared meaning, and that it does not necessarily come naturally (Bukowski, Newman, & Hartup, 1996; Burk, 1996; Lawhon, 1997). The arena in which children choose to build this knowledge is play that further enhances their social skills and leads to stable friendships (Lawhon, 1997).

Note subheadings for main topic: caring, agression, and friendship.

Comments

The title of the article is the research topic. The abstract provides a good overview and lead-in to the study, including a rationale for the study and a brief description of data collection. The introduction section contains a number of articles from the literature that provide an overview for study. This report has an atypically large literature review section. This is perfectly all right, although it is not common. The introduction provides a general context for the study's central question: Do boys use R&T to express care for one another and to develop friendships?

As you read the following segment of another qualitative article, from the *Qualitative Report,* and as you continue to read sections of it in chapters 7 and 8, note the use of common qualitative research terms and processes:

> abstract, emotive terminology, descriptive discussion, literature review, research focuses on advocates not the dispassionate, interviews, observation, survey, natural settings, participant, emerging themes, implications, Paula's Story (case study)

THE DISLOCATED TEXTILE WORKER IN RURAL ALABAMA: A PORTRAIT[11]

Sharon G. Lankford-Rice

Abstract

This is a study that delves into the attitudes of the rural Alabama textile worker at the point of being laid off. The methodology and findings are discussed and a personal interview transcribed from a former dislocated worker concerning her feelings, attitudes, and aspirations on how the Job Training Partnership Act (JTPA) program has impacted her life and career.

In keeping with much qualitative research, the abstract is brief.

Introduction

The sense of urgency is almost palpable as the guests enter the break room. The workers start filing into the room a short time later, at first in small groups and then in larger ones. Their comments are hurriedly whispered to each other and too low to be overheard. Some of the workers laugh nervously and others remain grim faced. Almost all of the workers in this group are women aged anywhere from 37 to 65 and some look much older than their questionnaires indicate; however they all have one thing in common regardless of age, background, gender, and marital status: they have all just been laid off from possibly the best job they have ever held. They ask the same questions of the guests that groups before them have asked and future groups are likely to ask as well. "What do we do now? How are we going to make a living? I don't know how to do anything else!"

Description of participants: their ages are listed, they are briefly described

The guests have come to help the workers find answers to their questions and hopefully solutions to their dilemmas. The author has been faced with this particular type of group many times and has been able to help the dislocated workers leave their closing factories with a plan of action formulating in their heads and a renewed sense of hope that all is not lost. The guests are representatives from local agencies such as the Employment Service, the Unemployment Compensation Office, Human Resources, Adult Basic Education Centers, area colleges, and local training programs, who make up what is called a Rapid Response Team.

Participants' statements and statement of guests' intent are examples of a principal feature of qualitative research: reporting on and from the perspective of the participants.

This team is called together whenever a factory announces a shutdown; they visit the closing facility, set up meetings, and detail dislocated workers' options upon becoming unemployed. As a member of this panel who travels from company to company, the researcher acts as a representative of the Job Training Partnership Act (JTPA) program and explains the benefits of retraining and education to groups of workers just like this one. The researcher acts as career counselor, mentor, and motivator in many of these workers' lives.

Note how this researcher is a part of the setting and interacts with participants.

This is just one of many meetings that has been arranged for this particular company. It is a local textile plant with well over 250 residents employed on the first, second, and third shifts. These workers are considered lucky in that they have been given notice of the closing and will receive a severance package. Many other plants in this rural area simply pack up and leave over the weekend shut-down leaving their workers to discover locked doors and bounced paychecks on Monday morning.

The qualitative researcher may take many roles.

While all the agencies play an important role in the dislocated workers' life, one agency that delivers a training program performs a very vital role in training the unemployed worker in a new capacity: The North Alabama Skills Center. JTPA or Job Training Partnership Act has retrained over 1000 dislocated workers from 1996–1998 through the local delivery agent. The agency provides training dollars, case management, career guidance, and moral support to the workers who choose to take advantage of the unique opportunity the program offers. The North Alabama Skills Center in the delivery of the JTPA program services [has] made a tremendous impact on the people in the community it serves. The researcher worked in the capacity of coordinator of the North Alabama Skills Center in the northeast corner of Alabama for 11 years delivering services to the dislocated workers of that region.

The introduction ends with a description of the study. →

This article will present a review of literature concerning women in the workplace and dislocated workers specifically relating to women's issues in the training arena, a description of the methodology, the findings surrounding the program which emerged through the study and, finally, an ethnographic case study of one dislocated worker and the impact of JTPA on her life.

Review of Related Literature

Women

The JTPA program was designed to serve many different groups of people in a structured training program. Originally the focus was on the economically disadvantaged, particularly those who needed supportive services and/or a mixed combination of training services (Solow & Walker, 1986). The Solow and Walker study showed that emphasis on a high number of low cost placements had displaced program focus toward women. Specifically tailored programs for females have been limited to a very small percentage of training dollars in JTPA. While that may have been true for the greater portion of the US, rural Alabama has had to shift training focus to female oriented training as a result of the large number of women being laid-off due to the loss of the textile industry. While non-traditional training was offered to the displaced workers in this southern state, very few opted for that choice. The General Accounting Office (GAO) in 1989 reported that women nationwide were more often trained in traditionally female oriented occupations such as clerical/typist and secretarial positions than any other types of training.

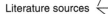

Literature sources ←→

The literature review describes the plight of women workers as background for this study. →

However, Pearce discovered in her study of four JTPA training sites in middle America that a significant number of women entering JTPA training programs chose a non-traditional curriculum for employment. The factors that appeared to contribute to the success of these women were: JTPA intake workers who brought their experiences to the participants, female mentors, and customized training to accommodate the non-traditional choice (1993). One reason for the lack of success was the lack of supportive services such as child care for women. One problem with training choices in JTPA that have been described in Middleton's 1986 study is women in low-paying non-technical occupations who often face discriminatory practices and attitudes and who lack a strong supportive services system. Middleton's 1986 study showed that only one site studied out of 13 used its entire supportive service budget of 15% to provide adequate supportive services to women and other participants.

The literature shows that women who have no supportive system in place run the high risk of dropping out of the training and not taking full advantage of the program. The North Alabama Skills Center has a strong supportive system in place that is designed to be "cradle to grave" in the training arena. A case manager is assigned from day one to the participant and stays with the client until he/she graduates from the program and finds a job. A major responsibility of the case manager is to help the client search for employment in that client's training field. Once employment is secured, the client is then tracked for 13 weeks to calculate retention rates.

Dislocated Workers

The dislocated worker has become a large area of focus in the JTPA program. Due to the high number of plant closings around the nation, the federal government enacted EDWAA (Economic Dislocation and Worker Assistance Act) to replace Title III services under JTPA in 1988. Upon enactment the amount spent on retraining dislocated workers jumped from $172.4 million in

1987 to \$246.5 million in 1988 (GAO, 1990). Prior to 1988 and the EDWAA replacement act, services varied greatly to Title III customers; however the predominant service was job placement assistance which comprised more than 80% of the services rendered. Fewer than half of the participants received occupational skills training and fewer than 25% received any supportive services. It was also indicated that fewer older dislocated workers aged 55 and older and fewer less educated workers were enrolled in the program. This study revealed that 69% of the participants were placed in jobs; however the wage at placement was lower than their previous wages had been (GAO, 1987). While it would appear that placing workers below their previous standard of pay may indicate unsuccessful rates, another study conducted revealed that while no significant differences existed for those who undertook short training programs, the workers themselves felt they had gained valuable training that would assist them in their future job search efforts. Most of these training programs were GED, basic skills, or short occupational curriculum and did provide wider employment options for the dislocated workers.

The majority of those workers studied stated they would go through the programs again even though many returned to manufacturing jobs at substantially lower wages than before their dislocation (Merrifield, 1991). Unfortunately in rural areas, manufacturing jobs are usually the highest paying positions in close proximity to the workers' homes. Too many times it is a matter of quality of life rather than free choice that brings the workers back to the factory in assembly work.

It is imperative that dislocated workers have the time necessary to train and strong cooperative efforts be made to assist the dislocated worker to place her back in the job market. Naylor in a 1989 study made recommendations to fortify the abilities of the local educational structures (JTPA included) to serve the needs of the dislocated worker. Some of those recommendations were to develop programs that are comprehensive, link programs with public and private agencies, to have aggressive managers who are closely aligned with local employers and who are dynamic in advertising the programs as well as promoting the participants.

The review of literature revealed that dislocated workers are very likely to return to the workforce with or without new skills, but do not regret any time spent in training regardless of the outcome. While most would prefer to secure employment in fields other than their previous fields, the workers are grateful to have had the opportunity to learn new skills they feel will help them in future endeavors. The North Alabama Skills Center has made learning new skills a reality for the dislocated workers in the rural community it serves.

The researcher has worked for years interviewing and retraining dislocated workers and heard the same sentiments expressed time and time again. Regardless of background, job status, or gender, dislocated workers have evinced similar feelings. The researcher was interested in categorizing these attitudes to come to a richer understanding and design "help" programs geared specifically for the workers. To achieve these objectives, an ethnographic study appeared the most appropriate form for such categorization. Each worker may have expressed similar feelings but each individual lent a different perspective on those comparable experiences. In order to capture the context of each worker's encountering, it was necessary to use a method that adequately allowed the workers to freely express their sentiments rather than just a method that allowed them to check off responses that did not truly express the depth and breadth of their emotions.

Margin notes:

◄ What the literature revealed.

Note that the researcher's "voice" is part of the study. This is common in qualitative research.

The researcher explains why she chose to conduct a study using ethnographic data collection methods. Descriptive terms are characteristic of this type of study.

◄ Given the features of this study, it is clear that the researcher was correct to employ qualitative methods.

Comments

The abstract is somewhat shorter than that of the prior example. There was much less literature examined, and most of the literature is aimed at allowing readers to understand the context in which the study takes place. The tone of the writing is much more emotive and rich than the prior example, describing loss of job, dislocation, and other difficulties related to JTPA. This study is an example of a qualitative research topic that exemplifies studies of inequities relating to race, gender, and class that face participants.

We will continue to examine these two qualitative examples in chapters 7 and 8 as we study and describe the remaining four qualitative research steps: selecting participants, collecting data, analyzing and interpreting data, and reporting and evaluating research.

GAINING ENTRY

As discussed in Chapter 3, before any study can begin, the researcher typically needs to submit a proposal to the college's or university's Institutional Review Board (IRB). Once the study has been approved, the researcher must negotiate entry into the research setting, such as a school, and obtain the cooperation of potential participants. Because data collection in qualitative research is generally lengthy and in depth, it involves a more than casual relationship between the researcher and participants. Thus, how the researcher enters the setting and makes contact with participants is extremely important. In fact, the method she or he uses to do this can influence the relationship between researcher and participants from the very beginning. For example, a poor initial impression can hamper the research study from start to finish, making participants hesitant to fully cooperate. Grandma was right: first impressions really *are* important and do influence the way others perceive you.

The first obstacle you will face in gaining entry is getting permission to carry out your research in the desired field setting. You have decided, at least in general, what your study will be about. If your research is to be conducted in a classroom, a clinic, or a hospital, you will likely have to deal with a **gatekeeper** who will either directly decide or strongly influence the decision to allow you to conduct your study in that setting. For example, in most schools, the principal is the most important gatekeeper in determining admission into the school for research. In large school districts there may be a central body that decides on the acceptability of proposed research study requests, although the school principal will still likely have substantial input. Note that principals usually will not approve your request unless they know that the teachers or other participants agree. Note also that if you plan to gather data from students, you will probably need parental agreement and informed consent. Most schools, hospitals, clinics, and other institutions have specific procedures that must be followed to gain entrance (see, for example, the discussion in Chapter 3). You should identify the gatekeepers, learn the procedures for requesting access to a desired site, and follow those procedures. You should also ask how long the decision process typically takes.

The process of obtaining entry to a field site can be tedious and lengthy. To avoid tedium and save time, you might be tempted to short circuit the process by studying participants you can access easily, such as people you supervise (teachers in your own school), students in your class, or acquaintances and friends whom you know will cooperate. This tempting alternative to school or site approval is not advised except, of course, when conducting action research. Acquaintances may be uncomfortable answering certain questions, and friends may assume they understand each other and thus not probe or question given responses.

Gaining permission to a site may require negotiation between yourself and the gatekeeper. For example, timing, access, use of results, and the like are common negotiation issues. You should be prepared to answer questions from both the gatekeeper and, subsequently, the research participants. Make every attempt to establish good rapport with everyone involved; it will serve you well. For example, they may wish to know the following:

- *What are you trying to do in your study?* This question is logical and your response is important; participants want to know what you're planning to do and find out. Notice, to answer this question, you must have some idea about the purpose of your study. Few people will give access or agree to be participants if all you can tell them about your study is, "It's about teachers (or students, or aides, or parent involvement), but I don't know more than that at this time." You don't have to know the specifics of your topic and methods, but you will need to provide some focus in your response. In describing your topic, avoid educational jargon. Anticipate their questions and prepare a two- or three-sentence description of your aims. If pushed by participants for more details, it is appropriate to respond that an important part of your study is to identify what's important and should be examined. It is advisable to put the topic in writing to provide interested parties with documentation.

- *How much will your presence disrupt my classroom and students?* Participants have rhythms and routines to their activities and want to minimize their disruption. It is important to be honest in answering this question. For example, don't water down what you expect teachers to do, because they will be resentful and uncooperative when they find out (during the study) that you were not truthful. However, you may also capitalize on the fact that much of qualitative research involves data gathering that is not disruptive.

- *What will you do with the findings?* Gatekeepers and participants may have concerns about how results of the study are reported, and to whom. For example, they may worry about bad publicity or political use of the findings against the research site or its participants. Respond honestly. In most cases you will be able to indicate that no participant's name or title will be published and the site and location will be disguised for publication. Two things that you might face are the gatekeeper demanding a copy of the results as a condition of providing the site and participants' demanding access to the data during and at the end of the study. Agreeing to the former may affect the responses of participants: if I know the principal will see the results, I may not give honest answers to questions or may change my teaching practices. Allowing teachers access to data at the end of the study can provide insights and corroboration of your interpretations, but may also make teachers self-conscious, leading to revisions of interpretations and descriptions. Don't show data to participants during the study unless you have a compelling reason to do so.

- *Why did you select this setting?* In answering this question try to say something positive about the setting as your basis for its selection. For example, I heard the teachers in this school are exceptional; there are many new teachers in this school and I wanted to work in such a setting; you have a unique science program that I wish to understand. It is important that you indicate that your focus is on teachers or programs as a group, not as individuals.

- *What do we get out of this?* This is a valid and reasonable question. This is a qualitative research study, so you will be spending a lot of time and asking a lot of your participants. It is reasonable that they expect something in return. Think carefully about what you are willing to provide in return for participation. Would you be willing to provide information about your results, to meet with teachers and parents to summarize and answer questions about the results, provide a written summary of the results? Would you teach teachers a course in teacher research? You should give thought to this question.

There are many aspects to gaining entrance, and negotiation and compromise usually are important aspects of the process. It might be useful for you to write brief answers to these five questions, just to make you think about how you will answer them when asked.

MIXED METHOD: INTEGRATING QUALITATIVE AND QUANTITATIVE METHODS

Now that you have gotten a flavor for qualitative research, and before we proceed much further, you need to be aware of something: You can mix quantitative and qualitative methods in a single study! Now, before you close your book in frustration, or decide right now would be a good time for a nap, stay with us for the next few pages for an introduction to mixed-method research. Your study may be better off if you know how to integrate both qualitative and quantitative aspects.

In Chapter 1 we introduced qualitative and quantitative research methods, and we have mentioned occasionally since then the possibilities of mixing them. Recall some of the characteristics of each approach:

1. Quantitative research methods are characterized by a deductive approach; qualitative methods are characterized by an inductive approach.
2. Quantitative researchers are concerned with objective reality that is "out there" to be discovered; qualitative researchers focus on interpreting their participants' perspectives.

3. Quantitative researchers focuses on cause–effect relationships; qualitative researchers focus on describing the process of their research.
4. Quantitative researchers identify hypotheses to test; qualitative research topics emerge slowly as a study progresses.
5. Quantitative researchers select participants as randomly as possible; qualitative researchers select research participants purposely based on their articulateness and experience in the research setting.

These distinctions do not completely define quantitative and qualitative approaches, but they do highlight important differences. As Krathwohl notes, "Research, however, is a creative act; don't confine your thinking to specific approaches. Researchers creatively combine the elements of methods in any way that makes the best sense for the study they want to do. Their own limits are their own imagination and the necessity of presenting their findings convincingly. The research question to be answered really determines the method."[12]

BRIEF BACKGROUND

In recent years, educational researchers have become increasingly interested in combining quantitative and qualitative research methods. However, although both quantitative and qualitative researchers support mixed-method or multimethod research studies, historically most educational researchers are primarily educated in quantitative research methods. Thus, many researchers are not experienced in carrying out multimethod research studies.

Support for the multimethod approach has come from some of the foremost proponents of experimental and quasi-experimental designs.[13] Mixed-method studies require dual competencies, in both qualitative and quantitative methods, and considerable time and resources.

THREE MODELS OF MIXED-METHOD RESEARCH

There are three common mixed-method approaches: (1) qualitative data are collected first and are more heavily weighted than quantitative; (2) quantitative data are collected first and are more heavily weighted than qualitative; and (3) qualitative and quantitative data are equally weighted and are collected concurrently. The third is the most difficult to implement.[14]

The QUAL-Quan Model

In the QUAL-Quan model, a qualitative study (or phase in a study) comes first, typically an "exploratory" study in which observation and open-ended interviews with individuals or groups are conducted and concepts and potential hypotheses are identified. In the second phase of the study, variables are identified from concepts derived from the qualitative analysis and hypotheses are tested with quantitative techniques. For example, the QUAL-Quan approach is useful for researchers who obtain results from multi-item scales to measure phenomena. The validity of the qualitative results can be enhanced by results from the second, quantitative study results.

---

[12]Krathwohl, D. R. (1998). *Methods of educational and social science research: An integrated approach,* 2nd ed. Reading, MA: Addison-Wesley, p. 27.

[13]See, for example, Campbell, D. T., and Stanley, J. C. (1971). *Experimental and quasi-experimental designs for research,* Chicago: Rand McNally; Cook, T. D., and Campbell, D. T. (1979), *Quasi-experimentation: Design and analysis issues for field settings,* Chicago: Rand McNally; and Creswell, J. W. (1994). *Research design: Qualitative and quantitative approaches,* Thousand Oaks, CA: Sage.

[14] The following discussion is adapted from Padgett, Deborah K. (1998). *Qualitative methods in social work research: Challenges and rewards.* Beverly Hills, CA: Sage (pp. 126–131) and from Creswell, J. W. (1994). *Research Design: Qualitative and Quantitative Approaches.* Thousand Oaks, CA: Sage (pp. 177–190).

The QUAN-Qual Model

In the QUAN-Qual model, the findings of the quantitative study are followed by—and determine the type of data collected in—a qualitative study. That is, the first study or phase is comprised of a hypothesis, quantitative data collection, and analysis. The second study or phase is comprised of qualitative data collection, analysis, and interpretation. This type of study is more heavily weighted toward the quantitative side, and the qualitative analysis and interpretation can help explain or elaborate on the quantitative results.

The QUAN-QUAL Model

The third type of mixed-method model, QUAN-QUAL, integrates simultaneous qualitative and quantitative methods, and with equal weight, *throughout the same study.* One method may be dominant over the other (QUAN-qual or QUAL-quan), or the two methods may be given equal weight throughout.[15] When following the QUAN-qual model, for example, researchers might enliven their quantitative findings by collecting and writing case vignettes. When using the QUAL-quan approach, qualitative researchers might decide to include survey, census, and Likert-scale data along with narrative data.

The most challenging type of multimethod research is the fully integrated QUAL-QUAN approach because it requires expertise in both quantitative and qualitative methods. In this model, quantitative and qualitative methods are given equal weight at *all* stages of the study.

The same issues in the general debate over qualitative versus quantitative paradigms arise in discussions of mixed-method evaluation. Qualitative researchers who are philosophically opposed to quantitative methods argue that these methods have taught us very little about how and why programs work. Quantitative studies are good at establishing *what,* but qualitative studies help us to understand *how* a program succeeds or fails. Both sides can benefit from collaboration. Note how triangulation occurs in mixed method studies—one set of data corroborates another.

TYPES OF MIXED-METHOD DESIGNS

To identify a study as a mixed-method design, ask yourself the following questions:[16]

1. Is there evidence in the title? Does the title include terms such as *quantitative and qualitative, mixed methods, integrated, triangular,* or other terms that suggest a mixture of methods?
2. What about in the data collection section? Does the procedure or methods section, where data analyses are shown, use more numbers or words?
3. Does the purpose statement or the research questions indicate the type(s) of method(s) used?
4. What priority does the research give to qualitative or quantitative elements?
5. What is the sequence of collecting qualitative and/or quantitative data? Which comes first?
6. How does the researcher actually analyze the data? Describe any distinction in analysis.

The following are some criteria for evaluating whether a study is mixed method:

1. Are both qualitative and quantitative methods in the study?
2. Does the researcher describe the kind of mixed methods applied?

---

[15]Our use of capitalization in this discussion follows Morse (1991) as cited in Creswell, J. W. (2002), *Educational research: Planning, conducting, and evaluating qualitative research,* Upper Saddle River, NJ: Merrill/Prentice Hall (p. 563). The method in uppercase letters is weighted more heavily than the method in lowercase. Where both are uppercase, they are in balance.

[16] Creswell, J. W. (2002). *Educational research: Planning, conducting, and evaluating quantitative and qualitative research.* Upper Saddle River, NJ: Merrill/Prentice Hall (p. 564).

TABLE 6.2   The Interaction of Qualitative Research Methods with Quantitative Research Designs

QUANTITATIVE DESIGN TYPE	ROLE OF ETHNOGRAPHY IN QUANTITATIVE RESEARCH DESIGNS
Cross-sectional research: Population and sample surveys	*Preparation for survey* — Identification of the problem and context — Identification of the range of responses — Identification of target population, characteristics, locations, and possible barriers to survey research *Complementary data* — Identification and exploration of social subgroups, explaining patterned variation in survey results
Experiments	*Preparation* — Identification of elements of the experiment — Identification of constraints in the field — Pilot testing for acceptability and feasibility — Developing and validating measures of change *Process* — Finding differences in implementation — Documenting content of intervention for comparison with outcome measures
Controlled field studies/ quasi-experiments	*Preparation* — Identification of elements of the treatment — Identification of potential differences among treatment and control groups — Identification of constraints to experimentation in the field — Pilot testing for acceptability and feasibility — Developing and validating measures of change *Process* — Finding differences in implementation — Documenting content of intervention for comparison with outcome measures

Source: From LeCompte, M. D., and Schensul, J. J. (1999). *Designing and Conducting Ethnographic Research: Ethnographer's Toolkit,* p. 93. Lanham, MD: Alta Mira/Bowman & Littlefield. Reprinted by permission.

Now go to the Companion Website accompanying this text at *www.prenhall.com/gay* to chook your understanding of chapter concepts in the following modules: Objectives, Practice Quiz, and Applying What You Know. Expand your research skills with Evaluating Articles, Analyzing Qualitative Data, Analyzing Quantitative Data, and Research Tools and Tips. Visit Web Links to broaden your knowledge about research.

3. Are questions for both qualitative and quantitative approaches stated or described?
4. Is the writing balanced in terms of qualitative and quantitative approaches?

Tables 6.2 and 6.3 illustrate (1) the interaction of quantitative methods with qualitative designs and, conversely, (2) the interaction of qualitative methods with quantitative designs. These tables illustrate the varied strategies available for linking qualitative and quantitative methods in the same research study.

Figure 6.3 is an example of an abstract for a combined qualitative and quantitative research study. The abstract provides an overview of how combined quantitative and qualitative research can work together to broaden educational research from a single to a multiple perspective.

TABLE 6.3   The Interaction of Quantitative Methods with Qualitative Research Designs

QUALITATIVE RESEARCH DESIGNS	ROLE OF QUANTITATIVE RESEARCH IN RELATION TO ETHNOGRAPHY
Case studies/ethnographies	— Survey to confirm and validate ethnographically defined patterns
	— "Case-control" matched sample to identify factors associated with presence/absence of element (e.g., disease, school performance, etc.)
Ethnographies	— Survey to confirm and validate ethnographically defined patterns
	— "Case-control" matched sample to identify factors associated with presence/absence of element (e.g., disease, school performance, etc.)
	— Time series design (repeated observations of the same units over time) to define change more accurately
Narratives	— Survey to demonstrate presence of patterns revealed by narratives, using language and concepts of respondents
Compressed or rapid ethnographic assessments or focused ethnography	— Brief cross-sectional surveys with small samples
	— Brief pre-post surveys and panel designs for assessing intervention
Action research	— Action research makes use of both qualitative and quantitative design features to accomplish the purpose designated by the problem and the partnership

Source: From LeCompte, M. D., and Schensul, J. J. (1999). *Designing and Conducting Ethnographic Research: Ethnographer's Toolkit,* p. 94. Lanham, MD: Alta Mira/Bowman & Littlefield. Reprinted by permission.

SUMMARY

The Nature of Qualitative Research

1. Qualitative researchers strive to capture the human meanings of social life as lived and experienced by the research participants.
2. Qualitative research approaches are rooted in the disciplines of sociology, anthropology, philosophy, and history.
3. Because qualitative researchers rely heavily on verbal description, researchers are their own main instrument of data collection, interpretation, and written narratives. It is commonly noted that in qualitative research "the researcher is the research method."

Six General Steps in Qualitative Research

4. The six steps in qualitative research are (1) identifying a topic or issue to study, (2) reviewing the literature related to the topic, (3) selecting research participants, (4) collecting data related to the topic, (5) analyzing and interpreting the data, and (6) developing a narrative to describe the results of the study.

Qualitative Research Methods

5. Qualitative research methods include ethnography, historical research, grounded theory, and action research. The primary difference among the methods are the social context examined and participants studied.

Ethnography

6. Ethnography seeks to describe and analyze all or part of the culture of a community by identifying and describing the participants' practices and beliefs.
7. Context, or background, is an important aspect of interpreting qualitative research results.

FIGURE 6.3 Abstract of a Mixed-Method Study.

Note that the title indicates that the research involves both qualitative and quantitative methods.

AUTHOR	Holbrook, Allyson; Bourke, Sid; Owen, John M.; McKenzie, Phil; Ainley, John
TITLE	Mapping Educational Research and Exploring Research Impact: A Holistic, Multi-Method Approach.
PUB DATE	2000
NOTE	31P.; Paper presented at the Annual Meeting of the American Educational Research Association (New Orleans, LA, April 24–26, 2000). "Mapping Educational Research and Its Impact on Schools" was one of three studies of the "Impact of Educational Research" commissioned and funded by the Australian Federal Dept. of Education, Training, and Youth Affairs in 1999 (Minister: The Honorable Dr. David Kemp, MP).
PUB TYPE	Reports—Research (143)—Speeches/Meeting Papers (150)
EDRS PRICE	MFOI/PCO2 Plus Postage.
DESCRIPTORS	Administrator Attitudes; Databases; Educational Administration; Educational Policy; *Educational Research; Elementary Secondary Education; Foreign Countries; *Graduate Students; Higher Education; *Principals; *Research Utilization; *Teacher Attitudes; Theory Practice Relationship
IDENTIFIERS	*Australia
ABSTRACT	This paper discusses the main analytical techniques used in "Mapping Educational Research and Its Impact on Schools." The study considered the impact of the outcomes of educational research on the practice of teaching and learning in Australian schools and on educational policy and administration. Mixed methods were used, beginning with a review of the literature and the exploration of the Australian Education Index (AEI) educational research database. Documents were collected from faculties of education in Australia, and questionnaires about the use of educational literature were developed for postgraduate students ($n = 1,267$), school principals ($n = 73$), and representatives of 72 professional associations. Interviews were then conducted with seven policymakers and selected respondents to the postgraduate student questionnaires. The study indicates that it is possible to use an existing database to monitor educational research in Australia. A clear majority of all three groups surveyed provided evidence of the awareness, acceptance, and valuing of educational research in Australia. Interviews with policymakers also showed the use of educational research in policy formation. The multiple perspectives of this study give a picture of the links between research and its use in schools and departments of education in Australia. An appendix summarizes the database descriptors from the database investigation. (Contains 3 tables, 3 figures, and 34 references.) (SLD)

The topic states that the study "considered the impact"—not "determined the impact"—giving the abstract a distinct qualitative flavor.

Note that the study used both questionnaires (quantitative) and interviews (qualitative) to collect data. It is common in mixed-method studies to combine these two data-collection methods.

Source: ERIC Document Reproduction Service No. ED 441 850.

Historical Research

8. Historical research is the systematic collection and evaluation of data related to past occurrences for the purpose of describing causes, effects, or trends of those events.

9. In conducting a historical study, the researcher can neither manipulate nor control any of the variables.

Grounded Theory

10. Grounded theory is a systematic qualitative method that aims at generating a theory that explains, at a conceptual level, a process, an action, or a concept.

11. The most common strategies used to carry out grounded theory are observation and interviews.

12. The key to success of grounded theory is the constant comparison method, an inductive strategy that "constantly compares" and integrates the data the researcher collects in numerous data collection forays. As data are continually examined and narrowed, theoretical propositions emerge that develop and link to other propositions.

Action Research

13. Action research is a systematic inquiry done by teachers and other educational personnel to collect and

study data that can help them to both understand and improve their practice. It is based on the view that teachers can serve as practical researchers who can help improve practice in school.

14. Any teacher- or school-based question, topic, or problem is pertinent to action research and may be the start of the process.

Qualitative Research Process

15. Five characteristics of qualitative research are (1) real-world setting for the study, (2) data are descriptive, not numerical, (3) the research emphsizes a holistic approach to the setting and participants, (4) inductive data analysis, and (5) the researcher strives to describe meaning as seen from the perspectives of the research participants.

Characteristics of Good Qualitative Research

16. Good qualitative research displays 10 features:
   - Researchers take a holistic stance.
   - Researchers avoid making premature decisions or assumptions about the study.
   - Methods focus on person-to-person interactions.
   - Researchers spend a good deal of time in the research setting.
   - Researchers gather data directly from participants.
   - Researchers remain open to alternative explanations of phenomena.
   - Researchers admit to and describe their biases and preferences.
   - Phenomena are described and explained from the viewpoint of, and in the voice of, the participants.
   - Researchers are responsible for obtaining participants' informed consent and ensuring their ethical treatment throughout the study.
   - The research focus is on discovery and understanding, rather than on confirmation of existing theory.

Qualitative Research Questions

17. Qualitative research questions encompass a range of topics, but most focus on participants' understanding of meanings and social life in a particular context.

18. These general topics must necessarily be more focused to become useful and researchable questions.

19. Qualitative research topics are usually more general and tentative than quantitative research topics, mainly because it is expected that a qualitative study will evolve in focus once the researcher is in the research setting and beginning to interact with the participants.

20. Although qualitative researchers seldom begin a study with a specific topic or plan, they must begin with at least a general idea of the topic and methods of their study. Qualitative proposals are not fixed contracts that cannot be altered, but neither are they so brief and general that they convey little about the proposed study.

Step 1: Selecting a Research Topic or Issue

21. The first step in qualitative research is to select a topic or issue to study. Qualitative researchers begin with an open-ended, broad research topic that will narrow and emerge as they learn more about the research participants, their thoughts, and their setting.

22. Qualitative researchers depend heavily on information provided by participants during the research.

23. The research topic may have a variety of functions. It can provide a voice for groups or individuals to be heard. It can identify new directions for research. It can help identify and examine gaps in educational practice and theory. It can help students develop their research knowledge and practice.

24. The most common sources of research topics are from testing existing theories, examining questions that pique researcher interest or curiosity, and carrying out replications of existing studies.

25. The ethnographic researcher should select a topic that (1) is of strong personal interest, and (2) can be carried out with a limited number of participants and a narrow research context.

26. The historical researcher should select a topic (1) that is *not* of strong personal interest, to reduce the effect of bias, and (2) for which sufficient sources of data are available.

27. The grounded theorist should select a topic that will lead to new insights and new understanding of what aspects of the topic are most important. The initial topic is a working model that will be altered and narrowed as the researcher applies an iterative process that seeks to help make sense of the data participants provide.

28. The action researcher should select a topic that derives from a perceived need to understand or correct an existing problem.

Step 2: Reviewing the Literature

29. Unlike quantitative researchers, who spend a great deal of time examining the research on their topic in

the early stages of the research process, some qualitative researchers tend not to delve deeply into their literature until data collection. Some qualitative researchers believe too much emphasis on the examination of literature can bias or influence the research and prematurely narrow the focus of the intended topic prior to interaction with the participants. Others believe researchers should review literature on all aspects of the topic at the outset of the study. Nevertheless, examining literature is flexible and typically lasts throughout data collection and data analysis.

30. Ethnographic, historical, and action research each have approach-specific types of literature available to the researcher. Grounded theory does not involve prior literature analysis, beginning instead directly with data collection and analysis.

Gaining Entry

31. Qualitative researchers should be prepared to answer in a general way the following questions that gatekeepers and potential participants may ask: (1) What is the purpose of your study? (2) How much will your presence disrupt my setting and activities? (3) What will you do with the findings? (4) Why did you select this setting? (5) What do we get out of this?

Mixed Method: Integrating Qualitative and Quantitative Methods

32. Mixed-method studies integrate both qualitative and quantitative methods. The research question determines the methods undertaken.

33. Mixed-method studies require competencies in conducting both quantitative and qualitative methods.

34. The three models of mixed-method research are (1) quantitative data are more heavily weighted and are collected before qualitative data, (2) qualitative data are more heavily weighted and collected before quantitative data, and (3) qualitative and quantitative data are equally weighted throughout the study.

"The key to 'sampling' in qualitative research is to choose good participants who can provide the insights and articulateness needed to attain the desired richness of qualitative data." (p. 195)

CHAPTER 7

QUALITATIVE RESEARCH: DATA COLLECTION

OBJECTIVES

After reading Chapter 7, you should be able to do the following:

1. Identify strategies for finding and selecting research participants.
2. Describe observation approaches for qualitative data collection.
3. Briefly describe two types of observational research.
4. Describe practices in obtaining and recording field notes.
5. Briefly describe the steps involved in conducting an observational study.
6. Describe interview approaches for qualitative data collection.

7. State strategies to enhance the validity of collected data.

In Chapter 6 we described a number of qualitative research types, and how you might go about choosing and narrowing a qualitative research topic. We also presented how and when literature may be read in qualitative approaches. Now, with your research topic in mind and having obtained entry into the research setting, you will need to identify potential research participants and collect data from them in the setting. Qualitative data takes many forms, and we describe these data sources and their methods of collection later in the chapter. We begin here by discussing how to select your research participants.

STEP 3: SELECTING RESEARCH PARTICIPANTS

After getting approval from the IRB at their institution, and receiving the gatekeeper's approval to conduct the study at the setting, researchers should identify potential research participants. They should do this firsthand, because the initial communication with potential participants is the start of a relationship with them throughout the study. However, it is helpful to use the advice of the gatekeeper regarding the best way to initiate meetings with identified participants. After getting a green light from the gatekeeper, go ahead and make contact with potential participants. Establish a day and time when you can meet with them to discuss the study. It will usually be more convenient for them if you visit them in the setting. This is also to your advantage because it gives you an initial look at the setting. If the participants are teachers, your chances of meeting their students also are quite good.

INITIAL MEETING TO SCREEN PARTICIPANTS

There are a number of benefits to the initial, face-to-face meeting. As noted, it gives you a view of the setting. It also shows potential participants that you are willing to make a separate contact with them to discuss the study, showing your interest in them as participants and starting the research relationship off in a positive and professional way. It allows you to explain your expectations for their participation and to find out if they are interested. A face-to-face discussion also lets you size up potential participants in terms of whether they are able to provide the data you seek. Finally, if potential participants are interested and can provide appropriate data, then you can arrange mutually agreed times and places for interviewing, observing, and meeting.

ETHICAL ISSUES

Potential participants will probably ask you, "Will your study disrupt my classroom and students?" "Will I be identified?" "Who will have access to the results?" and "What do you expect me to do for you?" Be prepared for such questions and answer them honestly. It is wise to assure teachers that they will not be identified by name and that their supervisors will not have access to their individual data. Ethically, you must protect the interests of potentially vulnerable participants. Be clear about issues of confidentiality or anonymity. *Confidentiality* means that you know the participants' names but promise not to divulge them, while *anonymity* means that no one will know the participants' names. Although it is true that the focus of a qualitative study grows and evolves as the study progresses, it is necessary that you have a reasonably clear conception of the key research questions and the methods of data collection. If not, gaining access and participants' cooperation will be difficult. Gaining access and identifying the appropriate participants are critical aspects of qualitative research, but if a gatekeeper or the participants are not comfortable with you or if they mistrust promises of confidentiality or anonymity, they may not provide or may even distort the information you seek, to protect themselves.

All researchers are bound to search out and avoid unethical treatment of research participants. Two basic and fundamental ethical principles relate to all forms of research activity: (1) both qualitative and quantitative researchers keep participants as informed as possible about the research study, and (2) they make every effort to protect participants from harm. Although it is difficult to identify all the potential problems that can arise in a research study, whether prior to, during, or after the study, it is the researcher's responsibility to be aware of and avoid threats to study participants. Figure 7.1 presents a number of common ethical concerns, which can blur the relationship between researcher and participants.

Recall from Chapter 3 that most professional organizations, such as the American Psychological Association, American Educational Research Association, and the American Sociological Society, have standards for ethical research. Virtually all colleges and universities require their faculty and students to have their research proposals approved by an institutional review board prior to conducting their study.

Obtaining Informed Consent

Once participants are selected, it is useful to obtain their formal, informed consent for being part of the study. While this might seem like overkill, informed consent is useful for both the participants and the researcher and ensures that both know their reciprocal rights and expectations. Further, the depth of personal and sensitive information collected in qualitative studies calls for researcher–participant understandings prior to beginning the study. The emphasis is on *informed consent*. Participants should know, at least in general terms, about the nature

FIGURE 7.1
Common ethical
concerns in research.

1. Have participants knowingly consented to be part of the study?
2. Do participants understand what their consent involves?
3. Are participants' rights and consents maintained during and after the study?
4. Were participants given a description of the study and its purpose?
5. Was a clear description given of the procedures in the study?
6. Were participants told what will happen to them if they agree to participate?
7. Were participants told how the researcher will protect their identities?
8. Were participants given the address or phone numbers of the researcher(s) and of the responsible individual at the research institution?

Source: Adapted from LeCompte, M. D., and Schensul, J. J. (1999). *Designing and Conducting Ethnographic Research: Ethnographer's Toolkit*, pp. 189–190. Lanham, MD: Alta Mira/Bowman & Littlefield. Adapted by permission.

and purpose of the study. Qualitative researchers should provide participants information about the study and the participants' expected roles and activities. They should know what they will be expected to do and any risks involved. They should know about the conditions under which they may withdraw from the study. Issues of anonymity, confidentiality, and dissemination of results also should be made clear. It is best if both the researcher and the participant sign the informed consent. (See also Chapter 3's discussion of "Informed Consent and Protection from Harm" and "Ethical Issues in Qualitative Research.")

In sum, gaining entry and identifying potential participants can be an ethically complex process, with many pitfalls. Much of a researcher's success depends on the personal characteristics of the researcher and how the participants perceive him or her. Mutual trust underlies all research studies, but especially so for qualitative research, because of the close and deep interactions between researcher and participants. Trust is earned, not given, and must be maintained throughout the study. The process begins with the first interaction with potential participants and carries on during and after the study is completed.

> Trust and rapport in fieldwork are not simply a matter of niceness; a non-coercive, mutually rewarding relationship with key informants is essential if the researcher is to gain valid insights into the informant's point of view. Since gaining a sense of the perspective of the informant is crucial to the success of the research enterprise, it is necessary to establish trust and maintain it throughout the course of the study.[1]

THE NATURE AND GOAL OF SELECTING PARTICIPANTS

As you may recall from Chapter 4, researchers conducting quantitative studies select samples of a population to study, whereas those conducting qualitative studies typically select actual, individual people—participants—to study. Qualitative research generally relies on purposive selection of participants; they are selected because they can provide pertinent information about the intended research topic and setting. Qualitative researchers emphasize in-depth inquiry in the research setting, and require different sampling approaches than those used in quantitative research, such as random sampling. Whereas the quantitative researcher seeks to obtain sample data to generalize to a larger population, the qualitative researcher seeks to obtain deep understanding of a relatively few participants in a single setting. Thus, qualitative researchers typically deal with small, purposely selected samples. The key to "sampling" in qualitative research is to choose good participants who can provide the insights and articulateness needed to attain the desired richness of qualitative data. The focus on participant selection is to identify those who can provide such information. Many purposive sampling strategies are useful in qualitative research, as shown in Table 7.1. Each of these strategies calls for different types of qualitative samples, depending on the aim of the research topic.

How Many Participants Are Enough?

Inevitably, all qualitative researchers face the question: How many participants are enough? As is usually the case with such questions, the answer is, "It depends." There are no hard and fast numbers that represent the "correct" number of participants in a study. It is usually true that sample sizes in quantitative research are larger than qualitative. Qualitative studies can be carried out with a single participant or, when studying multiple contexts, may have as many as 60 or 70 participants. However, rarely will qualitative studies have more than 20 or so participants, and in many cases will have fewer. The qualitative researcher's time, money, participant availability, participant interest, and other factors will influence the number of participants engaged in a research sample.

---

[1]Erickson, F. (1990). *Qualitative methods: Research on teaching and learning, volume 2.* New York: Macmillan (p. 141).

TABLE 7.1   Sampling Strategies in Qualitative Research

TYPE OF SAMPLING	PURPOSE
Maximum variation	Documents diverse variations and identifies important common patterns
Homogeneous	Focuses, reduces, simplifies, and facilitates group interviewing
Critical case	Permits logical generalization and maximum application of information to other cases
Theory-based	Finds examples of a theoretical construct and thereby elaborates on and examines it
Confirming and disconfirming cases	Elaborates on initial analysis, seeks exceptions, looks for variation
Snowball or chain	Identifies cases of interest from people who know people who know what cases are information-rich
Extreme or deviant case	Learns from highly unusual manifestations of the phenomenon of interest
Typical case	Highlights what is normal or average
Intensity	Looks at information-rich cases that manifest the phenomenon intensely but not extremely
Politically important cases	Attracts desired attention or avoids attracting undesired attention
Random purposeful	Adds credibility to sample when potential purposeful sample is too large
Stratified purposeful	Illustrates subgroups and facilitates comparisons
Criterion	Encompasses all cases that meet some criterion; useful for quality assurance
Opportunistic	Follows new leads; takes advantage of the unexpected
Combination or mixed	Triangulation, flexibility; meets multiple interests and needs
Convenience	Saves time, money, and effort, but at the expense of information and credibility

Source: Miles, M. B., and Huberman, A. M. (1994). *Qualitative Data Analysis: An Expanded Sourcebook,* 2nd ed. p. 28. Copyright 1994 Sage Publications. Reprinted by permission of Sage Publications, Inc.

Qualitative researchers have some options in sampling. They may select participants at the start of the study and deal only with them. They may start with a few participants and add new ones over time to corroborate and extend the perspectives of the initial participants. However, in picking participants, be careful of participants who are extremely eager to be included in the study. They may have an ax to grind or have prior strong feelings about what they perceive the study to be about. Including such zealots likely will produce preformed, not reflective, responses. In most cases, the researcher cannot identify good participants until after observing them for some time. The researcher may gain some sense of the qualities of individual potential participants by conversing with them prior to beginning the study. The researcher would seek individuals who can explain their thoughts and ideas clearly, who are familiar with the study's context, and who are open to exploring new perspectives on their experience.

Two general indicators are commonly used to determine when the number of participants is sufficient. The first is the extent to which the selected participants represent the range of potential participants in the setting. For example, if the research setting is a school with kindergarten to sixth graders and the researcher only includes teachers from grades K, 1, and 2, the selected participants do not represent those in the chosen setting. To rectify this problem, the researcher could change the focus to the lower grades or add participants at the higher grade levels. The second indicator is the redundancy of the information gathered from the participants. When the researcher begins to hear the same thoughts, perspectives, and responses from most or all of the participants, he or she will know that little more is being learned and additional participants are not needed, at least for that particular topic or issue. This point is commonly known as **data saturation.**

Later in this chapter, you will see how the description of the participants is written, in sample segments from two different published studies. Now, let us turn our attention to collecting qualitative data from our selected participants.

STEP 4: DATA COLLECTION

DATA COLLECTION TECHNIQUES

Observations, interviews, phone calls, personal and official documents, photographs, recordings, drawings, e-mail messages and responses, and informal conversations are all sources of qualitative data. The most commonly used sources are observations and interviews. Each of these data types shares one common aspect: the researcher is the primary source of data. The researcher's ability to integrate data and analyze it is key because collected data are typically narrative and are rich in both length and detail. In this section we examine qualitative data collection approaches, primarily observations and interviews. We examine these approaches individually for clarity, but in most cases, qualitative researchers employ more than one data collection method. Although the approaches we describe are the ones most commonly used, bear in mind that there are many options for data collection, including in some cases quantitative data (recall our discussions of mixed-method research in chapters 1 and 6). Any data collection approach that is ethical and feasible, and that contributes to understanding the phenomenon studied, may be used.

Getting Started

Having obtained entry into a setting and having selected participants, the qualitative researcher is ready to begin data collection, also commonly called *fieldwork*. Regardless of how much you read, think about, and discuss fieldwork you will not really know what it is like until you actually live it. Living an experience for the first time always means uncertainty in a new role—uncertainty about how to act and interact with others. It is common to feel nervous as you learn the ropes, try to establish rapport with participants, and get a feel for the setting. Bogdan and Biklen[2] suggest a number of cautions to make the initial days of entry into the setting less painful:

1. Do not take what happens in the field personally.
2. Set up your first visit so that someone is there to introduce you to the participants.
3. Don't try to accomplish too much in the first few days. Make your initial visit for observation short. You will have to take field notes after each data collection encounter, so start with brief data collection episodes to ease into the process of writing field notes.
4. Be relatively passive. Ask general, nonspecific, noncontroversial questions that allow participants to reply without being forced to provide answers they might find uncomfortable discussing with a relative "stranger." Ease your way into the context; don't storm in. The intent is for the participants to gradually become comfortable with you, and you with them. Then you can gradually increase your degree of involvement.

---

[2] Bogdan, R. C., and Biklen, S. K. (1998). *Qualitative research in education: An introduction to theory and methods,* 3rd ed. Needham Heights, MA: Allyn & Bacon (pp. 79–81).

5. Be friendly and polite. Answer questions participants and others ask, but try not to say too much about the specifics of your presence and purpose, lest it influence the participants.

Your demeanor and personal characteristics will be important in carrying out your research. That is one of the realities of most qualitative research. Decisions about methods and focus of data collection are usually made after selecting and examining the site and sizing up the participants. You may even want to "get the feel" of the setting and participants before deciding on the data collection techniques to employ.

OBSERVATION

In an observational study, the current status of a phenomenon is determined not by asking but by observing. For certain research questions, observation is clearly the most appropriate approach. For example, you could ask teachers how they handle discipline in their classrooms, but more objective information would probably be obtained by actually observing teachers' classes. The value of observational research is illustrated by a study conducted in the Southwest on the classroom interaction between teachers and Mexican American students. Many teachers claimed that Mexican American children are difficult to teach due to their lack of participation in classroom activities and their failure to ask or answer questions. However, systematic observation revealed that the main reason they did not answer questions was that they were not asked very many! Observation revealed that teachers tended to talk less often and less favorably to Mexican American children and to ask them fewer questions. Thus, observation not only provided more accurate information than teacher reports, but also made the teachers aware that they were unintentionally part of the problem.

Observational techniques may also be used to collect data in nondescriptive studies. For example, in an experimental study designed to determine the effect of behavior modification techniques on disruptive behavior, students could be observed prior to and following the introduction of behavior modification in order to determine if instances of disruptive behavior were reduced in number. In either case, an observational study must be planned and executed just as carefully as any other type of research study.

Types of Observers

Observation can take many forms in qualitative research, depending on the involvement of the observer. The observer can be a **participant observer,** who engages fully in the activities being studied but is known to the participants as a researcher. This type of observation is usually associated with qualitative research. Alternatively, the observer can be an **external** or **nonparticipant observer** of the activities of the group being studied, that is, one who watches but does not participate. The major type of quantitative observational research is nonparticipant observation. Between the participant and the nonparticipant observer there are a number of other possibilities, such as a combination of both approaches, as when acting as an external observer at the start of the study and a participant observer in the latter stages of the study. It is also possible for the observer to be covert, disguising his identity from participants. Although this approach may gather the most realistic data about participants and their setting, there are ethical issues regarding participants' lack of awareness. The covert observer is a member of the group under false and unknown premises. Avoid covert observation.

The advantages of participant observation include the ability to gain insights and develop relationships with participants that cannot be obtained in any other way. Being a participant and having a "residence" in the field provides both breadth and depth of information about participants and setting. The drawbacks to participant observation are that the researcher may lose objectivity and become emotionally involved with participants, and, more pragmatically, the researcher may have difficulty participating and taking detailed field notes simultaneously.

Nonparticipant observers are less intrusive and less likely to become emotionally involved with participants. On the other hand, information such as participants' opinions, attitudes, and emotional states are more difficult to obtain.

Most qualitative observational research is naturalistic, encompassing holistic inquiry about participants' understanding of their natural setting or environment. The emphasis is on understanding the natural environment as lived by the participants, with no intent on the researcher's part to alter or manipulate the natural environment. Altering or manipulating the natural research setting destroys the reality of the researched setting and the trust of the participants.

The amount and kind of observation that is appropriate for a given study will depend on the nature of the study. If it is not feasible for the researcher to become a true participant in the group being studied, it probably is best to be an external observer. For example, the researcher may not have the background or needed expertise to meaningfully act as a true participant. Or, in some cases, it might be awkward for a male researcher to enter as a participant observer in an all-female context or for a middle-aged researcher to be a true participant in a group of fifth graders. If the group studied is tight-knit and closely organized, participation may be difficult for both the researcher and the group. If participation is feasible, the researcher must decide how well she can simultaneously act as a participant and gather the desired data. In some measure the researcher's personality will influence whether she feels more comfortable being a participant or an external observer. Beginning qualitative researchers should consider this question carefully prior to deciding to adopt the role of a participant observer; balancing participation and observation can be difficult. There is much to think about in deciding the nature of observation to employ. Throughout observation of whatever type, Bogdan and Biklen provide an important reminder:

> Becoming a researcher means internalizing the research goal while collecting data in the field. As you conduct research you participate with the subjects in various ways. You joke with them and behave socially in many ways. You may even help them perform their duties. You do these things, but always from the purpose of promoting your research goals. You carry with you an imaginary sign that you hang over each subject and on every wall and tree. The sign says, "My primary purpose in being here is to collect data. How does what I am doing relate to that goal?"[3]

This quote emphasizes the difference between a participant and a participant observer: a participant participates while a participant observer participates and collects data. This is, of course, potentially difficult and confusing for the novice researcher. Observation is complex. What should be watched, written down, and ignored? How does one overcome this complexity? The same way one gets to Carnegie Hall: practice, practice, practice. With practice one learns to be aware of implicit agendas among participants, to try to experience the situation from the perspective of both observer and participant, to be introspective about what one sees, and to provide records that richly describe observed situations.

Field Notes

Field notes are the record of what the observer has specifically seen or heard. In addition to these literal descriptions, field notes contain personal reactions, or what the observer has experienced and thought about during an observation session. They contain a descriptive *and* a reflective aspect—the former describes what's seen or heard (**emic data**) and the latter provides the researcher's thoughts or ideas about the description (**etic data**). Field notes are the data that will be analyzed to provide the description and understanding of the research setting and participants. In each session, beginning with the first, observation should produce

---

[3] Bogdan, R. C., and Biklen, S. K. (1998). *Qualitative research in education: An introduction to theory and methods,* 3rd ed. Needham Heights, MA: Allyn & Bacon (p. 82).

field notes that are as detailed as possible. If possible, notes should be made in the field, during the observation, when they are fresh to the researcher. The longer the interval between the observation and writing field notes, the more likely that there will be some distortion from the original observation, especially if the researcher has an excellent, but short, memory.

Clearly, the longer an observation session lasts, the more there will be to digest and write up in the field notes. Although the researcher cannot always control the length of an observation (it may break up earlier or go on longer than anticipated), when possible, it will be easier to develop field notes on shorter observation sessions. Over time, with practice, researchers often are surprised at how lengthy and detailed field notes produced from an observation session can be. Field notes should be entered into a computer for future examination and used for data analysis.

Each observation session will have its unique focus and interactions, but it is useful to have a *protocol,* or list of issues, to guide observation. This has two benefits. It provides the researcher with a focus during the observation, and it provides a common framework for field notes, making it easier to organize and categorize data across field notes. A simple protocol for observation might include these topics:

- Who is being observed? How many people are involved, who are they, and what individual roles and mannerisms are evident?
- What is going on? What is the nature of conversation? What are people saying or doing? What is the physical setting like? How are people seated, and where? How do the participants interact with each other? What are the status or roles of people; who leads, who follows, who is decisive, who is not? What is the tone of the session? What beliefs, attitudes, values, etc., seem to emerge?
- How did the meeting end? Was the group divided, united, upset, bored, or relieved?
- What activities or interactions seemed unusual or significant?
- What was the observer doing during the session? What was the observer's level of participation in the observation (participant observer, nonparticipant observer, etc.)?

Certainly different studies with different participants in a different setting would have alternative protocol questions. The aim here is not to be exhaustive, but to encourage you to develop and refine some form of protocol for observations. Figure 7.2 illustrates a simple protocol.

However, protocols are not useful if field notes are not extensive and descriptive records. The term that describes extensive, clear field notes is *thick description.*[4] Thick description is partially influenced by what is seen, but mainly by the detail and language the researcher uses in constructing the notes. Be clear and descriptive. Don't write, "The class was happy." Instead, describe the activities of the students, the looks on their faces, their interactions with each other, the teachers' activities, and other observations that led you to think the class was happy. Don't write, "He turned to her and engaged her in conversation." Say instead, "Turning to face her, he asked, 'What are we doing here? Can't we leave now?' She seemed hardly to hear him and would not meet his eyes." Don't say that the teacher is "teaching." Provide a description that indicates what the teacher was doing and saying. Avoid such words as "good," "happy," "useful," and the like; replace them with what was actually seen or heard. Figure 7.3 gives a portion of field notes that represent thick description. Note that the figure shows the sixth set of notes in the study and appears to be produced by a researcher with prior experience in constructing field notes. The sections labeled "O.C." indicate the observer's (researcher's) comments.

---

[4] Clifford Geertz (1973) believed that writing ethnography is "an elaborate adventure in . . . 'thick description' " (p. 6). Geertz, C. (1973). "Thick description: Toward an interpretive theory of culture." In C. Geertz, *The Interpretation of Cultures* (pp. 3–30). New York: Basic Books.

Setting:
Individual Observed:
Observation #: (first observation, second, etc.)
Observer Involvement:

Date/Time:
Place:
Duration of Observation (indicate start/end times):

Descriptive Notes	**Reflective Notes**
(Detailed, chronological notes about what the observer sees, hears; what occurred; the physical setting)	(Concurrent notes about the observer's thoughts, personal reactions, experiences)

FIGURE 7.2   Sample of observation protocol.

Figure 7.3 shows both the descriptive (emic data) and the reflective (etic data) aspects of field notes. Each O.C. entry represents a reflection that the researcher had while writing up the descriptive field notes. In reflective notes, the observer is free to express personal thoughts and issues. They represent a more personal and subjective aspect of the field notes, and should be distinguished from the descriptive material in the notes themselves. In reading Figure 7.3 you probably will identify times when the researcher's entries (O.C.'s) were about something unusual, something that has recurred, something that had to be explored, and the like.

Memo Writing

Good qualitative research requires simultaneous data collection and analysis. In the process of observing, writing, and reflecting on field notes, qualitative researchers engage in a process of evolving data analysis. These ongoing analyses lead to a form of data analysis referred to as *memo writing*. A **memo** is a form of thinking on paper; researchers write memos to themselves that describe their mental exploration of their ideas, themes, hunches, and reflections about the research topic. They are "thought pieces" that can range from a few sentences to many pages, and help researchers elaborate or examine significant features of their data. The ideas, themes, hunches, and reflections contained in memos usually form the basis for much of the final research report. Figure 7.4 presents an example of a memo.

The reflective aspects of field notes serve a number of functions. First, they identify topics or issues the researcher wishes to explore in more detail (e.g., I have the feeling that tension among faculty members is growing). Second, they begin to identify areas that might be important to focus on in data analysis (e.g., I'm finding it hard to remain objective because of Mr. Hardnose's abrasive manner). Third, if categorized across field notes, they can be collected into reflective groups such as a group for reflections on method, on ethical issues, on areas for analysis, and on ways to improve data collection.

March 24, 1980
Joe McCloud
11:00 a.m. to 12:30 p.m.
Westwood High
6th Set of Notes

THE FOURTH-PERIOD CLASS IN MARGE'S ROOM

I arrived at Westwood High at five minutes to eleven, the time Marge told me her fourth period started. I was dressed as usual: sport shirt, chino pants, and a Woolrich parka. The fourth period is the only time during the day when all the students who are in the "neurologically impaired/learning disability" program, better known as "Marge's program," come together. During the other periods, certain students in the program, two or three or four at most, come to her room for help with the work they are getting in other regular high school classes.

It was a warm, fortyish, promise of a spring day. There was a police patrol wagon, the kind that has benches in the back that are used for large busts, parked in the back of the big parking lot that is in front of the school. No one was sitting in it and I never heard its reason for being there. In the circular drive in front of the school was parked a United States Army car. It had insignias on the side and was a khaki color. As I walked from my car, a balding fortyish man in an Army uniform came out of the building and went to the car and sat down. Four boys and a girl also walked out of the school. All were white. They had on old dungarees and colored stenciled t-shirts with spring jackets over them. One of the boys, the tallest of the four, called out, "oink, oink, oink." This was done as he sighted the police vehicle in the back.

O.C.: This was strange to me in that I didn't think that the kids were into "the police as pigs." Somehow I associated that with another time, the early 1970s. I'm going to have to come to grips with the assumptions I have about high school due to my own experience. Sometimes I feel like Westwood is entirely different from my high school and yet this police car incident reminded me of mine.

Classes were changing when I walked down the halls. As usual there was the boy with girl standing here and there by the lockers. There were three couples that I saw. There was the occasional shout. There were no teachers outside the doors.

O.C.: The halls generally seem to be relatively unsupervised during class changes.

Two black girls I remember walking down the hall together. They were tall and thin and had their hair elaborately braided with beads all through them. I stopped by the office to tell Mr. Talbor's (the principal) secretary that I was in the building. She gave me a warm smile.

O.C.: I feel quite comfortable in the school now. Somehow I feel like I belong. As I walk down the halls some teachers say hello. I have been going out of my way to say hello to kids that I pass. Twice I've been in a stare-down with kids passing in the hall. Saying, "How ya' doin'?" seems to disarm them.

I walked into Marge's class and she was standing in front of the room with more people than I had ever seen in the room save for her homeroom which is right after second period. She looked like she was talking to the class or was just about to start. She was dressed as she had been on my other visits—clean, neat, well-dressed but casual. Today she had on a striped blazer, a white blouse and dark slacks. She looked up at me, smiled, and said: "Oh, I have a lot more people here now than the last time."

O.C.: This was in reference to my other visits during other periods where there are only a few students. She seems self-conscious about having such a small group of students to be responsible for. Perhaps she compares herself with the regular teachers who have classes of thirty or so.

There were two women in their late twenties sitting in the room. There was only one chair left. Marge said to me something like: "We have two visitors from the central office today. One is a vocational counselor and the other is a physical therapist," but I don't remember if those were the words. I felt embarrassed coming in late. I sat down in the only chair available next to one of the women from the central office. They had on skirts and carried their pocketbooks, much more dressed up than the teachers I've seen. They sat there and observed.

FIGURE 7.3   Section of field notes.

202

Below is the seating arrangement of the class today:

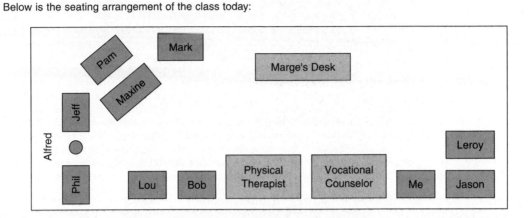

Alfred (Mr. Armstrong, the teacher's aide) walked around but when he stood in one place it was over by Phil and Jeff. Marge walked about near her desk during her talk which she started by saying to the class: "Now remember, tomorrow is a fieldtrip to the Rollway Company. We all meet in the usual place, by the bus, in front of the main entrance at 8:30. Mrs. Sharp wanted me to tell you that the tour of Rollway is not specifically for you. It's not like the trip to G.M. They took you to places where you were likely to be able to get jobs. Here, it's just a general tour that everybody goes on. Many of the jobs that you will see are not for you. Some are just for people with engineering degrees. You'd better wear comfortable shoes because you may be walking for two or three hours." Maxine and Mark said: "Ooh," in protest to the walking.

She paused and said in a demanding voice: "OK, any questions? You are all going to be there. (Pause) I want you to take a blank card and write down some questions so you have things to ask at the plant." She began passing out cards and at this point Jason, who was sitting next to me, made a tutting sound of disgust and said: "We got to do this?" Marge said: "I know this is too easy for you, Jason." This was said in a sarcastic way but not like a strong putdown.

O.C.: It was like sarcasm between two people who know each other well. Marge has known many of these kids for a few years. I have to explore the implications of that for her relations with them.

Marge continued: "OK, what are some of the questions you are going to ask?" Jason yelled out "Insurance," and Marge said: "I was asking Maxine not Jason." This was said matter of factly without anger toward Jason. Maxine said: "Hours—the hours you work, the wages." Somebody else yelled out: "Benefits." Marge wrote these things on the board. She got to Phil who was sitting there next to Jeff. I believe she skipped Jeff. Mr. Armstrong was standing right next to Phil. She said: "Have you got one?" Phil said: "I can't think of one." She said: "Honestly Phil. Wake up." Then she went to Joe, the white boy. Joe and Jeff are the only white boys I've seen in the program. The two girls are white. He said: "I can't think of any." She got to Jason and asked him if he could think of anything else. He said: "Yeah, you could ask 'em how many of the products they made each year." Marge said: "Yes, you could ask about production. How about Leroy, do you have any ideas, Leroy?" He said: "No." Mr. Armstrong was standing over in the corner and saying to Phil in a low voice: "Now you know what kinds of questions you ask when you go for a job?" Phil said: "Training, what kind of training do you have to have?" Marge said: "Oh yes, that's right, training." Jason said out loud but not yelling: "How much schooling you need to get it." Marge kept listing them.

O.C.: Marge was quite animated. If I hadn't seen her like this before I would think she was putting on a show for the people from central office.

Source: From R. C. Bogdan and S. K. Biklen, *Qualitative Research for Education: An Introduction to Theory and Methods, 3/e.* © 1998 by Allyn & Bacon. Reproduced by permission.

FIGURE 7.4   Example
of a researcher's memo.

> *2. Teachers' use of the concept of mainstreaming.* When I first started this study I thought that regular class teachers would or would not want to be involved with disabled children on the basis of their feelings and experiences with "labeled" kids. While this seems to be true in some cases, a lot of the disposition to the program seems unrelated to the particulars about it or the population served. Some teachers feel that the administration is in general not supportive and they approach what they consider "additional" problems with the disposition that "I have enough." When I say "the administration," I mean the central office, those whom they see as determining the outcome of the contract bargaining. Others concentrate on the principal and feel that he works hard to make things work for them so if he wants them to get involved in a new effort, they will. This needs a lot of working out but it may be fruitful to pursue looking at what one's position is on mainstreaming and how it is talked about as being a manifestation of conflict and competing interests in the school. Also, this reminds me of how particular teachers think of the various special education classes. Marge was telling me that she likes kids with learning disabilities because they aren't trouble-makers like those in the resource room who have emotional disturbances.

Source: From R. C. Bogdan and S. K. Biklen, *Qualitative Research for Education: An Introduction to Theory and Methods, 3/e.*
© 1998 by Allyn & Bacon. Reproduced by permission.

Guidelines for Field Notes

The following guidelines describe important aspects for successfully recording and organizing field notes in observational research.

- Start slowly. Do not assume you know what you're looking for until you "experience" the setting and participants for a while.
- Try to enter the field with no preconceptions. Try to recognize and dismiss your own assumptions and biases and remain open to what you see; try to see things through the participants' perspectives.
- Write up your field notes as soon as possible. When you're done, list the main ideas or themes you've observed and recorded. Don't discuss your observation until the field notes are written; discussion may alter your initial perspective.
- List the date, site, time, and topic on *every* set of field notes. Leave wide margins to write in your impressions next to sections of the descriptive field notes. Write only on one side of a page. This will save you much photocopying when the time comes to "cut and paste" the field notes into different categories. Draw diagrams of the site.
- In writing field notes, first list key words related to your observation, then outline what you saw and heard. Then, using the key words and outline, write your detailed field notes.
- Although collected together, keep the descriptive and reflective sections of field notes separate. Focus on writing detailed descriptive field notes.
- Write down your hunches, questions, and insights after each observation. Use memos.
- Number the lines or paragraphs of your field notes. This will help you find particular sections when needed.

Field notes are obviously of prime importance in qualitative research studies of most kinds. Thus, it is important to understand the complexity involved in developing accurate and descriptive field notes. To appreciate the complexity, imagine yourself trying to write, *in detail,* what happened during just one class of your research methods course. What was the physical setting like? Who was present? How did they act? What was the instructor doing and saying and how was he or she interacting with the students? What took place? What was usual and unusual? The task appears even more daunting when you consider that you are expected to provide sharp, detailed descriptions that represent what was happening, not your interpretation of what was happening. Qualitative researchers can produce rich, deep descriptions and understandings of settings and participants, but it takes a great deal of hard and detailed work to do so.

NONPARTICIPANT DATA COLLECTION METHODS FOR OBSERVATIONAL STUDIES

Earlier we mentioned that nonparticipant observers are on the outside, looking in. They typically record behaviors of the object of the observation; they do not interact with them. Nonparticipant observation includes both naturalistic observation and simulation observation, and typically involves observation of human subjects. The steps in conducting observational research are essentially the same as for other types of qualitative research. Selecting and defining the problem are essentially the same, as is participant selection. Like the interview technique (discussed in the next section) observation is time consuming and typically involves smaller samples than do quantitative methods such as questionnaire and interview studies.

Naturalistic Observation

Certain kinds of behavior can only be (or can best be) observed as they occur naturally. In such situations the observer purposely does not control or manipulate the setting being observed. In fact, the researcher works very hard at not affecting the observed situation in any way. **Naturalistic observation** is an important qualitative method. The main difference between a quantitative and qualitative approach to naturalistic observation is that the quantitative researcher approaches the observation with a predetermined idea of what behaviors will be observed, while the qualitative researcher tends not to have a preformed focus. The intent is to record and study behavior as it normally occurs. As an example, classroom behavior of the teacher, student, and the interactions between teacher and student can best be studied through naturalistic observation. Insights gained as a result of naturalistic observation often form the foundation for more controlled research in an area. The work of Piaget, for example, involved primarily naturalistic observation of children. His research and the research that it stimulated have provided education with many important findings regarding concept development in children.

Simulation Observation

In **simulation observation** the researcher creates a situation to be observed and tells participants what activities they are to engage in. This technique allows the researcher to observe behavior that occurs infrequently in natural situations or not at all—for example, having a teacher trainee role play a teacher–parent conference. The major disadvantage of this type of observation is that it is not natural, and the behaviors exhibited by those observed may not be the behaviors that would occur in a natural setting. Those being observed may behave the way they think they *should* behave, rather than the way they normally *would* behave. In reality, this problem is not as serious as it may sound. Individuals being observed often get carried away with their roles and often exhibit very true-to-life emotions. Besides, even if those observed "fake it," at least they show that they are aware of the correct way to behave or perform. A student teacher who demonstrates the correct way to interact with an irate parent at least knows what should be done.

Two major types of simulation are individual role playing and team role playing. In individual role playing the researcher is interested in the behavior of one person, although other "players" may be involved. The individual is given a role, a situation, and a problem to solve. The observer records and evaluates the person's solution to the problem and the way in which she or he executed it. As an example, a teacher trainee might be told,

> Yesterday Billy Bungle was caught drawing pictures on his desk. You made him stay after school and wash and wax all the desks. The principal has just informed you that a very upset Mrs. Bungle is on her way to see you. What will you say to Mrs. Bungle?

In a team role-playing situation, a small group is presented with a situation and a problem, and the group solution is recorded and evaluated. As an example, a group might be told, "The faculty has appointed you a committee of six. Your charge is to come up with possible solutions to the problem of student fights in the halls, an occurrence that has been increasing."

Definition of Observational Variables

There is no way that an observer can observe and record everything that goes on during an observation session, especially in a natural setting such as a classroom. The research hypothesis or question determines what will be observed. Thus, in a study concerned with the effectiveness of assertive discipline in reducing instances of disruptive behavior, attention would be focused only on "disruptive behavior." The term *disruptive behavior,* however, does not have universal meaning, so the researcher must clearly define (operationalize) what specific behaviors do and do not make up disruptive behavior. In the earlier example, "disruptive behavior" might include talking out of turn, making extraneous noises, throwing things, making offensive noises, and getting out of one's seat, whereas doodling during class would probably not be considered disruptive.

In quantitative research, once an observational topic is defined, observations must be quantified so that all observers will count the behavioral activities in the same way. If Gorgo screams and tips over his chair at the same time, that could be considered as one instance of disruptive behavior or as two instances. Researchers typically divide observation sessions into a number of specific observation periods. That is, they define a time unit for observation. The length of the time unit will usually be a function of both the behavior to be observed and the frequency with which it normally occurs. If observation is simply a matter of observing and recording a high-frequency behavior, the time unit may be as small as 10 seconds. If any judgments or inferences are required on the part of the observer, or if the behavior is a low-frequency behavior, the time unit is typically longer, perhaps 30 seconds or 1 minute. There should be correspondence between actual frequency and recorded frequency. Once the time unit has been established, the observer records what occurred in each observation period. If during a 15-second interval a student exhibits disruptive behavior, this would be indicated, regardless of how often disruptive behavior occurred. In contrast, qualitative researchers are more interested in describing the behavior itself, together with its antecedents and its effects on other participants.

Recording Observations

One point, which at first reading may seem obvious, is that quantitative observers should not only observe but also record observed behavior. Even if you are interested in two types of behavior (e.g., teacher behavior and student behavior), the observer should only have to make one decision at a time. Thus, if two types of behavior are to be observed they should probably be observed alternately. In other words, for the teacher–student observation example, teacher behavior might be observed during the first, third, fifth, seventh (and so forth) observation periods, and student behavior might be observed during the second, fourth, sixth, and eighth periods. Such a procedure would present a fairly accurate picture of what occurred in the observed classroom. It is also a good idea to alternate observation periods and recording periods, especially if any inference is required on the part of the observers. Thus, we might have the observers observe for 15 seconds, record for 5 seconds, observe for 15 seconds, record for 5 seconds, and so forth. This approach controls for the fact that the observer is not paying complete attention while recording, and tends to increase the reliability of observations. Qualitative researchers endeavor to record simultaneous observations of as many behaviors as they can attend to.

Although the point is debatable, as a general rule for both quantitative and qualitative research it is better to record observations at the time the behavior occurs. Since each quantitative observation must be made within a set period of time, for example, 15 seconds or 5 minutes, the recording process should be as simplified as possible. Most observation studies facilitate recording by using an agreed code and a recording instrument. Often the task is not just to determine whether a behavior occurred but to record what actually occurred. The classic Flanders System, for example, which is widely used for quantitative classroom observation, classifies all teacher behavior and all student behavior into 1 of 10 categories, each of which is represented by a number. Figure 7.5 describes the 10 categories. Thus, if a teacher praises a student, the observer records that behavior 2 occurred.

Both quantitative and qualitative researchers have developed some very good coding systems. Go to the ETS Test Collection Database and search under "observation" to see brief descriptions of many quantitative observational instruments.

There are a number of different types of quantitative observation recording forms. Probably the most often and easily used one is a checklist of all behaviors to be observed so that the observer can simply check each behavior as it occurs. This permits the observer to spend his or

Teacher Talk	Response	1. *Accepts feeling.* Accepts and clarifies an attitude or the feeling tone of a student in a nonthreatening manner. Feelings may be positive or negative. Predicting and recalling feelings are included. 2. *Praises or encourages.* Praises or encourages students; says "um hum" or "go on"; makes jokes that release tension, but not at the expense of a student. 3. *Accepts or uses ideas of students.* Acknowledges student talk. Clarifies, builds on, or asks questions based on student ideas.
		4. *Asks questions.* Asks questions about content or procedures, based on teacher ideas, with the intent that a student will answer.
	Initiation	5. *Lectures.* Offers facts or opinions about content or procedures; expresses *his* own ideas, gives *his* own explanation, or cites an authority other than a student. 6. *Gives directions.* Gives directions, commands, or orders with which a student is expected to comply. 7. *Criticizes students or justifies authority.* Makes statements intended to change student behavior from nonacceptable to acceptable patterns; corrects student behaviors; bawls someone out. Or states why the teacher is doing what he is doing; uses extreme self-reference.
Student Talk	Response	8. *Student talk—response.* Student talk in response to teacher contact which structures or limits the situation. Freedom to express own ideas is limited.
	Initiation	9. *Student talk—initiation.* Students initiate or express own ideas either spontaneously or in response to teacher's soliciting initiation. Freedom to develop opinions and a line of thought; going beyond existing structure.
Silence		10. *Silence or confusion.* Pauses, short periods of silence, and periods of confusion in which communication cannot be understood by the observer.

FIGURE 7.5 Flanders Interaction Analysis Categories (FIAC).

her time thinking about what is occurring rather than how to record it. Figure 7.6 shows the recording form for the Flanders observational instrument. It is basically a checklist in which the 10 categories shown in Figure 7.5 are listed on the vertical axis and the observation periods are indicated across the top (1–30). With the exception of categories 1 and 2, which must be described in writing, other categories are indicated with a checkmark. The time line shows the sequence of events that occurred over a period of time. During observation periods 1 and 2, the teacher was asking questions. During the next four periods students were expressing their ideas, and so forth. Thus, Figure 7.6 represents a classroom interaction in which the students are doing most of the talking and the teacher is encouraging and supporting their participation. In addition to time sampling, other data collection approaches include observing the duration of a behavior or the number of times a behavior occurs.

Rating scales are also sometimes used in observational research. These require the observer to observe, evaluate, and rate the observed performance. For example, an observer might rate a teacher's explanation to a student as 1 (not very clear), 2 (clear), or 3 (very clear). Although as many as five rating categories are used, three is probably the ideal number. Do not use more than five rating categories, because the more categories, the more difficult it becomes to reliably classify performance. An observer could probably discriminate between "not very clear" and "clear" fairly easily, but deciding between "very unclear" and "not very clear" would not be as simple and would lower reliability.

Before developing your own observation form, you should check to see if there is a standardized observation form that is appropriate for your study. Check the ETS Test Collection Database or other sources cited in Chapter 5. Using a standardized observation form has the same advantages as using a standardized test in terms of time saved, validity, and reliability. Also, as with standardized tests, the results of your study can be compared with the results of other studies that have used the same form. The Flanders System, for example, has been used in a number of quantitative studies.

Assessing Observer Reliability

Unreliable observations are as useless as an unreliable test. Determining observer reliability generally requires that at least two observers independently make observations so that their recorded judgments can then be compared to determine agreement. If we wanted to estimate the reliability of scoring for a short-answer test, we could correlate the scores resulting from two independent scorings of the same answers. In other words, all of the tests would be scored twice, and the correlation between the two sets of scores would be our estimate of the reliability of scoring. When we observe behavior, however, we are not typically dealing with scores. In quantitative research, we are dealing with frequencies, that is, how frequently certain behaviors occurred. In these cases reliability is generally calculated based on percent agreement. For example, we might have two independent observers recording the number of disruptive behaviors exhibited by a selected student during a 1-hour period. One observer recorded 20 incidents and the other observer recorded 25 incidents. We can compute interobserver reliability by dividing the total number of agreed observations by the total number of agreed and

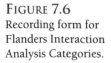

FIGURE 7.6
Recording form for
Flanders Interaction
Analysis Categories.

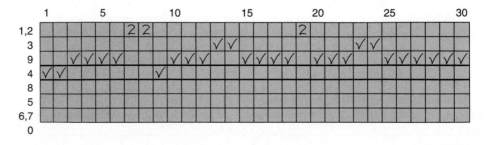

disagreed observations. That is, suppose that 18 observations were common across the two observers. That means that one observer had two disagreed upon observations and the other had seven disagreed observations. The percent agreement is 18 (number of agreements) divided by 27 (total of agreements and disagreements), or .67 reliability.

In qualitative research, the emphasis is on the observer's ability to accurately record the details of the observed behavior. One solution is to record the observation with a VCR or audiocassette recorder to play back at a later time. Another advantage to recording observations is that you can replay the recording as often as you like. If the behaviors observed are at all complex or occur at a fairly rapid rate, the recording may be difficult to obtain reliable observations from a single observation. If you record the behavior, you can play it back to your heart's content, as can other observers. This is especially useful if important judgments or evaluations are required of the observer. You want such judgments and evaluations to be as reliable as possible. Assuming usage of a valid, reliable observation system, regardless of whether observations are written as they occur or while viewing or listening to a tape, the best way to increase observer reliability is by thoroughly training and monitoring observers.

Training Observers.   The most important effect on the reliability and validity of observations is that of the observers. In order to determine agreement among observers, at least two observers are required. That means that there will be at least one other person besides yourself (or two, if you are not going to personally observe) who needs to be familiar with the observational procedures. Additional observers need to be trained to have assurance that all observers are observing and recording the same behaviors in the same way. Thus, they must be instructed as to what behaviors to observe, how behaviors are to be coded, how behaviors are to be recorded, and how often (time unit). Observers should participate in numerous practice sessions at which they observe and score situations similar to those to be involved in the study. Then observers should compare their recordings. Each point of disagreement should be discussed so that the observer who differs from the expected understands why. Practice sessions using recordings of behavior are most effective, because segments with which observers have difficulty can be replayed for discussion and feedback purposes. Estimates of observer reliability should be calculated periodically to determine the effectiveness of the training and practice; observer reliability should increase with each session. Training may be terminated when a satisfactory level of agreement is achieved (say, 80%).

Monitoring Observers.   Training observers only guarantees that the desired level of interobserver reliability is attained. It does not guarantee that this level will be maintained throughout the study. Observers can get tired, bored, overconfident, and forgetful over time. The major way to ensure continued satisfactory levels of reliability is to monitor the observers. The ideal would be to constantly monitor all observers, but this is usually not feasible. At the very least, however, spot checks of observer agreement should be made.

INTERVIEWS

A second important qualitative data collection approach is the interview. An **interview** is a purposeful interaction between two or more people focused on one person trying to get information from the other person. Interviews permit researchers to obtain important data they cannot acquire from observation. For example, observation cannot provide information about past events, or the way things used to be before Mr. Hardnosed became principal, or why Ms. Haddit has had it and is considering transferring to another school. Information about these events cannot be observed; they must be obtained from peoples' own words. Interviewers can explore and probe participants' responses to gather more in-depth data about their experiences and feelings. They can examine attitudes, interests, feelings, concerns, and values more easily than using observation.

It is important to consider two additional aspects of interviews. First, not all qualitative researchers who gather data through interviews would accept the definition of interview just stated. Many researchers would not view the interview as a process of "pulling out" information from respondents about the topic studied. They would say that interviewing is a joint construction of meaning between the researcher and the participant, not just a construction of the participant. Second, while the concept of an interview study seems straightforward, it can be a complex and difficult undertaking when the gender, culture, and life experiences of the interviewer and participant are quite different. Depending on the characteristics of the researcher and the participant, there can be issues of who "controls" the interview, the accuracy of responses provided, and the extent to which the language of the interviewee and the researcher are similar enough to permit meaningful inferences about the topic studied.

Interview methods can be a study's sole data collection method or may be used in conjunction with other data collection methods, such as participant observation. Combined with other data gathering approaches, interviews can lead to identifying new topics to explore and can help explain data collected from other methods. For example, issues that arise from observation may be clarified or expanded by interviewing participants.

Interviews vary in a number of ways. They may be a one-time interview or they may involve multiple interviews with the same participant. They may involve a single participant as in a case study, or a number of participants as in ethnographic research. Participants may be interviewed individually or in groups. Interviews may vary in length from a few minutes to a few hours. They may be **structured,** with a specified set of questions to be asked, or they may be **unstructured,** with questions being prompted by the flow of the interview. Some qualitative studies employ both structured and unstructured approaches. For example, structured interviews may be used to gather basic information or a career history from participants at the start of a study, while an unstructured interview may be used further into the study to obtain more complex or personal information. Semistructured interviews combine both structured and unstructured approaches. Interviews may be formal and planned (we'll meet Tuesday at 1:00 to discuss your perceptions) or informal and unplanned (I'm glad I caught you in the corridor; I've been meaning to ask you . . .). You should note that the interviewer will almost always be face to face with research participants. Therefore be cautious about entering the setting unobtrusively, build rapport and trust with participants before probing sensitive issues, and consider your demeanor. All of these will contribute to the success of your study.

Types of Interviews

Interviews range from open ended and spontaneous to closed ended and prescribed, with various intermediate levels. In general, qualitative interviews tend to be on the unstructured rather than the structured side of the continuum shown in Table 7.2. One of the emphases in qualitative research is its focus on depth of understanding. Usually the depth sought is more readily obtained from interviews that permit probing of participants' responses, exploring unplanned topics that arise, and obtaining clarification of participants' responses. Thus, qualitative interviews are more free flowing and open than are quantitative interviews.

Recognize, however, that it is easier to conduct structured interviews than less structured ones, because structured interviews contain the questions to be asked in the interview. Although an interviewer is always able to probe and explore during the interview, unstructured interviewing, even in small doses, requires insight, recognition of needed probing, and finesse in posing questions that will elicit the information sought. For researchers inexperienced in interviewing, an interview protocol is a helpful tool that can provide a safety net as they refine their sensitivity to participants and to interviewing technique (see Figure 7.7). The focus of the interview can be on one or many areas. For example, interviews may focus on a participants' prior history (Where and when have you taught?), attitudes (How do you feel about parents' involvement in your classroom?), perceptions (What do you think are the main strengths and

TABLE 7.2 Continuum of Interviews with Increasing Amounts of Structure

Unstructured	Partially Structured	Semistructured	Structured	Totally Structured
Exploratory, only area of interest is chosen, interviewer "follows his/her nose" in formulating and ordering questions. Impromptu conversations that occur during observation are of this nature.	Area is chosen and questions are formulated but order is up to interviewer. Interviewer may add questions or modify them as deemed appropriate. Questions are open-ended, and responses are recorded nearly verbatim, possibly taped.	Questions and order of presentation are determined. Questions have open ends; interviewer records the essence of each response.	Questions and order are predetermined, and responses are coded by the interviewer as they are given.	Questions, order, and coding are predetermined, and the respondent is presented with alternatives for each question so that phrasing of responses is structured. Questions are self-coding in that each choice is preassigned a code.

Source: D. Krathwohl, *Methods of Educational and Social Science Research, 2/e,* 1998, p. 287. Copyright 1998. Reprinted by permission of Addison Wesley Educational Publications, Inc.

Interview Protocol
Project: University Reaction to a Terrorist Incident

Time of interview:
Date:
Place:
Interviewer:
Interviewee:
Position of interviewee:

(Briefly describe the project)

Questions:
  1. What has been your role in the incident?

  2. What has happened since the event that you have been involved in?

  3. What has been the impact on the university community of this incident?

  4. What larger ramifications, if any, exist from the incident?

  5. To whom should we talk to find out more about campus reaction to the incident?

(Thank individual for participating in this interview. Assure him or her of confidentiality of responses and potential future interviews.)

FIGURE 7.7 Sample of interview protocol.

Source: Creswell, J. W. (1998). *Qualitative Inquiry and Research Design: Choosing among Five Traditions,* p. 127. Copyright 1998 Sage Publications. Reprinted by permission of Sage Publications, Inc.

weaknesses of the first- and second-year teachers in this school?), knowledge (How much do you know about the planned rearrangement of the fifth-grade teams?), concerns (Are there any school policies or emphases that concern you?), and interpersonal relations (How would you describe your relationships with the principal and vice principal?). Asking questions that deal with values, feelings, and opinions, such as, "How did you feel when you found out that Mr. Hardcase was going to be appointed principal?" and "How has teacher morale been affected?" require both methodological and interpersonal skills on the part of the interviewer.

A good interviewer is always looking for openings to probe deeper. Although interviews often start with mundane questions and gradually ease into more sensitive and complex questions, as an alert interviewer, you must respond to probing opportunities as they arise. If a response to an apparently innocuous question, "How long have you felt this way?" is "Too, too, too long!" your antennae should go up, prompting a followup question such as, "Why do you say that?" Similarly, avoid posing questions that produce a yes or no answer; or, if such questions are asked, follow up with "Why?" or "Tell me why you feel that way." Or, if a participant tells you that the reaction of the students today was "interesting," ask what the participant means by *interesting,* or ask for examples of what made the students' reactions interesting. Remember, the aim of the qualitative interview is to find out about the participants, where they are "coming from," what they believe, experienced, felt, and so forth.

In addition to the range of structure that interviews can have, other aspects of interviews can vary. For example, the length of an interview can be short or long, although it is not recommended that interviews last more than 1 to 2 hours. The nature of the interview (structured versus unstructured), the amount and nature of the information desired (factual demographic information versus attitude and value personal information), and the attention span of the interviewer and interviewee (short versus long) all influence the nature of the interview. Also, you may interview each participant only once or more than once during the study. Single interviews are efficient, but cannot usually provide depth of data, nor allow for followup questions. Multiple participant interviews allow for followup questions and can build on one another to probe deeply and reveal changes over time. However, they are time consuming and can produce voluminous data to organize and interpret. Interviews can be with a single participant or a group of participants (often called a *focus group*). A focus group is especially useful in obtaining a variety of views or opinions about a topic or issue, which can then be used in interviews with single participants. One downside to focus groups is that a few participants may be overly outspoken and overshadow quieter participants.

Collecting Data from Interviews

Interviewers have three basic choices for collecting their data: taking notes during the interview, writing notes after the interview, and audio- or videotaping the interview. The last choice is the most viable, although all can be used in a study. Taking notes during the interview is distracting and can alter the flow of the session. Writing notes after the interview is better than trying to write during the interview, but it is difficult to remember the contents of the interview. Plus, long interview sessions limit the usefulness of these two approaches. Thus, the data collection method of choice is audio- or videotape recording, which provides a verbatim account of the session. Also, tapes provide researchers with the original data for use at any time. Although a few participants may balk at recording the interview, most participants will not, especially if you promise them confidentiality. Make sure that the recording machine is in good working order (new batteries, too) prior to entering the interview setting.

To work most productively, it is useful to transcribe the tape recordings. This is a time-consuming task, especially for long interviews. If you choose to do the transcribing instead of hiring someone to transcribe (a costly alternative), it would help to use short interview sessions, if feasible. Transcribing one 60-minute tape may take 4 or 5 more hours. When transcribing, write the date, subject discussed, and participant (using a coded name) on the transcript. Number all pages. Make sure a different indicator is given and used to identify the various persons speaking on the tape.

The transcripts are the field notes for interview data. They should be reviewed against the tape for accuracy. Interview transcripts are voluminous and usually have to be reduced to focus on the data pertinent to the study. Sometimes this is difficult to do. During data analysis the transcript will be read and important (or thought to be important) sections labeled to indicate their importance. This process of culling the transcripts will be described in the next chapter.

Guidelines for Interviewing

A number of actions can improve the collection of interview data.[5]

- Listen more, talk less. Listening is the most important part of interviewing.
- Follow up on what participants say and ask questions when you don't understand.
- Avoid leading questions; ask open-ended questions.
- Don't interrupt. Learn how to wait.
- Keep participants focused and ask for concrete details.
- Tolerate silence. It means the participant is thinking.
- Don't be judgmental about participants' views or beliefs. You're there to learn about their perspectives, whether you agree with them or not.
- Don't debate with participants over their responses. You are a recorder, not a debater.

THREATS TO THE QUALITY OF OBSERVATIONS AND INTERVIEWS

Two main threats to the validity of observation and interview studies are observer bias and the observer effect. For example, the very presence of the researcher in the setting may create potential problems. The situation may be "seen" differently than it would have been through the eyes of a different researcher (observer bias) or may be a somewhat different situation than it would have been if the researcher were not present (observer effect). Although these problems are not unique to qualitative research, they are potentially more serious because of the more intimate involvement of researcher and participants.

Observer bias refers to invalid information that results from the perspective the researcher brings to the study. Each researcher brings to a setting a highly individual background, set of experiences, preferences, attitudes, and the like, which, in turn, affect not only what and how she or he observes, but also her or his personal reflections and interpretations. The qualitative researcher runs the risk of identifying with one or more participants or being negative toward others, which can influence the way the researcher weights information from different groups. For example, after attending a number of faculty meetings a researcher might tend to identify with the values of the teachers, and observations and interpretations of principal–teacher interactions would be affected by this role identification. In other words, no two researchers in the same situation would have identical field notes. (No, not even identical twins!) This apparently inevitable subjectivity is, however, both a weakness and a strength of participant observation. The more involved the researcher is, the greater the degree of subjectivity likely to creep into the observations. On the other hand, the greater the involvement, the greater the opportunity for acquiring in-depth understanding and insight.

Thus, qualitative researchers must walk a fine line in their attempt to be at the same time both involved and unbiased. What is important is that they be aware of this challenge and make every effort to meet it. For example, they may try to minimize the effects of their personal biases on their findings by conscientiously recording their thoughts, feelings, and

[5]Seidman, I. E. (1991). *Interviewing as qualitative research.* New York: Teachers College, Columbia University, adapted from pp. 56–71.

reactions about what they observe. Of course, detecting bias and eliminating it are not the same thing. Qualitative researchers, however, do not claim that they can eliminate bias. They do maintain, however, and rightfully so, that they have a number of strategies for minimizing its effect on the results of their research. These strategies are discussed in the next subsection.

Other types of observer bias are similar to those described as response sets in Chapter 5. A response set is the tendency of an observer to rate the majority of observees as above average, average, or below average regardless of the observees' actual behavior. A related problem is the **halo effect,** whereby initial impressions concerning an observee (positive or negative) affect subsequent observations. A final major source of observer bias occurs when the observer's knowledge of the observees or the purposes of the study affect observations. The observer might tend to see what she or he expected or wanted to see. In this instance, having observers view recordings rather than observe live behavior would help, since observers would not have to be told which recordings were made early and which were made late.

The other side of the coin is called the **observer effect** and refers to the impact of the observer's participation on the setting or participants being studied. In other words, the situation is somewhat different than it would have been if the observer did not participate; and, of course, the greater the researcher's participation, the greater the likely observer effect. It is not news that persons being observed may behave atypically simply because they are being observed. Would you behave exactly the same as you normally would on a given day if you knew you were being observed? Probably not! Again, while this problem is by no means unique to qualitative research, it is potentially more serious, since the researcher is trying to study how people naturally behave in their natural setting. The larger the observer effect, the less "natural" the setting is. The best way to handle the problem is to make observers aware of it so they can attempt to be as inconspicuous as possible.

Another strategy to lessen the observer effect is for the researcher to be excessively unassuming and nonthreatening initially, and only gradually increase participation and entry into the setting. Thus, for example, at the first faculty meeting the researcher may simply observe and appear cordial. By the fourth or fifth meeting, people will become used to his or her presence and tend to be their usual selves. As noted, it also helps if the exact nature of the researcher's inquiry is not described in any more detail than is necessary ethically or legally. The fact that persons being observed may initially behave differently than usual is a problem, but focusing participants on the specific research targets to be examined can be much worse! So, for example, it would probably be sufficient if the *official* reason given for the researcher's presence were "to observe high school faculty meetings," rather than "to observe principal–teacher interactions." Qualitative researchers are well aware that they cannot totally eliminate observer effects. They do, however, make every effort to recognize, minimize, record, and report them.

ENHANCING VALIDITY AND REDUCING BIAS

The data collected from and about participants in qualitative research studies are voluminous, generally nonquantitative, and rich in detail. Because qualitative data extend far beyond superficial issues, and because each researcher brings her or his own perspectives and biases to the study, important questions that all qualitative researchers must ask and answer are, "How much confidence can I place in the data I have collected?" "What is the quality of the data I have obtained from participants?" "Have my personal biases intruded into my data collection?" These questions relate to the validity of the data collected.

Qualitative researchers use several strategies to check on and enhance a study's validity. Used in combination, the following strategies can reduce researcher bias and improve the validity of the data collected.

- Extend the study by staying in the field for a longer period to obtain additional data that can be compared to earlier data or to compare participant's consistency of responses.
- Include additional participants to broaden the representativeness of the study and thus the database.
- Make a concerted effort to obtain participant trust and comfort, thus providing more detailed, honest information from participants.
- Try to recognize one's own biases and preferences and be honest with oneself in seeking them out.
- Work with another researcher, and independently gather and compare data collected from subgroups of the participants.
- Allow participants to review and critique field notes or tape recordings for accuracy and meaning, but only at the end of the entire data collection period. Doing this in the middle of data collection may influence participants' responses or actions in subsequent data collections. Note that the comments and reactions of participants at the end of the study provide additional research data.
- Use verbatim accounts of observations or interviews by collecting and recording data with tape recordings or detailed field notes, including quotes.
- Record in a journal one's own reflections, concerns, and uncertainties during the study and refer to them when examining the data collected.
- Examine unusual or contradictory results for explanations; ignoring such "outliers" may represent a bias in the researcher's perspective toward the more "conventional" data collected.
- Corroborate data by using **triangulation.** Researchers triangulate by using different data sources to confirm one another, as when an interview, related documents, and recollections of other participants produce the same descriptions of an event, or when a participant responds similarly to a personal question asked on three different occasions. Examining documents to corroborate participant information is useful because documents are "unobtrusive" measures that are not affected by the presence of the researcher. Participant absenteeism records, for example, might be one unobtrusive measure of stress that could be compared to the participant's interview comments on stress. It is not likely that data derived from different sources will all be biased in the same way.

In reality, it is virtually impossible to obtain totally unbiased and perfectly valid data in a qualitative research study. The same can be said for quantitative research studies. However, the evolving design of the study, the volume and nature of the data collected, and the personal interpretive role the researcher takes in qualitative research make bias and invalid data serious concerns. Interpretation is desired and expected of qualitative research, and efforts to change this would defeat the purpose of such research. Nonetheless, attention to issues of bias and validity are important for maintaining the integrity of qualitative research.

EXAMPLES OF QUALITATIVE RESEARCH: PARTICIPANTS, METHODOLOGY, AND DATA COLLECTION PROCEDURES

In Chapter 6 we examined features of two qualitative studies, "The Expression of Care in the Rough and Tumble Play of Boys" and "The Dislocated Textile Worker in Rural Alabama: A Portrait." In particular, we examined their abstracts, research topics, and introductory information. In this chapter we continue our examination by looking at the sections in them addressing methodology, procedures, and participants. First, we examine characteristics of "The Expression of Care in the Rough and Tumble Play of Boys."[6]

---

[6]Reed, T., and Brown, M. (2000). The expression of care in the rough and tumble play of boys. *Journal of Research in Childhood Education, 15*(1), 104–116. Copyright 2000 by the Association for Childhood Education. Reprinted by permission.

The Expression of Care in the Rough and Tumble Play of Boys

Research is carried out in participants' setting. →

Methodology

This qualitative study examined the way in which primary school age boys engage in R&T, and described their interactions and relationships with each other in their natural surroundings. The importance of this research was initially demonstrated by Karl Groos in 1901 and brought to mainstream research by Blurton-Jones in 1967 (Pellegrini, 1995). The value of qualitative research is well-documented in the literature (e.g., Eisner & Peshkin, 1990; Flinders & Mills, 1993; Noffke & Stevenson, 1995). A critical element in this research is the phenomenological interview, as described by Seidman (1991), which employs open-ended questions with the specific purpose of building upon the participants' responses. For this study, boys were videotaped while engaged in R&T; later, they were asked to view the tapes and give their personal interpretations of the R&T experience. Reliability and validity were achieved by using techniques described by Lincoln and Guba (1985).

Interview (open-ended questions) is one method of data collection. →

Many hours of observation and data collection. →

Prolonged engagement, which allowed for learning the culture and establishing trust, encompassed a total of 30 hours of observation over three weeks, resulting in the recording of 10 hours of play. Of those 10 hours, three consisted primarily of R&T. Persistent observation resulted in the recording of several types of R&T, including one game that would become the focus of this study. Triangulation involved the participants interpreting play previously videotaped by the researcher. This process was also audio- and video-recorded and later transcribed for further data analysis.

Finally, three early childhood researchers reviewed a segment of R&T (taken from this study), achieving an inter-rater reliability of 97.4% in recognizing R&T as described by Harlow (1962). While the participants initially "hammed it up" for the camera, they quickly fell into normal play routines. Any play that appeared to be contrived was omitted from this study. Due to unexpected and extremely loud noise interference, audio was not recorded during outdoor play.

Procedures

Videotaping play is another data collection method, which allows the researcher to examine the data multiple times. →

The criteria for identifying and recording an episode as R&T included reciprocal role taking, the play face, vigorous movement, and alternating between the roles of victim and victimizer (Pellegrini, 1995). The first step of the data collection was the videotaping of all play that included R&T (see Table 1). Play that was determined to consist of R&T was re-recorded on a separate videotape to be used at a later date. A specialized game, evident and identified by the participants as "Smear the Queer," became a primary source of R&T.

Table 1
Types of Behavior Demonstrated in R&T

Type of R&T Play	Frequency
Tackling	30
Chase and flee	22
Light touching	11
Pushing or shoving	7
Avoided tackling	5
Shadow boxing	5
Picking up and dropping a player	4
Throwing dirt, sand, ice cubes	5
Hiding	3
Juking (faking)	3
Kicking the ball at players against a wall	3
Kick behind knee	3
Pinching	2
Tripping	2
Climbing up wall with feet after running start	1
Running up the sliding board and jumping off	1
Arm wrestling	1
Grabbing feet on monkey bars	1
Total	119

The same procedure was followed by the researcher in the recording and re-recording of examples of care during R&T (see Table 2). It should be noted that although every attempt was made to avoid leading questions, occasionally the researcher did "tease" out answers when participants seemed to have difficulty finding words to describe their thoughts. The final step of the data collection was the creation of two separate videotapes that were viewed by the participants, one for examples of R&T and one for examples of caring behavior.

Table 2

Types and Instances of Care During R&T and the Game

Caring Experience	Frequency
Physical	
Helped the fallen player up	7
Hugged and/or had arms around shoulders	5
Lingering on the ground after a tackle	5
Brushed off clothing	4
Jumped up and down with hands on another's shoulder	2
Balanced player before giving a gentle shove	1
Placed hand on buttocks	1
Held hands	1
Subtotal Physical	26
Non Physical, but Close	
Checked to see if he was okay	11
Stopped the game until a player catches his breath	9
Held game up while boy composed himself	8
Called time out when a player falls accidentally	5
Helped find lost items	4
Walked with a player while he regains composure	3
Picked up glasses	3
Called for or took the player to the teacher	2
Took hurt child to teacher	1
Called for teacher	1
Subtotal Non Physical	47
Total Physical and Non Physical	73

Participants were involved in two individual interviews, plus one final group experience. During the first interview, the participants were asked to view and comment on R&T episodes in which they were featured. Each participant was asked specific questions (see Table 3) about the same episodes to determine whether or not they viewed the play episodes as R&T. The participants were videotaped watching the previously recorded play episodes. Later on, typewritten transcripts of the interview were made. During the second interview, the exact same process was repeated, except that it emphasized caring behaviors (see Table 4). In the third and final data-gathering experience, a group of children viewed episodes of caring behaviors in which the researcher allowed the participants to respond spontaneously in an uncontrolled environment.

Table 3
Questions Asked During the First Interview

Do you know who I am?
Do you know what I have been doing here?
What are they playing?
How do you play it?
Are they your friends?
Why didn't someone get hurt?
What would you do if someone were playing mean?
How can you tell?

Table 4
Questions Asked During the Second Interview

Do you know what we talked about last week?
Where was his hand?
Why didn't he hit him?
Why did he take him to the teacher?
What are these boys doing?
What can you tell by the look on his face?
What is happening with the boy's glasses?
How can you tell they are friends or care about each other?

Setting and Activity Schedule

Observations were conducted in a youth center for school-age children within an Air Force military installation located in the southeastern United States. Children were videotaped during a 10-day period from 2:30 p.m. until 5:30 p.m. during free play (supervised but unorganized). The director of the youth center announced to the students that they would be videotaped while playing, but gave no further directions or instructions. In addition, staff members were asked not to intervene in play that the researcher was videotaping. Parents were informed in writing that the research was taking place and were asked to grant permission to videotape their child. During this time the researcher acted as an observer and did not interact with the participants during the collection of data.

Participants

The student population of the youth center was composed from a diverse socioeconomic background, including Asian, Black, Hispanic, and White children. No specific figures regarding income levels or racial make-up were available. The youth center was strictly for "enlisted" personnel's children, however. Inclusion in the study was based on whether the child routinely decided to participate in R&T. Seven boys, whose ages ranged from 6 years through 9 years (mean age = 7.42), routinely engaged in R&T. Girls did not routinely choose to engage in R&T, although some were occasional participants for short periods of time. The racial makeup of the participants (four Caucasian and three African American) was incidental and dependent upon the self-selection of the participants.

The participants were those boys who routinely chose to engage in a game they called "Smear the Queer." They were selected as a result of their sustained play in a game that encompassed R&T behaviors and exhibited evidence of caring. The following is a brief description of each participant. Kevin (age 9) was the self-appointed leader, as he claimed he had control over who was invited to play. Indeed, Kevin controlled the tempo most of the time. Brian (age 8) enjoyed playing R&T, but was more tentative than the other players. When talking to the researcher, it seemed Brian was much more likely to say what he thought the researcher wanted to hear. Jake (age 8) played a passive role and was less definitive in discussing more intimate aspects of the game. Perry and Patrick (ages 7.5), identical twins, were very animated about their participation in R&T and very articulate during the interviews. Zach (age 8) was very descriptive and could clearly articulate what aggression looked like. Linden (at age 6,

Description of participants includes general ethnic backgrounds and SES, age, and gender.

The researchers hand-selected the boys to be studied. Note that this would *not* be the case in quantitative participant selection. Most likely, a quantitative researcher would randomly select participants.

the youngest participant) was very aggressive and enjoyed physical contact immensely. He liked Kevin the best (as did all of the other players) because "he can push all of us" and "The last time we jumped on his back, he fell down," referring to Kevin's playful nature and willingness to take his turn as the victim.

Comments

Participants

Qualitative research data collection is typically carried out in the setting of the research participants. This study identified its participants as seven males with a mean age of about 7-1/2 years, and described the participants by name, age, and play characteristics. We learned that the researchers collected their data in a youth center where the participants were in their natural surroundings, which made their activities unself-conscious after awhile. It is important and often difficult for qualitative researchers not to lead participants in providing research data, which was commented on in the study.

Data Collection

Common qualitative data collection approaches, as you have learned in this chapter, are observation, interviews, audio- and videotaping, and other face-to-face data collection methods. This study included observation, videotaping, and multiple levels of interviews, from which written transcripts were produced. Open-ended questions are also commonly used in qualitative data collection because the very nature of them require face-to-face contact with the participants. The questions posed in this study are listed in Tables 3 and 4. Triangulation was used in this study; data included previously videotaped play, observation, video recordings of a game the researchers identified, and additional segments of audio and video recordings of rough and tumble play. Data analyses emerged from lengthy data collection. In the next chapter, we will see the analysis of the data collected in this study, the study's findings, and its final write-up.

The Dislocated Textile Worker in Rural Alabama: A Portrait[7]

Methodology

Ethnography is the work of describing a culture (Hebert, 1995), in this case the culture of the workers in a rural Appalachian community. Rather than "studying people" as the word suggests, it is the researchers' aim to have learned from the people and understand their unique position through their native point of view. To truly understand the dislocated workers' standpoint, researchers would need to "walk a mile" in their shoes.

As a service delivery program administrator, the researcher understood the dislocation from a JTPA program performance context, however the researcher needed to fully understand the workers' feelings, emotions, and experiences as much as possible expressed in their own unique style. In order to relay those emotions and feelings accurately, an ethnographic methodology was appropriate.

Rationale for using ethnographic approach is explained.

Data collection methods explained. Note the difference between this study, in which interviews were conducted over a year, and "R&T," in which data collection was performed in 30 hours over a period of three weeks.

→ To capture the dislocated workers' feelings and perceptions, a combination of interviews, surveys, and observations were used to gather data. Participant observations were made in their natural settings—on the job before the plant shut down and in the aftermath of actually losing their jobs. While the observations had no specific structure, they were guided by procedures already in place within the Skills Center structure.

How interview questions were designed. The interviews let each participant provide her "voice" to the researcher. Open-ended questions encouraged them to offer their own thoughts and perspectives.

→ The in-depth interviews were conducted over a period of a year and spanned the time just before the worker became unemployed and in many instances ended just after the dislocated worker became gainfully employed again after training. These interviews had an open structure and consisted of open ended questions designed to draw the participant out and not only gather information about the participant's feelings but develop insight as well (Bogdan & Biklen, 1982, p. 135). Each participant had a unique view of their situation and these types of interviews allowed each participant to "draw his or her own picture" in regards to the closing of the textile plant. Questions designed to give the researcher the "grand tour" of the gamut of feelings and emotions (Spradley, 1979, p. 86) were asked of every participant and followed up with more specific questions; an example of this would be "Tell me what you think about the plant closing down," followed with "Tell me how this is going to affect you and your family." The participants' responses guided the interviews and the direction of the ensuing questions so that a deeper understanding could be obtained.

Data collection, tape transcription, data analysis, and theme emergence.

→ The total study transpired over the course of a year. Observation notes were taken as well as case notes on the conversations and interviews with each participant. Whenever the participant agreed to the tape recording of the interview it was done and transcribed verbatim. When the participant voiced reluctance at having the interview taped, notes were taken during the interview and immediately afterward to record specific comments and emotions. As themes began to emerge, they were noted, developed, and compared with the evolving hypotheses (Marshall & Rossman, 1989, p. 118). These interviews were then examined and unitized for "chunks of meaning." These chunks were then explored further and themes then emerged.

Participants

Participants' description includes age, educational attainment, test results, and survey results.

→ There were 35 participants in the study: all were white women between the ages of 35 to 65. Thirty-one already had their high school diplomas and 4 completed their GED in the JTPA program just prior to the commencement of their freshman year of college. All had tested with the JTPA program and placed high in the testing process. All participants indicated a college degree was among their goals when asked to list what they wanted to accomplish in the next two years. Each participant's interest inventory supported the training decision to go into the college referral program with the JTPA program.

Participants were chosen randomly (normally a quantitative procedure). It is not clear whether random selection was used to select a sample of all participants, or whether these were widely varied participant "stories" that had to be told. Note also that 35 participants would require lengthy periods of both data collection and analysis.

→ For the purpose of this study a dislocated worker was defined as a textile worker who had received her lay-off notice between January 1996 and January 1997. The participants were chosen at random using the random tables of numbers. Each participant was assigned a number and then selected accordingly. Approximately one half of the participants came from Jackson County's largest textile closing in January 1996 and the other half came form [sic] Dekalb County's largest textile closing in February 1996 and extending into April 1996.

Comments

Participants

The participants were chosen at random, and were described by age, race, and educational attainment. The researcher sought through this study to both understand participants' points of view and use her professional position to help them through their transition. There was a focus on describing the culture in this ethnographic study.

Data Collection

A combination of methods—interviews, surveys, and observation—was used to collect data. Observations were gathered in the natural context, at the Job and Skills Center. Open-ended questions were used to elicit participants' feelings. Note how "the participants' responses guided the interviews and the direction of the ensuing questions so that a deeper understanding could be obtained" (paragraph 4). The emotions and feelings expressed by the participants in this study could not have been recorded and gathered via a survey alone. Qualitative researchers typically conduct their research over long-term periods; the duration of data collection in this study was one year. Note how the themes emerged after a great deal of time spent collecting and analyzing data. Data analysis draws from a variety of qualitative data collection strategies.

LEAVING THE FIELD

There is always a quandary about when to exit the field. Sometimes the decision is easy (e.g., my sabbatical ends next week and I have to return home to Boston. Or school is ending for the year and my participants are about to disperse. Or I have no more money to support data gathering so I must quit). In most cases, the answer to the when-to-leave-the-field quandary is less clear. How much is enough data? How many pages of field notes are enough? These are hard questions to answer in general, since each study is different from others in some respects.

There are no simple rules for disengagement. Some say that the researcher will just "know" when it's time to stop. Others say that the search for the researcher's grail—that one more piece of evidence that will "make" the study—keeps many researchers in the field for too long. In the end, however, the more practical bases for leaving the field are when field notes become similar or redundant or when more recent data adds little to older data. In some circumstances, the researcher can also observe similar, but new, participants from the site to see whether the observations are similar to the prior participants. It may also be psychologically better for both the researcher and the research participants if the researcher "eases out" over time, rather than abruptly leaving.

HISTORICAL RESEARCH: DATA COLLECTION

The data collection techniques that we have so far discussed in this chapter apply primarily to ethnography, grounded theory, and action research. Each research type collects data in a manner best fitting its special requirements. The main ethnographic data collection techniques are observation, interviews, and artifacts. Sometimes the researcher will participate in the participants' lives and actions; sometimes the researcher will be strictly an observer. Grounded theory utilizes similar methods, but performs them in ever-narrowing iterations of constant comparison so as to distill from the data a testable theory. The primary action research data collection methods are observation interviews, questionnaires, and student artifacts. (We discuss action research in detail in Chapter 9.) In contrast, historical research by its very nature uses different data collection procedures. With the exception of interviewing participants to an event after the fact, historical research is limited to the study of artifacts and documents of various types.

In historical research, the review of related literature and the study procedures are part of the same process. The term *literature* takes on a broad meaning in a historical study and refers to all sorts of communications, including tape recordings, movies, photographs, documents, oral history, books, pamphlets, journal articles, and so on. The literature may be in the form of legal documents, records, minutes of meetings, letters, diaries, and other documents, many of which are not normally indexed alphabetically by subject, author, and title in a library. Thus, identifying such data often requires considerably more "detective work" on the part of the researcher. Further, given the nature of the topic, it is common for relevant literature to be available only at distant locations (e.g., in a special library collection). In such cases, proper examination of the data requires either considerable travel or, when feasible, extensive reproduction. Each of these approaches presents the researcher with problems. Travel requires that the researcher have a healthy bank account (which very few do!), unless, of course, the effort is supported by a funding agency. Acquiring photocopies of documents in a private collection can also become costly, and a 50-page document might turn out to contain only one or two paragraphs directly related to the research topic.

A historical research study in education might also involve interviews with persons who observed an event or knew a person being written about. Remember, however, that the use of interviews has limitations, especially when the researcher is studying events that occurred more than a lifetime previously. It would be tough to interview an observer of the Boston tea party! If a historical study focuses on changes in high school social studies textbooks from 1880 to 1945, artifacts such as the books themselves would be important data. The range of useful data in a historical study can be quite broad and varied.

Sources of data in a historical research study are classified as either primary or secondary sources. Primary sources include firsthand information, such as original documents and eyewitness observation reports. Secondary sources include secondhand information, such as encyclopedias or textbooks or reports by persons who were not actual participants or eyewitness observers. If you see an automobile crash on the highway, your description of it is a primary source. If you go home and tell your mother what you saw and she describes it to a newspaper reporter who had to talk with your mother because you were not home, her description is that of a secondary source. Similarly, a student who participated in the takeover of the president's office at Excellent U. would be a primary source of data concerning the event; the student's roommate who was not in the president's office would be a secondary source. Primary sources are definitely preferred; in general, the further removed from the primary source the evidence is, the less comprehensive and accurate the resulting data. You may have played a party game, usually called *telephone,* that illustrates how the facts get twisted as a story is passed from person to person. The first person hears the "true" story and whispers it to the second person, who whispers it to the third person, and so on until finally the last person tells out loud the story he or she was told. There is generally a considerable discrepancy between the first and the last version: "Greg and Muffy were seen holding hands at Bigger Burger" may well end up as "Greg and Muffy were kicked out of Club Yuppee because of their behavior on the dance floor!"

Because primary sources are often more difficult to acquire, a common criticism of historical research is excessive reliance on secondary sources. It is better to select a "less grand" problem for which primary sources are available and accessible than to inadequately investigate the "problem of the year." Of course the further back in time the event under study occurred, the more likely it is that secondary sources may also have to be used. As a rule, however, the more primary sources, the better.

We described in Chapter 2 the process of obtaining, reviewing, and abstracting data from primary and secondary sources, including assessing the source's relevancy to your topic; recording complete bibliographic information; coding the data from each source with respect to the areas of the study to which it relates; summarizing the pertinent information; and noting questions, comments, and quotations. Due to the nature of historical sources, several different note cards may be required for any one source. Also, one source may provide information for more than one aspect of the study. One critical aspect of historical sources is that they must be subjected to a careful analysis to determine both their authenticity and accuracy.

Now go to the Companion Website accompanying this text at *www.prenhall. com/gay* **to check your understanding of chapter concepts in the following modules: Objectives, Practice Quiz, and Applying What You Know. Expand your research skills with Evaluating Articles, Analyzing Qualitative Data, Analyzing Quantitative Data, and Research Tools and Tips. Visit Web Links to broaden your knowledge about research.**

SUMMARY

Step 3: Selecting Research Participants

1. Meet potential participants face to face and explain what is expected of them and what protections you will provide them (e.g., anonymity, confidentiality, no reporting to supervisors). Obtain a signed informed consent document from each selected participant.

2. Researchers must work to achieve rapport with gatekeepers and study participants, and to earn their trust. Trust is essential to the tone of the study and the quality of the data collected.

3. All researchers are bound to search out and avoid unethical treatment of research participants. Two basic and fundamental ethical principles relate to all forms of research activity: (1) both qualitative and quantitative researchers keep participants as informed as possible about the research study, and (2) they make every effort to protect participants from harm.

4. Participant selection is usually done using some form of purposive sampling. The key to sampling in qualitative research is to choose good participants who can provide the insights and articulateness needed to attain the desired richness of qualitative data.

Step 4: Data Collection

5. There are many sources of qualitative data, including observation, interviews, phone calls, personal and official documents, photographs, recordings, drawings, e-mails, and informal conversations. The most commonly used sources are observations and interviews.

6. In most cases, qualitative researchers employ more than one data collection method.

Observation

7. Observation takes many forms of interaction with participants. The researcher may take roles ranging from participant observer to nonparticipant observer to covert observer. Covert observation should be avoided.

8. Although participant observers can gain insights from their close contact, they also may lose objectivity and become emotionally engaged with participants.

9. Most qualitative observational research is naturalistic, encompassing holistic inquiry. The emphasis is on understanding the natural environment as lived by the participants, with no intent on the researcher's part to alter or manipulate that environment.

Field Notes

10. Field notes describe what the observer has heard, seen, experienced, and thought about during an observation. Because field notes are the basis for data collection and analysis, they must be detailed and descriptive, capturing the reality of the setting and participants.

11. The description (emic data) and reflection sections (etic data) should be separated. Both of these are important in data analysis. Field notes should be written as soon as possible after the observation, and should include the date, time, site, and topics recorded. Number all pages and keep them in order.

12. Novice observers should use a written *protocol*, or list of issues, to guide and focus their observations.

13. A memo is a form of thinking on paper; researchers write memos to themselves that describe their mental exploration of their ideas, themes, hunches, and reflections about the research topic.

Nonparticipant Data Collection Methods for Observational Studies

14. In nonparticipant observation, the observer is not directly involved in the situation to be observed.

15. In naturalistic observation, the observer purposely does not control or manipulate the setting so that observations will reveal the natural state of activity in the setting.

16. In simulation observation the researcher creates a situation to be observed and tells participants what activities they are to engage in. This technique allows the researcher to observe behavior that occurs infrequently in natural situations or not at all. Two major types of simulation are individual and team role playing.

17. The steps in conducting observational research are essentially the same as for other types of qualitative research. Once the behavior to be observed is determined, the researcher must clearly define what specific actions do and do not match the intended behavior.

Recording Observations

18. Observers should have to observe and record only one behavior at a time. It is also a good idea to alternate observation periods and recording periods, especially if inferences are required on the part of the observers.

19. As a general rule, it is probably better to record observations as the behavior occurs. Both qualitative and quantitative observation studies often facilitate recording by using an agreed code, or set of symbols, and a recording instrument.

20. Probably the most often and efficiently used type of recording form is a checklist that lists all behaviors to be observed so that the observer can simply check each behavior as it occurs. Rating scales are also sometimes used.

Assessing Observer Reliability

21. Determining observer reliability generally requires two observers independently making observations. Their recorded judgments about what occurred are compared to see how well they agree.

22. One approach to increasing reliability is to use shorter observation periods and to base reliability calculations on both observer agreements and disagreements. This approach makes it easier to determine whether observers are recording the same events at the same time.

23. In qualitative research, the emphasis is on the observer's ability to accurately record the details of the observed behavior.

24. Mechanical recording allows observers to play back tapes as often as needed. They can improve both validity and reliability.

25. Observers need to be trained to assure that all observers are observing and recording the same behaviors in the same way. Observers must be instructed as to what behaviors to observe, how behaviors are to be coded, how behaviors are to be recorded, and how often.

26. Practice sessions using recordings of behaviors are most effective since segments with which observers have difficulty can be replayed for discussion and feedback purposes. Training may be terminated when a satisfactory level of reliability is achieved (say, 80%).

27. The main way to ensure continued high levels of reliability is to periodically monitor the activities of observers. As a general rule, the more monitoring that can reasonably be managed, the better.

Interviews

28. An *interview* is a purposive interaction between two or more persons, with one trying to obtain information from the other. Interviews permit researchers to obtain information that cannot be obtained from observation, such as subjective reports of past events or participants' emotions.

29. Interviews vary in a number of ways: they may be focused on one or on many interviewees; the researcher may hold one or a number of interviews; interviews may vary in length from a few minutes to a few hours; they may be conducted using structured or unstructured questions.

30. Generally, qualitative interviews are free flowing and open ended, with the interviewer probing to clarify and extend the participant's comments. This interview format requires insight, tact, and timing to accomplish successfully. An important aspect of good interviewing is the interviewer's ability to "read" the interviewee. Inexperienced interviewers should have a general protocol of questions as a safety net.

31. Multiple-participant interviews, commonly called *focus groups,* are mainly useful for exploring ideas, topics, and perspectives of participants.

32. It is difficult to simultaneously interview participants and record the data they provide, so use of recording devices during interviews is recommended. Audio- or videotapes provide the researcher with a verbatim account of the interview.

33. Beginning researchers should keep their interviews relatively short.

34. It is expensive and time consuming to transcribe interview recordings, especially long ones. Nonetheless, transcribing is strongly encouraged; transcripts are the interview field notes, and become the data the researcher will analyze.

Threats to the Quality of Observations and Interviews

35. There are two main threats to the validity of qualitative data: observer bias and the observer effect.

36. Observer *bias* refers to invalid information that results from the perspective the researcher brings to the study. It occurs when the researcher consciously or unconsciously interprets data on the basis of attitudes or beliefs held prior to the research. While no researcher can be totally unbiased, all researchers must try as much as possible to avoid bias or prejudgment.

37. The observer *effect* occurs when the researcher's presence leads participants to behave atypically. The best way to handle the problem is to make observers aware of it so they can attempt to be as inconspicuous as possible.

Enhancing Validity and Reducing Bias

38. A number of strategies can be used to improve validity and reduce bias. The researcher can strive to obtain participants' trust, recognize his or her own biases, use verbatim observation and interview data, work with another researcher when collecting and reviewing data, examine unusual or contradictory results for explanations, and triangulate varied data sources.

Leaving the Field

39. Disengagement from the field and participants is not an easy task, either to decide when to leave or to actually leave. There are no simple rules to determine when to disengage, except when data collection

becomes redundant. However, whenever one leaves the setting and participants, it may be helpful to "ease out" gradually.

Historical Research: Data Collection

40. Historical research data collection differs from that of other types of research in that the sources are primarily artifacts and documents. In historical research, the review of related literature and the study procedures are part of the same process.

41. The term *literature* takes on a broad meaning in a historical study and refers to all sorts of communications, including tape recordings, movies, photographs, documents, oral history, books, pamphlets, journal articles, and other types of artifacts.

42. A historical research study might also involve interviews with persons who observed an event or knew a person being written about. However, the use of interviews has limitations in historical research, especially when the researcher is studying events that occurred more than a lifetime previously.

43. Sources of data in a historical research study are classified as either primary or secondary. Primary sources are definitely preferred; in general, the further removed from the primary source the evidence is, the less comprehensive and accurate the resulting data.

44. Because primary sources are often more difficult to acquire, a common criticism of historical research is excessive reliance on secondary sources.

"What does this remind me of?" "Is this activity like some other activity I'm familiar with?"
(p. 228)

CHAPTER 8

QUALITATIVE RESEARCH: DATA ANALYSIS

OBJECTIVES

After reading Chapter 8, you should be able to do the following:

1. Describe the purpose of qualitative research data analysis.
2. State approaches to qualitative data analysis.
3. Describe processes involved in analyzing, interpreting, and reporting data.
4. State the role of categories in structuring qualitative data analysis.
5. Describe the role of data analysis at various stages of the research process.
6. Distinguish between data *analysis* and data *interpretation.*
7. Identify guidelines that can provide information about the quality of the data analyzed.
8. Identify characteristics of a good qualitative narrative report.
9. List guidelines to be followed in verifying and storing qualitative data.

PREPARING TO ANALYZE DATA

Thus far in Part Two we have discussed four of the six main steps of qualitative research. We have examined selecting an initial topic for the research, and ways to handle the literature review in qualitative research. We have also considered issues of selecting research participants. And we have discussed the various qualitative data sources. In this chapter we focus on step 5, data analysis, and step 6, writing narratives about the research.

Analyzing qualitative data is a formidable task for all qualitative researchers, especially those just starting their qualitative careers. As a novice researcher, you have followed the urgings of your qualitative mentors who have emphasized the need to collect rich, thick, and deep data that reveal the perspectives and understandings of the research participants. You have learned that qualitative research is iterative. Unlike the quantitative researcher, who typically visits her participants once or maybe twice during the study, the qualitative researcher interacts with participants during the entire research process. And here you now stand (or sit), looking over piles of field notes, piles of memos, piles of verbatim interview or observation transcriptions, or piles of all three. You may even deal with all three forms of qualitative data: what participants do, what they say, and what they leave behind.

Your data are not only rich and thick and deep, they are voluminous and unorganized. Your task is to bring order to your data, to separate the wheat from the chaff among your field notes and transcripts. Unlike the quantitative researcher whose data produces numbers that can be organized and "crunched" in fairly routine ways, you must find your own, idiosyncratic path to the meaning of your data. However, it may be consoling to know that no qualitative researcher can be amazing enough, brilliant enough, or experienced enough to observe and grasp *everything* of interest in a given setting. As you go through this chapter, keep in mind the following seven characteristics of qualitative research: (1) there is no single way to come to know something, (2) there are numerous ways to report data,

(3) messages are not neutral, (4) language creates reality, (5) the researcher interrelates deeply with what and who is being studied, (6) affect and cognition are inextricably united, and (7) what we understand as social reality is not neat, linear, or fixed.

STEP 5: ANALYZING THE DATA

DATA ANALYSIS DURING DATA COLLECTION

Data analysis is lengthy and time consuming, not only because of the large quantity of data to be analyzed, but also because data typically are not organized in a manner that facilitates easy analysis. Thus, data analysis in qualitative research is not left until all data are collected, as is the case with quantitative research. The qualitative researcher begins data analysis from the initial interaction with participants, and continues that interaction throughout the entire study. During the study, the qualitative researcher tries to progressively narrow, and focus in on, the key aspects of the participants' data. Thus, the qualitative researcher goes through a series of steps and iterations: gathering data, examining data, comparing prior data to newer data, and developing new data to gather. There is simultaneous interaction of data collection and analysis, so that the researcher's emerging hunches or thoughts become the focus for the next data collection period. While gathering data, the researcher reviews and asks questions about it: "Why do participants act as they do?" "What does this focus mean?" "What else do I want to know about that participant's attitude?" "What new ideas have emerged in this round of data collection?" "Is this a new concept or is it the same as a previous one?" and so forth. This ongoing process—almost a protracted discussion with oneself—leads to adding new important data and eliminating other data. During these iterations the initial research topic may be altered or abandoned. While dealing with data analysis and data integration, it is important to bear in mind that in qualitative research the important concepts and issues are not the ones stated by the researcher, but the ones stated by the participants.

Bogdan and Biklen[1] suggest a number of steps to facilitate data analysis. For example, they recommend that during data collection the researcher try to progressively narrow the focus of the study. As the researcher observes aspects of the setting or characteristics of the participants, the focus of the study begins to emerge. Having such a focus is beneficial in determining which data are important and which are not. Also, having a focus or topic makes it possible to design data collection sessions that are built on prior sessions, thereby allowing the researcher to gather richer, more focused data for analysis. While not all qualitative researchers agree that the literature should be explored during data analysis, it is true that knowing what other researchers have found can help one conceptually and methodologically by guiding the direction of data analysis. It also is important to reexamine the research topic to identify if and how it should be modified during data collection.

Another important suggestion is for the researcher to write memos during data collection. Memos help organize and focus data analysis (Figure 7.3 illustrates one researcher's memo). Finally, the use of metaphors, analogies, and visual devices can provide alternative perspectives on the data collected. To make links between data the researcher asks questions such as, "What does this remind me of?" "Is this activity like some other activity I'm familiar with?" and so on. Also, making charts, diagrams, concept maps, or matrices is useful in identifying relations between or among the data. Visually displaying your data can help you to see it in a new light. You can create data displays informally during data analysis to aid your understanding and formally in your final written study. In sum, the point is to use data collection strategies that help you focus and think about aspects of your data analysis.

---

[1]Bogdan, R. C., and Biklen, S. K. (1998). *Qualitative research for education: An introduction to theory and methods,* 3rd ed. Needham Heights, MA: Allyn & Bacon.

DATA ANALYSIS AFTER DATA COLLECTION

After the data have begun to be collected and analyzed, the "romance" of field research is over and the difficult task of data analysis and interpretation begins. Guided by insights gained during data collection, data analysis is concerned with identifying what is in the data. The researcher's descriptions and analysis focus on making sense of what the descriptions mean. Qualitative data analysis is based on induction; the researcher constructs patterns that emerge from the data and makes sense of them. Starting with a large set of issues and data, the researcher seeks to progressively narrow them into small and important groups of key data. There are no predefined variables to focus analysis, as there are in quantitative research. The qualitative researcher identifies his own variables from the examination and analysis of the data obtained, based on the participants' information.

A problem that faces virtually all qualitative researchers is the lack of agreed-on approaches for analyzing and narrating qualitative data. There are some guidelines and general strategies for analysis, but few specific rules for their application. Thus, once data are collected, the qualitative researcher undertakes a multistage process of organizing, categorizing, synthesizing, interpreting, and writing about the data. Each of these processes is iterative; in most cases the researcher will cycle through the stages more than once, in a continual effort to narrow and make sense of what she has seen in the data.

STEPS IN ANALYZING QUALITATIVE RESEARCH DATA

In this section we examine four of the five steps for analyzing and interpreting qualitative data: data managing, reading/memoing, describing the context and participants, and classifying. (We discuss the fifth step, interpreting, later in this chapter.) Although these steps are not exhaustive of the many qualitative research approaches available, they are used in most qualitative approaches.

Bearing in mind that data analysis takes place with data collection, the first step is managing the data so they can be studied. Once the data are organized, data analysis begins in earnest. The researcher cannot fully interpret data until they are broken down and classified in some way, so the analysis itself requires four iterative steps: reading/memoing, describing what is going on in the setting, classifying research data, and interpreting. This cyclical process is shown in Figure 8.1. The process focuses on (1) becoming familiar with the data and identifying potential themes in it (reading/memoing); (2) examining the data in depth to provide detailed descriptions of the setting, participants, and activity (describing); (3) categorizing and coding pieces of data and grouping them into themes (classifying); and (4) interpreting and synthesizing the organized data into general written conclusions or understandings based on the data (interpreting).

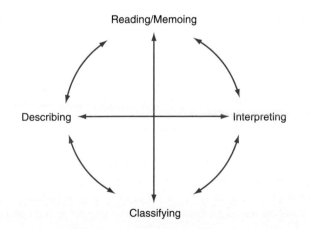

FIGURE 8.1   The integration of qualitative data.

Note that the interrelationships among these steps are not necessarily linear. At the start of data analysis, the logical sequence of activities goes from reading/memoing, to description, to classifying, and to interpretation. However, as the researcher begins to internalize and reflect on the data, the initial ordered sequence may lose its structure and become more flexible. For example, describing may lead to interpretation without the intermediate step of classifying. Or interpretation may lead to reclassifying some issues. If you've ever been driving home pondering some issue or problem you've not solved and out of the blue have had a sudden flash of understanding that provides a solution, you have a sense of how qualitative data analysis takes place. Once you are into the data, it is not the four steps that lead to understanding and interpretation; it is your ability to think, imagine, create, intuit, and analyze that guides the data analysis. Knowing the steps is not enough; the thinker, imaginer, and hypothesizer—that is, the researcher—is the data analyzer, and the quality of the research analysis will depend heavily on the intellectual qualities of the qualitative researcher. Stated in more blunt terms, if you are unable to integrate, analyze, and classify, you will find the inductive nature of qualitative research difficult to master and frustrating to pursue.

Let us be very clear about the process being discussed. It is a process of digesting the contents of qualitative data and finding related threads in it. You will not meaningfully accomplish these tasks with one or two or more readings of your collected data. To make the kinds of connections needed to analyze and interpret qualitative data, you must know your data—really know it, in your head, not just on paper. The process can be tedious, time consuming, and necessarily iterative. With this proviso in mind, we can discuss actions that help manage, describe, and classify qualitative data, always bearing in mind that the insights and qualities of the researcher are the key factors influencing the quality of the study.

Data Managing

Data managing involves creating and organizing the data collected during the study. Envision what the data from a qualitative observation or interview study looks like—piles of field notes or transcripts, memos, and numerous description awaiting organization. Recall from Chapter 7 that field notes are all the written information the researcher obtains while collecting data in the research settings. Field notes encompass what the researcher hears, sees, experiences, and thinks about in the research context (see Figure 7.2).

Before you can begin managing your data, you must put them in a form that will facilitate analysis. For example, you might need to "tidy up" the data you have collected to make sure that you have dated, organized, and sequenced all notes, transcripts, observer's comments, memos, and reflections. You can also organize your computer files and create separate folders for different data types and stages of analysis. You would probably want to make copies (at least two) of your field notes and transcripts so that you can mark or underline important sections while still retaining a clean, unmarked copy of your precious original data. Put one unmarked copy in a really safe place, making sure that *all* the data are there and ordered. It is also useful to make backup copies of any computer files containing your data in the event that you lose some data by mistake. You may also read through the data and note tentative issues or activities that relate to your research topic. Arranging the data so that they can be easily managed and "milked" is an important first step in analysis. Figure 8.2 shows some ways to "tidy up" your data.

There are two main purposes of data managing: organizing and checking the data for completeness and starting the process of analyzing and interpreting the data. In organizing the data, examine your field notes, memos, and other information. Also, begin your initial questioning of the data by noting themes, patterns, regularities, and issues that have previously emerged at earlier passes of data analysis. At these early stages, data analysis is general and rudimentary. Over time, increased analysis will be more specific and integrated.

- Write dates (month, day, year) on all notes.
- Sequence all notes with labels (e.g., 6th set of notes).
- Label notes according to type (such as observer's notes, memo to self, transcript from interview).
- Make two photocopies of all notes (field notes, transcripts, etc.) and retain original copies.
- Organize computer files into folders according to data type and stages of analysis.
- Make backup copies of all files.
- Read through data and make sure it is complete and legible before proceeding to analysis and interpretation.
- Begin to note themes and patterns that emerge.

FIGURE 8.2   Data organizing activities.

Reading/Memoing

As your first analytical step, you will read and write memos about all field notes, transcripts, memos, and observer comments to get an initial sense of the data. To begin, find a quiet place and plan on reading for a few hours at a time during your initial reading of the data. Krathwohl[2] wisely points out that "the first time you sit down to read your data is the only time you come to that particular set fresh." It is important that you write notes in the margins or underline sections or issues that seem important to you so that you will have a record of your initial thoughts and sense of the data. You might find that many of these early impressions will not be useful once you are deeper into analysis, but you will also find some initial impressions that do hold up throughout. In addition to recording initial impressions from the data, at this stage of analysis you also will begin the search for recurring themes or common threads.

Describing

Describing addresses what is going on in the setting and among the participants. It is based on your collected observations, questionnaires, and field notes. The aim is to provide a true picture of the setting and events that take place in it, so you will have an understanding of the context in which the study is taking place. Description is often held in less esteem than analytical or theoretical aspects of research, but in qualitative research description is an integral and important aspect. Early in your analysis, you develop thorough and comprehensive descriptions of the participants, the setting, and the phenomenon studied. Such description is often called *thick* or *thorough* description because it seeks to convey the rich complexity of the research, in contrast to *thin* description that contains only factual information. Description focuses on painting a verbal picture of the context, processes, and the world as viewed from the participants' perspective.

Attention to features of the research context is a common and important theme in qualitative research, because the context influences participants' actions and understandings. Meaning is influenced by context; without a thorough description of the context, actions, and interactions of participants, analysis (and therefore, interpretation) is hampered. An important concern of qualitative researchers is portraying the views of the research participants. It is crucial that your notes describe thoroughly how participants define situations and explain their actions. Also, ongoing descriptions of the interactions and social relations among the participants is important because social processes can change over time. The descriptions of the research contexts, meanings, and social relations can be presented in a number of forms. For example, you can use chronological ordering of setting and events, describe a typical "day in the life" of participants in their setting, focus on key contextual episodes, or illuminate different perspectives of the participants.

---

[2]Krathwohl, D. R. (1998). *Methods of educational and social science research.* New York: Longmans (p. 309).

Description also leads to the separation and grouping of pieces of data related to different aspects of the setting, events, and participants. As Dey notes,

> One distinctive feature of description is its integrative function. By summarizing data, for example, we strip away unnecessary detail and delineate more clearly the more central characteristics of the data. Moreover, it is in pulling together and relating these central characteristics through a reasoned account that description acquires its unity and force.[3]

Description enhances and leads to classifying the data.

Classifying

Qualitative data analysis is basically a process of breaking down data into smaller units, determining their import, and putting the pertinent units together in a more general, interpreted form. The typical way qualitative data are broken down is through the process of coding or classifying. A **category** is a classification of ideas or concepts. When concepts in the data are examined and compared to one another and connections are made, categories are formed. Categories are used to organize similar concepts into distinct groups.

To get a feel for the nature of classification, imagine you are in a large room that contains hundreds and hundreds of books. Your task is to organize the books into categories that differentiate among the many characteristics (concepts) of the books. Think about some possible categories that can be used to differentiate among book characteristics. You probably would identify categories of fiction and nonfiction, categories for each of the various book publishers, categories for the length of books, categories for the age of books, categories for children and adult books, and so on.

But did you identify categories for male and female authors, for the print type used in the books, or for the state in which they were published? Probably not, which points out the fact that there are many, many ways to categorize. There is not just one appropriate category. Now consider a researcher who is conducting a qualitative study on characteristics of fifth-grade students' study methods. Suppose the researcher had collected 20 observations or 20 interviews. The researcher's task is to read through all the observations or interviews and categorize the meanings or understandings that emerge from the data. Without data that are classified and grouped, there is no reasonable way for a researcher to analyze qualitative studies. The categories provide the basis for structuring analysis and interpretation. Are you beginning to get a sense of the meaning of *interpretive research*? Think of a 1,000-piece jigsaw puzzle when you don't have the picture on the front of the box to guide you.

However, unlike the jigsaw puzzle, the categories one researcher identified to organize data in qualitative research would not necessarily be the same ones another researcher would identify, even if they analyzed the same data. There is no one single "correct" way to organize and analyze the data. There are many reasons why different researchers would not produce the same categories from the same data. Some of these reasons are researcher biases, personal interests, style, and interpretive focus.

Analytic Strategies

Three main strategies are used to analyze qualitative data: negative case analysis, analytic induction, and constant comparison. Each is important in identifying and categorizing concepts related to research categories and patterns. Negative case and discrepant data methods are, as the names suggest, based on the search for data that are negative or discrepant from the main data collected in a study. A **negative case** is one that contradicts an emerging category, thereby providing a different perspective on the emerging category or pattern. It is often easy for a researcher (any researcher) to adopt or cling to an initial hypothesis or hunch

---

[3]Dey, I. (1993). *Qualitative data analysis.* New York: Routledge (p. 39).

and fail to examine alternative evidence that might negate or weaken the hypothesis or hunch. The search for negative or discrepant data provides an important counterbalance to a researcher's tendency to stick with her or his first impression or hunch.

Analytic induction is a process concerned with the development and test of a theory. It starts with a preliminary focus or explanation of a phenomenon that is being studied. For example, early in a study of teachers' perspectives on merit pay, the researcher may indicate that teachers who do not receive merit pay are those who have little allegiance to their school and students. A hypothetical explanation of the hypothesis is formed, for example, "Lack of merit pay angers teachers and their anger is taken out on the school and students." Given this explanation, data are gathered to test it. If the hypothesis is upheld, more data are gathered to determine whether it is still upheld. If the initial explanation is not upheld, it is reformulated based on the contrary evidence, for example, "Lack of merit pay does not make teachers angry; it lowers their self-esteem and this is translated into teachers distancing themselves from the school and students." Data are then gathered to examine the revised hypothesis. The process continues with the refining of the hypothesis until there are no examples of the revised hypothesis not being upheld. However, one failure to uphold requires additional revision. This process is very rigorous, but the explanation ultimately arrived at will contribute to our understanding of the phenomenon.

A third, very common type of qualitative data analysis is the *constant comparison* method, also called *grounded theory*. As its name suggests, this approach involves the constant comparison of identified data and concepts to determine their distinctive characteristics so that they can be placed in different and appropriate categories. As each new concept or piece of data is identified, it is compared to existing categories. The researcher asks, "Is this data or concept similar to, or different from, one or more existing categories?" Categories are modified as needed to fit new data and are further tested by additional new data, based on their key points as interpreted by the qualitative researcher. Categories can be compared to develop more general patterns of data. The aim of the constant comparative method is to understand and explain qualitative data.

Where do categories come from? One answer is from commonly used, predefined categories. For example, Miles and Huberman[4] suggest the use of the following categories to order qualitative data:

- participant acts
- activities
- participant meanings
- relationships among participants
- setting

Bogdan and Biklen[5] recommend the use of the following categories:

- research setting
- perspectives of participants
- participants' ways of thinking
- regularly occurring activities
- infrequently occurring activities
- methods

[4]Miles, M. B., and Huberman, A. M. (1994). *Qualitative data analysis: An expanded source book.* Thousand Oaks, CA: Sage (p. 51).

[5]Bogdan, R. C., and Biklen, S. K. (1998). *Qualitative research in education: An introduction to theory and methods,* 3rd ed. Needham Heights, MA: Allyn & Bacon (pp. 172–177).

Clearly, these categories could be subdivided into narrower ones. In fact, the researcher might start with Miles and Huberman's or Bogdan and Biklen's general categories (note that these are drawn from a sociological perspective) and put as many pieces of data as will fit into the selected general categories and then, in succeeding iterations, break down the contents of the more general categories into more specific and narrower ones. For example, "participant acts" could be subdivided into "group acts" and "individual acts." Or "regularly occurring activities" could be subdivided into "teacher regularities," "student regularities," and "joint regularities." Obviously, categories can also be defined by a combination of predefined and researcher-defined categories. Note, however, that relying on predefined categories may increase substantially the likelihood that researchers will overload or miss important categories in their own data.

For example, consider Figure 8.3, which shows a portion of a researcher's field notes obtained during an observation session. Two aspects of the field notes stand out: (1) some sections are underlined or bracketed, and (2) brief labels in the margins are linked to each underlined or bracketed section. The underlined/bracketed sections are individual pieces of data from the field session. Similar individual data pieces can and must be identified in all qualitative data. The marginal labels are the categories; that is, they are general placeholders for organizing and accumulating narrowed related data pieces. Thus, the data piece labeled "correcting papers" would fit into a more general category called "teachers' work." Other data pieces related to teachers' work (e.g., writing lesson plans, dealing with parents) found in additional field notes would also be placed in that category. Two different data pieces related to "parents" were identified in the last section of the field notes.

How were these data pieces and categories identified? What is the process that uncovers the important data pieces and categories from among all the possible pieces and categories that could be derived from a set of field notes or transcripts? The answer is that there are a number of ways and strategies for dissecting and reorganizing the data. For example, the topic or focus of the study can provide initial ideas about relevant data pieces and more general categories. Thus, the researcher in Figure 8.3 might have been interested in the activities of teachers and thus identified categories before analysis actually began. He or she would then scour the data seeking examples in the field notes that fit into these previously identified categories. In this case, the categories precede the data pieces. (Note again that when researchers predetermine categories they run the risk of only seeing those items in the data and may miss important items that could enhance their study.)

Alternatively, while reading through a few of the field notes, the researcher in Figure 8.3 might have encountered some themes or common issues that cut across the field notes. For example, the researcher might have noted that various kinds of teachers' work as well as parent comments showed up in a number of the notes. From these initial common multiple data pieces, general descriptive categories (e.g., teachers' work and parents) could be identified. In this case, the field notes precede the categories. Categories can also identify observer comments or memos. For example, a researcher's memo describing the large number of discipline cases teachers referred to the principal might suggest the need of a category for discipline. Reflections, anomalies, and commonalities noted during data analysis may also lead to useful categories.

Schatzman and Strauss make a strong argument for the emphasis on categories in qualitative research methods:

> Probably the most fundamental operation in the analysis of qualitative data is that of discovering significant *classes* of things, persons, and events and the *properties* which characterize them. In this process, which continues throughout the research, the analyst gradually comes to reveal his own "is's" and "because's": he names classes and links one with another, at first with "simple" statements (propositions) that express the linkages, and continues this process until his propositions fall into sets, in an ever-increasing density of linkages.[6]

---

[6]Schatzman, L., and Strauss, A. (1973). *Field research.* Upper Saddle River, NJ: Prentice Hall (p. 110).

FIGURE 8.3 Coded field notes.

Field Notes
Vista City Elementary School Teachers' Lounge
February 3, 1981

teachers' work

Then I went down to the teachers' lounge to see if anybody might happen to be there. I was in luck. Jill Martin sat at the first table, correcting papers; Kathy Thomas was also there, walking around and smoking. I said, "Hi Jill, hi Kathy. Okay if I join you?" "Sure," Jill said. "You and your husband have been to China, right?" I said, "Yes. Why?" Jill then turned to Kathy and said, "Have you studied China yet? Sari has slides that she can show." Kathy said to me that she was going to study world communities, even though "they" had taken them out of the sixth-grade social studies curriculum. "Now can you tell me who 'they' are?" I asked her. She said, "You know, 'them': 'they.'"

authority

autonomy

Both Jill and Kathy were upset at how they had mandated what the teachers could teach in their rooms. "They" turned out to be the central office who had communicated the state's revised sixth-grade social studies curriculum. The state has "taken out all the things that we think are important" from the curriculum and have substituted the theme of "economic geography" for the sixth-graders to study.

doing your own thing

Both Jill and Kathy think that "sixth-graders can't comprehend economic geography well," and think world communities of Africa and Asia are more important. They said they planned to teach what they wanted to anyway. Kathy said, "They'll come around one of these days." "Oh, Kathy, are you a rebel?" I asked. "No," she replied, "I'm just doing my own thing."

parents

After we chatted for a little while, Jill turned to me: "You're interested in what concerns us. I guess one thing is parents." She proceeded to describe a parent conference she had participated in yesterday afternoon with a child's parents and a child's psychiatrist.

parents

She said, "What really upsets me is how much responsibility they placed on me to change the child's behavior." They seemed to give lip service, she reported, to have "controls" come from the child when they said, "It's so difficult for parents to see that kids need to take responsibility for their actions."

Source: From R. C. Bogdan and S. K. Biklen, *Qualitative Research for Education: An Introduction to Theory and Methods,* 3/e. © 1998 by Allyn & Bacon. Reproduced by permission.

As we have said before, developing and verifying categories is not done with a single reading of the data. The quantity and complexity of qualitative data require more than one pass. In fact, one strategy that is useful for both learning about one's data and verifying the usefulness of potential categories is to stagger the reading of field notes and memos. For example, one quarter of the field notes or memos are read carefully. If a preexisting set of categories is available, the researcher can try to classify data pieces from the selected field notes or memos into the existing categories. If some of the data pieces cannot be classified, additional categories likely should be added.

The categories identified from these approaches should be considered provisional. One should not become overly attached to initial categories until they have been tested more rigorously, perhaps with negative case methods. For example, one approach to sharpen and validate categories is to apply the categories derived from the first quarter of the data to the second quarter of the data. Can one classify all data pieces in these categories? Are additional categories needed? Is one category so broad that it should be divided into two categories instead of one? As noted, data analysis is iterative.

Even when you have continued to refine and validate the categories by using them to examine additional data, the task may not be completed. If you have identified 60 categories, you probably should winnow the 60 down to no more than 10 or so. Too many categories, especially for beginning qualitative researchers, makes data analysis and description difficult, time consuming, and superficial. Ask yourself questions such as, "Can two or more categories be collapsed into one?" "Are some categories secondary to the main focus of the study?" "Is the category with only three data pieces really needed?" A great deal of data are generated in qualitative research; focusing on the most important data is sometimes difficult, but is very important. It may also be useful to reread the field notes or transcripts to make sure important data were not overlooked and that you are still "comfortable" with your categories after another reading.

We have seen that categories help organize data and that identifying the categories that best represent the data usually require multiple examinations. We have also seen that categories can be identified before, during, or after data analysis. In the end, the aim is to analyze data into a pyramid with at least three levels: data pieces, categories, and patterns. At each level, the pyramid narrows, signifying more integration and abstraction of the qualitative data. Just as some data pieces can be subsumed into categories, so too can some categories be subsumed into patterns. A **pattern** is a link between two or more categories that further organizes the data and that usually becomes the primary basis for organizing and reporting the outcomes of the study. Patterns are identified in the same way pieces of data are organized into categories—the researcher seeks and finds connections among the categories. There is, of course, no guarantee that there will be patterns to be induced from the categories, but seeking relations among activities, time usage, or links among categories can help focus the search for patterns.

As noted, qualitative data analysis is complex and iterative, which leads to an often-asked question: How long should data analysis of this type go on? Frankly, it's hard to say, since the analysis depends on the nature of the study, the amount of data collected, and the analytic and synthetic abilities of the researcher. The qualitative researcher must both deconstruct the field notes or transcriptions into data pieces and then reconstruct them into meaningful and relevant data categories and patterns. The ability of the researcher to induce or construct meaning from the data greatly influences the duration and quality of the data analysis. Qualitative data analysis typically requires substantially more time to complete than does quantitative data analysis.

Qualitative Analysis: An Example

This example is intended to provide a sense of qualitative analysis. The analysis conducted in a true qualitative study would entail more data analysis than shown here. However, the basic ideas represent the process a qualitative researcher would undertake to conduct a study. See Figure 8.4 for a diagram illustrating the categories and patterns that emerged from the data analysis.

- *Topic to be studied:* Concerns of parents on their first child's entering kindergarten. Teachers interactions with students and families.
- *Participants:* 4 parents, three female and one male; all children will be in the same school; first child of all participants.
- *Data collection:* interviews with the parents. Observations, interviews, and interviews with students and parents.

1. Initial data collection: from the field notes of your classroom observations, you begin to list some common items or topics that you noticed. You may have noted that during classroom instruction the teacher was using books, videos, and handouts. You also noted that at times, instruction was directed toward individual students, sometimes toward the whole class, and sometimes toward students who were working together in small groups.

FIGURE 8.4 Diagram of category levels and organization.

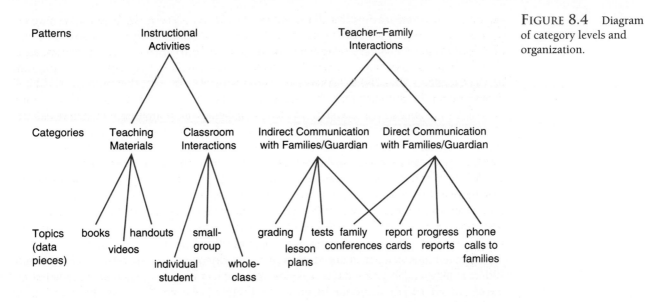

2. From your interviews with the teacher, you realize that she gave you information about how she communicated with families about the children. You note that she talked about how she indirectly communicates through grading and report cards, and how her lesson plans and tests were related to her overall assessment of the students' work. She also mentioned that she talked about report cards directly with families during conferences. Other ways that she communicated with families were through progress reports and phone calls about their child.

3. From your initial analysis, you decide how to group the individual items or topics together into categories that show how the items or topics are related. For example, you could group books, videos, and handouts under a category called "teaching materials." You could group together the ways in which the instruction was carried out—individual, small group, and whole class—and label this category as "classroom interactions." From the interviews, you could construct the categories "indirect communication with families" to include grading, report cards, lesson plans, and tests. A category of "direct communication with families" includes report cards, progress reports, family conferences, and phone calls to families. Notice that report cards appears in both "indirect" and "direct" categories.

4. Now, you organize these four categories into patterns. A pattern is made up of two or more categories. For example, the categories of "teaching materials" and "classroom interactions" indicate a pattern of "instructional activities." The categories of "indirect communication" and "direct communication" fit together under a pattern of "teacher–family interactions."

You then decide if you need to collect further data by interviewing students and parents about their experiences of interacting with the teacher to confirm your categories and patterns.

Using Computers in Qualitative Data Analysis

Many computer programs for both Mac and PC are available to aid in analyzing qualitative data. Although programs differ in the features they provide, one can expect a substantial number of common features when using a qualitative data analysis program. While computers can enhance and broaden qualitative research analysis, there are some drawbacks to their use. For example, the researcher must learn how to use the program. The more features the program provides, the longer it will take to master it. Programs differ in their features. Most programs provide little help with interpreting data, although their search capabilities can be a useful prod to researcher interpretation. However, one drawback of computer analyses is that they diminish the likelihood of the researcher's reexamination of the data set once the computer-generated organization is produced. A second drawback issues from the growing use of computer analysis, particularly among new qualitative researchers. While the computer is an exceptional research tool, you will appreciate and understand it more if your first qualitative analysis experience is a manual, noncomputer one.

It is important for novice qualitative researchers to remember that computers alone do not analyze or even code data. They are designed only to help expedite these operations when researchers are working with large bodies of text and other kinds of data. The process of coding, retrieving, and subsequently mulling over and making sense of data remains a laborious process completely controlled by researchers. Even if a computer is used, researchers still must go through the process of punching each code into the data on the computer as they read through their interviews, field notes, and audio- and videotapes. Computers are merely handy and extremely fast labeling and retrieval tools. Researchers also must remember that they alone can tell or program the computer to retrieve and count data in specific ways; the machines do not do these tasks automatically.

NUD-IST is one qualitative data analysis application that qualitative researchers use. Table 8.1 lists various data analysis elements, their manual tasks (writing objectives), and corresponding procedures that may be carried out or assisted by using NUD-IST.

TABLE 8.1   Data Analysis Elements, Writing Objectives, and NUD-IST Procedures

DATA ANALYSIS ELEMENT	WRITING OBJECTIVE	NUD-IST PROCEDURE
Create a template for analysis	Develop a visual of data analysis plan	Create a tree of steps in analysis into which data segments are placed
Create headings in the manuscript for major themes	Create four or five major themes in the study in words of participants	Create a node for each heading and put text that applies into the node
Title the manuscript	Create a title in words of the participants—to make report realistic, to catch attention of readers	Create a node based on short phrases found in the text; create alternative titles in this node as they appear in analyzing the texts
Include quotes in the manuscript	Identify good quotes that provide sound evidence for the themes, description, interpretation, and so forth	Create a general node and place all good quotes in that node; create a node for quotes under each theme or category of information
Phrase study in words of participants	Locate commonly used words or phrases and develop them into themes	Use word search procedure, string or pattern search, and place contents into a node; spread text around the word (or phrase) to capture the context of the word (or phrase)
Create a comparison table	Compare categories of information	Use matrix feature of program
Show levels of abstraction in the analysis	Present a visual of the categories in the analysis	Present the "tree" diagram
Discuss metaphors	Find text in which metaphors are presented and group into categories	Set up one node for metaphors with children of different types of metaphors; place text in nodes by types of metaphors

Source: Creswell, J. (1998). *Qualitative inquiry and research design: Choosing among five traditions*. Thousand Oaks, CA: Sage Publications, p. 162. Copyright 1998 Sage Publications. Reprinted by permission of Sage Publications, Inc.

EXAMPLES OF QUALITATIVE RESEARCH: DATA ANALYSIS

Once again, we return to the two sample articles we analyzed in Chapters 6 and 7. I know you can't wait to see how these stories end! Here, you will read the "Findings" section in "The Expression of Care in the Rough and Tumble Play of Boys" and the "Results of the Study" and "Implications" sections in "The Dislocated Textile Workers in Rural Alabama: A Portrait"—essentially the data analysis sections of each study. Here, we see how researchers answer the question, "What is in the data?" Later sections of these articles will address the *meanings* of the data.

The Expression of Care in the Rough and Tumble Play of Boys[7]

Findings

In all, 119 demonstrations of R&T (see Table 1 [Chapter 7]) were observed, taped, and analyzed. Selected episodes of R&T were viewed and discussed with the participants by the researcher. Sixty of the R&T episodes were observed during a game that followed the "tackle the boy with the ball" format and referred to by the participants as "Smear the Queer." It should be noted that despite the repugnant nature of the name Smear the Queer (hereafter referred to as "Smear"), it was the players who coined the term, which was not used in any other context.

An analysis of the data clearly indicates that R&T is indeed a means by which boys express care and intimacy for one another. There were 73 demonstrations of caring and intimate contact observed (see Table 2 [Chapter 7]) during the 119 episodes of R&T. In addition, these data indicate that all R&T episodes, except those involving non-playing intruders, occur within the context of friendships and caring relationships. The following findings were commonalities that emerged from the data and were shared by all the R&T episodes. More specifically, analysis of the data revealed the following six findings:

> **Clear statement about what analysis indicates.**

1. R&T provides the opportunity for the declaration of friendship and caring relations
2. R&T involves intimate contact that is met with understanding by the players
3. R&T resembles a ritualized type of play that requires specific knowledge
4. All of the regular R&T players knew or observed the rules
5. Knowledge of rules separated R&T players from intruders
6. R&T resulted in one minor injury.

> **Research findings are itemized.**

R&T Is a Declaration of Friendship and Caring

In choosing to play the game of Smear, the seven participants were declaring their friendship. They felt that R&T gave them an opportunity to show that they cared for each other. Kevin claimed that the seven who played Smear together were friends. The aggressive nature of Smear (which is very much like that in American football) is one of its attractions. For example, Linden and Jake liked playing Smear with their friends because they liked to be tackled. Linden also said, "When we play Smear we get to be with our friends." Patrick expressed similar feelings and remarked that during Smear, "We are all friends and we play together all of the time." However, not all of the players perceived the game in exactly the same way. Brian stated, "Most [of the players] are my friends; some aren't. It doesn't really matter. We are having fun."

There were several other things players did as an indication of care. For example, when one of the players fell or was knocked down, a delay of the game was called while the player gathered his composure. In another episode, Perry lost his glasses while being tackled. Zach

[7]Reed, T., and Brown, M. (2000). The expression of care in the rough and tumble play of boys. *Journal of Research in Childhood Education, 15*(1), 104–116. Copyright 2000 by the Association for Childhood Education. Reprinted by permission.

shook the sand off the glasses and handed them back to Perry. When asked if Zach cared about him, Perry smiled demurely and said, "Yes." When Linden observed Zach dusting off Perry's glasses, he described it as a "friendly" thing to do. Brian characterized the same scenario as friendship more cautiously: "Not if they are acting but if they're really good friends." While watching an extended play scenario involving Patrick and Zach, Linden was asked if the pair were friends; he agreed, stating, "They must [be] because they been playing for a long time." It appears that friendship was considered by the participants to be a prerequisite for participating in R&T.

Table 4
Questions Asked <u>During the Second</u> Interview

Do you know what we talked about last week?
Where was his hand?
Why didn't he hit him?
Why did he take him to the teacher?
What are these boys doing?
What can you tell by the look on his face?
What is happening with the boy's glasses?
How can you tell they are friends or care about each other?

The second interview broadened the researchers' knowledge of the participants. Questions emerged from observation and from the first interview.

Several of the tackles during Smear resulted in a pile of bodies on top of one another, which often resulted in the boys checking to see if the fallen were hurt. When asked why they wanted to check on each other so much, Perry thought for a moment and said, "Well, we're best friends" and "We're like brothers." Zach added, "Well, if they get hurt we take them to a grown-up." When asked why he did that, Zach simply stated, "He's my friend." Brian also thought that some boys checked on their fallen friends for reasons other than friendship: "Well, they don't want to get into any trouble so they act nice to either person." The trouble Brian was referring to was with teachers who were not supportive of boys playing Smear. Friendship also received credit for acts of forgiveness. One time, Kevin pushed Patrick rather aggressively into Zach. When asked why he did not retaliate, Patrick simply replied, "Because we're friends." Kevin was very concerned because he knew that he had pushed a little harder than necessary, and so he went to see if Patrick was hurt. In summary, R&T appears to be the vehicle in which friendships are nurtured.

R&T Involves Intimate Physical Contact

Each of the six findings are presented as headings.

These R&T participants seemed to display a healthy respect for personal boundaries expressed through physical contact that, at times, was quite intimate. The participants knew what was considered appropriate touching during R&T, but were less certain when outside of the play arena. This lack of certainty was evident in responses to questions regarding whether it was appropriate to touch when outside the realm of R&T and, if so, where on the body was touching permissible. While observing Smear, it became evident that physical contact was often more than just an incidental part of the experience. The participants would allow themselves to be grabbed by their arms, legs, and/or crotch area before a collapsing into what Kevin described as a "puppy pile." After being tackled, the boys would often linger on the ground, laughing, with their bodies remaining in physical contact. Other times, particularly during lulls in the action, participants would walk around with their arms around each other or, on at least one occasion, holding hands.

Quotes from participants. Their "voices" are heard here.

The participants were certain that the boys who were physically touching were friends, and that "hanging on" or walking arm-in-arm was perfectly acceptable within the context of play. Perry commented, "They have their arms around each other because they are friends." Brian contributed, "They look like buddies because they are hanging around together." When pressed by the interviewer, the players would agree that hanging on to each other was similar to hugging, but they would not choose that terminology themselves.

When asked if this type of touching is permissible outside of the play context, the answers varied by age. Linden (age 6) thought it was acceptable to put his arm around anyone at anytime he pleased. Jake (age 8) was noncommittal, claiming that he didn't know. Kevin (age 9) was positive that any time other than in the Smear or R&T arena was not a good time to have his arm around another boy. Because the number of participants was low, it is not possible to make a generalization about what could be an age-related finding.

The boys had a clear sense of what was appropriate touching by a friend within R&T. When shown a videotape of a boy being picked up by a friend who had his hand placed on the boy's derriere, the informants all agreed that this type of touching was okay as long as they were friends and just playing. It was quite another matter, however, when asked what they would do if someone who was not a friend touched them like that. The older boys would be more likely to take matters into their own hands, whereas the younger boys would be more likely to seek help. Perry and Zach both claimed that inappropriate touching would lead to a fight. Brian and Kevin were far more vehement, stating, "I'll kill him." Patrick simply said, "I won't let him do that." Linden said, "I would tell the teacher." Jake was also clear in what to do; he claimed he would "get him off." The intensity of physical contact was markedly different for those who were considered friends versus those who were not friends. Clearly, the boys enjoyed physical contact with their friends; however, that contact was limited primarily to R&T play.

R&T as a Stylized Type of Play

This finding supports Donaldson's (1976) conclusion that R&T is ritualized and symbolic of aggression, but not real aggression. There was a predictable rhythm or pattern to the game of Smear. In fact, the behaviors involved in this game were so routine and predictable that they could be considered almost ritual in nature. Despite the negative appearance of Smear, the participants respected the rules of engagement and the seemingly aggressive yet respectful style of play. Those who did not know the rules or were unfamiliar with the style of play had difficulty playing with those who did. Any interruption in the play by a participant who either did not know the rules, or tried to change them, met resistance from those who routinely played together. New players were accepted, but only if they were willing to learn and follow the rules.

Recognizing a "play face" was something all of the players were able to do. Eye contact and body language clued the players into whether or not a player was being aggressive. The boy adopting a play face smiles, laughs, and uses eye contact to signal that even though his behavior might appear aggressive, he is still playing (Blurton-Jones, 1976). The Smear players knew the difference between the "play face" and an "aggressive or hostile face." They evaluated eye contact, facial expressions, and body posture to help make this determination.

Each one of the informants easily identified what a person looks like when he is angry. Common descriptors included drawn lips, scrunched eyes, furrowed eyebrows, and running too fast. Kevin was able to further identify aggression, as when a person "has his hands turned inward and arms outstretched like he's going to choke you." Perry added, "His eyes look bad." Brian said this about an aggressor's eyes: "They're probably stretched out wide." Those who attempted to play Smear but who could not read or missed the nonverbal cues were rejected or ignored.

Other clues were used as invitations in R&T, such as juking (faking), hiding, and playful taunting. During Smear, a player would stand as though inattentive, as a way to get someone to chase him. Another player would hide behind a tree and peek out, trying to coax someone into chasing him. There would be playful teasing as simple as "You can't catch me," which often would be enough to get the others to give chase. Recognizing the play face, the invitation to play allowed each player not only to know that it was safe to play, but also to be vulnerable to others. This point was underscored by Kevin, who stated, "Well, what makes it fun is that we're all trying to work together to get somebody down. We're playing together." Brian further stated, "One person jumps on him and throws him down and everybody else goes after him. So we're working like a team." Clearly, recognizing the play face and knowing the style of play were critical to the success of Smear and other types of R&T.

Players Knew or Observed the Rules

All the regular Smear players knew the rules that governed conduct and behavior. The major rules to Smear, as described by the participants, included: (1) taking turns tackling and being tackled

---

The researcher notes an unanticipated finding that suggests possible further research.

Voices of participants are presented and interpreted by the researcher.

Note the depth of the data collected.

while using only minimal force; (2) retaining possession of the ball when a player falls down accidentally; (3) tending to a player who gets hurt, and calling a teacher if needed; (4) waiting until the ball is thrown and caught before tackling a player; (5) chastising a player taking unfair advantage of a fallen player; and (6) recognizing that play face is an integral part of the R&T experience. Since the rules for Smear are not written, players recommitted to them daily. At times, a new rule could govern the game, such as a new boundary. However, unless embraced by the players, the new rule rarely lasted for more than a day.

The rules governing Smear were articulated verbally by older boys and understood by the younger ones. Linden, a younger participant, knew that the rules were not written down and that "somebody just taught us and you remember after the other day, after the other day" (meaning day after day). Linden knew that taking the ball when a player fell down accidentally was not fair, stating that "He gets to keep the ball." Kevin (the oldest and physically dominant) was the self-proclaimed rule-enforcer and chooser of players; he stretched the rules to his advantage, often hitting the players with more force while tackling or carrying the ball. When asked about this privilege, Kevin simply said, "I am the oldest and get to make the rules." Occasionally, an older and more physically developed boy would enter the game of Smear and instantly become the object of intense physical contact. This player was now granted the allowance of being more physical in tackling the younger players, as well as in being tackled, thus replacing Kevin in this leadership role. Again, Kevin understood his place, stating, "He is bigger than me and gets to make the rules." . . .

Knowledge of Rules Separated Players from Intruders

The participants were asked how they knew if a player was an intruder or going to be aggressive. Linden knew aggressive players "because they start pushing and stuff when they get mean." Jake claimed that an aggressor's eyes would be "weird," and "If they are knocking you down and taking the ball, this would not be fair." Other characteristics included frowning, arguing, anger, and retaliating when tackled. When asked what he would do if a person who did not follow the rules fell, Patrick said he would "just let him lay there and get stepped on." Brian had similar thoughts on the matter (although he was a little more civil), claiming, "We don't get real mad," and "If somebody's not playing fair, sometimes we tell them not to do it." Smear players as a group would try to ignore the intruders, ask them to leave, or, as a last resort, disband until the unwanted player(s) left.

On at least one occasion, a few known aggressive players attempted to join in Smear and try to fool the participants by either displaying a play face or verbalizing their intent to follow the rules. Experience taught the players to be aware of this tactic and of individuals who had used it in the past. David and Malachi had a reputation for hitting too hard and not stopping the game when someone had fallen. Although the pair promised to abide by the rules, they did not, and so the game was stopped until this uninvited and unwelcome twosome left. Patrick spoke for all the Smear players when he said, "We'd all have to agree on this," indicating that a group decision had been made and all were in agreement as to how to handle intruders.

R&T Rarely Results in Injury

An evaluation of the 119 episodes and three hours of R&T reveals only one instance of injury requiring adult attention: Brian stepped into a low spot in the sand and twisted his ankle. This injury resulted from running and not from direct contact with another player. It also occurred at a time when no one was chasing him. Three other players came by to ask Brian if he was okay; another player, recognizing that Brian was in pain, scurried off to get a supervisor. The players believed that they would not get hurt playing Smear, but also acknowledged that teachers did not like them to play this game, because they feared someone would get hurt. Brian affirmed this view by stating that when it came to playing Smear in school, "Teachers won't let us." Kevin was of a like mind: "Teachers sometimes don't understand how we play, and they are afraid that we will get hurt."

Note how the "voices" of the boys add a sense of reality to the research. Readers get to "know" the boys more than superficially.

Comments

Data were collected by both observation and interview methods. Note that quantitative data was collected as part of the qualitative study. Data were collected, described, and analyzed within the organization of six main "findings," or categories. Each finding provides a detailed description of its rationale. The "voices" of the boy participants are included in both the presentation of the data and its analysis.

The Dislocated Textile Workers in Rural Alabama: A Portrait[8]

Results of the Study

Many themes emerged during the course of the study. The dislocated workers expressed a myriad of concerns during this time in their lives. However two themes readily emerged early in the interview process and then continually throughout the life of the study. Each theme will be discussed separately.

The emerged themes are stated clearly.

"All One Happy Family"

As the interviews evolved it became clear that many of the participants were having the same feelings about specific issues. Several participants voiced concern about leaving their "family" of co-workers. The researcher found the interviews reinforced Hebert's familial concept when he interviewed students who worked closely in swim teams who developed the same type of "family" relationships (1995). One worker cried as she described her relationship with her co-workers, "I don't know what I'm going to do . . . these women are like my sisters. I have gone through my married life with them, a divorce, my kids growing up and everything. I am used to seeing these people every day . . . I tell them everything." Another woman was very frank about her co-workers, "Some of them I can live without but the girls in my group are my family, hell, they've gone through two husbands with me!"

Theme 1

Quotes support first theme.

All the participants voiced concern at having their support system being taken from them in such an abrupt manner. Most of the women had worked together for an extensive amount of time and felt their co-workers were part of their immediate family unit. The core of the group at each plant appeared to have remained intact over the years with a minimal amount of transition through the workforce. Many of the older women felt very maternal towards the younger members of the group. They felt responsible for the younger, more inexperienced workers and took them under their wing as well as mentored them. In fact the researcher saw generations working at the same factory. It was not unusual to find the grandmother-mother-daughter all working in the same textile plant in different departments.

"I Can't Do Anything Else, I'm Not Smart Enough"

Another theme that emerged rather quickly was the assumption by all the dislocated workers that they were "not smart enough" to make it outside the textile plant industry. All the workers had been out of school for at least 18 years and were reluctant to return to the classroom. Many of the participants discussed how they had been told by family members, husbands in particular, that they were not smart enough to get a GED, a college degree, or a different job. Many of the participants had no self-confidence in their own skills and self-esteem appeared to be in shreds.

Theme 2

An interesting spin-off on this theme was the results of the testing that was required of all participants. Test results indicated all participants had high levels of intelligence and academic skill, yet none seemed to accept that concept. When the results were revealed most participants asked for copies of scores to take home to family members to "prove they were smart." During

Note the researcher's subjectivity.

Note that tests are a quantitative data collection method.

[8]Lankford-Rice, S. G. (2000). The dislocated textile worker in rural Alabama: A portrait. *The Qualitative Report* [online], 4(1/2). Available at http://www.nova.edu/ssss/QR/QR4-1/lankford.html. Copyright ©2000. Reprinted by permission of the author and the Qualitative Report.

Note the researcher's
subjectivity.   ⟶

the interview process, a transformation seemed to take place in the participants when an independent test imparted the knowledge that the workers could be very successful in the classroom. To have an unbiased party express confidence in their abilities seemed to bolster their own self-confidence and esteem.

These two themes were the major two motifs that emerged through the interview process: the feeling of strong familial ties with the co-workers and the overwhelming lack of confidence in their own academic abilities. The 35 participants all divulged a myriad of feelings and emotions throughout the entire process, but the aforementioned themes seemed to be a part of all the interviews. It was interesting to note the metamorphosis all the participants affected as their confidence grew throughout their program of study. As the participants progressed in their studies, their own view of their abilities evolved. With each quarter and each grade sheet, all the ladies expressed a more independent nature. One participant grew so self-confident that she triumphantly announced her divorce decree in the office during one visit. She told the researcher that she had always been told she "was stupid" and through the JTPA college program she realized she wasn't. In every case, the participant "blossomed" while participating in the study; not every party confirmed it with a divorce, however.

Implications

JTPA addressed both motifs that evolved in the interviews. Many women were reluctant to embark on a new academic experience without at least one co-worker. Because the JTPA program scheduled departments together for interviews and testing, the workers felt more secure in their support network and more apt to take risks. Risks included working toward a GED and even going to college. The dislocated worker was able to transfer her support system from the workplace to the classroom with little disruption.

JTPA also addressed the "I'm stupid" theme by administering tests that proved to the participant she could succeed in the academic arena. These tests were the tangible evidence of intelligence for the women. These scores became badges of honor among the participants; even so much so that several ladies carried copies in their purses for reinforcement of the concept. While the testing remained competitive among the dislocated workers, it also cemented their camaraderie. It was proof in their own minds they knew each other better than their own family members.

Comments

Two research themes *emerged* from the research data: "We are a family" and "I can't do this." There was substantial use of participants' own descriptions of their perspective. Data from interviews evolved over a lengthy period of time. The interviews of the participants evidence emotive words, both from the interviewees and the researcher, such as "stupid," "badges of honor," and "blossomed." There is emphasis on the participants' emotional understanding of their plight.

INTERPRETATION

What you cannot explain to others, you do not understand yourself. Producing an account of our analysis is not just something we do for an audience. It is also something we do for ourselves. Producing an account is not just a question of reporting results; it is also another method of producing these results. Through the challenge of explaining ourselves to others, we can help to clarify and integrate the concepts and relationships we have identified in our analysis.[9]

---

[9]Dey, I. (1993). *Qualitative data analysis*. New York: Routledge (p. 237).

These comments contain a number of important insights about data analysis, interpretation, and writing. Dey emphasizes the need to understand one's own data in order to describe it to others. He notes that data interpretation continues on after the data collection, analysis, and interpretive stages of a study; interpretation is also a part of the process of writing the results of the study. *Interpreting* is the reflective, integrative, and explanatory aspect of dealing with a study's data. At this stage, the question is not, "What is in the data?" but rather, "What are the *meanings* in the data?" As we saw in our textile worker example, the interview data was analyzed and two clear themes emerged; we learned what was in the data. Later, we'll see how the researcher interpreted the study's findings—what did it all mean?

Data interpretation is based heavily on the connections, common aspects, and linkages among the data, especially the identified categories and patterns. One cannot classify data into categories without thinking about the meaning of the categories. Thus, implicitly or explicitly, the researcher is interpreting data whenever she or he uses some conceptual basis or understanding to cluster a variety of data pieces into a category. To aid interpretation, it is important to make explicit what the conceptual bases or understandings of the categories are and what makes one category different from another. Interpretation requires more conceptual and integrative thinking than data analysis, because interpretation involves identifying and abstracting important understandings from the detail and complexity of the data.

All researchers, and qualitative researchers in particular, must face the prospect of not being able to report in their analysis all of the data they have collected. This is a difficult reality for any researcher, but more so for qualitative researchers because of the time and effort it typically takes them to obtain and understand their data. Rarely is every piece of data used in the report of a study. Remember, the task of interpreting data is to identify the important themes or meanings in the data, not necessarily *every* theme.

It is also important to note that the nature of the qualitative research employed in a study strongly influences what areas of interpretation the study will emphasize. For example, if the study is ethnographic, interpretation will focus on the cultural patterns and perspectives of the participants. If the study is a case study, interpretation will focus on the characteristics of a single person or group. If the study is phenomenological, the focus will be on how individuals experienced a given phenomenon. If the study is based on a grounded theory design, the focus will be on generating a theoretical model or process of something its participants do. If the study is historical, the focus will be on understanding something that occurred in the past. Thus, as noted earlier in this chapter, the processes used among many qualitative approaches are quite similar, but the focuses of the studies vary.

Regardless of the research approach, the implicit issue in data interpretation is the answer to these three questions: "What is important in the data? Why is it important? What can be learned from it?"

The researcher's task, then, is to determine how one identifies what is important, why it is important, and what it indicates about the participants and context studied. As noted at numerous times, the process for answering these three questions is to a large extent idiosyncratic. Interpretation is personal. Thus, the process is difficult to teach because there are no hard and fast rules for how to go about the task of interpreting the meaning of data. As in most qualitative studies, it depends on the perspective and interpretive abilities of the researcher. Look back at the "Findings" section of the "Rough and Tumble Play" article and the "Results of the Study" section of the "Dislocated Textile Workers" article. Do these sections answer these three questions?

Lucky for you, there are some strategies that can help guide data interpretation. For example, pay attention to your topic or research focus; it should guide you when selecting important portions of your data for interpretation. Examine closely categories that contain large amounts of data; they are likely to identify important concepts for interpretation. Also, because they contain a great deal of data, look within the categories for links or sequences. Patterns represent the highest level of data integration, so identify the interrelations between categories that link to a pattern. "What do the links suggest? How do they relate to one another? What meaning do they have for the study's topic?" Also, examining existing studies related to your topic may identify interpretations pertinent to your study. Talk with colleagues or co-investigators about the data and its meaning, focusing on discussion of areas of agreement and disagreement. Finally, step back from the data every now and then to give yourself time to reflect on what you've seen and thought. All of these strategies are merely suggestions that may help in deriving interpretations from the data. In the end, these or other approaches to making sense of the data will only be as successful as your interpretive and integrative skills.

ENSURING CREDIBILITY IN YOUR STUDY

Throughout this chapter we have emphasized the centrality of the researcher as the integrator and interpreter of data. You might infer that this emphasis means that researchers have carte blanche when analyzing and interpreting data; that is, they can rely strictly on their personal feelings or preferences. This is definitely not the case. If qualitative research were based solely on producing unsubstantiated opinions, ignoring data that did not confirm the researcher's expectations, and failing to examine biases of research participants, it would be of little value. Thus, while researchers do have substantial control over data analysis and interpretations, that control should be exercised within guidelines. For example, Dey identifies six questions intended to help researchers check the quality of their data:[10]

- Are the data based on one's own observation, or is it hearsay?
- Is there corroboration by others of one's observation?
- In what circumstances was an observation made or reported?
- How reliable are those providing the data?
- What motivations might have influenced a participant's report?
- What biases might have influenced how an observation was made or reported?

As we discussed in earlier sections, prolonged research engagement, peer examination of meaning, and negative case analysis are tools that enhance analysis. Triangulation is another important and powerful approach used to establish the credibility of a qualitative research study. Triangulation is a form of cross-validation that seeks regularities in the data by comparing different participants, comments, settings, and methods to identify recurring results. The aim is to obtain similar information from different independent sources. Denzin[11] identifies three types of triangulation: (1) comparing multiple sources of data across participants, times, and sites, (2) comparing the results of multiple independent investigators, and (3) comparing multiple methods of data analysis. Other approaches to triangulation include observing participants' consistency in different situations or comparing participants' consistency in their verbal statements and actual performance. In each case, the ability to produce similar results from different times or methods enhances the credibility of the data.

Credibility of data can be attained by demonstrating that the concepts used to describe the study are congruent with the data selected to gather information about the concepts. For example, if the purpose of a study was to examine perceptions of participants' social justice in a community college, credibility would be demonstrated by showing that the data gathered matched the researcher's definition of social justice. Credibility also may be attained by eliminating rival explanations of the data and by showing that the study results are similar

---

[10]Dey, I. (1993). *Qualitative data analysis*. New York: Routledge (p. 224).

[11]Denzin, N. (1978). *The research act*. Newbury Park, CA: Sage.

to other, similar studies. Of course, triangulation is a paramount criterion for establishing qualitative research credibility.

A second criterion is *transferability,* which is concerned with transferring or generalizing the results of a study to other contexts. Transferability may relate to demonstrating that the results generalize to others in the original research context or to contexts beyond the original study. Recognize, however, that many qualitative researchers have no desire to generalize beyond the research setting, not feeling the necessity to leap beyond the initial study. In qualitative studies conducted in multiple settings, in which findings may be varied, generalization may be an important intent.

A third criterion is *including a methods section* that describes in depth the processes and methods used in the study. This criterion is commonly required of quantitative studies and is beginning to be recognized as an important aspect of qualitative research. In order to judge the credibility, transferability, and conclusions of a research study, it is important to know the methods applied to collect and interpret data. Without this information, it is difficult to judge the quality of the study and the meaningfulness of the results. For example, without information about how participants were selected, why particular data collection methods were chosen, how and how much data were collected, and how data were organized and analyzed, it is difficult to judge the quality and usefulness of the reported results. Thus, while data analysis and interpretation are heavily determined by the researcher, there are criteria that researchers should respect and respond to in conducting their own studies.

STEP 6: WRITING THE REPORT

The final stage in qualitative research is writing a report to describe the study and its findings. Of course, the characteristics and length of the report will depend on the type of report being written. If you are writing a dissertation, the report will be lengthy and structured by the dissertation format at your university. If you are preparing a journal article or a conference paper, it will be relatively short, often limited by the number of pages available to the journal's editor or minutes you have to present your report. Oddly, in most instances, the shorter the report, the harder it is to write because of the large amounts of data obtained in qualitative studies. There are a variety of qualitative research approaches to your report, such as ethnographic prose, biographical and autobiographical, oral or written historical, personal stories or activities, and many others.

Regardless of the form of writing you choose, it will serve a dual purpose. In addition to producing the report, the process will inevitably force you to reexamine your data interpretations. Unless you are astoundingly atypical, you probably have found that the writing process raises questions, concerns, and anomalies that were not questions, concerns, and anomalies when you were planning your writing. The concrete process of writing your thoughts in a logical and explanatory manner inevitably identifies flaws in your thinking, missing links in your descriptions, and new interpretations of your concepts and understandings. That is the reality and the importance of writing a report. So, as you strive to produce your report, recognize that your writing is also a test of your thoughts and interpretations. If something you write doesn't "feel" right or doesn't logically fit into a chain of reasoning you are developing, go back to your data and interpretations to try to understand why, so you can provide a more coherent, logical description.

There are many types of information that can be included in a research report. Obviously, the type of report will influence the number and depth of these. Typically, elements such as an introduction, purpose or focus of the study, information about existing literature, and the background of the study are placed in the introductory section of the report. Pieces such as descriptions of the data, the methods used to collect it, descriptions of the participants and context, development of categories and patterns, quotes and examples to illustrate the data, methods of data analysis, and major interpretations and findings are usually included in the body of the report. Finally, major conclusions, implications of your findings, and perhaps suggestions for future research belong in the ending or conclusion section of the report. Resist the temptation to summarize your findings; the conclusion is not a summary.

TELL A STORY

Dey[12] provides a useful metaphor relating writing a qualitative report to storytelling. He notes that qualitative report writing has three main features analogous to storytelling: a setting in which data are collected, characters who are informants, and a plot in the form of the social action in which the characters are engaged. Continuing the metaphor, he describes a good report as one that "provides an authentic context in which characters and plot can unfold," one that "engages our attention by making us care about what happens to the characters," and one in which there is "evolution of the plot toward some sort of climax or resolution." To keep the "story" coherent, the researcher must keep track of major activities and decisions made as the story unfolds and must integrate them into a report that flows logically and ends with some resolution or generalization. Note that keeping the story coherent and integrated may require elimination of data that are not central to the "plot."

To make the metaphor more descriptive, Dey provides six guidelines for writing the report:

1. Engage interest through description and dramatization.
2. Trace the evolution of the account.
3. Develop overall coherence.
4. Select key themes.
5. Use simple language.
6. Make concepts and connections explicit.[13]

Researchers conducting a qualitative study frequently ask if using the pronoun "I" in their written report is alright. First-person voice is perfectly acceptable. Qualitative reports can be organized in numerous ways, all intended to aid the readers' understanding. Some organizational techniques[14] include presenting data and findings as they unfolded for the researcher, thus recreating for the reader the fieldwork process of exploration and discovery; as a chronology, if time was important in the study; narrowing and expanding the focus, moving between theory and generalities to specifics; separating narration and analysis; and by themes or topics, as we see in our two qualitative articles in this chapter.

Although the style of the report is one matter, the issue of what makes an acceptable qualitative report is another. Throughout this chapter, characteristics of what makes an acceptable report have been identified, particularly in the section on "Interpretation." Figure 8.5 provides a more comprehensive list of characteristics that are important in producing an acceptable report. Although not every qualitative study will require each of the criteria listed in Figure 8.5, it will be useful for qualitative researchers to consider the list when planning a report in order to identify the criteria that should be addressed.

EXAMPLES OF QUALITATIVE RESEARCH: NARRATIVE

Now let us read the concluding sections of our two qualitative articles that we have examined in these chapters. In the first, "The Expression of Care in the Rough and Tumble Play of Boys," we examine the "Discussion" and "Implications" sections, and in "The Dislocated Textile

---

[12]Dey, I. (1993). *Qualitative data analysis.* New York: Routledge (pp. 238–249).

[13]Dey, I. (1993), p. 247.

[14]Glesne, C. (1999). *Becoming qualitative researchers: An introduction,* 2nd ed., New York: Longman (pp. 165–166).

FIGURE 8.5 Common criteria for qualitative reports.

(1) The method is explicated in detail so the reader can judge whether it was adequate and makes sense. An articulate rationale for the use of qualitative methods is given so that skeptics will accept the approach. The methods for attaining entry and managing role, data collection, recording, analysis, ethics, and exit are discussed. There is an audability trail—a running record of procedures (often done in an appendix)—and there is description of how the site and sample were selected. Data collection and analysis procedures are public, not magical.

(2) Assumptions are stated. Biases are expressed, and the researcher does a kind of self-analysis for personal biases and a framework analysis for theoretical biases.

(3) The research guards against value judgments in data collection and in analysis.

(4) There is abundant evidence from raw data to demonstrate the connection between the presented findings and the real world, and the data are presented in readable, accessible form, perhaps aided by graphics, models, charts, and figures.

(5) The research questions are stated, and the study answers those questions and generates further questions.

(6) The relationship between this study and previous studies is explicit. Definitions of phenomena are provided, with explicit reference to previously identified phenomena, but it is clear that the research goes beyond previously established frameworks—challenging old ways of thinking.

(7) The study is reported in a manner that is accessible to other researchers, practitioners, and policy makers. It makes adequate translation of findings so that others will be able to use the findings in a timely way.

(8) Evidence is presented showing that the research was tolerant of ambiguity, searched for alternative explanations, checked out negative instances, and used a variety of methods to check the findings (i.e., triangulation).

(9) The report acknowledges the limitations of generalizability while assisting the readers in seeing the transferability of findings.

(10) It is clear that there was a phase of "first days in the field" in which a problem focus was generated from observation, not from library research. In other words, it is a study that is an exploration, not merely a study to find contextual data to verify old theories.

(11) Observations are made (or sampled) of a full range of activities over a full cycle of activities.

(12) Data are preserved and available for reanalysis.

(13) Methods are devised for checking data quality (e.g., informants' knowledgeability, ulterior motives, and truthfulness) and for guarding against ethnocentric explanations.

(14) In-field work analysis is documented.

(15) Meaning is elicited from cross-cultural perspectives.

(16) The researcher is careful about sensitivity of those being researched—ethical standards are maintained.

(17) People in the research setting benefit in some way (ranging from getting a free meal or an hour of sympathetic listening to being empowered to throw off their chains).

(18) Data collection strategies are the most adequate and efficient available. There is evidence that the researcher is a finely tuned research instrument, whose personal talents, experiential biases, and insights are used consciously. The researcher is careful to be self-analytical and recognize when she or he is getting subjective or going native.

(19) The study is tied into "the big picture." The reasearcher looks holistically at the setting to understand linkages among systems.

(20) The researcher traces the historical context to understand how institutions and roles have evolved.

Source: Marshall, C., and Rossman, G. (1995). *Designing qualitative research* (2nd ed.), Thousand Oaks, CA: Sage Publications, (pp. 146–148). Copyright 1995 Sage Publications. Reprinted by permission of Sage Publications, Inc.

Workers . . ." we look at the "Discussion" and "Paula's Story" sections to get an idea of how these researchers wrote the narrative to sum up their study's findings. Remember to look for what is important in the data, why it is important, and what can be learned from it.

The Expression of Care in the Rough and Tumble Play of Boys[15]

Discussion

R&T generally, and the game of Smear specifically, appear to be a staging area for caring friendships. To these participants, R&T is also a place for negotiation, problem solving, fulfilling their need to belong to a group, having intimate contact with friends, experiencing friendly competition, and developing a sense of community somewhere between the warmth and closeness of family and the isolation and indifference of the adult masculine world. The observations in this study clearly support both Donaldson's (1976) suggestion that intimate contact is established in R&T and Pellegrini's (1989) assertion that social competence is being developed. Only those boys who were trusted friends and competent in following the rules were welcomed into the game.

Early childhood literature, most notably that in the area of developmentally appropriate practice (DAP), seems to have adopted society's fear in not permitting intimate contact among males. Ignoring the research on R&T, some writers consider R&T to be a form of antisocial behavior (Ladd, 1983) that should be discouraged. In the first edition of the National Association for the Education of Young Children handbook on developmentally appropriate practice, Bredekamp (1986, p. 74) calls for intervention when children "get carried away" with chasing or wrestling. Yet, chasing and wrestling are two salient characteristics of R&T. Ward (1996) further suggests that aggressive play should be eliminated, failing to make a distinction between real aggression and play that appears aggressive.

This attitude may be changing. The latest edition of NAEYC's developmentally appropriate practice guidelines suggests that R&T is acceptable, but only for preschool-age children (Bredekamp & Copple, 1997). The frequently expressed concern that R&T is too rough was not supported by the data in this study. Brian, the only child to be injured in three hours of R&T play, turned his ankle when he accidentally stepped in a low spot on the ground. Pellegrini (1989) asserts that aggressive play amounts to less than 5% of all play on the playground. Therefore, the often expressed fear that "someone will get hurt" is proven to be of low probability, with the benefits of R&T far outweighing the possibility of injury.

Boys in early childhood are very affectionate and enjoy physical and emotional closeness with their parents (Gilligan, 1982). Gilligan asserts, however, that boys as early as age 3 begin to gradually withhold outward expressions of feelings. Males are taught that "big boys don't cry," and that to "be a man" one must hold in one's feelings. Indeed, being the "strong silent type" is viewed as an attractive feature. This also may be the point at which males begin to hide their true feelings, and their voices go "underground" in a similar fashion to that which Gilligan (1982) speaks of for girls. The affectionate and emotionally expressive male finds that he will pay a price among his peers. As expressions of feelings and intimate contact are driven underground, they seem to resurface in R&T. Goldstein (1998) suggests that if more men were involved in the giving and receiving of care as an ongoing, central, and valued part of their lives, they would be as likely to espouse this viewpoint in a similar fashion as women. Present research clearly demonstrates that although males do care for one another, societal pressures force them to express that caring in a much different way than females. This attitude also may be changing as parents and society in general have become more aware of gender stereotyping, and fathers are becoming more aware of their sensitive side.

R&T appears to be used by boys as camouflage for expressions of intimacy and care. The very name chosen by the boys for their game, "Smear the Queer," is an act of camouflage. Fine (1986)

Literature review. Note how the researchers integrate their study data with statements taken from the literature, to support or refute these statements.

---

[15]Reed, T., and Brown, M. (2000). The expression of care in the rough and tumble play of boys. *Journal of Research in Childhood Education, 15*(1), 104–116. Copyright 2000 by the Association for Childhood Education. Reprinted by permission.

suggests that the word "queer" may be used to indicate "sissy" or "cry baby," rather than a homosexual. In any event, by using the name Smear the Queer, the boys declare that the game is only for the masculine. Yet, the underlying behaviors are in fact acts of intimacy, which in a different context could and probably would be misconstrued as homosexual in nature. The participants, except for the youngest, fully understand that touching each other is only acceptable in the context of play. Imagine, for a moment, two 7-year-old girls who are best friends kissing each other as they part company. Now imagine two 7-year-old boys who are also best friends doing the same thing. The boys will likely be shamed for this behavior and taught that the masculine thing to do is "shake hands" and that boys do not kiss each other. This unwarranted fear of intimacy among boys (homophobia) may actually retard intimate contact and, consequently, boys' emotional development. Suppression of R&T may be a further illustration of our culture's homophobia.

Survey from literature cited.

A survey of over 200 early childhood and elementary teachers suggests that they often interpret R&T play as aggressive, and that they attempt to discourage it (Reed, Brown, & Roth, in press). These teachers seem to be less interested in the potential benefits to children engaging in R&T and more concerned with controlling play. When teachers and administrators deny children the opportunity to participate in R&T, however, they deny them an opportunity to care for one another. Noddings (1992) stresses the importance of such opportunities to acquire skills in care giving and to experience care. For boys, there is much care expressed in R&T that does not fit within the framework of traditional means of expressing care. The authors join Noddings in suggesting that school personnel need to help students increase their self-understanding through reflection on their recreational choices. When boys are denied the opportunity to experience R&T, they are also denied one of the few socially acceptable ways to express care and intimacy for another male. Miller (1994) refers to schools' denial of such opportunities as poisonous pedagogy; in other words, while ostensibly acting in children's best interests, schools may be doing harm to children.

Researcher states agreement with literature.

Implications

An implication of this study is that early childhood and elementary literature should encourage R&T, recommending that schools design playground space suitable for its rough nature and allot time for R&T for those who choose this method of self-expression. Teacher education programs and programs for educating administrators should include information on the difference between R&T and aggressive behavior, as well as the nature of caring among preadolescent boys. Preservice and inservice educators should be led to examine society's stereotypes regarding gender and the concept of gender-appropriate behaviors. This study's findings also suggest that further research is needed to determine how children of different ages perceive intimate touching.

Boulton and Smith (1989) found that confusion between real fighting and play fighting can occur from misinterpretations of the play signal or because of cheating. Pellegrini (1995) found that play tutoring can enhance the development of social, cognitive, and linguistic abilities (Saltz, Dixon, & Johnson, 1977; Smilansky, 1968). A particularly interesting and potentially fruitful exploration would be to study the use of R&T to improve aggressive children's social competence. A baseline of the attitudes and values of educators and parents toward R&T should be established so that any changes could be documented. Finally, R&T among girls and cross-gender groups should be observed, to describe and assess what this type of play means to them.

Suggestions for further research.

Although there are many and varied definitions of play, there is at least one essential characteristic: legitimate forms of play (including R&T) must not purposely result in children's psychological or physical victimization (MacDonald, 1992). A child should never be unmercifully teased, pushed around by older or more physically dominating children, verbally abused, or made to perform rituals that are not appropriate for the situation. This is not tolerable. This study and its findings add to the growing body of literature supporting R&T as a legitimate form of play beneficial for the participants. Rough and tumble play, as well as other aspects of childhood, need to be examined in the context of childhood, not adulthood. Educators must learn to evaluate R&T's meaning for the participants. If educators are to develop a greater respect for childhood, they must respect the rights of children to be childish and to express themselves more openly through play.

Comments

There is a heavy use of the existing literature in describing the research results. Here, literature is used to aid data analysis and interpretation. These researchers examined the literature both to corroborate the study results and to link them to the literature; this gives the study validity. There is a good explanation in this narrative for why and how the boys engage in R&T, and justification for the study's overall conclusion that R&T is good for early childhood and elementary pupils.

The Dislocated Textile Workers in Rural Alabama: A Portrait[16]

Discussion

The dislocated workers' emotions and feelings ran high during the course of their participation in the program as well as the study. The findings in this research were significant to the Skills Center because it helped the staff understand the emotions of such a turbulent time for the workers. Many staff members had not experienced a layoff with few or no options and the research helped them empathize with the workers on a deeper level. Too many times, participants in programs such as this become "numbers" rather than people and this study helped affix a face and a story behind each statistic. The research guided the staff in this center in designing the types of activities needed for the participant as well as choosing the types of counseling techniques employed in one-on-one sessions.

Follow-up studies are imperative to gauge the lay-off trends prevalent in the area. Future studies would be able to better assess the needs of future dislocated workers as well as study the long term impacts of the JTPA program in the lives of the participants of this particular study. Specific studies could focus on the accomplishments of this group and how retraining shaped their lives and the explicit effects upon their families. Further studies could be made into the effects of a parent returning to school on the children. Such a study would be significant in other areas and could impact reforms regarding those areas such as welfare to work.

A case study follows that epitomizes the dislocated female workers in the Jackson-Dekalb county area. Paula's story mirrors the stories of all 35 participants in this study.

Paula's Story

Paula lived in rural Dekalb county all her life and met her husband while both were in high school. She dated him all through school and on the day she graduated from high school set her wedding day. Immediately upon marrying she became pregnant with her first child and worked to help put her husband through college. After her second child was born she stopped working and became a full-time mom. Paula continued to stay at home until after her fifth child started school. It was then she went back to work in a textile plant. It was this job she liked most because her co-workers took her in and treated her like a family member. Paula shared the details of her life with her co-workers and the kinship grew. "I spent 8 hours a day with these women; that was more time than I spent with my family during the week!" She invited these fellow workers into her home and life. She bought gifts and even baby-sat for the workers who delivered babies; she invited them to her daughter's wedding. They helped her through the trying time when her parents died. They were the friends who were there for her in the "worst of times and best of times." "These women were like my sisters. I could always count on them."

When the plant closing was announced, Paula was concerned, of course, about her extended family and the loss of income, but her main concern was about the kind of job she would get next. "I didn't know what I would do after the plant shut down. I had my husband and my kids, of course, but what was I going to do? To me losing my job and my co-workers was like losing family members." On the last day of work, Paula and her co-workers cried and promised to get together at least once a week as a support group. In the following weeks, they remained a close knit

Margin notes (left side):

Note the findings' practical value.

Future studies suggested. Researchers typically plan and carry out a number of related studies to deepen their understanding of a topic.

Including a case study in narrative to illustrate a viewpoint.

Concern of the participant. Participants' "voices" are heard.

---

[16]Lankford-Rice, S. G. (2000). The dislocated textile worker in rural Alabama: A portrait. *The Qualitative Report* [online], 4(1/2). Available at http://www.nova.edu/ssss/QR/QR4-1/lankford.html. Copyright ©2000. Reprinted by permission of the author and *The Qualitative Report*.

group until the different members began finding other work. Others took advantage of the JTPA program and started training for new jobs. Paula herself decided to give it a shot and see if she could make it in college. It was a new environment for her and she thrived in her new academic environment. The JTPA program provided Paula with the opportunity to return to school and earn her degree. "That was the other really scary move for me; I had been a stay at home mom for so long I just wasn't sure if I could hack it in school. Everybody encouraged me including my old friends from the plant, so I am glad I really did well." While many work friends dropped out of touch along the two years Paula was in school, there were a few who remained in her inner circle of friends. These friends remained by her side as she studied hard and maintained a 4.0 average while raising a family and watched her walk across the stage to receive her degree. "I had a case worker at the JTPA office who was always there when I felt down. I knew I could go there and be encouraged. Even when I wanted to throw my hands up and just give up, I knew that JTPA would help me through whatever crisis I was having at the time."

Paula has since graduated from college and started to work for the Director of the Technical Division of her alma mater. Her office handles all the JTPA students at the college. Part of her duties consists of maintaining records for JTPA students and acting as liaison for the students. She gives encouragement to people just like herself who come back to school after being dislocated. Paula credits JTPA with giving her the opportunity to change the direction of her life, but credits her family and herself for having the determination to continue. "The people at the JTPA program made me believe in myself again. If it weren't for the people at JTPA I don't think I would have had the courage to go back to school after such a long time. My family told me I could do it and I believed them. But I also know they love me and wanted me to be happy. The people at the JTPA office showed me I could do it with my test scores—that's what made me know I could be successful."

When asked how she likes her new career, she smiles a wide grin and says, "Oh I love it . . . and the best part is when I see a dislocated worker from JTPA. I can honestly tell them that it is going to be all right because I know from experience. I can look in their eyes and see myself when I first got laid off; I just hope they can look at me and see themselves when they finally graduate!"

Comments

This study focuses on a socially undesirable theme: the plight and layoffs of female workers. The emotions of the participants are prominent in the study. The case of Paula is presented in depth, with deep, rich data about Paula and her family. Much of Paula's story is told in her own voice and we get to know Paula and her circumstance in a way we would not if the study was quantitative. Also note, in the Discussion section, the suggested topics for future studies.

POSTANALYSIS CONSIDERATIONS

Whether you do your analyses by hand or computer, all data should be thoroughly checked and stored in an organized manner.

VERIFICATION AND DATA CHECKING

Verification involves double-checking the data and organizing it, and evaluating the research conclusion. Double-checking qualitative data (observation notes, interview and recording transcriptions, and so forth) may seem a bit excessive, but conclusions are only valid to the degree that data are accurate. Remember the saying "GIGO"—garbage in . . . garbage out. Thus, the original data should be rechecked, preferably all but at least a high percentage of it. If raw data were coded into a smaller number of categories, the coded data should be compared to the initial uncoded data to make sure coding was done properly. If data are kept in a computer, they should be printed and examined for thoroughness—in file names, to make sure no data was lost, for dates, times, participants' names, and so forth. Considering that a study is worthless if inaccurate data are analyzed, and considering all the effort that has been expended to this point of the study, time rechecking data is time well spent. It is better for you to find any errors, than for your advisor or a reader to find them.

When analyses are done, typically by hand, the reasonableness of the results (patterns, categories) should be checked. When data are analyzed by computer, output must be checked very carefully. Usually (but not always), if the data have been entered correctly into a computer, the results of the computer analysis will be accurate. Some people are under the mistaken impression that if a result was produced by a computer, it is automatically correct. "The results must be right; the computer did them." Wrong! Computers may not make mistakes but people do, and people are who input data. So, spot check your data to ensure accuracy. If you end up with a result that just does not look right, it is a lot easier to find an error if every step is in front of you. Computer analyses rarely show each step in the analysis process, only the final result. This is a disadvantage of computer usage, especially if the software is new to the researcher.

STORAGE

When you are convinced that your work is accurate, data should be labeled, organized, and filed in a safe place. You never know when you might need your data again. Sometimes an additional analysis is desired either by the original researcher, an advisor, or another researcher who wishes to analyze the data using a different approach. Also, it is not unusual to reuse data from one study in a later study. Therefore, all of the data should be carefully labeled with as many identification labels as possible, such as the dates of the study, names and contact information for each participant and gatekeeper, data source, and so forth. Find a safe place and guard it very carefully. If you use a computer, keep one set of data in your computer or hard drive, but also keep a labeled, backup floppy disk in case your computer or hard drive crashes.

Now go to the Companion Website accompanying this text at www.prenhall.com/gay to check your understanding of chapter concepts in the following modules: Objectives, Practice Quiz, and Applying What You Know. Expand your research skills with Evaluating Articles, Analyzing Qualitative Data, Analyzing Quantitative Data, and Research Tools and Tips. Visit Web Links to broaden your knowledge about research.

SUMMARY

Preparing to Analyze Data

1. Qualitative data analysis requires the researcher to systematically search, categorize, integrate, and interpret the data collected in a study.

2. Because qualitative data are typically voluminous, the researcher should try to narrow the focus of the study to facilitate analysis.

3. A great deal of data analysis occurs before data collection is complete. Researchers think about and make hunches about what they see and hear during data collection.

4. *Analysis* involves describing what's in the data. *Interpretation* involves making sense of what the data mean.

5. There is no single, agreed-on approach for qualitative data analysis. The method selected will depend in part on the topic chosen and the researcher's analytic abilities. The researcher has the key role in data analysis.

Step 5: Analyzing the Data

6. Data analysis typically involves five processes: data managing; reading/memoing; describing; classifying; and finally, interpreting. These processes do not have to be applied sequentially during analysis.

7. Data analysis is a cyclical, iterative process of reviewing data for common topics or themes. The analytic focus is on the context, events, and participants, with a focus on describing from the perspective of the participants. Three approaches to data analysis are the constant comparative, negative case, and analytic induction approaches.

8. Classifying small pieces of data into more general categories is the qualitative researcher's way to make sense and find connections among the data.

9. Field notes and transcriptions are broken down into small pieces of data, and these pieces are integrated into categories and often to more general patterns.

10. Typically, data analysis results in a pyramid, with small *data pieces* at the bottom layer linked to larger and more general *categories*, and categories linked to even more general *patterns*.

11. The length of data analysis is difficult to state. It depends mainly on the nature of the study, the amount of data to be analyzed, and the analytic and synthetic abilities of the researcher.

12. Data interpretation is based heavily on the connections, common aspects, and linkages among the data pieces, categories, and patterns. Interpretation cannot be meaningfully accomplished unless the researcher knows the data in great detail.

13. The aim of interpretation is to answer three questions: "What is important in the data? Why is it important? What can be learned from it?"

14. There are some strategies that can help answer these questions: pay attention to your research topic when searching for interpretations; examine closely categories that contain a large amount of data pieces because they likely identify important concepts or practices; examine the findings of other researchers to identify interpretations; and talk to co-investigators and colleagues.

15. Much of analysis and interpretation relies on the skills of the researcher. However, while the researcher is the main analyst and interpreter, she or he must act within guidelines that help maintain the integrity of the analysis and interpretation.

16. Guidelines for analysis and interpretations include (1) the credibility of the link between the topic studied and the data used to examine the topic; (2) the description of the methods used to collect, analyze, and interpret the data; (3) expressing researcher and participant biases; and (4) checking data quality.

17. Many computer programs are available for qualitative data analysis.

Step 6: Writing the Report

18. The nature of the final report of the qualitative study differs with the type of report needed (e.g., dissertation, speech, journal article, etc.).

19. Data analysis and interpretation also go on during the writing of the report. Writing tests the quality and meaningfulness of ideas and logic. Inevitably the writer must return to the data to clarify a thought or to verify a logical connection in the report.

20. The report should focus on the key themes and interpretations in the data, not on every theme or interpretation. Language should be straightforward and not contain jargon. First-person voice is acceptable. Qualitative reports are often more like a story than a formal report.

TASK 6   PERFORMANCE CRITERIA

The qualitative research topic or problem should be open ended and exploratory in nature. Your qualitative research questions should be worded to illuminate an issue and provide understanding of a topic, not answer specific questions. You should mention the type of research approach you will use, whether it is a case study, a grounded theory study, an ethnography, or historical research. The reason you chose this topic, or the nature of its importance, should be mentioned.

Qualitative studies may include literature citations in the introduction of a study to provide background information for the reader and to build a case for the need for the study. Literature relevant to the research topic should be presented in your example, and citations should follow APA style (i.e., Smith, 2002). Despite the fact that your study may not require a literature review until data collection begins, cite some related texts anyway to get practice weaving the literature into the plan.

The description of participants should include the number of participants, how they were selected, and major characteristics (for example, occupation). Participants are ideally interviewed or observed in their natural setting to keep the interview or observation as authentic as possible. The description of the setting should be included.

Data collection methods should be described, and there may be more than one data collection method in a study. Qualitative data are descriptive; they are collected as words. Data may be in the form of interview notes and transcriptions, observation field notes, and the like. The researcher will be immersed in the data and participate in data collection. Instruments may be video cameras, audio tape recorders, notepads, researcher-created observation records, and so forth. The description of instruments should also describe their validity and reliability. Also see Figure 8.5 for other criteria for qualitative reports.

The following pages present an example that illustrates the performance called for by Task 6. (See Task 6 Example.) The Task Example is representative of the level of understanding that you should have after studying chapters 6, 7, and 8. This researcher still needs to choose his core participants, carry out data collection and data analysis, and write the final study. He constructed his plan taking into consideration the six steps in the research process. Note that not all plans or proposals require a results section.

TASK 6 EXAMPLE

Research Plan for: How Do Teachers Grade Student Essays?

The Research Aim

The purpose of this study was to examine the ways that freshman and sophomore high school English teachers grade their students' essays. I chose this topic to study because students in my school complain that their essays are graded unfairly. For example, one student said, "Teachers give the same scores for essays of different length." Other comments I hear include, "Teachers don't provide enough information about the number of examples they want included in an essay" and "Teachers don't give enough information about features they want included in essays so I can never match what they expect." I wanted to understand how teachers actually grade student essays. I also wanted to find out what criteria teachers use and whether they explain their essay grading criteria to their students, or whether the students' complaints are legitimate.

At the beginning of my exploration, my topic was stated generally, but through my initial investigations, it has narrowed a bit. Because qualitative research involves recurring study and examination, the topic may narrow some more. My approach is to carry out an ethnographic study. The research context is participants' classrooms.

Literature Review

An initial concern was the decision of whether to obtain and study existing literature, and if so, at what point in the study. For this study, I have consulted two assessment books frequently read by teachers in teacher education programs, Nitko (2001) and Linn and Gronlund (2000), to find out what sort of training teachers receive in scoring essays. Having some understanding of the following will help me to recognize scoring practices in the teachers I plan to interview: forms and uses of essay questions, their advantages and limitations, how essay questions should be constructed to measure the attainment of learning outcomes, and essay question scoring criteria. Later in the study, I may find a need to examine additional literature, but for now, this has been sufficient.

Choosing Participants

I identified teachers in freshman and sophomore English classes in an urban high school as participants for the study. The high school is the context for the ethnographic setting of the study. I contacted the school principal initially to propose the study and receive her approval before proceeding and contacting potential participants. She was cordial, and asked for more information about the role that the teachers and students would have. We discussed her concerns and she consented. She indicated that she would send informed consent forms to the parents involved in the study. All but two of the students' parents agreed to let their children participate. There was no indication why the parents declined the request.

The principal of the school also provided me with copies of the school's Human Subject Review Form to give to the teachers to sign when I explained their part in the study to them. I contacted the freshman and sophomore English teachers in the school, and described the project to them as an exploratory study about how teachers plan lessons and assess their students. I also told them, and the principal concurred, that each teacher participant would be identified by a number rather than by a name in the final written study. Only I would know the identities of the teachers. I thought this would allow the teachers to be more open when providing data. All but three teachers agreed to become participants in the study. Two of these teachers asked for more information about what would be asked of them. One of the two teachers agreed to participate after more discussion, but the remaining two teachers still opted not to participate. I thought this final number, 8 teacher participants, was a good sample for the study. The principal has been a helpful gatekeeper and interested observer. In general, the school personnel are supportive.

I will identify approximately 10 students to participate in the study and provide comments about essay items and graded essays. I suspect that this number will decrease once data collection begins and I determine which participants can provide the most helpful comments.

As the research data are collected, I will note the comments of the teachers, not only to obtain their comments on grading essays, but also to identify the most articulate and conceptual teachers to focus on during data collection. Ultimately, I will have a smaller number of core participants than I began with.

Data Collection

The teachers will be studied in their own context, in each teacher's own classroom. If this is not possible, data collection will take place somewhere else in the school. Ethnographic data collection relies heavily on asking questions, interviewing, and observing participants. Each of these methods will be applied over a period of 12 weeks. I plan to collect data in the form of completed and graded student essays from the teachers. I expect to collect approximately 7 to 9 essays per teacher over the 12 weeks. I think this will be sufficient to capture and integrate the data.

I have arranged to receive a copy of each essay exam or assignment. The purpose of this form of data collection is to assess the characteristics of the essay items. I plan to examine the essay items to evaluate whether students understand what is expected of them in this type of performance assessment. I will also look at samples of the teachers' essay items that will be critiqued by students. Again, the names of the students will be confidential.

I also plan to informally interview teachers and ask questions such as "Tell me how you grade your essays and why," "What do you consider to be the best feature of your essay grading?" "What do you consider to be the weakest feature of your essay grading?" Similar questions will be asked of the students in informal interviews.

During the 12-week period, I plan to hold several focus groups, one with teachers, and one with students, in which grading is discussed. The focus groups will be audiotaped and then transcribed. Finally, I will employ observation to obtain data. I will observe teachers grading student essays, question them about why they assign the grade they do, note the time it takes them to grade the items, and so forth. If written feedback is provided for the graded essays, I will collect a copy as data, for later analysis. I will also follow these graded essays and ask the students whether they feel the essay items are fairly graded. Therefore, my data will include student artifacts, audiotapes, field notes and memos from informal questioning and interviews, and field notes from observations.

Data Analysis

As data are collected from the participants, I will examine and reexamine the data in search of themes and integration in the data to arrive at a number of themes. I anticipate that analyzing and synthesizing the data will take approximately three to four weeks, eight hours a day, after data collection ends. Triangulation among asking questions, observing, interviewing, and analyzing essays will help to integrate the analysis.

Results

The final step will be to describe the procedures and interpretation in a written format for others to examine and critique. Before writing up the study, it will be important to spend time thinking about the data analysis and interpret what the data reveal. I hope to be able to express a contribution or insight that emerges from this study.

"Undertaken by teacher-practioners, action research involves one or more teachers (or counselors or administrators) looking at their own practice or a situation involving students' development or behavior." (p. 261)

CHAPTER 9

ACTION RESEARCH

OBJECTIVES

After reading Chapter 9, you should be able to do the following:

1. Describe the purposes of action research.
2. Describe the benefits of action research.
3. Identify the four basic steps in conducting action research.
4. Identify common data collection sources and strategies used to carry out action research in schools.

Action research, also called teacher research and teacher-as-researcher, is an approach designed to develop and improve teaching and learning. The essence of action research is teachers' solving everyday problems in schools to improve both student learning and teacher effectiveness.

The linking of the terms *action* and *research* highlight the essential features of the method: (1) seeking out aspects in teaching as a means for increasing knowledge and (2) improving practice. Undertaken by teacher-practitioners, action research involves one or more teachers (or counselors or administrators) looking at their own practice or a situation involving students' development or behavior. Action research is a structured process in which teachers identify, examine, and improve aspects of their practice.

TASK 7

Develop a design for an action research study to answer a school-based research question. (See Performance Criteria, p. 273.)

SCHOOL-BASED ACTION RESEARCH

Interest in teacher action research is growing, partly because it provides teachers the opportunity to study and improve their own practice and because it provides them an opportunity to work together on common issues or everyday concerns in their classrooms. Good action research integrates theory, practice, and meaningful applications of research results. Action research encourages change in schools, empowers individuals through collaboration with one another, encourages teacher reflection, and examines new methods and ideas. Action research is typically focused on a particular issue or concern that is examined in a single school. The results tend to be localized to a given school, department, or classroom. Table 9.1 compares action research with traditional educational research.

Varied views of action research have over the years shown a common perspective. Kurt Lewin[1] describes action research as a three-step spiral process of (1) planning that involves reconnaissance; (2) taking action; and (3) fact-finding about the results of the action. Stephen Corey[2] states that action research is the process by which practitioners attempt to study their problems scientifically in order to guide, correct, and evaluate their decisions and actions. Carl Glickman[3] says that action research in education is study conducted by colleagues in a school setting of the results of their activities to improve instruction. Emily

---

[1]Lewin, K. (1947). Frontiers in group dynamics. II. Channels of group life: social planning and action research. *Human Relations, 1,* 143–153.

[2]Corey, S. M. (1953). *Action research to improve school practices.* New York: Bureau of Publications, Teachers College, Columbia University.

[3]Glickman, C. D. (1992). The essence of school renewal: the prose has begun. *Educational Leadership, 50*(1), 24–27.

TABLE 9.1   A Comparison of Traditional Research and Action Research

WHAT?	TRADITIONAL RESEARCH	ACTION RESEARCH
Who?	Conducted by university professors, scholars, and graduate students on experimental and control groups.	Conducted by teachers and principals on children in their care.
Where?	In environments where variables can be controlled.	In schools and classrooms.
How?	Using quantitative methods to show, to some predetermined degree of statistical significance, a cause-effect relationship between variables.	Using qualitative methods to describe what is happening and to understand the effects of some educational intervention.
Why?	To report and publish conclusions that can be generalized to larger populations.	To take action and effect positive educational change in the specific school environment that was studied.

Source: From Mills, G. (2003). *Action Research: A Guide for the Teacher Researcher,* 2nd ed., p. 5. Upper Saddle River, NJ: Merrill/Prentice Hall. Reprinted by permission.

Calhoun[4] describes action research as a fancy way of saying "let's study what's happening in our school and decide how to make it a better place." For practical purposes, we will summarize these findings with our own simple definition: action research involves teachers identifying a school-based topic or problem to study, collecting and analyzing information to solve or understand a teaching problem, or helping teachers understand aspects of their practice. Action research is educative, focuses on teachers and schools, focuses on problems of practice, and aims at improving practice.

Increasingly, teachers are understanding that knowledge can be found in their own experiences and meaning. Teachers' action research emerges from the areas they consider problematic and from the discrepancies between what is intended and what actually occurs in their teaching. The increase in site-based and shared decision making is growing, particularly in schools, providing and encouraging teachers to examine their own classroom problems and issues. With this newly acquired autonomy, however, comes new responsibilities. Teachers, local schools, and school districts are accountable to stakeholders for the policies, programs, and practices they implement. It is not enough for teachers merely to make decisions; they will be called on to make *informed* decisions—decisions that are data driven. Therefore, it is necessary for teachers to be much more deliberate in documenting and evaluating their efforts. Action research is one means to that end. Action research assists practitioners and other stakeholders in identifying needs, assessing development processes, and evaluating outcomes of the changes they define and implement. The self-evaluation aspect of teacher research by educators is congruent with the present focus on constructivism. Although both qualitative and quantitative research methods are used in action research, it is clear that in action research qualitative methods are used most frequently.

Several benefits ensue from the use of action research.[5]

---

[4]Calhoun, E. F. (1994). *How to use action research in the self-renewing school.* Alexandria, VA: Association for Supervision and Curriculum Instruction.

[5]Adapted from Borgia, E. T., and Schuler, D. (1996). *Action research in early childhood education.* University of Illinois at Urbana-Champaign: ERIC Clearinghouse on Elementary and Early Childhood Education (p. 2). Adapted by permission.

1. Teachers investigate their own practice in new ways, looking deeper in what they and their students actually do and fail to do.
2. Teachers develop a deeper understanding of students, the teacher learning process, and their role in the education of both teachers and students.
3. Teachers are viewed as equal partners in deciding what works best and what needs improvement in their classroom or classrooms.
4. In most cases, solutions for identified problems are arrived at cooperatively among teachers.
5. Teachers are often more committed to action research because they identify the areas *they* view as problematical and in need of change.
6. Action research is an ongoing process and its strategies can be widely applied.
7. Professional development and school improvement are core aspects for any teacher who engages in action research.
8. Teacher reflection can be conducted individually or in a school-based team composed of students, teachers, and administrators.

LEVELS OF ACTION RESEARCH

Educational action research focuses on three levels of action research: individual teacher research, small teacher groups or teams in a single school or a single department, and schoolwide research. In keeping with qualitative research, in which the focus is on a particular setting, most action research studies take place in a single school. Thus, teachers rarely carry out action research involving multiple schools because of the organizational complexity and the uniqueness of the many settings or schools.

It also is likely that in a single school, action research is carried out by groups of teachers, rather than an individual teacher, who all seek to understand and improve a common issue. For example, it is understandable that a group of high school math teachers might wish to work together to implement a promising "hands-on" math strategy for students who are lagging in math performance and determine its impact on student math performance. Similar, shared goals are surely voiced by teachers in other content areas as well. This does not imply that teachers never collaborate across subject areas, just that it is more common and interesting for teachers to focus their action research in their own disciplines. As another example, elementary teachers might form a small group and design a study to answer questions about such varied strategies as inclusion of special education students, inquiry-based learning, or literary clubs, which cross content area and grade lines. Or some teachers might work with university-based researchers in their classrooms doing collaborative or participatory research. For example, teachers may study their own research questions along with similar or related questions that the university has.

In schoolwide action research, the majority of the school community identifies a problem and conducts research together with a common, focused goal in mind. For example, a schoolwide emphasis on reading is a common goal of many elementary schools. Or counselors, teachers, and administrators may band together in a middle school and try strategies to integrate cliques or groups of students to create a more cooperative environment.

One way that action research is conducted is by individual teachers who seek to improve their understanding and practice in their classrooms. Quite often, individual teachers seek to study aspects of their classroom that are unique to them and their students. As an example of carrying out action research individually, a teacher may gather information by observing students to better understand their interests or behaviors in a particular subject area. Alternatively, the teacher may select or construct simple instruments or tests to collect student information pertaining to the issue or topic under study. Individual teacher action research can be a useful tool to solve educational problems in one's own setting.

CHARACTERISTICS OF ACTION RESEARCH

Many steps in action research are steps in other qualitative research approaches, as described in chapters 6, 7, and 8. Keep in mind, however, that action researchers can collect both quantitative and qualitative data to analyze and interpret and solve their problem. In this chapter, we focus particularly on individual or small-group action research as applied by teachers. Borgia and Schuler[6] describe the components of action research as the "Five C's": commitment, collaboration, concern, consideration, and change:

- *Commitment.* Action research takes time. The participants need time to get to know and trust each other and to observe practice, consider changes, try new approaches, and document, reflect, and interpret the results. Those who agree to participate should know that they will be involved with the project for some time and that the time commitment is a factor that all participants should consider carefully.
- *Collaboration.* In action research, the power relations among participants are equal; each person contributes, and each person has a stake. Collaboration is not the same as compromise, but it involves a cyclical process of sharing, of giving, and of taking. The ideas and suggestions of each person should be listened to, reflected on, and respected.
- *Concern.* The interpretive nature of action research (for example, relying on personal dialogue and a close working relationship) means that the participants will develop a support group of "critical friends." Trust in each other and in the value of the project is important.
- *Consideration.* Reflective practice is the mindful review of one's actions, specifically, one's professional actions. Reflection requires concentration and careful consideration as one seeks patterns and relationships that will generate meaning within the investigation. Reflection is a challenging, focused, and critical assessment of one's own behavior as a means of developing one's craftsmanship.
- *Change.* For humans, growing and changing are part of the developmental cycle of life. Change is ongoing and, at times, difficult, but it is an important element in remaining effective as a teacher.

Other characteristics and examples of action research can be found in Table 9.2. Some characteristics of action research are listed in the left column of this table. Examples of these characteristics are listed in the right column of the table. We can gain a deeper understanding of action research by analyzing what the teachers in the examples actually did. Read these examples carefully. What action does the teacher take in each of these situations? The first example is not very specific, but we can see that the teacher *investigated the impact of his intervention.* In the second example, the teacher learned about teaching strategies and *implemented* them. In the third, the teacher *monitored the impact* of a new curriculum, and in the last example, the teacher implemented a new policy and then *monitored its impact.* In action research, teachers take action *in* their studies, not only after their study has concluded. Each of these teachers identified a problem and subsequently studied an intervention or an implementation to better understand teaching and learning.

---

[6]Adapted from Borgia, E. T., and Schuler, D. (1996). *Action research in early childhood education.* University of Illinois at Urbana-Champaign: ERIC Clearinghouse on Elementary and Early Childhood Education (p. 3). Adapted by permission.

TABLE 9.2   Some Characteristics of Action Research

KEY CONCEPT	EXAMPLE
Action research is participatory and democratic.	You have identified an area in your teaching that you believe can be improved (based on data from your students). You decide to investigate the impact of your intervention and to monitor if it makes a difference.
Action research is socially responsive and takes place in context.	You are concerned that minority children (for example, ESL [English as a Second Language] students) in your classroom are not being presented with curriculum and teaching strategies that are culturally sensitive. You decide to learn more about how best to teach ESL children and to implement some of these strategies.
Action research helps teacher researchers examine the everyday, taken-for-granted ways in which they carry out professional practice.	You have adopted a new mathematics problem-solving curriculum and decide to monitor its impact on student performance on open-ended problem-solving questions and students' attitudes toward mathematics in general.
Knowledge gained through action research can liberate students, teachers, and administrators and enhance learning, teaching, and policy making.	Your school has a high incidence of student absenteeism in spite of a newly adopted district-wide policy on absenteeism. You investigate the perceptions of colleagues, children, and parents toward absenteeism to more fully understand why the existing policy is not having the desired outcome. Based on what you learn, you implement a new policy and systematically monitor its impact on absenteeism levels and students' attitudes toward school.

Source: From Mills, G. (2003). *Action Research: A Guide for the Teacher Researcher,* 2nd ed., p. 8. Upper Saddle River, NJ: Merrill/Prentice Hall. Reprinted by permission.

RATIONALES FOR ACTION RESEARCH

Osterman and Kottkamp[7] provide a rationale for action research that focuses on the professional growth opportunity and responsibility for teachers. They suggest that everyone needs professional growth opportunities; all professionals want to improve; all professionals can learn; all professionals are capable of assuming responsibility for their own professional growth and development; people need and want information about their own performance; and that collaboration enriches professional development. These activities are closely related to teacher professionalism.

CONDUCTING ACTION RESEARCH

The basic steps in action research are (1) identify a topic or issue to study, (2) collect data related to the chosen topic or issue, (3) analyze and interpret the collected data, and (4) carry out action planning, which represents the application of the action research results.[8]

---

[7]Osterman K. F., and Kottkamp, R. B. (1993). *Reflective practice for educators: improving schools through professional development.* Newbury Park, CA: Corwin (p. 46).

[8]The following discussion is based in large part on Padak, N., and Padak, G. (2001), Research to practice: Guidelines for planning action research projects. Kent, OH: Ohio Literacy Resource Center. Accessed online at LINCS—Literacy Information and Communication System (http://literacy.kent.edu/Oasis/Pubs/0200-08.htm).

Identify the Topic or Issue

What makes a good action research topic or issue? First, the topic or issue should be important to the teacher, the team of teachers, or the school or district team that is undertaking the study. It must be relevant to their professional lives. Typically, action research involves issues that are a pressing problem or a new teaching strategy or assessment instrument that researchers think or hypothesize will improve the problem. To identify topics, researchers can reflect on their daily professional lives and ask themselves, "What classroom problem or issue do I need to solve (or improve)?" Counselors and administrators can ask this same question to identify topics to study, to address issues they deal with on a day-to-day basis. If a problem does not readily come to mind (usually one does for many of us!), try brainstorming to arrive at a real-life issue to study. You should make sure the topic is truly substantive and if a solution is found, that it might improve your practice.

Researchers also must consider whether the type of information needed to solve the problem is available. For example, it would be very difficult to study a group of students who no longer attend the school because they've graduated or moved. Early in the process, researchers must be sure they can obtain the data needed to carry out the action research. Topics can also be evaluated and refined by discussing them with a colleague, mentor, or school principal.

Following are some examples of the type of topics studied in action research:

- How can we find ways to encourage slow readers to engage in more reading?
- Are we helping or hurting students by letting them invent their own spelling?
- What are the best strategies to settle students down quickly at the start of class?

Conducting a Literature Review

Once the topic or general problem is identified, you will need to narrow the topic to put it into a researchable form—a research question. Often, in order to do this, you may need to read literature to learn more about your topic. (Chapter 2 discusses the literature review in depth, and these strategies apply to action research studies.) The literature review can provide ideas for strategies in identifying promising practices. For example, if your problem is, "What are the best strategies to settle students down quickly at the start of class?" then a literature review can inform you about commonly used methods to get students quiet in order to begin instruction, how to handle transitions, and other classroom management strategies. Once you have sufficient information about your topic, you can narrow the topic and form a researchable question.

Some research problems or topics already are researchable, or involve an intervention or some action. These problems may not require a literature search. For example, if your problem is whether X curriculum is better than Y curriculum, you may not need to conduct a literature search because you know what your variables are—X and Y. You know that your study will involve comparing the effects of X and the effects of Y. Whereas if your topic was "What strategies are most helpful for helping fourth graders to turn in homework on time?" you might need to research these strategies. Therefore, the necessity of the literature search simply depends on the nature of the research topic.

Developing Research Questions

A well-written action research question relates directly to the identified topic. If multiple research questions are involved in the study, researchers should make sure that they are closely related to each other. The more broad and complex the research topic, the more difficult and time consuming the research process will be and the longer it will take to obtain helpful information. Keep in mind that action research usually focuses on posing and answering questions in a *particular* classroom or school. In an action research study, you want your questions to address *your* problems, not those of your colleague or your sister in another state. Generalization is not a major feature of action research, and general questions should not be asked.

When you write your questions, keep them narrow in scope. What, exactly, do you want to "fix," evaluate, compare, improve, or better understand? Researchable, answerable questions usually begin with "Why," "How," and "What." Rule out questions that can be answered by "yes" or "no." Include an intervention in your question. What action will you take—or what implementation will you make—to try to improve the situation? Following are some examples of narrowed, researchable research questions:

- What is the impact of math manipulatives on second-grade students' achievement of subtraction skills?
- How effective has the peer tutoring program in honors English been on improving student essays?
- What is the effect of self-selection of books on increasing students' interest in reading?

Note that these questions are all ones that would be of interest to teachers, counselors, and administrators. The topics are narrow and defined so as to be solved in a relatively short time span. Also, these questions all include a common characteristic—some sort of intervention, some variable being evaluated in the study. "What is the impact of X on Y?" "How effective has X been on Y?" and "What is the effect of X on Y?" are typical scripts you can follow to frame your research question. For practice, write three of your own action research questions.

COLLECT THE DATA

As Padak and Padak observe, "Any information that can help you answer your questions is data." The best data are directly related to the topic or issue; they provide answers pertinent to the intended research. If possible, you should try to use a variety of data collection tools—quantitative, qualitative, or both, as appropriate—for *each* topic or issue, helping to ensure the validity of your results. The concept of triangulation introduced in Chapter 7 is useful in action research. Triangulation seeks regularities in data by comparing different participants, settings, and activities to identify recurring results. This corroboration strengthens a study's results. For example, suppose you were interested in studying the effect of literary clubs in your reading program on student attitudes toward reading. After initiating literary clubs, you could ask members questions about their participation in the club, but you would probably also want to observe their interactions during their club meetings. You could also give the students an attitude survey. If the data match from your interviews, observations, and surveys, you can be more confident that your research results are valid.

Data Sources

The number of potential data sources in an action research study is very broad. We can group them into four general types of data: observations, interviews, questionnaires/surveys, and readily available data. In the qualitative chapters, we had fairly strict definitions for data sources that constituted observations and interviews. For our purposes in describing action research data sources, these categories expand to include other, similar data sources.

Observation.   Observing participants in action and recording your observations is a common way to collect data in action research. For example, you may observe students or teachers as they work with a new curriculum. Your observation record may then help you determine the curriculum's effectiveness. As noted in Chapter 7, remembering your observations is the hardest part. Consequently, you will need to either keep a daily journal or take field notes. Your handwritten field notes (narrative, qualitative data) or tallies or checkmarks on an observation record (numerical, quantitative data) become your data sources. Observation also includes videotaped samples of teacher performance, student interactions, student-teacher interactions, and so forth. The videotaped recordings and, if a transcript is produced from the recording, the transcript are both data sources. *External* or *peer observation* involves having a peer or colleague observe (and later assess and provide suggestions about) an aspect of the teacher's practice such as questioning behavior, lesson organization, or feedback to students. Some student performance data—watching students do something, such as play a musical instrument, play basketball, or give a speech—that is observable can be used to help teachers assess their own instructional effectiveness.

Interviews or Recorded Conversations.   Interviews or conversations can be either planned (formal) or spontaneous (informal); you may develop questions beforehand or simply invite an open-ended exchange. In any event, you must either transcribe or record the conversation. If you take written notes, make them as complete as possible. Reread them while your memory is fresh so that you can fill in any missing information and add your own insights. You can also tape record (audio or video) interviews or conversations and then transcribe them (see Chapter 7). One helpful source of action research data that falls under the informal interview umbrella is that of *collegial dialogue, experience sharing,* and *joint problem solving.* In other words, conversations among teachers to discuss common problems or issues, share procedures and promising practices, and compare perceptions encourage collaboration and the confidence to improve practice. These conversations may be recorded by hand or tape recorded and serve as data in your study.

Questionnaires and Attitude Scales.   Another common data source is teacher-administered questionnaires and attitude scales completed by students or, sometimes, parents of students. Questionnaires can be used when there is not time to individually question students or small groups of students. Also, they are advantageous when a large number of responses are needed, such as a questionnaire mailed home for completion by a parent of every student in the school. Questionnaires may include closed-end items, in which respondents are given a limited number of responses, and open-ended items, in which a question is asked and respondents must create their own response. Both can supply information about a program's perceived effectiveness, for example, including specific responses that may be counted, and narrative comments from the open-ended questions. Writing questionnaires is a skill, and is something that should be done with thought and care. (See a full discussion of questionnaires in Chapter 10.) Attitude scales, as discussed in Chapter 5, determine "what an individual believes, perceives, or feels about self, others, and a variety of activities, institutions, and situations." Scales that are typically used in action research include Likert scales, semantic differential scales, and rating scales. Data from attitude scales are numeric, and are accompanied by narrative comments.

Readily Available Data.   To be efficient, and to add validity to your analysis, seek readily available information, or *naturally occuring data,* that can serve as data. For example, although you could study changes in students' math skills using a series of standardized tests, a more focused, efficient alternative might be to analyze homework samples or quiz results from students in your program. No extra time or cost is involved, and the samples are likely to match your interests exactly. Other examples of data that could be collected include tallies (e.g., lists of books read or projects completed), demographic information, test results, student grades, report cards, attendance records, contents of journals (teacher's self-reflections or students'), writing samples, contents of teacher or student portfolios, illness records, medical records, lists of out-of-class activities, and parent information. Note from this list that although action research focuses on use of qualitative data, researchers also use quantitative data.

Characteristics of Data Collection in Action Research

Because action research is often focused on a single classroom in which students and teachers are continually interacting, data collection should have four important characteristics.

First, when students are asked to complete checklists, rating scales, or questionnaires as part of the action research process, they should be allowed to respond anonymously to protect students and to improve the validity of the data gathered. Second, because the teacher is the interpreter of the data collected, it is a good idea for the teacher researcher to build a comparison into data collection. For example, if a teacher is planning to ask students to complete a checklist about the teacher's fairness in grading, *before administering the checklist* the teacher should write a prediction of how he or she thinks the students will respond in their replies. After the anonymous student responses are collected, the teacher can compare the student results to his or her prechecklist projection. Large discrepancies between the teacher's prediction and student responses should be a red flag for the teacher to reexamine current practice.

Third, when data collection is carried out using techniques such as video- or audiotaping or peer observations, teachers should identify the specific aspects of performance that will be examined. A set of criteria that focuses observations and interpretations on a limited number of specific performances provides more relevant information than general, unstructured data collection. For example, if a teacher were videotaping a cooperative learning lesson, or if a peer were observing the teacher teach the lesson, focusing criteria such as "appropriateness of the topic for students," "desired activities explained clearly to students," "all teams visited at least once," and "lesson summarized at end of lesson" will provide more specific feedback to the teacher than unfocused, general feedback. Also, stating criteria helps teachers gather information about their specific concerns and makes it easier to carry out changes in practice.

Fourth, no single data collection approach can provide appropriate data for all of a teacher's questions or topics. Different approaches inform different types of questions. For example, questionnaires are useful for providing information about respondents' attitudes and points of view, while observation or videotaping is useful for providing direct information about teachers' actual teaching activities. The data collection method should fit the type of information needed to examine the problem or topic.

The Spiraling Nature of Data Collection.   To understand the spiraling nature of data collection in action research, try this exercise: Review the action research topics listed on page 267 and identify data sources for at least two. If you were to actually carry out one of these studies, your next step would be to collect and review the data from your identified sources. For this exercise, briefly review the sources you have chosen. Note that as you continue to review, key underlying concepts begin to emerge. In an actual study, identifying key concepts typically takes a few iterations. Figure 9.1 graphically portrays the spiraling iterations in action research. The researcher observes the setting and the participants (looking), interprets the observations (thinking), and identifies a solution (acting). The researcher typically proceeds through a number of iterations before arriving at a core solution.

Ethical Considerations in Action Research Data Collection

Research ethics must be fully implemented throughout any study. You must ask your principal whether you need to obtain permission and informed consent from every participant. In most cases, especially if the study is being conducted in your classroom, you will need only to explain that you are doing a research project, describe the information you want to use, emphasize that any participation is voluntary, and promise participants full confidentiality. However, complex issues arise. For example, what is the school's requirement about using a video camera in the classroom and capturing the faces of minors on tape? What is the district's rule? Investigate questions such as these fully before beginning data collection so that it is ethical. See the sections that discuss research ethics in chapters 3 and 7.

FIGURE 9.1
Action research
interacting spiral.

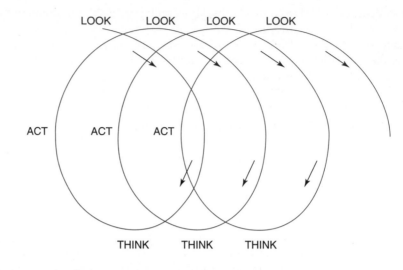

LOOK   LOOK   LOOK   LOOK

ACT   ACT   ACT

THINK   THINK   THINK

Source: From Stringer, E. (1996). *Action Research: A Handbook for Practitioners*, p. 17. Copyright ©1996 by Sage Publications. Reprinted by Permission of Sage Publications, Inc.

ANALYZE THE DATA

You will know when you have gathered enough information. In practical terms, you will have reached what researchers call *redundancy* or *data saturation* when you no longer learn anything new or identify new themes or patterns. It is then time to stop collecting and start analyzing. (See Chapter 8 for more about redundancy and data saturation.)

First, make sure all your data are organized and legible. If you have asked more than one question, sort the data according to question. Reread everything at least once. Keep in mind that you probably will have been analyzing all along, if the data is qualitative. If one type of data is numerical or quantitative, such as from an attitude survey, analysis cannot be done until that data is complete. Set aside data that do not directly relate to your research questions.

Most analysis involves creating categories (see Chapter 8). One way to create categories is to sort data according to shared characteristics. You can then summarize the essence of these characteristics. These summaries should answer the research questions.

The collected data must be summarized and interpreted in order to help teachers, counselors, and administrators make decisions about their practices. This activity is the same as, though often less complex than, qualitative and quantitative data interpretation procedures (see chapters 8 and 16). The goal of analysis is to interpret the data and make decisions for teacher understanding or improvement.

CARRY OUT ACTION PLANNING AND SHARE THE FINDINGS

Research results can suggest program refinements or may lead to more questions. In any event, one of your final tasks as researcher is to share your findings with others, in both formal and informal settings. Results can be shared with other teachers, both in a given school or in other schools. You may share information verbally, in presentations and conversations, and also may write about your results. Writing can lead to further analysis, interpretation, and deeper understanding of the problem—and how to act on your findings. Writing also creates a permanent record of the research that others may use. Fellow teachers, administrators, other researchers, and current or potential funders for your program may be in a position to benefit from your results. Refer to the section, "Step 6: Writing the Report," in Chapter 8 for more information on writing up your action research.

TAKING ACTION

As the name suggests, *action research* is action oriented. The purpose of action research is to affect teachers' actions, activities, beliefs, and effects; action research is directed toward both understanding and improving practice. Thus, the last step is deciding what steps, if any, need to be taken to alter or improve practice.

Action research is typically carried out with the intent of using the data collected to help educators understand or try out new or needed methods or paradigms for teaching or administrating. Much action research is focused on evaluating new strategies or promising practices for their potential use in instruction. There are many ways to implement action research results in schools. For example, study results can be used in the classroom, school, or district to improve instruction, procedures, and outcomes of education, and aid teacher understanding of instruction, deportment, and applications. Often, action research leads to new questions to examine, thus forging new forms of understanding and deeper insights in practice. It is the practical nature of action research that fosters much of the teacher-based improvement in schools.

Now go to the Companion Website accompanying this text at *www.prenhall.com/gay* to check your understanding of chapter concepts in the following modules: Objectives, Practice Quiz, and Applying What You Know. Expand your research skills with Evaluating Articles, Analyzing Qualitative Data, Analyzing Quantitative Data, and Research Tools and Tips. Visit Web Links to broaden your knowledge about research.

SUMMARY

1. Good action research integrates theory, practice, and application.

School-Based Action Research

2. Key aspects of action research are conducted by educators, in schools and classrooms, applying mainly qualitative research, and seek to focus on understanding and improvement of teaching.
3. Action research is typically focused on a particular issue within a single school.

Levels of Action Research

4. There are three levels of action research: individual researcher level, small groups of researchers, and schoolwide research. The first two levels are the most commonly used.

Conducting Action Research

5. The four steps in action research are (1) select a topic or issue to study, (2) collect pertinent data related to the topic, (3) analyze and interpret the data, and (4) apply the research results.

Identify the Topic or Issue

6. A good action research topic involves either a pressing problem or learning about a promising practice. Good topics and research questions relate directly to the identified problem or issue.
7. Brainstorming is a good way to develop answerable questions. Answerable questions usually begin with "Why," "How," or "What." Include an intervention or implementation in a research question.

Collect the Data

8. Many data sources, both qualitative and quantitative, are pertinent to action research, including tallies, demographic information, test results, student work samples, observation notes, interview transcripts, surveys, questionnaires, and many others.
9. Observations and interviews are two of the most common data sources.
10. When possible, use readily available data to increase a study's efficiency and overall validity.
11. Research ethics must be fully implemented throughout any study. Researchers generally must still obtain

permission and informed consent from all research participants. Consult the building principal or district office to be sure.

Analyze the Data

12. Analyzing action research is similar to that for other forms of qualitative research. It is a cyclical process, ultimately narrowing the findings to a few key categories or features.
13. Most analysis involves creating categories. Use quantitative data analysis procedures when quantitative data is collected.

Carry Out Action Plan and Share the Findings

14. The final step in action research is to write up the results of the study so that other researchers can examine and critique the research process and its results.
15. The purpose of action research is to affect understanding and behavior. Although research results often lead to new questions to examine, the primary intent of action research is to use collected data to alter or improve teaching practice.

PERFORMANCE CRITERIA   TASK 7

Develop a design for an action research study to answer a school-based question. Use the following headings in your written plan:

Topic
Research Questions
Intervention
Participants
Data Collection

To get started selecting your topic, use the beginning words or phrases in the list of questions in the chapter ("How can I . . . " "What is the best way . . . " or "Why . . . "). Brainstorming is a good way to choose a topic: "What classroom problem or issue do you need to improve or resolve?" Eventually narrow your topic to "The purpose of this study is . . . " (see Task 7 Example).

Research questions should be narrow enough to be answerable. Your question or questions should contain language that indicates what action or change you are implementing in the study to improve teaching or learning. For example, "What is the impact of X on Y?" is more action-oriented and specific than "How can I improve Y?"

The intervention should describe what you or your group of researchers will implement in the classroom to study. For example, if you are implementing a new teaching strategy, explain what it is and why you want to implement and evaluate it.

The participants section should describe the participants and the context of the study.

The description of data collection should include multiple data sources, collection methods, the timeframe of the study, and duration of data collection.

See the *Student Study Guide* that accompanies this text for more examples of action research.

1

Action Research Plan:

Do Graphic Displays Aid Understanding in Expository Text?

Dick Kendrick

Topic

The purpose of this study is to learn whether students gain a better understanding of expository text when they are given strategies to understand accompanying graphic displays (maps, charts, tables, diagrams, illustrations, etc.).

Research Questions

Do students make sense out of graphic displays in textbooks or other reading material? Will teaching students strategies to decipher meaning from graphic displays lead to a better understanding of the text that the displays illustrate?

Participants

Twenty-seven students in a fifth-grade classroom will participate in this study. Twelve of these students are reading below grade level, eight are reading at grade level, and seven are reading above grade level. Included in this group are two ESL students, two TAG students, four students with an IEP, and one student with a 504.

Intervention

I will teach strategies to enhance students' abilities to gain understanding from graphic displays during expository reading over a three-week period.

Data Collection

At the beginning of the study, I will give students a one-page article with graphic displays and text from *Scholastic News* to read, followed by a simple quiz over the contents and a survey about how they approached the graphic displays and text. After the three-week period of teaching strategies to the students, I will give them an additional *Scholastic News* one-page article with graphic displays and text to read, followed by another quiz over the contents and a post survey. The surveys will focus on questions such as whether they look at or use the visuals, whether they think it is important to understand the visuals, whether they feel confident in their ability to derive information from the visuals, and so forth. Quiz scores will be recorded and survey data tallied for analysis.

PART 3

QUANTITATIVE RESEARCH

Part Two described and differentiated a number of qualitative research approaches. It provided examples of both qualitative and mixed-method research. In Part Three, we examine in detail quantitative research methods. The goal of Part Three is for you to be able to develop a quantitative research topic, carry out its data collection, and develop data analysis procedures for the chosen topic. Note that the six general steps are similar for both quantitative and qualitative research, but their applications are different.

Chapter 10 focuses on survey research. The subject of Chapter 11 is correlational research. Chapter 12 explores causal–comparative research. In Chapter 13 we discuss experimental research.

"The responses given by a respondent may be biased and affected by her or his reaction to the interviewer. . . ." (p. 291)

SURVEY RESEARCH

OBJECTIVES

After reading Chapter 10, you should be able to do the following:

1. Briefly state the purpose of survey research.
2. List the major steps involved in designing and conducting a survey research study.
3. State the major difference between self-report and observational research.
4. List and briefly describe the steps involved in conducting a questionnaire study.
5. Identify and briefly describe four major differences between an interview study and a questionnaire study.

Task 8 builds on previous tasks in Chapters 2, 3, 4, and 5. The goal of this task is for you to be able to describe the data collection and analysis procedures involved in quantitative research methods. After you have read Chapters 10–13, you should be able to perform the following task.

TASK 8

Having stated a problem, formulate one or more hypotheses (if appropriate), describe a sample, select one or more ways to collect data, and develop the methods section of your research report. Include a description of participants, data collection methods, and research design. (See Performance Criteria, p. 405.)

SURVEY RESEARCH: DEFINITION AND PURPOSE

Although some people refer to this research approach as *descriptive research,* in this context we will refer to it as *survey research.* A survey study, also referred to as a descriptive study, determines and describes the way things are. It may also compare how subgroups such as males and females or experienced and inexperienced teachers view issues and topics. We discuss survey research in some detail for two major reasons. First, a high percentage of research studies rely on surveys for data and, as a result, are descriptive in nature. Survey research influences what television programs we see, the type of automobiles that will be produced, the foods found on grocery shelves, the fashions we wear, and what issues and topics we will be confronted with. Second, the survey method is useful for investigating a variety of educational problems and issues. Typical survey studies are concerned with assessing attitudes, opinions, preferences, demographics, practices, and procedures. Examples of educational survey topics are, How do teachers in our school district rate the qualities of our new teacher evaluation program? and What do high school principals consider their most pressing administrative problems? Survey data are usually collected by questionnaire, interview, telephone, or observation.

Chapter 7 also discussed issues of descriptive research, mainly interviews and observations, as they pertain to qualitative research. There is some overlap between Chapter 7 and this chapter, but there also are important differences that highlight distinctions between qualitative and quantitative research approaches. For example, the survey research plan as described in this chapter is much more structured and standardized than that described in Chapter 7. Further, while the qualitative researchers described in Chapter 7 interviewed and observed research participants, they did so primarily to identify what the important issues to study were from the participants' perspective. (See the section in that chapter, "Nonparticipant Data Collection Methods for Observational Studies," for a side-by-side comparison of quantitative and qualitative procedures when used with these forms of observational research.) In this more quantitatively oriented chapter, we observe that the researcher predetermines what variables will be surveyed before selecting or observing the research participants. The two approaches have a different conception of whose view is more important, the researcher's or the participants'. Also, sample sizes and the methods of data analysis differ. It is important to recognize these differences, and it also is important to understand that both are different yet viable approaches to descriptive research.

Survey research sounds very simple—just ask some people some questions and count responses—but there is considerably more to it than just asking questions and reporting answers. A set of basic steps should guide survey research studies, just as in the qualitative methods we examined in Part Two. Each step must be conscientiously executed: identify a topic or problem, review the literature, select an appropriate sample of participants, collect valid and reliable data, analyze data, and report conclusions. In addition, survey studies involve a number of unique problems. For example, self-report studies, such as those utilizing questionnaires or interviews, often suffer from lack of participant response; many potential participants do not return mailed questionnaires or attend scheduled interviews. This makes it difficult to interpret findings, since people who do not respond may feel very differently than those who do. Twenty percent of survey participants might feel very negatively about the year-round school concept and might avail themselves of every opportunity to express their unhappiness, including on your questionnaire. The other 80%, who feel neutrally or positively, might not be as motivated to respond. Thus, if conclusions were based only on those who responded, very wrong conclusions might be drawn concerning the population's feelings about year-round schooling. Further, the researcher is seldom able to explain to research participants who are filling out a questionnaire what exactly a particular question or word really means. One of the hardest things questionnaire researchers must do is to write or select questions that are clear and unambiguous. Survey studies that utilize observational techniques often require training observers and developing recording forms that permit data to be collected objectively and reliably. There is more to survey research than first meets the eye.

Once you have defined a survey problem, reviewed related literature, and, if appropriate, stated hypotheses or questions, you must give careful thought to selection of the research participants and data collection procedures. Identifying the population that has the desired information, for example, is not always easy and must be thought through ahead of time. Also, there are many alternative methods for collecting data, and finding the most appropriate requires thought. Suppose, for example, your problem was concerned with how elementary school teachers spend their time during the school day. You might hypothesize that they spend one-quarter of their time on noninstructional activities such as collecting book money and maintaining order. Your first thought might be to mail to a sample of principals a questionnaire about how teachers spend their time. Doing this, however, assumes that principals *know* how teachers spend their daily time. While principals would of course be familiar with the duties and responsibilities of their teachers, it is not likely that they could provide the data needed for the study. Thus, directly asking the teachers themselves would probably result in more accurate information. However, it is possible that teachers might tend to subconsciously exaggerate the amount of time they spend on activities they consider to be distasteful, such as clerical operations like grading papers. (More to think about!) Further thought might suggest that direct observation would probably yield the most accurate data (but would be very time consuming), or that allowing teachers to respond anonymously would increase the likelihood of accurate answers.

Having decided on a target population and a data collection strategy, your next steps are to identify your accessible population, determine needed sample size, select an appropriate sampling technique, and select or develop a data collection instrument. Because survey studies often seek information that is not already available, the development of an appropriate instrument is usually needed. Of course if there is a valid and reliable instrument available, it can be used, but using an instrument just "because it is there" is not a good idea. If you want the appropriate answers, you have to ask the appropriate questions. If instrument development is necessary, the instrument should be tried out and revised where necessary before it is used in the actual study. Having identified an appropriate sample of participants, and selected or developed a valid data collection instrument, the next step is to carefully plan and execute the specific procedures of the study (when the instrument will be administered, to whom, and how) and the data analysis procedures. In general, the basic steps in conducting a survey study will be similar across studies, with specific details such as the research question, the participants, and data collection instruments differing across studies.

Surveys are often viewed with some disdain because many people have encountered poorly planned and poorly executed survey studies utilizing poorly developed instruments. You should not condemn survey research, however, just because it is often misused. Survey research at its best can provide very valuable data.

TYPES OF SURVEYS

Surveys are used in many fields, including political science, sociology, economics, and education. In education their most common use is for the collection of data by schools or about schools. Surveys conducted by schools are usually prompted by a need for certain kinds of information related to the instruction, facilities, or student population. For example, school surveys may examine variables such as community attitudes toward schools, institutional and administrative personnel, curriculum and instruction, finances, and physical facilities. School surveys can provide necessary and valuable information to both the schools studied and to other agencies and groups whose operations are school related.

The results of various public opinion polls are frequently reported by the media. Such polls represent an attempt to determine how all the members of a population (be it the American public in general or citizens of Skunk Hollow) feel about political, social, educational, or economic issues. Public opinion polls are almost always **sample surveys.** Samples are selected to properly represent relevant subgroups (in terms of such variables as socioeconomic status, gender, and geographic location) and results are often reported separately for each of those subgroups as well as for the total group.

Developmental surveys are concerned primarily with variables that differentiate children at different levels of age, growth, or maturation. Developmental studies may investigate progression along a number of dimensions, such as intellectual, physical, emotional, or social development. The children studied may be a relatively heterogeneous group, such as fourth graders in general, or a more narrowly defined homogeneous group, such as the study of academically gifted children. Knowledge of developmental patterns of various student groups can be used to make curriculum and instruction more appropriate and relevant for students. Knowing that 4-year-old and 5-year-old children typically enjoy skill-testing games (such as jumping rope and bouncing balls) but do not enjoy group activities involving competition would certainly be helpful to a preschool teacher in developing lesson plans.

Followup studies are conducted to determine the status of a group after some period of time. Like school surveys, followup studies are often conducted by educational institutions for the purpose of internal or external evaluation of their instructional program. Colleges and accreditation agencies, for example, typically require systematic followup of their graduates. Such efforts seek objective information regarding the current status of former students (Are you presently employed?) as well as attitudinal and opinion data concerning graduates' perceptions of the adequacy of their education. If a majority of graduates should indicate that

TABULATING QUESTIONNAIRE RESPONSES

The easiest way to tabulate questionnaire responses is to have participants mark responses to closed-ended questions on a scannable answer sheet. This option involves locating a scanner and possibly paying a fee to have questionnaires scanned.

If scannable answer sheets are not an option, then each respondent's answers will have to be entered one by one into a computer spreadsheet (e.g., Excel or Lotus) or a statistical program (e.g., SPSS or SAS). Remember this when designing your questionnaire. Make sure that the format is easy to follow and allows respondents to mark answers clearly. This will ensure that you can enter data quickly, without having to search for information.

If your questionnaire contains open-ended questions, you will need to code answers according to patterns in the responses provided. It is very useful to use a qualitative software program to examine your textual data, code it, and generate information regarding the frequency and nature of various codes. Many qualitative software programs also allow the researcher to export coded qualitative data into statistical programs, where advanced statistical analyses can be performed.

they feel the career counseling they received at old Alma Mater University was poor, this would suggest an area for improvement. Followup studies may also be conducted solely for research purposes. A researcher may be interested, for example, in assessing the degree to which initial treatment effects have been maintained over time. A study might demonstrate that students participating in preschool education are better adjusted socially and demonstrate higher academic achievement in the first grade. A followup study could be conducted to determine if this initial advantage is still in evidence at the end of the third grade. Often, treatments have an initial impact that does not last; initial differences "wash out" or disappear after some period of time. Conversely, some treatments do not result in initial differences but may produce long-range effects. In many areas of research, a followup study is essential to a more complete understanding of the effects of a given approach or technique.

CLASSIFYING SURVEY RESEARCH

There are many ways to classify survey research, but the two most common are in terms of how data are collected and how often a particular group is surveyed. Survey data are collected in two main ways: self-report instruments and observation. As noted in Chapter 5, self-report approaches require individuals to respond to a series of statements or questions about themselves. For example, a survey about local schools might ask respondents questions such as, "Do you believe the cost for the education of children in our community is too high?" Respondents would self-report their views by marking "yes," "uncertain," or "no." Note that questionnaires, telephone surveys, and interviews are all self-report methods, differing only in the ways the self-report data are collected.

Conversely, in an observation study, individuals are not directly asked for information; rather, the researcher obtains the desired data by watching participants. As stated in Chapter 7, observation permits various levels of involvement, ranging from participant observer (very involved) to nonparticipant observer (least involved). In survey research, observers tend to be uninvolved with the participants. Also, the survey researcher typically observes predetermined activities, unlike the qualitative researcher who usually does not have predetermined topics to observe. It is possible, but not typical, for a survey study to employ both self-report and observation methods.

The second general classification of descriptive research differentiates cross-sectional surveys from longitudinal surveys. A *cross-sectional* survey involves collecting data from selected individuals in a single time period (however long it takes to collect data from the participants). It is a single, stand-alone study. One limitation of cross-sectional studies is that often, a single point in time does not provide sufficient perspective to make needed decisions. When a cross-sectional study includes the entire population, as in the U.S. census, the survey is called, oddly enough, a **census survey.** *Longitudinal* surveys collect data at two or more times to measure changes over time. Developmental surveys frequently rely on longitudinal data to measure growth or development. There are four kinds of longitudinal surveys. All collect data multiple times, but all study different sample groups. To illustrate the difference among the four types, consider how each could be used to collect information about California female valedictorians' attitudes toward female/male equality.

1. A *trend* survey would sample from the general population of female valedictorians in California. To provide information about the trend of the valedictorians' attitudes, the researcher would annually select a sample of the female valedictorians in the current year. Each succeeding annual sample would be made up of that year's female valedictorians. A trend survey consists of different groups and different samples over time.

2. A *cohort* survey would select a specific population of female California valedictorians, such as the valedictorians in 1997. Over time, the researcher would select samples of the 1997 valedictorians. Each sample would be composed of different valedictorians, but all samples would be selected only from the 1997 valedictorian group. The members stay the same, but different groups of them are sampled over time. A cohort survey consists of the same group but different samples from that group over time.

3. A *panel* survey would select a single sample of valedictorians from a particular year and study the attitudes of that sample over time. If the researcher were conducting a three-year panel study, the same individuals would respond in each of the three years of the study. A panel survey consists of the same group and the same sample over time. A frequent problem with panel studies and, to a lesser degree, cohort studies is loss of individuals from the study because of their relocation, name change, lack of interest, or death. This is especially problematic the longer the longitudinal survey continues.

4. A *followup* survey is similar to a panel study, except that it is undertaken after the panel study is completed and seeks to examine subsequent development or change. It typically is undertaken to determine subsequent development or perceptions. For example, a researcher who wished to study female valedictorians in California a number of years after the original study was concluded would find individuals from the prior study and survey them to examine changes in their attitudes.

Longitudinal surveys are useful for studying the dynamics of a topic or issue over time. Suppose, for example, you were interested in studying the development of abstract thinking in elementary school students in grades one to four. If you used a cross-sectional approach, you could study samples of children at each of the four grade levels, first graders to fourth graders. The children studied at one grade level would be different children from those studied at another grade level. The advantage of the cross-sectional method is convenience. If you used a longitudinal approach such as a panel study, you could select a sample of first graders and study the development of their abstract thinking as they progressed from grade to grade; the children who were studied at the fourth-grade level would be the same children who were studied in the first, second, and third grades. In longitudinal studies, samples tend to shrink as time goes by; keeping track of participants over time can be difficult, as can maintaining their participation in the study. A major concern in a cross-sectional study is selecting samples of children that truly represent children at their level. A further related problem is selecting samples at different levels that are comparable on relevant variables such as intelligence. An advantage of the longitudinal method is that this latter concern about comparability is not a problem in that the same group is involved at each level. A major disadvantage of the longitudinal method is that an extended commitment must be made by the researcher, the subjects, and all others involved.

CONDUCTING SELF-REPORT RESEARCH

Self-report research requires the collection of standardized, quantifiable information from all members of a population or sample. To obtain comparable data from all participants, the researcher must ask them each the same questions. Many of the types of tests described in Chapter 5 are used in survey self-report research studies. A collection of such questions is called a **questionnaire.**

CONDUCTING A QUESTIONNAIRE STUDY

Most criticisms of questionnaires are related not to their use but to their misuse. Carelessly and incompetently constructed questionnaires have unfortunately been administered and distributed too often. Development of a sound questionnaire requires both skill and time. The use of a paper-and-pencil questionnaire has some definite advantages over other methods of collecting data such as interviews. In comparison to an interview a questionnaire requires less time, is less expensive, and permits collection of data from a much larger sample. Questionnaires may be individually administered to each respondent, but for efficiency are usually mailed. Although a personally administered questionnaire has some of the same advantages as an interview, such as the opportunity to establish rapport with respondents and explain unclear items, it also has some drawbacks. It is very time consuming, especially if the number of respondents is large and geographically scattered. An often-used alternative to the mailed questionnaire is the telephone interview. The steps in conducting a questionnaire study are essentially the same as for other types of research, although data collection involves some unique considerations.

Stating the Problem

The problem or topic studied and the contents of the questionnaire must be of sufficient significance both to motivate potential respondents to respond and to justify the research effort in the first place. Questionnaires dealing with trivial issues such as what color pencils do fifth graders prefer or what make of car do teachers most favor usually end up in potential respondents' circular file. Further, the topic must be defined in terms of specific objectives indicating the kind of information needed. Specific aspects of the topic should be described, as well as the kind of questions to be formulated.

Suppose a school superintendent wants to know how high school teachers perceive their schools. She wants to conduct a study to help identify areas in the high schools that might be improved. Because a survey questionnaire is made up of a number of questions related to the research topic, it would be useful for the superintendent to identify important aspects of her general question. For example, she might focus the study on the following four subareas of the topic: (1) respondent demographics (to compare the perceptions of males and females, experienced and new teachers and teachers in different departments); (2) teacher perceptions of the quality of teaching; (3) teacher perceptions of available educational resources; and (4) teacher perceptions of the school curriculum. Breaking the general topic into a few main areas helps to focus the survey and aid decision making in succeeding steps in the research sequence.

Selecting Participants

Survey participants should be selected using an appropriate sampling technique. Although simple random and stratified random sampling are most commonly used in survey research, cluster, systematic, and nonrandom samples are also used. (Refresh your memory about these types of samples by reviewing Chapter 4.) In some rare cases, when the population is small, the entire group may make up the sample. The selected research participants must be (1) able to provide the desired information sought and (2) willing to provide it to the researcher. Individuals who possess the desired information but are not sufficiently interested, or for whom the topic under study has little meaning, are not likely to respond. It is sometimes worth the effort to do a preliminary check of a few potential respondents to determine their receptivity.

The target population for our superintendent's study is likely to be all high school teachers in the state. Practically speaking, this may be too large a group to reasonably survey, so the superintendent will select participants from the accessible population. In this case, the likely accessible population would be high school teachers from the schools in the superintendent's district. A sample, perhaps stratified by gender and department, would be randomly selected and asked to complete the questionnaire.

In some cases it is useful to send the questionnaire to a person of authority, rather than directly to the person with the desired information. If a person's boss passes along a questionnaire and asks the person to complete and return it, that person may be more likely to do so than if you ask him or her directly. However, this assumes both that the boss cares enough to pass the questionnaire along and that the fact that the boss requested its completion does not influence the respondent's responses.

Constructing the Questionnaire

As a general guideline, the questionnaire should be attractive, brief, and easy to respond to. Respondents are turned off by sloppy, crowded, misspelled, and lengthy questionnaires, especially ones that require long written responses to each question. Turning people off is certainly not the way to get them to respond. To meet this guideline you must carefully plan both the content and the format of the questionnaire. No item should be included that does not directly relate to the topic of the study, and structured, selection-type items should be used if at all possible. It is easier to respond by circling a letter or word than writing out a lengthy response. Identifying subareas of the research topic can greatly help in developing the questionnaire. For example, the four areas our superintendent identified could make up the four sections of a questionnaire.

An important decision faced by all survey researchers is, What method should I use to collect data? There are five available approaches: mail, e-mail, telephone, personal administration, and interview. Each approach has its advantages and disadvantages. The bulk of educational surveys rely on mailed questionnaires. Although they are inexpensive, easily standardized, confidential, and easy to score, they are also subject to low response rates and suffer from the researcher's inability to ask probing or followup questions. E-mailing questionnaires has recently become a popular alternative. In addition to being speedy and efficient, this method shares both the advantages and disadvantages of mail questionnaires, with the additional disadvantage that not all potential respondents have e-mail. Telephone surveys tend to have high response rates and fairly quick data collection, but require lists of target phone numbers and administrator training. Personal administration is efficient if participants are closely situated, but requires time and again, administrators must be trained. Personal interviews allow rich, more complete responses, but have the least standardization and take the longest to administer. Table 10.1 summarizes the strengths and weaknesses of the five survey methods.

Many types of items are commonly used in questionnaires, including scaled items (Likert and semantic differential), ranked items (rank the following activities in order of their importance), checklist items (check all of the following that characterize your principal), and free response items (write in your own words the main reasons you became a teacher). These item types are all self-report measures. Most surveys consist of **structured items** (also called *closed-ended* items), that is, items that are answered by circling a letter, checking a list, or numbering preferences.

TABLE 10.1   Comparison of Survey Data Collection Methods

METHOD	ADVANTAGES	DISADVANTAGES
mail	inexpensive can be confidential or anonymous easy to score most items standardized items and procedures	response rate may be small cannot probe, explain, or follow up items limited to respondents who can read possibility of response sets
e-mail	speedy results easy to target respondents other advantages same as mail	not everyone has e-mail possibility of multiple replies from single participant other disadvantages same as mail
telephone	high response rates quick data collection can reach a range of locations and respondents	requires phone number lists difficult to get in-depth data administrators must be trained
personal administration	efficient when respondents are closely situated	time consuming administrators must be trained
interview	can probe, follow up, and explain questions usually high return rate may be recorded for later transcription and analysis flexibility of use	time consuming no anonymity possible interviewer bias complex scoring of unstructured items administrators must be trained

Questionnaires rarely contain large numbers of free response items, but in many cases one or two can be included to give respondents opportunity to add information not tapped by the closed-ended items. An **unstructured item** format, in which the responder has complete freedom of response (questions are posed and the responder must construct her or his own responses), is sometimes defended on the grounds that it permits greater depth of response and insight into the reasons for responses. While this may be true, and unstructured items are simpler to construct, their disadvantages generally outweigh their advantages. Heavy reliance on free response items creates two important problems for the researcher: (1) many respondents won't take the time to respond to free response items and many that do will give unclear or useless responses, and (2) scoring such items is more difficult and time consuming than scoring closed-ended items. For certain topics or purposes unstructured items may be necessary and some questionnaires do contain both structured and unstructured items. In general, however, structured items are to be preferred.

Consider our superintendent, who wishes to conduct a survey to identify areas in high schools that could be improved. She is interested in four areas: the demographics of high school teachers, and teachers' perceptions of teaching quality, educational resources, and school curriculum. She might develop questionnaire items like those shown on p. 285. Each item type relates to one of the superintendent's area of interest. Note that these items are examples and the full questionnaire would likely have more items under each of the four areas. It is also desirable to include an open-ended question for respondents to provide additional information.

Test items should also be constructed according to a set of guidelines. Include only items that relate to the purpose of the study. Collect demographic information about the sample if you plan to make comparisons between different subgroups. Each question should deal with a single concept and be worded as clearly as possible. The item, "Although labor unions are desirable in most fields, they have no place in the teaching profession. Agree or disagree," really is asking two questions: do you agree or disagree that labor unions are desirable and do you agree or disagree that there should be no teachers' unions? This creates a problem for both respondent and researcher. If the respondent agrees with one part of the item but disagrees with the other, how should he or she respond? Also, if a respondent selects "agree," can the researcher assume that means agreement to both statements or to only one—and which one?

DEMOGRAPHIC INFORMATION

For each of the following items, put an X beside the choice that best describes you.
1. Gender: Male ___ Female ___
2. Total years teaching: 1–5 ___ 6–10 ___ 11–15 ___ 16–20 ___ 21–25 ___ more than 25 ___
3. Department (please list) _____

CHECKLIST

Below is a list of educational resources. Put a check in front of each resource you think is adequately available in your school.
4. ___ up-to-date textbooks
5. ___ VCRs
6. ___ classroom computers
7. ___ games
8. ___ trade books

LIKERT

Following are a number of statements describing a school's curriculum. Read each statement and circle whether you strongly agree (SA), agree (A), are uncertain (U), disagree (D), or strongly disagree (SD) that it describes your school.
In my school the curriculum:

9.	is up to date	SA	A	U	D	SD
10.	emphasizes outcomes more complex than memory	SA	A	U	D	SD
11.	is familiar to all teachers	SA	A	U	D	SD
12.	is followed by most teachers	SA	A	U	D	SD
13.	can be adapted to meet student needs	SA	A	U	D	SD

FREE RESPONSE

14. Circle how you would rate the quality of teaching in your school:
    very good   good   fair   poor
15. Write a brief explanation of why you feel as you do about the quality of teaching in your school.
16. Please make any additional comments you have about this topic.

Avoid jargon! Any term or concept that might mean different things to different people should be defined or restated. Be specific! Do not ask, "Do you spend a lot of time each week preparing for your classes?" because one teacher might consider one hour per day "a lot," while another might consider one hour per week "a lot." Instead, ask, "How many hours per week do you spend preparing for your classes?" or "How much time do you spend per week preparing for your classes? (a) less than 30 minutes, (b) between 30 minutes and an hour, (c) between 1 and 3 hours, (d) between 3 and 5 hours, (e) more than 5 hours."

Also, when necessary, questions should indicate a point of reference. For example, do not ask, "How much time do you spend preparing for your classes?" Instead, specify a particular time reference such as, "How much time do you spend per day (or week) preparing for your classes?" Or, if you were interested in how many hours were actually spent in preparation and also in teachers' perceptions concerning that time, you would not ask, "Do you think you spend a lot of time preparing for classes?" Instead, you would ask, "Compared to other teachers in your department, do you think you spend a lot of time preparing for your classes?" If you don't provide a point of reference, different respondents will use different points, thereby confusing interpretations of responses. Avoid words like *several* or *usually;* be specific about what you mean by *several,* for example. Underlining (in a typed questionnaire) or italicizing (in a printed one) key phrases may also help to clarify questions.

There are a few more "don'ts" to keep in mind when constructing items. First, avoid leading questions, which suggest that one response may be more appropriate than another. Don't use items that say, "Don't you agree with the experts that . . ." or "Would you agree with most people that . . ." Second, avoid touchy questions to which the respondent might not reply honestly or at all. For example, asking a teacher if she or he sets high standards for achievement is like asking a mother if she loves her children; the answer in both cases is going to be "of course!" Don't ask a question that assumes a fact not necessarily true. For example, suppose you ask, "Have you stopped stealing from the church poor box?" The question calls for a simple "yes" or "no" response, but how do those who have never stolen respond? If they answer "yes," it suggests that they used to steal but have stopped; if they answer "no," it suggests that they are still stealing! Typically, unwarranted assumptions are more subtle and difficult to spot. For example, a questionnaire item sent to high school foreign language teachers in a state asked, "How many hours per week do you use your foreign language laboratory?" This question assumes that all high schools in the state have a foreign language lab. A better way to ask this question is first to ask whether the school has a language lab and then ask those who do have one to indicate how many hours per week it is used.

Remember that the questionnaire items must stand on their own. In most cases you will not be present to explain to respondents what you meant by a particular word or item. That is why it is important to make your questions clear and unambiguous. Figure 10.1 summarizes important aspects of writing questionnaire items.

After the questionnaire items have been constructed, they must be placed in the questionnaire and directions for respondents must be written. Even though respondents will have received a cover letter describing the study and asking for their participation, it is good practice to include a brief statement describing the study and its purpose at the top of the questionnaire. Ask general items first and then move to more specific items. Start with a few interesting and nonthreatening items. If possible—and it often is not—put similar item types together. Provide information about how to respond to items, for example, "Select the choice that you most agree with," "Circle the letter of choice," "Rank the choices from 1 to 5, where 1 is the most desirable and 5 the least," and "Darken your choice on the answer sheet provided. Please use a pencil to record your choices." Standardized directions promote standardized, comparable responses. Also, providing clear directions for respondents helps them in completing the questionnaire and you in getting ready to conduct data analysis. Don't jam items together; a lot of white should show on questionnaire pages. Number pages and items to help with organizing your data for analysis. Don't put very important questions at the end; respondents often do not finish questionnaires.

Preparing the Cover Letter

Every mailed questionnaire must be accompanied by a cover letter that explains what is being asked of the respondent and why. The letter should be brief, neat, and if at all possible, addressed specifically to the potential responder (Dear Dr. Jekyll, not Dear Sir). Mercifully,

FIGURE 10.1
Criteria for writing
questionnaire items.

- Know what information you need
- Know why you need each item
- Write items that make sense
- Define or explain ambiguous terms
- Include only items respondents can answer
- Focus items on a single topic or idea
- Use short questions; do not require a great deal of reading
- Word questions as briefly and clearly as possible
- Word questions in positive, not negative, terms
- Avoid leading questions
- Organize items from general to specific
- Use examples if item format is unusual
- Try to keep items that are clustered on a single page; if a second page is needed, put the response options at the top of the second page
- If using open-ended items, leave sufficient space for respondents to write their responses
- Avoid or carefully word items that are potentially controversial or embarrassing
- Subject items to a pretest review of the questionnaire

there are database management computer programs that can assist you with the chore of personalizing your letters. However, recognize that it is not always possible to identify each potential respondent by name. The letter should also explain the purpose of the study, emphasizing its importance and significance. Give the responder a good reason for cooperating—the fact that you need the data for your thesis or dissertation is *not* a good reason. Good reasons relate to how the data gathered will help the respondent and/or the field in general. If at all possible, the letter should state a commitment to share the results of the study when completed. Include a mailing address, phone number, or e-mail address where you can be reached in case potential respondents want to ask questions. In some cases, prior contact with potential research participants is useful; a brief letter or phone call indicating that they will be receiving a request for participation in a study is useful. The letter or phone call should briefly note the nature of the study, explain who the researcher(s) is (are), and give an indication of when the formal request is likely to arrive.

It usually helps and adds credibility if you can obtain the endorsement of an organization, institution, group, or administrator that the responder is likely to know or recognize. For example, if you are seeking principals as respondents, you should try to get a principals' professional organization or the state's chief school officer to endorse your study. If you are seeking parents as respondents, then school principals or school committees would be helpful endorsers of your study. Ideally, you would like to have them cosign the cover letter, but even having them agree to state their endorsement in the cover letter will be helpful. If the planned respondents are very heterogeneous, or have no identifiable affiliation in common, you may make a general appeal to professionalism.

If the questions to be asked are at all threatening (such as items dealing with gender or attitudes toward colleagues or the local administrators), anonymity or confidentiality of responses must be assured. As stated previously, *anonymity* means that no one, including the researcher, knows who completed a given questionnaire. *Confidentiality* means that the researcher knows who completed each survey, but promises not to divulge that information. We highly recommend that one of these approaches be used and explained in the cover letter. The promise of anonymity or confidentiality will increase the truthfulness of responses as well as the percentage of returns. One way to promise anonymity and still be able to utilize followup efforts with nonrespondents is to include a preaddressed stamped post card with the questionnaire sent to respondents. Request that they sign their name on the postcard and mail it separately from the questionnaire. The post cards allow the researcher to know who has and has not responded, but maintains the anonymity of the separately mailed questionnaire. Anonymity also makes subgroup comparisons impossible unless specific demographic items such as grade taught, gender, and years on the job are included in the questionnaire.

Give respondents a specific deadline date by which the completed questionnaire is to be returned. This date should give participants enough time to respond but discourage procrastination; two to three weeks will usually be sufficient. Sign individually each letter you send. When many questionnaires are to be sent, individually signing each letter will admittedly take considerably more time than making copies of one signed letter, but it adds a personal touch that might make a difference in a potential responder's decision to comply or not comply. Finally, the act of responding should be made as painless as possible. Include a stamped, addressed, return envelope; if you do not, your letter and questionnaire will very likely be placed into the circular file along with the mail addressed to "Occupant"! Figure 10.2 shows an example of a cover letter.

Pretesting the Questionnaire

Before distributing the questionnaire to participants, try it out in a pilot study. The cover letter can be pilot tested at the same time. Few things are more disconcerting and injurious to a survey than sending out a questionnaire only to discover that participants didn't understand

FIGURE 10.2
Sample cover letter.

SCHOOL OF EDUCATION

BOSTON COLLEGE

January 16, 2002

Mr. Dennis Yacubian
Vice-Principal
Westside High School
Westside, MA 00001

Dear Mr. Yacubian,

The Department of Measurement and Evaluation at Boston College is interested in determining the types of testing, evaluation, research and statistical needs high school administrators in Massachusetts have. Our intent is to develop a Master's level program that provides graduates who can meet the methodological need of high school administrators. The enclosed questionnaire is designed to obtain information about your needs in the areas of testing, evaluation, research, and statistics. Your responses will be anonymous and seriously considered in developing the planned program. We will also provide you a summary of the results of the survey so that you can examine the responses of other high school administrators. This study has been approved by the university's Human Subjects Review Committee.

We would appreciate your completion of the questionnaire by January 31. We have provided a stamped, addressed envelope for you to use in returning the questionnaire. You do not need to put your name on the questionnaire, but we request that you sign your name on the enclosed postcard and mail it separately from the questionnaire. That way we will know you have replied and will not have to bother you with followup letters.

We realize that your schedule is busy and your time is valuable. However, we hope that the 15 minutes it will take you to complete the questionnaire will help lead to a program that will provide a useful service to school administrators.

Thank you in advance for your participation. If you have questions about the study, you can contact me at 555-555-4444.

Yours truly,

James Jones
Department Chair

the directions or many of the questions. Pretesting the questionnaire provides information about deficiencies and suggestions for improvement. Having three or four individuals read the cover letter and complete the questionnaire will help identify problems. Choose individuals who are thoughtful and critical, as well as similar to the research participants. That is, if research participants are superintendents, then individuals critiquing the cover letter and questionnaire should be superintendents. Encourage your pretest group to make comments and state suggestions concerning the survey directions, recording procedures, and specific items. They should note issues of both commission and omission. For example, if they feel that certain important questions have been left out or if they feel that some existing topics are not relevant, they should note this. Having reviewers examine the completeness of the questionnaire is one way to determine its content validity. All feedback provided should be carefully studied and considered. The end product of the pretest will be a revised instrument and cover letter ready to be mailed to the already selected research participants.

Followup Activities

Not everyone to whom you send a questionnaire is going to return it (what an understatement!). Some recipients will have no intention of completing it; others mean to but put it off so long that they either forget it or lose it. It is for this latter group that followup activities are mainly conducted. The higher your percentage of returned questionnaires, the better your data. Although you should not expect 100% responses, you should not be satisfied with whatever you get after your first mailing. Given all the work you have already done, it makes no sense to end up with a study of limited value because of low returns when some additional effort on your part can make a big difference.

An initial followup strategy is to simply send out a reminder postcard. Remember, if you decide on anonymity in your survey, you will have to send out reminders and questionnaires to all participants, unless you use some procedure that allows you to know who has responded, but not what their responses were. If responses are confidential but not anonymous you can mail a card only to those who have not responded. Followup will prompt those who meant to fill it out but put it off and have not yet lost it! Include a statement like the ones used by finance companies—"If you have already responded, please disregard this reminder and thank you for your cooperation." Followup activities are usually begun shortly after the cover letter deadline for responding has passed. A second set of questionnaires is sent to participants who have not responded, but with a new cover letter, and of course another stamped envelope. The new letter should suggest that you know they meant to respond but that they may have misplaced the questionnaire or maybe they never even received it. In other words, do not scold them; provide them with an acceptable reason for their nonresponse. Repeat the significance and purpose of the study and reemphasize the importance of their input. The letter should suggest subtly that many others are responding, thus implying that their peers have found the study to be important and so should they.

If the second mailing does not result in an overall acceptable percentage of return, be creative. Magazine subscription agencies have developed followup procedures to a science and have become very creative, using gentle reminders and "sensational one-time-only offers," as well as phone calls from sweet-voiced representatives suggesting that your mail was apparently not getting through since you failed to renew your subscription. The point is that phone calls, if feasible, may be used with any other method of written, verbal, or personal communication that might induce additional participants to respond. They may grow to admire your persistence!

If your topic is of interest, your questionnaire well constructed, and your cover letter well written, you should get at least an adequate response rate. Research suggests that first mailings will typically result in a 30 to 50% return rate, and a second mailing will increase the percentage by about 20%; mailings beyond a second are generally not cost effective, in that they each increase the percentage by about 10% or less. After a second mailing, it is usually better to use other approaches to obtain an acceptable percentage of returns.

Dealing with Nonresponse

Despite all your efforts and followups, you may find yourself with an overall response rate of 60%. This raises concern about the generalizability of results, since you do not know how well the 60% responding represent the population from which the sample was originally selected or from the sample actually surveyed. If you knew that those responding were quite similar to the total sample, there would be no problem with generalizablilty; but you do not know that. Those who responded may be different in some systematic way from the nonresponders. After all, they chose not to reply, which already makes them different. They may be better educated, feel more strongly about the issue, or be more concerned about other issues than those responding.

The usual approach to dealing with such nonresponders is to try to determine if they are different from responders in some systematic way. This can be done by randomly selecting a small sample of nonresponders and interviewing them, either in person or by phone. This allows you to not only obtain responses to questionnaire items but also gather demographic information to determine if nonrespondents are similar to respondents. If responses are essentially the same for the two groups, you may assume that the response group is representative of the whole sample and that the results are generalizable. If the groups are significantly different, the generalizability across both groups is not present and must be discussed in the research report. Information describing the return rate and its impact on study interpretations should be provided in the final report.

In addition to nonresponse to the questionnaire in general, there also can be nonresponse to individual items in the questionnaire. If respondents do not understand an item or if they find it offensive in some way, they may not respond to it. Nonresponse to the entire questionnaire is usually more frequent and more critical than individual item nonresponse. The best defense for item nonresponse is careful examination of the questionnaire during your pretest. It is at that time that problems with items are most likely to show up. If you follow the item-writing suggestions in Figure 10.1 and subject the questionnaire to rigorous examination, item nonresponses will be few and will pose no problem in analysis.

Analyzing Results

When presenting the results of a questionnaire study, the response rate for each item should be given as well as the total sample size and the overall percentage of returns, since not all respondents will answer all questions. The simplest way to present the results is to indicate the percentage of responders who selected each alternative for each item. For example, "On item 4 dealing with possession of a master's degree, 50% said yes, 30% said no, and 20% said they were working on one." In addition to simply determining choices, comparisons can be investigated by examining the responses of different subgroups in the sample. For example, it might be determined that 80% of those reporting possession of a master's degree expressed favorable attitudes toward personalized instruction, while only 40% of those reporting lack of a master's degree expressed a favorable attitude. Thus, possible explanations for certain attitudes and behaviors can be explored by identifying factors that seem to be related to certain responses. Note that the questionnaire must obtain demographic information about the respondents in order to make desired comparisons.

While item-by-item descriptions provide one form of reporting the results of a survey, it can produce an overload of information that is difficult to absorb and condense. A better way to report is to group items into clusters that address the same issue and develop total scores across an item cluster. For example, recall the four issues our school superintendent had, and also recall the nature of the items she included for the four issues, especially the ones related to Likert and checklist items (see p. 285). Instead of reporting each Likert or checklist item separately, each type can be summed into a total score. For example, if the Likert items were scored from 5 (SA) to 1 (SD), a score for each item can be obtained and the scores could be summed across the Likert items. The total scores or their average could be reported and demographic comparisons could be made using the average score of each group being compared, for example, males and females. Not only does developing and analyzing clusters of items related to the same issue make it easier and more meaningful to report survey results, it also improves the reliability of the scores themselves—in general, the more items, the higher the reliability.

CONDUCTING AN INTERVIEW STUDY

An **interview** is essentially the oral, in-person administration of a questionnaire to each member of a sample. The interview has a number of unique advantages and disadvantages. When conducted well it can produce in-depth data not possible with a questionnaire; on the other hand, it is expensive and time consuming. The interview is most appropriate for asking questions that cannot effectively be structured into a multiple-choice format, such as questions of a personal nature or those that require lengthy responses. In contrast to the questionnaire, the interview is flexible; the interviewer can adapt the situation to each subject. By establishing rapport and a trust relationship, the interviewer can often obtain data that respondents would not give on a questionnaire. The interview may also result in more accurate and honest responses since the interviewer can explain and clarify both the purposes of the research and individual questions. Another advantage of the interview is that it allows followup on incomplete or unclear responses by asking additional probing questions. Reasons for particular responses can also be determined.

Direct interviewer-interviewee contact also has disadvantages. The responses given by a respondent may be biased and affected by her or his reaction to the interviewer, especially if there is not a long-time relationship with the interviewer. For example, a respondent may become hostile or uncooperative if the interviewer reminds him of the dentist who performed five root canals on him last Wednesday! However, another respondent may try hard to please the interviewer because she looks like her sister. Another disadvantage is that interviews are time consuming and expensive, with the consequence that the number of respondents is generally a great deal fewer than the number that can be surveyed with a questionnaire. Interviewing 500 people would be a monumental task compared to mailing 500 questionnaires.

Also, the interview requires a level of skill usually beyond that of the beginning researcher. It requires not only research skills, such as knowledge of sampling and instrument development, but also a variety of communication and interpersonal relation skills.

An alternative to face-to-face interviewing that is widely used is telephone interviewing. The telephone interview is most useful and effective when the interview is short, specific, and not too personal, and contains mainly selection-type questions. Other advantages of telephone interviews are that they are less expensive because there is no travel; they can be used to gather data from national samples; and data is collected and summarized easily in a single location. Telephone interviews also have some drawbacks. For example, it is difficult to build rapport with the interviewee; it is difficult to obtain detailed information over the telephone; interviewees are often bombarded by phone interviews and unwilling to participate. In general, telephone interviews, like face-to-face interviews, require a clearly stated interview questionnaire and training for interviewers.

The steps in conducting an interview study are basically the same as for a questionnaire study, with some unique differences. The process of selecting and defining a problem and formulating hypotheses is essentially the same. Potential respondents who possess the desired information are selected using an appropriate sampling method. An extra effort must be made to get a commitment of cooperation from selected respondents, because their failure to attend interviews is more serious since the interview sample size is small to begin with. The major differences between an interview study and a questionnaire study are the nature of the instrument involved (an interview guide versus a questionnaire), the need for human relations and communication skills, the methods of recording responses, and the nature of pretest activities.

Constructing the Interview Guide

The interviewer must have a written protocol, or guide, that indicates what questions are to be asked, in what order, and how much additional prompting or probing is permitted. In order to obtain standardized, comparable data from each respondent, all interviews must be conducted in essentially the same manner. As with a questionnaire, each question in the interview should relate to a specific study topic. Also, as with a questionnaire, interview questions may be structured, semistructured, or unstructured, but generally are semi- or unstructured to take advantage of the strengths of interviews. Structured questions tend to defeat the purpose of an interview. Completely unstructured questions, such as "What do you think about life in general?" or "Tell me about yourself," allow absolute freedom of response, but tend to be time consuming and unproductive. Therefore, most interviews use a semistructured approach that focuses respondents on more narrow questions and issues. However, sometimes it is useful to ask a structured question to focus in on a desired topic and then use semistructured questions to follow up on the structured question. For example, "Are you in favor of or against the death penalty?" "Why do you feel that way?" Semistructured questions may facilitate explanation and understanding of the responses to the structured question. Thus, a combination of objectivity and depth can be obtained, and results can be tabulated as well as explained.

Many of the guidelines for constructing questionnaires apply to constructing interview guides. The interview should be as brief as possible and questions should be worded as clearly as possible. Terms should be defined when necessary and a point of reference given when appropriate. Also, leading questions should be avoided, as should questions based on the assumption of a fact not in evidence ("Tell me, are you still stealing from the church poor box?").

Communication During the Interview

Effective communication during the interview is critical, and interviewers should be well trained before the study begins. Since first impressions are important, getting the interview "off on the right foot" is desirable. Before asking the first formal question, spend some time establishing rapport and putting the interviewee at ease. The purpose of the study should be explained and strict confidentiality of responses assured. Note that it is hard to provide anonymity when you are face-to-face with the respondent. As the interview proceeds, make full use of the advantages of the interview situation. You can, for example, explain the purpose of any question that is unclear to the respondent. You should also be sensitive to the reactions of the respondent and proceed accordingly. For example, if a respondent appears to be threatened by a particular line of questioning, move on to other questions and return to the threatening questions later, when perhaps the interviewee is more relaxed. Or, if the subject gets carried away with a question and gets "off the track," gently get him or her back on target. Above all, avoid words or actions that may make the respondent unhappy or feel threatened. Frowns and disapproving looks have no place in an interview!

Recording Responses

Responses made during an interview can be recorded manually by the interviewer or mechanically by a recording device. If the interviewer writes the responses, space on the interview form should be provided after each question. Responses can be written during the interview or shortly after the interview is completed. Writing responses during the interview may tend to slow things down, especially if responses are at all lengthy. It also may make some respondents nervous to have someone writing down the words they say. If responses are written after the interview, the interviewer is not likely to recall every response exactly as given, especially if many questions are asked. On the other hand, if an audiocassette recorder or video camcorder is used, the interview moves more quickly, and responses are recorded exactly as given. If a response needs clarifying, several persons can listen to or view the recordings independently and make judgments about the response. Of course, a recorder or VCR may make respondents nervous, but they tend to forget its presence as the interview progresses. In general, mechanical recording leads to more objective interpretations and scoring. However, if a mechanical recording device is used it is very important that the respondent know that and agree to its use.

Pretesting the Interview Procedure

The interview guide, procedures, and planned analysis should be tried out before the main study begins, using a small group from the same or a very similar population to the one being studied. As with written questionnaires, feedback from a small pilot study can be used to add, remove, or revise interview questions. Insights into better ways to handle certain questions can also be acquired. Finally, the pilot study will determine whether the resulting data can be quantified and analyzed in the manner intended. As with the pretesting of a questionnaire, feedback should be sought from the pilot group as well as from the interviewers. As always, a pretest is a good use of the researcher's time.

OBSERVATIONAL RESEARCH

One form of descriptive research is **observational research.** In an observational study, the current status of a phenomenon is determined not by asking, as with a survey or through an interview, but by observing. For certain research questions, observation is clearly the most appropriate approach. For example, you could ask teachers how they handle discipline in their classrooms, but more objective information would probably be obtained by actually observing several of each teacher's classes. An observational study must be planned and executed just as carefully as any other type of research study.

MAIN TYPE OF OBSERVATIONAL RESEARCH

The major type of quantitative observational research is nonparticipant observation. Recall from Chapter 7 that participant observation is usually associated with qualitative research. Nonparticipant observation includes both naturalistic observation and simulation observation, and typically involves observation of human subjects.

Nonparticipant Observation

In nonparticipant observation, the observer is not directly involved in the situation to be observed. In other words, the observer is on the outside looking in and does not intentionally interact with, or affect, the object of the observation. (See the discussion in Chapter 7 on data collection methods in nonparticipant observation.)

Naturalistic Observation

Certain kinds of behavior can only be (or best be) observed as they occur naturally. In such situations the observer purposely does not control or manipulate the setting being observed. In fact, the researcher works very hard at not affecting the observed situation in any way. As noted in Chapter 7, naturalistic observation is also an important qualitative method. The main difference between a quantitative and qualitative approach to naturalistic observation is that the quantitative researcher approaches the observation with a predetermined idea of what behaviors will be observed, while the qualitative researcher tends not to have a predetermined focus. The intent is to record and study behavior as it normally occurs. (Review Chapter 7 for information on conducting observational research, recording observations, and monitoring and training observers, and reread the extracts from the study, "The Expression of Care in the Rough and Tumble Play of Boys" in chapters 6, 7, and 8.)

META-ANALYSIS

Meta-analysis is a statistical approach to summarizing the results of many studies that have investigated basically the same problem. Given a number of studies, meta-analysis provides a numerical way of expressing the "average" result of the studies. As you may have noticed when you reviewed the literature related to your problem, there are numerous variables that have been the subject of literally hundreds of studies—ability grouping and cheating, for example. Traditional attempts to summarize the results of many related studies have basically involved classifying the studies in some defined way, noting the number of studies in which a variable was and was not significant, and drawing one or more conclusions. Thus, it might be stated that since in 45 of 57 studies the Warmfuzzy approach resulted in greater student self-esteem than the Nononsense approach, the Warmfuzzy approach appears to be an effective method for promoting self-esteem.

There are two major problems associated with this traditional approach to summarizing studies. The first is that subjectivity is involved. Different authors use different criteria for selecting the studies to be summarized. They apply different review strategies and often come to different (sometimes opposite) conclusions. Thus, for example, some reviewers might conclude that the Warmfuzzy method is superior to the Nononsense method, while other reviewers might conclude that the results are inconclusive. The second major problem is that as the number of research studies available on a topic increases, so does the difficulty of the reviewing task. During the 1970s, the need for a more efficient and more objective approach to research integration, or summarization, became increasingly apparent.

Meta-analysis is the alternative that was developed by Glass and his colleagues.[1] While much has been written on the subject, Glass's *Meta-Analysis in Social Research* remains the classic work in the field. It delineates specific procedures for finding, describing, classifying, and coding the research studies to be included in a meta-analytic review, and for measuring and analyzing study findings. A central characteristic that distinguishes meta-analysis from more traditional approaches is the emphasis placed on having the review be as inclusive as possible. Thus, reviewers are encouraged to include results typically excluded, such as those presented in dissertation reports and unpublished works. Critics of meta-analysis claim that this strategy results in the inclusion in a review of a number of "poor" studies. Glass and his colleagues counter that there is no evidence that such is the case or that final conclusions are negatively affected, and that further, there is evidence that on average, dissertations exhibit higher design quality than many published journal articles. They also note that experimental effects reported in journals are generally larger than those presented in dissertations; thus, if dissertations are excluded, effects will appear to be greater than they actually are.

The key feature of meta-analysis is that each study's results are translated into an effect size (ES), symbolized as Δ. *Effect size* is a numerical way of expressing the strength or magnitude of a reported relationship, be it causal or not. For example, in an experimental study the effect size expresses how much better (or worse) the experimental group performed as compared to the control group. The basic formula for effect size is

$$ES = \frac{\overline{X}_e - \overline{X}_c}{SD_c}$$

where

$\overline{X}_e$ = the mean (average) score for the experimental group
$\overline{X}_c$ = the mean (average) score for the control group
SD_c = the standard deviation (variability) of the scores for the control group

The formula may differ, depending on the statistics actually presented in a study, but the objective is the same. After effect size has been calculated for each study, the results are averaged, yielding one number that summarizes the overall effect of the studies. Effect size is expressed as a decimal number and, while numbers greater than 1.00 are possible, they do not occur very often. Thus, an effect size near .00 means that, on average, experimental and control groups performed the same; a positive effect size means that, on average, the experimental group performed better; and a negative effect size means that, on average, the control group did better. For positive effect sizes, the larger the number the more effective the experimental treatment.

Although there are no hard and fast rules, it is generally agreed that an effect size in the twenties (e.g., .28) indicates a treatment that produces a relatively small effect, whereas an

[1]Glass, G. V., McGaw, B., & Smith, M. L. (1981). *Meta-analysis in social research*. Beverly Hills, CA: Sage.

effect size in the eighties (e.g., .81) indicates a powerful treatment. Just to give you a couple of examples, Walberg[2] has reported that for cooperative learning studies the effect size is .76. This indicates that cooperative learning is a very effective instructional strategy. Walberg also reports that the effect size for assigned homework is .28, and for graded homework, .79. This suggests that homework makes a relatively small difference in achievement but that graded homework makes a big difference. (Many of you can probably use this information to your advantage!) As suggested earlier, meta-analysis is not without its critics. It must be recognized, however, that despite its perceived shortcomings, it still represents a significant improvement over traditional methods of summarizing literature. Further, it is not a fait accompli, but rather an approach in the process of refinement.

On the following pages, we present an example of survey research. Note that the study involved a stratified random sample, a mailed questionnaire, a procedure for assuring anonymity of responses, a followup mailing, and telephone interviews to assess response bias (i.e., differences between mail responders and nonresponders).

Now go to the Companion Website accompanying this text at www.prenhall.com/gay to check your understanding of chapter concepts in the following modules: Objectives, Practice Quiz, and Applying What You Know. Expand your research skills with Evaluating Articles, Analyzing Qualitative Data, Analyzing Quantitative Data, and Research Tools and Tips. Visit Web Links to broaden your knowledge about research.

---

[2]Walberg, H. J. (1984). Improving the productivity of America's schools. *Educational Leadership, 41*(8), 19–27.

READING INSTRUCTION:
PERCEPTIONS OF ELEMENTARY SCHOOL PRINCIPALS

JOHN JACOBSON
The University of Texas at Arlington

D. RAY REUTZEL
Brigham Young University

PAUL M. HOLLINGSWORTH
Brigham Young University

ABSTRACT   A stratified random sample of 1,244 U.S. elementary public school principals was surveyed to determine perceptions of their understanding of current issues in elementary reading instruction and the information sources that they use to learn about current issues in reading. The principals reported four major unresolved reading issues: (a) whole language versus basal approaches; (b) assessment of students' reading progress; (c) the use of tradebooks in place of basals; and (d) ability grouping students for reading instruction. Principals' priority ranking of the four most important unresolved reading issues were (a) whole language versus basal approaches; (b) effective alternative assessment of students' reading progress; (c) alternatives to ability grouping students for reading instruction; and (d) the necessity of phonics instruction as a prerequisite to formal reading instruction. The most frequently consulted reading information sources used by elementary school principals within the past 12 months included (a) professional education magazines, (b) personal contacts with specialists and colleagues, and (c) newspapers. Although college classes were the least used information resource of U.S. elementary school principals within the past 12 months, college courses in reading education rated high in utility along with personal contacts with reading specialists. The study concluded that U.S. elementary school principals report awareness of the important reading issues of the day, but that they may need readily accessible and practical information to significantly impact implementation of the current innovations in reading education.

No other area of the curriculum receives as much attention and generates as much debate as does reading instruction. For many years, research and practice have indicated that the success or failure of a school's reading program depends largely upon the quality of school principals' knowledge of and involvement in the school reading program (Ellis, 1986; McNinch & Richmond, 1983; McWilliams, 1981; Weber, 1971). One may conclude, then, that it is important for elementary principals to be informed, active participants in the national conversation about reading instructional issues. It is also an ipso facto conclusion that the quality of school principals' instructional leadership in school reading programs is directly linked to the quality of their knowledge about reading instruction (Barnard & Hetzel, 1982; Kean, Summers, Raivetz, & Tarber, 1979; McNinch & Richmond, 1983; Nufrio, 1987; Rausch & Sanacore, 1984). When principals lack necessary understanding of reading instruction, they tend to shun or delegate responsibility to others for the school reading program (Nufrio). Even worse, some researchers have determined that principals who lack sufficient knowledge of reading instruction tend to resort to misguided means for making decisions instead of grounding their decisions in reliable information and research (Roser, 1974; Zinski, 1975).

A synthesis of past and current research strongly suggests that elementary school principals should bear a major responsibility for the school reading program and have an ethical and professional obligation to be conversant in the same curriculum areas as those expected of elementary classroom teachers (Wilkerson, 1988). To do this, elementary school administrators must stay abreast of current critical reading issues to be effective instructional leaders in their own school's reading programs.

Past research related to elementary school principals' understanding of reading instruction has been based primarily on surveys of teachers' impressions of principals' reading leadership capabilities. In other related studies, elementary school administrators have been queried about their familiarity with specific reading instructional concepts, their professional reading instruction preparation, and the amount of their own classroom reading teaching experience. Some past research has determined that principals understand reading instructional concepts fairly well (Aldridge, 1973; Gehring, 1977; Panchyshyn, 1971; Shelton, Rafferty, and Rose, 1990), while other research concluded that principals' reading instructional understanding is insufficient and their preparation inadequate to assume leadership roles for elementary school reading programs (Berger & Andolina, 1977; Kurth, 1985; Laffey & Kelly, 1983; Lilly, 1982; Moss, 1985; Nufrio, 1987; Rausch & Sanacore, 1984; Zinski, 1975).

Several problems have been associated with past attempts to research principals' knowledge of reading instruction. First, most past studies have been limited to a local area or single state. Few past studies go beyond state lines, and none of them have attempted to describe elementary school principals' perceived knowledge of reading instructional issues nationwide. Second, past survey studies have generally had marginally acceptable return rates, and no checks for response bias by comparing responders with nonresponders were made, thus severely limiting the generalizability of their conclusions.

Address correspondence to Paul M. Hollingsworth, Brigham Young University, Department of Elementary Education, 215 McKay Building, Provo, UT 84602.

An exhaustive search of the extant literature indicated that no national research study of principals' perceived knowledge of current critical issues in reading education has been conducted to date. Thus, little is known about the state of contemporary elementary school administrators' perceptions of current, critical issues in reading education. Furthermore, no research data are available on how these important leaders of school reading programs commonly access information regarding current issues in reading education. Thus, the purpose of this study focused on three research questions: (a) What do practicing elementary principals perceive are the critical and unresolved issues in reading education? (b) What level of understanding do practicing elementary principals perceive that they have of each issue? (c) What sources do practicing elementary principals use and find helpful to inform themselves about current issues in reading education?

METHOD

Survey Instrument

A survey questionnaire consisting of several sections was constructed (see Appendix A). The first section requested the following standard demographic information from the elementary school principals surveyed: (a) school size and type (1–299, 300–599, or 600 or more students, and Grades K–3, K–6, etc.), (b) years of experience as a principal and educator, (c) state, and (d) type of reading approaches used in their schools. The second section of the survey instrument included three tasks. Task 1 presented principals with 11 reading issues and asked them to indicate whether each issue was resolved, unresolved, or never had been an issue in their own minds, experiences, or schools.[1] Task 2 requested that principals rank order from 1 to 3 the top three issues that they had classified as unresolved in Task 1. Task 3 requested that the principals perform a self-rating of their understanding level of each reading issue on a 4-point forced-choice scale: (a) understand well enough to describe underlying issues and give a reasoned argument, (b) understand most of the underlying issues and give a rationale in taking a position, (c) know problem exists, but not sure of basic issue, and (d) not aware of a problem.

In the third section of the questionnaire, Task 4 listed 16 different information sources that principals could use to learn about current reading instructional issues and related research. Principals were asked to respond whether they "had" or "had not" used each of the 16 information sources within the past 12 months. Finally, Task 5 asked principals to rate the usefulness of each reading information resource that they had used on a 3-point forced-choice scale: (1) quite helpful, (2) moderately helpful, and (3) not very helpful.

Procedures

Subjects for this study were randomly selected from a computerized list obtained from Quality Educational Data (QED) of elementary public school principals in the United States during the 1989–90 school year. A total of 1,261 principals from a possible population of 41,467 were selected. The sample represented ap-

proximately 3% of the total target population. A stratified random sampling design was used to increase the precision of variable estimates (Fowler, 1988). Elementary school principals were proportionately selected from school size and school types to yield 95% confidence intervals of within ± 1% for the total population from schools with a population of 1 through 299, 300 through 599, and 600 or more. Other subject schools included those having only Grades K through 3 and K through 6 (Fowler, 1988, p. 42).

To track the responses anonymously, we included a postcard (giving the principal's name and a code indicating the size of school) in the mailing. Respondents were asked to return the questionnaire and postcard to separate return addresses. The first mailing was sent in February 1990. Four weeks later, a second mailing (with an updated cover letter and survey form) was sent to those who had not responded to the initial mailing (Heberlein & Baumgartner, 1981).

Return rates on mailed educational survey instruments are frequently in the 40 to 60% range (Could-Silva & Sadoski, 1987). An unbiased final sample of 500 responses would still yield 95% confidence intervals of within ± 3% for the entire target population of U.S. elementary school administrators surveyed (Asher, 1976). To check for response bias among responders, a trained graduate student randomly selected and interviewed over the telephone a sample of 31 (5%) of the nonrespondents (Frey, 1989). The telephone interview consisted of 16 questions selected from the mailed questionnaire (11 questions relating to reading issues and 5 questions on reading information sources used). Telephone responses were then compared with mailed responses by using chi-square analyses of each item to learn if any systematic differences existed between the answers of the two groups. If significant differences were not found between the two groups, then responses for those who returned their survey by mail may be generalizable to the larger population of elementary school principals (Borg & Gall, 1989).

RESULTS

Of the 1,261 surveys sent, 17 were returned because of inaccurate addresses. Thus, a total of 1,244 possible responses remained. Thirty percent (373) of the principals responded to the first mailing. The second mailing yielded an additional 17% or 208 principals, giving a total response rate of 47%, or 581 principals. In Table 1, we report the number of principals receiving and returning questionnaires from each state.

Because a 47% survey return rate is a figure that is minimally adequate to accurately reflect the perceptions of the target population (Dillman, 1978), a follow-up telephone interview of 5% of the nonrespondents was conducted. Responses to the telephone interview were compared with the mailed responses by constructing contingency tables from the responses of the two groups (responders and nonresponders). Chi-square statistics were calculated for each of the 16 questions. No significant differences ($p < .05$) were found for responses on 7 of 11 reading issues and 4 of 5 reading information sources. In other words, 64% of the responses between those who responded by telephone and those who responded by mail did

Table 1.
Number of Principals Receiving and Returning Questionnaires, by State

State	Sent	Returned	State	Sent	Returned	State	Sent	Returned
Alabama	21	5	Kentucky	16	8	North Dakota	4	1
Alaska	5	3	Louisiana	23	8	Ohio	62	28
Arizona	14	6	Maine	9	3	Oklahoma	21	10
Arkansas	17	6	Maryland	24	12	Oregon	21	8
California	125	38	Massachusetts	32	11	Pennsylvania	57	30
Colorado	23	12	Michigan	56	24	Rhode Island	7	3
Connecticut	18	7	Minnesota	24	12	South Carolina	17	5
Delaware	2	0	Mississippi	12	6	South Dakota	17	4
District of Columbia	3	2	Missouri	29	16	Tennessee	22	8
Florida	39	16	Montana	7	3	Texas	92	45
Georgia	27	16	Nebraska	17	7	Utah	10	7
Hawaii	4	3	Nevada	6	2	Vermont	7	2
Idaho	9	8	New Hampshire	7	4	Virginia	21	10
Illinois	53	30	New Jersey	36	13	Washington	24	12
Indiana	33	19	New Mexico	11	8	West Virginia	19	10
Iowa	25	12	New York	68	27	Wisconsin	23	11
Kansas	22	7	North Carolina	31	12	Total	1,244[a]	581

not vary significantly on the 11 reading issues. And 80% of the responses between those who responded by telephone and those who responded by mail did not vary significantly on the sources of information that principals use to remain informed about reading issues. The differences between responders and nonresponders are described in Table 2.

In addition, chi-square analyses of responders from the first and second mailings yielded no significant differences, nor were measurable differences found between respondents resulting from school type or size ($p < .05$). Overall, the similarities between the two groups were determined sufficient to enable reasonably confident generalizations to the target population to be made by using the mail responses only (deVaus, 1986). Therefore, only the mail response data are reported.

Summary of Research Questions

Research Question 1: What do practicing elementary school principals perceive are the critical and unresolved issues in reading education? Of the 11 issues surveyed, 40% or more of the principals perceived 6 issues as *unresolved:* (a) use of whole language approaches instead of basal-reader approaches (73%); (b) assessment of students' reading progress (63%); (c) use of trade books instead of basal readers (56%); (d) use of ability grouping for reading instruction (48%); (e) whether kindergarten children should pass a screening test to enter kindergarten (46%); (f) whether at-risk readers should spend increased time reading or practicing skills (40%).

Of the 11 issues, 40% or more of the principals surveyed perceived the following 6 issues as *resolved:* (a) whether reading skills should be taught in isolation or integrated with the remaining language arts (63%); (b) whether phonics should be taught as a prerequisite to formal reading instruction (48%); (c) whether at-risk

readers should spend increased time reading or practicing skills (47%); (d) whether reading instruction should be mastery based (46%); (e) use of ability grouping for reading instruction (43%); and (f) whether schools should be required to use the same reading instructional program in all grades (41%).

In 24% or more of the principals' responses, they indicated that certain reading issues had never been an issue in their perception. In order of *never been an issue,* the principals indicated (a) whether schools should be required to adopt basal reading series (26%); (b) whether tradebooks should be used in place of basal readers (25%); (c) whether kindergarten children should pass a screening test to enter kindergarten (25%); and (d) whether schools should be required to use the same reading instructional program in all grades (24%).

Of the issues that principals rated as unresolved, the top four items receiving the highest *priority ranking* in terms of their relative importance to improving reading instruction were (a) use of whole language approaches instead of basal reader approaches; (b) assessment of students' reading progress; (c) use of ability grouping for reading instruction; and (d) whether phonics should be taught as a prerequisite to formal reading instruction. Of the 11 reading issues surveyed, the principals perceived the issue of requiring schools to use the same program in all grades (e.g., the same basal series) to be the issue of least importance. Table 3 gives the rankings of the surveyed elementary school principals for each reading issue.[2]

In summary, from among the 11 reading issues surveyed, elementary school principals rated the following as the single most important *unresolved* issue: use of whole language approaches instead of basal reader approaches (73%). The issue that the principals perceived as most *resolved* was whether reading skills should be taught in isolation or integrated with the remaining language arts (63%). The *unresolved* issue that the

Table 2.

Percentage of Responders and Nonresponders Whose Answers Differed Significantly
(Chi-Square) for the Resolvedness Question About Reading

Issue	Unresolved (%)	Resolved (%)	Never an issue (%)	No response	Total
Should schools be required to adopt a basal series?					
Responders	38.9	35.1	26.0	3	581
Nonresponders	48.4	51.6	.0	0	31
Should reading instruction be mastery based?					
Responders	37.3	46.0	16.7	5	581
Nonresponders	38.7	61.3	0.0	0	31
Should children's entry into kindergarten be delayed until they perform successfully on a screening test?					
Responders	45.7	29.1	25.3	3	581
Nonresponders	45.2	48.4	6.5	0	31
Should schools be required to use the same program in all grades (e.g., same basal series)?					
Responders	35.0	41.1	23.9	7	581
Nonresponders	51.6	45.2	3.2	0	31

Note. Critical value of chi-square $= 5.99$, $df = 2$, $p < .05$.

principals ranked highest in relative importance was use of whole language approaches instead of basal reader approaches. Finally, the issue that most of the principals felt had *never been an issue* was whether schools should be required to adopt basal reading series (26%).

Research Question 2: What level of understanding do practicing elementary principals perceive they have of each issue? After the principals were asked to rank order the unresolved issues in terms of importance, we requested that they rate their understanding level for each of the 11 reading issues using a 4-point scale (1 being the highest). Therefore, the lower the mean score, the higher the principals rated their personal understanding of each reading issue. Percentages, along with means and standard deviations, are also presented in Table 3.

Principals expressed *greatest* understanding of the following four issues: (a) teaching reading skills in isolation or integrated with other language arts curriculum ($M = 1.34$); (b) grouping students by reading ability for instruction in reading ($M = 1.42$); (c) teaching phonics as a prerequisite to reading instruction ($M = 1.42$); and (d) assessing students' reading progress. Principals expressed *least* confidence in their understanding of the following three issues: (a) using tradebooks in place of basals ($M = 1.93$); (b) using mastery-based reading instruction ($M = 1.76$); and (c) requiring schools to adopt a basal series ($M = 1.72$). Though principals reported a lack of confidence in their understanding of certain reading education issues, an overall mean score of 1.59 indicated that, generally, elementary school principals believed they understood most of the underlying issues, but, according to the survey criteria, they did not feel confident enough in their understanding of reading issues to give a good rationale for taking one side or the other.

Research Question 3: What sources do practicing elementary principals use and find helpful to inform themselves about current issues in reading education? Sixteen different information sources were listed on the questionnaire. Principals were to indicate if they had used each of the information sources in the past 12 months. They were asked also to rate the helpfulness of the sources that they had used. Percentages, along with means and standard deviations, were calculated and are reported in Table 4.

The principals reported that the top four reading information sources *used most* were (a) magazines for professional educators that carry articles about reading and literacy (96.6%); (b) personal contacts with specialists in the field (95.9%); (c) newspaper articles about reading issues (93.6%); and (d) magazines or newsletters focusing on reading issues (88.6%). The five reading information sources *used least* were, in order, (a) college or university reading courses (14.3%); (b) college textbooks focused on reading (24.9%); (c) reading articles in professional handbooks (38.8%); (d) reading reports from research agencies (42.3%); and (e) journal research articles (49.3%).

Also shown in Table 4 are the principals' rankings of the relative helpfulness of each used source. To calculate means and standard deviations for the relative helpfulness rating of each information resource, we converted category responses to numeric values, using a 3-point scale. The closer each mean approximated the value of 1, the higher the mean helpfulness utility rating for the information source. From an examination of the means, the following five reading information sources were reported as *most helpful:* (a) personal contacts with specialists in the field ($M = 1.2$); (b) workshops or organized study groups focused on reading ($M = 1.3$); (c) attendance at professional

Table 3.
Classification, Rating, and Ranking of Reading Issues by U.S. Elementary School Principals

Reading issues	Unresolved (%)	Resolved (%)	Never an issue (%)	Issue ranking	Understanding of the issues[a]					
					1 (%)	2 (%)	3 (%)	4 (%)	M	SD
How should student reading progress be assessed?	65	26	9	2	60	33	5	2	1.48	.68
Should the whole language approach be used instead of the basal reader approach?	73	21	6	1	52	39	8	1	1.58	.67
Should tradebooks be used in place of basals?	56	19	25	7	43	15	31	11	1.93	1.0
Should reading skills be taught in isolation or integrated with other language arts curriculum?	23	63	14	8	76	18	3	3	1.34	.70
Should phonics be taught as a prerequisite to formal reading instruction?	39	48	13	4	67	27	4	2	1.42	.67
Should students be grouped by ability for reading instruction?	48	43	9	3	67	28	2	3	1.42	.69
Should schools be required to adopt a basal series?	39	35	26	10	57	26	6	11	1.72	1.0
Should at-risk readers spend more time reading connected text or on practicing isolated reading skills?	40	47	13	6	57	33	8	2	1.54	.71
Should reading instruction be mastery based?	37	46	17	9	45	39	11	5	1.76	.84
Should children's entrance into kindergarten be delayed until they perform successfully on a screening test?	46	29	25	5	58	28	9	5	1.62	.86
Should schools be required to use the same program in all grades (e.g., the same basal series)?	35	41	24	11	61	24	5	10	1.64	.96

[a]1 = understand well enough to describe underlying issues and give a reasoned argument; 2 = understand most of underlying issues and give a rationale in taking a position; 3 = know problem exists, but not sure of basic issue; 4 = not aware of problem.

association conventions ($M = 1.4$); (d) literacy articles in magazines for professional educators ($M = 1.4$); and (e) college or university reading courses ($M = 1.4$). Three information sources rated *least helpful* by elementary principals were (a) reading articles in popular national magazines ($M = 2.1$); (b) watching or listening to TV or radio broadcasts about reading issues ($M = 2.1$); and (c) reading newspaper articles about reading issues ($M = 2.1$).

DISCUSSION

Among elementary school principals surveyed across the United States, the most unresolved reading issue is the controversy between the whole language versus basal approaches to reading instruction. The reading education issue rated least understood by

principals was the use of tradebooks in place of basals. These findings are most interesting because of their immediate relationship to each other and to the whole language versus basal reader approaches to reading instruction issue. Explaining this finding is difficult because principals were not asked *why* they indicated that this issue is unresolved. One speculation might be that, in the minds of principals, part of the problem associated with deciding whether to implement tradebooks in reading instruction is the question of *how* to use tradebooks either to supplant or supplement the basal reader. However, further research is needed to determine the reasons *why* the issue surrounding the use of whole language versus basal readers is an issue of such great importance.

Also of note, the principals ranked as the second and third most important *unresolved* national reading issues, assessment of reading progress and use of ability grouping. Yet, when asked to rank their understanding of reading issues, the principals gave the

Table 4.
Utility of Reading Education Information Sources as Rated by U.S. Elementary School Principals

| | | Rated utility in percentages | | | | |
Source	Percentage used	Quite	Moderately	Not very	M	SD
Personal contacts with specialists in the field	95.9	79.1	20.7	.2	1.2	.41
Professional association conventions	61.0	62.0	35.4	2.5	1.4	.54
Magazines or newsletters focusing on reading issues	88.6	52.5	46.3	1.2	1.5	.52
Literacy articles in magazines for professional educators	96.6	61.3	36.6	2.1	1.4	.53
Reading articles in magazines focused on techniques and instructional methods	81.3	46.2	51.5	2.3	1.6	.54
Reading articles in popular national magazines	74.4	17.6	55.4	27.0	2.1	.66
Journal articles reporting results of research	49.3	53.3	42.1	4.6	1.5	.59
Reading articles in professional handbooks	38.8	50.0	46.4	3.6	1.5	.57
College textbooks focused on reading	24.9	42.0	49.0	9.1	1.7	.64
Books about reading published by popular press	64.4	36.3	53.8	9.9	1.7	.63
TV or radio broadcasts about reading issues	77.7	19.3	55.6	25.1	2.1	.67
Newspaper articles about reading issues	93.6	18.3	55.8	25.9	2.1	.66
Reading reports from research agencies	42.3	49.6	46.7	3.7	1.5	.57
Reading reports and publications sponsored by governmental agencies	76.2	47.0	46.6	6.4	1.6	.61
College or university reading courses	14.3	61.3	35.0	3.8	1.4	.57
Workshops or organized study groups focused on reading issues	67.5	71.5	27.9	.5	1.3	.47

Note. Data represent only those principals who reported using the information resources in the past 12 months.

second and most important unresolved issue, assessment of student reading progress, the fourth highest rating of understanding, indicating that although it is an unresolved issue, they understand it well. Additionally, the third most important unresolved issue, ability grouping students for reading instruction, received the second highest rating of understanding. Though principals rated their perceived understanding of the issue of ability grouping as being high, it remains an unresolved issue in the minds of principals nationally. Again, these issues share close philosophical proximity with the whole language versus basal reader issue. Because tradebook use calls into question accepted assessment practices and the use of ability groups, one can understand that these issues would loom as critical issues in the minds of U.S. principals.

Principals' perceived lack of understanding and priority rating of the whole language versus basal reader issue as unresolved reflects a widespread concern among principals nationally regarding this issue. One positive sign that principals may be attempting to deal with the whole language versus basal reader issue is the fact that only 77% of the principals surveyed reported that their schools used the basal reader as the major approach for reading instruction, as compared with other recent estimates indicating that basal reader use in American schools exceeds 90% (Goodman, Shannon, Freeman, & Murphy, 1988).

Although the principals rated their understanding of the whole language versus basal reader issue as one of the least understood issues, they reported less use of basal readers and greater use of trade-

books in schools than previous national estimates indicated. This finding suggests that the principals' perceived lack of understanding regarding the whole language versus basal reader issue may not be precluding their attempts to make greater use of tradebooks in their school reading programs. The means by which principals are learning to make these changes *may* be related to their use of reading information resources.

With respect to the information resources used and valued most by principals, this study revealed that the majority of principals surveyed relied on (a) professional education magazines, (b) personal contacts with specialists in reading, and (c) newspapers as their major sources for gaining information about reading education issues and practices. Nearly 90% of those principals surveyed indicated that they had used one of those top three information sources about reading education in the past 12 months. Of note, those sources tend to be interpretive sources and may give only surface-level information, as opposed to more in-depth original research sources. However, considering the constraints exigent upon principals' time, less formal research synthesis may be the most pragmatic means of acquiring current information regarding critical reading instructional issues and promising practices. This fact is substantiated in part by the information sources that the principals used last.

During the past 12 months, the information sources that principals used least were (a) college or university reading courses, (b) college textbooks on reading, (c) articles in professional handbooks, and (d) research reports from research agencies. Those sources tend to focus on theories, practices, techniques, and approaches verified by in-depth original research studies, and they require greater time commitments than do the less formal information resources used most by practicing principals. The finding that enrolling in college or university reading courses was least used was rather curious when juxtaposed against principals' rankings of the most helpful information sources. Although the principals tended not to enroll in college and university reading course work during the past 12 months, they ranked college and university reading courses in the top four reading information sources as most helpful ($M = 1.4$, on a 3-point, with 1 being the highest).

In summary, the principals chose print informational sources that were interpretive, informal, and less technical information sources, that is, newsletters, newspaper articles, and magazines. They tended not to use detailed research reports found in texts, journals, handbooks, and reading reports from research agencies. However, the principals' selection and use of less technical, more interpretive reading information sources, as well as accessible reading specialists, seems logical given the constraints upon their time. Although the principals tended to rate college courses as extremely helpful, enrolling in university course work might not always be accessible, convenient, or even feasible for many practicing principals.

IMPLICATIONS

From this study, one might conclude that the vast majority of U.S. elementary school principals do attempt to keep current on issues related to reading education. Although principals appear to be aware of current trends and issues in reading education, they may not feel sufficiently confident about their understanding of the issues to implement innovative changes in school reading programs. This conclusion is sustained by the principals' ranking of the issue regarding using whole language versus basal readers as the most unresolved issue while also ranking this issue as least understood.

The conclusion of this study, that U.S. elementary school principals prefer obtaining information about critical reading issues and practices from practical and accessible sources, suggests that authors of educational literature and reading specialists should be aware that principals not only need to understand the issues but also to receive specific guidance on *how* to select promising reading practices for use in their schools and *how* to implement reading program changes.

One paradoxical finding should give strong signals to colleges and universities. Although the principals valued university-level reading courses, many of them had not used that information resource within the past 12 months. This finding may indicate a need for institutions of higher learning to design more accessible means for disseminating current, practical information into schools and classrooms.

In conclusion, the majority of U.S. elementary principals perceived that they were aware of current, critical, and unresolved issues in reading education, that is, tradebooks, reading assessment, and ability grouping. However, according to the survey criteria, many principals did not have enough confidence in their understanding of reading issues to give a reasoned rationale for taking one side or the other. Finally, if principals are to remain informed, information related to innovative reading practices must be disseminated in easily accessible and understandable ways.

APPENDIX A

Reading Education in the United States: Elementary Principals' Involvement
Elementary School Principals' Questionnaire
(This questionnaire takes approximately 10–15 minutes to complete)

Section 1. Important Demographic Information
Please complete the following:
(Check)
School Size: _____1–299 _____300–599 _____6001
School Type: _____K–3 _____K–6 _____Other _____
                                                   (Specify)

Years of experience as an elementary school prinicipal____
Total years of experience as an educator_____
State in which your school is located_____
Give, in percentage, the kinds of reading approaches that are currently being used in your school.
(e.g., 70% basal   20% literature based   10% whole language   _____other_____)
_____basal   _____literature based   _____whole language   _____other _____
                                                                   (Specify)

SECTION 2. THIS SECTION ASKS YOU TO CONSIDER ELEVEN READING INSTRUCTION ISSUES. YOU WILL BE ASKED TO COMPLETE THREE TASKS RELATED TO THESE ELEVEN ISSUES.

Task 1. Classify
Eleven reading education issues are listed below. In your mind, which of these are:
UI: An Unresolved Issue (research is conclusive—was once an issue but is no longer)
NI: Never has been an issue as far as I am concerned.
For each concern, circle the letter which designates the category you selected.

Task 2. Rank
After you have classified each statement, rank order the top three unresolved issues in terms of their relative importance to improving reading instruction from your point of view. Use the number "1" to indicate the issue which you believe is most important. Then use the numbers "2," "3," and so on to indicate the issues that are second, third. . . . Rank only the issues you classified as unresolved.

Task 3. Rate
Please rate your understanding of each issue (including any issues you added) as follows:
A. I understand this problem well enough to describe the underlying issues and can give a reasoned argument explaining my position.
B. I believe that I understand most of the underlying issues, but I can't give a good rationale for taking one side or the other.
C. I know that this problem exists, but I'm unsure of what the basic issues are.
D. I'm not aware of any problems in this area.

Reading Issues:

Reading Issue	Task 1: Classify			Task 2: Rank	Task 3: Rate
1. How should students' reading progress be assessed?	UI	RI	NI	____	____
2. Should the whole language approach be used instead of the basal reader approach?	UI	RI	NI	____	____
3. Should tradebooks be used in place of basals?	UI	RI	NI	____	____
4. Should reading skills be taught in isolation or integrated with other language arts curriculum?	UI	RI	NI	____	____
5. Should phonics be taught as a prerequisite to reading instruction?	UI	RI	NI	____	____
6. Should students be grouped by reading ability for instruction in reading?	UI	RI	NI	____	____
7. Should schools be required to adopt a basal reading series?	UI	RI	NI	____	____
8. Should at-risk readers spend more time on reading connected text or on practicing isolated reading skills?	UI	RI	NI	____	____
9. Should reading instruction be mastery based?	UI	RI	NI	____	____
10. Should children's entry into kindergarten be delayed until they perform successfully on a screening test?	UI	RI	NI	____	____
11. Should schools be required to use the same program in all grades (e.g., the same basal series)?	UI	RI	NI	____	____
12. (Other)_____	UI	RI	NI	____	____

SECTION 3. THIS SECTION ASKS YOU TO CONSIDER SIXTEEN READING INFORMATION SOURCES AVAILABLE TO PRINCIPALS. YOU WILL BE ASKED TO DO TWO TASKS IN THIS SECTION.

Task 4

Which of the activities listed below have you personally participated in during the past 12 months as a means of keeping yourself informed about current issues in reading. Mark an "X" in the blank "Have Done" or "Have Not Done" for each source.

Task 5

After completing Task 4, rate the degree to which each source you have used was helpful by placing an "X" in the blank "Quite Helpful," "Moderately Helpful," or "Not Very Helpful." **DO NOT** rate sources that you have not used in the last 12 months. Sources:

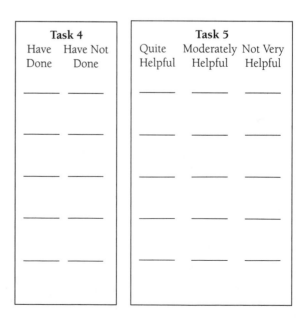

Source	Task 4 Have Done	Task 4 Have Not Done	Task 5 Quite Helpful	Task 5 Moderately Helpful	Task 5 Not Very Helpful
1. Personal contacts with specialists in the field (e.g., informal contacts with friends, colleagues, professors, and educators who have specialized in reading education)	____	____	____	____	____
2. Attendance at conventions of professional associations (e.g., local, state, or national: International Reading Association, National Reading Conference)	____	____	____	____	____
3. Reading magazines or newsletters which focus on reading issues (e.g., Language Arts, Reading Teacher, Journal of Reading, Reading Horizons)	____	____	____	____	____
4. Reading articles about literacy issues in magazines for professional educators (e.g., Phi Delta Kappan, The Principal, Elementary School Journal, Educational Leadership)	____	____	____	____	____
5. Reading articles in magazines focused on teaching techniques and instructional methods (e.g., Instructor, Teacher, K–12 Learning)	____	____	____	____	____

| | Task 4 | | Task 5 | | |
	Have Done	Have Not Done	Quite Helpful	Moderately Helpful	Not Very Helpful
6. Reading articles in popular national magazines (e.g., Atlantic Monthly, Time, U.S. News, Reader's Digest, Parents, Family Circle)	___	___		___	___
7. Reading journal articles which focus on reporting the results of reading research (e.g., Reading Research Quarterly, Journal of Reading Behavior, Journal of Educational Psychology, Journal of Educational Research)	___	___	___	___	___
8. Reading articles in professional handbooks (e.g., Handbook of Reading Research, Handbook of Research on Teaching, Encyclopedia of Educational Research, Review of Research in Education)	___	___	___	___	___
9. Reading college textbooks focused on reading (e.g., Books on teaching language arts, reading)	___	___	___	___	___
10. Books about reading which have been published by popular press (e.g., Cultural Literacy, Illiterate American, Why Johnny Still Can't Read, Closing of the American Mind, All I Ever Needed to Know I Learned in Kindergarten)	___	___	___	___	___
11. Watching or listening to radio and television broadcasts about reading issues (e.g., news reports, documentaries, debates, interviews, commentaries)	___	___	___	___	___
12. Reading newspaper articles about reading issues.	___	___	___	___	___
13. Reading reports about reading from research agencies (e.g., Center for the Study of Reading, regional labs)	___	___	___	___	___
14. Reading reports and publications about reading sponsored by governmental agencies (e.g., What Works, Becoming a Nation of Readers)	___	___	___	___	___
15. Enrollment in college or university courses related to reading education.	___	___	___	___	___
16. Participation in college or university courses related to reading education.	___	___	___	___	___
17. Other:_____	___	___	___	___	___

NOTES

1. The 11 issues included in the survey were selected by a panel of reading experts. Issues were selected based on attention that each has received in the recent reading education and research literature.

2. In the ranking of the reading issues, some respondents did not follow directions. They ranked all issues, instead of ranking only issues that they felt were unresolved. To adjust for the problem, we included only unresolved issues in the data analysis.

REFERENCES

Aldridge, T. (1973). *The elementary principal as an instructional leader for reading instruction.* Unpublished doctoral dissertation, University of Missouri.

Asher, J. W. (1976). *Educational research and evaluation methods.* Boston: Little, Brown.

Barnard, D., & Hetzel, R. (1982). *Principals handbook to improve reading instruction.* Lexington, MA: Ginn and Company.

Berger, A., & Andolina, C. (1977). How administrators keep abreast of trends and research in reading. *Journal of Reading, 21,* 121–125.

Borg, W. R., & Gall, M. D. (1989). *Educational research,* 5th ed. New York: Longman.

Could-Silva, C., & Sadoski, M. (1987). Reading teachers' attitudes toward basal reader use and state adoption policies. *Journal of Educational Research, 81,* (1), 5–16.

deVaus, D. A. (1986). *Surveys in social research.* Boston: George Allen and Unwin.

Dillman, D. A. (1978). *Mail and telephone surveys: The total design method.* New York: Wiley.

Ellis, T. (1986). The principal as instructional leader. *Research-Roundup, 3*(1), 6.

Fowler, F. J. (1988). *Survey research methods.* Newbury Park, CA: Sage.

Frey, J. H. (1989). *Survey research by telephone* (2nd ed.). Newbury Park, CA: Sage.

Gehring, R. (1977). *An investigation of knowledge of Clark County, Nevada, elementary school principals about the teaching of reading in primary grades.* Unpublished doctoral dissertation, University of Colorado, Boulder.

Goodman, K., Shannon, P., Freeman, Y., & Murphy, S. (1988). *Report card on basal readers.* Katonah, NY: Richard C. Owen Publishers.

Heberlein, T. A., & Baumgartner, R. (1981). Is a questionnaire necessary in a second mailing? *Public Opinion Quarterly, 45,* 102–108.

Kean, M., Summers, A., Raivetz, M., & Tarber, I. (1979). *What works in reading.* Office of Research and Evaluation, School Districts of Philadelphia, PA.

Kurth, R. J. (1985, December). *Problems court: The role of the reading educator in the training of elementary school principals.* Paper presented at the annual meeting of the American Reading Forum, Sarasota, FL.

Laffey, J., & Kelly, D. (1983). Survey of elementary principals. *The Journal of the Virginia State Reading Association* (a special edition), James Madison University, Harrisonburg, VA.

Lilly, E. R. (1982, September). *Administrative leadership in reading: A professional quagmire.* Paper presented at the meeting of the District of Columbia Reading Council of the International Reading Association, Washington, DC.

McNinch, G. H., & Richmond, M. G. (1983). Defining the principals' roles in reading instruction. *Reading Improvement, 18,* 235–242.

McWilliams, D. R. (1981). *The role of the elementary principal in the management of the primary reading program.* Unpublished doctoral dissertation, University of Pittsburgh, PA.

Moss, R. K. (1985). *More than facilitator: A principal's job in educating new and experienced reading teachers.* Paper presented at the annual meeting of the National Council of Teachers of English Spring Conference, Houston, TX. (ERIC Document Reproduction Service No. ED 253 856)

Nufrio, R. M. (1987). *An administrator's overview for teaching reading.* Opinion paper. (ERIC Document Reproduction Service No. ED 286 287)

Panchyshyn, R. (1971). *An investigation of the knowledge of elementary school principals about the teaching of reading in primary grades.* Unpublished doctoral dissertation, University of Iowa, Iowa City.

Rausch, S., & Sanacore, J. (1984). The administrator and the reading program: An annotated bibliography on reading leadership. *Reading World, 23,* 388–393.

Roser, N. L. (1974, February). Evaluation and the administrator: How decisions are made. *Journal of Education, 156,* 48–49.

Shelton, M., Rafferty, C., & Rose, L. (1990, Winter). The state of reading: What Michigan administrators know. *Michigan Reading Journal, 23,* 3–14.

Weber, G. (1971). *Inner-city children can be taught to read: Four successful schools.* New York: Council for Basic Education, Occasional Papers No. 18.

Wilkerson, B. (1988). A principal's perspective. In J. L. Davidson (Ed.), *Counterpoint and beyond: A response to becoming a nation of readers.* Urbana, IL: National Council of Teachers of English.

Zinski, R. (1975). *The elementary school principals and the administration of a total reading program.* Unpublished doctoral dissertation, University of Wisconsin, Madison.

Jacobson, J., Reutzel, D. R., & Hollingsworth, P. M. (1992). Reading perceptions of elementary school principals. The Journal of Educational Research, 85, 370–380. Reprinted with the permission of the Helen Dwight Reid Educational Foundation. Published by Heldref Publications, 1319 Eighteenth St., N.W., Washington, DC 20036-1802. Copyright © 1992.

SUMMARY

Survey Research: Definition and Purpose

1. Survey research involves collecting data to test hypotheses or to answer questions about the opinions of people about some topic or issue. Survey research is also called descriptive research.

2. A high percentage of all research studies are descriptive in nature. Surveys are used in many fields, including education, political science, sociology, and economics.

3. Survey research is not as simple as it appears.

4. Descriptive studies are commonly classified in terms of how data are collected, through self-report or observation. The most common self-report approaches are questionnaires, telephone surveys, and interviews. Self-report research requires the collection of standardized, quantifiable information from all members of a population or sample.

5. Survey research is also categorized in terms of cross-sectional or longitudinal. Cross-sectional research collects data at one point in time, whereas longitudinal research collects data at more than one time in order to measure growth or change.

Conducting a Questionnaire Study

6. In comparison to an interview, a questionnaire is much more efficient in that it requires less time, is less expensive, and permits collection of data from a much larger sample.

7. Questionnaires may be administered to respondents by mail, telephone, or in person, but are usually mailed.

Stating the Problem

8. The problem under investigation, and the topic of the questionnaire, must be of sufficient significance to motivate subjects to respond.

9. The problem must be defined in terms of specific objectives or subtopics concerning the kind of information needed; questions must be formulated and every item on the questionnaire should directly relate to them.

Selecting Participants

10. Participants should be selected using an appropriate sampling technique (or an entire population may be used), and identified participants must be persons who (1) have the desired information and (2) are likely to be willing to give it.

Constructing the Questionnaire

11. As a general guideline, the questionnaire should be attractive, brief, and easy to respond to. No item should be included that does not directly relate to the objectives of the study.

12. Structured, or closed-form, items should be used if at all possible. A *structured* item consists of a question and a list of alternative responses from which the respondent selects. In addition to facilitating responses, structured items also facilitate data analysis; scoring is very objective and efficient.

13. Common structured items used in questionnaires are scaled items (Likert and semantic differential), ranked items, and checklists. Often it is useful to obtain demographic information about the participants (e.g., gender, occupation, years teaching) to make comparisons of the respondents in different subgroups.

14. In an *unstructured* item format, respondents have complete freedom of response; questions are asked but respondents must construct their own answers. Unstructured items permit greater depth of response that may permit insight into the reasons for responses, but they often are difficult to analyze and interpret.

15. With respect to item construction, the number one rule is that each question should deal with a single concept and be worded as clearly as possible. Any term or concept that might mean different things to different people should be defined.

16. Avoid leading questions, questions that assume a fact not necessarily in evidence, and questions that do not indicate a point of reference.

Preparing the Cover Letter

17. Every mailed questionnaire must be accompanied by a cover letter that explains what is being asked of the respondent, and why. The cover letter should be brief, neat, and addressed specifically to the potential responder, if possible.

18. The letter should explain the purpose of the study, emphasizing its importance and significance, and give the responder a good reason for cooperating.

19. It usually helps to obtain the endorsement of an organization, institution, group, or administrator with which the responder is associated or views with respect (such as a professional organization).

20. It should be made clear whether anonymity or confidentiality of responses is assured.

21. A specific deadline date by which the completed questionnaire is to be returned should be given. Include a stamped, addressed return envelope for the respondents to return their surveys.

Pretesting the Questionnaire

22. The questionnaire and cover letter should be tried out in a field test using a few respondents who are similar to those who will respond to the questionnaire.
23. Pretesting the questionnaire yields data concerning instrument deficiencies as well as suggestions for improvement. Omissions or unclear or irrelevant items should be revised.
24. A too-often-neglected procedure is validation of the questionnaire to determine if it measures what it was developed to measure.

Followup Activities

25. If your percentage of returns is low, the validity of your conclusions may be weak. An initial followup strategy is to simply send out a reminder post card.
26. Full-scale followup activities are usually begun shortly after the deadline for responding has passed.

Dealing with Nonresponse

27. If your total response rate is quite low (40% or lower) you may have a problem with the generalizability of your results. You should try to determine if the persons who did not respond are similar to the persons who did respond. This can be done by randomly selecting a small subsample of nonresponders and interviewing them, either in person or by phone.

Analyzing Results

28. The simplest way to present the results is to indicate the percentage of responders who selected each alternative for each item. However, analyzing summed item clusters, that is, groups of items focused on the same issue, is more meaningful and reliable.
29. Relationships between variables can be investigated by comparing the summed cluster scores of different subgroups (e.g., male–female).

Conducting an Interview Study

30. An *interview* is essentially the oral, in-person administration of a questionnaire to each member of a sample.
31. When well conducted, an interview can produce in-depth data not possible with a questionnaire; but it is expensive and time consuming, and generally involves smaller samples.

Constructing the Interview Guide

32. The interviewer must have a protocol, a written guide that indicates what questions are to be asked, in what order, and what additional prompting or probing is permitted. In order to obtain standardized, comparable data from each subject, all interviews must be conducted in essentially the same manner.
33. As with a questionnaire, each question in the interview should relate to a specific study objective. Most interviews use a semistructured approach, first asking structured questions and following them up with explanatory, open-ended questions.
34. Many of the guidelines for constructing a questionnaire apply to constructing interview guides.

Communication During the Interview

35. Before the first formal question is asked, some time should be spent establishing rapport and putting the interviewee at ease. The interviewer should also be sensitive to the reactions of the respondent and proceed accordingly.
36. Responses made during an interview can be recorded manually by the interviewer or mechanically by a recording device. In general, mechanical recording is more objective and efficient. Respondents must both be aware of and consent to being recorded.

Pretesting the Interview Procedure

37. Feedback from a small pilot study can be used to revise questions in the interview guide. Insights into better ways to handle certain questions can also be acquired.
38. The pilot study will determine whether the resulting data can be quantified and analyzed in the manner intended.

Observational Research

39. In nonparticipant observation, the observer is not directly involved in the situation to be observed.
40. In naturalistic observation the observer purposely does not control or manipulate the setting so that observations will reveal the natural state of activity in the setting.

Meta-Analysis

41. Meta-analysis is a statistical approach to summarizing the results of many studies that have investigated a similar topic problem. Given a number of studies, it provides a numerical way of expressing the "average" result.

42. The key feature of meta-analysis is that the results of each study are translated into an effect size (ES), symbolized as Δ. Effect size is a numerical way of expressing the strength, or magnitude, of a reported relationship, be it causal or not.

43. After effect size has been calculated for each study, the results are averaged, yielding one number that summarizes the overall, or typical, effect. Low effect scores (0.00 to 0.30) indicate that a treatment does not make a difference, whereas a high effect size (0.70 to 1.00) indicates a strong treatment effect.

"Correlational research involves collecting data to determine whether, and to what degree, a relationship exists. . . ." (p. 311)

CORRELATIONAL RESEARCH

OBJECTIVES

After reading Chapter 11, you should be able to do the following:

1. Briefly state the purpose of correlational research.
2. List and briefly describe the major steps involved in basic correlational research.
3. Describe the size and direction of values associated with a correlation coefficient.
4. Describe how the size of a correlation coefficient affects its interpretation with respect to (1) statistical significance, (2) its use in prediction, and (3) its use as an index of validity and reliability.
5. State two major purposes of relationship studies.
6. Identify and briefly describe the steps involved in conducting a relationship study.

7. Briefly describe four different types of correlation and the nature of the variables they are used to correlate.
8. Describe the difference between a *linear* and a *curvilinear* relationship.
9. Identify and briefly describe two factors that may contribute to an inaccurate estimate of relationship.
10. Briefly define or describe *predictor variables* and *criterion variables*.
11. State purposes of prediction studies.
12. State the major difference between data collection procedures in a prediction study and a relationship study.

CORRELATIONAL RESEARCH: DEFINITION AND PURPOSE

Correlational research is sometimes treated as a type of descriptive research, primarily because it does describe an existing condition. However, the condition it describes is distinctly different from the conditions typically described in survey or observational studies. Correlational research involves collecting data to determine whether, and to what degree, a relationship exists between two or more quantifiable variables. The degree of relationship is expressed as a correlation coefficient. If a relationship exists between two variables, it means that scores within a certain range on one variable are associated with scores within a certain range on the other variable. For example, there is a relationship between intelligence and academic achievement; persons who get high scores on intelligence tests tend to have high grade-point averages, and persons who get low scores on intelligence tests tend to have low grade-point averages.

The purpose of a correlational study may be to determine relationships between variables or to use these relationships to make predictions. Correlational studies typically investigate a number of variables believed to be related to a major, complex variable, such as achievement. Variables found not to be highly related to achievement will be dropped from further examination, while variables that are highly related to achievement may be examined in causal–comparative or experimental studies to determine the nature of the relationships. As noted in Chapter 1, the fact that there is a high correlation between two variables does not imply that one causes the other. A high correlation between self-concept and achievement does not mean that achievement causes self-concept or that self-concept causes achievement. However, even though correlational relationships are not cause–effect ones, the existence of a high correlation does permit prediction. For example, high school grade-point average (GPA) and college GPA are highly related; students who have high GPAs in high school tend to have high GPAs in college, and students who have low GPAs in high school tend to have low GPAs in college. Therefore, high school GPA can be and is used in college admission to predict college GPA. As discussed in Chapter 5, correlational procedures are also used to determine various types of validity and reliability.

Correlational studies provide a numerical estimate of how related two variables are. Clearly, the higher the correlation, the higher the two variables are related and the more accurate are predictions based on the relationship. Rarely are two variables perfectly correlated or perfectly uncorrelated, but many are sufficiently related to permit useful predictions.

THE CORRELATIONAL RESEARCH PROCESS

Although relationship and prediction studies have unique features that differentiate them, their basic processes are very similar.

PROBLEM SELECTION

Correlational studies may be designed either to determine whether and how a set of variables are related, or to test hypotheses regarding expected relationships. Variables to be correlated should be selected on the basis of some rationale. That is, the relationship to be investigated should be a logical one, suggested by theory or derived from experience. Having a theoretical or experiential basis for selecting variables to be correlated makes interpretation of results more meaningful. Correlational "treasure hunts" in which the researcher correlates all sorts of variables to see "what turns up" are strongly discouraged. This research strategy (appropriately referred to as a *shotgun* or *fishing* approach) is both very inefficient and difficult to interpret.

PARTICIPANT AND INSTRUMENT SELECTION

The sample for a correlational study is selected using an acceptable sampling method, and 30 participants are generally considered to be a minimally acceptable sample size. There are, however, some factors that influence the size of the sample. The higher the validity and reliability of the variables to be correlated, the smaller the sample can be, but not less than 30. If validity and reliability are low, a larger sample is needed, because errors of measurement may mask the true relationship. As in any study, it is important to select or develop valid and reliable measures of the variables being studied. Also, if the measures used in correlation do not represent the intended variables, the resulting correlation coefficient will not accurately indicate the degree of relationship. Suppose, for example, you wanted to determine the relationship between achievement in mathematics and achievement in physics. If you administered a valid, reliable test of math computational skill and a valid, reliable test of physics achievement, the resulting correlation coefficient would not be an accurate estimate of the intended relationship, since computational skill is only one aspect of mathematical achievement. The resulting coefficient would indicate the relationship between physics achievement and only one aspect of mathematical achievement, computational skill. Thus, care must be taken to select measures that are valid and reliable for your purposes.

DESIGN AND PROCEDURE

The basic correlational research design is not complicated; two (or more) scores are obtained for each member of the sample, one score for each variable of interest, and the paired scores are then correlated. The result is expressed as a correlation coefficient that indicates the degree of relationship between the two variables. Different studies investigate different numbers of variables, and some utilize complex statistical procedures, but the basic design is similar in all correlational studies.

DATA ANALYSIS AND INTERPRETATION

When two variables are correlated the result is a correlation coefficient. A correlation *coefficient* indicates the size and direction of a relationship. A correlation coefficient is a decimal number ranging from +1.00 to 0.00 to −1.00. A coefficient near +1.00 has a high size and a positive direction. This means that a person with a high score on one of the variables is likely to have a high score on the other variable, and a person with a low score on one variable is likely to have a low score on the other. An increase on one variable is associated with an increase on the other variable. If the coefficient is near .00, the variables are not related. This means that a person's score on one variable provides no indication of what the person's score is on the other variable. A coefficient near −1.00 has a high size and a negative or inverse direction. This means that a person with a high score on one variable is likely to have a low score on the other variable, and a person with a low score on one is likely to have a high score on the other. An increase on one variable is associated with a decrease on the other variable, and vice versa. Note that correlations near +1.00 and near −1.00 represent the same size of relationship. The + and − represent different directions of relationship.

Table 11.1 presents four scores for each of eight 12th grade students: IQ, GPA, weight, and errors on a 20-item final exam. The table shows that IQ is highly and positively related to GPA (*r* = +.95), not related to weight (*r* = +.13), and negatively, or inversely, related to errors (*r* = −.89). The students with progressively higher IQs have progressively higher GPAs. On the other hand, students with higher IQs tend to make fewer errors (makes sense!). The relationships are not perfect, but then again, variables rarely are perfectly related or unrelated. One's GPA, for example, is related to other variables besides intelligence, such as motivation. The data do indicate, however, that IQ is one major variable related to both GPA and examination errors. The data also illustrate an important concept that is often misunderstood. A high negative relationship is just as strong as a high positive relationship; −1.00 and +1.00 indicate equally perfect relationships. They have the same size of relationship, but different directions. A coefficient near .00 indicates no relationship; the further away from .00 the coefficient

TABLE 11.1 Hypothetical Sets of Data Illustrating a High Positive Relationship Between Two Variables, No Relationship, and a High Negative Relationship

	HIGH POSITIVE RELATIONSHIP		NO RELATIONSHIP		HIGH NEGATIVE RELATIONSHIP	
	IQ	GPA	IQ	WEIGHT	IQ	ERRORS
1. Iggie	85	1.0	85	156	85	16
2. Hermie	90	1.2	90	140	90	10
3. Fifi	100	2.4	100	120	100	8
4. Teenie	110	2.2	110	116	110	5
5. tiny	120	2.8	120	160	120	9
6. Tillie	130	3.4	130	110	130	3
7. Millie	135	3.2	135	140	135	2
8. Jane	140	3.8	140	166	140	1
correlation	*r* = +.95		*r* = +.13		*r* = −.89	

is, in either direction, the stronger the relationship. Both high positive and high negative relationships are equally useful for making predictions; knowing that Iggie has a low IQ score would enable you to predict both a low GPA and a high number of errors.

Figure 11.1 shows a scatterplot for each of the three correlations shown in Table 11.1. The top left scatterplot shows that students who score low on IQ also tend to score low on GPA, while students who score high on IQ also tend to score high on GPA. This pattern illustrates a high positive correlation. The bottom scatterplot shows that students who score high on IQ tend to score low on errors, while students who score low on IQ tend to score high on errors. This pattern illustrates a high negative correlation. The lack of any systematic relationship between IQ and weight in the top right scatterplot illustrates a lack of relation between the two variables.

One way to interpret correlation coefficients is this: coefficient below plus or minus .35, low or not related; coefficient between plus or minus .35 and .65, moderately related; and coefficient higher than plus or minus .65, highly related. These figures are approximations and should not be blindly used. A correlation coefficient much below plus or minus .50 is generally useless for either group prediction or individual prediction, although a combination of several variables in this range may yield a reasonably satisfactory prediction. Coefficients of plus or minus .60 or .70 are usually considered adequate for group prediction purposes, as are coefficients of plus or minus .80 and above for individual prediction purposes. A correlational criterion-related validity of .60 for an affective measuring instrument may be considered high, since many affective instruments have lower validities. Conversely, we would consider a stability reliability of .74 for an achievement test to be low. A researcher would be very happy with observer reliabilities in the .90s, satisfied with the .80s, minimally accepting of the .70s, and would be progressively more unhappy with the .60s, .50s, and so forth. Thus, a correlation coefficient of .40, for example, would be considered useful in a relationship study, not useful in a prediction study, and terrible in a reliability study. A coefficient of .60 would be considered useful in a prediction study but would still probably be considered unsatisfactory as an estimate of reliability.

What a correlation coefficient means is difficult to explain. However, one thing it does *not* indicate is the percentage of relationship between variables. Unfortunately, many beginning researchers erroneously think that a correlation coefficient of .50 means that two variables are 50% related. Not true. In research talk, a correlation coefficient squared indicates the amount of common variance shared by the variables (WHAT??!!). Now, in English. When two or more

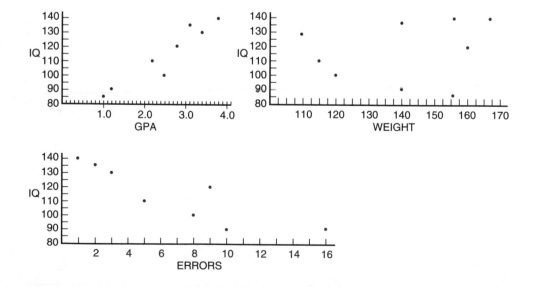

FIGURE 11.1 Data points for scores presented in Table 11.1 illustrating a high positive relationship (IQ and GPA), no relationship (IQ and weight), and a high negative relationship (IQ and errors).

variables are correlated, each variable will have a range of scores. Each variable will have score variance; that is, everyone will not get the same score. In Table 11.1, for example, IQ scores vary from 85 to 140 and GPAs from 1.0 to 3.8. **Common, or shared, variance** indicates the extent to which variables vary in a systematic way. The more systematically two variables vary, the higher the correlation coefficient. If two variables do not systematically vary, then the scores on one variable are unrelated to the scores on the other variable. In this case, there is no common variance and the correlation coefficient will be near .00. If two variables are perfectly related (positively or negatively), then the variability of one set of scores is very similar to the variability in the other set of scores. There is a great deal of common variance and the correlation coefficient will be near plus or minus 1.00. Thus, the more the common variance, the higher the correlation coefficient. In Table 11.1, a great deal of the score variance of IQ and GPA and IQ and errors is common, whereas the shared variance of IQ and weight is quite small.

The percent of common variance is less than the numerical value of the correlation coefficient. In fact, to determine common variance you simply square the correlation coefficient. A correlation coefficient of .80 indicates $(.80)^2$ or .64, or 64% common variance. A correlation coefficient of .00 indicates $(.00)^2$ or .00, or 00% common variance, and a coefficient of 1.00 indicates $(1.00)^2$ or 1.00, or 100% common variance. Thus, a correlation coefficient of .50 may look pretty good at first but it actually means that the variables have 25% common variance; 75% of the variance is unexplained, not common variance.

Interpretation of a correlation coefficient depends upon how it is to be used. In other words, how large it needs to be in order to be useful depends on the purpose for which it was computed. In a prediction study, the value of the correlation coefficient in facilitating accurate predictions is important. In a study designed to explore or test hypothesized relationships, a correlation coefficient is interpreted in terms of its statistical significance. Heads up! Statistical significance is an important new concept that you will be seeing more of in the next few chapters. It refers to whether an obtained correlation coefficient is really different from a correlation of zero, or no relation. That is, does a correlation reflect a true statistical relationship or is it only a chance one with no meaning? Decisions concerning statistical significance are made at a given level of probability.[1] Based on a correlation with a sample of a given size, a statistical significance test does not allow you to determine with perfect certainty that there is or is not a true, meaningful relationship between the variables. However, the statistical test does indicate the probability that there is or is not a significant, true relationship. To determine statistical significance, you only have to consult a table that tells you how large your coefficient must be to be significant at a given probability level and given sample size. (See Table A.2 in Appendix A. See also the article at the end of this chapter, especially Tables 2 and 3.)

Statistical significance depends on the sample size. To demonstrate a true relationship, small sample sizes require higher correlation coefficients than large sample sizes. This is because we can generally have a lot more confidence in a correlation coefficient based on 100 participants than one based on only 10 participants. Thus, for example, to be 95% confident that a correlation represents a true relationship (not a chance one), with a sample of 12 participants you would need a correlation of at least .58 to conclude the existence of a significant relationship. On the other hand, using a sample of 102 participants you would need a correlation of only .19 to conclude that the relationship is significant.[2] This concept makes sense if you consider the case when you could collect data on every member of a population. In this case, no inference would be needed because the whole population was in the sample. Thus,

---

[1]The concepts of statistical significance, level of significance, and degrees of freedom will be discussed further in Chapter 16.

[2]In case you are trying to read Table A.2, a 95% level of confidence corresponds to $p = .05$, and 12 cases correspond to $df = 8$; degrees of freedom, df, are equal to N (number in the sample) $- 2$, thus, $12 - 2 = 10$. For 102 cases, df equals $102 - 2 = 100$.

regardless of how small the actual correlation coefficient was, it would represent the true degree of relationship between the variables *for that population.* Even if the coefficient were only .11, for example, it would still indicate the existence of a significant relationship. As noted, the larger the sample, the more closely it approximates the population and therefore the more probable it is that a given correlation coefficient represents a significant relationship.

You may also have noticed that for a given sample size, the value of the correlation coefficient needed for significance increases as the level of confidence increases. The level of confidence, commonly called the *significance level,* indicates how confident we wish to be that we have a significant relationship. Usually we choose a significance level or .05 or .01, meaning that we wish to be 95% or 99% sure that we have a real, significant relationship. As the significance level increases, the p value (probability level) in the table gets smaller; the 95% confidence level corresponds to $p = .05$ and the 99% level to $p = .01$. Thus for a sample of 12 ($df = 10$), and $p = .05$, a coefficient of .58 is required; for a sample of 12 and $p = .01$, a correlation of .71 is required. In other words, the more confident you wish to be that your decision concerning significance is the correct one, the larger the coefficient must be. Beware, however, of confusing significance with strength. No matter how significant a coefficient is, a low coefficient represents a low relationship. The level of significance only indicates the probability that a given relationship is a true one, regardless of whether it is a weak or a strong relationship.

When interpreting a correlation coefficient you must always keep in mind that you are talking about relationship, not causality. When one observes a high relationship between two variables it is often very tempting to conclude that variable one "causes" the other. In fact, it may be that neither one is the cause of the other; there may be a third variable that "causes" both of them. The existence of a positive relationship between self-concept and achievement could mean one of three things: a higher self-concept leads to higher achievement, higher achievement leads to higher self-concept, or there is a variable, such as parent–child interaction, that underlies both self-concept and higher achievement. A significant correlation coefficient may suggest a cause–effect relationship but does not establish one. As you carry on your correlation and causal–comparative research (discussed in the next chapter), recognize that neither correlation nor causal–comparative research provides true experimental data. The only way to establish a cause–effect relationship is by conducting experimental research (the subject of Chapter 13).

RELATIONSHIP STUDIES

Relationship studies attempt to gain insight into variables that are related to complex variables such as academic achievement, motivation, and self-concept. For example, a researcher may be interested in whether a variable such as hyperactivity is related to motivation, or whether parental punishment is related to elementary school children's self-concept. Identifying related variables serves several purposes. First, correlational studies suggest subsequent examination using causal–comparative and experimental studies to determine whether there is a causal connection between the variables. Since experimental studies are costly and often time consuming, the use of correlational studies to suggest potentially productive experimental studies is efficient. Second, in both causal–comparative and experimental research studies, the researcher may need to control for variables that might be related to performance on the dependent variable. In other words, the researcher identifies variables that are correlated with the dependent variable and removes their influence so that they will not be confused with that of the independent variable. Relationship studies help the researcher to identify such variables and to control for them, and therefore to investigate the effects of the intended variable. For example, if you were interested in comparing the effectiveness of different methods of reading instruction on first graders, you would probably want to control for initial differences in reading readiness. You could do this by selecting first graders who were homogeneous in reading readiness or by using stratified sampling to ensure similar levels of reading readiness in each method.

The strategy of attempting to understand a complex variable such as self-concept by identifying variables correlated with it has been more successful for some variables than others. For example, while a number of variables correlated with achievement have been identified, factors significantly related to success in areas such as administration and teaching have not been as easy to pin down. If nothing else, however, relationship studies that have not uncovered useful relationships have at least identified variables that can be excluded from future studies, a necessary step in science.

DATA COLLECTION

In a correlational study the researcher first identifies the variables to be correlated. For example, if you were interested in factors related to self-concept, you might identify variables such as introversion, academic achievement, and socioeconomic status. As noted previously, you should have a reason for selecting variables in the study. A "shotgun approach" is very inefficient and often misleading. Also, the more correlation coefficients that are computed at one time, the more likely it is that some wrong conclusions about the existence of a relationship will be reached. If only 10 or 15 correlation coefficients are computed, this is not a major problem. On the other hand, if 100 coefficients are computed, it is likely that there will be relationships that are erroneously suggested as true. Thus, a smaller number of carefully selected variables is much preferred to a larger number of carelessly selected variables.

The next step in data collection is to identify an appropriate population of participants from which to select a sample. The population must be one for which data on each of the identified variables can be collected. Although data on some variables such as past achievement can be collected without direct access to participants, many relationship studies require the administration of one or more instruments and, in some cases, observations. Any of the types of measuring instruments so far discussed in this text can be used in a correlation study. One advantage of a relationship study is that all the data may be collected within a relatively short period of time. Instruments may be administered at one session or several sessions in close succession. If school children are the subjects, as is often the case, time demands on students and teachers are relatively small compared to those required for experimental studies, and it is usually easier to obtain administrative approval.

DATA ANALYSIS AND INTERPRETATION

In a correlational study, the scores for one variable are correlated with the scores for another variable. If a number of variables are to be correlated with some particular variable of primary interest, each of the variables would be correlated with that variable; each correlation coefficient then represents the relationship between a particular variable and the variable of primary interest. The end result of data analysis is a number of correlation coefficients, ranging between -1.00 and $+1.00$. There are a number of different methods of computing a correlation coefficient. Which is appropriate depends on the type of data represented by each variable. The most commonly used technique is the product moment correlation coefficient, usually referred to as the **Pearson r.** The Pearson r is used when both variables to be correlated are expressed as continuous data such as ratio or interval data. Since most instruments used in education, such as achievement measures and personality measures, are treated as being interval data, the Pearson r is usually the appropriate coefficient for determining relationship. Further, since the Pearson r results in the most precise estimate of correlation, its use is preferred even when other methods may be applied.

If the data for a variable are expressed as rank or ordinal data, the appropriate correlation coefficient to use is the rank difference correlation, usually referred to as the **Spearman rho.** Rank data are used when participants are arranged in order of score and each subject is assigned a rank from 1 to however many subjects there are. For a group of 30 participants, for example, the subject with the highest score would be assigned a rank of 1, the subject with the second highest score 2, and the subject with the lowest score 30. If two subjects have the same score, their ranks are averaged. Thus, if two participants have the same highest score they are each assigned the average of rank 1 and rank 2, namely 1.5. If only one of the variables to be correlated is in rank order, such as class standing at the time of graduation, the other variable or variables to be correlated with it must also be expressed in terms of ranks in order to use the Spearman rho technique. For example, if intelligence were to be correlated with class standing, students would have to be ranked from high to low in terms of intelligence. Actual IQ scores would not be used. Although the Pearson r is more precise, with a small number of subjects (less than 30) the Spearman rho is much easier to compute and results in a coefficient very close to the one that would have been obtained had a Pearson r been computed. When the number of subjects is large, however, the process of ranking becomes more time consuming and the Spearman rho loses its only advantage over the Pearson r.

There are also a number of other correlational techniques that are encountered less often but that should be used when appropriate. Some variables can only be expressed in terms of a categorical dichotomy, such as gender (male or female). Other variables that may be expressed as a dichotomy include political affiliation (Democrat versus Republican), smoking status (smoker versus nonsmoker), and educational status (high school graduate versus high school dropout). The two parts typically are labeled 1 or 0 (female versus male) or 1 or 2 (female versus male). Recall that for nominal variables, a 2 does not mean more of something than a 1, and 1 does not mean more than 0. The numbers only indicate different categories, not different amounts. The above examples illustrate "true" dichotomies in that a person is or is not a female, a Democrat, a smoker, or a high school graduate. Such dichotomies are correlated using a phi coefficient.

Artificial dichotomies may also be created by operationally defining a midpoint and categorizing subjects as falling above it or below it. For example, participants with test scores over 50 or above could be classified as "high achievers" and those below 50 as "low achievers." Such artificial classifications are typically translated into a "scores" of 1 and 0. These are called "artificial" dichotomies because variables that were ordinal, interval, or ratio are artificially turned into nominal variables. Table 11.2 describes a number of different correlations and the conditions under which they are used.

TABLE 11.2   Types of Correlation Coefficients

Name	Variable 1	Variable 2	Comments
Pearson r	continuous	continuous	most common correlation
Spearman's rho; or rank difference	rank	rank	easy to compute for small samples
Kendall's tau	rank	rank	used with samples less than 10
Biserial	artificial dichotomy	continuous	used to analyze test items; may have r greater than 1.00 if score distribution is oddly shaped
Point biserial	genuine dichotomy	continuous	maximum when dichotomous variable split 50–50
Tetrachoric	artificial dichotomy	artificial dichotomy	should not be used with extreme splits or sample
Phi coefficient	true dichotomy	true dichotomy	used in determining inter-item relationships
Intraclass	continuous	continuous	useful in judging rater agreement
Correlation ratio or eta	continuous	continuous	used for nonlinear relationships

Most correlational techniques are based on the assumption that the relationship being investigated is a linear one. If a relationship is **linear,** then plotting the scores of the two variables will result in a straight line. If a relationship is perfect (+1.00 or −1.00), the line will be perfectly straight, but if there is no relationship, the points will form a scattered, random plot. Refer back to Figure 11.1, which plots the data presented in Table 11.1. The top left and bottom scatterplots illustrate the concept of a linear relationship. However, not all relationships are linear; some are curvilinear. If a relationship is **curvilinear,** an increase in one variable is associated with a corresponding increase in another variable up to a point, at which further increases in the first variable result in corresponding decreases in the other variable (or vice versa). For example, the relationship between age and agility is a curvilinear one. As Figure 11.2 illustrates, agility increasingly improves with age, peaks or reaches its maximum somewhere in the twenties, and then progressively decreases as age increases. Two other examples of curvilinear relationships are age of car and dollar value, and anxiety and achievement. A car decreases in value as soon as it leaves the lot and continues to do so over time until it becomes an antique (!) and then it increases in value as time goes by. In contrast, increases in anxiety are associated with increases in achievement to a point; but at some point, anxiety becomes counterproductive and interferes with learning in that as anxiety increases, achievement decreases. If a relationship is suspected of being curvilinear, then an eta correlation is appropriate. If you try to use a correlational technique that assumes a linear relationship when the relationship is in fact curvilinear, your measure of the degree of relationship will be way off base. Use of a linear correlation coefficient to determine a curvilinear correlation will reveal little or no relationship.

In addition to computing correlation coefficients for a total participant group, it is sometimes useful to examine relationships separately for certain defined subgroups. For example, the relationship between two variables may be different for females and males, college graduates and non–college graduates, or high-ability and low-ability students. When the subgroups are lumped together and correlated, differential relationships may be obscured. However, regardless of whatever worthwhile knowledge may come from subdividing a sample and correlating the subgroups separately, a few cautions must be recognized. For example, subdivision and correlation can only be carried out if the original sample is large enough to permit sufficient numbers in the subgroups. Suppose a researcher starts with a correlation sample of 30 participants (15 males and 15 females) and subsequently wishes to compare separately the correlations of males and females on the selected variables. Upon subdividing the sample into male and female groups, the researcher has only 15 participants per group to study. The resulting samples are too small to obtain stable results. Sometimes researchers recognize this problem and select a larger sample to permit analysis of subgroups. However, if there are unequal numbers in the subgroups (for example, 55 females and 15 males), comparative analyses still cannot be carried out. If you think you want to study subgroups of your sample, select larger samples and use stratified samples to ensure similar numbers in the subgroups.

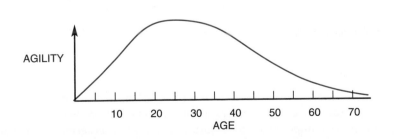

FIGURE 11.2 The curvilinear relationship between age and agility.

Other factors also may contribute to inaccurate estimates of relationship. **Attenuation,** for example, refers to the fact that correlation coefficients tend to be lowered if the measures being correlated have low reliability. In correlational studies a correction for attenuation (unreliability) can be applied that provides an estimate of what the coefficient would be if both measures were perfectly reliable. If such a correction is used, it must be kept in mind that the resulting coefficient does not represent what was actually found. Such a correction should not be used in prediction studies since predictions must be made based on existing measures, not hypothetical, perfectly reliable measures. Another factor that may lead to a correlation coefficient being an underestimate of the true relationship between two variables is a restricted range of scores. The more variability (spread) there is in each set of scores, the higher the coefficient is likely to be. The correlation coefficient for IQ and grades, for example, tends to decrease as these variables are measured at higher educational levels. Thus, the correlation will not be as high for college seniors as for high school seniors. The reason is that there are not many low-IQ college seniors; low-IQ individuals either do not enter college or drop out long before their senior year. In other words, the range of IQ scores is smaller, or more restricted, for college seniors, and a correlation coefficient based on a narrow range of scores will tend to be lowered. There is also a correction for restriction in range that may be applied to obtain an estimate of what the coefficient would be if the range of scores were not restricted. It should be interpreted with the same caution as the correction for attenuation since it, too, does not represent what was actually found.

PREDICTION STUDIES

If two variables are highly related, scores on one variable can be used to predict scores on the other variable. High school grades, for example, can be used to predict college grades. Or scores on a teacher certification exam can be used to predict principals' evaluation of teachers' classroom performance. The variable used to predict (high school grades or certification exam) is called the *predictor,* and the variable that is predicted (college grades or principals' evaluations) is called the *criterion.* **Prediction studies** are conducted to facilitate decisions about individuals or to aid in various types of selection. Prediction studies are also conducted to test variables believed to be good predictors of a criterion, and to determine the predictive validity of measuring instruments. Prediction studies are used to predict an individual's likely level of success in a specific course such as first-year algebra, to predict which of a number of individuals are likely to succeed in college or in a vocational training program, and to predict in which area of study an individual is most likely to be successful. Thus, the results of prediction studies are used by a number of groups such as counselors, admissions directors, and employers, in addition to researchers.

More than one variable can be used to make predictions. If several predictor variables each correlate well with a criterion, then a prediction based on a combination of those variables will be more accurate than a prediction based on any one of them. For example, a prediction of probable level of GPA success in college based on high school grades will be less predictive than basing the prediction on high school grade, rank in graduating class, and scores on college entrance exams. Although there are several major differences between prediction studies and relationship studies, both involve determining the relationship among a number of identified variables.

DATA COLLECTION

As in all correlation studies, research participants must be able to provide the desired data and be available to the researcher. Valid measuring instruments should be selected to represent the variables. It is especially important that the measure used as the criterion variable be valid. If the criterion were "success on the job," the researcher would have to carefully define "success" in quantifiable terms in order to carry out the prediction study. For example, size of desk would probably not be a valid measure of job success (although you never know!), whereas number of promotions or salary increases probably would be. The major difference in data collection procedures for a relationship study and a prediction study is that in a relationship study all variables are collected within a relatively short period of time, whereas in a prediction study the predictor variables are generally obtained earlier than the criterion variable. The researcher must have data that spans a sometimes lengthy time period, which in turn can create problems of participant loss. In determining the predictive validity of a physics aptitude test, for example, success in physics would probably be measured by end-of-course grade, whereas the aptitude test itself would be administered some time prior to the beginning of the course.

Once the strength of the predictor variable is established, the predictive relationship will be tested on a new group of participants to determine how well it will predict for other groups. An interesting characteristic of prediction studies is **shrinkage,** that is, the tendency of a prediction equation to become less accurate when used with a group other than the one on which the equation was originally developed. The reason for shrinkage is that an initial equation may be the result of chance relationships that will not be found again with another group of participants. Thus, any prediction equation should be validated with at least one other group, and variables no longer found to be related to the criterion measure should be taken out of the equation. This procedure is referred to as **cross-validation.**

DATA ANALYSIS AND INTERPRETATION

Data analysis in prediction studies differs somewhat from that of relational studies. It is beyond the scope of this text to discuss the statistical processes related to the analysis of prediction studies, but we will provide examples of how to interpret them. There are two types of prediction studies, single prediction studies and multiple prediction studies. The former predicts using a single predictive variable and the latter predicts using more than one predictive variable. In both cases, data analysis is based on a prediction equation.

For single variable predictions, the form of the prediction equation is

$$Y = a + bX$$

where

> Y = the predicted criterion score for an individual
> X = an individual's score on the predictor variable
> a = a constant calculated from the scores of all participants
> b = a coefficient that indicates the contribution of the predictor variable to the criterion variable

Suppose, for example, that we wished to predict a student's college GPA using the student's high school GPA. We want to know the student's predicted score. Suppose that the student's high school grade average is 3.0, the coefficient b is .87, and the constant a is .15. The student's predicted score would be

$$Y = .15 + .87(3.0) = .15 + 2.61 = 2.76 \text{ predicted college GPA}$$

We can compare the student's predicted college GPA to the student's actual college GPA at some subsequent time to determine how accurate the prediction equation is.

A **multiple regression equation**—also called a multiple prediction equation—is similar to a single predictive equation except that it contains more predictors. For example, suppose we wished to predict college GPA from high school GPA, SAT verbal score, and the rated quality of the student's admission essay. The student's high school GPA is 3.0, SAT verbal score is 450, and rated admission essay is 10. If a is .15, and the coefficients b for the three predictors are .87, .0003, and .4, the multiple regression equation would be

$$Y = .15 + .87(3.0) + .0003(450) + .4(10)$$
$$= .15 + 2.61 + .135 + .2 = 3.095 \text{ predicted college GPA}$$

We would validate the accuracy of the equation by comparing the predicted GPA of 3.095 to the student's actual college GPA.

Predictive studies are influenced by factors that affect the accuracy of prediction. For example, if the predictor and criterion variables are not reliable, error of measurement is introduced and the accuracy of the prediction is diminished. Also, the longer the length of time between the measurement of the predictor and the criterion, the lower the prediction accuracy is. This is because many **intervening variables** that influence the link between predictor and criterion variables can occur over time. Finally, general criterion variables such as success in business or teacher effectiveness tend to have lower prediction accuracy than narrower criterion variables because so many factors make up broad, general criterion variables.

Because relationships are rarely perfect, predictions made by single or multiple prediction equations are not perfect. Thus, predicted scores are generally reported as a range of predicted scores using a statistic called the *standard error*. For example, a predicted college GPA of 2.20 might be placed in an interval of 1.80 to 2.60. In other words, students with a predicted GPA of 2.20 would be predicted to earn a GPA somewhere in the range between 1.80 and 2.60. Thus, for most useful interpretation, the prediction should be viewed as a range of possible scores, not any single score. A college that does not accept all applicants will probably as a general rule fail to accept any applicants with such a projected GPA range even though it is very likely that some of those students would be successful if admitted. Although the predictions for any given individual might be way off (either too high or too low), for the total group of applicants predictions are quite accurate on the whole; most applicants predicted to succeed, do so. As with relationship studies, and for similar reasons, prediction equations may be formulated for each of a number of subgroups as well as for a total group.

As in relational studies, predictive studies can provide an indication of the common variance shared by the predictor(s) and the criterion variables. This statistic is called the *coefficient of determination* and indicates the percentage of variance in the criterion variable that is predicted by the predictor(s) variable. The coefficient of determination is the squared correlation of the predictor and the criterion. For example, if the correlation between high school GPA and college GPA is .80, the coefficient of determination is $.80 \times .80 = .64$ or 64%. This is a moderately high coefficient of determination, and the higher the coefficient of determination, the better the prediction.

OTHER CORRELATION-BASED ANALYSES

There are many sophisticated statistical analyses that are based on correlational data. We will briefly describe a number of these, recognizing that they are statistically complex. *Discriminant function analysis* is quite similar to multiple regression analysis, with one major difference: the criterion variable is categorical, not continuous. In multiple regression, continuous predictor variables are used to predict a continuous criterion variable. In discriminant function analysis, continuous predictor variables are used to predict a categorical variable, such as introverted/extroverted, high anxiety/low anxiety, or achiever/nonachiever. Thus, the predictions made are about categorical group membership. For example, based on the predictor variables, discriminant function analysis allows us to classify whether an individual manifests the characteristic of an introvert or an extrovert. Having identified groups who are introverts and extroverts, a researcher might want to compare the two groups on other variables.

Path analysis allows us to see the relationships and patterns among a number of variables. The outcome of a path analysis is a diagram that shows how variables are related to each other. Suppose, for example, that we wanted to examine the connections (paths) between variable *X* and variables *A, B,* and *C.* A path analysis based on the correlations among the variables will produce a path diagram such as that shown in Figure 11.3. In this diagram, single arrows indicate connections among variables and double arrows (*A* to *B*) indicate no direct link. Thus, variables *A* and *B* are individually linked to *D* and *A* and *B* are linked to variable *C. C* is not linked to *D.* Path analyses are useful in both showing what variables influence a given variable (like *X*) and also as a way to test theories about the ways groups of variables are related to a given variable. An extension of path analysis that is more sophisticated and powerful is called *structural equation modeling,* or LISREL, for the computer program used to perform the analysis. This approach provides more theoretical validity and statistical precision in the model diagrams it produces than those of path analysis. Like path analysis, it clarifies the direct and indirect interrelations among variables relative to a given variable.

Canonical correlation is an extension of multiple regression analysis. As noted, multiple regression uses multiple predictors to predict a single criterion variable. Canonical correlation produces a correlation based on a group of predictor variables and a group of criterion variables. For example, if we had a group of predictors related to achievement (GPA, SAT scores, teachers' ratings of ability, and number of AP courses passed) and we wanted to see how these predictors related to a group of criterion variables also related to achievement (job success, work income, and college GPA) we would use canonical correlation. A single correlation will be produced to indicate the correlation among both groups of variables.

Trying to make sense of a large number of variables is difficult, simply because there are so many variables to be considered. *Factor analysis* is a way to take a large number of variables and group them into a smaller number of clusters called *factors.* Factor analysis computes the correlations among all the variables and then derives factors by finding groups of variables that are correlated highly among each other, but lowly with other variables. The factors identified, not the many individual items within the factors, are then used as variables. Factor analysis produces a manageable number of factor variables to deal with and analyze.

PROBLEMS TO CONSIDER IN INTERPRETING CORRELATION COEFFICIENTS

The quality of the information provided in correlation coefficients depends on the data they are calculated from. It is important to ask the following questions when interpreting correlation coefficients:

- Was the proper correlation method used to calculate the correlation? (See Table 11.2.)
- Do the variables being correlated have high reliabilities? Low reliabilities lower the chance of finding significant relationships.
- Is the validity of the variables strong? Invalid variables produce meaningless results.
- Is the range of scores to be correlated restricted or extended? Narrow or restricted score ranges lower correlation coefficients while broad or extended score ranges raise them.

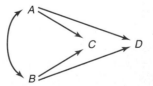

FIGURE 11.3
Example of a path analysis model: The connections of variables *A, B,* and *C* to variable *D.*

Now go to the Companion Website accompanying this text at www.prenhall.com/gay to check your understanding of chapter concepts in the following modules: Objectives, Practice Quiz, and Applying What You Know. Expand your research skills with Evaluating Articles, Analyzing Qualitative Data, Analyzing Quantitative Data, and Research Tools and Tips. Visit Web Links to broaden your knowledge about research.

- How large is the sample size? The larger the sample size, the smaller the value needed to reach statistical significance. Large sample sizes may be statistically significant, but practically unimportant.

On the following pages we present an example of correlational research. Note that the alpha reliability coefficients for the instruments used are given and they are satisfactory.

Explorations in Parent-School Relations

KATHLEEN V. HOOVER-DEMPSEY
OTTO C. BASSLER
JANE S. BRISSIE
Peabody College of Vanderbilt University

ABSTRACT   Grounded in Bandura's (1976, 1986) work, parent efficacy was defined as a parent's belief that he or she is capable of exerting a positive influence on children's school outcomes. Parents' sense of efficacy and its relationship to parent involvement were examined in this study. Parents ($n = 390$) of children in kindergarten through fourth grade in a metropolitan public school district responded to questionnaires assessing parent efficacy and parent involvement in five types of activities: help with homework, educational activities, classroom volunteering, conference participation, and telephone calls with teachers. Teachers ($n = 50$) from the same schools also participated, responding to questionnaires assessing teacher efficacy, perceptions of parent efficacy, and estimates of parent involvement. Findings revealed small but significant relationships between self-reported parent efficacy and three of the five indicators of parent involvement. Results for teachers revealed significant relationships among teacher efficacy, teacher perceptions of parent efficacy, and teacher reports of parent involvement in four areas. Results are discussed in relation to the patterns of involvement activities reported by parents and implications for research and intervention in parent-school relationships.

Bandura's (1977, 1984, 1986) work on personal efficacy considers the influence of beliefs that one is capable of achieving specific outcomes on behavior choices. In general, his work suggests that persons higher in efficacy will be more likely to engage in behaviors leading to a goal and will be more persistent in the face of obstacles than will persons with a lower sense of efficacy.

Hoover-Dempsey, Bassler, and Brissie (1987) earlier examined relationships between teacher efficacy and parent involvement. Building on Bandura's work and studies of the role of teacher efficacy in various educational outcomes (Ashton, Webb, & Doda, 1983; Dembo & Gibson, 1985), the authors defined teacher efficacy as "teachers' certainty that their instructional skills are effective" (p. 425). Hoover-Dempsey, Bassler, and Brissie found that teacher efficacy was significantly related to teacher reports of parents' involvement in conferences, volunteering, and home tutoring, as well as teacher perceptions of parent support.

Examination of specific parent variables often related to children's school performance suggests a complementary avenue of exploration in efforts to understand and improve parent-school relations. Some evidence that *parent* efficacy beliefs may be important in parent behaviors and child outcomes are reported in Baumrind's (1971, 1973) work on parenting styles, which established clear linkages between patterns of parenting behaviors and patterns of children's social and cognitive development. For example, the characteristics of Baumrind's authoritative style include consistent parental willingness to give reasons and explanations for requests and to consider and discuss alternative points of view. Because children of authoritative parents have consistent access to their parents' thinking—and because authoritative parents listen and take into account their children's reasoning—the children tend to develop higher levels of social and cognitive competence than do peers raised in other parenting styles.

Dornbusch, Ritter, Leiderman, Roberts, and Fraleigh (1987) recently demonstrated another specific outcome of an authoritative parenting style; they found that adolescents raised by authoritative parents, when compared with adolescents raised by authoritarian parents, have higher levels of academic performance in high school. In a related line of inquiry, Mondell and Tyler (1981) reported significant positive relationships between elements of parental competence and characteristics of parents' teaching interactions with their children, for example, more competent parents treat the child as an "origin," offer more approval and acceptance, and offer more helpful problem-solving questions and strategies.

In each set of findings, the qualities of parental behavior suggest the presence of strong parental beliefs in the abilities and "worthiness" of the child, for example, giving children reasons for requests and treating them as capable of solving problems. These behaviors suggest that parents believe in the abilities of the child and have confidence in their own ability to guide the child's learning. Such attitudes and the behaviors that they enable are central to a parental sense of efficacy—parents' belief and knowledge that they can teach their children (content, processes, attitudes, and values) and that their children can learn what they teach.

Applied in this manner, Bandura's (1977, 1984, 1986) theory suggests that parents will hold personal efficacy beliefs about their ability to help their children learn. These efficacy beliefs will influence their decisions about the avenues and timing of efforts to become involved in their children's education. For ex-

Address correspondence to Kathleen V. Hoover-Dempsey, Department of Psychology and Human Development, Box 512, Peabody College, Vanderbilt University, Nashville, TN 37203.

ample, parents with a strong sense of efficacy are more likely than low-efficacy parents are to help their children resolve a misunderstanding with the teacher, because they believe that they are capable of offering, and helping their child to act on, appropriate guidance. Overall, parents most likely become involved when they believe that their involvement will "make a difference" for their children.

Following Bandura's (1986) suggestion that assessments of perceived self-efficacy are appropriately "tailored to the domains of functioning being analyzed" (p. 360), the present study was designed to explore parent efficacy and the nature of its relationship to specific indicators of parents' involvement in their elementary school children's education. Although parent efficacy is likely only one of several contributors to parents' involvement decisions (Bandura 1986), we believe that it may operate as a fundamentally important mechanism, explaining variations in involvement decisions more fully than do some of the more frequently referenced status variables (e.g., parent income, education, employment). We believe that self-efficacy is more significant than such status variables because self-efficacy beliefs, far more than variables describing an individual's status, "function as an important set of proximal determinants of human motivation, affect, and action" (Bandura, 1989, p. 1175). Support for this position comes from related bodies of work, for example, Greenberger and Goldberg's (1989) findings that adults' commitment to parenting is "more consequential" for other parenting practices than is their involvement in work (30).

We also explored the replicability of previous results indicating a significant positive relationship between teachers' sense of efficacy and parent involvement. That relationship is grounded in the logical probability that teachers with a higher sense of personal teaching efficacy, being more confident of their teaching skills, are more likely to invite parent involvement and to accept parents' initiation of involvement activities (Hoover-Dempsey et al., 1987). Finally, we explored teachers' perceptions of parents' efficacy and involvement, based, in part, on earlier findings of a significant relationship between an "other's" perceptions of teacher efficacy and selected teacher outcomes (Brissie, Hoover-Dempsey, & Bassler, 1988). In general, we expected that higher levels of parent involvement would be associated with higher levels of parent efficacy, teacher efficacy, and teacher perceptions of parent efficacy. We expected to find those relationships because higher efficacy parents and teachers, being more confident of their skills and abilities related to children's learning, would more likely initiate and invite parent involvement in children's school-related learning activities.

Sample, Methods, and Procedures

Four elementary schools in a large public school district participated in the study. The schools varied in geographic location within the district, size (300 to 500 students), and mean annual family income reported by parents ($15,000 to $37,000). Because the purpose of the study was to examine a group of parents across varied school settings, data are not reported for individual schools.

We contacted principals from each school and obtained permission to solicit parent and teacher participation. Letters de-

scribing the study were put in teacher mailboxes at each school. Teachers choosing to participate were asked to complete a questionnaire that contained all teacher data needed for the study and to leave it in a sealed envelope in a collection box in the school office. All the teachers at each school, whether they choose to participate in the study or not, were asked to send parent letters and questionnaire packets home with students in their classes. The letter explained the study, solicited voluntary participation, and asked parents to complete an accompanying questionnaire and return it to school in a sealed envelope. We collected the sealed return envelopes from parents and teachers at the schools.

Parent Sample

Three hundred ninety parents participated in the study. The number represented approximately 30% of the children served by the four schools. Individual school response rates ranged from 24% to 36%. Given the relatively low response rate, the results must be interpreted with caution. It seemed probable that bias in the sample favored participation by parents who had stronger opinions about the issues involved. As a check on that possibility, we reviewed parents' comments at the end of the questionnaire (in a "comments" space used by approximately half of the participants). The comments revealed a wide range of positive and negative statements, indicating a varied set of parent experiences and attitudes (e.g., "I would appreciate more news on what the children are doing and why from teachers to parents, plus how to assist with that at home." "Conference times are inaccessible to people who work. Teachers do not like phone calls from parents in their off time and I understand this. You never hear from the schoolteacher unless they have a complaint or want something." "Our son's teacher this year and last has been a very positive influence on him. We're grateful for her caring the way she does." "She never has homework. What is this teacher's problem? Is she too lazy to grade extra papers? My child is making Cs and Ds. Please help.") Although the respondents may have had a higher-than-average level of interest in parent involvement issues, the variety of experiences reflected in their comments suggested that their reports would be useful in understanding many parents' patterns of school-related involvement.

In general, the respondents appeared to be an average group of elementary school parents (Table 1). Most of the respondents were mothers, most were married, and most were employed outside of the home. Education and income levels spanned a wide range. A comparison of that group with national data suggests that those parents were typical of many public school districts' parent population (e.g., compare Table 1 figures with national percentages for marital status in 1987—63% married, 36% not married—and for education—among the 25- to 34-year-old age group in 1984, 34% had a high school education and 16% had a college degree; U.S. Bureau of the Census, 1989).

Teacher Sample

Fifty teachers in the four schools (63% of the total possible) participated in the study and returned usable questionnaires. All the teachers were women, and their class enrollments averaged 21.06 ($SD = 5.20$). They had been teaching for an average

Table 1.
Parent Characteristics

Elementary school parents	n	% of sample
Sex		
Female	326	84
Male	54	14
No response	8	2
Education		
Grade school	27	7
High school	131	34
Some college	125	32
BA/BS degree	50	13
Some graduate work	22	6
Graduate degree (MA/MS, PhD/MD)	24	7
No response	9	2
Marital status		
Married	259	67
Not married (includes single, separated, divorced, widowed)	124	32
No response	5	1
Employment status		
Employed out of the home	253	65
Not employed out of the home	118	30
No response	17	4
Family income		
≤ $5,000	25	6
$5,001–$10,000	42	11
$10,001–$20,000	78	20
$20,001–$30,000	76	20
$30,001–$40,000	75	20
$40,001–$50,000	36	9
$50,001 +	23	6
No response	10	8
Age of respondent	$M = 33.37$	$SD = 6.61$

status, education, family income, marital status, age, and sex) and estimates of their levels of involvement in various forms of parent-school activities—help with homework (hours in average week); other educational activities with children (hours in average week); volunteer work at school (hours in average week); telephone calls with teachers (number in average month); and parent-teacher conferences (average number in semester). Similar estimation procedures have been used successfully in other investigations (Grolnick & Ryan, 1989; Hoover-Dempsey, et al., 1987; Stevenson & Baker, 1987).

The Parent Questionnaire contained Likert-scale response items designed to assess parents' perceptions of their own efficacy. We developed the 12-item Parent Perceptions of Parent Efficacy Scale on the basis of the teaching efficacy and parenting literature cited earlier. Although efforts to develop an assessment of general parenting efficacy have been reported (Johnston & Mash, 1989), the teaching efficacy literature was used as the basis for this measure because interest in this study focused on parents' perceptions of personal efficacy specifically in relation to children's school learning. The scale included such items as "I know how to help my child do well in school" and "If I try hard, I can get through to my child even when he/she has trouble understanding something." Following the model set by previously reported scales of teacher efficacy, items in this scale focused on assessment of parents' general abilities to influence children's school outcomes and specific effectiveness in influencing children's school learning. Items were scored on a 5-point scale ranging from strongly disagree (1) to strongly agree (5). Negatively worded items were subsequently rescored so that higher scores uniformly reflected higher efficacy. Possible total scores for the scale ranged from 12 to 60. Similarity to selected items of the Teacher Perceptions of Efficacy Scale (see below) and its grounding in related literature support the validity of this scale. Alpha reliability for this sample, .81, was judged satisfactory.

Teacher Questionnaire. The Teacher Questionnaire asked for specific information about teachers and their classes (grade, enrollment, percentage of students qualifying for free lunch, total years taught, years at present school, highest degree earned, sex, and age). Teachers were also asked to estimate the number of students in their classes whose parents participated in scheduled conferences, volunteer work at school, regular assistance with homework, regular involvement in other educational activities with children (e.g., reading and playing games), and telephone calls with the teacher. Again, such procedures have been used successfully in other investigations (Hoover-Dempsey et al., 1987; Stevenson & Baker, 1987).

We developed a seven-item Teacher Perceptions of Parent Efficacy Scale on the basis of the literature cited earlier. Items included such statements as "My students' parents help their children learn," and "My students' parents have little influence on their children's academic performance." All the items were scored on a scale ranging from strongly disagree (1) to strongly agree (5); negatively worded items were rescored so that higher scores consistently reflected more positive teacher perceptions of parent efficacy. Possible scores for the scale ranged from 7 to 35. Similarity to selected items of the Parent Perceptions of Parent Efficacy Scale and its

of 15.76 years (SD = 7.57) and had been in their present schools for approximately 6.5 years (SD = 5.73). Their average age was 41.21 years (SD = 8.73). The majority of the teachers held a master's degree, and many had credits beyond the MA/MS degrees.

Measures

All data on the parents and teachers were derived from questionnaires returned by the respondents. The questionnaire for each set of respondents contained demographic items, a set of requests for estimates of participation in specific parent involvement activities, and a series of items designed to assess respondents' perceptions of parent or teacher efficacy.

Parent Questionnaire. The Parent Questionnaire asked participants to give specific information about themselves (employment grounding in the literature reviewed earlier support the validity of this scale. Alpha reliability of .79 for this sample was adequate.

Items on the 12-item Teacher Perceptions of Teacher Efficacy Scale (Hoover-Dempsey et al., 1987) included such statements as "I am successful with the students in my class" and "I feel that I am making a significant educational difference in the lives of my students." Items were scored on a scale ranging from *strongly disagree* (1) to *strongly agree* (5); negatively worded items were subsequently rescored so that higher scores uniformly reflected higher efficacy. Total scale scores ranged from 12 to 60. The scale's grounding in related literature, and its earlier successful use after substantial pretesting for clarity and content, support the validity of the scale. An alpha reliability of .83 for the scale with this sample was judged satisfactory.

RESULTS

Correlations between parent efficacy and three indicators of parent involvement were statistically significant. Higher levels of parent efficacy were associated with more hours of classroom volunteering, more hours spent in educational activities with children, and fewer telephone calls with the teacher (see Table 2).

Parent efficacy scores did not reveal significant variations related to parents' sex, marital status, employment status, or family income. Parent education, however, was linked to some variations in efficacy scores, $F(5, 353) = 4.59$, $p < .01$. Parents with a grade school education had significantly lower efficacy scores than did parents with all levels of college education,

and parents with a high school education were significantly lower than parents with some college work beyond the bachelor's degree.

Parent reports of involvement were linked to some parent status characteristics. More hours of classroom volunteering were reported by females (0.74 hours per week v. 0.25 for males, $F[1, 352] = 8.53$, $p < .01$), married parents (0.81 hours per week v. 0.32 for not married, $F[1, 352] = 7.90$, $p < .01$), and unemployed parents (1.27 hours per week v. 0.34 for employed, $F[1, 352] = 8.82$, $p < .01$). More hours of homework help were reported by parents with lower education (high school at 4.80 hours per week v. college degree at 3.33, $F[5, 348] = 3.18$, $p < .01$), lower family income (3 lower income groups = $6.52 - 5.33$ hours per week v. 3 higher income groups = $3.62 - 3.09$ $F[6, 326] = 7.97$, $p < .01$), and single parent status (not married = 5.51 hours per week v. married = 4.05, $F[1, 352] = 13.83$, $p < .01$). More phone calls were reported by the lowest income parents (lowest income group = 1.38 calls per month v. $0.58 - 0.20$ for all other income groups, $F[6, 326] = 3.90$, $p < .01$).

Teacher efficacy and teacher perceptions of parents' efficacy were both positively linked to teacher reports of parent involvement in homework, educational activities, volunteering, and conference participation (see Table 3). Teacher efficacy was also positively linked to teacher perceptions of parent efficacy. Although teacher efficacy did not show a significant relationship with the number of students qualifying for free lunch ($r = -.16$, *ns*), teacher perceptions of parent efficacy were significantly linked to the free lunch figure ($r = -.59$, $p < .01$).

Table 2.
Means, Standard Deviations, and Intercorrelations: Parent Involvement Variables and Parent Efficacy ($n = 354$)

	Homework	Educational activities	Volunteering	Telephone calls	Conferences	Parent efficacy
Homework (hours per week)	—					
Educational activities (hours per week)	.38**	—				
Volunteering (hours per week)	.07	.14**	—			
Telephone calls (number per month)	.09	.02	.02	—		
Conferences (number per semester)	.10*	.08	.08	.34**	—	
Parent efficacy	.06	.11*	.15**	−.14**	.02	—
M	4.54	4.84	.66	.49	1.45	45.71
SD	3.58	3.58	.21	1.06	1.99	5.82

*$p < .05(.11)$. ** $p < .01(.14)$.

Table 3.
Means, Standard Deviations, and Intercorrelations Among Teacher Variables

	Homework	Educational activities	Volunteering	Telephone calls	Conferences	Free lunch	Teacher efficacy	Perceptions of parent efficacy
Parents help with homework (number of students)	—							
Parents engage in educational activities with children (number of students)	.69**	—						
Parents do volunteer work at school (number of students)	.58**	.67**	—					
Telephone calls with parents (average number per month)	.25	.30	.12	—				
Parents attend scheduled conferences (number of students)	.62**	.52**	.49**	.10	—			
Number of students qualifying for free lunch	−.34*	−.48**	−.45**	−.25	−.38**	—		
Teacher efficacy	.42**	.39**	.54**	.17	.41**	−.16	—	
Perceptions of parent efficacy	.56**	.75**	.65**	.27	.59**	.44**	−.59**	—
M	8.72	8.06	2.96	4.74	9.98	9.94	43.28	24.09
SD	4.59	4.58	2.48	5.03	5.83	8.39	6.38	4.57

*$p < .05$ (.30). **$p < .11$ (.38).

DISCUSSION

The finding that parent efficacy is related, at modest but significant levels, to volunteering, educational activities, and telephone calls suggests that the construct may contribute to an understanding of variables that influence parents' involvement in decisions and choices. Defined as a set of beliefs that one is capable of achieving desired outcomes through one's efforts and the effects of those efforts on others, parent efficacy appears to facilitate increased levels of parent activity in some areas of parent involvement. The correlational nature of our results suggests that just as efficacy may influence involvement choices, these varied forms of involvement may influence parents' sense of efficacy (e.g., parents may feel increased effectiveness when they observe, during their involvement activities, that their children are successful). Regardless of the direction of influence, however, the observed linkages seem logically based in dynamic aspects of the relationship between many parents and teachers.

Classroom volunteering, for example, may be linked to efficacy, because the decision to volunteer requires some sense that one has educationally relevant skills that can and will be used effectively. Similarly, the experiences implicit in classroom volunteering may offer parents new and positive information about their effectiveness with their own child. The decision to engage in educational activities with one's children at home may reflect a sense of personal efficacy ("I will do this because it will help my child learn."); in like manner, the activities undertaken may show up, from the parent's perspective, in improved school perform-

ance that, in turn, may enhance parent efficacy. The negative relationship between efficacy and telephone calls probably reflects the still-prevalent reality that calls to and from the school signal child difficulties. Lower efficacy parents, less certain of their ability to exert positive influence on their children's learning, may seek contact more often. Similarly, more school-initiated calls may signal to the parent that he or she is offering the child less-than-adequate help.

Overall, our findings suggest that the construct of parent efficacy warrants further investigation. Grounded in the teaching efficacy literature and theoretical work on personal efficacy, the Parent Perceptions of Parent Efficacy Scale achieved satisfactory reliability with this sample and emerged, as predicted, with modest but significant relationships with some indicators of parent involvement. Parents' average efficacy score, 45.71 ($SD = 5.82$) in a scale range of 12 to 60, indicated that those parents as a group had relatively positive perceptions of their own efficacy. The variations in efficacy by parental status characteristics suggested that, at least in this group, sex, marital status, employment status, and family income were *not* related to efficacy. The finding that parental education was significantly linked to efficacy is not surprising, given the probability that parents' own school experiences contribute to their sense of school-focused efficacy in relation to their children.

Parent efficacy may differ from parent education in the way it operates, however. Whereas higher levels of education may give parents a higher level of skill and knowledge, efficacy—a set of attitudes about one's ability to get necessary resources and offer effective help—increases the likelihood that a parent will *act* on his or her knowledge (or seek more information when available resources are insufficient). The explanatory function of efficacy is suggested by the finding that parent education was related to fewer and different outcomes than parent efficacy was. Parent efficacy was related to educational activities, volunteering and telephone calls, whereas education was significantly linked to homework alone. In that finding, parents with a high school education reported spending more time helping their children with homework than did parents with a college education. The fact that a group with lower education reported *more* homework help may reflect several different possibilities: the lower efficacy parents may be more determined to see their children succeed; they may use a set of less efficient helping strategies; or they may be responding to a pattern of greater school difficulty experienced by their children.

Although our data do not permit an assessment of those possibilities, we suspect that the finding reflects less adequate knowledge of effective helping strategies. Because many of our low-education parents were also unemployed, the finding may also reflect that they simply had more time for their children's homework activities than did the other parent groups. Whatever the explanations, the finding that education was related to fewer and different outcomes than efficacy suggests that the construct of parent efficacy warrants further investigation, perhaps particularly as it is distinguished from parent education

Results for teachers support earlier findings (Hoover-Dempsey et al., 1987) of significant positive relationships between teacher efficacy and teacher reports of parent involvement. The general pattern—higher efficacy teachers reported high levels of parent participation in help with homework, educational activities, volunteering, and conferences—suggests that higher efficacy teachers may invite and receive more parent involvement or, conversely, that teachers who perceive and report higher levels of parent involvement develop higher judgments of personal teaching efficacy. It is also possible that both perceptions are operating. The absence of a significant positive relationship between teacher efficacy and the number of students in a school using the free lunch program also supports previous findings, suggesting again that teachers' personal efficacy judgments are to some extent independent of school socioeconomic status (SES). We suspect that the absence of a significant relationship reflects the probability that teacher judgments of personal ability to "make a difference" are related more powerfully to variables other than the status characteristics of their students—for example, teaching skills, organizational support, and relations with colleagues (Brissie et al., 1988).

The strong positive linkages between teacher judgments of parents' efficacy and teacher reports of parent involvement likely point to the important role that parents' involvement efforts (and perhaps the visibility of those efforts) play in teachers' judgments of parents' effectiveness. In contrast to the absence of a significant relationship between teacher efficacy and school SES, teachers' judgments of *parent* efficacy were strongly and positively linked to school SES. Thus, although teachers appeared to distinguish between their own efficacy and the socioeconomic circumstances of the families that they serve, they did not appear to draw such boundaries between parents' SES and their judgments of parents' efficacy.

The further linkage between teacher efficacy and teacher judgments of parent efficacy suggests both that teachers with higher efficacy were likely to judge parents as more efficacious and that teachers who see their students' parents as more effective experience higher levels of efficacy themselves. We suspect that this relationship is an interactive one in reality, because, for example, high efficacy in each party would tend to allow each to act with more confidence and less defensiveness in the many forms of interaction that parents and teachers often routinely undertake.

The relationships between parent efficacy and some parent involvement outcomes, as well as those between teacher perceptions of parent efficacy and teacher efficacy, suggest the potential importance of intervention strategies designed to increase parents' sense of efficacy and involvement. Bandura's (1977, 1984, 1986) work offers specific points of entry into the development of such interventions. For example, parents' *outcome expectancies*—their general beliefs that engaging in certain involvement behaviors will usually yield certain outcomes—should be examined in relation to parents' *personal efficacy* expectancies (beliefs that one's *own* involvement behaviors will yield desired outcomes). Future investigations might focus on parents' expectations about the outcomes of involvement, for example, do most parents really believe that their involvement is directly linked to child outcomes? If they believe so, what makes parents think that their *own* involvement choices are—or are not—important?

The findings reported here suggest the possibility that high-efficacy parents are more likely than those with low efficacy to believe that their efforts pay off. Therefore, the schools' best interests may be served by designing parent involvement approaches that focus specifically on increasing parents' sense of positive influence in their children's school success. This could be accomplished in a number of ways. For example, schools might regularly send home relatively specific instructions for parents about strategies for helping children with specific types of homework assignments. Schools might issue specific invitations related to volunteering for specific assignments (e.g., making posters, doing classroom aide work) and follow up with brief notes of thanks for a valued job well done. Teachers might routinely link some student accomplishments and positive characteristics to parent efforts as they conduct scheduled conference discussions. Many schools already engage in such practices, but the frequency and focus of such efforts might be increased in other schools as one means of communicating a basic efficacy-linked message to parents: "We think you're doing a good job of _____, and this is helping your child learn."

Similarly, the role and functions of teacher efficacy in the parent involvement process should be explored further. Is it the case, for instance, that higher efficacy teachers—more secure in and confident of their own roles in children's learning—invite (explicitly and implicitly) more frequent and significant parent involvement? Do more efficacious teachers, aware of children's specific learning needs, offer more specific suggestions or tasks for parent-child interaction? It may be true that teachers in schools with stronger parent involvement programs tend to receive more (and more positive) feedback on the value and impact of their teaching efforts. Also, teachers with varying levels of teaching efficacy perceive parent involvement and comments from parents differently (e.g., high-efficacy teachers may hear legitimate questions in a parent comment, whereas low-efficacy teachers hear criticism and threat).

The role and function of teachers' perceptions of parent efficacy also appear to warrant further examination. Teachers in this sample appeared able to give reliable estimates of their assessments of parents' efficacy. Of future interest would be an examination of the bases on which teachers make such evaluations and the role of those evaluations in teacher interactions with parents. Lightfoot (1978) suggested that parents and teachers participate in children's schooling with different interests and roles; the roles often engender conflict, but they may also be construed as complementary. Implicit in these relationships, whatever their form, is the assumption that parents and teachers watch and evaluate the actions of the other, equally essential, players in the child's school success. Closer examination of teachers' and parents' perceptions of their own roles and the "others'" roles in children's learning may yield information about an important source of influence on parent involvement and its outcomes.

The many calls over recent decades for increased parent involvement in children's education (Hess & Holloway, 1984; Hobbs, Dokecki, Hoover-Dempsey, Moroney, Shayne, & Weeks, 1984; Phi Delta Kappa, 1980) appear to have produced public and professional belief that parent involvement is one means of increasing positive educational outcomes for children. As yet, however, there has been little specific examination of the ways in which parent involvement—in general or in its varied forms—functions to produce those outcomes. With few exceptions (Epstein, 1986), little information on patterns of specific forms of parent involvement is available, underscoring the relatively unexamined nature of the causes, manifestations, and outcomes of parent involvement. The findings of this study suggest that further examination of parents' and teachers' sense of efficacy in relation to children's educational outcomes may yield useful information as both sets of participants work to increase the probabilities of children's school success.

NOTES

We appreciate the cooperation and support of the parents, teachers, principals, and other administrators who participated in this research.

We also gratefully acknowledge support from the H. G. Hill Fund of Peabody College, Vanderbilt University.

REFERENCES

Ashton, P. T., Webb, R. B., & Doda, N. (1983). *A study of teachers' sense of efficacy: Final report, executive summary.* Gainesville, FL: University of Florida.

Bandura, A. (1977). Self-efficacy: Toward a unifying theory of behavioral change. *Psychological Review, 84,* 191–215.

Bandura, A. (1984). Recycling misconceptions of perceived self-efficacy. *Cognitive Therapy and Research, 8,* 231–255.

Bandura, A. (1986). The explanatory and predictive scope of self-efficacy theory. *Journal of Social and Clinical Psychology, 4,* 359–373.

Bandura, A. (1989). Human agency in social cognitive theory. *American Psychologist, 44,* 1175–1184.

Baumrind, D. (1971). Current patterns of parental authority. *Developmental Psychology Monographs, 4,* 1–103.

Baumrind, D. (1973). The development of instrumental competence through socialization. In A. D. Pick (Ed.), *Minnesota Symposium on Child Psychology, Vol. 7,* 3–46. Minneapolis, MN: University of Minnesota Press.

Brissie, J. S., Hoover-Dempsey, K. V., & Bassler, O. C. (1988). Individual and situational contributors to teacher burnout. *Journal of Educational Research, 82,* 106–112.

Dembo, M. H., & Gibson, S. (1985). Teachers' sense of efficacy: An important factor in school achievement. *The Elementary School Journal, 86,* 173–184.

Dornbusch, S. M., Ritter, P. L., Leiderman, P. H., Roberts, D. F., & Fraleigh, M. J. (1987). The relation of parenting style to adolescent school performance. *Child Development, 58,* 1244–1257.

Epstein, J. L. (1986). Parents' reactions to teacher practices of parent involvement. *Elementary School Journal, 86,* 277–294.

Greenberger, E., & Goldberg, W. A. (1989). Work, parenting and the socialization of children. *Developmental Psychology, 25,* 22–35.

Grolnick, W. S., & Ryan, R. M. (1989). Parent styles associated with children's self-regulation and competence in school. *Journal of Educational Psychology, 81,* 143–154.

Hess, R. D., & Holloway, S. D. (1984). Family and school as educational institutions. In R. D. Parke, R. M. Emde, H. P. McAdoo, & G. P. Sackett (Eds.), *Review of child development research: Vol. 7. The family* (pp. 179–222). Chicago: University of Chicago Press.

Hobbs, N., Dokecki, P. R., Hoover-Dempsey, K. V., Moroney, R. M., Shayne, M. W., & Weeks, K. A. (1984). *Strengthening families.* San Francisco: Jossey-Bass.

Hoover-Dempsey, K. V., Bassler, O. C., & Brissie, J. S. (1987). Parent involvement: contributions of teacher efficacy, school socioeconomic status, and other school characteristics. *American Educational Research Journal, 24,* 417–435.

Johnston, C., & Mash, E. J. (1989). A measure of parenting satisfaction and efficacy. *Journal of Clinical Child Psychology, 18,* 167–175.

Lightfoot, S. L. (1978). *Worlds apart: Relationships between families and schools.* New York: Basic Books.

Mondell, S., & Tyler, F. B. (1981). Parental competence and styles of problem-solving/play behavior with children. *Developmental Psychology, 17,* 73–78.

Phi Delta Kappa (1980). *Why do some urban schools succeed?* Bloomington, IN: Author.

Stevenson, D. L., & Baker, D. P. (1987). The family-school relation and the child's school performance. *Child Development, 58,* 1348–1357.

U.S. Bureau of the Census (1989). *Statistical abstract of the United States.* Washington, U.S. Government Printing Office. DC:

Hoover-Dempsey, K. V., Bassler, O. C., & Brissie, J. S. (1992). *Explorations in parent-school relations.* The Journal of Educational Research, 85, 287–294. Reprinted with the permission of the Helen Dwight Reid Educational Foundation. Published by Heldref Publications, 1319 Eighteenth St., N.W., Washington, DC 20036-1802. Copyright © 1992.

SUMMARY

Correlational Research: Definition and Purpose

1. Correlational research involves collecting data to determine whether and to what degree a relationship exists between two or more variables. The degree of relationship is expressed as a correlation coefficient.

2. If a relationship exists between two variables, it means that the scores on the variables vary in some nonrandom, related way.

3. The fact that there is a relationship between variables does not imply that one is the cause of the other. Correlations do not describe causal relationships. You cannot prove that one variable causes another with correlational data.

4. If two variables are highly related, a correlation coefficient near +1.00 (or −1.00) will be obtained; if two variables are not related, a coefficient near .00 will be obtained. The more highly related two variables are, the more accurate are predictions based on their relationship.

The Correlational Research Process

Problem Selection

5. Correlational studies may be designed either to determine which variables of a list of likely candidates are related or to test hypotheses regarding expected relationships. The variables to be correlated should have some theoretical or experimental basis for selection.

Participant and Instrument Selection

6. A common, minimally accepted sample size for a correlational study is 30 participants. However, if the variables correlated have low reliabilities and validities or if the participants will be subdivided and correlated, a higher sample size is necessary.

Design and Procedure

7. The basic correlational design obtains two (or more) scores from all members of a selected sample, one score for each variable, and the paired scores are correlated.

Data Analysis and Interpretation

8. A correlation coefficient describes both the size and direction of a relationship. A decimal number between −1.00 and +1.00 indicates the size of the relationship between the two variables. If the correlation coefficient is near .00, the variables are not related.

9. A correlation coefficient near +1.00 indicates that the variables are highly and positively related. A person with a high score on one variable is likely to have a high score on the other variable, and a person with a low score on one is likely to have a low score on the other. An increase on one variable is associated with an increase on the other.

10. If the correlation coefficient is near −1.00, the variables are highly and negatively or inversely related. A person with a high score on one variable is likely to have a low score on the other variable, and a person with a low score on one is likely to have a high score on the other. An increase on one variable is associated with a decrease on the other variable.

11. Correlations of +1.00 and −1.00 represent the same high degree of association, but in different directions.

12. Squaring the correlation coefficient indicates the amount of common or shared variation between the variables. The higher the shared variation, the higher the correlation.

13. How large a correlation coefficient must be to be useful depends on the purpose for which it was computed. Exploring or testing hypothesized relationships, predicting future performance, or determining validity and reliability require different correlation sizes.

14. Statistical significance refers to whether the obtained coefficient is really different from zero and reflects a true relationship, not a chance relationship. To determine statistical significance you consult a table that tells you how large your correlation coefficient needs to be to be significant, given a level of significance and the size of your sample.

15. For a given level of significance, the smaller the sample size, the larger the coefficient required. For a given sample size, the value of the correlation coefficient needed for significance increases as the level of confidence increases.

16. No matter how significant a coefficient is, a low coefficient represents a low relationship.

17. A correlation coefficient much below .50 is not generally useful for either group prediction or individual prediction. However, using a combination of correlations below .50 may yield a useful prediction.

18. Coefficients in the .60s and .70s are usually considered adequate for group prediction purposes, and coefficients in the .80s and above are adequate for individual prediction purposes.
19. While all reliabilities in the .90s are acceptable, for certain kinds ofum instrents, such as personality mea-sures, a reliability in the low .70s might be acceptable.
20. When interpreting any correlation coefficient you must always keep in mind that you are talking about a relationship only, not a cause–effect relationship.

Relationship Studies

21. Relationship studies are conducted to gain insight into the variables that are related to complex variables such as academic achievement, motivation, and self-concept. Such studies give direction to subsequent causal-comparative and experimental studies.

Data Collection

22. In a relationship study the researcher first identifies, either inductively or deductively, the variables to be related. An approach that involves unexamined collection and correlation of large numbers of variables is very inefficient and often misleading. A smaller number of carefully selected variables is much to be preferred to a large number of carelessly selected variables.
23. The population must be one for which data on each of the identified variables can be collected, and one whose members are available to the researcher. One advantage of a relationship study is that all the data may be collected within a relatively short period of time.

Data Analysis and Interpretation

24. In a relationship study, the scores for each variable are correlated among themselves or with the scores of a complex variable of interest.
25. There are many types of correlation, distinguished mainly by the type of data that are being correlated. The most commonly used correlation is the product moment correlation coefficient (Pearson r), which is used when both variables are continuous, that is, ratio or interval data. The Spearman rho correlation is used when ordinal data (ranks) are being correlated. See Table 11.2.
26. Most correlational techniques are concerned with investigating linear relationships. If a relationship is curvilinear, an increase in one variable is associated with a corresponding increase in another variable to a point, at which point further increase in the first variable results in a corresponding decrease in the other variable (or vice versa).

27. In addition to computing correlation coefficients for a total sample group, it is sometimes profitable to examine relationships separately for certain defined subgroups. In doing this you must be sure you have a large enough sample size to obtain reliable results.
28. Attenuation refers to the fact that correlation coefficients tend to be lowered due to the use of less-than-perfectly-reliable measures. In relationship studies, a correction for attenuation can be applied that indicates what the correlation coefficient would be if both measures were perfectly reliable.
29. A narrow or restricted range of scores is another factor that can lead to a correlation coefficient underrepresenting the true relationship. There is a correction for restriction in range that may be applied to obtain an estimate of what the coefficient would be if the range of scores were not restricted.

Prediction Studies

30. If two variables are highly related, scores on one variable can be used to predict scores on the other variable. Prediction studies are often conducted to facilitate decision making concerning individuals or to aid in the selection of individuals.
31. The variable on which the prediction is made is referred to as the *predictor,* and the variable predicted is referred to as the *criterion.*
32. If several predictor variables each correlate well with a criterion, then a prediction based on a combination of those variables will be more accurate than a prediction based on any one of them.

Data Collection

33. As with a relationship study, participants must be selected from whom the desired data can be collected and who are available to the researcher.
34. The major difference in data collection procedures for a relationship study and a prediction study is that in a relationship study data on all variables are collected within a relatively short period of time, whereas in a prediction study predictor variables are measured some period of time before the criterion variable is measured.
35. Once a prediction study is completed, it should be cross-validated on a new group of participants to determine its usefulness for groups other than the original one.

Data Analysis and Interpretation

36. As with a relationship study, each predictor variable is correlated with the criterion variable.

37. There are two types of prediction studies, single prediction studies and multiple prediction studies.

38. Since a combination of variables usually results in a more accurate prediction than any one variable, prediction studies often result in a prediction equation referred to as a multiple regression equation. A multiple regression equation uses all variables that individually predict the criterion to make a more accurate prediction.

39. The accuracy of prediction can be lowered by unreliable variables, length of time between gathering data about the predictor(s) and the criterion variable, and broadness of the criterion.

40. Since relationships are not perfect, predictions made by multiple regression equations are not perfect. Predictive studies can provide an indication of the common variance shared by the predictor(s) and the criterion variables by using the coefficient of determination.

41. Predicted scores should be interpreted as intervals, not as a single number.

42. As with relationship studies, and for similar reasons, prediction equations may be used for both the total group and subgroups.

43. *Shrinkage* is the tendency of a prediction equation to become less accurate when used with a group other than the one on which the equation was originally formulated. Thus, any prediction equation should be validated with at least one other group to assess shrinkage.

Other Correlation-Based Analyses

44. There are a number of more complex correlation-based analyses, including discriminant function analysis, path analysis, canonical analysis, and factor analysis.

". . . the resulting matched groups are identical or very similar with respect to the identified extraneous variable." (p. 342)

CAUSAL–COMPARATIVE RESEARCH

OBJECTIVES

After reading Chapter 12, you should be able to do the following:

1. Briefly state the purpose of causal–comparative research.
2. State the major differences between causal–comparative and correlational research.
3. State one major way in which causal–comparative and experimental research are the same and one major way in which they are different.
4. Diagram and describe the basic causal–comparative design.
5. Identify and describe three types of control procedures that can be used in a causal–comparative study.
6. Explain why the results of causal–comparative studies must be interpreted very cautiously.

CAUSAL–COMPARATIVE RESEARCH: DEFINITION AND PURPOSE

Like correlational research, causal–comparative research is sometimes treated as a type of descriptive research since it, too, describes conditions that already exist. Causal–comparative research, however, also attempts to determine reasons, or causes, for the existing condition. This emphasis, as well as differences in research procedures, qualifies causal–comparative as a unique type of research.

In causal–comparative, or ex post facto, research the researcher attempts to determine the cause, or reason, for preexisting differences in groups of individuals. In other words, it is observed that groups are different on some variable and the researcher attempts to identify the main factor that has led to this difference. Such research is referred to as *ex post facto* (Latin for "after the fact"), since both the effect and the alleged cause have already occurred and must be studied in retrospect. For example, a researcher might hypothesize that participation in preschool education is the major contributing factor for differences in the social adjustment of first graders. To examine this hypothesis the researcher would select a sample of first graders who had participated in preschool education and a sample of first graders who had not, and then compare the social adjustment of the two groups. If the group that did participate in preschool education exhibited a higher level of social adjustment, the researcher's hypothesis would be supported. Thus, the basic causal–comparative approach involves starting with an effect and seeking possible causes.

A variation of the basic approach starts with a cause and investigates its effect on some variable. Such research is concerned with questions of "What is the effect of X?" For example, a researcher might wish to investigate what long-range effect failure to be promoted to the seventh grade has on the self-concept of children not promoted. The researcher might hypothesize that children who are "socially promoted" have higher self-concepts at the end

337

of the seventh grade than children who are retained or "held back" in the sixth grade. At the end of a school year, the researcher would identify a group of seventh graders who had been socially promoted to the seventh grade the year before, and a group of sixth graders who had been made to repeat the sixth grade. The self-concepts of the two groups would be compared. If the socially promoted group exhibited a higher level of self-concept, the researcher's hypothesis would be supported. The basic approach is sometimes referred to as **retrospective causal–comparative research** (since it starts with effects and investigates causes), and the variation as **prospective causal–comparative research** (since it starts with causes and investigates effects). Retrospective causal–comparative studies are by far more common in educational research.

Beginning researchers often confuse causal–comparative research with both correlational research and experimental research. Correlational and causal–comparative research are probably confused because of the lack of manipulation common to both and the similar cautions regarding interpretation of results. There are definite differences, however. Causal–comparative studies *attempt* to identify cause–effect relationships; correlational studies do not. Causal–comparative studies typically involve two (or more) groups and one independent variable, whereas correlational studies typically involve two (or more) variables and one group. Also, causal–comparative studies involve comparison, whereas correlational studies involve relationship. A common misconception that beginning and even more experienced researchers have is that causal–comparative research is "better" or more rigorous than correlational research. Perhaps it is because the term *causal–comparative* sounds more "research-ey" than *correlation,* as if it might prove the cause of something. We all have heard the research mantra: "Correlation does not imply causation." In fact, *both* causal–comparative and correlation methods fail to produce true experiments. As you continue your causal–comparative and correlation research, realize that neither method provides researchers with true experimental data.

It is understandable that causal–comparative and experimental research are at first difficult to distinguish, since both *attempt to establish* cause–effect relationships and both involve group comparisons. In an experimental study the researcher selects a random sample from a population and then randomly divides the sample into two or more groups. These groups are assigned to the treatments by the researcher and the study is carried out. In causal–comparative research there is also a comparison, but individuals are not randomly assigned to treatment groups because they already were selected into groups before the research began. To put it as simply as possible, the major difference is that in experimental research the independent variable, the alleged cause, is manipulated by the researcher, whereas in causal–comparative research it is not because it has already occurred. In experimental research, the researcher can randomly form groups and manipulate the independent variable; that is, she can determine "who" is going to get "what treatment" of the independent variable. In causal–comparative research, the groups are *already formed* and already different on the independent variable. The difference between the groups (the independent variable) was not brought about by the researcher.

Independent variables in causal–comparative studies are variables that cannot be manipulated (such as socioeconomic status), should not be manipulated (such as number of cigarettes smoked per day), or simply are not manipulated but could be (such as method of reading instruction). There are a number of important educational problems for which it is impossible or not feasible to manipulate the independent variable. For example, it is not possible to manipulate **organismic variables** such as age or gender. Ethical considerations often prevent manipulation of a variable that *could be* manipulated but *should not be,* such as smoking or drug use. If the nature of the independent variable is such that it may cause physical or mental harm to participants, the ethics of research dictate that it should not be manipulated. For example, if a researcher were interested in determining the effect of mothers' prenatal care on the developmental status of their children at age one, it would not be ethical to deprive a group of mothers-to-be of prenatal care for the sake of a research study when such care is considered to be

ORGANISMIC VARIABLES	PERSONALITY VARIABLES	FAMILY-RELATED VARIABLES	SCHOOL-RELATED VARIABLES
Age	Anxiety level	Family income	Preschool attendance
Sex	Introversion/extroversion	Socioeconomic status	Size of school
Ethnicity	Agression level	Employment status (of)	Type of school (e.g., public
	Self-concept	Student	vs. private)
ABILITY VARIABLES	Self-esteem	Mother	Per pupil expenditure
Intelligence	Aspiration level	Father	Type of curriculum
Scholastic aptitude	Brain dominance	Marital status of parents	Leadership style
Specific aptitudes	Learning style (e.g.,	Family environment	Teaching style
Perceptual ability	field independence/	Birth order	Peer pressure
	field dependence)	Number of siblings	

Note: A few of the variables *can be* manipulated (e.g., type of curriculum), but are frequently the object of causal–comparative research.

FIGURE 12.1

Examples of independent variables investigated in causal–comparative studies.

extremely important to both the mother's and the child's welfare. Thus, causal–comparative research permits investigation of a number of variables that cannot be studied experimentally.

Figure 12.1 shows independent variables often studied in causal–comparative research. In causal–comparative studies, these variables are used to compare two or more levels of a given variable. For example, a causal–comparative study might compare participants younger than 50 to participants older than 50 in terms of their retention of facts. Students with high anxiety could be compared to students of low anxiety on attention span, or the difference in achievement between first graders who attended preschool and first graders who did not could be examined. In each case, preexisting participant groups are compared on a dependent variable.

As mentioned previously, experimental studies are costly in more ways than one and should be conducted only when there is good reason to believe the effort will be fruitful. Like correlational studies, causal–comparative studies help to identify variables worthy of experimental investigation. In fact, causal–comparative studies are sometimes conducted solely for the purpose of identifying the probable outcome of an experimental study. Suppose, for example, a superintendent was considering implementing computer-assisted remedial math instruction in his school system. Before initiating total implementation, the superintendent might consider trying it out on an experimental basis for a year in a number of schools or classrooms. However, even such limited adoption would be costly in terms of equipment and teacher training. Thus, as a preliminary measure to inform his decision, the superintendent might conduct a causal–comparative study and compare the math achievement of students in school districts or classrooms currently using computer-assisted remedial math instruction with the math achievement of students in school districts or classrooms not currently using it. Since most districts have yearly testing programs to assess students' achievements, including math, obtaining information on math achievement would not be difficult. If the results indicated that students learning through computer-assisted remedial math instruction were achieving higher scores, the superintendent would probably decide to go ahead with an experimental tryout of computer-assisted remedial math instruction in his own district. If no differences were found, the superintendent would probably not go ahead with the experimental tryout, preferring not to waste time, money, and effort.

Despite its many advantages, causal–comparative research does have some serious limitations that should also be kept in mind. Since the independent variable has already occurred, the same kinds of controls cannot be exercised as in an experimental study. Extreme caution must be applied in interpreting results. An apparent cause–effect relationship may not be as it appears. As with a correlational study, only a relationship is established, not necessarily a causal connection. The alleged cause of an observed effect may in fact be the effect itself, or there may be a third variable that has "caused" both the identified cause and the effect. For example, suppose a researcher hypothesized that self-concept is a determinant of reading achievement. The researcher would identify two groups: one group with high self-concepts and one group with low self-concepts. The dependent variable would be reading achievement. If the high self-concept group did indeed show higher reading achievement, the temptation would be to conclude that self-concept influences high reading achievement. However, this conclusion would not be warranted since it is not possible to establish whether self-concept precedes achievement or vice versa. It might be that achievement influences self-concept. Since both the independent and dependent variables would have already occurred, it would not be possible to determine which came first, and thus, which influences the other. If the study were reversed, and a group of high achievers was compared with a group of low achievers, it might well be that they would be different on self-concept, thus suggesting that achievement causes self-concept. Even worse, it would be possible (in fact, plausible) that some third variable, such as parental attitude, might be the main influence on *both* self-concept and achievement. Parents who praise and encourage their children might produce high self-concept and high academic achievement. Thus, caution must be exercised in attributing cause–effect relationships based on causal–comparative research. Only in experimental research is the degree of control sufficient to establish cause–effect relationships. Only in experimental research does the researcher randomly assign participants to treatment groups. In causal–comparative research the researcher cannot assign participants to treatment groups because they are already in those groups. However, despite these limitations, causal–comparative studies *do* permit investigation of variables that cannot or should not be investigated experimentally, facilitate decision making, provide guidance for experimental studies, and are less costly on all dimensions.

CONDUCTING A CAUSAL–COMPARATIVE STUDY

The basic causal–comparative design is quite simple, and although the independent variable is not manipulated, there are control procedures that can be exercised to improve interpretation of results. Causal–comparative studies also involve a wider variety of statistical techniques than the other types of research thus far discussed.

DESIGN AND PROCEDURE

The basic causal–comparative design involves selecting two groups differing on some independent variable and comparing them on some dependent variable (Table 12.1). As Table 12.1 indicates, the researcher selects two groups of participants referred to as **experimental** and **control groups,** but more accurately referred to as *comparison groups*. The groups may differ in two ways. First, one group possesses a characteristic that the other does not (case A), and second, each group has the characteristic but to differing degrees or amounts (case B). An example of case A would be a comparison of two groups, one of which was composed of brain-injured children and the other that was composed of non–brain-injured children. An example of case B would be a comparison of two groups, one group composed of high self-concept individuals and one group composed of low self-concept individuals. Another case B example is a comparison of the algebra achievement of two groups, one which had learned algebra via traditional instruction and one which had learned algebra via computer-assisted instruction. In both case A and case B, the performance of the groups should be compared using some valid dependent variable measure selected from the types of instruments discussed in Chapter 5.

Definition and selection of the comparison groups are very important parts of the causal–comparative procedure. The independent variable differentiating the groups must be clearly and operationally defined, since each group represents a different population. The way in which the groups are defined will affect the generalizability of the results. If a researcher were

TABLE 12.1   The Basic Causal–Comparative Design

	GROUP	INDEPENDENT VARIABLE	DEPENDENT VARIABLE
Case A	(E)	(X)	O
	(C)		O
		OR	
	GROUP	INDEPENDENT VARIABLE	DEPENDENT VARIABLE
Case B	(E)	(X_1)	O
	(C)	(X_2)	O

Symbols:

(E) = Experimental group; ( ) indicates no manipulation

(C) = Control group

(X) = Independent variable

O = Dependent variable

to compare a group of students with an "unstable" home life to a group of students with a "stable" home life, the terms *unstable* and *stable* would have to be operationally defined. An unstable home life could refer to any number of things, such as a home with a parent with an alcohol problem, a violent parent(s), child neglect, or a combination of such factors. The operational definitions will help define the populations and guide sample selection.

Random selection from the defined populations is generally the preferred method of participant selection. The important consideration is to select samples that are representative of their respective populations. Note that in causal–comparative research the random sample is selected from two already existing populations, not from a single population as in experimental research. This difference is key in differentiating the two approaches. As in experimental studies, the goal is to have groups that are as similar as possible on all relevant variables except the independent variable. To determine the equality of groups, information on a number of background and current status variables may be collected and compared for each group. For example, information on age, years of experience, gender, prior knowledge, and the like, may be obtained and examined for the groups being compared. The more similar the two groups are on such variables, the more homogeneous they are on everything but the independent variable. This makes a stronger study and reduces the possible alternative explanations of the research findings. There are a number of control procedures to correct for identified inequalities on such variables.

CONTROL PROCEDURES

Lack of randomization, manipulation, and control are all sources of weakness in a causal–comparative study. Random assignment of participants to groups is probably the single best way to try to insure equality of groups. This is not possible in causal–comparative studies since the groups already exist and have already received the independent variable. A problem already discussed is the possibility that the groups are different on some other important variable (e.g., gender, experience, age) besides the identified independent variable. It may be that this other variable is the real cause of the observed difference between the causal–comparative groups.

For example, if a researcher simply compared a group of students who had received preschool education to a group who had not, she might draw the conclusion that preschool education results in higher first-grade reading achievement. However, what if all preschool programs in the region in which the study was conducted were private and required high tuition? If this were the case, the researcher would really be investigating the effects not just of preschool education, but also of membership in a well-to-do family. It might very well be that parents in such families provide early informal reading instruction for their children. This could make it very difficult to disentangle the effects of attending preschool from the effects of affluent families on first grade reading. If, however, the researcher was aware of the situation, she could control for the affluence variable by studying only children of well-to-do parents. Thus, the two groups to be compared would be equated with respect to the extraneous variable of parents' income level. The above example is but one illustration of a number of statistical and nonstatistical methods that can be applied in an attempt to control for extraneous variables.[1]

Matching

Matching is another control technique. If a researcher has identified a variable likely to influence performance on the dependent variable, she may control for that variable by *pair-wise matching* of participants. In other words, for each participant in one group, the researcher finds a participant in the other group with the same or very similar score on the control variable. If a participant in either group does not have a suitable match, the participant is eliminated from the study. Thus, the resulting matched groups are identical or very similar with respect to the identified extraneous variable. For example, if a researcher matched participants in each group on IQ, a participant in one group with an IQ of 140 would have a matched participant with an IQ at or near 140. As you may have deduced (if you have an IQ of 140!), a major problem with pair-wise matching is that there are invariably participants who have no match and must therefore be eliminated from the study. The problem becomes even more serious when the researcher attempts to simultaneously match participants on two or more variables.

Comparing Homogeneous Groups or Subgroups

Another way to control extraneous variables is to compare groups that are homogeneous with respect to the extraneous variable. For example, if IQ were an identified extraneous variable, the researcher might limit the groups to only subjects with IQs between 85 and 115 (average IQ). Of course, this procedure may lower the numbers of participants in the study and, of course, limits the generalizability of the findings because only a limited range of IQ participants was studied.

A similar but more satisfactory approach is to form subgroups within each group that represent all levels of the control variable. For example, each group might be divided into high (116 and above), average (85 to 115), and low (84 and below) IQ subgroups. The existence of comparable subgroups in each group controls for IQ. In addition to controlling for the variable, this approach also permits the researcher to determine whether the independent variable affects the dependent variable differently at different levels of IQ, the control variable. That is, the researcher can examine whether the effect on the dependent variable is different for the different subgroups. If this information is of interest, the best approach is not to do separate analyses for each of the subgroups but to build the control variable right into the research design and analyze the results with a statistical technique called **factorial analysis of variance.** A factorial analysis (discussed in Chapter 13) allows the researcher to determine the effect of the independent variable and the control variable on the dependent variable both separately

---

[1]Several of these methods will be discussed further, and in more detail, in regard to their use in experimental research (Chapter 13).

and in combination. In other words, it permits him to determine if there is an interaction between the independent variable and the control variable such that the independent variable operates differently at different levels of the control variable. For example, IQ might be a control variable in a causal–comparative study of the effects of two different methods of learning fractions. It might be found that a method involving manipulation of blocks is more effective for low-IQ students who may have difficulty thinking abstractly.

Analysis of Covariance

Analysis of covariance is used to adjust initial group differences on variables used in causal–comparative and experimental research studies. In essence, **analysis of covariance** adjusts scores on a dependent variable for initial differences on some other variable related to performance on the dependent. For example, suppose we were doing a study to compare two methods, X and Y, of teaching fifth graders to solve math problems. When we gave the two groups a pretest of math ability, we found that the group in method Y scored much higher than the group in method X. This difference suggests that method Y will be superior to method X at the end of the study just because it has higher math ability than the other group. Covariate analysis statistically adjusts the scores of method Y to remove the initial advantage so that the results at the end of the study can be fairly compared as if the two groups started equally.

DATA ANALYSIS AND INTERPRETATION

Analysis of data in causal–comparative studies involves a variety of descriptive and inferential statistics. All of the statistics that may be used in a causal–comparative study may also be used in an experimental study, and a number of them will be described in chapters 14 and 15. Briefly, however, the most commonly used descriptive statistics are the **mean,** which indicates the average performance of a group on a measure of some variable, and the **standard deviation,** which indicates how spread out a set of scores is around the mean, that is, whether the scores are relatively homogeneous or heterogeneous around the mean. The most commonly used inferential statistics are the ***t* test**, used to determine whether the means of two groups are significantly different from one another; **analysis of variance,** used to determine if there is significant difference among the means of three or more groups; and **chi square,** used to compare group frequencies, that is, to see if an event occurs more frequently in one group than another.

As repeatedly pointed out, interpreting the findings in a causal–comparative study requires considerable caution. Due to lack of randomization, manipulation, and control factors, it is difficult to establish cause–effect relationships with any great degree of confidence. The cause–effect relationship may in fact be the reverse of the one hypothesized (the alleged cause may be the effect and vice versa), or there may be a third factor that is the "real" underlying cause of both the independent and dependent variables. Note, however, that there are some cases in which reversed causality is not a reasonable alternative. For example, preschool training may "cause" increased reading achievement in third grade but reading achievement in third grade cannot "cause" preschool training. Similarly, one's gender may affect one's achievement in mathematics, but one's achievement in mathematics certainly does not affect one's gender! In other cases, however, reversed causality is more plausible and should be investigated. For example, as pointed out, it is equally plausible that achievement affects self-concept as it is that self-concept affects achievement. It is also equally plausible that excessive absenteeism produces, or leads to, involvement in criminal activities as it is that involvement in criminal activity produces, or leads to, excessive absenteeism. The way to determine the correct order of causality—which variable caused which—is to determine which one occurred first. If, in the above example, it could be demonstrated that a period of excessive absenteeism was frequently followed by a student getting in trouble with the law, then it could more reasonably be concluded that excessive absenteeism leads to involvement in criminal activities. On the other

Now go to the Companion Website accompanying this text at www.prenhall.com/gay to check your understanding of chapter concepts in the following modules: Objectives, Practice Quiz, and Applying What You Know. Expand your research skills with Evaluating Articles, Analyzing Qualitative Data, Analyzing Quantitative Data, and Research Tools and Tips. Visit Web Links to broaden your knowledge about research.

hand, if it were determined that prior to a student's first involvement in criminal activities her attendance was good, but following it, poor, then the hypothesis that involvement in criminal activities leads to excessive absenteeism would be more reasonable.

The possibility of a third, common explanation in causal–comparative research is plausible in many situations. Recall the example of parental attitude affecting both self-concept and achievement. One way to control for a potential common cause is to equate groups on that variable. For example, if students in both the high self-concept group and the low self-concept group could be selected from parents who had similar attitudes, the effects of parents' attitudes are removed because both groups have the same parental attitudes. It is clear that to investigate or control for alternative hypotheses, the researcher must be aware of them and must present evidence that they are not in fact the true explanation for the behavioral differences being investigated.

The following pages present an example of causal–comparative research. Note that even though survey forms were used to collect data, the study was not descriptive because the purpose of the study was to investigate existing differences between groups.

Differing Opinions on Testing Between Preservice and Inservice Teachers

KATHY E. GREEN
University of Denver

ABSTRACT   Studies of teachers' use of tests suggest that classroom tests are widely used and that standardized test results are rarely used. What is the genesis of this lack of use? A previous comparison of pre- and inservice teachers' attitudes toward assessment suggested no differences. This study assessed the different opinions among sophomores ($n = 84$), seniors ($n = 152$), and inservice teachers ($n = 553$) about the use of classroom and standardized tests. Significant differences were found; preservice teachers had less favorable attitudes toward classroom testing than teachers did and more favorable attitudes toward standardized testing.

This study assessed differences among college students entering a teacher education program, students finishing a teacher education program, and inservice teachers concerning their opinions of some aspects of classroom and standardized testing. Although numerous studies of inservice teachers' attitudes toward testing have been conducted, little research is available regarding preservice teachers' views of testing and of the genesis of teachers' views of testing.

Interest in this topic stemmed from research findings suggesting that the results of standardized tests are not used by most teachers. If standardized testing is to continue, the failure to use results is wasteful. Other studies have identified some of the reasons for the lack of use. This study's purpose was to determine whether opinions about the usefulness of standardized and other tests were negative for students before they even entered the teaching profession. When were those attitudes developed? Are attitudes fixed by students' educational experiences *prior* to entry into a teacher education program? Are preservice teachers socialized by their educational programs into resistance to testing? Do negative attitudes appear upon entry into the profession because of socialization into the school culture? Or do they appear after several years of service as a teacher because of personal experiences in the classroom?

I found only one study that addressed differences in opinions of pre- and inservice teachers (Reeves & Kazelskis, 1985). That study examined a broad range of issues salient to first-year teachers; only one item addressed testing specifically. Reeves and Kazelskis found no significant differences between pre- and inservice teachers' opinions about testing, as measured by that item. In this study, I sought more information pertinent to the development of opinions about testing.

Test use in U.S. schools has been and continues to be extensive. It has been estimated that from 10 to 15% of class time is spent dealing with tests (Carlberg, 1981; Newman & Stallings, 1982). Gullickson (1982) found that 95% of the teachers he surveyed gave tests at least once every 2 weeks. The estimated percentage of students' course grades that are based on test scores is 40 to 50%, ranging from 0 to 100% (Gullickson, 1984; McKee & Manning-Curtis, 1982; Newman & Stallings). Classroom tests, thus, are used frequently and may, at times, be used almost exclusively in determining students' grades.

In contrast, a review of past practice suggests minimal teacher use of *standardized* test results in making instructional decisons (Fennessey, 1982; Green & Williams, 1989; Lazar-Morrison, Polin, Moy, & Burry, 1980; Ruddell, 1985). Stetz and Beck (1979) conducted a national study of over 3,000 teachers' opinions about standardized tests. They noted that 41% of the teachers surveyed reported making little use of test results, a finding consistent with that of Goslin (1967) from several decades ago and that of Boyd, McKenna, Stake, and Yachinsky (1975). Test results were viewed as providing information that was supplemental to the wider variety of information that the teachers already possessed. Reasons offered for why standardized tests are given but results not always used by teachers include resistance to a perceived narrowing of the curriculum, resistance to management control, accountability avoidance (Darling-Hammond, 1985), and a limited understanding of score interpretation resulting from inadequate preservice training (Cramer & Slakter, 1968; Gullickson & Hopkins, 1987). Marso and Pigge (1988) found that teachers perceive a lower need for standardized testing skills than for classroom testing skills. They also found that teachers reported lower proficiencies in standardized test score use and interpretation than in classroom test score use and interpretation.

The results of those studies suggest that inservice teachers use classroom tests extensively but make little use of standardized test results. This suggests that inservice teachers, in general, hold positive attitudes toward classroom tests and less positive attitudes toward standardized tests. The literature does not lead to any predictions about preservice teachers' attitudes toward tests.

Address correspondence to Kathy E. Green, University of Denver, School of Education, Denver, CO 80208.

This study assessed differences between preservice and inservice teachers' opinions about testing and test use. The following research hypotheses were formulated to direct the study.

H1. There are significant differences in opinions about the testing and test use between preservice and inservice teachers.
H2. There are significant differences in opinions about testing between students beginning their preparation (sophomores) and students finishing their preparation (seniors).
H3. There are significant differences among inservice teachers with differing years of experience.

METHOD

Samples

Three samples were drawn for this study. They were samples of (a) practicing teachers, (b) college sophomores beginning a teacher education program, and (c) college seniors completing a teacher education program (but prior to student teaching). For the first sample, survey forms were mailed in a rural western state to 700 teachers randomly selected from the State Department of Education list of all licensed educators. During the spring semester of 1986, teachers were sent a letter explaining the nature of the study, a survey form, and a stamped return envelope. With two follow-up mailings, a total of 555 questionnaires were received, or 81% of the deliverable envelopes. (Twelve questionnaires were undeliverable, 4 persons refused to respond, and 133 persons did not reply.) No compulsory statewide standardized testing program was in place in the state.

The second sample was a convenience sample of three sections of an educational foundations class typically taken by college sophomores who have just enrolled in a teacher preparation program ($n = 84$). The course examines educational thought and practice in the United States. The classes were taught in an 8-week block, meeting for 50 min per day, 4 days per week. Survey forms were distributed in class and completed during class time.

The third sample was also a convenience sample of four sections of a tests and measurement class taken by college seniors ($n = 152$). The course is typically taken after coursework is almost complete, but prior to student teaching. The course provides instruction in basic statistics, classroom test construction and analysis, and standardized test use and interpretation. The course was also taught in an 8-week block, with the same schedule as the foundations course. Survey forms were distributed during the first week of class and completed during class time. Survey forms took from 10 to 30 min to complete. Responses were anonymous. Both sophomores and seniors were attending a public university in a small western town.

Table 1 presents descriptive information for the three samples.

Instruments

Three different forms with overlapping questions were used in this study. The survey form sent to the teachers contained ques-

tions regarding training in tests and measurement, subject and grades taught, tests given, and attitudes toward both standardized and classroom tests. The questionnaire was two pages in length, double-sided and contained 49 questions. The form given to the sophomores had 43 questions and was one page in length, double-sided. The form given to the seniors was three pages in length, single-sided. The latter two forms differed by the inclusion of an evaluation anxiety scale and items eliciting importance of contemporary measurement practices for the seniors. Although different formats may have affected responses to some extent, all the forms began with several demographic questions followed by the items relevant to this study. Any form differences would, then, likely be minimized for those initial items.

There were 18 items common to the three forms. Sixteen of the items were Likert items with a 1 to 6 (*strongly disagree* to *strongly agree*) response format. Likert-scale items were drawn from a previously developed measure of attitudes toward both standardized and classroom testing (Green & Stager, 1986). Internal consistency reliabilities of the measures ranged from .63 to .75. The remaining two items asked how many hours per week teachers spend in testing activities and how much of a student's grade should be based on test results. The study examined differences found among groups on those items. Item content is presented in Table 2, in which items are grouped by content (opinions about standardized tests, classroom tests, and about personal liking for tests).

Data were analyzed using multivariate analyses of variance, followed by univariate analyses of variance. If univariate results were significant, I used Tukey's HSD test to assess the significance of pairwise post hoc differences. Samples of both items and persons were limited; therefore, results may not be widely generalizable.

Results

Significant multivariate differences were found across opinion items (Wilks's lambda = .70, $p < .001$) when the three samples were compared (Table 2). Hypothesis 1 was supported. Differences were found between teachers and students for all items, with significance levels varying from .02 to .001 for individual items. Opinions were not consistently more positive across all items for teachers or for students. For instance, whereas teachers were most likely to feel that standardized tests address important educational outcomes, teachers were least likely to find that standardized tests serve a useful purpose. In general, though, students favored use of standardized tests for student or

Table 1.
Description of Samples

Item	Sophomores ($n = 84$)	Seniors ($n = 152$)	Teachers ($n = 553$)
Percentage female	84	152	553
Mean age	73.0	75.9	63.6
Age range	18–33	20–45	—
Mean years in teaching	—	—	12

Table 2.
Means and Standard Deviations for Opinions About Testing by Group

Variable	Sophomores (n = 84)	Seniors (n = 152)	Teachers (n = 553)	p	1	2	3
Hours spent in testing/week	10.43 (6.72)	9.18 (6.43)	4.37 (4.05)	.001	*	*	—
Percentage grade based on test	49.63 (15.48)	46.94 (18.71)	41.31 (22.68)	.001	*	*	—
Standardized test items							
Standardized tests are the best way to evaluate a teacher's effectiveness.	2.79 (1.03)	2.83 (1.10)	2.12 (1.18)	.001	*	*	—
Teachers whose students score higher on standardized tests should receive higher salaries.	2.53 (1.07)	2.33 (1.17)	1.74 (1.01)	.001	*	*	—
Requiring *students* to pass competency tests would raise educational standards.	4.14 (1.13)	3.89 (1.09)	3.69 (1.26)	.001	*	*	—
Requiring *teachers* to pass competency tests would raise. educational standards	4.35 (.90)	4.09 (1.27)	3.30 (1.34)	.001	*	*	—
Standardized tests assess important educational outcomes.	3.47 (1.04)	3.54 (.87)	3.95 (.88)	.001	*	*	—
Standardized tests serve a useful purpose.	4.02 (.83)	3.97 (.81)	2.93 (.97)	.001	*	*	—
Standardized tests force teachers to "teach to the test."	3.05 (1.19)	2.74 (.98)	3.11 (1.22)	.02	—	*	—
Classroom test items							
Test construction takes too much teacher time.	4.57 (1.02)	4.36 (.85)	3.97 (.88)	.001	*	*	—
Test scores are a fair way to grade students.	3.42 (1.02)	3.32 (1.13)	4.04 (.84)	.001	*	*	—
Testing has a favorable impact on student motivation.	4.00 (.71)	3.88 (1.00)	4.16 (.88)	.01	—	*	—
Tests are of little value in identifying learning problems.	1.76 (.96)	1.43 (.84)	1.44 (1.05)	.01	*	—	*
It is relatively easy to construct tests in my subject area.	4.11 (1.25)	3.51 (1.34)	4.35 (.89)	.001	—	*	*
Tests measure only minor aspects of what students can learn.	2.92 (1.13)	3.01 (1.13)	3.24 (1.00)	.01	*	—	—
Personal reflections							
I do(did) well on tests.	4.05 (1.04)	4.00 (1.10)	4.46 (.94)	.001	*	*	—
I personally dislike taking tests.	3.13 (1.35)	3.12 (1.14)	3.46 (1.16)	.01	—	*	—
The tests I have taken were generally good assessments of my knowledge of an area.	3.65 (1.08)	3.41 (1.10)	4.09 (.82)	.001	*	*	—

Note. For opinion items, the scale ranged from *strongly disagree* (1) to *strongly agree* (6). Standard deviations are presented in parentheses. Asterisks (*) indicate significant ($p < .05$) differences between groups: 1 = teachers versus sophomores, 2 = teachers versus seniors, 3 = sophomores versus seniors.

teacher evaluation more than teachers did. Although the students were less likely to say that they do well on tests and that tests previously taken were good assessments of their ability, the students were also less likely to say that they disliked taking tests. Students' opinions about classroom testing were less favorable than were teachers' opinions for all but one item. Differences were also found between teachers and students in estimates of time spent in testing and in the percentage of students' grades based on test scores.

Hypothesis 2 was not supported. Only two significant differences in means were found between the sophomores and the seniors. One difference was found for the item "It is relatively easy to construct tests in my subject area." Sophomores tended to agree with that statement more than the seniors did. Because the seniors were required to complete a task involving test construction, the impending course requirement may have influenced their opinions. The second difference was found for the item "Tests are of little value in identifying learning problems," with more positive opinions expressed by seniors than by sophomores.

Hypothesis 3 was tested by dividing teachers into three groups: 0 to 1 years, 2 to 5 years, and 5+ years of experience as a teacher. No significant multivariate or univariate differences were found, so Hypothesis 3 was not supported. However, there were few teachers with 0 to 1 years of experience in the sample. Because of the small number of teachers with 0 to 1 years of teaching (46 teachers; 8.7% of the data file), groups were reformed as follows: 0 to 3 years, 4 to 6 years, and 6+ years of experience. Still, no significant multivariate or univariate differences were found. (In addition, no differences were found between teachers with 0 to 3 years of experience and those with 6 or more years of experience.)

DISCUSSION

This study was undertaken to examine whether differences in opinions about testing would be discerned between preservice and inservice teachers and whether those differences would suggest a progression. The differences found suggest that teacher education students are less favorable to classroom testing and more favorable to standardized testing than teachers are. Differences were *not* found between sophomores and seniors, however. Nor were opinions about testing found to depend upon years of experience in teaching. Those results do not reflect a developmental progression. The shift in opinion seems to occur when beginning a teaching position, suggesting effects that result from job requirements or socialization as a teacher more than from a developmental trend. Differences between students and teachers, then, seem likely to be caused by direct teacher experience with creating, administering, and using tests or by acculturation into life as a teacher in a school. That conclusion suggests that if one wishes to affect teachers' opinions about testing, provision of inservice experiences may be a more profitable avenue than additional preservice education.

Test use. The teachers sampled in this study reported spending an average of about 11% of their time in testing, which is consistent with estimates reported in the literature (10 to 15%). The finding in this study that an average of 41% of the students' grades was based on test results is also consistent with estimates reported in the literature (40 to 50%). Estimates of the time needed for testing activities obtained from students sampled in this study were much higher (23% and 26% for seniors and sophomores, respectively) than the estimates obtained from the teachers' reports. Although students' estimates of the percentage of grade based on test scores were significantly higher than those of teachers, they were within the range reported in the literature. Students, then, who lack an experiential base, seem either to have exaggerated views regarding the time that teachers spend on testing-related activities or think that it will take them longer to construct tests.

Beginning teachers also lack an experiential base. One might ask whether beginning teachers spend more time in test-related activities than do teachers with more experience, because beginning teachers may not have files of tests to draw upon. Mean reported time spent in testing was higher for first- and second-year teachers (means of 5.4 and 5.7 hours per week) than for teachers with more experience (mean for third year = 2.3, 4th year = 2.8, 5th year = 3.8). Thus, students may be accurate in their perception of the time needed by novices for testing-related activities.

Standardized testing. The students' opinions ranged from neutral to positive regarding the use of standardized tests and were, on average, significantly more positive than the teachers' opinions. One explanation for the positive opinions may be that students have extremely limited personal experience with standardized tests (their own or their friends) and so have a limited basis upon which to judge test effectiveness. By college level, most students have taken a number of standardized tests but may not be aware of the results, may not have been directly affected by the results, or may have been affected by the results at a time when they were too young to understand or argue. Students may believe that the tests must be useful because "authorities and experts" sanction their administration. Students' opinions may, then, be shaped by the positive *public* value placed on tests, as well as by their educational programs. The tests and measurement course taken by many preservice teachers emphasizes how tests can be valuable if used properly. One can argue that most students view themselves as intending to use tests properly. In contrast, many teachers are required to give standardized tests, and they may also be required to take them.

Preservice–inservice differences might be even more extreme in states where the stakes attached to standardized test use are higher—where the teacher's job or salary depends upon test results. Teachers develop a broader base of experience with standardized testing, and they may be more aware of the limitations of the tests and of the controversy surrounding standardized testing. The measurement profession is unclear about the value of standardized testing; it is not surprising that teachers also have reservations.

Classroom testing. Differences were also found between teachers and teacher education students for most classroom test items, though differences were not as pronounced for these items. The result is in contrast to Reeves and Kazelski's (1985) finding of no differences between similar groups. The result of somewhat less favorable opinions of preservice than inservice teachers toward classroom testing may have stemmed from the frequent test taking by students versus the frequent use of tests by teachers. By the time students are seniors in college, they will have taken a larger number of classroom tests than standardized tests and thus will have considerably more experience in evaluating their effectiveness. Students undoubtedly encounter classroom tests and test questions that they consider to be unfair assessments of their knowledge. Such experiences may temper their opinions toward classroom tests. In contrast, because most teachers rely to some extent on test results in assigning grades and in evaluating instruction, opinions may change to conform with this behavior. Teachers' opinions may also be influenced by an experiential understanding of testing gained through learning how informative test results can be.

Because it is unlikely that the widespread use of classroom and standardized tests will diminish, teachers will continue to be called upon to use tests to make decisions that are important in the lives of students. Teachers need to be competent in test construction and interpretation. However, if tests are to be used effectively as part of the instructional process, teachers must perceive the positive aspects of test use. If a teacher finds that task impossible, that teacher should discontinue traditional test use and seek alternative assessment techniques, within the boundaries allowed by the district. Teachers should communicate positive feelings about the tests they give to their students. Teachers will probably be more likely to do so if they have positive opinions of tests. Tests are often viewed as evaluative; they may more effectively be viewed as informative and prescriptive.

If teacher educators wish to affect prospective teachers' views, they may need to both clarify their own views about the place of testing in instruction and clearly present arguments about testing, pro and con, to their classes. Well-constructed classroom assessments, whether paper-and-pencil, portfolio, or performance measures, provide diagnostic and prescriptive information about the students' progress and about the effectiveness of instruction. This information is valuable. Poorly constructed or standardized measures that do not address the curriculum provide little information of use in the classroom. The reasons for giving tests that do not provide information useful in instruction must be clearly explained. Such tests may be mandated to provide legitimate administrative, state, or national information.

But to what extent can teacher educators shape *prospective* teachers' views? The results of this study suggest that opinions held prior to and following preservice instruction may not survive the transition to the real world of the classroom. If this is the case, the preservice course—no matter how good it is—would be ineffective in influencing attitudes. (It may, however, be highly effective in influencing the quality of testing practices by providing basic skills in test construction and interpretation.) Inservice instruction may be a better vehicle to use to produce attitude change.

This study was cross-sectional in design. A longitudinal study that examined opinions over time (from preservice to inservice) is required to identify the extent to which opinions are shaped by school requirements. Additional information regarding school characteristics affecting preservice and inservice teachers' attitudes toward testing would be of interest, as would information about differences in testing skill levels between pre- and inservice teachers.

NOTES

An earlier version of this paper was presented at the 1990 annual meeting of the National Council on Measurement in Education, held April 1990 in Boston.

Appreciation is expressed to the *Journal of Educational Research* reviewers for their helpful suggestions.

REFERENCES

Boyd, J., McKenna, B. H., Stake, R. E., & Yachinsky, J. (1975). *A study of testing practices in the Royal Oak (MI) public schools.* Royal Oak, MI: Royal Oak City School District. (ERIC Reproduction Service No. 117 161)

Carlberg, C. (1981). South Dakota study report. Denver, CO: Midcontinent Regional Educational Laboratory.

Cramer, S., & Slakter, M. (1968). A scale to assess attitudes toward aptitude testing. *Measurement and Evaluation in Guidance, 1*(2).

Darling-Hammond, L., & Wise, A. E. (1985). Beyond standardization: State standards and school improvement. *Elementary School Journal, 85,* 315–336.

Fennessey, D. (1982). Primary teachers' assessment practices: Some implications for teacher training. Paper presented at the annual conference of the South Pacific Association for Teacher Education, Frankston, Victoria, Australia.

Goslin, D. A. (1967). *Teachers and testing.* New York: Russell Sage Foundation.

Green, K. E., & Stager, S. F. (1986–87). Testing: Coursework, attitudes, and practices. *Educational Research Quarterly, 11*(2), 48–55.

Green, K. E., & Stager, S. F. (1986). Measuring attitudes of teachers toward testing. *Measurement and Evaluation in Counseling and Development, 19,* 141–150.

Green, K. E., & Williams, E. J. (1989, March). Standardized test use by classroom teachers: Effects of training and grade level taught. Paper presented at the annual meeting of the National Council on Measurement in Education, San Francisco.

Gullickson, A. R. (1982). The practice of testing in elementary and secondary schools. (ERIC Reproduction Service No. ED 229 391)

Gullickson, A. R. (1984). Teacher perspectives of their instructional use of tests. *Journal of Educational Research, 77,* 244–248.

Gullickson, A. R., & Hopkins, K. D. (1987). The context of educational measurement instruction for preservice teachers: Professor perspectives. *Educational Measurement: Issues and Practice, 6,* 12–16.

Karmos, A. H., & Karmos, J. S. (1984). Attitudes toward standardized achievement tests and their relation to achievement test performance. *Measurement and Evaluation in Counseling and Development, 17,* 56–66.

Lazar-Morison, C., Polin, L., Moy, R., & Burry, J. (1980). A review of the literature on test use. Los Angeles: Center for the Study of Evaluation, California State University. (ERIC Reproduction Service No. 204 411)

Marso, R. N., & Pigge, F. L. (1988). Ohio secondary teachers' testing needs and proficiencies: Assessments by teachers, supervisors, and principals. *American Secondary Education, 17,* 2–9.

McKee, B. G., & Manning-Curtis, C. (1982, March). Teacher-constructed classroom tests: The stepchild of measurement research. Paper presented at the National Council on Measurement in Education annual conference, New York.

Newman, D. C., & Stallings, W. M. (1982). Teacher competency in classroom testing, measurement preparation, and classroom testing practices. Paper presented at the American Educational Research Association annual meeting. New York. (ERIC Reproduction Service No. ED 220 491)

Reeves, C. K., & Kazelskis, R. (1985). Concerns of preservice and inservice teachers. *Journal of Educational Research, 78,* 267–271.

Ruddell, R. B. (1985). Knowledge and attitudes toward testing: Field educators and legislators. *Reading Teacher, 38,* 538–543.

Stetz, F. P., & Beck, M. D. (1979). Comments from the classroom: Teachers' and students' opinions of achievement tests. Paper presented at the annual meeting of the National Council on Measurement in Education, San Francisco.

SUMMARY

Causal–Comparative Research: Definition and Purpose

1. In causal–comparative, or ex post facto, research, the researcher attempts to determine the cause, or reason, for existing differences in the behavior or status of groups.
2. The basic causal–comparative approach is retrospective; that is, it starts with an effect and seeks its possible causes. A variation of the basic approach is prospective, that is, starting with a cause and investigating its effect on some variable.
3. An important difference between causal–comparative and correlational research is that causal–comparative studies involve two or more groups and one independent variable while correlation studies involve two or more variables and one group.
4. The major difference between experimental research and causal–comparative research is that in experimental research the independent variable, the alleged cause, is manipulated, and in causal–comparative research it is not, because it has already occurred. In experimental research the researcher can randomly form groups and manipulate the independent variable. In causal–comparative research the groups are already formed and already divided on the independent variable. Note that *neither* causal–comparative nor correlational research produces true experimental data.
5. Independent variables in causal–comparative studies are variables that cannot be manipulated (such as socioeconomic status), should not be manipulated (such as number of cigarettes smoked per day), or simply are not manipulated, though they could be (such as method of reading instruction).
6. Causal–comparative studies identify relationships that may lead to experimental studies, but only a relationship is established. Cause–effect relationships established through causal–comparative research are at best tenuous and tentative. Only experimental research can truly establish cause–effect relationships.
7. The alleged cause of an observed causal–comparative effect may in fact be the effect, the supposed cause, or a third variable that has "caused" both the identified cause and effect.

Conducting a Causal–Comparative Study

Design and Procedure

8. The basic causal–comparative design involves selecting two groups differing on some independent variable and comparing them on some dependent variable.
9. The groups may differ in a number of ways. One group may possess a characteristic that the other does not, one group may possess more of a characteristic than the other, or the two groups may have had different kinds of experiences.
10. It is important to select samples that are representative of their respective populations and similar with respect to critical variables other than the independent variable.

Control Procedures

11. Lack of randomization, manipulation, and control are all sources of weakness in a causal–comparative design. A threat is the possibility that the groups are different on some other major variable besides the identified independent variable, and it is this other variable that is the real cause of the observed difference between the groups.
12. A number of strategies are available to overcome problems of initial group differences on an extraneous variable. Three approaches to overcome such group differences are matching, comparing homogeneous groups or subgroups, and covariate analysis.
13. Analysis of covariance adjusts scores on a dependent variable for initial differences on some other variable (assuming that performance on the "other variable" is related to performance on the dependent variable, which is what control is all about anyway).

Data Analysis and Interpretation

14. Analysis of data in causal–comparative studies involves a variety of descriptive and inferential statistics.
15. The most commonly used descriptive statistics are the mean, which indicates the average performance of a group on a measure of some variable, and the standard deviation, which indicates how spread out a set of scores is, that is, whether the scores are clustered together around the mean or widely spread out around the mean.

16. The most commonly used inferential statistics are the *t* test, which is used to determine if there is a significant difference between the means of two groups; analysis of variance, which is used to determine if there is a significant difference among the means of three or more groups; and chi square, which is used to compare group frequencies, that is, to see if an event occurs more frequently in one group than another.

17. As repeatedly pointed out, interpreting the findings in a causal–comparative study requires considerable caution. The alleged cause may be the effect, and vice versa. There may be a third factor that is the real "cause" of both the independent and dependent variable.

18. The way to determine the correct order of causality, which variable caused which, is to determine which one occurred first.

19. One way to control for a potential common cause is to equate groups on the suspected variable.

Single-subject experimental designs "are typically used to study the behavior change an individual exhibits as a result of some treatment." (p. 383)

EXPERIMENTAL RESEARCH

OBJECTIVES

After reading Chapter 13, you should be able to do the following:

1. Briefly state the purpose of experimental research.
2. List the basic steps involved in conducting an experiment.
3. Explain the purpose of control.
4. Briefly define or describe *internal validity* and *external validity*.
5. Identify and briefly describe eight major threats to the internal validity of an experiment.
6. Identify and briefly describe six major threats to the external validity of an experiment.
7. Briefly discuss the purpose of experimental design.
8. Identify and briefly describe five ways to control extraneous variables (and you'd better not leave out randomization!).

9. For each of the pre-experimental, true experimental, and quasi-experimental group designs discussed in this chapter, (1) draw a diagram, (2) list the steps involved in its application, and (3) identify major problems of invalidity.
10. Briefly define and describe the purpose of a *factorial design*.
11. Briefly explain what is meant by the term *interaction*.
12. For each of the A-B-A single-subject designs discussed in this chapter, (1) draw a diagram, (2) list the steps involved in its application, and (3) identify major problems with which it is associated.
13. Briefly describe the procedures involved in using a multiple-baseline design.
14. Briefly describe an *alternating treatments design*.
15. Briefly describe three types of replication involved in single-subject research.

EXPERIMENTAL RESEARCH: DEFINITION AND PURPOSE

Experimental research is the only type of research that can test hypotheses to establish cause-and-effect relationships. It represents the strongest chain of reasoning about the links between variables. In an experimental study, the researcher manipulates at least one independent variable, controls other relevant variables, and observes the effect on one or more dependent variables. The researcher determines "who gets what"; that is, she has control over the selection and assignment of groups to treatments. The manipulation of the independent variable is the one characteristic that differentiates experimental research from other types of research. The independent variable, also called the *treatment, causal,* or *experimental* variable, is that treatment or characteristic believed to make a difference. In educational research, independent variables that are frequently manipulated include method of instruction, type of reinforcement, arrangement of learning environment, type of learning materials, and length of treatment. This list is by no means exhaustive. The dependent variable, also called the *criterion, effect,* or *posttest* variable, is the outcome of the study, the change or difference in groups that occurs as a result of the independent variable. It is referred to as the *dependent* variable because it is "dependent" on the independent variable. The dependent variable may be measured by a test or some other quantitative measure or by variables such as attendance, number of suspensions, and attention span. The only restriction on the dependent variable is that it represents a measurable outcome.

Experimental research is the most structured of all research types. When well conducted, experimental studies produce the soundest evidence concerning cause–effect relationships. The results of experimental research permit prediction, but not the kind that is characteristic of correlational research. A correlational prediction predicts a particular score for a particular individual. Predictions based on experimental findings are more global and often take the form, "If you use approach X you will probably get better results than if you use approach Y." Of course, it is unusual for a single experimental study to produce broad generalization of results, because any single study is limited in context and participants. However, replications of a study using different contexts and participants often produce cause–effect results that can be generalized widely.

THE EXPERIMENTAL PROCESS

The steps in an experimental study are basically the same as in other types of research: selecting and defining a problem, selecting participants and measuring instruments, selecting a research plan, executing the plan, analyzing the data, and formulating conclusions. An experimental study is guided by at least one hypothesis that states an expected causal relationship between two variables. The experiment is conducted to confirm (support) or disconfirm (refute) the experimental hypothesis. In an experimental study, the researcher is in on the action from the very beginning. He selects the groups, decides what treatment will go to which group, controls extraneous variables, and measures the effect of the treatment at the end of the study.

It is important to note that the experimental researcher controls *both* the selection and the assignment of the research participants. That is, the researcher randomly selects participants from a single, well-defined population and then randomly assigns these participants into the different treatment conditions. It is the ability to randomly select and randomly assign participants to treatments that makes experimental research unique. The random assignment of participants to treatments, which is also called the *researcher's manipulation of the treatments,* is the distinguishing aspect of experimental research and the feature that distinguishes it from causal–comparative research. It is important for you to understand the difference between random selection and random assignment. Experimental research has both, whereas causal–comparative research has only random selection, not assignment, because causal–comparative participants are obtained from two already existing populations. There can be no random assignment to treatment *from a single population* in causal–comparative studies.

An experiment typically involves a comparison of two groups (although as you will see later, there may be only one group, or there may be three or more groups). The experimental comparison is usually one of three types: (1) comparison of two different approaches (A versus B); (2) comparison of a new approach and the existing approach (A versus no A); and (3) comparison of different amounts of a single approach (a little of A versus a lot of A). An example of an A versus B comparison would be a study that compared the effects of a computer-based and a teacher-based approach to teaching first-grade reading. An example of an A versus no A comparison would be a study that compared a new handwriting method and the classroom teachers' existing handwriting approach. An example of a little of A versus a lot of A comparison would be a study that compared the effect of 20 minutes of daily science instruction versus 40 minutes of daily science instruction on fifth graders' attitudes toward science. Experimental designs may get quite complex and involve simultaneous manipulation of several independent variables. At this stage of the game, however, we recommend that you stick to just one!

The group that receives the new or novel treatment is often called the *experimental* group while the other group is called the *control* group. An alternative to using experimental and control groups is to simply describe the treatments as comparison groups, treatment groups, or groups A and B. The terms are commonly used interchangeably. A common misconception is that a control group always receives no treatment. This is not true and would hardly provide a fair comparison. For example, if the independent variable was type of reading instruction, the experimental group might be instructed with a new method, while the control group might continue instruction with the currently used method. The control group would still receive reading instruction; members would not sit in a closet while the study was being conducted. Otherwise, you would not be evaluating the effectiveness of a new method as compared to a traditional method, but rather the effectiveness of a new method as compared to no reading instruction at all! Any method of instruction is bound to be more effective than no instruction at all.

The groups that are to receive the different treatments should be equated on all variables that might influence performance on the dependent variable. For example, in the previous reading example, initial reading readiness should be equated or be very similar in each treatment group at the start of the study. In other words, the researcher makes every effort to ensure that the two groups start as equivalently as possible on all variables except the independent variable. The main way that groups are equated is through simple random or stratified random sampling (see Chapter 4).

After the groups have been exposed to the treatment for some period, the researcher collects data on the dependent variable from the groups and determines whether there is a real or significant difference between their performance. In other words, using statistical analysis, the researcher determines whether the treatment made a real difference. Chapters 14 and 15 discuss statistical analysis of experimental studies in detail. For now, suppose that at the end of an experimental study one group had an average score of 29 on the dependent variable and the other group had an average score of 27. There clearly is a difference between the groups, but is a two-point difference a meaningful or significant difference, or is it just a chance difference produced by measurement error? Statistical analysis helps answer this question.

Experimental studies in education often encounter two problems: a lack of sufficient exposure to treatments and failure to make the treatments substantially different from each other. In most cases, no matter how effective a treatment is, it is not likely to be effective if students are exposed to it for only a brief period. To adequately test a hypothesis concerning the effectiveness of a treatment, the experimental group would need to be exposed to it over a period of time so that the treatment is given a fair chance to work. Also of concern is the difference between treatments. In a study comparing team teaching and traditional lecture teaching it would be vital that team teaching be operationalized in a manner that clearly differentiated it from the traditional method. If team teaching meant two teachers taking turns lecturing, it would not be very different from traditional teaching and the researcher would be very unlikely to find a meaningful difference between the two study treatments. Also, if teachers using different treatments converse with and borrow from each other's treatments, the original treatments become diluted and similar to each other. These problems have detrimental effects on the outcome of the study.

MANIPULATION AND CONTROL

Direct manipulation by the researcher of at least one independent variable is the one single characteristic that differentiates experimental research from other types of research. Manipulation of an independent variable is often a difficult concept to grasp. Quite simply it means that the researcher decides what treatments will make up the independent variable and which group will get which treatment. For example, if the independent variable was number of annual teacher reviews, the researcher might decide that there should be three groups, one group receiving no review, a second group receiving one review, and a third group receiving two reviews. In addition, having selected research participants from a single, well-defined population, the researcher would randomly assign participants to treatments. Thus, manipulation means being able to select the number and type of treatments and to randomly assign participants to treatments.

Independent variables in education are either manipulated (active variables) or not manipulated (assigned variables). You can manipulate such variables as method of instruction, number of reviews, and size of group. You cannot manipulate variables such as gender, age, or socioeconomic status. You can place participants into one method of instruction or another (active), but you cannot place participants into male or female categories because they already are male or female (assigned). Although the design of an experimental study may or may not include assigned variables, at least one active variable that can be manipulated must be present.

Control refers to the researcher's efforts to remove the influence of any extraneous variable (other than the independent variable itself) that might affect scores on the dependent variable. In other words, the researcher wants the groups to be as similar as possible, so that the only major difference between them is the treatment variables as manipulated. To illustrate the importance of research control, suppose you conducted a study to compare the effectiveness of student tutors versus parent tutors in teaching first graders to read. Student tutors might be older children from higher grade levels, and parent tutors might be members of the PTA. Suppose also that student tutors helped each member of their group for 1 hour per day for a month, while the parent tutors helped each member of their group for 2 hours per week for a month. Would the comparison be fair? Certainly not. Participants with the student tutors would have received two and one half times as much help as from the parents group (5 hours per week versus 2 hours per week). Thus, one variable that would need to be controlled would be amount of tutoring. If this variable were not controlled, you could be confronted with a dilemma. If the student tutors produced higher reading scores than the parent tutors, you would not know whether this result indicated that student tutors were more effective than parent tutors, that longer periods of tutoring were more effective than shorter periods, or that type and amount of tutoring combined are more effective. For the comparison to be fair and interpretable, both students and parents should tutor for the same amount of time. Then time of tutoring would be controlled and you could truly compare the effectiveness of student and parent tutors.

This example is just one of the many kinds of factors that must be considered in planning an experimental study. Some variables that need controlling may be relatively obvious; in the example, in addition to time tutoring, other variables such as reading readiness and prior reading instruction also would need to be examined and controlled if necessary. Some variables that need to be controlled may not be as obvious; for example, you would need to ensure that both groups used similar reading texts and materials. Thus, there are really two different kinds of variables that need to be controlled: **participant variables** (such as reading readiness) on which participants in the different groups might differ; and **environmental variables** (such as learning materials) that might cause unwanted differences between groups. The researcher strives to ensure that the characteristics and experiences of the groups are as equal as possible on all important variables except the independent variable. If relevant variables can be controlled, group differences on the dependent variable can be attributed to the independent variable.

Control is not easy in an experiment, especially in educational studies where real live participants are involved. It certainly is a lot easier to control solids, liquids, and gases! Our task is not an impossible one, however, since we can concentrate on identifying and controlling only those variables whose **interactions** might really affect the dependent variable. For example, if two groups differed significantly with respect to shoe size or height, the results of most education studies would probably not be affected by these differences. There are a number of techniques at the researcher's disposal that can be used to control for extraneous variables, and we will discuss them later in this chapter. Bear in mind, however, that even though experimental research is the only type of research that can truly establish cause–effect relationships, it is not universally appropriate for all educational research problems or studies. The experimental method is only one of many ways to examine important educational questions and problems.

THREATS TO EXPERIMENTAL VALIDITY

As noted, any uncontrolled extraneous variables affecting performance on the dependent variable are threats to the validity of an experiment. An experiment is valid if results obtained are due only to the manipulated independent variable and if they are generalizable to individuals or contexts beyond the experimental setting. These two criteria are referred to, respectively, as the internal validity and external validity of an experiment. **Internal validity** is concerned with threats or factors other than the independent variable that affect the dependent variable. In other words, internal validity focuses on threats or rival explanations that influence the outcomes of an experimental study but are not part of the independent variable. In the former example of student and parent tutors, a plausible threat or rival explanation for the research results would have been differences in the amount of time the two groups tutored. The degree to which experimental research results are attributable to the independent variable and not to some other rival explanation is the degree to which an experimental study is internally valid.

External validity, also called **ecological validity,** is concerned with the extent to which the study results can be generalized to groups and settings beyond those of the experiment. In other words, external validity focuses on threats or rival explanations that would not permit the results of a study to be generalized to other settings or groups. For example, if a study was conducted using groups of gifted ninth graders, the results should be applicable to other groups of gifted ninth graders. If research results are not generalizable outside the experimental setting, then no one could profit from the research. Each and every study would have to be reestablished over and over and over. An experimental study can only contribute to educational theory or practice if there is some assurance that results and effects are replicable and generalize to other places and groups. If results cannot be replicated in other settings by other researchers, the study has low external or ecological validity.

So, all one has to do in order to conduct a valid experiment is to maximize internal and maximize external validity, right? Wrong. Unfortunately, there is a "catch-22" complicating the researcher's experimental life. Maximizing internal validity requires the use of very rigid controls over participants and conditions, similar to a laboratory-like environment. However, the more a research situation is narrowed and controlled, the less realistic and generalizable it becomes. A study can contribute little to educational practice if there is no assurance that a technique effective in a highly controlled setting will also be effective in a less controlled classroom setting. On the other hand, the more natural the experimental setting becomes, the more difficult it is to control extraneous variables. It is very difficult, for example, to conduct a well-controlled study in an actual classroom. Thus, the researcher must strive for balance between control and realism. If a choice is involved, the researcher should err on the side of control rather than realism,[1] since a study that is not internally valid is worthless. A useful strategy to address this problem is first to demonstrate an effect in a highly controlled environment (with maximum internal validity) and then to redo the study in a more natural setting (to examine external validity). In the final analysis, however, the researcher seeks a compromise between a highly controlled and highly natural environment.

In the following pages we discuss many threats to internal and external validity. Some extraneous variables are threats to internal validity, some are threats to external validity, and some may be threats to both. How potential threats are classified is not of great importance; what is important is that you be aware of their existence and how to control for them. As you read, you may begin to feel that there are just too many threats for one little researcher to control. However, the task is not as formidable as it may at first appear, since there are a number of experimental designs that do control many or most of the threats you are likely to encounter. Also, remember that each threat to be discussed is only a potential threat that may not be a problem in a particular study.

---

[1] This is a clear distinction between the emphases of quantitative and qualitative research.

Threats to Internal Validity

Probably the most authoritative source regarding experimental design and threats to experimental validity is the work of Donald Campbell and Julian Stanley and Thomas Cook and Donald Campbell.[2] They have identified eight main threats to internal validity: history, maturation, testing, instrumentation, statistical regression, differential selection of participants, mortality, and selection–maturation interaction. However, before describing these threats to internal validity, it is useful to note the role of experimental research in overcoming these threats. You are not rendered helpless when faced with them. Quite the contrary, the use of random selection of participants, the researcher's assignment of participants to treatments, and control of other variables are powerful approaches to overcoming the threats. As you read the threats, note how experimental research's random selection and assignment to treatments can control most threats.

History

History refers to the occurrence of events that are not part of the experimental treatment but that occur during the study and affect the dependent variable. The longer a study lasts, the more likely it is that history will be a threat. Happenings such as a bomb scare, an epidemic of measles, or even general current events are examples of the history effect. For example, suppose you conducted a series of inservice workshops designed to increase the morale of teacher participants. Suppose that between the time you conducted the workshops and the time you administered a posttest measure of morale, the news media announced that, due to state-level budget problems, funding to the local school district was going to be significantly reduced and that it was likely that promised pay raises for teachers would have to be postponed. Such an event could easily wipe out any effect the workshops might have had, and posttest morale scores might well be considerably lower than they otherwise might have been (to say the least!).

Maturation

Maturation refers to natural physical, intellectual, and emotional changes that occur in participants over a period of time. These changes may affect participants' performance on the dependent variable. Especially in studies that last a long time, participants may become older, more coordinated, unmotivated, anxious, or just plain bored. Maturation is more likely to be a problem in a study designed to test the effectiveness of a psychomotor training program on three-year-olds than in a study designed to compare two methods of teaching algebra. Young participants would typically be undergoing rapid biological changes during the training program, raising the question of whether changes were due to the training program or to maturation.

Testing

Testing, also called **pretest sensitization,** refers to improved scores on a posttest as a result of having taken a pretest. Taking a pretest may improve performance on a posttest, regardless of whether there is any treatment or instruction in between. Testing is more likely to be a threat when the time between testings is short; a pretest taken in September is not likely to affect performance on a posttest taken in June. The testing threat to internal validity is more likely to occur in studies that measure factual information that can be recalled. For example, taking a pretest on algebraic equations is less likely to improve performance on a similar posttest than if the information were factual.

---

[2]Campbell, D. T., and Stanley, J. C. (1971). *Experimental and quasi-experimental designs for research.* Chicago: Rand McNally; Cook, T. D, and Campbell, D. T. (1979). *Quasi-experimentation: Design and analysis issues for field settings.* Chicago: Rand McNally.

Instrumentation

The **instrumentation** threat refers to unreliability, or lack of consistency, in measuring instruments that can result in an invalid assessment of performance. Instrumentation may occur in several different ways. If two different tests are used, one for pretesting and one for posttesting, and if the tests are not of equal difficulty, instrumentation may become a threat. For example, if the posttest is more difficult than the pretest, it may mask improvement that is actually present. Alternatively, if the posttest is less difficult than the pretest, it may indicate improvement that is not really present. If data are collected through observation, the observers may not be observing or evaluating behavior the same way at the end of the study as at the beginning. In fact, if they are aware of the nature of the study, they may unconsciously tend to see and record what they know the researcher is hypothesizing. If data are collected through the use of a mechanical device, the device may be poorly calibrated, resulting in inaccurate measurement. Thus, the researcher must take care in selecting tests, observers, and mechanical devices to measure the dependent variable.

Statistical Regression

Statistical regression usually occurs when participants are selected on the basis of their extremely high or extremely low scores. It refers to the tendency of participants who score highest on a test to score lower on a second, similar test, and of subjects who score lowest on a test to score higher on a second, similar test. The tendency is for scores to *regress,* or move, toward a mean (average) or expected score. Thus, extremely high scorers regress (lower) to the mean and extremely low scorers regress (higher) to the mean. For example, suppose a researcher wished to determine the effectiveness of a new method of instruction on the spelling ability of poor spellers. The researcher might administer a 100-item, 4-alternative, multiple-choice spelling pretest. Each question might read, "Which of the following four words is spelled incorrectly?" The researcher might then select for the study the 30 students who scored lowest. Now suppose none of the pretested students knew any of the words and guessed on every single question. With 100 items, and 4 choices for each item, a student would be expected to receive a score of 25 just by guessing. Some students, however, just due to rotten guessing, would receive scores much lower than 25, and other students, equally by chance, would receive much higher scores than 25. If they were administered the test a second time, without any instruction intervening, their expected score would still be 25. Thus students who scored very low the first time would be expected to have a second score closer to 25, and students who scored very high the first time would also be expected to score closer to 25 the second time. Whenever participants are selected on the basis of their extremely high or extremely low performance, statistical regression is a viable threat to internal validity.

Differential Selection of Participants

Differential selection of participants usually occurs when already formed groups are compared, thereby raising the threat that the groups were different before the study even begins. Initial group differences may account for posttest differences. Suppose, for example, you received permission to use two of Ms. Hynee's English classes in your study. There is no guarantee that the two classes are at all equivalent. If your luck was really bad, one class might be the honors English class and the other class might be the remedial English class. It would not be too surprising if the first class did much better on the posttest! Thus using already formed groups should be avoided if possible. If they must be used, groups should be selected that are as similar as possible, and a pretest should be administered to check for initial equivalence.

Mortality

First, let us make it perfectly clear that mortality does not mean that subjects die! **Mortality,** or **attrition,** refers to the case in which participants drop out of a study. Mortality is a particular problem when different groups drop out for different reasons and with different frequency. The change in the characteristics of the groups due to mortality can have a significant effect on the results of the study. For example, participants who drop out of a study may be less motivated or uninterested in the study than those who remain. This is especially a problem when volunteers are used or when a study compares a new treatment to an existing treatment. Participants rarely drop out of control groups or existing treatments because few or no additional demands are made on them. However, volunteers or participants using the new, experimental treatment may drop out because too much effort is required for participation. The experimental group that remains at the end of the study then represents a more motivated group than the control group. As another example of mortality, suppose Suzy Shiningstar (a high IQ and all that student) got the measles and dropped out of your control group. Suppose that before Suzy dropped out she managed to infect her friends in the control group. Since birds of a feather often flock together, Suzy's control group friends might also be the "high IQ and all that" type students. The experimental group might end up looking pretty good when compared to the control group simply because many of the good students dropped out of the control group. The researcher cannot assume that participants drop out of a study in a random fashion and should, if possible, select a design that controls for mortality.

One way to assess the mortality of groups is to obtain demographic information about the participant groups prior to the start of the study and compare the groups at the end of the study. Another approach is to provide some incentive to participants to remain in the study. Finally, one can identify the kinds of participants who drop out of the study and remove similar portions from the other groups.

Selection–Maturation Interaction, Etc.

The *etc.* means that selection may also interact with history and testing as well as maturation, although the **selection–maturation interaction** is most common. What this means is that if already formed groups are used, one group may profit more (or less) from a treatment, or have an initial advantage, because of maturation, history, or testing factors. Suppose, for example, that you received permission to use two of Ms. Hynee's English classes, and both classes were average and apparently equivalent on all relevant variables. Suppose, however, that for some reason Ms. Hynee had to miss one of her classes but not the other (maybe she had to have a root canal), and Ms. Alma Mater took over Ms. Hynee's class. Suppose further that as luck would have it, Ms. Mater covered much of the material now included in your posttest (remember history?). Unbeknownst to you, your experimental group would have a definite advantage to begin with, and it might be this initial advantage, not the independent variable, that caused posttest differences in the dependent variable. Thus, the researcher must select a design that controls for this potential problem or make every effort to determine if it is operating in the study. Table 13.1 summarizes the threats to internal validity.

THREATS TO EXTERNAL VALIDITY

There are several major threats to external validity that can limit generalization of experimental results to other populations. Building on the work of Campbell and Stanley, Bracht and Glass[3] refined and expanded discussion of threats to external validity. Bracht and Glass classified these threats into two categories. Threats affecting "generalizing to whom," that is, to what groups can research results be generalized, make up threats to population validity. Threats affecting "generalizing to what," that is, to what settings, conditions, variables, and contexts results can be generalized, are referred to as threats to ecological validity. The following dis-

---

[3]Bracht, G. H., and Glass, G. V. (1968). The external validity of experiments. *American Education Research Journal, 5,* 437–474.

TABLE 13.1   Threats to Internal Validity

history	Unexpected events occur between the pre- and posttest, affecting the dependent variable.
maturation	Changes occur in the participants, from growing older, wiser, more experienced, etc., during the study.
testing	Taking a pretest alters the result of the posttest.
instrumentation	The measuring instrument is changed between pre- and posttesting, or a single measuring instrument is unreliable.
statistical regression	Extremely high or extremely low scorers tend to regress to the mean on retesting.
differential selection of participants	Participants in the experimental and control groups have different characteristics that affect the dependent variable differently.
mortality	Different participants drop out of the study in different numbers, altering the composition of the treatment groups.
selection–maturation interaction	The participants selected into treatment groups have different maturation rates. Selection interactions also occur with history and instrumentation.

cussion incorporates the contributions of Bracht and Glass into Campbell and Stanley's original (1971) conceptualizations.

Pretest–Treatment Interaction

Pretest–treatment interaction occurs when participants respond or react differently to a treatment because they have been pretested. Pretesting may sensitize or alert subjects to the nature of the treatment, potentially making the treatment effect different than had subjects not been pretested. Thus, the research results would only be generalizable to other pretested groups. The results are not even generalizable to the unpretested population from which the sample was selected. The seriousness of the pretest–treatment interaction threat is dependent on the research participants, the nature of the independent and dependent variables, and the duration of the study. Studies involving self-report measures such as attitude and interest are especially susceptible to this threat. Campbell and Stanley illustrate this effect by pointing out the probable lack of comparability of a group viewing the antiprejudice film *Gentleman's Agreement* right after taking a lengthy pretest dealing with anti-Semitism, and another group viewing the movie without a pretest. Individuals not pretested could conceivably enjoy the movie as a good love story and be unaware that it deals with a social issue. Pretested individuals would be much more likely to see a connection between the pretest and the message of the film. Conversely, taking a pretest on algebraic algorithms would probably have very little impact on a group's responsiveness to a new method of teaching algebra. The pretest–treatment interaction would also be expected to be minimized in studies involving very young children, who would probably not see or remember a connection between the pretest and the subsequent treatment. Similarly, for studies conducted over a period of months or longer, the effects of the pretest would probably have worn off or been greatly diminished by the time a posttest was given. Thus, for some studies the potential interactive effect of a pretest is a more serious consideration than others. In such cases the researcher should select a design which either controls for the effect or allows her to determine the magnitude of the effect. In studies in which there is a strong possibility that pretest sensitization may occur, **unobtrusive measures** (gathering data from records, transcripts, and other inanimate sources) are recommended, if feasible.

Multiple-Treatment Interference

Multiple-treatment interference occurs when the same research participants receive more than one treatment in succession. The carryover effects from an earlier treatment may make it difficult to assess the effectiveness of a later treatment. Suppose you were interested in comparing two different approaches to improving classroom behavior—behavior modification and corporal punishment (admittedly an extreme example used to make a point!). Let us say that for 2 months behavior modification techniques were systematically applied to the participants, and at the end of this period you found behavior to be significantly better than before the study began. Now suppose that for the next 2 months the same participants were physically punished whenever they misbehaved (hand slappings, spankings, and the like), and at the end of the 2 months behavior was equally as good as after the 2 months of behavior modification. Could you then conclude that behavior modification and corporal punishment are equally effective methods of behavior control? Cer-tain-ly not. In fact, the goal of behavior modification is to produce self-maintaining behavior, that is, behavior that continues after direct intervention is stopped. Thus, the good behavior exhibited by the participants at the end of the corporal punishment period could well be due to the effectiveness of previous exposure to behavior modification and exist in spite of, rather than because of, exposure to corporal punishment. If it is not possible to select a design in which each group receives only one treatment, the researcher should try to minimize potential multiple-treatment interference by allowing sufficient time to elapse between treatments and by investigating distinctly different types of independent variables. Multiple-treatment interference may also occur when participants who have already participated in a study are selected for inclusion in another, apparently unrelated study. If the accessible population for a study is one whose members are likely to have participated in other studies (psychology majors, for example), then information on previous participation should be collected and evaluated before subjects are selected for the current study. If any members of the accessible population are eliminated from consideration because of previous research activities, a note should be made of this limitation in the research report.

Selection–Treatment Interaction

Selection–treatment interaction is similar to the "differential selection of participants" problem associated with internal invalidity. It mainly occurs when participants are not randomly selected for treatments. Interaction effects aside, the very fact that participants are not randomly selected from a population severely limits the researcher's ability to generalize, because what population the sample represents is in question. Even if intact groups are randomly selected, the possibility exists that the experimental group is in some important way different from the control group and/or from the larger population.

Nonrepresentativeness of groups may also result in a selection–treatment interaction such that the results of a study apply only to the groups involved and are not representative of the treatment effect in the extended population. The interaction of personological variables and treatment effects creates another population validity threat. This interaction occurs when *actual* study participants at one level of a variable react differently to a treatment than other *potential* participants in the population, at another level, would have reacted. For example, a researcher might conduct a study on the effectiveness of microcomputer-assisted instruction on the math achievement of junior high students. Classes available to the researcher (the accessible population) may represent an overall ability level at the lower end of the ability spectrum for all junior high students (the target population). If a positive effect is found, it may be that it would not have been found if the subjects were truly representative of the target population. And similarly, if an effect is not found, it might have been. Thus, extra caution must be taken in stating conclusions and generalizations based on studies involving existing, nonrandomized groups.

Selection–treatment interaction is also an uncontrolled variable in designs involving randomization. For example, one's accessible population is often quite different from one's target population, creating another population validity problem when one attempts to generalize the results of the accessible population to the target population. Thus, the way a given population becomes available to a researcher may make generalizability of findings questionable, no matter how internally valid an experiment may be. If, in seeking a sample, a researcher is turned down by 9 school systems and finally accepted by a 10th, the accepting system is very likely to be different from both the other 9 and the population of schools to which the researcher would like to generalize the results. Administrators and instructional personnel in the 10th school likely have higher morale, less fear of being inspected, and more zeal for improvement than personnel in the other 9 schools. It is recommended that researchers report problems involved in acquiring participants, including the number of times they were turned down, so that the reader can judge the seriousness of a possible selection–treatment interaction.

Specificity of Variables

Like selection–treatment interaction, specificity of variables is a threat to generalizability of research results regardless of the particular experimental design used. **Specificity of variables** refers to the fact that any given study is conducted (1) with a specific kind of participant; (2) based on a particular operational definition of the independent variable; (3) using specific dependent variables; (4) at a specific time; and (5) under a specific set of circumstances. We have also discussed the need to describe research procedures in sufficient detail to permit another researcher to replicate the study. Such detailed descriptions also permit interested readers to assess how applicable findings are to their situation. Experimental procedures require operational definition of the variables. When a group of studies that supposedly manipulated the same independent variable get quite different results, it is often difficult to determine the reasons for the differences because researchers have not provided a clear, operational description of their independent variables. When clearly stated, operational descriptions of independent variables are available, it often is found that two independent variables with the same name are quite differently operationalized, thus explaining why results differed. Because such terms as *discovery method, whole language,* and *computer-based instruction* mean different things to different people, it is impossible to know what a researcher means by these terms without clear operationalized descriptions. Without operationalized descriptions it is not clear to what populations a study can be generalized. Generalizability of results is also tied to the clear definition of the dependent variable, although in most cases the specific measure selected (e.g., the Baloney Achievement Test) is the operational definition. When there is a number of dependent variable measures to select from, questions about the comparability of these instruments are raised, just as with the definition of the independent variables.

Generalizability of results may also be affected by short- or long-term events that occur while the study is taking place. This threat is referred to as the *interaction of history and treatment effects.* It describes the situation in which events extraneous to the study alter the research results. Short-term, emotion-packed events, such as the firing of a superintendent, the release of district test scores, or the impeachment of a president might affect the behavior of participants. Usually, however, the researcher is aware of such happenings and can assess their possible impact on results. Of course, accounts of such events should also be included in the research report. The impact of more long-term events, such as wars and economic depressions, however, is more subtle and tougher to evaluate. Another threat to external validity is the *interaction of time of measurement and treatment effect.* This threat results from the fact that posttesting may yield different results depending on when it is done. A treatment effect based on the administration of a posttest immediately following the treatment may not be the same if a delayed posttest is given some time after treatment. Conversely, a treatment may have a long-term, but not a short-term, effect. Thus, the only way to assess the generalizability of findings over time is to measure the dependent variable at various times following treatment. To deal with the threats associated with specificity, the researcher must (1) operationally define variables in a way that has meaning outside the experimental setting and (2) be careful in stating conclusions and generalizations.

Treatment Diffusion

Treatment diffusion occurs when different treatment groups communicate with and learn from each other. Knowledge of each other's treatments often leads to the groups borrowing aspects from each other so that the study no longer has two distinctly different treatments, but two overlapping ones. The integrity of each treatment is diffused. Often, it is the more desirable treatment, the experimental treatment or the treatment with additional resources, that is diffused into the less desirable treatment. For example, Mr. Darth and Ms. Vader's classes were trying out two different treatments to improve spelling. Mr. Darth's class received videos, new and colorful spelling texts, and prizes for improved spelling. Ms. Vader's class received the traditional approach to spelling—list words on the board, copy them into notebooks, use each word in a sentence, and study at home. After the first week of treatments, the students began talking to their teachers about the different ways spelling was being taught. Ms. Vader heard about Mr. Darth's spelling treatment and asked if she could try out the videos in her class. Her students liked them so well that she incorporated them into her spelling program. The diffusion of Mr. Darth's treatment into Ms. Vader's treatment produced two overlapping treatments that did not represent the initial intended treatments. Strategies to reduce treatment diffusion include requesting teachers who are implementing different treatments not to communicate with each other about their treatments until the study is completed, or carrying out the study in different locales.

Experimenter Effects

There is evidence that researchers themselves may present potential threats to the external validity of their own studies. In a number of ways the experimenter may unintentionally affect study procedures, the behavior of participants, or the assessment of their performance. **Experimenter effects** may be passive or active. Passive elements include characteristics or personality traits of the experimenter such as gender, age, race, anxiety level, and hostility level. These influences are collectively called the *experimenter personal-attributes effects*. Active experimenter effects occur when the researcher's expectations of the study results affect his behavior and the research outcomes. This effect is referred to as the *experimenter bias effect*. Thus, the way an experimenter looks, feels, or acts may unintentionally affect study results, typically in the direction desired by the researcher. One form of **experimenter bias** occurs when the researcher affects participants' behavior because of previous knowledge of the participants. Suppose a researcher hypothesizes that a new reading approach will improve reading skills. If the researcher knows that Suzy Shiningstar is in the experimental group and that Suzy is a good student, she may give Suzy's reading skills a higher rating than they actually warrant. This example illustrates another way a researcher's expectations may actually contribute to producing those outcomes: Knowing which participants are in the experimental and control groups may cause the researcher to unintentionally evaluate their performances differently. It is difficult to identify experimenter bias in a study, which is all the more reason for researchers to be aware of its consequences on the external validity of their study. The moral is that the researcher should strive to avoid communicating emotions and expectations to participants in the study. Experimenter bias effects can be reduced by doing things such as scoring dependent variables "blind," that is, without the researcher knowing whose variable is being scored.

Reactive Arrangements

Reactive arrangements, also called **participant effects**, refer to a number of factors associated with the way in which a study is conducted and the feelings and attitudes of the participants involved. As discussed previously, in order to maintain a high degree of control and thus obtain internal validity, a researcher may create an experimental environment that is highly artificial and hinders generalizability to nonexperimental settings. Another type of reactive arrangement results from participants' knowledge that they are involved in an experiment or their feeling that they are in some way receiving "special" attention. The effect that such knowledge or feelings can have on the participants was demonstrated at the Hawthorne Plant of the Western Electric Company in Chicago some years ago. Studies were conducted to investigate the relationship between various working conditions and productivity. As part of their study, researchers investigated the effect of light intensity and worker output. The researchers increased light intensity and production went up. They increased it some more and production went up some more. The brighter the place became, the more production rose. As a check, the researchers decreased the light intensity, and guess what, production went up! The darker it got, the more workers produced. The researchers soon realized that it was the attention given the workers, and not the illumination, that was affecting production. To this day, the term **Hawthorne effect** is used to describe any situation in which participants' behavior is affected not by the treatment per se, but by their knowledge of participating in a study.

A related reactive effect is known as **compensatory rivalry** or the **John Henry effect.** Folk hero John Henry, you may recall, was a "steel drivin' man" who worked for a railroad. When he heard that a steam drill was going to replace him and his fellow steel drivers, he challenged, and set out to beat, the machine. Through tremendous effort he managed to win the ensuing contest, dropping dead at the finish line. Compensatory rivalry occurs when the control group is informed that they will be the control group for a new, experimental method. Like John Henry, they decide to challenge the new method by putting extra effort into their work, essentially saying (to themselves), "We'll show them that our old ways are as effective as their newfangled ways!" By doing this, however, the control group performs atypically and thus becomes a rival explanation for the study results. When this effect occurs, the treatment under investigation does not appear to be very effective, since posttest performance of the experimental group is not much (if at all) better than that of the control group.

A so-called **placebo effect** is often used as an antidote to the Hawthorne and John Henry effects. Medical researchers discovered that any "medication," even sugar and water, could make subjects feel better. To counteract this effect, a placebo approach was developed in which half of the subjects receive the true medication and half receive a placebo (sugar and water, for example). The use of a placebo is, of course, not known by the participants; both groups think they are taking a real medicine. The application of the placebo effect in educational research is that all groups in an experiment should appear to be treated the same. Suppose, for example, you have four groups of ninth graders, two experimental and two control, and the treatment is a film designed to promote a positive attitude toward a vocational career. If the experimental participants are to be excused from several of their classes to view the film, then the control participants should also be excused and shown another film whose content is unrelated to the purpose of the study (*Drugs and You: Just Say No!*, would do). As an added control you might have all the participants told that there are two movies and that eventually all of them will see both movies. In other words, it should appear as if all the students are doing the same thing.

Another related participant effect is the **novelty effect,** which refers to increased interest, motivation, or engagement on the part of participants simply because they are doing something different. In other words, a treatment may be effective because it is different, not because it is better. To counteract the novelty effect, the study should be conducted over a period of time sufficient to allow the treatment "newness" to wear off. This is especially true if the treatment involves activities very different from the subjects' usual routine. Table 13.2 summarizes the threats to external validity.

TABLE 13.2   Threats to External Validity

pretest–treatment interaction	The pretest sensitizes participants to aspects of the treatment and thus influences posttest scores.
selection–treatment interaction	The nonrandom or volunteer selection of participants limits the generalizability of the study.
multiple-treatment interference	When participants receive more than one treatment, the effect of prior treatment can affect or interact with later treatments, limiting generalizability.
specificity of variables	Poorly operationalized variables make it difficult to identify the setting and procedures to which the variables can be generalized.
treatment diffusion	Treatment groups communicate and adopt pieces of each other's treatment, altering the initial status of the treatments' comparison.
experimenter effects	Conscious or unconscious actions of the researcher affects participants' performance and responses.
reactive effects	The fact of being in a study affects participants so that they act differently from their normal behavior. The Hawthorne and John Henry effects are reactive responses to being in a study.

Obviously there are many internal and external threats to the validity of an experimental (and causal–comparative) study. You should be aware of likely validity threats to validity of your research study and strive to nullify them. One main way to overcome many threats to validity is to choose a research design that controls for such threats. We examine some of these designs in the following sections.

GROUP EXPERIMENTAL DESIGNS

The validity of an experiment is a direct function of the degree to which internal and external variables are controlled. If such variables are not controlled, it is difficult to interpret the results of a study and the groups it can be generalized to. The term *confounding* is sometimes used to refer to the fact that the effects of the independent variable may be intertwined with extraneous variables that make it difficult to determine the unique effects of each. This is what experimental design is all about: the control of extraneous variables. Good designs control many sources of invalidity; poor designs control few. If you recall, two types of extraneous variables in need of control are participant variables and environmental variables. Participant variables are characteristics of the participants (such as gender) that cannot be altered but that can be controlled. Environmental variables are variables that intervene between the independent and the dependent variables (such as anxiety or boredom) that cannot be directly observed, but can be controlled.

CONTROL OF EXTRANEOUS VARIABLES

Randomization is the best single way to simultaneously control for many extraneous variables. Thus, randomization should be used whenever possible; participants should be randomly selected from a population and they should be randomly assigned to treatment groups. Recall that random selection and assignment mean that participants' selection and assignment to treatments are done by pure chance, usually with a table of random numbers. Other randomization methods are also available. For example, a researcher could flip a coin or use odd and even numbers on a die to assign participants to two treatments; heads or even number to treatment 1 and tails or odd number to treatment 2.

Randomization is effective in creating equivalent, representative groups that are essentially the same on all relevant variables. As noted, randomly formed treatment groups are a unique characteristic of experimental research; it is a control factor not possible with causal–comparative research. The underlying rationale for randomization is that if subjects are assigned at random (by chance) to groups, there is no reason to believe that the groups will be greatly different in any systematic way. Thus, the groups would be expected to perform essentially the same on the dependent variable if the independent variable makes no difference. Therefore, if the groups perform differently at the end of the study, the difference can be attributed to the independent variable. It is important to remember that the larger the groups, the more confidence the researcher can have in the effectiveness of randomization. Randomly assigning 6 participants to two treatments is much less likely to equalize extraneous variables than assigning 50 participants to two treatments. In addition to equating groups on variables such as ability, gender, or prior experience, randomization can also equalize groups on environmental variables. Teachers, for example, can be randomly assigned to treatment groups so that the experimental groups will not have all the "Carmel Kandee" teachers or all the "Hester Hartless" teachers (and likewise for the control groups). Clearly, the researcher should use as much randomization as possible. If subjects cannot be randomly selected, those available should at least be randomly assigned. If participants cannot be randomly assigned to groups, then at least treatment conditions should be randomly assigned to the existing groups.

In addition to randomization, there are other ways to control for extraneous variables. Certain environmental variables, for example, can be controlled by holding them constant for all groups. Recall the example of the student tutor versus parent tutor study. In that example, help time was an important variable that had to be held constant, that is, made the same for both groups for them to be fairly compared. Other such variables that might need to be held constant include learning materials, prior exposure, meeting place and time (students might be more alert in the morning than in the afternoon), and years of teacher experience. Controlling participant variables is critical. If the groups are not the same to start with, you have not even given yourself a fighting chance to obtain valid, interpretable research results. Even if groups cannot be randomly formed, there are a number of techniques that can be used to try to equate groups.

Matching

Matching is a technique for equating groups on one or more variables, usually ones highly related to performance on the dependent variable. The most commonly used approach to matching involves random assignment of pairs, one participant to each group. In other words, the researcher attempts to find pairs of participants similar on the variable or variables to be controlled. If the researcher is matching on gender, obviously the matched pairs must be of the same gender. However, if the researcher is matching on variables such as pretest, GRE, or ability scores, the pairs should be based on having similar scores. Unless the number of participants is very large, it is unreasonable to try to make exact matches or matches on more than one or two variables. Once a matched pair is identified, one member of the pair is randomly assigned to one treatment group and the other member to the other treatment group. A participant who does not have a suitable match is excluded from the study. The resulting matched groups are identical or very similar with respect to the variable being controlled. A major problem with such matching is that there are invariably participants who do not have a match and must be eliminated from the study. This may cost the researcher many subjects, especially if matching is attempted on two or more variables (imagine trying to find a match for a male with an IQ near 140 and a GPA between 1.00 and 1.50!). Of course, one way to combat loss of participants is to match less stringently. For example, the researcher might decide that if two ability test scores are within 20 points, they will constitute an acceptable match. This procedure may increase the number of subjects but it tends to defeat the purpose of matching.

A related matching procedure is to rank all of the participants, from highest to lowest, based on their scores on the variable to be matched. The two highest ranking participants, regardless of score, are the first pair. One member of the first pair is randomly assigned to one group and the other member to the other group. The next two highest ranked participants (third and fourth ranked) are pair two, and so on. The major advantage of this approach is that no participants are lost. The major disadvantage is that it is a lot less precise than pair-wise matching. Advanced statistical procedures, such as analysis of covariance, have greatly reduced the research use of matching.

Comparing Homogeneous Groups or Subgroups

Another previously discussed way to control an extraneous variable is to compare groups that are homogeneous with respect to that variable. For example, if IQ were an identified extraneous variable, the researcher might select only participants with IQs between 85 and 115 (average IQ). The researcher would then randomly assign half the selected participants to the experimental group and half to the control group. Of course this procedure also lowers the number of participants in the population and additionally restricts the generalizability of the findings to participants with IQs between 85 and 115. As noted in the discussion of causal–comparative research (Chapter 12), a similar, more satisfactory approach is to form different subgroups representing all levels of the control variable. For example, the available participants might be divided into high (116 or above), average (85 to 115), and low (84 and below) IQ subgroups. Half of the participants from each of the subgroups could then be randomly assigned to the experimental group and half to the control group. This procedure should sound familiar, since it describes stratified sampling. (You knew that!) If the researcher is interested not just in controlling the variable but also in seeing if the independent variable affects the dependent variable differently at different levels of IQ, the best approach is to build the control variable right into the design. Thus, the research design would have six cells, two treatments by three IQ levels. Draw the design for yourself, and label each cell with its treatment and IQ level.

Using Participants as Their Own Controls

Using participants as their own controls involves exposing a single group to different treatments one treatment at a time. This strategy helps to control for participant differences, since the same participants get both treatments. Of course this approach is not always feasible; you cannot teach the same algebraic concepts to the same group twice using two different methods of instruction (well, you could, but it would not make much sense). A problem with this approach is a carryover effect from one treatment to the next. To use a previous example, it would be very difficult to evaluate the effectiveness of corporal punishment in improving behavior if the group receiving corporal punishment was the same group that had previously been exposed to behavior modification. If only one group is available, a better approach, if feasible, is to randomly divide the group into two smaller groups, each of which receives both treatments but in a different order. Thus, the researcher could at least get some idea of the effectiveness of corporal punishment because there would be a group that received it before behavior modification. In situations in which the effect of the dependent variable disappears quickly after treatment, or when a single participant is the focus of the research, participants can be used as their own control.

Analysis of Covariance

The analysis of covariance is a statistical method for equating randomly formed groups on one or more variables. In essence, analysis of covariance adjusts scores on a dependent variable for initial differences on some other variable, such as pretest scores, IQ, reading readiness, or musical aptitude. The covariate variable should be one related to performance on the dependent variable. Although analysis of covariance can be used in studies when groups cannot be randomly formed, its use is most appropriate when randomization is used. In spite of randomization it might be found that two groups still differ significantly in terms of pretest scores. Analysis of covariance can be used in such cases to "correct" or adjust posttest scores for initial pretest differences. However, analysis of covariance is not universally useful. For example, the relationship between the independent and covariate variables must be linear (straight line). If the relationship is curvilinear, analysis of covariance is not useful. Also, analysis of covariance is often used when a study deals with intact groups, uncontrolled variables, and nonrandom assignment to treatments, all of which weaken its results. Calculation of an analysis of covariance is a complex procedure.

Types of Group Designs

The experimental design you select to a great extent dictates the specific procedures of your study. Selection of a given design influences factors such as whether there will be a control group, whether participants will be randomly selected and assigned to groups, whether the groups will be pretested, and how data will be analyzed. Particular combinations of such factors produce different designs that are appropriate for testing different types of hypotheses. Designs vary widely in the degree to which they control various threats to internal and external validity. Of course there are certain threats to validity, such as experimenter bias, that no design can control for. However, some designs clearly do a better job than others. In selecting a design, you first determine which designs are appropriate for your study and for testing your hypothesis. You then determine which of these are also feasible given the constraints under which you may be operating. If, for example, you must use existing groups, a number of designs will automatically be eliminated. From the designs that are appropriate and feasible, you select the one that will control the most sources of internal and external invalidity and will yield the data you need to test your hypothesis or hypotheses.

There are two major classes of experimental designs: single-variable designs, which involve one manipulated independent variable, and factorial designs, which involve two or more independent variables with at least one being manipulated. **Single-variable designs** are classified as pre-experimental, true experimental, or quasi-experimental, depending on the degree of control they provide for threats to internal and external invalidity. *Pre-experimental designs* do not do a very good job of controlling threats to validity and should be avoided. In fact, the results of a study based on a pre-experimental design are so questionable they are not useful for most purposes except, perhaps, as a preliminary investigation of a problem. *True experimental designs* provide a very high degree of control and are always to be preferred. *Quasi-experimental designs* do not control as well as true experimental designs but do a much better job than the pre-experimental designs. If we were to assign letter grades to experimental designs, true experimental designs would get an A, quasi-experimental designs would get a B or a C (some are better than others), and pre-experimental designs would get a D or an F. Thus, if you have a choice between a true experimental design and a quasi-experimental design, select the true design. If your choice is between a quasi-experimental design and a pre-experimental design, select the quasi-experimental design. If your choice is between a pre-experimental design or not doing the study at all, do not do the study at all, or do a followup study using an acceptable (C or better!) design. The less useful designs are discussed here only so that (1) you will know what not to do, and (2) you will recognize their use in published research reports and be appropriately critical of their findings.

Factorial designs are basically elaborations of single-variable experimental designs except that they permit investigation of two or more variables, individually and in interaction with each other. After an independent variable has been investigated using a single-variable design, it is often useful to then study the variable in combination with one or more other variables. Some variables work differently when paired with different levels of another variable.

The designs to be discussed represent the basic designs in each category. Campbell and Stanley and Cook and Campbell[4] present a number of variations (for those of you who are getting "hooked" on research).

Pre-Experimental Designs

Here is a research riddle for you: Can you do an experiment with only one group? The answer is . . . yes, but not a really good one. As Figure 13.1 illustrates, none of the pre-experimental designs does a very good job of controlling extraneous variables that jeopardize validity.

The One-Shot Case Study.   The **one-shot case study** (it even sounds shoddy) involves a single group that is exposed to a treatment (X) and then posttested (O). None of the sources of invalidity are controlled in this design. As Figure 13.1 indicates, the only threats to validity that are controlled are those that are automatically controlled because they are irrelevant in this design. None of the validity threats that are relevant, such as history, maturation, and mortality, are controlled. Even if the research participants score high on the posttest, you cannot attribute their performance to the treatment since you do not even know what they knew before you administered the treatment. So, if you have a choice between using this design and not doing a study—select another study.

The One-Group Pretest-Posttest Design.   The **one-group pretest-posttest design** involves a single group that is pretested (O), exposed to a treatment (X), and posttested (O). The success of the treatment is determined by comparing pretest and posttest scores. This design controls some areas of invalidity not controlled by the one-shot case study, but a number of additional factors relevant to this design are not controlled. If participants do significantly better on the posttest than on the pretest, it cannot be assumed that the improvement is due to the treatment. History and maturation are not controlled. Something may happen to the participants that makes them perform better the second time, and the longer the study takes, the more likely these become threats. Testing and instrumentation also are not controlled; the participants may learn something on the pretest that helps them on the posttest, or unreliability of the measures may be responsible for the apparent improvement. Statistical regression is also not controlled. Even if subjects are not selected on the basis of extreme scores (high or low), it is possible that a group may do very poorly on the pretest, just by poor luck. For example, participants may guess badly just by chance on a multiple-choice pretest and improve on a posttest simply because their score based on guessing is more in line with an expected score. The external validity threat pretest–treatment interaction is also not controlled. Pretest–treatment interaction may cause participants to react differently to the treatment than they would have if they had not been pretested.

   To illustrate the problems associated with this design let us examine a hypothetical study. Suppose a professor teaches a very "heavy" statistics course and is concerned that the high anxiety level of students interferes with their learning. The kindly professor (aren't they all?) prepares a 100-page booklet that explains the course, tries to convince students that they will have no problems, and promises all the help they need to successfully complete the course, even if they have a poor math background. The professor wants to see if the booklet "works." At the beginning of the term she administers an anxiety test and then gives each student a copy of the booklet with instructions to read it as soon as possible. Two weeks later she administers the anxiety scale again and, sure enough, the students' scores indicate much less anxiety than at

---

[4]Campbell, D. T., and Stanley, J. C. (1971). *Experimental and quasi-experimental designs for research.* Chicago: Rand McNally; Cook, T. D., and Campbell, D. T. (1979). *Quasi-experimentation: Design and analysis issues for field settings.* Chicago: Rand McNally.

Designs	Sources of Invalidity									
	Internal								External	
	History	Maturation	Testing	Instrumentation	Regression	Selection	Mortality	Selection Interactions	Pretest-X Interaction	Multiple-X Interference
One-Shot Case Study X O	–	–	(+)	(+)	(+)	(+)	–	(+)	(+)	(+)
One-Group Pretest–Posttest Design O X O	–	–	–	–	–	(+)	+	(+)	–	(+)
Static Group Comparison X_1 O X_2 O	+	–	(+)	(+)	(+)	–	–	–	(+)	(+)

FIGURE 13.1
Sources of invalidity for
pre-experimental designs.

Symbols:

X or X_1 = Unusual treatment   + = Factor controlled for
X_2 = Control treatment   (+) = Factor controlled for because not relevant
O = Test, pretest or posttest   – = Factor not controlled for

Each line of Xs and Os represents a group.

Note: Figures 13.1 and 13.2 basically follow the format used by Campbell and Stanley and are presented with a similar note of caution: The figures are intended to be supplements to, not substitutes for, textual discussions. You *should not* totally accept or reject designs because of their +s and –s; you *should* also be aware that which design is most appropriate for a given study is determined not only by the controls provided by the various designs but also by the nature of the study and the setting in which it is to be conducted.

While the symbols used in these figures, and their placement, vary somewhat from Campbell and Stanley's format, the intent, interpretations, and textual discussions of the two presentations are in agreement (Personal communication with Donald T. Campbell, April 22, 1975).

the beginning of the term. The professor is satisfied and prides herself on the booklet's effectiveness in reducing anxiety. But wait, is this self-satisfaction warranted? If you think about it, you will see that there are a number of alternative factors or threats that could explain the students' decreased anxiety. For example, students are typically more anxious at the beginning of a course because they do not know exactly what they are in for (fear of the unknown!). After being in a course for a couple of weeks students usually find that it is not as bad as they imagined (right?), or they have dropped it (remember mortality?). Also, the professor doesn't even know whether the students read her masterpiece! The only situations for which the one-group pretest-posttest design is even remotely appropriate is when the behavior to be measured is not likely to change all by itself. Certain prejudices, for example, are not likely to change unless a concerted effort is made.

The Static-Group Comparison. The **static-group comparison** at least involves two groups: one that receives a new, or experimental, treatment and another that receives a traditional, or control, treatment. Both groups are posttested. In this case, although the terms *experimental* and *control* groups are commonly used, it is probably more appropriate to call both groups *comparison* groups, since each really serves as the comparison for the other. Each group receives some form of the independent variable (the treatments). So, for example, if the independent variable is type of drill and practice, the "experimental" group (X_1) may receive computer-assisted drill and practice, and the "control" group may receive worksheet drill and practice. Occasionally, but not often, the experimental group may receive something while the control group receives nothing. For example, a group of teachers may receive some type of inservice education while the comparison group of teachers does not. In this case, X_1 = inservice training and X_2 = no inservice training. The purpose of a control group is to indicate what the performance of the experimental group would have been if it had not received the experimental treatment. Of course, this purpose is fulfilled only to the degree that the control group is equivalent to the experimental group.

The static-group comparison design can be expanded to deal with any number of groups. For three groups the design would take the following form:

$$X_1 \qquad O$$
$$X_2 \qquad O$$
$$X_3 \qquad O$$

Which group is the control group? Basically, each group serves as a control or comparison group for the other two. For example, if the independent variable were number of minutes of review at the end of math lessons, then X_1 might represent 6 minutes of review, X_2 might represent 3 minutes of review, and X_3 no minutes of review. Thus X_3 (no minutes) would help us to assess the impact of X_2 (3 minutes), and X_2 would help us to assess the impact of X_1 (6 minutes). As already emphasized, but worthy of repeating, the degree to which the groups are equivalent is the degree to which their comparison is reasonable. In this design, participants are not randomly assigned to groups, and since there are no pretest data, it is difficult to determine just how equivalent the groups are. That is, it is possible that posttest differences are due to initial group differences in maturation, selection, and selection interactions, rather than the treatment effects. Mortality is also a problem, since if you lose participants from the study you have no information regarding what you have lost because you have no pretest data. On the positive side, the presence of a comparison group does control for history, since it is assumed that events occurring outside the experimental setting will equally affect both groups.

In spite of its limitations, the static-group comparison design is occasionally employed in a preliminary or exploratory study. For example, one semester, early in the term, a teacher wondered if the kind of test items given to educational research students affects their retention of course concepts. For the rest of the term students in one section of the course were given multiple-choice tests, and students in another section were given short-answer tests. At the end of the term, group performances were compared. The group receiving short-answer test items had higher total scores than the multiple-choice item group. Based on this exploratory study, a formal investigation of this issue was undertaken (with randomly formed groups and everything!).

True Experimental Designs

True experimental designs control for nearly all sources of internal and external invalidity. As Figure 13.2 indicates, all of the true experimental designs have one characteristic in common that none of the other designs have—random assignment of participants to treatment groups. Ideally, participants should be randomly selected and randomly assigned; however, to qualify as a true design, at least random assignment must be involved. Notice too that all the true designs have a control group. Finally, although the posttest-only control group design looks like the static-group comparison design, random assignment in the former makes it very different in terms of control.

Designs	Sources of Invalidity									
	Internal								External	
	History	Maturation	Testing	Instrumentation	Regression	Selection	Mortality	Selection Interactions	Pretest-X Interaction	Multiple-X Interference
TRUE EXPERIMENTAL DESIGNS										
1. Pretest–Posttest Control Group Design $R \ O \ X_1 \ O$ $R \ O \ X_2 \ O$	+	+	+	+	+	+	+	+	−	(+)
2. Posttest-Only Control Group Design $R \ \ \ \ X_1 \ O$ $R \ \ \ \ X_2 \ O$	+	+	(+)	(+)	(+)	+	−	+	(+)	(+)
3. Solomon Four-Group Design $R \ O \ X_1 \ O$ $R \ O \ X_2 \ O$ $R \ \ \ \ X_1 \ O$ $R \ \ \ \ X_2 \ O$	+	+	+	+	+	+	+	+	+	(+)
QUASI-EXPERIMENTAL DESIGNS										
4. Nonequivalent Control Group Design $O \ X_1 \ O$ $O \ X_2 \ O$	+	+	+	+	−	+	+	−	−	(+)
5. Time Series Design $O \ O \ O \ O \ X \ O \ O \ O \ O$	−	+	+	−	+	(+)	+	(+)	−	(+)
6. Counterbalanced Design $X_1 O \ X_2 O \ X_3 O$ $X_3 O \ X_1 O \ X_2 O$ $X_2 O \ X_3 O \ X_1 O$	+	+	+	+	+	+	+	−	−	−

FIGURE 13.2 Sources of invalidity for true experimental designs and quasi-experimental designs.

New Symbol:

R = Random assignment of subjects to groups

The Pretest-Posttest Control Group Design. The **pretest-posttest control group design** requires at least two groups, each of which is formed by random assignment. Both groups are administered a pretest and each group receives a different treatment. Both groups are posttested at the end of the study. Posttest scores are compared to determine the effectiveness of the treatment. The pretest-posttest control group design may also be expanded to include any number of treatment groups. For three groups, for example, this design would take the following form:

$$
\begin{array}{cccc}
R & O & X_1 & O \\
R & O & X_2 & O \\
R & O & X_3 & O
\end{array}
$$

The combination of random assignment and the presence of a pretest and a control group serve to control for all sources of internal invalidity. Random assignment controls for regression and selection factors; the pretest controls for mortality; randomization and the control group control for maturation; and the control group controls for history, testing, and instrumentation. Testing is controlled because if pretesting leads to higher posttest scores, the advantage should be equal for both the experimental and control groups. The only weakness in this design is a possible interaction between the pretest and the treatment, which may make the results generalizable only to other pretested groups. The seriousness of this potential weakness depends on the nature of the pretest, the nature of the treatment, and the length of the study. When this design is used, the researcher should assess and report the probability of a pretest–treatment interaction. For example, a researcher might indicate that possible pretest interaction was likely to be minimized by the nonreactive nature of the pretest (chemical equations), and by the length of the study (9 months).

There are a number of ways in which the data from this and other experimental designs can be analyzed to test the research hypothesis regarding the effectiveness of the treatments. The best way to analyze these data is to compare the posttest scores of the two treatment groups. The pretest is used to see if the groups are essentially the same on the dependent variable at the start of the study. If they are, posttest scores can be directly compared using a statistic called the t test. If the groups are not essentially the same on the pretest (random assignment does not guarantee equality), posttest scores can be analyzed using analysis of covariance. Recall that covariance adjusts posttest scores for initial differences on any variable, including pretest scores. This approach is superior to using gain or difference scores (posttest minus pretest) to determine the treatment effects.

A variation of the pretest-posttest control group design involves random assignment of matched pairs to the treatment groups, in order to more closely control for one or more extraneous variables. There is really no advantage to this technique, however, since any variable that can be controlled through matching can be better controlled using other procedures such as analysis of covariance.

Another variation of this design involves one or more additional posttests. For example:

$$
\begin{array}{ccccc}
R & O & X_2 & O & O \\
R & O & X_3 & O & O
\end{array}
$$

This variation has the advantage of providing information about the effect of the independent variable both immediately following treatment and at a later date. Recall that the interaction of time of measurement and treatment effects is a threat to external validity because posttesting may yield different results depending on when it is done. A treatment effect (or lack of same) that is based on the administration of a posttest immediately following the treatment may not be found if a delayed posttest is given after treatment. While the above variation does not completely solve the problem, it does greatly minimize it by providing information about group performance subsequent to the initial posttest.

The Posttest-Only Control Group Design.   The **posttest-only control group design** is exactly the same as the pretest-posttest control group design except there is no pretest. Participants are randomly assigned to groups, exposed to the different treatments, and posttested.

Posttest scores are then compared to determine the effectiveness of the treatment. As with the pretest-posttest control group design, the posttest-only control group design can be expanded to include more than two groups. The combination of random assignment and the presence of a control group serves to control for all sources of internal invalidity except mortality. Mortality is not controlled because of the absence of pretest data on participants. However, bear in mind that mortality may or may not be a problem, depending on the duration of the study. In this case the researcher may report that while mortality is a potential threat to validity with this design, it did not prove to be a threat in this study since the group sizes remained constant or nearly constant throughout the study. If the probability of differential mortality is low, the posttest-only design can be very effective. However, if there is any chance that the groups may be different with respect to pretreatment knowledge related to the dependent variable, the pretest-posttest control group design should be used. Which design is "best" depends on the study. If the study is to be short, and if it can be assumed that neither group has any knowledge related to the dependent variable, then the posttest-only design may be the "best" choice. If the study is to be lengthy (good chance of mortality), or if there is a chance that the two groups differ on initial knowledge related to the dependent variable, then the pretest-posttest control group design may be the best.

What if, however, you face the following dilemma?

1. The study is going to last 2 months.
2. Information about initial knowledge is essential.
3. The pretest is an attitude test and the treatment is designed to change attitudes.

This is a classic case where pretest–treatment interaction is probable. Do we throw our hands up in despair? Of course not. One solution is to select the lesser of the two evils by taking our chances that mortality will not be a threat. Another solution, if enough participants are available, is to use the Solomon four-group design, which we will discuss next. As Figure 13.2 shows, the Solomon four-group design is simply a combination of the pretest-posttest control group design (the top two lines) and the posttest-only control group design (the third and fourth lines). A variation of the posttest-only control group design involves random assignment of matched pairs to the treatment groups, one member to each group, to control for one or more extraneous variables. However, there is really no advantage to this technique, since any variable that can be controlled by matching can better be controlled using other procedures.

The Solomon Four-Group Design. The **Solomon four-group design** involves random assignment of participants to one of four groups. Two of the groups are pretested and two are not. One of the pretested groups and one of the unpretested groups receive the experimental treatment. All four groups are posttested with the dependent variable. As Figure 13.2 indicates, this design is a combination of the pretest-posttest control group design and the posttest-only control group design, each of which has its own major source of invalidity (pretest–treatment interaction and mortality, respectively). The combination of these two designs results in a design that controls for pretest–treatment interaction and for mortality. The correct way to analyze data resulting from application of this design is to use a 2 × 2 (two by two) factorial with treatment and control groups crossed with pretesting and nonpretesting. There are two independent variables in this design: treatment/control and pretest/no pretest. The 2 × 2 factorial analysis tells the researcher whether the treatment is effective and whether there is an interaction between the treatment and the pretest. To put it simply, if the pretested experimental group performs differently on the posttest than the unpretested experimental group, there is probably a pretest–treatment interaction. If no pretest–treatment interaction is found, then the researcher can have more confidence in the generalizability of treatment differences across pretested and nonpretested treatments.

A common misconception is that since the Solomon four-group design controls for so many sources of invalidity, it is always the "best" design to choose. This is not true. For one thing, this design requires twice as many participants as most other true experimental designs, and participants are often hard to find. Further, if mortality is not likely to be a problem, and pretest data are not needed, then the posttest-only design may be the best choice. If pretest–treatment interaction is unlikely, and testing is a normal part of the subjects' environment (such as when classroom tests are used), then the pretest-posttest control group design may be the "best." Thus, which design is the "best" depends on the nature of the study and the conditions under which it is to be conducted.

Quasi-Experimental Designs

Sometimes it is just not possible to randomly assign individual participants to groups. For example, to receive permission to use school children in a study, a researcher often has to agree to keep students in existing classrooms intact. Thus, entire classrooms, not individual students, are assigned to treatments. When this situation occurs there are still a number of designs that provide adequate control of sources of invalidity. These designs are referred to as *quasi-experimental designs*. Although there are many such designs, we discuss only three of the major ones here. Keep in mind that designs such as these are only to be used when it is not feasible to use a true experimental design.

The Nonequivalent Control Group Design.   This design should be familiar to you since it looks very much like the pretest-posttest control group design. The only difference is that the **nonequivalent control group design** involves random assignment of intact groups to treatments, not random assignment of individuals. Two (or more) treatment groups are pretested, administered a treatment, and posttested. For example, suppose a school volunteered six intact classrooms for a study. Three of six classrooms may be randomly assigned to the experimental group (X_1) and the remaining three assigned to the control group (X_2). The inability to randomly assign individuals to treatments (we're stuck with whole classes), adds validity threats such as regression and interactions between selection, maturation, history, and testing. The more similar the intact groups are, the stronger the study, so the researcher should make every effort to use groups that are as equivalent as possible. Comparing an advanced algebra class to a remedial algebra class, for example, would not be comparing equivalent groups. If differences between the groups on any major extraneous variable are identified, analysis of covariance can be used to statistically equate the groups. An advantage of this design is that since classes are selected "as is," possible effects from reactive arrangements are minimized. Groups may not even be aware that they are involved in a study. As with the pretest-posttest control group design, the nonequivalent control group design may be extended to include more than two groups.

The Time-Series Design.   The **time-series design** is actually an elaboration of the one-group pretest-posttest design. One group is repeatedly pretested until pretest scores are stable; then the group is exposed to a treatment, and after treatment implementation, repeatedly posttested. If a group scores essentially the same on a number of pretests and then significantly improves following a treatment, the researcher can be more confident about the effectiveness of the treatment than if just one pretest and one posttest were administered. To use a former example, if our statistics professor measured anxiety several times before giving the students her booklet, she would be able to see if anxiety was declining naturally, and thus not a result of the booklet per se. History is still a problem with this design since some event or activity might occur between the last pretest and the first posttest. Instrumentation may also be a problem but only if the researcher changes measuring instruments during the study. Pretest–treatment interaction is also a validity problem. If one pretest can interact with a treatment, more

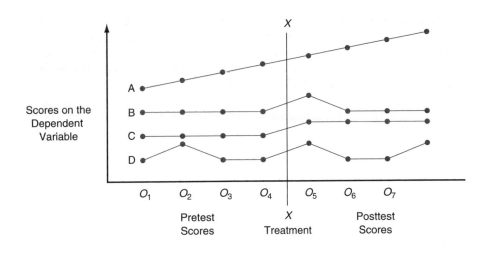

FIGURE 13.3   Possible
patterns for the results of
a study based on a time-
series design.

than one pretest can only make matters worse. If instrumentation or pretest–treatment interaction occurs, however, you will probably be aware of the problem because scores will change
prior to treatment.

While statistical analyses appropriate for this design are quite advanced, determining the
effectiveness of the treatment basically involves analysis of the pattern of the test scores. Figure 13.3 illustrates some of the possible patterns that might be found with the time-series design. In Figure 13.3 the vertical line between O_4 and O_5 indicates the point at which the
treatment was introduced. Pattern A does not indicate a treatment effect; performance was increasing before the treatment was introduced, and continued to increase at the same rate following introduction of the treatment. In fact pattern A represents the reverse situation to that
encountered by our statistics professor with her anxiety-reducing booklet. Patterns B and C do
indicate a treatment effect, with pattern C more permanent than in pattern B. Pattern D does
not indicate a treatment effect even though student scores are higher on O_5 than O_4. The pattern is too erratic to make a decision about treatment effect. Scores appear to be fluctuating up
and down, so the O_4 to O_5 fluctuation cannot be attributed to the treatment. These four patterns illustrate that just comparing O_4 and O_5 is not sufficient; in all four cases O_5 indicates a
higher score than O_4, but only in two of the patterns does it appear that the difference is due
to a treatment effect.

A variation of the time-series design is the **multiple time-series design**, which involves
the addition of a control group as shown:

$$O \quad O \quad O \quad O \quad X_1 \quad O \quad O \quad O \quad O$$
$$O \quad O \quad O \quad O \quad X_2 \quad O \quad O \quad O \quad O$$

This variation eliminates history and instrumentation as validity threats and thus represents
a design with no likely sources of internal invalidity. This design can be more effectively used
in situations where testing is a naturally occurring event, such as research involving school
classrooms.

Counterbalanced Designs.   In a **counterbalanced design**, all groups receive all treatments
but in a different order. Although the sixth example in Figure 13.2 represents the design for
three groups and three treatments, any number of groups more than one may be studied. The
only restriction is that the number of groups be equal to the number of treatments. The order
in which the groups receive the treatments is randomly determined. While participants may be
pretested, this design is usually employed when intact groups must be used and when administration of a pretest is not possible. The pre-experimental static group comparison also can be

used in such situations, but the counterbalanced design controls several additional sources of invalidity. Figure 13.2 shows that there are three treatment groups and three treatments. The first horizontal line indicates that group A receives treatment 1 and is posttested, then receives treatment 2 and is posttested, and then receives treatment 3 and is posttested. The second line indicates that group B receives treatment 3, then treatment 1, and then treatment 2, and is posttested after each treatment. The third line indicates that group C receives treatment 2, then treatment 3, then treatment 1, and is posttested after each treatment. To put it another way, the first column indicates that at time 1, while group A is receiving treatment 1, group B is receiving treatment 3 and group C is receiving treatment 2. All three groups are posttested and the treatments are shifted to produce the second column. The second column indicates that at time 2, while group A is receiving treatment 2, group B is receiving treatment 1, and group C is receiving treatment 3. The groups are then posttested again and the treatments are again shifted to produce the third column showing that at time 3, group A is receiving treatment 3, group B is receiving treatment 2, and group C is receiving treatment 1. All groups are posttested again. (Note that this design is not a research variation of the old comedy routine "Who's on First?") To determine the effectiveness of the treatments, the average performance of the groups on each treatment can be calculated and compared. In other words, the posttest scores for all the groups for the first treatment can be compared to the posttest scores of all the groups for the second treatment, and so forth, depending on the number of groups and treatments.

A unique weakness of this design is potential multiple-treatment interference that results when the same group receives more than one treatment. Thus, a counterbalanced design should really only be used when the treatments are such that exposure to one will not affect the effectiveness of another. Unfortunately, there are not too many situations in education where this condition can be met. You cannot, for example, teach the same geometric concepts to the same group using several different methods of instruction. Sophisticated analysis procedures that are beyond the scope of this text can be applied to determine both the effects of treatments and the effects of the order of treatments.

Factorial Designs

Factorial designs involve two or more independent variables, at least one of which is manipulated by the researcher. Factorial designs are basically elaborations of single-variable true experimental designs that permit investigation of two or more variables individually and in interaction with each other. In education, variables rarely operate in isolation. After an independent variable has been investigated using a single-variable design, it is often useful to study that variable in combination with one or more other variables. Some variables work differently at different levels of another variable. For example, one method of math instruction may be more effective for high-aptitude students while a different method may be more effective for low-aptitude students. The term *factorial* refers to a design that has more than one independent variable, or factor. In the preceding example, method of instruction is one independent variable or factor and student aptitude is another independent variable or factor. In the example, the factor "method of instruction" has two levels since there are two types of instruction, and the factor "student aptitude" also has two levels, high aptitude and low aptitude. Thus, a 2 × 2 (two by two) factorial design has two factors and each factor has two levels. This four-celled design is the simplest possible factorial design. As another example, a 2 × 3 factorial design has two factors; one factor has two levels and the other factor has three levels (such as high, average, and low aptitude). Suppose we have three independent variables, or factors: homework (required homework, voluntary homework, no homework); ability (high, average, low); and gender (male, female). How would you symbolize this study? Right, it is a 3 × 3 × 2 factorial design. Note that multiplying the factors indicates the total number of cells in the factorial design. For example, a 2 × 2 design will have four cells and a 3 × 3 × 2 design will have 18 cells.

Figure 13.4 illustrates the simplest 2 × 2 factorial design. In Figure 13.4 there are two factors: type of instruction has two levels, personalized and traditional, and IQ has two levels, high and low. Each of the groups in the four design cells represents a combination of a level of one factor and a level of the other factor. Thus, group 1 is composed of high IQ students receiving personalized instruction (PI), group 2 is composed of high IQ students receiving traditional instruction (TI), group 3 is composed of low IQ students receiving PI, and group 4 is composed of low IQ students receiving TI. To implement this design, high IQ students would be randomly assigned to either group 1 or group 2, and a similar number of low IQ students would be randomly assigned to either group 3 or group 4. This approach should be familiar, since it involves stratified sampling. Also, in case the question crossed your mind, the study shown in Figure 13.4 would not necessarily require four classes; there could be two classes, the personalized class and the traditional class, and each of these two classes could be subdivided to obtain similar numbers of high and low IQ students. In a 2 × 2 design both variables may be manipulated or one group may be a manipulated variable and the other a nonmanipulated variable. The nonmanipulated variable is often referred to as a **control variable.** In this example, IQ is a nonmanipulated control variable. Control variables are usually physical or mental characteristics of the subjects such as gender, years of experience, or aptitude. When describing and symbolizing such designs, the manipulated variable is traditionally placed first. Thus, a study with two independent variables, type of instruction (three types, manipulated) and gender (male, female), would be symbolized as 3 × 2, not 2 × 3.

The purpose of a factorial design is to determine whether the effects of an independent variable are generalizable across all levels or whether the effects are specific to particular levels. A factorial design also can demonstrate relationships that a single-variable design cannot. For example, a variable found not to be effective in a single-variable study may be found to interact significantly with another variable. The second example in Figure 13.5 illustrates this possibility.

Figure 13.5 represents two possible outcomes for an experiment involving a 2 × 2 factorial design. The number in each box, or cell, represents the average posttest score of that group. Thus, the high IQ students under method A had an average posttest score of 80 and the low IQ students under method B had an average score of 20. The row and column numbers outside the boxes represent average scores across boxes, or cells. Thus, in the top example, the average score for high IQ students was 60 (found by averaging the scores for all high IQ subjects regardless of treatment; 80 + 40 = 120/2 = 60), and for low IQ students the average score was 40. The average score for students under method A was 70 (found by averaging the scores of all the subjects under method A regardless of IQ level; 80 + 60 = 140/2 = 70), and for students under method B, 30. By examining the cell averages, we see that method A was better than method B for high IQ students (80 versus 40), and method A was also better for low IQ students (60 versus 20). Thus, method A was better, regardless of IQ level; there was no interaction between method and IQ. The high IQ students in each method outperformed the low IQ students in each method (no big surprise), and the subjects in method A outperformed the subjects in method B at each IQ level. The graph to the right of the results illustrates the lack of interaction.

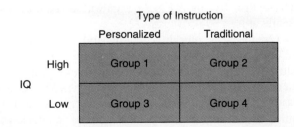

Type of Instruction

FIGURE 13.4 An example of the basic 2 × 2 factorial design.

FIGURE 13.5
Illustration of interaction
and no interaction in a 2
× 2 factorial experiment.

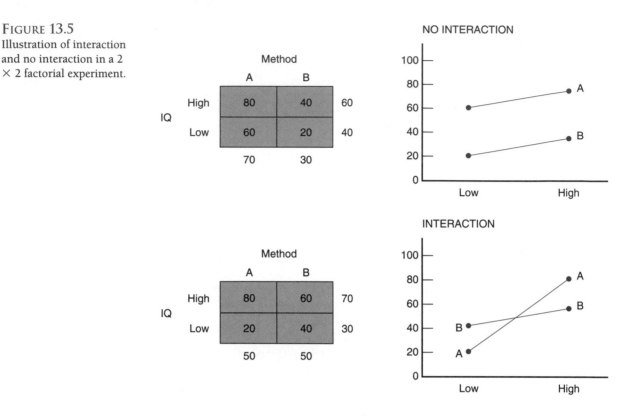

In the bottom example of Figure 13.5, which method was better, A or B? The answer, as is frequently the case, is that "It depends!" On what? On which IQ level we are talking about. For high IQ students, method A was better (80 versus 60); for low IQ students, method B was better (20 versus 40). Even though high IQ students did better than low IQ students regardless of method, how well they did depended on which method they were in. It cannot be said that either method was generally better since which method was better depends on which IQ level one focuses on. Now suppose the study had not used a factorial design but had simply compared two groups of subjects, one group receiving method A and one group receiving method B. High and low IQ students were not separated as in the factorial design. What would the researcher have concluded? The researcher would have concluded that method A and method B were equally effective, since the overall average score for both methods A and B was 50! Using a factorial design it was determined that an interaction existed between the variables such that the methods are differentially effective depending on the IQ level of the participants. The crossed lines in the graph to the right of the results illustrate an interaction effect.

There are many possible factorial designs depending on the nature and the number of independent variables. Theoretically, a researcher could simultaneously investigate 10 factors in a 2 × 2 × 2 × 2 × 2 × 2 × 2 × 2 × 2 × 2 design. In reality, however, more than 3 factors are rarely used because each additional factor increases the number of participants needed to fill the cells. Four cells are easier to fill than 10 cells. A 2 × 2 design with 20 participants per cell (a relatively small number) requires at least 80 participants (2 × 2 = 4 × 20 = 80). It is easy to see that as the number of cells increases things quickly get out of hand, and the results of studies with small sample sizes in each cell require extra-cautious interpretations. Moreover, when too many factors are included, resulting interactions become difficult, if not impossible, to interpret. Interpretation of a two-way interaction, such as the one illustrated in Figure 13.5, is relatively straightforward. But how, for example, would you interpret a five-way interaction between teaching method, IQ, gender, aptitude, and anxiety? Not only is it difficult to graph five-way interactions, they also tend to be uninterpretable! When used reasonably, factorial designs are very effective for testing research hypotheses that cannot be tested with a single-variable design.

SINGLE-SUBJECT EXPERIMENTAL DESIGNS

As you would probably guess, **single-subject experimental designs** (also referred to as *single-case* experimental designs) are designs that can be applied when the sample size is one or when a number of individuals are considered as one group. These designs are typically used to study the behavior change an individual exhibits as a result of some treatment. In single-subject designs, each participant serves as her or his own control, similar to a time-series design. Basically, the participant is exposed to a nontreatment and a treatment phase and performance is measured during each phase. The nontreatment condition is symbolized as A and the treatment condition is symbolized as B. For example, if we (1) observed and recorded a student's out-of-seat behavior on five occasions, (2) applied a behavior modification procedure and observed behavior on five more occasions, and (3) stopped the behavior modification procedure and observed behavior five more times, our design would be symbolized as A-B-A. While single-subject designs have their roots in clinical psychology and psychiatry, they are useful in many educational settings, particularly those involving studies of students with disabilities.

SINGLE-SUBJECT VERSUS GROUP DESIGNS

As single-subject designs have become progressively refined and capable of dealing with threats to validity, they are increasingly viewed as acceptable substitutes for traditional group designs in a number of situations. Most traditional experimental research studies use group designs. This is mainly because the desired results are intended to be generalized to other groups. As an example, if we were investigating the comparative effectiveness of two approaches to teaching reading, we would be interested in which approach generally produces better reading achievement, since schools usually seek strategies that are beneficial for groups of students, not individual students. Thus, group comparison designs are widely used. A single-subject design would not be very practical for this research study, since they focus on single students and require multiple measurements over the course of the study. Remember the earlier example of 15 separate observations, 5 for each phase. It would be highly impractical to administer a reading achievement test 15 times to the same students.

There are, however, some research questions for which traditional group designs are not appropriate. First, group comparison designs are sometimes opposed on ethical or philosophical grounds because such designs include a control group that does not receive the experimental treatment. Withholding students with a demonstrated need from a potentially beneficial program may be opposed or prohibited, as in the case with certain federally funded programs. If the treatment is potentially effective, it may raise objections when eligible participants are denied it. Second, group comparison designs are not possible in many cases because of the size of the population of interest. There may simply not be enough potential participants to permit the formulation of two equivalent groups. If, for example, the treatment is aimed at improving the social skills of profoundly emotionally disturbed children, the number of such children available in any one locale is probably too small to conduct comparative research. A single-subject design is clearly preferable to the formulation of two more-or-less equivalent treatment groups composed of 5 children each. Further, single-subject designs are most frequently applied in clinical settings where the primary emphasis is on therapeutic impact, not contribution to a research base. In such settings, the overriding objective is the identification of intervention strategies that will change the behavior of a specific individual, who might, for example, be engaging in self-abusive or aggressive behavior.

EXTERNAL VALIDITY

A major criticism of single-subject research studies is that they suffer from low external validity; results cannot be generalized to a population of interest. While this criticism is basically true, it is also true that the results of a study using a group design cannot be directly generalized to any individual within the group. Thus, group designs and single-subject designs each have their own generalizability problems. If your aim is to improve the functioning of an individual, a group design is not going to be appropriate.

Nonetheless, we usually are interested in generalizing the results of our research to persons other than those directly involved in the study. For single-subject designs, the key to generalizability is replication. If a researcher applies the same treatment using the same single-subject design individually to a number of participants and gets essentially the same results in every case (or even in most cases), confidence in the generalizability of the findings is increased. Different students respond similarly to the treatment. The more diverse the replications are (i.e., different kinds of subjects, different behaviors, different settings), the more generalizable the results are.

One important generalizability problem associated with many single-subject designs is the effect of the baseline condition on the subsequent effects of the treatment condition. We can never be sure that the treatment effects are the same as they would have been if the treatment phase had come before the baseline phase. This problem parallels the pretest–treatment interaction problem associated with a number of the group designs.

INTERNAL VALIDITY

If proper controls are exercised in connection with the application of a single-subject design, the internal validity of the resulting study may be quite good.

Repeated and Reliable Measurement

In a time-series design, pretest performance is measured a number of times prior to implementation of the treatment. In single-subject designs similar multiple measures of pretest performance are referred to as **baseline measures.** By obtaining baseline measures over a period of time, sources of invalidity such as maturation are controlled in the same way that they are for the time-series design. However, unlike the time-series design, the single-subject design measures performance at various points in time while the treatment is being applied. This added dimension greatly reduces the potential threat to validity from history, a threat to internal validity in time-series design.

One very real threat to the internal validity of most single-subject designs is instrumentation, the unreliability or inconsistency of measuring instruments. Because repeated measurement is a characteristic of all single-subject designs, it is especially important that measurements of participants' performance be as consistent as possible. Every effort should be made to obtain observer reliability by clearly defining and measuring the dependent variable. Since single-subject designs often rely on some type of observed behavior as the dependent variable, it is critical that the observation conditions (e.g., location, time of day) be standardized. If a single observer makes all the observations, intraobserver reliability should be obtained. If more than one observer makes observations, interobserver reliability should be obtained. Measurement consistency is especially crucial when moving from phase to phase. If a change in measurement procedures occurs at the same time a new phase is begun, the result can be invalid assessment of the treatment effect.

Also, the nature and conditions of the treatment should be specified in sufficient detail to permit replication. For example, an A-B-A-B design has a baseline phase, a treatment phase, a return to baseline conditions (withdrawal of the treatment), and a second treatment phase. If effects at each phase are to be validly assessed, the treatment must have the same procedures each time it is introduced. Also, since the key to the generalizability of single-subject designs is replication, it is clearly a necessity for the treatment to be sufficiently standardized to permit other researchers to apply it as it was originally applied.

Baseline Stability

The length of the baseline and treatment phases can influence the internal validity of single-subject designs. A key question is, "How many measurements of behavior should be taken before treatment is introduced?" There is no single answer to this question. The purpose of baseline measurements is to provide a description of the target behavior as it naturally occurs before the treatment is applied. The baseline serves as the comparison for determining the effectiveness of the treatment. If most behaviors were stable, there would be no problem with the baseline phase. But human behavior is variable, often very variable. For example, if a student's disruptive behavior were being measured, we would not expect that student to exhibit exactly the same number of disruptive acts in each observation period. The student would likely be more disruptive at some times than at others. Fortunately, such fluctuations usually fall within some consistent range, permitting the researcher to establish a pattern or range of student baseline performance. We might observe, for example, that the child normally exhibits 5 to 10 disruptive behaviors during a 30-minute period. These figures then become our basis of comparison for assessing the effectiveness of the treatment. If during the treatment phase the number of disruptive behaviors ranges from, say, 0 to 3, or steadily decreases until it reaches 0, and if the number of disruptive behaviors increases when treatment is withdrawn, the effectiveness of the treatment is demonstrated.

The existence of a trend can affect the number of baseline data points needed. If the baseline behavior is observed to be getting progressively worse, fewer measurements are required to establish the baseline pattern. If, on the other hand, the baseline behavior is getting progressively better, there is no point in introducing the treatment until, or unless, the behavior stabilizes. Three data points are usually considered the minimum number of measurements necessary to establish baseline stability, but as noted, more than three are often required. Normally, the length of the treatment phase and the number of measurements taken during the treatment phase should parallel the length and measurements of the baseline phase. If baseline stability is established after 10 observation periods, then the treatment phase should include 10 observation periods.

The Single Variable Rule

An important principle of single-subject research is the **single variable rule,** which states that only one variable at a time should be manipulated. In other words, as we move from phase to phase only one variable should be added or withdrawn at any phase. Sometimes an attempt is made to simultaneously manipulate two variables to assess their interactive effects. This is not sound practice in single-subject designs because it prevents us from assessing adequately the effects of either variable.

TYPES OF SINGLE-SUBJECT DESIGNS

Single-subject designs are classified into three major categories: A-B-A withdrawal, multiple-baseline, and alternating treatments designs. A-B-A designs involve alternating phases of baseline (A) and treatment (B). Multiple-baseline designs entail the systematic addition of behaviors, subjects, or settings for intervention. They are utilized mainly for cases in which a baseline cannot be recovered once treatment is introduced, and for cases in which treatment cannot or should not be withdrawn once it is applied. Alternating treatment designs involve the relatively rapid alternating of treatments for a single subject. Their purpose is to assess the relative effectiveness of two (or more) treatment conditions. This section describes these basic designs and some common variations.

A-B-A Withdrawal Designs

There are a number of variations of the basic A-B-A withdrawal design, the least complex of which is the **A-B design**. Although this design is an improvement over the simple **case study**, its internal validity is suspect. When this design is used, baseline measurements (O) are repeatedly made until stability is established. Then the treatment (X) is introduced and an appropriate number of measurements (O) are made during treatment implementation. If behavior improves during the treatment phase, the effectiveness of the treatment is allegedly demonstrated. The specific number of measurements involved in each phase will vary from experiment to experiment. We could symbolize this design as follows:

$$
\begin{array}{c|c}
\text{O   O   O   O} & \text{X   O   X   O   X   O   X   O} \\
\text{baseline phase} & \text{treatment phase} \\
\text{A} & \text{B}
\end{array}
$$

The problem with this design is that we don't know if behavior improved because of the treatment or for some other nontreatment reason. It is possible that the observed behavior change occurred as a result of some other, unknown variable or that the behavior would have improved naturally without the treatment. Using an **additive design** (as discussed in the following subsections) improves the researcher's ability to make such determinations.

The A-B-A Design.   By simply adding a second baseline phase to the A-B design we get a much improved design, the **A-B-A design.** If the behavior is better during the treatment phase than during either baseline phase, the effectiveness of the treatment has been demonstrated. Symbolically, we can represent this design in the following way:

$$
\begin{array}{c|c|c}
\text{O   O   O   O} & \text{X   O   X   O   X   O   X   O} & \text{O   O   O   O} \\
\text{baseline} & \text{treatment} & \text{baseline} \\
\text{phase} & \text{phase} & \text{phase} \\
\text{A} & \text{B} & \text{A}
\end{array}
$$

During the initial baseline phase we might observe on-task behaviors during 5 observation sessions. We might then introduce tangible reinforcement in the form of small toys for on-task behaviors and observe on-task behaviors during 5 observation periods in the treatment phase. Lastly, we might stop the tangible reinforcement and observe on-task behaviors during an additional 5 sessions. If on-task behavior was greater during the treatment phase, we would conclude that the tangible reinforcement was the probable cause. A variation on this design is the **changing criterion design**, in which the baseline phase is followed by successive treatment phases, each of which has a more stringent criterion for acceptable (improved) behavior.

The impact of positive reinforcement on the attending behavior of an easily distracted 9-year-old boy was studied using the A-B-A designs.[5] A reinforcement program was developed for the student. Prior to actual data collection, observer training was conducted until interrater reliability was .90 or above for 5 randomly selected attending behavior observations of 10 minutes each. Figure 13.6 shows the three stages of the design: baseline, treatment, and baseline. Each dot represents a data collection point. The reinforcement program established for the student improved his attending behaviors a great deal compared to the initial baseline. When the treatment was removed, attending behavior decreased, demonstrating the effectiveness of the reinforcement program.

---

[5]Walker, H. M., and Buckley, N. K. (1968). The use of positive reinforcement in conditioning attending behavior. *Journal of Applied Behavior Analysis, 1*(3), 245–250.

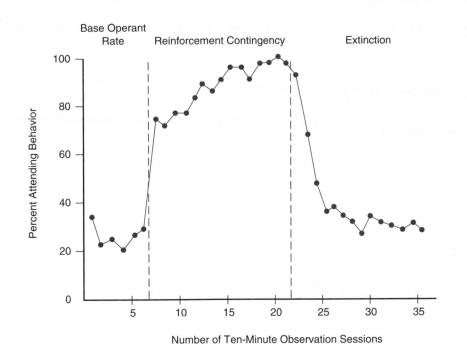

FIGURE 13.6

Percentage of attending behavior of a subject during successive observation periods in a study utilizing an A-B-A design.

Source: Reprinted from Walker, H. M., and Buckley, N. K. (1968). The use of positive reinforcement in conditioning attending behavior. *Journal of Applied Behavior Analysis, 1*(3), 247. Reprinted by permission.

It should be noted that there is some terminology confusion in the literature concerning A-B-A designs. A-B-A withdrawal designs are frequently referred to as *reversal designs,* which they are not, since treatment is generally withdrawn following baseline assessment, not reversed. You should be alert to this distinction.

The internal validity of the A-B-A design is superior to that of the A-B design. With the A B design it is possible that behaviors improved without treatment intervention. It is very unlikely, however, that behavior would coincidentally improve during the treatment phase and coincidentally deteriorate during the subsequent baseline phase, as is the case in A-B-A designs. The major problem with this design is an ethical one, since the experiment ends with the subject not receiving the treatment. Of course if the treatment has not been shown to be effective, there is no problem. But if it has been found to be beneficial, the desirability of removing it is questionable.

A variation of the A-B-A design that eliminates this problem is the B-A-B design, which involves a treatment phase (B), a withdrawal phase (A), and a return to treatment phase (B). Although this design provides an experiment that ends with the subject receiving treatment, the lack of an initial baseline phase makes it very difficult to assess the effectiveness of the treatment. Some studies have involved a short baseline phase prior to application of the B-A-B design, but this strategy only approximates a better solution, which is application of an A-B-A-B design.

The A-B-A-B Design.   The **A-B-A-B design** is the A-B-A design with the addition of a second treatment phase. Not only does this design overcome ethical objections to the A-B-A design, it also greatly strengthens the research conclusions by demonstrating the effects of the treatment twice. If treatment effects are essentially the same during both treatment phases, the possibility that the effects are a result of extraneous variables is greatly reduced. The A-B-A-B design can be symbolized as follows:

O O O O | X O X O X O X O | O O O O | X O X O X O X O
baseline phase A | treatment phase B | baseline phase A | treatment phase B

When application of this design is feasible, it provides very convincing evidence of treatment effectiveness.

Figure 13.7 shows a hypothetical example of the A-B-A-B design. The figure shows the summarized results of five days of observations in each of the four design phases. Baseline A_1 shows the student's average talking out behavior for a five-day period. Treatment B_1 shows the effect of a reinforcement program designed to diminish talking out behavior. The figure shows that talking out behavior diminished greatly with the treatment. Baseline A_2 shows that removal of the treatment led to increased talking out behavior. The reintroduction of treatment B_2 again led to diminished talking out behavior. These patterns strongly suggest the efficacy of the treatment.

Multiple-Baseline Designs

Multiple-baseline designs are used when it is not possible to withdraw a treatment and have performance return to baseline. They are also used when a treatment can be withdrawn but the effects of the treatment "carry over" so that a return to baseline conditions is difficult or impossible. The effects of many treatments do not disappear when a treatment is removed (see Figure 13.3, pattern C). In many cases it is highly desirable for treatment effects to sustain. Reinforcement techniques, for example, are designed to produce improved behavior that will be maintained when external reinforcements are withdrawn.

The three basic types of multiple-baseline designs are across behaviors, across subjects, and across settings designs. With a **multiple-baseline design,** instead of collecting baseline data on one specific behavior, data are collected on (1) several behaviors for one subject, (2) one behavior for several subjects, or (3) one behavior and one subject in several settings. Then, over a period of time, the treatment is systematically applied to each behavior (or subject, or setting) one at a time until all behaviors (or subjects, or settings) are exposed to the treatment. The "multiple" part of a multiple-baseline design refers to the study of more than one behavior, subject, or setting. For example, a study might seek to sequentially change three

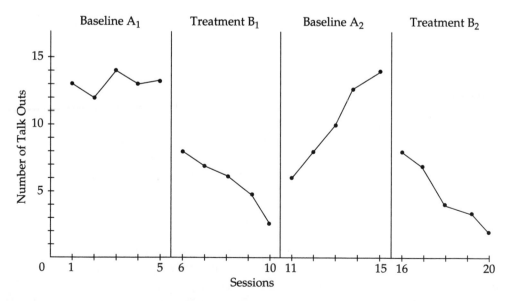

FIGURE 13.7 Talking out behavior during four 5-day observations of a student: baseline 1, treatment 1 (reinforcement program), baseline 2 (no treatment), and treatment 2 (reinforcement program).

different behaviors using the multiple-baseline design. If measured performance improves only after a treatment is introduced, then that treatment is judged to be effective. There are, of course, variations that can be applied. We might, for example, collect data on one target behavior for several participants in several settings. In this case, performance for the group of participants in each setting would be summed or averaged, and results would be presented for the group as well as for each individual.

The multiple-baseline design can be symbolized as follows:

behavior 1   O O OXOXOXOXOXOXOXOXOXOXOXOXO
behavior 2   O O O O O OXOXOXOXOXOXOXOXOXO
behavior 3   O O O O O O O O OXOXOXOXOXOXO

In this example, a treatment was applied to three different behaviors, behavior 1 first, then behavior 2, and then behavior 3, until all three behaviors were under treatment. If measured performance improved for each behavior only after the treatment was introduced, the treatment would be judged to be effective. We could symbolize examination of different participants or settings in the same manner. In all cases, the more behaviors, subjects, or settings involved, the more convincing the evidence is for the effectiveness of the treatment. What constitutes a sufficient minimum number of replications, however, is another issue. While some investigators believe that four or more are necessary, three replications are generally accepted to be an adequate minimum.

When applying treatments across behaviors, it is important that the behaviors be independent of one another. If we apply treatment to behavior 1, behaviors 2 and 3 should remain at baseline levels. If the other behaviors change when behavior 1 is treated, the design is not valid for assessing treatment effectiveness. When applying treatment across participants, they should be as similar as possible (matched on key variables such as age and gender), and the experimental setting should be as identical as possible for each participant. When applying treatment across settings, it is preferable that the settings be natural, not artificial. We might, for example, systematically apply a treatment (e.g., tangible reinforcement) to successive class periods. Or we might apply the treatment first in a clinical setting, then at school, and then at home. Sometimes it is necessary, due to the nature of the target behavior, to evaluate the treatment in a contrived, or simulation, setting. The target behavior may be an important one, but one which does not often occur naturally. For example, if we are teaching a child who is mentally challenged how to behave in various emergency situations (e.g., fires, injuries, intruders), simulated settings may be the only feasible approach.

Figure 13.8 shows a study using a hypothetical multiple-baseline design. The treatment, a program for improving social awareness, was applied to three behaviors: (1) social behaviors, (2) seeking help, and (3) handling criticism. The figure shows that performance increased for each of the three behaviors, after each treatment, thus indicating that the treatment was effective.

Although multiple-baseline designs are generally used when there is a problem with returning to baseline conditions, they also can be used very effectively for situations in which baseline conditions are recoverable. We could, for example, target talking out behavior, out-of-seat behavior, and aggressive behavior, which over time could return to baseline conditions. If we applied an A-B-A design within a multiple-baseline framework, the result could be symbolized as follows:

talking out behavior   A-B-A-A-A
out-of-seat behavior   A-A-B-A-A
aggressive behavior   A-A-A-B-A

or

talking out behavior   O O OXOXOXO O O O O O O O O O
out-of-seat behavior   O O O O O OXOXOXO O O O O O O
aggressive behavior   O O O O O O O O OXOXOXO O O O

FIGURE 13.8
Multiple-baseline
analysis of social
awareness training on
a student's social
behaviors, seeking help,
and handling criticism.

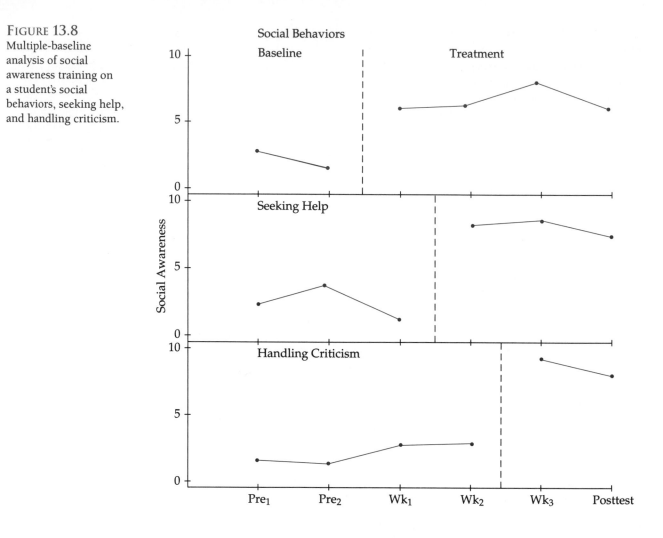

Such a design would combine the best features of the A-B-A and the multiple-baseline design and would provide very convincing evidence regarding treatment effects. In essence it would represent three replications of an A-B-A experiment. Whenever baseline is recoverable and there are no carryover effects, any of the A-B-A designs can be applied within a multiple-baseline framework.

Alternating Treatments Design

The **alternating treatments design** is very useful in assessing the relative effectiveness of two (or more) treatments, in a single-subject context. While the alternating treatments design has many names (multiple schedule design, multi-element baseline design, multi-element manipulation design, and simultaneous treatment design), there is some consensus that "alternating treatments" most accurately describes the nature of the design. The name of the design describes what it involves, namely, the relatively rapid alternation of treatments for a single subject. The qualifier *relatively* is attached to *rapid* because alternation does not necessarily occur within fixed intervals of time. If a child with behavior problems saw a therapist who used an alternating treatment design every Tuesday, the design would

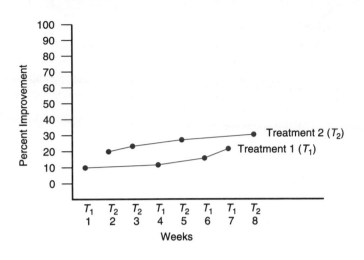

FIGURE 13.9

Hypothetical example of
an alternating treatments
design comparing
treatments T_1 and T_2.

Source: Reprinted from Barlow,
D. M., and Hersen, M. (1992).
*Single case experimental designs:
Strategies for studying behavior
change*, p. 254. Boston, Allyn &
Bacon. Reprinted by permission.

require that on some Tuesdays the child would receive one treatment (e.g., verbal rein-forcement), and on other Tuesdays another treatment (e.g., tangible reinforcement). The treatments (call them T_1 and T_2) would not be alternated in a regular, ordered pattern (T_1-T_2-T_1-T_2). Rather, to avoid potential validity threats, the treatments would be alternated on a random basis, e.g., T_1-T_2-T_2-T_1-T_2-T_1-T_1-T_2. Figure 13.9 illustrates this random appli-cation of two treatments. In this example, treatment T_2 appears to be more effective for this participant than T_1, since the data points are consistently higher for treatment T_2 than for T_1. To determine whether T_2 would be more effective for other participants would require replication.

This design has several pluses that make it attractive to investigators. First, no withdrawal is necessary; thus, if one treatment is found to be more effective, it may be continued. Second, no baseline phase is necessary since we are usually attempting to determine which treatment is more effective, not whether a treatment is better than no treatment. Another major advan-tage is that a number of treatments can be studied more quickly and efficiently than with other designs. However, one potential problem with this design is multiple-treatment interference—that is, carryover effects from one treatment to the other.

DATA ANALYSIS AND INTERPRETATION

Data analysis in single-subject research typically is based on visual inspection and analysis of a graphic presentation of results. First, an evaluation is made concerning the adequacy of the design. Second, assuming a sufficiently valid design, an assessment of treatment effectiveness is made. The primary criterion of effectiveness is typically clinical significance, not statistical significance. Clinical effects that are small may not be large enough to make a sufficient dif-ference in the behavior of a participant. As an example, suppose the participant is an 8-year-old male who exhibits dangerous, aggressive behavior toward other children. A treatment that produced a 5% reduction in such behavior may be statistically significant, but it is clearly not clinically significant. There are a number of statistical analyses available to the single-subject researcher, including t and F tests (to be discussed in Chapter 15). Whether statistical tests should be used in single-subject research is currently debated. To date, they have not been widely used in this type of research.

REPLICATION

Replication is a vital part of all research and especially for single-subject research, since initial findings are generally based on one or a small number of participants. The more results are replicated, the more confidence we have in the procedures that produced those results. This is true for all types of research. Replication also serves to establish the generalizability of findings by providing data about participants' behaviors and settings to which results are applicable. There are three basic types of replication of single-subject experiments: direct, systematic, and clinical. **Direct replication** refers to replication by the same investigator, with the same or different participants, in a specific setting (e.g., a classroom). Generalizability is promoted when replication is done with other participants who share the same problem, matched closely on relevant variables. When replication is done on a number of participants with the same problem, location, or time, the process is referred to as **simultaneous replication. Systematic replication** refers to replication that follows direct replication and that involves different investigators, behaviors, or settings. Over time, techniques are identified that are consistently effective in a variety of situations. We know, for example, that teacher attention can be a powerful factor in behavior change. At some point, enough data are amassed to permit the third stage of replication, clinical replication. **Clinical replication** involves the development of treatment packages, composed of two or more interventions that have been found to be effective individually, designed for persons with complex behavior disorders. Individuals with autism, for example, exhibit a number of characteristics, including apparent sensory deficit, mutism, and self-injurious behavior. Clinical replication would utilize research on each of these individually to develop a total program to apply to individuals with autism. Regardless of the type, replication is critically important in establishing the generalizability of single-subject research.

The following pages present an example of experimental research. See if you can figure out which experimental design was used. Hint: Students were randomly assigned to one of three treatment groups. Also, don't be concerned because you don't understand the statistics; focus on the problem, the procedures, and the conclusions.

Now go to the Companion Website accompanying this text at www.prenhall.com/gay to check your understanding of chapter concepts in the following modules: Objectives, Practice Quiz, and Applying What You Know. Expand your research skills with Evaluating Articles, Analyzing Qualitative Data, Analyzing Quantitative Data, and Research Tools and Tips. Visit Web Links to broaden your knowledge about research.

Effects of Word Processing on Sixth Graders' Holistic Writing and Revisions

GAIL F. GREJDA
Clarion University of Pennsylvania

MICHAEL J. HANNAFIN
Florida State University

ABSTRACT   The purpose of this study was to examine the effects of word processing on overall writing quality and revision patterns of sixth graders. Participants included 66 students who were randomly assigned to one of three revision treatments: paper and pencil, word processing, and a combination of the two techniques. Training in word processing was provided, and instruction was subsequently given during the 3-week study. The students were given a standard composition to revise and were also required to write and revise an original composition. Significant differences were found for both mechanical and organizational revisions in favor of the word-processing group. In addition, word-processing students tended to correct more first-draft errors and to make fewer new errors than their counterparts did. Although a similar pattern was found, no significant differences were discovered for holistic writing quality.

Interest in the potential of word processors to improve writing has grown substantially during the past decade. Various authorities have lauded the capability to increase writer productivity (Zaharias, 1983), to reduce the tediousness of recopying written work (Bean, 1983; Daiute, 1983; Moran, 1983), to increase the frequency of revising (Bridwell, Sirc, & Brooke, 1985; Daiute, 1986), and to improve both attitudes toward writing (Rodriguez, 1985) and the writing process (McKenzie, 1984; Olds, 1982). Some researchers have argued that word processors alter both individuals' writing styles and the methods used to teach writing (Bertram, Michaels, & Watson-Geges, 1985).

Yet, research findings on the effects of word processing have proved inconsistent (Fitzgerald, 1987). Some researchers have reported positive effects on writing (Daiute, 1985), whereas others have reported mixed effects (Wheeler, 1985). Although word processing seems to increase the frequency of revision, the revisions are often surface level and do little to improve the overall quality of composition (Collier, 1983; Hawisher, 1987). In some cases, word processing has actually hampered different aspects of writing (Grejda & Hannafin, in press; Perl, 1978).

However, comparatively little has been demonstrated conclusively. Attempts to study word processing have been confounded by both typing requirements and limited word-processing proficiency. Inadequate definition has also plagued word-processing research. Many studies have isolated only mechanical attributes of revision, such as punctuation, requiring only proofreading rather than sophisticated revision skills (Collier, 1983; Dalton & Hannafin, 1987). Other research has focused only on global writing measures, with little attribution possible for observed changes in writing quality (Boone, 1985; Woodruff, Bereiter, & Scardamalia, 1981–82). Both mechanical and holistic aspects of writing are important, but they are rarely considered concurrently (cf. Humes, 1983).

Although comparatively few studies have focused on young writers, the results have been encouraging. Daiute (1986) reported that junior high school students using word processors were more likely to expand their compositions, as well as to identify and correct existing errors, than were paper-and-pencil students. Likewise, word-processing students were more likely than paper-and-pencil students were to revise their language-experience stories (Barber, 1984; Bradley, 1982). Boone (1985) reported that the compositions of fourth, fifth, and sixth graders became increasingly sophisticated through revisions focusing on both mechanics and higher level organizations. In contrast, despite improving students' attitudes, word processing has failed to improve overall compositions based upon holistic ratings of writing quality (Woodruff, Bereiter, & Scardamalia, 1981–82).

The purpose of this study was to examine the effects of word processing on the holistic writing quality and revision patterns of sixth graders. We predicted that word processing would improve both the accuracy of revisions as well as the overall holistic quality of student writing.

METHODS

Subjects

The subjects included 66 sixth graders (23 girls and 43 boys), and 3 classroom teachers. The students were enrolled in a school in a rural university community. Overall language achievement of the participating students, based upon the Language Scale of the Stanford Achievement Test, was at the 79th percentile.

Address correspondence to Gail F. Grejda, Education Department, 110 Stevens Hall, Clarion University of Pennsylvania, Clarion, PA 16214.

Preliminary Training

Prior to the study, the sixth-grade teachers and the students in word-processing groups received 1 hour of word-processing training during each of 5 days. The *Bank Street Writer* was used because of its widespread availability and popularity among elementary school teachers. The training included entering text, deleting and inserting characters, capitalizing letters, moving the cursor, centering, indenting, making corrections, moving and returning blocks of text, erasing and unerasing, saving, retrieving, and printing. In addition, the purpose and design of the study, as well as procedural information and materials required, were presented.

Revision Instruction

An hour of daily instruction on mechanical and organizational revisions was provided for 10 days of the 3-week study. The instruction reviewed previously taught revision rules commonly found in sixth-grade language books and focused on errors typical of those in the compositions of young writers.

The first 5 days included instruction on five mechanical error categories: capitalization, commas, punctuation, possessive nouns, and sentence structure. Daily lessons included rules for the error category under consideration, pertinent examples of each rule, and a paragraph containing numerous violations of the rules that were subsequently identified and revised by the students. During the next 5 days, the subjects focused on revising the following organizational errors, phrasing the main idea, adding relevant detail sentences, deleting irrelevant sentences. sequencing or ordering sentences, and, finally, applying the rhetorical devices vital to paragraph unity and coherence.

Original Writing Sample

All the students were allotted 60 min to write an original composition on a given topic. The task was to describe a planned trip itinerary to Canada, a topic based on a recently completed unit of study. The writing sample was obtained to provide a unique composition for each student, and it was subsequently used to identify and to make needed revisions in individual writing. All the students used paper and pencil to create the initial compositions.

Standard Composition

A standard composition was developed to determine each student's ability to identify and revise typical mechanical and organizational errors. The writing yielded a common metric from which revision comparisons could be made across students. The composition contained 57 mechanical errors and eight organizational writing errors. The errors, violations of rules found in typical sixth-grade language books, required the application of rules stressed during the daily lessons.

Instructional Groups

The students were assigned to one of three groups, depending on how revisions were made: exclusively with computer word processing (C-C); exclusively with paper and pencil (P-P); or a combination of the two techniques (C-P). All the treatment groups received identical revision instruction.

In the C-C group, the students used word-processing software during all phases of the study. That group examined the influence of continuous access to word processing on student editing, revising, and writing quality. The students in the P-P treatment group used paper and pencil to make all revisions on both compositions throughout the 10 days of instruction. That group approximated writing without the aid of the word processor. In the C-P treatment, the students used a word processor to revise the 10 daily lessons and paper and pencil to revise the compositions. That method examined the potential transfer of word-processing skills to non-computer writing and approximated the circumstances encountered when word processors were provided for some, but not all, of a student's writing needs.

Design and Data Analysis

In this study we used a one-way design, featuring three word-processing groups: pencil-pencil (P-P), computer-computer (C-C), and computer-pencil (C-P). Individual scores on the Stanford Achievement Test–Language Scale were used as a covariate in the analysis to adjust for potential prestudy writing differences. In addition, because of the relatively high prior achievement in the sample (only 4 students scored below the 50th percentile on the language scale) and the high correlation between writing and general language, the use of the standardized test scores as a covariate in the analysis permitted greater precision in isolating true treatment effects. The highly significant effect for the covariate, paired with the nonsignificant preliminary test for homogeneity of slopes, further supported the analysis.

A one-way multivariate analysis of covariance (MANCOVA), with the four composition subscale scores and the holistic writing rating, was run to test for treatment group effects. Analysis of covariance (ANCOVA) procedures were subsequently executed for each measure: a priori contrasts were constructed to test for differences between the C-C group and each of the other word-processing groups. The remaining scores were used to provide descriptive data related to revision strategies.

Procedures

Regularly assigned sixth-grade classroom teachers were presented an overview of the purpose and design of the study, procedural information, and required materials. The students were randomly assigned to one of the three treatment groups. The students and teachers in both word-processing groups (C-C and C-P) were then given word-processing training.

The students in each group were allotted 60 min to write their original composition. All students wrote the preliminary composition with pencil and paper. The compositions of students in the C-C group were subsequently entered electronically by a typist, because those students were required to revise the writing via word processing.

Next, instruction on revising mechanical and organizational writing error categories was provided. Each lesson included rules for the error category under consideration, pertinent examples of each rule, and a paragraph containing violations of the rules to be identified and revised by the students. After discussing the rules and examples of applications, the students revised the given paragraph, using their designated writing instrument. Upon completion, the students were given an errorless copy of the paragraph and were instructed to correct any existing errors. On subsequent days the subjects followed the same format, each day focusing on another of the mechanical and organizational error categories. During the study, the first author scheduled regular conferences with the classroom teachers to ensure compliance with current instruction topics as well as to preview upcoming lessons. In addition, the first author randomly rotated among the classes to ensure that planned activities were implemented as scheduled.

After the 10 daily lessons were completed, the students revised both the standard composition and the original composition. On the standard composition, students were allotted 60 min to revise mechanical errors in capitalization, punctuation, commas, possessive nouns, sentence structure, and organizational errors, including rephrasing the main idea, adding relevant detail sentences, deleting irrelevant sentences, sequencing sentences, and applying rhetorical devices vital to paragraph unity and coherence. None of the mechanical or organizational errors were cued in any way. The score for each measure was a percentage of the number of correct revisions to the total possible errors (57 mechanical, 8 organizational) on the standard composition.

The students were also provided 60 min to revise the mechanical and organizational errors on their original composition. The number of possible errors varied in each student's composition, so percentage correction scores were derived to account for differences in the number of mechanical and organizational errors. The score was a percentage of the correct revisions versus the total number of initial mechanical and organizational errors on the students' original composition.

Each original composition was then evaluated holistically for overall writing quality based on the procedures developed by Myers (1980) and Potkewitz (1984). Three trained composition instructors, experienced in both process writing and holistic scoring, served as raters; none of them were participants in the study. Each composition was evaluated "blind" by at least two of the raters by comparing the works to a rubric consisting of six competency levels ranging from lowest (1) to highest (6). If the two ratings were within one point of one another, the ratings were summed to yield a total rating score. If discrepancies of greater than one point were found, the third evaluator rated the composition independently, and the most discrepant rating of the three was discarded. Interrater agreement, based upon the percentage of rating pairs identical or within one point of one another, was .91. Discrepancies of more than one point in the initial ratings occurred on only 6 of the 66 compositions.

The students inadvertently introduced additional errors in their revisions, so new errors in the final compositions were also tallied. New errors, mechanical as well as organizational, were computed beyond those provided in the standard composition or generated by the students in the original composition. The errors were tallied according to the same criteria established for mistakes in the standard and original compositions.

Finally, revisions on both the standard and original compositions were classified to examine the nature of editorial revisions made by different writing groups. The instructors tallied word insertions and deletions, sentence insertions and deletions, sentences moved, sentence fragments and run-on-sentences inserted, and sentence fragments or run-on sentences corrected.

All compositions were typed, printed, coded, and randomized to prevent rater bias. In addition, that step allowed the students to work with comparably "clean" copies, and equalized the time spent revising versus recopying: To isolate specific revision skills without the confounding of either excessive typing or manual recopying, we provided the students with typed versions of their work.

RESULTS

The means for each of the subscales, adjusted for the influence of the covariate, are contained in Table 1. The one-way MANCOVA revealed a significant difference among word-processing groups, $F(2, 62) = 9.28, p < .001$. ANCOVA results, shown in Table 2, revealed a significant difference among treatment groups for all scales except for the mechanical revisions on the original composition.

Table 1.
Adjusted Percentage Means for Composition Subscales

Source	C-C	C-P	P-P
Standard composition			
Mechanical revisions	74.86	68.59	68.23
Organizational revisions	81.14	58.82	66.18
Original composition			
Mechanical revisions	57.32	42.91	45.00
Organizational revisions	63.64	48.55	42.73

Table 2.
ANCOVA Source Data for Composition Subscales

Source	df	M	F	p<
Standard composition				
Mechanical revisions				
Covariate (prior achievement)	1	7,915.55	76.11	.0001
Writing group	2	459.58	4.42	.016
Error	62	104.00		
Organizational revisions				
Covariate (prior achievement)	1	8,463.83	13.62	.0001
Writing group	2	3,353.83	5.40	.007
Error	62	621.48		
Original composition				
Mechanical revisions				
Covariate (prior achievement)	1	5,156.74	6.27	.015
Writing group	2	1,590.89	1.93	nsd
Error	62	822.93		
Organizational revisions				
Covariate (prior achievement)	1	5,027.33	7.69	.007
Writing group	2	2,818.37	4.31	.018
Error	62	653.86		

A priori contrasts for each significant difference indicated that the C-C students corrected a higher percentage of mechanical and organizational errors than the C-P or P-P groups did, on both the standard and original compositions (min. $p < .05$ in each case). No differences were found between the C-P and P-P groups for any of the subscales. In addition, although not statistically significant, the performance pattern for the mechanical revisions on original compositions was similar to the other subscales, with the C-C group performing best.

A profile of revision errors is shown in Table 3. The C-C word-processing group made fewer new mechanical and organizational errors than the other groups on both the standard and the original compositions. The C-C students also made fewer new errors on their own compositions. Paper-and-pencil and mixed-writing groups corrected a comparable percentage of organizational errors on both compositions.

Table 3.
Frequency of New Errors Introduced
During Final Revision

Revision type	C-C	C-P	P-P
Original			
Mechanical	12	20	39
Organizational	2	45	56
Standard			
Mechanical	0	7	12
Organizational	5	38	43

Table 4.
Revision Types for Original and Standard Compositions

Revision activity	C-C	C-P	P-P
Original composition			
Words inserted	167	52	31
Words deleted	13	9	17
Sentences inserted	121	47	64
Sentences deleted	9	14	3
Sentences moved	27	3	0
Sentence fragments/run-on sentences inserted	2	19	13
Sentence fragments/run-on sentences corrected	26	12	18
Standard composition			
Words inserted	9	0	0
Words deleted	0	15	23
Sentences inserted	0	1	0
Sentences deleted	59	43	38
Sentences moved	31	3	0
Sentence fragments/run-on sentences inserted	0	4	5
Sentence fragments/run-on sentences corrected	37	29	23

Revision patterns, summarized in Table 4, suggest different strategies among the three groups. On the original composition, word-processing students inserted more words and sentences, moved more sentences, and corrected more sentence fragments or run-on sentences than did students in the remaining groups. On the standard composition, word-processing students were more likely to insert words and move sentences, but less likely to delete words, than their counterparts.

Students in all groups revised the standard composition more effectively than their original compositions; that was true for both mechanical and organizational revisions. Comparatively few new mechanical and organization errors were made by the word-processing students, whereas new errors were substantially more common for the other writing groups.

Although adjusted means for holistic ratings fell in the predicted direction, there were only marginal differences in overall writing quality, $F(2, 62) = 2.31, p > .107$. Computer word-processing students (6.36) and the mixed-treatment group (6.27) were marginally higher than the paper-and-pencil group (5.00).

DISCUSSION

Several findings warrant further discussion. Consistent with much research on revising (Bridwell, Sirc, & Brooke, 1985; Daiute, 1986), word-processing students performed consistently better than other students did. Those students were more successful in revising existing as well as original writing, and they made more revisions to their work. In the present study, face evidence for improving editing via word processing is strong.

Yet, consistent with other researchers (Collier, 1983; Hawisher, 1987), overall quality did not improve significantly. Though word-processing groups performed marginally better than the paper-and-pencil group did, reliable differences were not detected. Despite strong evidence that mechanical and organizational revisions improved significantly, holistic writing quality was only marginally affected. Overall quality improvements may require substantially more time to develop (Riel, 1984). Word processing may, in the absence of concerted efforts to offset the tendency, inadvertently direct proportionately more attention to structural than holistic aspects of writing. Structural skills are important and yield the most visible features of composition, but they do not, by themselves, ensure improvement in the holistic quality of compositions (Flower & Hayes, 1981).

Editing is a necessary, but not sufficient, skill for effective writing (cf. Hodges, 1982; Sommers, 1980). The conceptual aspects of holistic writing, although not diminished in our study by word processing, require more than simple mechanical and even organizational changes in written products (Hairston, 1986; Humes, 1983; Kintsch & van Dijk, 1978). Yet, word processors seem to bias students toward mechanical editing. A spelling or capitalization error is substantially more apparent than an error of logic, argumentation, or internal inconsistency. Process-writing advocates promote recursive methods in the teaching of writing—methods designed to promote writer-level problem solving in their expression. Though such goals are likely attainable and supportable through well-constructed writing-via-word-processing efforts, they are less likely to be supported directly in typical word-processing software. Mechanical improvements may be necessary to overall quality, but they are clearly insufficient when emphasized exclusively.

Contrary to the findings of some researchers (Bartlett, 1982), more revisions were made and a higher proportion of initial errors were detected on the standard composition than on the original composition. That finding is not surprising because the standard composition was essentially an editing task. On the other hand, the students were more likely to embellish their own compositions by inserting words and sentences. In this study, in which we used both types of composition, different revision patterns clearly emerged for student- versus instructor-generated compositions.

In contrast to the findings of others, the students in this study focused principally on in-text revisions, and they made few new additions during revisions. Daiute (1986) noted that word-processing students appended words to their text rather than making corrections within the text. In this study, however, word-processing students made both mechanical and organizational revisions throughout the text. They also corrected more first-draft errors and made fewer new errors than did students in the other treatment groups. The emphasis on identifying and revising in-text errors rather than on adding new text during the instructional phase of the study might account for that difference.

Various authorities have expressed concern that providing writing instruction exclusively via word processors may ultimately interfere with conventional writing (Keifer & Smith, 1983). The rationale has been that students develop writing strategies that are dependent upon technological capabilities of limited accessibility. The combined word-processing and paper-and-pencil group was designed to test the transfer of revision skills developed via word processing to traditional writing tools. Consistent with previous research (Grejda & Hannafin, in press), intermittent word processing neither improved nor impeded transfer to paper-and-pencil formats.

Several other aspects of the present study are noteworthy. The initial training provided to both students and teachers, paired with control of supporting instruction, permitted increased precision in localizing those effects reasonably attributable to word processing. The short-term effects of word processing appear most pronounced for structural revisions; the long-term effects on both structural and holistic aspects remain unproved. Likewise, examining revision skills on both standard and student-generated compositions allowed us to focus on both specific editing and the constructive aspects of process writing.

Considerable work is needed to refine both research methods and instructional practices. Keyboarding, although not a major issue in our study, remains a concern. Young students can be trained nominally, but few of them actually develop proficiency. Daiute (1983) suggested that sustained word-processing training, for as much as 1 year, may be needed before sufficient technical proficiency is acquired to improve writing. In addition, the potential antagonism between the structural versus holistic approaches to word processing is troublesome. Methods designed to optimize both are needed, but the present findings suggest that one often benefits at the expense of the other.

From a research perspective, we have not generated clear-cut answers but, rather, clarifications regarding the relevant questions and needed methods of study. Neither writing nor the tools available to improve writing are likely to be advanced appreciably through studies that simplify complex processes artificially or control everyday factors unrealistically. From an academic perspective, educators must temper the enthusiasm for technologies and tools of such high-face validity with the sobering reality that a word processor "does not a writer make."

REFERENCES

Barber, B. (1984). Creating Bytes of language. *Language Arts, 59*, 472–475.

Bartlett, E. J. (1982). Learning to revise. In M. Nystrand (Ed.), *What writers know* (pp. 345–363). New York: Academic Press.

Bean, H. C. (1983). Computerized word processing as an aid to revision. *College Composition and Communication, 34*, 146–148.

Bertram, B., Michaels, S., & Watson-Geges, K. (1985). How computers can change the writing process. *Language Arts, 2*, 143–149.

Boone, R. A. (1985). *The revision processes of elementary school students who write using a word processing computer program.* Unpublished doctoral dissertation. University of Oregon, Eugene, OR.

Bradley, V. (1982). Improving students' writing with microcomputers. *Language Arts, 59*, 732–743.

Bridwell, L., Sirc, G., & Brooke, R. (1985). Revising and computing: Case studies of student writers. In S. W. Fredman (Ed.), *The acquisition of written language: Response and revision* (pp. 172–194). Norwood, NJ: Ablex.

Collier, R. M. (1983). The word processor and revision strategies. *College Composition and Communication, 34*, 149–155.

Daiute, C. (1983). The computer as stylus and audience. *College Composition and Communication, 34*, 134–145.

Daiute, C. (1985). *Writing and computers.* Reading, MA: Addison-Wesley.

Daiute, C. (1986). Physical and cognitive factors in revising: Insights from studies with computers. *Research in the Teaching of English, 20*, 141–159.

Dalton, D., & Hannafin, M. J. (1987). The effects of word processing on written composition. *Journal of Educational Research, 80*, 338–342.

Fitzgerald, J. (1987). Research on revision in writing. *Review of Educational Research, 57*(4), 481–506.

Flower, L., & Hayes, J. (1981). A cognitive process theory of writing. *College Composition and Communication, 32*, 365–387.

Grejda, G. F., & Hannafin, M. J. (in press). The influence of word processing on the revisions of fifth graders. *Computers in the Schools.*

Hairston, M. (1986). Different products, different processes: A theory about writing. *College Composition and Communication, 37*, 12.

Hawisher, G. (1987). The effects of word processing on the revision strategies of college freshmen. *Research in the Teaching of English, 21*, 145–159.

Hodges, K. (1982). A history of revision: Theory versus practice. In R. Sudol (Ed.), *Revising: New essays for teachers of writing* (pp. 24–42). Urbana, IL: National Council of Teachers of English.

Humes, A. (1983). Research on the composing process. *Review of Educational Research, 53*, 201–216.

Keifer, K., & Smith, C. (1983). Textual analysis with computers: Tests of Bell Laboratories' computer software. *Research in the Teaching of English, 17*, 201–214.

Kintsch, W., & van Dijk, T. (1978). Toward a model of text comprehension and production. *Psychological Review, 85*, 363–394.

McKenzie, J. (1984). Accordion writing: Expository composition with the word processor. *English Journal, 73*, 56–58.

Moran, C. (1983). Word processing and the teaching of writing. *English Journal, 72*, 113–115.

Myers, M. (1980). *A procedure for writing assessment and holistic scoring.* Urbana, IL: National Council of Teachers of English.

Olds, H. (1982). Word processing: How will it shape the student as writer? *Classroom Computer News, 3*, 24–26.

Perl, S. (1979). The composing process of unskilled college writers. *Research in the Teaching of English, 13,* 317–336.

Potkewitz, R. (1984). *The effect of writing instruction on the written language proficiency of fifth and sixth grade pupils in remedial reading programs.* Unpublished doctoral dissertation.

Riel, M. M. (1984). *The computer chronicles newswire: A functional learning environment for acquiring skills.* Paper developed for Laboratory of Comparative Human Cognition, San Diego, CA.

Rodrigues, D. (1985). Computers and basic writers. *College Composition and Communication, 36,* 336–339.

Sommers, N. (1980). Revision strategies of student writers and experienced adult writers. *College Composition and Communication, 31,* 378–388.

Wheeler, F. (1985). "Can word processing help the writing process?" *Learning, 3,* 54–62.

Woodruff, E., Bereiter, C., & Scardamalia, M. (1981–82). On the road to computer-assisted composition. *Journal of Educational Technology Systems, 10,* 133–148.

Zaharias, J. (1983). Microcomputers in the language arts classroom: Promises and pitfalls. *Language Arts, 60,* 990–995.

Grejda, G. F., & Hannafin, M. J. (1992). Effects of word processing on sixth graders' holistic writing and revisions. The Journal of Educational Research, 85, 144–149. Reprinted with the permission of the Helen Dwight Reid Educational Foundation. Published by Heldref Publications, 1319 Eighteenth St., N.W., Washington, DC 20036-1802, Copyright © 1992.

SUMMARY

Experimental Research: Definition and Purpose

1. In an experimental study, the researcher manipulates at least one independent variable, controls other relevant variables, and observes the effect on one or more dependent variables.

2. The independent variable, also called the experimental variable, the cause, or the treatment, is that process or activity believed to make a difference in performance. The dependent variable, also called the criterion variable, effect, or posttest, is the outcome of the study, the measure of the change or difference resulting from manipulation of the independent variable.

3. When conducted well, experimental studies produce the soundest evidence concerning hypothesized cause–effect relationships.

The Experimental Process

4. The steps in an experimental study are basically the same as for other types of research: selecting and defining a problem, selecting participants and measuring instruments, selecting a design, executing procedures, analyzing data, and formulating conclusions.

5. An experimental study is guided by at least one hypothesis that states an expected causal relationship between two treatment variables.

6. In an experimental study, the researcher forms or selects the groups, decides what treatments each group receives, controls extraneous variables, and observes or measures the effect on the groups at the end of the study.

7. The experimental group typically receives a new, or novel, treatment, while the control group either receives a different treatment or is treated as usual.

8. The two groups that are to receive different treatments are equated on all other variables that might be related to performance on the dependent variable.

9. After the groups have been exposed to the treatment for some period, the researcher administers the dependent variable and then determines whether there is a significant difference between the groups.

Manipulation and Control

10. Direct manipulation by the researcher of at least one independent variable is the one single characteristic that differentiates experimental research from other types of research.

11. The three different forms of the independent variable are presence versus absence (A versus no A), presence in varying degrees (a lot of A versus a little A), and presence of one kind versus presence of another kind (A versus B).

12. *Control* refers to efforts to remove the influence of any variable (other than the independent variable) that might affect performance on the dependent variable.

13. Two different kinds of variables need to be controlled: subject variables, on which subjects in the different groups might differ, and environmental variables, which might cause unwanted differences between groups.

Threats to Experimental Validity

14. Any uncontrolled extraneous variables that affect performance on the dependent variable are threats to the validity of an experiment. An experiment is valid if results obtained are due only to the manipulated independent variable, and if they are generalizable to situations outside the experimental setting.

15. Internal validity is concerned with ensuring that observed differences on the dependent variable are a direct result of manipulation of the independent variable, not some other variable. External validity is concerned with ensuring that results are generalizable to groups and environments outside the experimental setting.

16. The researcher must strive for a balance between control and realism, but if a choice is involved, the researcher should err on the side of control.

Threats to Internal Validity

17. History refers to the occurrence of an event that is not part of the experimental treatment but that may affect performance on the dependent variable.

18. Maturation refers to physical or mental changes that may occur within participants over a period of time. These changes may affect participants' performance on the measure of the dependent variable.

19. Testing refers to improved scores on a posttest resulting from participants having taken a pretest.

20. Instrumentation refers to unreliability, or lack of consistency, in measuring instruments that may result in invalid assessment of performance.

21. Statistical regression usually occurs when participants are selected on the basis of their extreme scores

and refers to the tendency of participants who score highest on a pretest to score lower on a posttest, and of those who score lowest on a pretest to score higher on a posttest.

22. Differential selection usually occurs when already formed groups are used and refers to the fact that the groups may be different before the study begins, and this initial difference influences posttest differences.

23. Mortality, or attrition, refers to the fact that participants who drop out of a study may alter the characteristics of the treatment groups.

24. Selection may also interact with factors such as maturation, history, and testing. This means that if already formed groups are used, one group may profit more (or less) from a treatment or have an initial advantage (or disadvantage) because of maturation, history, or testing factors.

Threats to External Validity

25. Threats affecting to whom research results can be generalized are called threats to external validity.

26. Pretest–treatment interaction occurs when subjects respond or react differently to a treatment because they have been pretested.

27. Posttest sensitization refers to the possibility that treatment effects may be affected by giving a pretest. The pretest may provide information that influences the posttest results.

28. Multiple-treatment interference can occur when the same subjects receive more than one treatment in succession and when the carryover effects from an earlier treatment influence a later treatment.

29. Selection–treatment interaction occurs when subjects are not randomly selected for treatments. Interaction effects aside, the very fact that subjects are not randomly selected from a population severely limits the researcher's ability to generalize since representativeness of the sample is in question.

30. Specificity is a threat to generalizability when the treatment variables are not clearly operationalized, making it unclear to whom the variable generalizes.

31. Generalizability of results may be affected by short-term or long-term events that occur while the study is taking place. This potential threat is referred to as interaction of history and treatment effects.

32. Interaction of time of measurement and treatment effects results from the fact that posttesting may yield different results depending on when it is done.

33. Passive and active researcher bias or expectations can influence participants. Examples of experimenter effects are when the researcher affects participants' behavior or is unintentionally biased when scoring different treatment groups.

34. Reactive arrangements refer to a number of factors associated with participants performing atypically because they are aware of being in a study. The Hawthorne, John Henry, and novelty effects are examples of reactive arrangements.

35. The placebo effect is sort of the antidote for the Hawthorne and John Henry effects. Its application in educational research is that all groups in an experiment should appear to be treated the same.

Group Experimental Designs

36. The validity of an experiment is a direct function of the degree to which extraneous variables are controlled. Participant variables include organismic variables and intervening variables. Organismic variables are characteristics of the subject, or organism (such as gender), which cannot be directly controlled, but that can be controlled for.

37. Intervening variables intervene between the independent variable and the dependent variable (such as anxiety or boredom), which cannot be directly observed or controlled, but that can be controlled for.

Control of Extraneous Variables

38. Randomization is the best single way to control for extraneous variables. Randomization is effective in creating equivalent, representative groups that are essentially the same on all relevant variables thought of by the researcher, and probably even a few not thought of. Randomly formed groups are a characteristic unique to experimental research; they are a control factor not possible with causal–comparative research.

39. Randomization should be used whenever possible; participants should be randomly selected from a population and be randomly assigned to groups, and treatments should be randomly assigned to groups.

40. Certain environmental variables can be controlled by holding them constant for all groups. Controlling subject variables is critical.

41. Matching is a technique for equating groups. The most commonly used approach to matching involves random assignment of pair members, one member to each group.

42. A major problem with such matching is that there are invariably subjects who do not have a match and must be eliminated from the study. One way to combat loss of subjects is to match less closely. A related

procedure is to rank all of the subjects, from highest to lowest, based on their scores on the control variable; each two adjacent scores constitute a pair.

43. Another way of controlling an extraneous variable is to compare groups that are homogeneous with respect to that variable. A similar but more satisfactory approach is to form subgroups representing all levels of the control variable.

44. If the researcher is interested not just in controlling the variable but also in seeing if the independent variable affects the dependent variable differently at different levels of the control variable, the best approach is to build the control variable right into the design.

45. Using participants as their own controls involves exposing the same group to the different treatments, one treatment at a time.

46. The analysis of covariance is a statistical method for equating randomly formed groups on one or more variables. It adjusts scores on a dependent variable for initial differences on some other variable related to the dependent variable.

Types of Group Designs

47. Selection of a given design dictates such factors as whether there will be a control group, whether subjects will be randomly assigned to groups, whether each group will be pretested, and how resulting data will be analyzed.

48. Different designs are appropriate for testing different types of hypotheses, and designs vary widely in the degree to which they control the various threats to internal and external validity. From the designs that are appropriate and feasible, you select the one that controls the most sources of internal and external invalidity.

49. There are two major classes of experimental designs: single-variable designs, which involve one independent variable (which is manipulated), and factorial designs, which involve two or more independent variables (at least one of which is manipulated).

50. Single-variable designs are classified as pre-experimental, true experimental, or quasi-experimental, depending on the control they provide for sources of internal and external invalidity. Pre-experimental designs do not do a very good job of controlling threats to validity and should be avoided. True experimental designs represent a very high degree of control and are always to be preferred. Quasi-experimental designs do not control as well as true experimental designs but do a much better job than the pre-experimental designs.

51. Factorial designs are basically elaborations of true experimental designs and permit investigation of two or more variables, individually and in interaction with each other.

Pre-Experimental Designs

52. The one-shot case study involves one group that is exposed to a treatment (X) and then posttested (O). None of the threats to validity that are relevant is controlled.

53. The one-group pretest-posttest design involves one group that is pretested (O), exposed to a treatment (X), and posttested (O). It controls several sources of invalidity not controlled by the one-shot case study, but additional factors are not controlled.

54. The static-group comparison involves at least two groups; one receives a new, or unusual, treatment and both groups are posttested. Since participants are not randomly assigned to groups, and since there is no pretest data, it is difficult to determine just how equivalent the treatment groups are.

True Experimental Designs

55. True experimental designs control for nearly all sources of internal and external invalidity. True experimental designs have one characteristic in common that none of the other designs has—random assignment of participants to groups. Ideally, participants should be randomly selected and randomly assigned to treatments.

56. All the true designs have a control group.

57. The pretest-posttest control group design involves at least two groups, both of which are formed by random assignment. Both groups are administered a pretest of the dependent variable; one group receives a new, or unusual, treatment; and both groups are posttested. The combination of random assignment and the presence of a pretest and a control group serves to control for all sources of internal invalidity.

58. The only definite weakness with this design is a possible interaction between the pretest and the treatment, which may make the results generalizable only to other pretested groups. A variation of this design involves random assignment of members of matched pairs to the groups to more closely control extraneous variables.

59. The posttest-only control group design is the same as the pretest-posttest control group design except there is no pretest. Participants are randomly assigned to groups, exposed to the independent variable, and posttested to determine the effectiveness of the treatment. The combination of random assignment and

the presence of a control group serves to control for all sources of invalidity except mortality, which is not controlled because of the absence of pretest data. A variation of this design is random assignment of matched pairs.

60. The Solomon four-group design involves random assignment of subjects to one of four groups. Two of the groups are pretested and two are not; one of the pretested groups and one of the unpretested groups receive the experimental treatment. All four groups are posttested. This design controls all threats to internal validity.

61. The best way to analyze data resulting from the Solomon four-group design is to use a 2 × 2 factorial analysis of variance. This procedure indicates whether there is an interaction between the treatment and the pretest.

Quasi-Experimental Designs

62. When it is not possible to randomly assign subjects to groups, quasi-experimental designs are available to the researcher. They provide adequate control of sources of invalidity.

63. The nonequivalent control group design looks very much like the pretest-posttest control group design, except that the nonequivalent control group design does not involve random assignment. The lack of random assignment raises the possibility of interactions between selection and variables such as maturation, history, and testing. Reactive effects are minimized.

64. In this design, every effort should be made to use groups that are as equivalent as possible. If differences between the groups on any major extraneous variable are identified, analysis of covariance can be used to statistically equate the groups.

65. In the time-series design, one group is repeatedly pretested, exposed to a treatment, and then repeatedly posttested. If a group scores essentially the same on a number of pretests and then significantly improves following a treatment, the researcher has more confidence in the effectiveness of the treatment than if just one pretest and one posttest are administered. History is a problem, as is pretest–treatment interaction.

66. Determining the effectiveness of the treatment in the time-series design basically involves analysis of the pattern of the test scores. A variation of the time-series design, which is referred to as the multiple time-series design, involves the addition of a control group to the basic design. This variation eliminates all threats to internal invalidity.

67. In a counterbalanced design, all groups receive all treatments but in a different order. The number of groups should equal the number of treatments. This design is usually employed when intact groups must be used and when administration of a pretest is not possible. A weakness of this design is potential multiple-treatment interference.

68. Factorial designs involve two or more independent variables, at least one of which is manipulated by the researcher. They permit investigation of two or more variables, individually and in interaction with each other. The term *factorial* indicates that the design has several factors, each with two or more levels. The 2 × 2 is the simplest factorial design.

69. The purpose of a factorial design is to determine whether an interaction between the independent variables exists. If one value of the independent variable is more effective regardless of level of the control variable, there is no interaction. If an interaction exists between the variables, different values of the independent variable are differentially effective depending on the level of the control variable. Rarely are more than three factors in a factorial design.

Single-Subject Experimental Designs

70. Single-subject experimental designs, also referred to as single-case experimental designs, can be applied when the sample size is one; they are typically used to study the behavior change an individual exhibits as a result of some intervention, or treatment.

71. Basically, the participant is alternately exposed to a nontreatment and a treatment condition, or phase, and performance is repeatedly measured during each phase. The nontreatment condition is symbolized as A and the treatment condition is symbolized as B.

72. At the very least, single-subject designs are considered to be valuable complements to group designs. There are two limitations of traditional group designs: (1) they are frequently opposed on ethical or philosophical grounds since by definition such designs involve a control group that does not receive the experimental treatment and (2) application of a group comparison design is not possible in many cases because of the small sample sizes. Single-subject designs are most frequently applied in clinical settings where the primary emphasis is on therapeutic, not statistical, outcomes.

External Validity

73. Results of single-subject research cannot be generalized to the population of interest as they can with group design research. For single-subject designs, the key to generalizability is replication. A main threat to these designs is the possible effect of the baseline condition on the subsequent effects of the treatment condition.

Internal Validity

74. Single-subject designs require repeated and reliable measurements or observations. Pretest performance is measured or observed a number of times prior to implementation of the treatment to obtain a stable baseline. Performance is also obtained at various points while the treatment is being applied. Since repeated data collection is a fundamental characteristic of all single-subject designs, it is especially important that measurement or observation of performance be standardized. Intraobserver and interobserver reliability should be estimated.

75. Also, the nature and conditions of the treatment should be specified in sufficient detail to permit replication. If its effects are to be validly assessed, the treatment must involve the same procedures each time it is introduced.

76. The purpose of the baseline measurements is to provide a description of the target behavior as it naturally occurs prior to the treatment. The baseline serves as the basis of comparison for assessing the effectiveness of the treatment. The establishment of a baseline pattern is referred to as baseline stability.

77. Normally, the length of the treatment phase and the number of measurements taken during it should parallel the length and measurements of the baseline phase.

78. An important principle of single-subject research is that only one variable at a time should be manipulated.

Types of Single-Subject Designs

79. When the A-B design is used, baseline measurements are repeatedly made until stability is established. Treatment is then introduced and multiple measurements are made during treatment. If behavior improves during the treatment phase, the effectiveness of the treatment is allegedly demonstrated. This design is open to many internal and external validity threats.

80. By simply adding a second baseline phase to the A-B design we obtain a much improved design, the A-B-A design. The internal validity of the A-B-A design is superior to that of the A-B design. It is unlikely that behavior would coincidentally improve during the treatment phase and coincidentally deteriorate during the subsequent baseline phase. A problem with this design is the ethical concern that the experiment ends with the treatment being removed.

81. The B-A-B design involves a treatment phase (B), a withdrawal phase (A), and a return to treatment phase (B). Although the B-A-B design does yield an experiment that ends with the subject receiving treatment, the lack of an initial baseline phase makes it difficult to assess the effectiveness of treatment.

82. The A-B-A-B design is basically the A-B-A design with the addition of a second treatment phase. This design overcomes the ethical objection to the A-B-A design and greatly strengthens the conclusions of the study by demonstrating the effects of the treatment twice. When application of the A-B-A-B design is feasible, it provides very convincing evidence of treatment effectiveness. The second treatment phase can be extended beyond the termination of the actual study to examine stability of treatment.

83. Multiple-baseline designs are used when the treatment is such that it is not possible to withdraw or return it to baseline or when it would not be ethical to withdraw it or reverse it. They are also used when treatment can be withdrawn but the effects of the treatment "carry over" into other phases of the study.

84. There are three basic types of multiple-baseline designs: across behaviors, across subjects, and across settings.

85. In a multiple-baseline design, data are collected on several behaviors for one subject, one behavior for several subjects, or one behavior and one subject in several settings. Systematically, over a period of time, the treatment is applied to each behavior (or subject, or setting) one at a time until all behaviors (or subjects, or settings) are under treatment. If performance improves in each case only after a treatment is introduced, then the treatment is judged to be effective.

86. When applying a treatment across behaviors, it is important that the behaviors treated be independent of each other. When applying treatment across participants, they and the setting should be as similar as possible. When applying treatment across settings, it is preferable that the settings be natural, although this is not always possible.

87. Whenever baseline is recoverable and there are no carryover effects, any of the A-B-A designs can be applied within a multiple-baseline framework.

88. The alternating treatments design represents a highly valid approach to assessing the relative effectiveness of two (or more) treatments, within a single-subject context. The alternating treatments design involves the relatively rapid alternation of treatments for a single subject. To avoid potential validity threats such as ordering effects, treatments are alternated on a random basis, e.g., T_1-T_2-T_2-T_1-T_2-T_1-T_1-T_2.

89. This design has several pluses that make it attractive to investigators. First, no withdrawal is necessary. Second, no baseline phase is necessary. Third, a number of treatments can be studied more quickly and efficiently than with other designs. One potential problem with this design is multiple-treatment interference (carryover effects from one treatment to the other).

Data Analysis and Interpretation

90. Data analysis in single-subject research usually involves visual and graphical analysis. Given the small sample size, the primary criterion is the clinical significance of the results, rather than the statistical significance. Effects that are small, but statistically significant, may not be large enough to make a sufficient difference in the behavior of a subject. Statistical analyses may supplement visual and graphical analysis.

91. In all the designs discussed, the key to sound data evaluation is judgment. The use of statistical analyses does not remove this responsibility from the researcher.

Replication

92. The more results are replicated, the more confidence that can be placed in the procedures that produced those results. Also, replication serves to delimit the generalizability of findings.

93. There are three types of replication. Direct replication refers to replication by the same investigator, with the same subject or with different subjects, in a specific setting (e.g., a classroom). Systematic replication refers to replication that follows direct replication, and that involves different investigators, behaviors, or settings. Clinical replication involves the development of a treatment package, composed of two or more interventions that have been found to be effective individually, designed for persons with complex behavior disorders.

PERFORMANCE CRITERIA   TASK 8

The description of participants should describe the population from which the sample was selected (allegedly, of course!), including its size and major characteristics.

The description of the instrument(s) should describe the purpose of the instrument (what it is intended to measure), and available validity and reliability coefficients.

The description of the design should indicate why it was selected, potential threats to validity associated with the design, and aspects of the study that are believed to have minimized their potential effects. A figure should be included illustrating how the selected design was applied in the study. For example, you might say: Since random assignment of participants to groups was possible, and since administration of a pretest was not advisable due to the reactive nature of the dependent variable (attitudes toward school), the posttest-only control group design was selected for this study (see Figure 1).

The description of procedures should describe in detail all steps that were executed in conducting the study. The description should include (1) the manner in which the sample was selected and the groups formed; (2) how and when pretest data were collected (if applicable); (3) the ways in which the groups were different (the independent variable, or treatment); (4) aspects of the study that were the same or similar for all groups; and (5) how and when posttest data were collected. (Note: If the dependent variable was measured with a test, the specific test or tests administered should be named. If a test was administered strictly for selection-of-subjects purposes, that is, not as a pretest of the dependent variable, it too should be described.)

On the following pages, Task 8 Example illustrates the performance called for by Task 8 at the beginning of Chapter 10. Again, the task was prepared by the same student who developed previous task examples, and you should therefore be able to see how Task 8 builds on previous tasks. Note especially how Task 3, the research plan, has been refined and expanded. Keep in mind that Tasks 3, 4, and 5 will not appear in your final research report; Task 8 will. Therefore, all of the important points in those previous tasks should be included in Task 8. Additional examples for this and subsequent tasks are included in the *Student Guide* that accompanies this text.

FIGURE 1   Experimental design.

Group	Assignment	N	Treatment	Posttest
I	Random	25	Daily Homework	So-so Attitude Scale
II	Random	25	No Homework	So-so Attitude Scale

1

Effect of Interactive Multimedia on the Achievement of 10th-Grade Biology Students

Method

Participants

The sample for this study was selected from the total population of 213 10th-grade students at an upper middle class all-girls Catholic high school in Miami, Florida. The population was 90% Hispanic, mainly of Cuban-American descent, 9% Caucasian non-Hispanic and 1% African-American. Sixty students were randomly selected (using a table of random numbers) and randomly assigned to two groups of 30 each.

Instrument

The biology test of the National Proficiency Survey Series (NPSS) was used as the measuring instrument. The test was designed to measure individual student performance in biology at the high school level but the publishers also recommended it as an evaluation of instructional programs. Content validity is good; items were selected from a large item bank provided by classroom teachers and curriculum experts. High school instructional materials and a national curriculum survey were extensively reviewed before objectives were written. The test objectives and those of the biology classes in the study were highly correlated. Although the standard error of measurement is not given for the biology test, the range of KR-20s for the entire battery is from .82 to .91 with a median of .86. This is satisfactory since the purpose of the test was to evaluate instructional programs not to make decisions concerning individuals. Catholic school students were included in the battery norming and its procedures were carried out in April and May of 1988 using 22,616 students in grades 9–12 from 45 high schools in 20 states.

Experimental Design

The design used in this study was the posttest-only control group design (see Figure 1). This design was selected because it provides control for most sources of invalidity and random assignment to groups was possible. A pretest was not necessary since the final science grades from June 1993 were available to check initial group equivalence and to help control mortality, a potential threat to internal validity with this design. Mortality, however, was not a problem as no students dropped from either group.

Group	Assignment	n	Treatment	Posttest
1	Random	30	IMM instruction	NPSS:B[a]
2	Random	30	Traditional instruction	NPSS:B

[a]National Proficiency Survey Series: Biology

Figure 1. Experimental design.

Procedure

Prior to the beginning of the 1993–94 school year, before classes were scheduled, 60 of the 213 10th-grade students were randomly selected and randomly assigned to two groups of 30 each, the average biology class size; each group became a biology class. One of the classes was randomly chosen to receive IMM instruction. The same teacher taught both classes.

The study was designed to last eight months beginning on the first day of class. The control group was taught using traditional methods of lecturing and open class discussions. The students worked in pairs for laboratory investigations which included the use of microscopes. The teacher's role was one of information disseminator.

The experimental classroom had 15 workstations for student use, each one consisting of a laser disc player, a video recorder, a 27-inch monitor, and a Macintosh computer with a 40 MB hard drive, 10 MB RAM, and a CD-ROM drive. The teacher's workstation incorporated a Macintosh computer with CD-ROM drive, a videodisc player, and a 27-inch monitor. The workstations were networked to the school library so students had access to online services such as Prodigy and Infotrac as well as to the card catalogue. Two laser printers were available through the network for the students' use.

In the experimental class the teacher used a videodisc correlated to the textbook. When barcodes provided in the text were scanned a section of the videodisc was activated and appeared on the monitor. The section might be a motion picture demonstrating a process or a still picture offering more detail than the text. The role of the teacher in the experimental group was that of facilitator and guide. After the teacher had introduced a new topic, the students worked in pairs at the workstations investigating topics connected to the main idea presented in the lesson. Videodiscs, CD-ROMs, and online services were all available as sources of information. The students used HyperStudio to prepare multimedia reports, which they presented to the class.

Throughout the study the same subject matter was covered and the two classes used the same text. Although the students of the experimental group paired up at the workstations, the other group worked in pairs during lab time, thus equalizing any effect from cooperative learning. The classes could not meet at the same time as they were taught by the same teacher, so they met during second and third periods. First period was not chosen as the school sometimes has a special schedule that interferes with first period. Both classes had the same homework reading assignments, which were reviewed in class the following school day. Academic objectives were the same for each class and all tests measuring achievement were identical.

During the first week of May, the biology test of the NPSS was administered to both classes to compare their achievement in biology.

"Looks bad, right?" (p. 428)

DESCRIPTIVE STATISTICS

OBJECTIVES

After reading Chapter 14, you should be able to do the following:

1. List the steps involved in scoring standardized and self-developed tests.
2. Describe the process of coding data, and give three examples of variables that would require coding.
3. List the steps involved in constructing a frequency polygon.
4. Define or describe three measures of central tendency.
5. Define or describe three measures of variability.
6. List four characteristics of normal distributions.
7. List two characteristics of positively skewed distributions and negatively skewed distributions.
8. Define or describe two measures of relationship.
9. Define or describe four measures of relative position.
10. Generate (in other words, make up) a column of 10 numbers, each between 1 and 10. You may use any number more than once. Assume those numbers represent scores on a posttest. Using these "scores," give the formula and compute the following (show your work): mean, standard deviation, z scores, and Pearson r (divide the column in half and make two columns of five scores each).

The goal of chapters 14 and 15 is for you to be able to select, apply, and correctly interpret analyses appropriate for a given study. After you have read Chapter 15, you should be able to perform the following task.

TASK 9

Based on Tasks 2–5, which you have already completed, write the results section of a quantitative research report. Specifically,

1. Generate data for each of the participants in your study.
2. Summarize and describe data using descriptive statistics.
3. Statistically analyze data using inferential statistics.
4. Interpret the results in terms of your original research hypothesis.
5. Present the results of your data analyses in a summary table.

If SPSS is available to you, use it to check your work (see Task 9 Performance Criteria, p. 498).

THE WORD IS "STATISTICS," NOT "SADISTICS"

Statistics is a set of procedures for describing, synthesizing, analyzing, and interpreting quantitative data. For example, 1,000 scores can be represented by a single number. As another example, you would not expect two groups to perform exactly the same on a posttest, even if they were essentially equal. Application of the appropriate statistic helps you to decide if the difference between two groups' scores is big enough to represent a true rather than a chance difference.

Choice of appropriate statistical techniques is determined to a great extent by your research design, hypothesis, and the kind of data that will be collected. Thus, different research focuses lead to different statistical analyses. The statistical procedures and techniques of the study should be identified and described in detail in the research plan. Data analysis is as important as any other component of research. Regardless of how well the study is conducted, inappropriate analyses can lead to inappropriate research conclusions. Note, however, the complexity of the analysis is *not* necessarily an indication of its "goodness" or appropriateness.

There are many statistical approaches available to a researcher. This chapter and Chapter 15 will describe and explain those commonly used in educational research. The focus is on your ability to apply and interpret these statistics, not your ability to describe their theoretical rationale and mathematical derivation. Despite what you have heard, statistics is easy. To calculate the statistics in these chapters, you only need to know how to add, subtract, multiply, and divide. That is all. No matter how gross or complex a formula is, it can be turned into an arithmetic problem when applied to your data. The arithmetic problems involve only addition, subtraction, multiplication, and division; the formulas tell you how often, and in what order, to perform those operations. Even if you haven't had a math course since junior high school, you will be able to calculate statistics. The hardest formula requires arithmetic at the sixth-grade level. In fact, you are encouraged to use a calculator! All you have to do is follow the steps we present. Trust us. You are going to be pleasantly surprised to see just how easy statistics is.

PREPARING DATA FOR ANALYSIS

A research study usually produces a mass of raw data, such as the responses of participants to an achievement, ability, interest, or attitude test. Collected data must be accurately scored and systematically organized to facilitate data analysis.

SCORING PROCEDURES

All instruments administered should be scored accurately and consistently; each participant's test results should be scored in the same way and with one criterion. When a standardized instrument is used, scoring is greatly facilitated. The test manual usually spells out the steps to follow in scoring each test, and a scoring key is usually provided. If the manual is followed conscientiously and each test is scored carefully, errors are minimized. It is usually a good idea to recheck all or at least some of the tests for consistency of scoring (say, 25% or every third test).

Scoring self-developed instruments is more complex, especially if open-ended items are involved. There is no manual to follow, and the researcher has to develop and refine a scoring procedure. Steps for scoring each item and for arriving at a total score must be delineated and carefully followed. If other than objective-type items (such as multiple-choice questions) are to be scored, it is advisable to have at least one other person independently score some or all of the tests as a reliability check. Planned scoring procedures should be tried out by administering the instrument to some individuals from the same or a similar population as the one from which research participants will be selected for the actual study. In this way, problems with the instrument or its scoring can be identified and corrected prior to the start of the study. The procedure ultimately used to score study data should be described in detail in the final research report.

Test questions that can be responded to on a standard, machine-scorable answer sheet can save a lot of time and increase the accuracy of the scoring process. If tests are to be machine scored, answer sheets should be checked carefully for stray pencil marks and a percentage of them should be scored by hand just to make sure that the key is correct and that the machine is scoring properly. The fact that the tests are being scored by a machine does not relieve the researcher of the responsibility of carefully checking data before and after processing.

TABULATION AND CODING PROCEDURES

After instruments have been scored, the results are transferred to summary data sheets, or more likely to a computer. Tabulation involves organizing the data. Recording the scores in a systematic manner facilitates examination and analysis of the data. If analysis consists of comparing the posttest scores of two or more groups, data would generally be placed in columns, one for each group, with the data arranged in ascending or descending order. If pretest scores are involved, additional columns should be formed. If analyses involve subgroup comparisons, scores should be tabulated separately for each subgroup. For example, in a study investigating the interaction between two types of mathematics instruction and two levels of aptitude (a 2 × 2 factorial design), four subgroups are involved, as shown in Table 14.1. This is the common method of dealing with quantitative data. If the data to be analyzed are categorical, tabulation usually involves counting responses. For example, a

TABLE 14.1   **Hypothetical Results of a Study Based on a 2 × 2 Factorial Design**

	METHOD A	METHOD B
	68	55
	72	60
	76	65
	78	70
	80	72
	84	74
	84	74
High Aptitude	85	75
	86	75
	86	76
	88	76
	90	76
	91	78
	92	82
	96	87
	METHOD A	**METHOD B**
	50	60
	58	66
	60	67
	62	68
	64	69
	64	69
	65	70
Low Aptitude	65	70
	66	71
	67	71
	70	72
	72	75
	72	76
	75	77
	78	79

superintendent might be interested in comparing the attitude toward unions of elementary and secondary teachers. Thus, for a question such as, "Would you join a union if given the opportunity?" the superintendent would tally the number of "yes," "no," and "undecided" responses separately for elementary and secondary teachers.

When a number of different kinds of data are collected from each participant, such as demographic information and several different test scores, both the variable names and the actual data are frequently coded. The variable "pretest reading comprehension scores," for example, may be coded as PRC, and gender of participants may be recorded as "M" or "F" or "1" or "2." Use of a computer for tabulating data and doing data analysis is recommended in general, but particularly if complex or multiple analyses are to be performed, or if a large number of participants are involved. In these cases, coding the data is especially important. The major advantage of using a computer to organize and analyze data is the capacity to rearrange data by subgroups and extract information without reentering all the data.

The first step in coding data is to give each participant an ID number. If there are 50 participants, for example, number them from 01 to 50. As this example illustrates, if the highest value for a variable is 2 digits (e.g., 50), then all represented values must be 2 digits. Thus, the first participant is 01, not 1. Similarly, achievement scores that range from 75 to 132 are coded 075 to 132. The next step is to make decisions as to how nonnumerical, or categorical, data will be coded. Nominal or categorical data include variables such as gender, group membership, and college level (e.g., sophomore). Thus, if the study involves 50 participants, with 2 groups of 25, then group membership may be coded "1" or "2" or "experimental" or "control." Categorical data also occur in survey instruments on which participants choose from a small number of alternatives representing a wider range of values. For example, teachers might be asked the following question:

How many hours of classroom time do you spend per week in nonteaching activities?
(a) 0–5   (b) 6–10   (c) 11–15   (d) 16–20

Responses might be coded (a) = 1, (b) = 2, (c) = 3, and (d) = 4.

Once the data have been prepared for analysis, the choice of statistical procedures to be applied is determined not only by the research hypothesis and design, but also by the type of measurement scale (categorical, ordinal, interval, ratio) represented by the data.

USING A COMPUTER

Generally the computer is a logical choice for data analysis. However, a good guideline for beginning researchers is, do not use the computer to perform an analysis that you have never done yourself by hand, or at least studied extensively. For example, after you have performed several analyses of variance on various sets of data, you will have the experience to understand the information produced by a computer analysis. In addition, instructions for preparing data for computer processing will make sense to you and you will know what the resulting output should look like.

Rapid advances and the development of "user friendly" computers have made it possible for researchers to perform a variety of analyses efficiently and accurately. One of the most popular statistical packages, commonly used in many colleges and universities, is the Statistical Package for the Social Sciences (SPSS). SPSS is used widely in quantitative research and is relatively easy to learn. We will demonstrate the usefulness of SPSS in this chapter and the next.

TYPES OF DESCRIPTIVE STATISTICS

The first step in data analysis is to describe, or summarize, the data using descriptive statistics. In some studies, particularly survey ones, the entire data analysis procedure may consist solely of calculating and interpreting descriptive statistics. **Descriptive statistics** permit the researcher to meaningfully describe many pieces of data with a few indices. If such indices are calculated for a sample drawn from a population, the resulting values are referred to as statistics; if they are calculated for an entire population, they are referred to as parameters. Most of the statistics used in educational research are based on data collected from well-defined samples, so most analyses deal with statistics, not parameters. Restated, a **statistic** is a quantitative index that describes performance of a sample or samples, and a **parameter** is a quantitative index describing the performance of a population.

The major types of descriptive statistics are measures of central tendency, measures of variability, measures of relative position, and measures of relationship. **Measures of central tendency** are used to determine the typical or average score of a group of scores. **Measures of variability** indicate how spread out a group of scores are. Measures of *relative position* describe a participant's performance compared to the performance of all other participants. Measures of *relationship* indicate the degree to which two sets of scores are related (remember correlation?). Before actually calculating any of these measures, it is often useful to present the data in graphic form.

GRAPHING DATA

As discussed, data are usually recorded on summary sheets or in computers—in columns, placed in ascending order. Data in this form are easily graphed, permitting the researcher to see what the distribution of scores looks like. The shape of the distribution may not be self-evident, especially if a large number of scores are involved, and, as we shall see later, the shape of the distribution may influence the researcher's choice of certain descriptive statistics.

The most common method of graphing data is to construct a frequency polygon. The first step is to list all scores and to tabulate how many subjects received each score. If 85 10th-grade students were administered an achievement test, the results might be as shown in Table 14.2.

TABLE 14.2   Frequency Distribution Based on 85 Hypothetical Achievement Test Scores

SCORE	FREQUENCY OF SCORE
78	1
79	4
80	5
81	7
82	7
83	9
84	9
85	12
86	10
87	7
88	6
89	3
90	4
91	1
	Total: 85 students

Once the scores are tallied, the steps are as follows:

1. Place all the scores on a horizontal axis, at equal intervals, from lowest score to highest.
2. Place the frequencies of scores at equal intervals on the vertical axis, starting with zero.
3. For each score, find the point where the score intersects with its frequency of occurrence and make a dot.
4. Connect all the dots with straight lines.

From Figure 14.1 we can see that most of the 10th graders scored at or near 85, with progressively fewer students achieving higher or lower scores. In other words, the scores appear to form a relatively normal or bell-shaped distribution, a concept we will discuss a little later. This knowledge would be helpful in selecting an appropriate measure of central tendency.

There are many types of other data-graphing approaches such as bar graphs, pie graphs, scatter plots (see Figure 11.1), box plots, and stem-and-leaf charts.[1] Examining a picture of the data can give some clues about which statistics are appropriate analyses.

MEASURES OF CENTRAL TENDENCY

Measures of central tendency provide a convenient way of describing a set of data with a single number. The number resulting from computation of a measure of central tendency represents the average or typical score attained by a group of subjects. The three most frequently encountered indices of central tendency are the mode, the median, and the mean. Each of these indices is used with a different scale of measurement: the mode is appropriate for describing nominal data, the median for describing ordinal data, and the mean for describing interval or ratio data. Since most quantitative measurement in educational research uses an interval scale, the mean is the most frequently used measure of central tendency.

The Mode

The **mode** is the score that is attained by more subjects than any other score. The data presented in Figure 14.1, for example, shows that the group mode is 85, since more participants (12) achieved that score than any other. The mode is not established through calculation; it is determined by looking at a set of scores or at a graph of scores and seeing which score occurs most frequently. There are several problems associated with the mode, and it is therefore of limited value and seldom used. For one thing, a set of scores may have two (or more) modes, in which case they are referred to as *bimodal*. Another problem with the mode is that it is an unstable measure of central tendency; equal-sized samples randomly selected from the same accessible population are likely to have different modes. However, when nominal data are being analyzed, the mode is the only appropriate measure of central tendency.

The Median

The **median** is that point, after scores are organized from low to high or high to low, above and below which are 50% of the scores. In other words, the median is the midpoint (like the median strip on a highway). If there are an odd number of scores, the median is the middle score (assuming the scores are arranged in order). For example, for the scores 75, 80, 82, 83, 87, the median is 82, because it is the middle score. If there is an even number of scores, the median is the point halfway between the two middle scores. For example, for the scores 21, 23, 24, 25, 26, 30, the median is 24.5; for the scores 50, 52, 55, 57, 59, 61, the median is 56.

---

[1]Wallgren, A., Wallgren, B., Persson, R., Jorner, U., and Haaland, J. (1996). *Graphing statistics and data*. Thousand Oaks, CA: Sage.

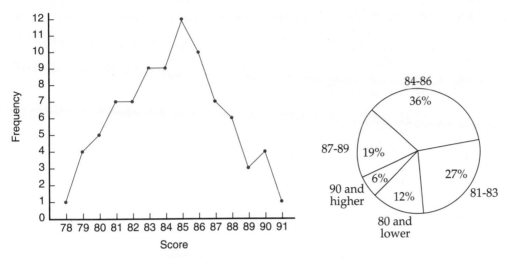

FIGURE 14.1
Frequency polygon and
pie chart based on 85
hypothetical achievement
test scores.

Thus, the median is not necessarily the same as one of the scores. There is no calculation for the median except finding the midpoint when there are an even number of scores.

The median does not take into account each and every score; it focuses on the middle scores. Two quite different sets of scores may have the same median. For example, for the scores 60, 62, 65, 67, 72, the median is 65; for the scores 30, 55, 65, 72, 89, the median is also 65. As we shall see shortly, this apparent lack of precision can be advantageous at times.

The median is the appropriate measure of central tendency when the data represent an ordinal scale. For certain distributions, the median may be the most appropriate measure of central tendency even though the data represent an interval or ratio scale. Although the median appears to be a rather simple index to determine, it cannot always be arrived at by simply looking at the scores; it does not always neatly fall between two different scores. For example, determining the median for the scores 80, 82, 84, 84, 84, 88 would require application of a relatively complex formula.

The Mean

The *mean* is the arithmetic average of the scores and is the most frequently used measure of central tendency. It is calculated by adding up all of the scores and dividing that total by the number of scores. In general, the mean is the preferred measure of central tendency. It is appropriate when the data represent either an interval or ratio score and is more precise than the median and the mode, because if equal-sized samples are randomly selected from the same population, the means of those samples will be more similar to each other than either the medians or the modes. By the very nature of the way in which it is computed, the mean takes into account, or is based on, each and every participant's score. Because all scores count, the mean can be affected by extreme scores. Thus, in certain cases, the median may actually give a more accurate estimate of the typical score.

When there are one or more extreme scores, the median will not be the most accurate representation of the performance of the total group but it will be the best index of typical performance. As an example, suppose you had the following IQ scores: 96, 96, 97, 99, 100, 101, 102, 104, 195. For these scores, the three measures of central tendency are

mode = 96 (most frequent score)
median = 100 (middle score)
mean = 110.6 (arithmetic average)

In this case, the median clearly best represents the typical score. The mode is too low, and the mean is higher than all of the scores except one. The mean is "pulled up" in the direction of the 195 score, whereas the median essentially ignores it. The different pictures presented by the different measures are part of the reason for the phrase, "lying with statistics." And in fact, selecting one index of central tendency over another one may present a particular point of view in a stronger light. In a labor-versus-management union dispute over salary, for example, very different estimates of typical employee salaries will be obtained depending on which index of central tendency is used. Let us say that the following are typical employee salaries in a union company: $12,000, $13,000, $13,000, $15,000, $16,000, $18,000, $45,000. For these salaries, the measures of central tendency are

mode = $13,000 (most frequent score)
median = $15,000 (middle salary)
mean = $18,857 (arithmetic average)

Both labor and management could overstate their case, labor by using the mode and management by using the mean. The mean is higher than every salary except one, $45,000, which in all likelihood would be the salary of a company manager. Thus, in this case, the most appropriate, and most accurate, index of typical salary would be the median. In research, we are not interested in "making cases" but rather in describing the data in the most accurate way. For the majority of sets of data the mean is the appropriate measure of central tendency.

MEASURES OF VARIABILITY

Although measures of central tendency are very useful statistics for describing a set of data, they are not sufficient. Two sets of data that are very different can have identical means or medians. As an example, consider the following sets of data:

set A:	79	79	79	80	81	81	81
set B:	50	60	70	80	90	100	110

The mean of both sets of scores is 80 and the median of both is 80, but set A is very different from set B. In set A the scores are all very close together and clustered around the mean. In set B the scores are much more spread out; in other words, there is much more variation or variability in set B. Thus, there is a need for a measure that indicates how spread out the scores are, that is, how much variability there is. There are a number of descriptive statistics that serve this purpose, and they are referred to as measures of variability. The three most frequently encountered are the range, the quartile deviation, and the standard deviation. Although the standard deviation is by far the most often used, the range is the only appropriate measure of variability for nominal data, and the quartile deviation is the appropriate index of variability for ordinal data. As with measures of central tendency, measures of variability appropriate for nominal and ordinal data may be used with interval or ratio data even though the standard deviation is generally the preferred index for such data.

The Range

The **range** is simply the difference between the highest and the lowest score and is determined by subtraction. As an example, the range for the scores 79, 79, 79, 80, 81, 81, 81, is 2, while the range for the scores 50, 60, 70, 80, 90, 100, 110 is 60. Thus, if the range is small, the scores are close together; if it is large, the scores are more spread out. Like the mode, the range is not a very stable measure of variability, and its chief advantage is that it gives a quick, rough estimate of variability.

The Quartile Deviation

In "research talk" the **quartile deviation** is one half of the difference between the upper quartile and the lower quartile in a distribution. In English, the upper quartile is the 75th percentile, that point below which are 75% of the scores. Correspondingly, the lower quartile is the 25th percentile, that point below which are 25% of the scores. By subtracting the lower quartile from the upper quartile and then dividing the result by two, we get a measure of variability. If the quartile deviation is small, the scores are close together; if it is large, the scores are more spread out. The quartile deviation is a more stable measure of variability than the range and is appropriate whenever the median is appropriate. Calculation of the quartile deviation involves a process very similar to that used to calculate the median, which just happens to be the second quartile or the 50th percentile.

Variance

Variance indicates the amount of spread among test scores. If the variance is small, the scores are close together; if it is large, the scores are more spread out. The square root of the variance is called the *standard deviation* and, like variance, a small standard deviation indicates that scores are close together and a large one indicates that the scores are more spread out.

Calculation of the variance is quite simple. For example, five students took a test and received scores of 25, 25, 30, 40, and 30. The mean of these scores is—what? Right, 32. The difference of each student's score from the mean is

$$35 - 32 = 3$$
$$25 - 32 = -7$$
$$30 - 32 = -2$$
$$40 - 32 = 8$$
$$30 - 32 = -2 \text{ (Notice that the sum of the differences is 0. That's why}$$

we have to square the differences in the next step.)

Squaring each difference gives $9 + 49 + 4 + 64 + 2 = 130$. Dividing the squared differences by the number of scores gives us $130/5 = 26$. This is called the variance of the scores. Variance is seldom used itself, but is used to obtain the standard deviation. The standard deviation is the square root of the variance (26). Get your calculator out. The square root of 26 is 5.1, and this is the standard deviation of the five scores.

The Standard Deviation

The standard deviation is used when the data are interval or ratio, and is by far the most frequently used index of variability. Like the mean, its central tendency counterpart, the standard deviation is the most stable measure of variability and includes every score in its calculation. In fact, the first step in calculating the standard deviation is to find out how far away each score is from the mean by subtracting the mean from each score. If you know the mean and the standard deviation of a set of scores you have a pretty good picture of what the distribution looks like. If the distribution of scores is relatively normal or bell-shaped (about which we will have more to say shortly), then the mean plus 3 standard deviations and the mean minus 3 standard deviations encompass over 99% of the scores. In other words, each score distribution has its own mean and its own standard deviation that are calculated based on the scores. The number 3 is a constant. For any normal distribution of scores, the standard deviation multiplied by 3 and then added to the mean and subtracted from the mean will include almost all the scores in the distribution. The symbol for the mean is $\overline{X}$ and the standard deviation is usually abbreviated as *SD*. Thus, the concept described here can be expressed as follows: $\overline{X} \pm 3\,SD = 99+\%$ of the scores.

As an example, suppose that the mean of a set of scores ($\overline{X}$) is calculated to be 80 and the standard deviation (*SD*) to be 1. In this case the mean plus 3 standard deviations, $\overline{X}$ + 3 *SD*, is equal to 80 + 3(1) = 80 + 3 = 83. The mean minus 3 standard deviations, $\overline{X}$ − 3 *SD*, is equal to 80 − 3(1) = 80 − 3 = 77. Thus, almost all the scores fall between 77 and 83. This makes sense since, as we mentioned before, a small standard deviation (in this case *SD* = 1) indicates that the scores are close together, not very spread out.

As another example, suppose that a different set of scores had a mean ($\overline{X}$) calculated to be 80, but this time the standard deviation (*SD*) is calculated to be 4. In this case the mean plus three standard deviations, $\overline{X}$ + 3 *SD*, is equal to 80 + 3(4) = 80 + 12 = 92. In case you still do not see,

$$80 + 1\ SD = 80 + 4 = 84$$
$$80 + 2\ SD = 80 + 4 + 4 = 88$$
$$80 + 3\ SD = 80 + 4 + 4 + 4 = 92$$

Or, to explain it another way, 80 plus 1 *SD* = 80 + 4 = 84, plus another *SD* = 84 + 4 = 88, plus one more (the third) *SD* = 88 + 4 = 92. Now, the mean minus three standard deviations, $\overline{X}$ − 3 *SD*, is equal to 80 − 3(4) = 80 − 12 = 68. In other words,

$$80 - 1\ SD = 80 - 4 = 76$$
$$80 - 2\ SD = 80 - 4 - 4 = 72$$
$$80 - 3\ SD = 80 - 4 - 4 - 4 = 68$$

Or, to explain it another way, 80 minus 1 *SD* = 80 − 4 = 76, minus another *SD* = 76 − 4 = 72, minus one more (the third) *SD* = 72 − 4 = 68. Thus, almost all the scores fall between 68 and 92. This makes sense since a larger standard deviation (in this case *SD* = 4) indicates that the scores are more spread out. Clearly, if you know the mean and standard deviation of a set of scores, you have a pretty good idea of what the scores look like. You know the mean score and you know how spread out or variable the scores are. Using both, you can describe a set of data quite well.

The Normal Curve

The plus and minus 3 concept is valid only when the scores are normally distributed, that is, form a normal, or bell-shaped, score distribution. Many, many variables, such as height, weight, IQ scores, and achievement scores yield a normal curve if a sufficient number of participants are measured.

If a variable is *normally distributed*, that is, forms a *normal* or *bell-shaped curve,* then several things are true:

1. Fifty percent of the scores are above the mean and 50% are below the mean.
2. The mean, the median, and the mode are the same value.
3. Most scores are near the mean and the farther from the mean a score is, the fewer the number of participants who attained that score.
4. The same number, or percentage, of scores is between the mean and plus one standard deviation ($\overline{X}$ + 1 *SD*) as is between the mean and minus one standard deviation ($\overline{X}$ − 1 *SD*), and similarly for $\overline{X}$ ± 2 *SD* and $\overline{X}$ ± 3 *SD* (Figure 14.2).

In Figure 14.2, the symbol σ (the Greek letter sigma) is used to represent the standard deviation, that is, 1 σ = 1 *SD*, and the mean ($\overline{X}$) is designated as 0 (zero). The vertical lines at each of the *SD* (σ) points delineate a certain percentage of the total area under the curve. As Figure 14.2 indicates, if a set of scores forms a normal distribution, the $\overline{X}$ + 1 *SD* includes

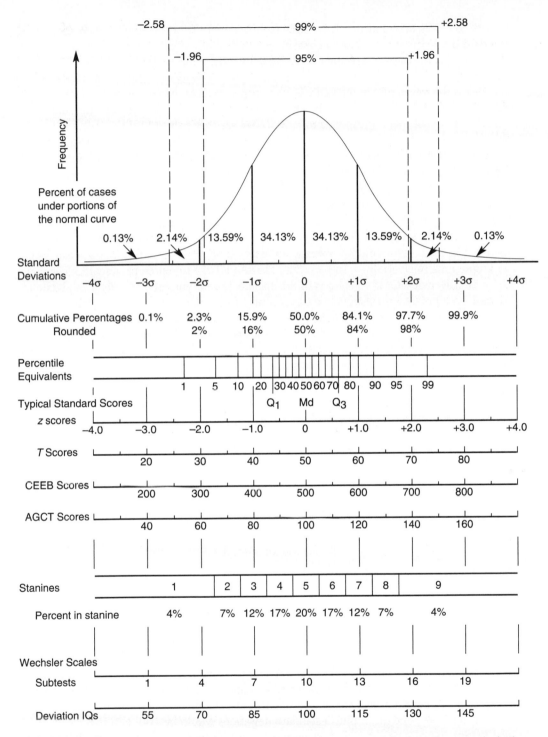

Note. This chart cannot be used to equate scores on one test to scores on another test. For example, both 600 on the CEEB and 120 on the AGCT are one standard deviation above their respective means, but they do not represent "equal" standings because the scores were obtained from different groups.

FIGURE 14.2 Characteristics of the normal curve (*Note:* Based on a figure appearing in *Test Service Bulletin* No. 48, January, 1955, of The Psychological Corporation.)

34.13% of the scores and the $\overline{X} - 1\,SD$ includes 34.13% of the scores. Each succeeding standard deviation encompasses a constant percentage of the cases. Since $\overline{X} \pm 2.58\,SD$ includes 99% of the cases, we see that $\overline{X} \pm 3\,SD$ includes almost all the scores, as pointed out previously.

Below the row of SDs in the figure is a row of percentages. As you move from left to right, from point to point, the cumulative percentage of scores that fall below each point is indicated. Thus, at the point that corresponds to $-3\,SD$, we see that only .1% of the scores fall below this point. The numerical value corresponding to $+1\,SD$, on the other hand, is a figure higher than 84.1% (rounded to 84% on the next row) of the scores. Relatedly, the next row, percentile equivalents, also involves cumulative percentages. The figure 20 in this row, for example, indicates that 20% of the scores fall below this point. While we will discuss percentiles and the remaining rows further as we proceed through this chapter, we will look at one more row at this time. Near the bottom of Figure 14.2, under Wechsler Scales, is a row labeled Deviation IQs. This row indicates that the mean IQ for the Wechsler Scale is 100 and the standard deviation is 15 (115 is in the column corresponding to $+1\,SD$ [$+1\,\sigma$]) and since the mean is 100, 115 represents $\overline{X} + 1\,SD = 100 + 15 = 115$. An IQ of 145 represents a score 3 SDs above the mean (average) IQ. If your IQ is in this neighborhood, you are certainly a candidate for Mensa! An IQ of 145 corresponds to a percentile of 99.9. On the other side of the curve we see that an IQ of 85 corresponds to a score one standard deviation below the mean ($\overline{X} - 1\,SD = 100 - 15 = 85$) and to the 16th percentile. Note that the mean *always* corresponds to the 50th percentile. In other words, the average score is always that point above which are 50% of the cases and below which are 50% of the cases. Thus, if scores are normally distributed the following statements are true:

$$\overline{X} \pm 1.0\,SD = \text{approximately } 68\% \text{ of the scores}$$
$$\overline{X} \pm 2.0\,SD = \text{approximately } 95\% \text{ of the scores}$$
$$(1.96\,SD \text{ is exactly } 95\%)$$
$$\overline{X} \pm 2.5\,SD = \text{approximately } 99\% \text{ of the scores}$$
$$(2.58\,SD \text{ is exactly } 99\%)$$
$$\overline{X} \pm 3.0\,SD = \text{approximately } 99+\% \text{ of the scores}$$

And similarly, the following are always true:

$$\overline{X} - 3.0\,SD = \text{approximately the .1 percentile}$$
$$\overline{X} - 2.0\,SD = \text{approximately the 2nd percentile}$$
$$\overline{X} - 1.0\,SD = \text{approximately the 16th percentile}$$
$$\overline{X} = \text{the 50th percentile}$$
$$\overline{X} + 1.0\,SD = \text{approximately the 84th percentile}$$
$$\overline{X} + 2.0\,SD = \text{approximately the 98th percentile}$$
$$\overline{X} + 3.0\,SD = \text{approximately the 99th}+ \text{ percentile}$$

You may have noticed that the ends of the curve never touch the baseline and that there is no definite number of standard deviations that corresponds to 100%. This is because the curve allows for the existence of unexpected extremes at either end and because each additional standard deviation includes only a tiny fraction of a percent of the scores. As an example, for the IQ test the mean plus 5 standard deviations would be $100 + 5(15) = 100 + 75 = 175$. Surely 5 SDs would include everyone. Wrong! There has been a very small number of persons who have scored near 200, which corresponds to $+6.67\,SD$s. Thus, while $\pm 3\,SD$s includes just about everyone, the exact number of standard deviations required to include every score varies from variable to variable.

As mentioned earlier, many variables form a normal distribution, including physical measures, such as height and weight, and psychological measures, such as intelligence and aptitude.

In fact, most variables measured in education form normal distributions if enough subjects are tested. Note, however, that a variable that is normally distributed in a population may not be normally distributed in smaller samples from the population. In Figure 14.2 the standard deviation is symbolized as σ, instead of *SD*, to indicate that the curve represents the scores of a population, not a sample; thus, σ represents a population parameter, whereas *SD* represents a sample-based statistic. Depending on the size and nature of a particular sample, the assumption of a normal curve may or may not be a valid one. Since research studies deal with a finite number of participants, and often not a very large number, research data only more or less approximate a normal curve. Correspondingly, all of the equivalencies (standard deviation, percentage of cases, and percentile) are also only approximations. This is an important point, since most statistics used in educational research are based on the assumption that the variable is normally distributed. If this assumption is badly violated in a given sample, then certain statistics should not be used. In general, however, the fact that most variables are normally distributed allows us to quickly determine many useful pieces of information concerning a set of data.

Skewed Distributions

When a distribution is not normal, it is said to be skewed. A normal distribution is symmetrical and the values of the mean, the median, and the mode are the same. A **skewed distribution** is not symmetrical, and the values of the mean, the median, and the mode are different. In a symmetrical distribution, there are approximately the same number of extreme scores (very high and very low) at each end of the distribution. In a skewed distribution there are more extreme scores at one end than the other. If the extreme scores are at the lower end of the distribution, the distribution is said to be **negatively skewed,** and if the extreme scores are at the higher end of the distribution, the distribution is said to be **positively skewed** (Figure 14.3).

As we can see by looking at the negatively skewed distribution, most of the participants did well but a few did very poorly. Conversely, in the positively skewed distribution, most of the participants did poorly but a few did very well. In both cases, the mean is "pulled" in the direction of the extreme scores. Since the mean is affected by extreme scores (all scores are used) and the median is not (only the middle score(s) are used), the mean is always closer to the extreme scores than the median. Thus, for a negatively skewed distribution the mean ($\overline{X}$) is always lower, or smaller, than the median (md); for a positively skewed distribution the mean is always higher or greater than the median. Since the mode is not affected by extreme scores, no "always" statements can be made concerning its relationship to the mean and the median in a skewed distribution. Usually, however, as Figure 14.3 indicates, in a negatively skewed distribution the mean and the median are lower, or smaller, than the mode, whereas in a positively skewed distribution the mean and the median are higher, or greater, than the mode.

To summarize:

negatively skewed: mean < median < mode
positively skewed: mean > median > mode

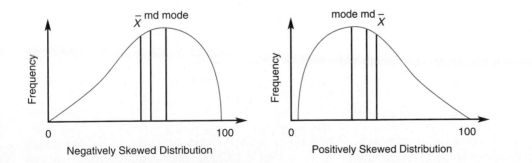

FIGURE 14.3 A positively skewed distribution and a negatively skewed distribution, each resulting from the administration of a 100-item test.
(*Note.* $\overline{X}$ = mean; md = median)

Because the relationship between the mean and the median is a constant, the skewness of a distribution can be determined without constructing a frequency polygon. If the mean is less than the median, the distribution is negatively skewed; if the mean and the median are the same, or very close, the distribution is symmetrical; if the mean is greater than the median, the distribution is positively skewed. The farther apart the mean and the median are, the more skewed is the distribution. If the distribution is very skewed, then the assumption of normality required for many statistics is violated.

MEASURES OF RELATIVE POSITION

Measures of relative position indicate where a score is in relation to all other scores in the distribution. In other words, measures of relative position permit one to express how well an individual has performed as compared to all other individuals in the sample who have been measured on the same variable. In Chapter 5 this was called *norm-referenced measurement*. A major advantage of such measures is that they make it possible to compare the performance of an individual on two or more different tests. For example, if Ziggy's score in reading is 40 and his score in math is 35, it does not follow that he did better in reading; 40 may have been the lowest score on the reading test and 35 the highest score on the math test! Measures of relative position express different scores on a common scale. The two most frequently used measures of relative position are percentile ranks and standard scores.

Percentile Ranks

A *percentile rank* indicates the percentage of scores that fall at or below a given score. If Matt Mathphobia's score of 65 corresponds to a percentile rank of 80, the 80th percentile, this means that 80 percent of the scores in the distribution are lower than 65. Matt scored higher than 80 percent of those taking the test. Conversely, if Dudley Veridull scored at the 7th percentile, this would mean that Dudley only did better than, or received a higher score than, 7% of the test takers.

Percentiles are appropriate for data representing an ordinal scale, although they are mainly computed for interval data. The median of a set of scores corresponds to the 50th percentile, which makes sense since the median is the middle point and therefore the point below which are 50% of the scores. While percentile ranks are not used very often in research studies, they are frequently used in the public schools to report test results of students in a form that is understandable to most audiences.

Standard Scores

Figure 14.2 depicts a number of standard scores. Basically, a *standard score* is a derived score that expresses how far a given raw score is from some reference point, typically the mean, in terms of standard deviation units. A standard score is a measure of relative position which is appropriate when the test data represent an interval or ratio scale of measurement. The most commonly reported and used standard scores are z scores, T scores (or Z scores), and stanines. Standard scores allow scores from different tests to be compared on a common scale and, unlike percentiles, permit valid mathematical operations such as averages to be computed. Averaging nonstandard scores on a series of tests in order to obtain an overall average score is like averaging apples and oranges and getting an "orapple." Such tests are likely to vary in level of difficulty and variability of scores. By converting test scores to standard scores, however, we can average them and arrive at a valid final index of average performance.

The normal curve equivalencies indicated in Figure 14.2 for the various standard scores are accurate only to the degree to which the distribution is normal. Further, standard scores can be compared only if all the derived scores are based on the raw scores (number correct) of the same group. For example, a CEEB (College Entrance Examination

Board) score of 700 is not equivalent to a Wechsler IQ of 130 because the tests were normed on different groups. If a set of raw scores is normally distributed, then so are the standard score equivalents. But, as noted, all distributions are not normal. For example, height is normally distributed, but the measured heights of the girls in a seventh-grade gym class may not be. There is a procedure for transforming raw scores that ensures that the distribution of standard scores will be normal. Raw scores thus transformed are referred to as *normalized* scores. All resulting standard scores are normally distributed and the normal curve equivalencies are accurate.

z **Scores.**   A *z* **score** is the most basic standard score. It expresses how far a score is from the mean in terms of standard deviation units. A score that is exactly "on" the mean corresponds to a *z* score of 0. A score that is exactly 1 standard deviation above the mean corresponds to a *z* score of +1.00 and a *z* score that is exactly 2 standard deviations below the mean corresponds to a *z* score of −2.00. Get it? As Figure 14.2 indicates, if a set of scores is transformed into a set of *z* scores (each score is expressed as a *z* score), the new distribution has a mean of 0 and a standard deviation of 1.

The major advantage of *z* scores is that they allow scores from different tests or subtests to be compared. As an example, suppose Bobby Bonker's mother, a woman who is really on top of things, comes in and asks his teacher, "How is Bobby doing in the basic skills area?" If the teacher tells her that Bobby's reading score was 50 and his math score was 40, she still does not know how well Bobby is doing. In fact, she might get the false impression that he is better in reading when in fact 50 might be a very low score on the reading test and 40 may be a very good score on the math test. Now suppose Bobby's teacher also tells his mother that the average score (the mean, $\overline{X}$) on the reading test was 60, and the average score on the math test was 30. Aha! Now it looks as if Bobby is better in math than in reading. Further, if the standard deviation (*SD*) on both tests was 10, Bobby's true status becomes even more evident. Since his score in reading is exactly 1 *SD* below the mean (60 − 10 = 50), his *z* score is −1.00. On the other hand, his score in math is 1 *SD* above the mean (30 + 10 = 40) and his *z* score is +1.00. As shown, *z* scores can be translated into percentiles to show that Bobby is clearly better in math than in reading.[2]

	Raw Score	$\overline{X}$	SD	*z*	Percentile
Reading	50	60	10	−1.00	16th
Math	40	30	10	+1.00	84th

We can use Figure 14.2 to estimate percentile equivalents for given *z* scores, but this becomes more difficult for *z* scores that fall between the values given in the figure, for example, *z* scores of .63 or −1.78. A better approach is to use Table A.3 in Appendix A. For each *z* between −3.00 and +3.00 in the column labeled Area, Table A.3 gives the proportion of cases that are included up to that point. In other words, for any value of *z*, the area created to the left of the line on the curve represents the proportion of cases that falls below that *z* score. Thus, for *z* = .00 (the mean score), we go down the *z* columns until we come to .00 and we see that the corresponding area to the left is .5000, representing 50% of the cases and the 50th percentile. For Bobby, we simply go down the *z* columns until we come to −1.00 (his *z* score for reading), and we see that the corresponding area under the curve is .1587. By multiplying by 100 and rounding, we see that Bobby's reading score corresponds to approximately the 16th percentile (16% of the cases fall below *z* = −1.00). Similarly, for his math score of +1.00, the area is .8413, or approximately the 84th percentile.

---

[2]This analysis is based on the assumption that the same groups took the test and that the tests were normally distributed.

Of course there are lots of other fun things we can do with Table A.3. If we want to know the proportion of cases in the area to the right of a given z score, for example, we simply subtract the left area value from 1.00, since the total area under the curve equals all, or 1.00 (100% of the cases). So, if we want to know the percentage of students who did better than Bobby on the reading test, we subtract .1587 from 1.00 and we get .8413, or approximately 84%. Similarly, if we want to know the percentage of scores for any test that falls between $z = -1.00$ and $z = +1.00$, we subtract .1587 from .8413 and we get .6826, or approximately 68%. In other words, approximately 68% (68.26% to be exact) of the scores fall between $z = -1.00$ and $z = +1.00$ (as indicated by Figure 14.2, 34.13% + 34.13% = 68.26%). Thus, we can find the percentage of cases that falls between any two z scores by subtracting their Table A.3 area values.

Also by subtraction, we can find the percentage of cases that falls between the mean ($z = .00$, area = .5000) and any other z score. And, we can also reverse the process to find, for example, the z score that corresponds to a given percentile. To become a member of Mensa, for example, you have to have an IQ at or higher than the 98th percentile. The closest area value in Table A.3 that reflects 98th percentile is .9803, which corresponds to $z = 2.06$. In other words, your IQ has to be approximately two standard deviations ($+2\ \sigma$) above average, which corresponds to an IQ of 130 (see Figure 14.2).

Of course, as mentioned previously and as Table A.3 indicates, scores are not always exactly 1 SD (or 2 SD or 3 SD) above or below the mean. Usually we have to apply the following formula to convert a raw score to a z score:

$$z = \frac{X - \overline{X}}{SD}, \text{ where } X \text{ is the raw score}$$

The only problem with z scores is that they involve negative numbers and decimals. It would be pretty hard to explain to Mrs. Bonker that her son was a -1.00. How do you tell a mother her son is a negative?! A simple solution is to transform z scores into T (or Z) scores. As Figure 14.2 indicates, z scores are actually the building blocks for a number of standard scores. Other standard scores represent transformations of z scores that communicate the same information in a more generally understandable form by eliminating negatives and/or decimals.

T Scores. A **T score** (also called a **Z score**) is nothing more than a z score expressed in a different form. To transform a z score to a T score, you simply multiply the z score by 10 and add 50. In other words, $T = 10z + 50$. Thus, a z score of 0 (the mean score) becomes a T score of 50 [$T = 10(0) + 50 = 0 + 50 = 50$]. A z score of $+1.00$ becomes a T score of 60 [$T = 10(1.00) + 50 = 10 + 50 = 60$], and a z score of -1.00 becomes a T score of 40 [$T = 10(-1.00) + 50 = -10 + 50 = 40$]. Thus, when scores are transformed to T scores, the new distribution has a mean of 50 and a standard deviation of 10 (see Figure 14.2). It would clearly be much easier to communicate to Mrs. Bonker that Bobby is a 40 in reading and a 60 in math and that the average score is 50 than to tell her that he is a $+1.00$ and a -1.00 and the average score is .00.

If the raw score distribution is normal, then so is the z score distribution and the T score distribution. If, on the other hand, the original distribution is not normal (such as when a small sample group is involved), then neither are the z and T score distributions. In such cases the distribution resulting from the $10z + 50$ transformation is more accurately referred to as a Z distribution. However, even with a set of raw scores that are not normally distributed, we can produce a set of normalized Z scores. In either case, we can use the normal curve equivalencies to convert such scores into corresponding percentiles, or vice versa. As Figure 14.2 indicates, for example, a T of 50 = a percentile of 50%. Similarly, a T of 30 corresponds to a percentile of 2 and a T of 60 corresponds to the 84th percentile. The same is true for the other standard score transformations illustrated in Figure 14.2. The CEEB distribution is formed by multiplying T scores by 10 to eliminate decimals; it is calculated directly using CEEB = $100z$ + 500. The AGCT (Army General Classification Test) distribution is formed by multiplying T scores by 2, and is formed directly using AGCT = $20z$ + 100. In both cases, given values can be converted to percentiles (and vice versa) using normal curve equivalencies. Thus, a CEEB score of 400 corresponds to the 16th percentile and the 98th percentile corresponds to an AGCT score of 140.

Stanines.   *Stanines* are standard scores that divide a distribution into nine parts. Stanine (short for "standard nine") equivalencies are derived using the formula $2z + 5$ and rounding resulting values to the nearest whole number. Stanines 2 through 8 each represent $\frac{1}{2}$ SD of the distribution; stanines 1 and 9 include the remainder. In other words, stanine 5 includes $\frac{1}{2}$ SD around the mean ($\overline{X}$); that is, it equals $\overline{X} \pm \frac{1}{4}$ SD. Stanine 6 goes from $+\frac{1}{4}$ SD to $+\frac{3}{4}$ SD ($\frac{1}{4}$ SD $+ \frac{1}{2}$ SD $= \frac{3}{4}$ SD), and so forth. Stanine 1 includes any score that is less than $-1\frac{3}{4}$ SD (-1.75 SD) below the mean, and stanine 9 includes any score that is greater than $+1\frac{3}{4}$ SD ($+1.75$ SD) above the mean. As Figure 14.2 indicates (see the row of figures directly beneath the stanines), stanine 5 includes 20% of the scores, stanines 4 and 6 each contain 17%, stanines 3 and 7 each contain 12%, 2 and 8 each contain 7%, and 1 and 9 each contain 4% of the scores (percentages approximate). Thus, if a student was at the 7th stanine her percentile would be approximately $4 + 7 + 12 + 17 + 20 + 17 + 12 =$ 89th percentile.

Like percentiles, stanines are very frequently reported in norms tables for standardized tests. They are very popular with school systems because they are so easy to understand and to explain to others. They are not as exact as other standard scores, but are useful for a variety of purposes. They are frequently used as a basis for grouping and are also used as a criterion for selecting students for special programs. A remediation program, for example, may select students who scored in the first and second stanine on a standardized reading test.

Use Figure 14.2 and Appendix A, Table A.3 to answer the following questions:

1. What percentile corresponds to a z score of $+2.00$?
2. What z score corresponds to a percentile of $-.20$?
3. Approximately what percentile corresponds to a stanine of 3?
4. What range of z scores encompasses 95% of the area in a normal curve?
5. What is the relationship of the mean, median, and mode in the normal distribution?

MEASURES OF RELATIONSHIP

Correlational research, the examination of the relationships between variables, was discussed in detail in Chapter 11. You will recall that correlational research involves collecting data to determine whether and to what degree a relationship exists between two or more quantifiable variables—not a causal relationship, just a relationship. Degree of relationship is expressed as a correlation coefficient, which is computed using two sets of scores from a single group of participants. The correlation coefficient provides an estimate of just how related two variables are. If two variables are highly related, a correlation coefficient near $+1.00$ (or -1.00) will be obtained; if two variables are not related, a coefficient near .00 will be obtained. There are a number of different methods of computing a correlation coefficient; which one is appropriate depends on the scale of measurement represented by the data. The two most frequently used correlational analyses are the rank difference correlation coefficient, usually referred to as the Spearman rho, and the product moment correlation coefficient, usually referred to as the Pearson *r*. See Table 11.2 for other correlational approaches, including the phi coefficient, biserial, and intraclass correlations, among others.

The Spearman Rho

The Spearman rho coefficient is used to correlate ranked data. The Spearman rho is thus appropriate when the data represent an ordinal scale (although it may be used with interval data) and is used when the median and quartile deviation are used. If only one of the variables to be correlated is ranked, the other variable to be correlated must also be expressed in terms of ranks. Thus, if intelligence were to be correlated with class rank, students' intelligence scores would have to be translated into ranks. If more than one participant receives the same score, then the corresponding ranks are averaged. So, for example, if two participants have the same highest score, they are each assigned the average of rank 1 and rank 2, namely, rank 1.5, and the next highest score is assigned rank 3. Similarly, the 24th and 25th highest scores, if identical, would each be assigned the rank 24.5. Like most other correlation coefficients, the Spearman rho produces a coefficient somewhere between -1.00 and $+1.00$. If, for example, a group of participants achieves identical ranks on both variables the coefficient will be $+1.00$.

The Pearson r

The Pearson r correlation coefficient is the most appropriate measure when the variables to be correlated are either interval or ratio. Like the mean and the standard deviation, the Pearson r takes into account each and every score in both distributions; it is also the most stable measure of correlation. Since most educational measures represent interval scales, the Pearson r is usually the most used coefficient for determining relationship. An assumption associated with the application of the Pearson r is that the relationship between the variables being correlated is a linear one. If this is not the case, the Pearson r will not yield a valid indication of relationship. If there is any question concerning the linearity of the relationship, the two sets of data should be plotted as previously shown in Figure 11.1.

CALCULATION FOR INTERVAL DATA

Because most educational data are represented in interval scales, we will calculate the measure of central tendency, variability, relationship, and relative position appropriate for interval data. There are several alternate formulas available for computing each of these measures; in each case, however, we will use the easiest, raw score formula. At first glance some of the formulas may look scary but they are really easy. The only reason they look hard is because they involve symbols with which you may be unfamiliar. As promised, however, each formula transforms "magically" into an arithmetic problem; all you have to do is substitute the correct numbers for the correct symbols.

Thus far most of this chapter has introduced varied types of statistics such as means, central tendency, variables, normal curves, and measures of relationship. These and other statistics are used to analyze various types of quantitative data. The remainder of this chapter and Chapter 15 will focus on quantitative data analysis. We will demonstrate aspects of data analysis in two ways. The first will be based on data analysis by following step-by-step procedures; the second will entail analysis by computer.

Although computer-based data analysis can be more efficient, it is important to work through data analyses for yourself to obtain a basic understanding of the research results. Once you are familiar with the step-by-step examples, you should also carry out analyses by computer.

For our computer analysis, we will use the SPSS student version 10.0 for Windows. SPSS is the most commonly used quantitative desktop computer analysis application. Please bear in mind that this is not a statistics course; our purpose is not to teach you how to use SPSS, but rather to illustrate how to use it to perform your quantitative data analysis. We will not examine all the analyses available in SPSS, but we will look at many of the basic ones commonly used in quantitative research. You will be able to compare the two types of analysis and see how they each can be used to produce the same results. (Note that the step-by-step and SPSS analyses do produce slightly different results due to the fact that the step-by-step analyses are worked out to two decimal places and the SPSS analyses are worked out variously to up to five decimal places. These differences do not significantly affect the results.)

SYMBOLS

Before we start calculating let's get acquainted with a few basic statistical symbols. First, X (without a bar) is usually used to symbolize a score. If you see a column of numbers, and at the top of that column is an X, you know that the column represents a set of scores. If there are two sets of scores they may be labeled X_1 and X_2 or X and Y, it does not matter which.

Another symbol used frequently is the Greek letter Σ, which is used to indicate addition. Σ means "the sum of," or "add them all up." Thus ΣX means "add up all the Xs" and ΣY means "add up all the Ys." Isn't this easy? Now, if any symbol has a bar over it, such as $\overline{X}$, that indicates the mean, or arithmetic average, of the scores. Thus $\overline{X}$ refers to the mean of the X scores and $\overline{Y}$ refers to the mean of the Y scores.

A capital N refers to the number of participants; $N = 20$ means that there are 20 participants (N is for number; makes sense, doesn't it?). If one analysis involves several groups, the number of participants in each group is indicated with a lowercase letter n and a subscript indicating the group. If there are three groups, and the first group has 15 participants, the second group has 18, and the third group has 20, this is symbolized as $n_1 = 15$, $n_2 = 18$, and $n_3 = 20$. The total number of subjects is represented with a capital $N = 53$ ($15 + 18 + 20 = 53$).

Finally, you must get straight the difference between ΣX^2 and $(\Sigma X)^2$; they do not mean the same thing. Different formulas may include one or the other or both and it is very important to interpret each correctly, since a formula tells you what to do and you must do exactly what it tells you. Now let us look at ΣX^2. What does it tell you? The Σ tells you that you are supposed to add something up. What you are supposed to add up are X^2s. What do you suppose X^2 means? Right. It means the square of the score; if $X = 4$, then $X^2 = 4 \times 4 = 16$. Thus, ΣX^2 says, square each score and then add up all the squares. Now let us look at $(\Sigma X)^2$. Since whatever is in the parentheses is always done first, the first thing we do is ΣX. You already know what that means: "add up all the scores." And then what? Right. You add up all the scores and then you square the total. As an example:

X	X^2	
1	1	
2	4	$\Sigma X^2 = 55$
3	9	
4	16	$(\Sigma X)^2 = 225$
5	25	
$\Sigma X = 15$	$\Sigma X^2 = 55$	

As you can see, there is a big difference between ΣX^2 and $(\Sigma X)^2$, so watch out! To summarize, symbols commonly used in statistical formulas are as follows:

X = a score
Σ = the sum of; add them up
ΣX = the sum of all the scores
$\overline{X}$ = the mean, or arithmetic average, of the scores
N = total number of subjects
n = number of subjects in a particular group
ΣX^2 = the sum of the squares; square each score and add up all the squares
$(\Sigma X)^2$ = the square of the sum; add up the scores and square the sum, or total

If you approach each statistic in an orderly fashion, it makes your statistical life easier. A suggested procedure is as follows:

1. Make the columns required by the formula (e.g., X, X^2, as just shown) and find the sum of each column.
2. Label the sum of each column; in the previous example, the label for the sum of the X column = ΣX, and the label for the sum of the X^2 column = ΣX^2.
3. Write the formula.
4. Write the arithmetic equivalent of the formula (e.g., $(\Sigma X)^2 = (15)^2$).
5. Solve the arithmetic problem (e.g., $(15)^2 = 225$).

THE MEAN

Although sample sizes of 5 are hardly ever considered to be acceptable, we will use this number of participants for illustration purposes. Our calculations will be based on the scores of 5 participants so that you can concentrate on how the calculation is being done and will not get lost in the numbers. For the same reason we will also use small numbers. Now, assume we have the following scores for some old friends of ours and we want to compute the mean, or arithmetic average.

$$X$$

Iggie	1
Hermie	2
Fifi	3
Teenie	4
Tiny	5

Remember that a column labeled X means "here come the scores!"

The formula for the mean is $\overline{X} = \dfrac{\Sigma X}{N}$

You are now looking at a statistic. Looks bad, right? Now let us first see what it really says. It reads "the mean ($\overline{X}$) is equal to the sum of the scores (ΣX) divided by the number of participants (N)." So, to find X we need ΣX and N.

X
1
2
3
4
5
$\Sigma X = 15$

Clearly, $\Sigma X = 1 + 2 + 3 + 4 + 5 = 15$
$N = 5$ (there are 5 participants, right?)

Now we have everything we need to find the mean and all we have to do is substitute the correct number for each symbol.

$$\overline{X} = \frac{\Sigma X}{N} = \frac{15}{5} = 3$$

Now what do we have? Right! An arithmetic problem. And hardly a difficult one! More like an elementary school arithmetic problem. And all we did was to substitute each symbol with the appropriate number. Thus,

$$\overline{X} = \frac{\Sigma X}{N} = \frac{15}{5} = 3(3.00)$$

and the mean is equal to 3.00. If you look at the scores you can see that 3 is clearly the average score. Since traditionally statistical results are given with 2 decimal places, our "official" answer is 3.00.

Was that hard? Cer-tain-ly not! And guess what—you just learned how to do a statistic! Are they all going to be that easy? Of course!

THE STANDARD DEVIATION

Earlier we explained the fact that the standard deviation is the square root of the variance, which is based on the distance of each score from the mean. To calculate the standard deviation (SD), however, we do not have to calculate variance scores; we can use a raw score formula that gives us the same answer with less grief. Now, before you look at the formula, remember that no matter how bad it looks, it is going to turn into an easy arithmetic problem. Ready?

$$SD = \sqrt{\frac{SS}{N-1}} \text{ where } SS = \Sigma X^2 - \frac{(\Sigma X)^2}{N}$$

or

$$SD = \sqrt{\frac{\Sigma X^2 - \frac{(\Sigma X)^2}{N}}{N-1}}$$

In other words, the SD is equal to the square root of the sum of squares (SS) divided by $N - 1$.

If the standard deviation of a population is being calculated, the formula is exactly the same, except we divide sum of squares by N, instead of $N - 1$. The reason is that a sample standard deviation is considered to be a biased estimate of the population standard deviation. When we select a sample, especially a small sample, the probability is that participants will come from the middle of the distribution and that extreme scores will not be represented. Thus, the range of sample scores will be smaller than the population range, as will be the sample standard deviation. As the sample size increases, so do the chances of getting extreme scores; thus, the smaller the sample, the more important it is to correct for the downward bias. By dividing by $N - 1$ instead of N, we make the denominator (bottom part!) smaller, and thus $\frac{SS}{N-1}$ is larger, closer to the population SD than $\frac{SS}{N}$. For example, if $SS = 18$ and $N = 10$, then

$$\frac{SS}{N-1} = \frac{18}{9} = 2.00 \qquad \frac{SS}{N} = \frac{18}{8} = 1.80$$

Now just relax and look at each piece of the formula; you already know what each one means. Starting with the easy one, N refers to what? Right—the number of subjects. How about (ΣX)? Right—the sum of the scores. And $(\Sigma X)^2$? Right—the square of the sum of the scores. That leaves ΣX^2, which means the sum of what? . . . Fantastic. The sum of the squares. Okay, let us use the same scores we used to calculate the mean. The first thing we need to do is to square each score and then add those squares up—while we are at it we can also go ahead and add up all the scores.

	X	X^2	
Iggie	1	1	
Hermie	2	4	$\Sigma X = 15$
Fifi	3	9	$\Sigma X^2 = 55$
Teenie	4	16	$N = 5$
Tiny	5	25	$N - 1 = 4$
	$\Sigma X = 15$	$\Sigma X^2 = 55$	

Do we have everything we need? Yes. Does the formula ask for anything else? No. We are in business. Substituting each symbol with its numerical equivalent we get

$$SS = \frac{(\Sigma X)^2}{N} = 55 - \frac{(15)^2}{5}$$

Now what do we have? A statistic? No! An arithmetic problem? Yes! A hard arithmetic problem? No! It is harder than 15/5 but it is not hard. If we just do what the formula tells us to do we will have no problem at all. The first thing it tells us to do is to square 15:

$$SS = \Sigma X^2 \frac{(\Sigma X)^2}{N} = 55 - \frac{(15)^2}{5} = 55 - \frac{225}{5}$$

So far so good. The next thing the formula tells us to do is divide 225 by 5, which equals 45. It is looking a lot better; now it is really an easy arithmetic problem. Okay, the next step is to subtract 45 from 55 and we get a sum of squares (SS) equal to 10.00.

Mere child's play. Think you can figure out the next step? Terrific! Now that we have SS, we simply substitute it into the SD formula as follows:

$$SD = \sqrt{\frac{SS}{N-1}} = \sqrt{\frac{10}{4}} = \sqrt{2.5}$$

To find the square root of 2.5, simply enter 2.5 into your calculator and hit the square root button ($\sqrt{\ }$); the square root of 2.5 is 1.58. Substituting in our square root we have

$$SD = \sqrt{2.5} = 1.58$$

and the standard deviation is 1.58. If we had calculated the standard deviation for the IQ distribution shown in Figure 14.2, what would we have gotten? Right, 15. Now you know how to do two useful descriptive statistics.

STANDARD SCORES

Your brain has earned a rest, and the formula for a z score is a piece of cake:

$$z = \frac{X - \overline{X}}{SD}$$

To convert scores to z scores we simply apply that formula to each score. We have already computed the mean and the standard deviation for the following scores:

	X	
Iggie	1	
Hermie	2	X = 3
Fifi	3	
Teenie	4	SD = 1.58
Tiny	5	

Let's see how Iggie's z score works out:

$$\text{Iggie} \quad z = \frac{X - \overline{X}}{SD} = \frac{1-3}{1.58} = \frac{-2}{1.58} = -1.26$$

This tells us that Iggie's standard score was 1.26 standard deviations below average. In case you have forgotten, if the signs are the same (two positives or two negatives), the answer in a multiplication or division problem is a positive number; if the signs are different, the answer is a negative number, as in Iggie's case. For the rest of our friends, the results are

$$\text{Hermie} \quad z = \frac{X - \bar{X}}{SD} = \frac{-1}{1.58} = -.63$$

$$\text{Fifi} \quad z = \frac{X - \bar{X}}{SD} = \frac{0}{1.58} = 0.0$$

$$\text{Teenie} \quad z = \frac{X - \bar{X}}{SD} = \frac{1}{1.58} = +.63$$

$$\text{Tiny} \quad z = \frac{X - \bar{X}}{SD} = \frac{2}{1.58} = +1.26$$

Notice that Fifi's score was the same as the mean score. Her z score is .00, meaning that her score is no distance from the mean (it's on the mean). On the other hand, Iggie's and Hermie's scores were below the mean so their z scores are negative, whereas Teenie and Tiny scored above the mean and their z scores are positive. If we want to eliminate the negatives, we can convert each z score to a Z score. Remember those? Multiplying each z score by 10 and adding 50 gives $Z = 10z + 50$. If we apply the z score formula we get

$$
\begin{aligned}
\text{Iggie} \quad Z &= 10z + 50 = 10(-1.26) + 50 \\
&= -12.6 + 50 \\
&= 50 - 12.6 \\
&= 37.40 \\
\text{Hermie} \quad Z &= 10z + 50 = 10(-.63) + 50 \\
&= -6.3 + 50 \\
&= 50 - 6.3 \\
&= 43.70 \\
\text{Fifi} \quad Z &= 10z + 50 = 10(.00) + 50 \\
&= .00 + 50 \\
&= 50 + .00 \\
&= 50.00 \\
\text{Teenie} \quad Z &= 10z + 50 = 10(+.63) + 50 \\
&= 6.3 + 50 \\
&= 50 + 6.3 \\
&= 56.30 \\
\text{Tiny} \quad Z &= 10z + 50 = 10(+1.26) + 50 \\
&= 12.6 + 50 \\
&= 50 + 12.6 \\
&= 62.60
\end{aligned}
$$

Note the analyses produced by these three common statistics: the mean = 3; the standard deviation = 1.58; and standard scores are -1.26, $-.63$, .00; .63., and 1.26. Now we will illustrate the use of SPSS to obtain the same results from the previous analysis. In this chapter and the next, we will show you both the analyses generated by the step-by-step approach and the SPSS approach.

OBTAINING DESCRIPTIVE STATISTICS WITH SPSS 10.0

When the data set is large, it is often easier to input, or type, the scores into a spreadsheet and generate the statistics you want using a computer program such as the Statistical Package for the Social Sciences (SPSS.) Figure 14.4 shows the same five scores for our friends as we just discussed. This time they have been entered into the SPSS spreadsheet.

To generate the descriptive statistics you want click on the "Analyze" menu and choose the "Descriptive Statistics" option as shown in Figure 14.5. In the Descriptive Statistics menu choose the "Descriptives . . ." option.

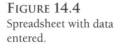

FIGURE 14.4
Spreadsheet with data
entered.

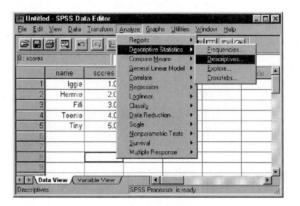

FIGURE 14.5 SPSS
menu options for
descriptive statistics.

Analyze
Descriptive Statistics
Descriptives . . .

Now, SPSS shows you the window displayed in Figure 14.6, where you are able to choose
the variables you wish to generate statistics on and where you select the statistics you would
like generated.

All variables appropriate for computing statistics are listed in the left section of the window. Notice that the variable containing the name of our friends is not included in the list because statistics cannot be computed on names of people. The first thing you need to do is select
the variable(s) in the left section of the window by clicking on them and move them to the
right section of the window by using the arrow button in the center of the window.

Once you have done this you are ready to choose the statistics you want to generate. To
make your selections click on the "Options . . ." button at the bottom right corner of the "Descriptives" window. In the "Options" window shown in Figure 14.7, you just click on the but-
tons to the left of the statistics you would like to see generated. Keep in mind that often there
are more statistics than you need or want shown in the SPSS window; choose only those you
think you will need. Once you have done this click on the "Continue" button in the upper right
corner of the window.

Once you are back to the "Descriptives" window, you will notice a button on the bottom
left corner of the window with a label that reads "Save standardized values as variables" (Figure 14.8). By clicking on this button the z scores will be saved for each score in the data set in
another variable labeled "z scores."

Once you click the "OK" button to generate the statistics, the new variable containing the
z scores will be visible in your data set.

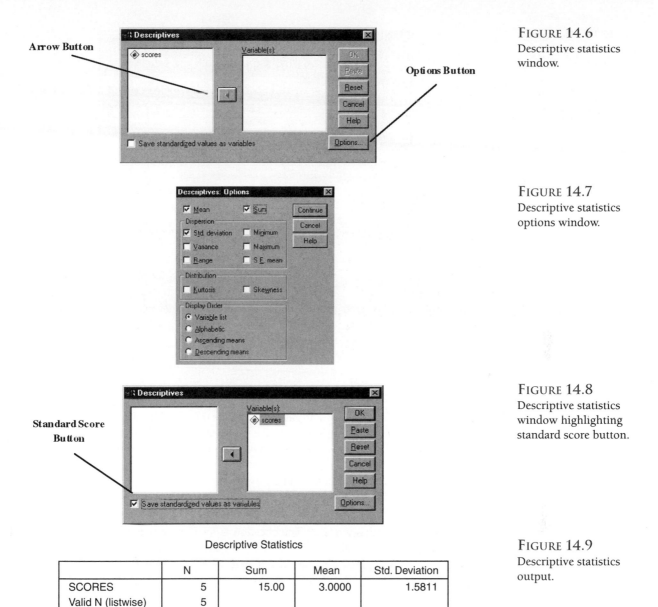

FIGURE 14.6
Descriptive statistics window.

FIGURE 14.7
Descriptive statistics options window.

FIGURE 14.8
Descriptive statistics window highlighting standard score button.

FIGURE 14.9
Descriptive statistics output.

Descriptive Statistics

	N	Sum	Mean	Std. Deviation
SCORES	5	15.00	3.0000	1.5811
Valid N (listwise)	5			

Figure 14.9 shows the output SPSS generates containing the statistics. In the first column the variable used to generate the statistics is listed; in this case it is the variable labeled "SCORES." Just below the name is a section labeled "Valid N (listwise)," which indicates the number of our friends that had an actual score in the data set. This number indicates the number of scores used in generating the statistics you selected. The second column in the output lists the number of cases in the data set. The second number in this column shows the number of cases that had actual values or scores. As you can see there are five cases with scores. The third column shows the sum of scores equal to 15.00, which is consistent with the earlier computations. The third and fourth columns show the mean and standard deviation for the scores. Compare these numbers with those found earlier.

Now, if we look at the spreadsheet shown in Figure 14.10, with the names and scores for our friends, you can see that z scores for all of the people have been added to the list of variables.

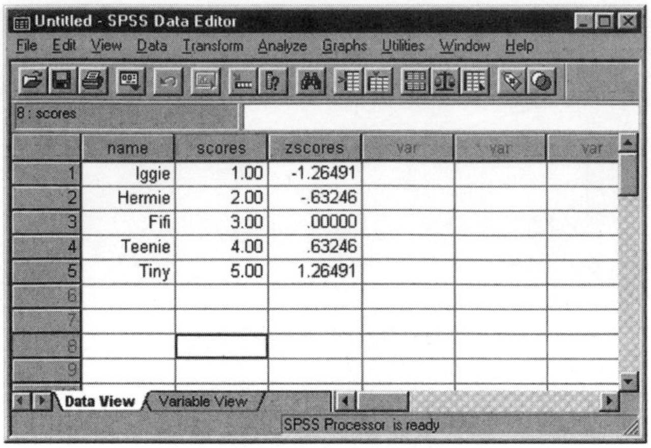

	name	scores	zscores	var	var	var
1	Iggie	1.00	-1.26491			
2	Hermie	2.00	-.63246			
3	Fifi	3.00	.00000			
4	Teenie	4.00	.63246			
5	Tiny	5.00	1.26491			
6						
7						
8						
9						

FIGURE 14.10
SPSS spreadsheet with standard scores added.

Congratulations! The step-by-step analysis and the SPSS analysis give the same results, although the SPSS analysis reports results to five decimal places, and the step-by-step analysis reports to only two (see p. 431).

THE P.EARSON *r*

Now that your brain is rested, you are ready for the Pearson *r*. The formula for the Pearson *r* looks very, very complicated, but it is not (have we lied to you so far?). It looks tough because it has a lot of pieces, but each piece is quite simple to calculate. To calculate correlations including a Pearson *r* we need two sets of scores. Let us assume we have the following sets of scores for two variables for our old friends:

	X	Y
Iggie	1	2
Hermie	2	3
Fifi	3	4
Teenie	4	3
Tiny	5	5

The question is, "Are these two variables related?" Positively? Negatively? Not at all?

To answer those questions we apply the formula for the Pearson *r* to the data. Here goes!

$$r = \frac{\Sigma XY - \dfrac{(\Sigma X)(\Sigma Y)}{N}}{\sqrt{\left[\Sigma X^2 - \dfrac{(\Sigma X)^2}{N}\right]\left[\Sigma Y^2 - \dfrac{(\Sigma Y)^2}{N}\right]}}$$

Now, if you look at each piece you will see that you already know how to calculate all of them except one. You should have no problem with ΣX, ΣY, ΣX^2, or ΣY^2. And even though there are 10 scores there are only 5 participants, so $N = 5$. What is left? The only new symbol in the formula is ΣXY. What could that mean? Well, you know that it is the sum of something, namely, the *XY*s, whatever they are. An *XY* is just what you would guess it is—the product of an *X* score and its corresponding *Y* score. Thus, Iggie's *XY* score is $1 \times 2 = 2$, and Teenie's *XY* score is $4 \times 3 = 12$. Okay, let us get all the pieces we need:

	X	Y	X²	Y²	XY
Iggie	1	2	1	4	2
Hermie	2	3	4	9	6
Fifi	3	4	9	16	12
Teenie	4	3	16	9	12
Tiny	5	5	25	25	25
	15	17	55	63	57
	ΣX	ΣY	ΣX²	ΣY²	ΣXY

Now guess what we are going to do. Right! We are going to turn that horrible-looking statistic into a horrible-looking arithmetic problem! Just kidding. Of course it will really be an easy arithmetic problem if we do it one step at a time.

$$r = \frac{\Sigma XY - \frac{(\Sigma X)(\Sigma Y)}{N}}{\sqrt{\left[\Sigma X^2 - \frac{(\Sigma X)^2}{N}\right]\left[\Sigma Y^2 - \frac{(\Sigma Y)^2}{N}\right]}} = \frac{57 - \frac{(15)(17)}{5}}{\sqrt{\left[55 - \frac{(15)^2}{5}\right]\left[63 - \frac{(17)^2}{5}\right]}}$$

It still doesn't look good, but you have to admit it looks better! Let's start with the numerator (for you nonmathematical types, the top part). The first thing the formula tells you to do is multiply 15 by 17:

$$= \frac{57 - \frac{255}{5}}{\sqrt{\left[55 - \frac{(15)^2}{5}\right]\left[63 - \frac{(17)^2}{5}\right]}}$$

The next step is to divide 255 by 5:

$$= \frac{57 - 51}{\sqrt{\left[55 - \frac{(15)^2}{5}\right]\left[63 - \frac{(17)^2}{5}\right]}}$$

The next step is a real snap. All you have to do is subtract 51 from 57:

$$= \frac{6}{\sqrt{\left[55 - \frac{(15)^2}{5}\right]\left[63 - \frac{(17)^2}{5}\right]}}$$

So much for the numerator. Was that hard? NO! *Au contraire,* it was very easy. Right? Right. Now for the denominator (the bottom part). If you think hard, you will realize that you have seen part of the denominator before. Hint: It was not in connection with the mean. Let us go through it step by step anyway just in case you did not really understand what we were doing the last time we did it. The first thing the formula says to do is to square 15:

$$= \frac{6}{\sqrt{\left[55 - \frac{225}{5}\right]\left[63 - \frac{(17)^2}{5}\right]}}$$

Now we divide 225 by 5:

$$= \frac{6}{\sqrt{\left[55 - 45\right]\left[63 - \frac{(17)^2}{5}\right]}}$$

Did you get that? All we did was divide 225 by 5 and we got 45. Can you figure out the next step? Good. We substract 45 from 55:

$$= \frac{6}{\sqrt{\left[10\right]\left[63 - \frac{(17)^2}{5}\right]}}$$

It is looking a lot better, isn't it? Okay, now we need to square 17; $17 \times 17 = 289$.

$$= \frac{6}{\sqrt{\left[10\right]\left[63 - \frac{289}{5}\right]}}$$

Next, we divide 289 by 5 (sorry, life doesn't always come out even):

$$= \frac{6}{\sqrt{[10][63 - 57.8]}}$$

We are getting there. Now we subtract 57.8 from 63. Do not let the decimals scare you:

$$= \frac{6}{\sqrt{[10][63 - 57.8]}} = \frac{6}{\sqrt{[10][5.2]}}$$

Can you figure out what to do next? If you find this difficult, hang in there, we're almost finished. If you find this easy, also hang in there. Next, we multiply 10 by 5.2:

$$= \frac{6}{\sqrt{[10][5.2]}} = \frac{6}{\sqrt{52}}$$

Next, we find the square root of 52:

$$= \frac{6}{\sqrt{52}} = \frac{6}{7.2}$$

Almost done. All we have to do is to divide 6 by 7.2:

$$\frac{6}{7.2} = .83$$

Thus, the Pearson *r* correlation coefficient is .83. Well done! Is .83 good? Does it represent a true relationship? Is .83 significantly different from .00? If you recall the related discussion in Chapter 11 you know that a correlation coefficient of .83 indicates a high positive relationship between the variables. To determine whether .83 represents a true relationship we need a table. We need a table that indicates how large our correlation needs to be to be significant, that is, different from zero, given the number of participants we have and the level of significance at which we are working (see Table A.2 in Appendix A). The number of participants affects the degrees of freedom, which for the Pearson *r* are always computed by the formula $N - 2$. Thus, for our example, degrees of freedom $(df) = N - 2 = 5 - 2 = 3$. If we select $\alpha = .05$ as our level of significance, we are now ready to use Table A.2. Degrees of freedom and level of significance are among the coming attractions of Chapter 15.

Look at Table A.2 and find the column labeled *df* and run your left index finger down the column until you hit 3, the *df* associated with our Pearson *r*; keep your left finger right there for the time being. Now run your right index finger across the top of the table until you come to .05, the significance level we have selected. Now, run your left finger straight across the table and your right finger straight down the table until they meet. If you follow directions well, you should have ended up at .8783, which rounds off to .88. Now we compare our coefficient to the table value. Is .83 greater than .88? No, .83 is not greater than or equal to .88. Therefore, our coefficient does not indicate a true relationship between variables X and Y. Even though the correlation looks big, it is not big enough, given that we only have five subjects. We are not absolutely positive that there is no relationship (remember measurement error), but the odds are against it. Note that if we had had just one more participant ($N = 6$) our df would have been 4 ($N - 2 = 6 - 2 = 4$) and Table A.2 would have indicated a significant relationship (.83 is greater than .81). Note, too, that the same table would have been used if r had been a negative number, $-.83$. The table does not know or care whether the r is positive or negative. It only tells you how large r must be to indicate a true relationship, that is, a relationship significantly different from .00.

Do not forget, however, that even if a correlation coefficient is statistically significant, it does not imply a causal relationship nor does it necessarily mean that the coefficient has any practical significance. Whether the coefficient is useful depends upon the use to which it will be put; a coefficient to be used in a prediction study needs to be much higher than a coefficient to be used in a relationship study.

Obtaining the Pearson r Using SPSS 10.0

To obtain the Pearson r correlation coefficient in SPSS, one follows similar procedures as when looking for the mean and standard deviation. First, find the "Analyze" menu in the SPSS data editor window. Now look for the "Correlate" option. When you click on the Correlate option another submenu will appear. Within this submenu choose the "Bivariate" option. This will give you the correlation between two sets of scores (between two variables). Figure 14.11 shows the menu options to choose. In summary, the options are as follows:

Analyze
Correlate
Bivariate . . .

Once you have followed this procedure you will get the Bivariate Correlation window shown in Figure 14.12. This is where you will select the variables you wish to correlate. In the upper left side of the window you will see a list of variables that may be correlated. Here, one can see the variables for the first and the second set of scores for our friends. With the cursor,

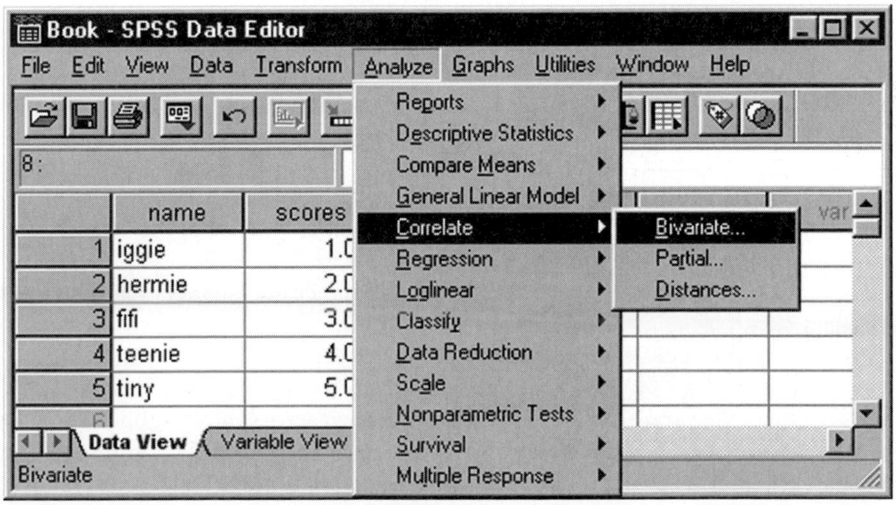

FIGURE 14.11
SPSS menu options for correlations.

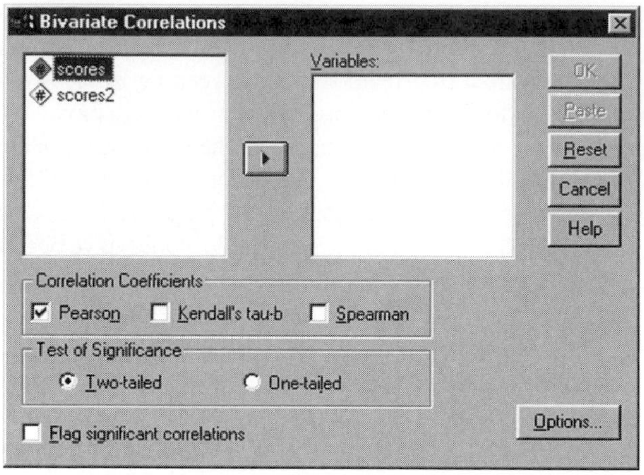

FIGURE 14.12
Bivariate correlation
window.

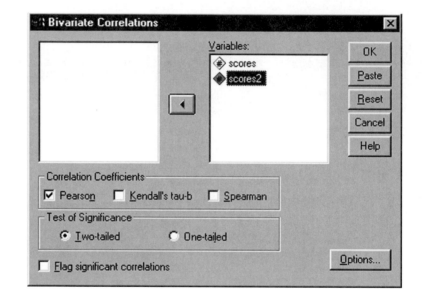

FIGURE 14.13
Illustrating correlation
coefficient options.

highlight each variable and move them to the "Variables" section of the window using the arrow button in the middle of the window.

Once you have chosen the variables you wish to correlate, make sure you are asking for the Pearson correlation. To do this, find the section of the window labeled "Correlation Coefficients." Figure 14.13 shows this section in the correlation window where you will find the option labeled "Pearson." Click on the box to the left of the word *Pearson* to select it.

Once you have selected the variables and checked the Pearson correlation coefficient option you can click on the "OK" button in the upper right corner to run your analysis. You should get output that looks like that shown in Figure 14.14.

The figure shows a 2 × 2 matrix with four cells. The cells contain the correlation coefficients between the variables. Two variables are shown across the top and two are shown down the left side. As you can see they are the same sets of variables. In the column labeled "Scores" you can see that the first cell is the correlation with the variable "Scores." Note that the Pearson correlation is equal to one. Since this is the correlation of the vari-

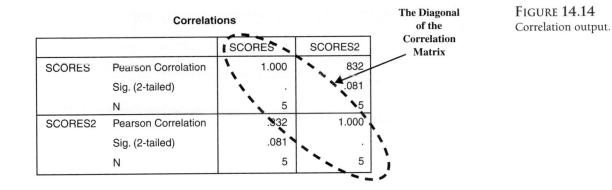

FIGURE 14.14
Correlation output.

able "Scores" with itself it makes sense that there would be a perfect correlation. This is also the case in the second cell of the second column of the 2 × 2 matrix. Here the variable "Scores2" is correlated with itself. This set of perfect correlations is called the "Diagonal" of the matrix.

The other cells in the matrix are called the "off diagonal" cells. These cells show the Pearson correlation of one variable with the other. Since there are only two variables in this analysis both "off diagonal" boxes represent the same information. As you can see the Pearson correlation coefficient represented in the bottom cell in the first column is the same as that computed earlier; that is, the Pearson *r* equals 0.83 (.832 rounded off).

Congratulations!

POSTSCRIPT

Almost always in a research study, descriptive statistics such as the mean and standard deviation are computed separately for each group in the study. A correlation coefficient is usually only computed in a correlational study (unless it is used to compute the reliability of an instrument used in a causal–comparative or experimental study). Standard scores are rarely used in research studies. However, to test our hypothesis we almost always need more than descriptive statistics; we need the application of one or more inferential statistics to test hypotheses and determine the significance of results. We discuss inferential statistics in the next chapter.

Now go to the Companion Website accompanying this text at www.prenhall.com/gay to check your understanding of chapter concepts in the following modules: Objectives, Practice Quiz, and Applying What You Know. Expand your research skills with Evaluating Articles, Analyzing Qualitative Data, Analyzing Quantitative Data, and Research Tools and Tips. Visit Web Links to broaden your knowledge about research.

SUMMARY

Preparing Data for Analysis

1. All instruments administered should be scored accurately and consistently, using the same procedures and criteria.
2. When a standardized instrument is used the test manual usually spells out the steps to be followed in scoring and a scoring key is often provided.
3. Scoring self-developed instruments is more complex, especially if open-ended items are involved. Steps for scoring each item and for arriving at a to-

tal score must be delineated and carefully followed. If open-ended items are to be scored, have at least one other person score the tests as a reliability check. Tentative scoring procedures should always be tried out beforehand by administering the instrument to individuals similar to but not among the study participants.
4. After instruments have been scored, the results are transferred to summary data sheets or, more commonly, to a computer program. If planned analyses

involve subgroup comparisons, scores should be tabulated for each subgroup.

5. The more complex the data are, the more useful computer record keeping and analysis can be.

6. Computers can facilitate data analysis and should be used when possible. However, a good guideline is that you should not use the computer to perform an analysis that you have never done yourself by hand, or at least studied extensively.

Types of Descriptive Statistics

7. The first step in data analysis is to describe, or summarize, the data using descriptive statistics, which permit you to meaningfully describe many, many scores with a small number of indices.

8. The values calculated for a sample drawn from a population are referred to as *statistics*. The values calculated for an entire population are referred to as *parameters*.

Graphing Data

9. The shape of the distribution may not be self-evident, especially if a large number of scores are involved. The most common method of graphing research data is to construct a frequency polygon. Other methods include the boxplot, pie chart, and the stem-and-leaf chart.

Measures of Central Tendency

10. Measures of central tendency are a convenient way of describing a set of data with a single number.

11. The number resulting from computation of a measure of central tendency represents the average or typical score attained by a group of participants. Each index of central tendency is appropriate for a different scale of measurement; the mode is appropriate for nominal data, the median for ordinal data, and the mean for interval or ratio data.

12. The mode is the score that is attained by more subjects than any other score. It is determined by looking at a set of scores or at a graph of scores and seeing which score occurs most frequently. A set of scores may have two (or more) modes. When nominal data are involved, however, the mode is the only appropriate measure of central tendency.

13. The median is that point in a distribution above and below which are 50% of the scores; in other words, the median is the midpoint. The median does not take into account each and every score; it ignores,

for example, extremely high scores and extremely low scores.

14. The mean is the arithmetic average of the scores and is the most frequently used measure of central tendency. The mean takes into account, or includes, each and every score in its computation. It is a more precise, stable index than both the median and the mode except in situations in which there are extreme scores, making the median the best index of typical performance.

Measures of Variability

15. Two sets of data that are very different can have identical means or medians, thus creating a need for a measure that indicates how spread out the scores are—how much variability there is.

16. Although the standard deviation is used with interval and ratio data and is the most commonly used measure of variation, the range is the only appropriate measure of variability for nominal data, and the quartile deviation is the appropriate index of variability for ordinal data.

17. The range is simply the difference between the highest and lowest score in a distribution and is determined by subtraction. It is not a very stable measure of variability, but its chief advantage is that it gives a quick, rough estimate of variability.

18. The quartile deviation is one half of the difference between the upper quartile (the 75th percentile) and lower quartile (the 25th percentile) in a distribution. The quartile deviation is a more stable measure of variability than the range and is appropriate whenever the median is appropriate.

19. Like the mean, the standard deviation is the most stable measure of variability and takes into account each and every score. If you know the mean and the standard deviation of a set of scores, you have a pretty good picture of the distribution.

20. If the score distribution is relatively normal, then the mean plus 3 standard deviations and the mean minus 3 standard deviations encompasses just about all the scores, over 99% of them.

The Normal Curve

21. Many variables do yield a normal, bell-shaped curve if a sufficient number of subjects are measured.

22. If a variable is normally distributed, then several things are true. First, 50% of the scores are above the mean and 50% of the scores are below the mean.

Second, the mean, the median, and the mode are the same. Third, most scores are near the mean and the further from the mean a score is, the fewer the number of subjects who attained that score. Fourth, the same number, or percentage, of scores is between the mean and plus one standard deviation ($\overline{X} + 1\,SD$) as is between the mean and minus one standard deviation ($\overline{X} - 1\,SD$), and similarly for $\overline{X} \pm 2\,SD$ and $\overline{X} \pm 3\,SD$.

23. If scores are normally distributed, the following are true statements:

    $\overline{X} \pm 1.0\,SD$ = approximately 68% of the scores
    $\overline{X} \pm 2.0\,SD$ = approximately 95% of the scores
    $\qquad$ (1.96 SD is exactly 95%)
    $\overline{X} \pm 2.5\,SD$ = approximately 99% of the scores
    $\qquad$ (2.58 SD is exactly 99%)
    $\overline{X} \pm 3.0\,SD$ = approximately 99+% of the scores

    And similarly, the following are always true:

    $\overline{X} - 3.0\,SD$ = approximately the 0.1 percentile
    $\overline{X} - 2.0\,SD$ = approximately the 2nd percentile
    $\overline{X} - 1.0\,SD$ = approximately the 16th percentile
    $\qquad \overline{X}$ = the 50th percentile
    $\overline{X} + 1.0\,SD$ = approximately the 84th percentile
    $\overline{X} + 2.0\,SD$ = approximately the 98th percentile
    $\overline{X} + 3.0\,SD$ = approximately the 99th + percentile

24. Because research studies deal with a finite number of subjects, and often a not very large number, research data only more or less approximate a normal curve.

Skewed Distributions

25. When a distribution is not normal, it is said to be skewed, and the values of the mean, the median, and the mode are different.

26. In a skewed distribution, there are more extreme scores at one end than the other. If the extreme scores are at the lower end of the distribution, the distribution is said to be negatively skewed; if the extreme scores are at the upper, or higher, end of the distribution, the distribution is said to be positively skewed. In both cases, the mean is "pulled" in the direction of the extreme scores.

27. For a negatively skewed distribution the mean ($\overline{X}$) is always lower, or smaller, than the median (md); for a positively skewed distribution the mean is always higher, or greater, than the median.

Measures of Relative Position

28. Measures of relative position indicate where a score is in relation to all other scores in the distri-

bution. They make it possible to compare the performance of an individual on two or more different tests.

29. A percentile rank indicates the percentage of scores that fall at or below a given score. Percentiles are appropriate for data representing an ordinal scale, although they are frequently computed for interval data. The median of a set of scores corresponds to the 50th percentile.

30. A standard score is a measure of relative position that is appropriate when the data represent an interval or ratio scale. A z score expresses how far a score is from the mean in terms of standard deviation units. If a set of scores is transformed into a set of z scores, the new distribution has a mean of 0 and a standard deviation of 1. The z score allows scores from different tests to be compared.

31. A table of normal curve areas corresponding to various z scores can be used to determine the proportion (and percentage) of cases that fall below a given z score, above a given z score, and between any two z scores.

32. A problem with z scores is that they can involve negative numbers and decimals. A simple solution is to transform z scores into Z scores by multiplying the z score by 10 and adding 50.

33. Stanines are standard scores that divide a distribution into nine parts.

Measures of Relationship

34. Degree of relationship is expressed as a correlation coefficient, which is computed from two sets of scores from a single group of participants. If two variables are highly related, a correlation coefficient near +1.00 (or −1.00) will be obtained; if two variables are not related, a coefficient near .00 will be obtained.

35. The Spearman rho is the appropriate measure of correlation when the variables are expressed as ranks instead of scores. It is appropriate when the data represent an ordinal scale (although it may be used with interval data) and is used when the median and quartile deviation are used.

36. The Spearman rho is interpreted in the same way as the Pearson r and produces a coefficient somewhere between −1.00 and +1.00. If more than one subject receives the same score, then their corresponding ranks are averaged.

37. The Pearson r is the most appropriate measure of correlation when the sets of data to be correlated

represent either interval or ratio scales, as most educational measures are. An assumption associated with the application of the Pearson r is that the relationship between the variables being correlated is a linear one.

Calculation for Interval Data

Symbols

38. Symbols commonly used in statistical formulas are as follows:

X = any score
Σ = the sum of; add them up
ΣX = the sum of all the scores
$\overline{X}$ = the mean, or arithmetic average, of the scores
N = total number of subjects
n = number of subjects in a particular group
ΣX^2 = the sum of the squares; square each score and add up all the squares
$(\Sigma X)^2$ = the square of the sum; add up the scores and square the sum, or total

The Mean

39. The formula for the mean is $\overline{X} = \dfrac{\Sigma X}{N}$

The Standard Deviation

40. The formula for the standard deviation is

$$SD = \sqrt{\frac{SS}{N-1}} \text{ where } SS = \Sigma X^2 - \frac{(\Sigma X)^2}{N}$$

Standard Scores

41. The formula for a z score is $z = \dfrac{X - \overline{X}}{SD}$

The formula for a Z score is $Z = 10z + 50$.

The Pearson r

42. The formula for the Pearson r is

$$r = \frac{\Sigma XY - \dfrac{(\Sigma X)(\Sigma Y)}{N}}{\sqrt{\left[\Sigma X^2 - \dfrac{(\Sigma X)^2}{N}\right]\left[\Sigma Y^2 - \dfrac{(\Sigma Y)^2}{N}\right]}}$$

43. The formula for degrees of freedom for the Pearson r is $N - 2$.

". . . once in a while, just by chance, we will get a sample that is quite different from the population, but not very often." (p. 447)

INFERENTIAL STATISTICS

OBJECTIVES

After reading Chapter 15, you should be able to do the following:

1. Explain the concept of standard error.
2. Describe how sample size affects standard error.
3. Describe the null hypothesis.
4. State the purpose of a test of significance.
5. Describe Type I and Type II errors.
6. Describe the concept of significance level (probability level).
7. Describe one-tailed and two-tailed tests.
8. Explain the difference between parametric tests and nonparametric tests.
9. State the purpose, and explain the strategy, of the t test.
10. Describe independent and nonindependent samples.
11. State the purpose and appropriate use of the t test for independent samples.
12. State the purpose and appropriate use of the t test for nonindependent samples.
13. Describe one major problem associated with analyzing gain or difference scores.
14. State the purpose of the simple analysis of variance.
15. State the purpose of multiple comparison procedures.
16. State the purpose of a factorial analysis of variance.
17. State the purpose of analysis of covariance.
18. State two (2) uses of multiple regression.
19. State the purpose of chi square.
20. Generate three columns of five one-digit numbers ("scores"), compute each of the following statistics (give the formula and show your work), state whether each result is statistically significant at $\alpha = .05$, and interpret each result:

   a. t test for independent samples
   b. t test for nonindependent samples
   c. simple analysis of variance for three groups
   d. the Scheffé test
   e. chi square (Sum the numbers in each column and treat them as if they were the total number of people responding "yes," "no," and "undecided," respectively, in a survey.)

CONCEPTS UNDERLYING INFERENTIAL STATISTICS

Inferential statistics deal with, of all things, inferences. Inferences about what? Inferences about populations based on the results of samples. Inferential statistics allow researchers to generalize to a population of individuals based on information obtained from a limited number of research participants. Most educational research studies deal with samples from larger populations. Recall that the appropriateness of the various sampling techniques discussed in Chapter 4 is based on their effectiveness in producing representative samples. Representative samples of what? Right, of the populations they are drawn from. The more representative a sample is, the more generalizable its results will be to the population from which the sample was selected. Results that are representative only of that particular sample are of very limited research use. Consequently, random samples are preferred.

Inferential statistics are concerned with determining whether results obtained from a sample or samples are the same as would have been obtained for the entire population. As mentioned in Chapter 14, sample values, such as the mean, are referred to as *statistics*. The corresponding values in the population are referred to as *parameters*. Thus, if a mean is based on a sample, it is a statistic; if it is based on an entire population, it is a parameter. Inferential statistics are used to make inferences about parameters, based on the statistics from a sample. If a difference between means is found for two groups at the end of a study, the question of interest is whether a similar difference exists in the population from which the samples were selected. That is, can the results of the study be generalized to the larger population? It could be that no real difference exists in the population and that the difference found for the samples was a chance one (remember sampling error?).

And now we get to the heart of inferential statistics, the concept of "how likely is it?" If your study indicates a difference between two sample means (say $\overline{X}_1 = 35$ and $\overline{X}_2 = 43$) how likely is it that this difference is a real one in the population? What kind of process can you use to determine whether the difference between $\overline{X}_1$ and $\overline{X}_2$ is a real, significant one rather than one attributable to sampling error? It is important to understand that using samples to make inferences about populations produces only probability statements about the populations. The degree to which the results of a sample can be generalized to a population is expressed in terms of probabilities; analyses do not "prove" results are true or false. There are many concepts underlying the application of inferential statistics that must be discussed prior to describing and illustrating types of these statistics.

STANDARD ERROR

Inferences about populations are based on information from samples. However, the chances of any sample being exactly identical to its population are virtually nil. Even when random samples are used, we cannot expect that the sample characteristics will be exactly the same as those of the population. For example, if we randomly select a number of samples from the same population and compute the mean for each, it is very likely that the means will be somewhat different from each other and that none of the means will be identical to the population mean. This expected random, or chance, variation among the means is referred to as *sampling error*. Recall that in Chapter 4 we discussed the fact that unlike sampling bias, sampling error is not the researcher's fault. Sampling error just happens and is as inevitable as taxes and educational research courses! Thus, if a difference is found between two sample means, the important question is whether the difference is a true or significant one or just the result of sampling error.

A useful characteristic of sampling errors is that they are usually normally distributed. As discussed in Chapter 14, sampling errors vary in size (small errors versus large errors) and these errors tend to form a normal, bell-shaped curve. Thus, if a large number of samples of the same size are randomly selected from a population, we know that all the samples will not be the same but that the means of all these samples should form a normal distribution around the population mean. Further, the mean of all these sample means will yield a good estimate of the population mean.[1] Most of the sample means will be close to the population mean and the number of means that are considerably different from the population mean will decrease as the size of the difference increases. In other words, very few means will be much higher or much lower than the population mean. An example may help to clarify this concept.

Let us suppose that we do not know what the population mean IQ is for the Stanford-Binet, Form L.M (although we do know from Figure 14.2). To determine the population mean, suppose we randomly select 100 samples of the same size from the possible Stanford-Binet scores (the population of scores). We might get the following 100 means:

---

[1]To find the mean of the sample means, simply sum the sample means and divide by the number of means, as long as each sample is the same size.

So why not set α at .000000001 and hardly ever be wrong? Good question; glad you asked it. If you select α to be very, very small, you definitely decrease your chances of committing a Type I error; you will hardly ever reject a true null hypothesis. But, guess what happens to your chances of committing a Type II error? Right. As you decrease the probability of committing a Type I error, you increase the probability of committing a Type II error, that is, of not rejecting a null hypothesis when you should (another catch-22!). For example, you might conduct a study for which a mean difference of 9.5 represents a true difference. If you set α at .0001, however, you might require a mean difference of 20.0 to reach significance. If the difference actually found was 11.0, you would not reject the null hypothesis (11.0 is less than 20.0) although there really is a difference (11.0 is greater than 9.5). How do you decide which level to work at, and when do you decide?

The choice of a probability level, α, is made prior to execution of the study. The researcher considers the relative seriousness of committing a Type I versus a Type II error and selects α accordingly. In other words, the researcher compares the consequences of making the two possible wrong decisions. As an example, suppose you are a teacher and one day your principal comes up to you and says, "I understand you have research training and I want you to do a study for me. I'm considering implementing the Whoopee-Do Reading method in the school next year. This program is very costly, and if implemented, we will have to spend a great deal of money on materials and inservice training. I don't want to do that unless it really works. I want you to conduct a pilot study this year with several groups and then tell me if the Whoopee-Do program really results in better reading achievement. You have my complete support in setting up the groups the way you want to and in implementing the study."

In this case, which would be more serious, a Type I error or a Type II error? Suppose you conclude that the groups are significantly different, that the Whoopee-Do program really works. But suppose it really does not. Suppose you make a Type I error. In this case, the principal is going to be very upset if a big investment is made based on your decision and at the end of a year's period there is no difference in achievement. On the other hand, suppose you conclude that the groups are not significantly different, that the Whoopee-Do program does not really make a difference. Suppose it really does. Suppose you make a Type II error. In this case, what will happen? Nothing. You will tell the principal the program does not work, you will be thanked for the input, the program will not be implemented, and life will go on as usual. Therefore, for this situation, which would you rather commit, a Type I error or a Type II error? Obviously, a Type II error. You want to be very sure you do not commit a Type I error. Therefore you would select a very small α, perhaps $\alpha = .01$ or even $\alpha = .001$. You want to be pretty darn sure there is a real difference before you say there is.

As another example, suppose you are going to conduct an exploratory study to investigate the effectiveness of a new counseling technique. If you conclude that it is more effective (does make a difference), further research will be conducted. If you conclude that it does not make a difference, the new technique will be labeled "not very promising." Now, which would be more serious, a Type I error or a Type II error? If you conclude there is a difference, and there really is not (Type I error), no real harm will be done and the only real consequence will be that further research will probably disconfirm your finding. If, on the other hand, you conclude that the technique makes no difference, and it really does (Type II error), a technique may be prematurely abandoned; with a little refinement, this new technique might make a real difference. In this case, you would probably rather commit a Type I error than a Type II error. Therefore, you might select an α level as high as .10.

For most studies, $\alpha = .05$ is a reasonable probability level. The consequences of committing a Type I error are usually not too serious. However, a no-no in selecting a probability level is to first compute a test of significance to see "how significant it is" and then select a probability level. If the results just happen to be significant at $\alpha = .01$ you do not say "Oh goodie!" and report that the t was significant at the .01 level. In most cases you must put your cards on the table *before* you play the game, by stating a probability level for the significance test prior to data analysis. However, some researchers do not state a probability level before the study, preferring to report the exact probability level of the significance test at the end. This approach lets the reader of the study judge whether the results are "significant" for their purpose or use. We recommend that you stick to stating your α value at the start of your study.

A common misconception is the notion that if you reject a null hypothesis you have "proven" your research hypothesis. However, as stated, rejection or lack of rejection of a null hypothesis supports or does not support a research hypothesis. It does not prove it. If you reject a null hypothesis and conclude that the groups are really different, it does not necessarily mean that they are different for the reason you hypothesized. They may be different for some other reason. On the other hand, if you fail to reject the null hypothesis, it does not necessarily mean that your research hypothesis is wrong. The study, for example, may not have represented a fair test of your hypothesis. To use a former example, if you were investigating cooperative learning and the cooperative learning group and the control group each received its respective treatment for one day only, you probably would not find any differences between the groups. This would not mean that cooperative learning is not effective. If your study were conducted over a 6-month period, it might very well make a difference.

TWO-TAILED AND ONE-TAILED TESTS

Tests of significance are almost always two-tailed. The null hypothesis states that there is no difference between the groups (A = B), and a two-tailed test allows for the possibility that a difference may occur in either direction: either group mean may be higher than the other (A > B or B > A). A one-tailed test assumes that a difference can only occur in one direction. The null hypothesis states that one group is not better than another, and the one-tailed test assumes that if a difference occurs it will be in favor of that particular group (A > B). Remember, that the "tail" or "tails" represent the region of rejection. As an example, suppose a research hypothesis were

> Kindergarten children who receive a midmorning snack exhibit better behavior during the hour before lunch than kindergarten students who do not receive a midmorning snack.

For this research hypothesis the null hypothesis would state

> There is no difference between the behavior during the hour before lunch of kindergarten students who receive a midmorning snack and kindergarten students who do not receive a midmorning snack.

A two-tailed test of significance would allow for the possibility that either the group that received a snack or the group that did not might exhibit better behavior. For a one-tailed test, the null hypothesis might state

> Kindergarten children who receive a midmorning snack do not exhibit better behavior during the hour before lunch than kindergarten children who do not receive a midmorning snack.

In this case, the assumption would be that if a difference were found between the groups it would be in favor of the group that received the snack. In other words, the researcher would consider it highly unlikely that not receiving a snack could result in better behavior than receiving one (although it could if they were fed super sugar-coated chocolate twinkos!).

Tests of significance are almost always two-tailed. To select a one-tailed test of significance the researcher has to be pretty darn sure that a difference will only occur in one direction, and this is not very often the case. When appropriate, a one-tailed test has one major advantage: The score difference required for significance is smaller than for a two-tailed test. In other words, it is "easier" to obtain a significant difference. It is difficult to explain simply why this is so, but it has to do with α. Suppose you are computing a test of significance at $\alpha = .05$. If your test is two-tailed, you are allowing for the possibility of a positive t or a negative t; in other words, you are allowing that the mean of the first group may be higher than the mean of the second group ($X_1 - \overline{X}_2$ = a positive number), or that the mean of the second group may be higher than the mean of the first group ($\overline{X}_1 - \overline{X}_2$ = a negative number). Thus, our significance level, say .05, has to be divided into two halves (.025 and .025) to cover both possible outcomes ($\overline{X}_1 - \overline{X}_2$ is positive and $\overline{X}_1 - \overline{X}_2$ is negative). For a one-tailed test, the entire significance level, say .05, is concentrated on only one side of the normal curve. Since .025 has a smaller probability of committing a Type I error than .05, a larger t value is required. The above explanation applies to any α value and to other tests of significance besides the t test. While the above is definitely not the most scientific explanation of two-tailed and one-tailed tests, it should give you some conceptual understanding. The darkened areas of Figure 15.3 compare the significance areas of a one- and two-tailed test at $\alpha = .05$.

DEGREES OF FREEDOM

After you have determined whether your significance test will be two-tailed or one-tailed, selected a probability level, and computed a test of significance, you must consult the appropriate table to determine the significance of your results. (Most statistical computer programs provide information about the significance of the results computed in their output.) As you no doubt recall from our discussion of the significance of a correlation coefficient in Chapter 11, the appropriate table is usually entered at the intersection of your probability level and your degrees of freedom (df). Degrees of freedom are dependent on the number of participants and the number of groups. Recall that for the correlation coefficient, r, the appropriate

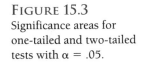

FIGURE 15.3
Significance areas for one-tailed and two-tailed tests with $\alpha = .05$.

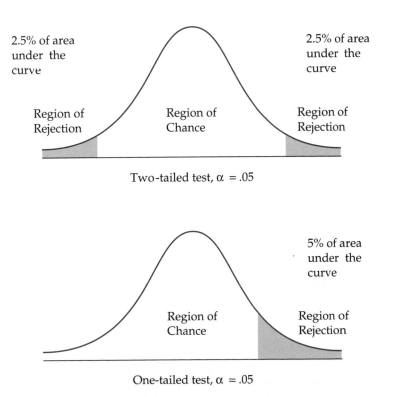

2.5% of area under the curve

2.5% of area under the curve

Region of Rejection

Region of Chance

Region of Rejection

Two-tailed test, $\alpha = .05$

5% of area under the curve

Region of Chance

Region of Rejection

One-tailed test, $\alpha = .05$

degrees of freedom were determined by the formula $N - 2$, number of participants minus 2. An illustration may help explain the concept of degrees of freedom. Suppose I ask you to name any five numbers. You agree and say "1, 2, 3, 4, 5." In this case N is equal to 5, you had 5 choices or 5 degrees of freedom to select the numbers. Now suppose I tell you to name 5 numbers and you say "1, 2, 3, 4, . . . ," and I say "Wait! The mean of the five numbers you choose must be 4." Now you have no choice—your last number must be 10 because $1 + 2 + 3 + 4 + 10 = 20$ and 20 divided by $5 = 4$. You lost one degree of freedom because of the restriction (lack of freedom) that the mean must be 4. In other words, instead of having $N = 5$ degrees of freedom, you only had $N = 4$ $(5 - 1)$ degrees of freedom. Got the idea?

Each test of significance has its own formula for determining degrees of freedom. For the correlation coefficient, r, the formula is $N - 2$. The number 2 is a constant, requiring that degrees of freedom for r are always determined by subtracting 2 from N, the number of participants. Each of the inferential statistics we are about to discuss also has its own formula for degrees of freedom.

TESTS OF SIGNIFICANCE: TYPES

Different tests of significance are appropriate for different types of data. It is important that the researcher select the appropriate test, since an incorrect test can lead to incorrect conclusions. The first decision in selecting an appropriate test of significance is whether a parametric or nonparametric test must be selected. Parametric tests are usually more powerful and generally to be preferred. "More powerful" in this case means more likely to reject a null hypothesis that is false; in other words, the researcher is less likely to commit a Type II error—less likely to not reject a null hypothesis that should be rejected.

Parametric tests, however, require that certain assumptions be met in order for them to be valid. One of the major assumptions underlying use of parametric tests is that the variable measured is normally distributed in the population (or at least that the form of the distribution is known). Since many variables studied in education are normally distributed, this assumption is often met. A second major assumption is that the data represent an interval or ratio scale of measurement. Again, since most measures used in education are or assumed to be interval data, this assumption is usually met. In fact, this is one major advantage of using an interval scale—it permits the use of a parametric test. A third assumption is that the selection of participants is independent. In other words, the selection of one subject in no way affects selection of any other subject. Recall that random sampling is sampling in which every member of the population has an equal and independent chance to be selected for the sample. Thus, if randomization is used in participant selection, the assumption of independence is met. Another assumption is that the variances of the population comparison groups are equal (or at least that the ratio of the variances is known). Remember, the variance of a group of scores is nothing more than the standard deviation squared.

With the exception of independence, some violation of one or more of these assumptions usually does not make too much difference in the statistical significance of the results. However, if one or more assumptions are greatly violated, such as if the distribution is extremely skewed, parametric statistics should not be used. In such cases, a nonparametric test should be used. **Nonparametric tests** make no assumptions about the shape of the distribution. They are usually used when the data represent an ordinal or nominal scale, when a parametric assumption has been greatly violated, or when the nature of the distribution is not known.

If the data represent an interval or ratio scale, a parametric test should be used unless one of the assumptions is greatly violated. As mentioned, parametric tests are more powerful. A nonparametric test is more difficult than a parametric test to reject a null hypothesis at a given level of significance. A nonparametric test usually takes a larger sample size to reach the same level of significance as a parametric test. Another advantage of parametric statistics is that they permit tests of a number of hypotheses that cannot be tested with a nonparametric test, since there are a number of parametric statistics that have no counterpart among nonparametric statistics. Because parametric statistics seem to be relatively hardy, that is, do their job even with moderate assumption violation, they will usually be selected for analysis of research data.

In the following sections we examine both parametric and nonparametric statistics. Of course, we are not going to discuss each and every statistical test available to the researcher. A number of useful, commonly used statistics will be described, and a smaller number of frequently used statistics will be calculated.

THE *t* TEST

The *t* test is used to determine whether two means are significantly different at a selected probability level. In determining significance, the *t* test makes adjustments for the fact that the distribution of scores for small samples becomes increasingly different from the normal distribution as sample sizes become increasingly smaller. For example, distributions for smaller samples tend to be higher at the mean and at the two ends of the distribution. Because of this, the *t* values required to reject a null hypothesis are higher for small samples. As the size of the samples becomes larger, the score distribution approaches normality. Table A.4 in Appendix A shows the values needed to reject the null hypothesis for different sample sizes (indicated by the degrees of freedom column on the extreme left). As the number of participants increases (*df*), the value needed to reject the null hypothesis becomes smaller. As previously discussed, Table A.4 also shows that as the probability or significance level becomes smaller (.10, .05, .01, .001), it takes a larger value to reject the null hypothesis.

The strategy of the *t* test is to compare the actual mean difference observed $(\overline{X}_1 - \overline{X}_2)$ with the difference expected by chance. The *t* test involves forming the ratio of these two values. In other words, the numerator for a *t* test is the difference between the sample means $\overline{X}_1$ and $\overline{X}_2$, and the denominator is the chance difference that would be expected if the null hypothesis were true. Thus, the denominator is the standard error of the difference between the means. The denominator, or error term, is a function of both sample size and group variance. Smaller sample sizes and greater variation within groups are associated with greater random differences between groups. To explain it one more way, even if the null hypothesis is true you do not expect two sample means to be identical; there is going to be some chance variation. The *t* test determines whether the observed difference is sufficiently larger than a difference that would be expected solely by chance. After the numerator is divided by the denominator, the resulting *t* value is compared to the appropriate *t* table value (depending on the probability level and the degrees of freedom). If the *t* value is equal to or greater than the table value, then the null hypothesis is rejected. There are two different types of *t* tests, the *t* test for independent samples and the *t* test for nonindependent samples.

Calculating the *t* Test for Independent Samples

Independent samples are two samples that are randomly formed without any type of matching. The members of one sample are not related to members of the other sample in any systematic way other than that they are selected from the same population. If two groups are randomly formed, the expectation is that at the beginning of a study they are essentially the same with respect to performance on the dependent variable. Therefore, if they are also essentially the same at the end of the study (their means are close), the null hypothesis is probably true. If, on the other hand, their means are not close at the end of the study, the null hypothesis is probably false and should be rejected. The key word is *essentially*. We do not expect the means to be identical at the end of the study—they are bound to be somewhat different. The question of interest, of course, is whether they are significantly different. The **t test for independent samples** is used to determine whether there is probably a significant difference between the means of two independent samples.

Suppose we have the following sets of posttest scores for two randomly formed groups. (Recognize that samples of five participants in each group are not considered acceptable, but will be used here for simplicity and clarity.)

Group 1 Posttest Scores	Group 2 Posttest Scores
3	2
4	3
5	3
6	3
7	4

Are these two sets of scores significantly different? They are different, but are they *significantly* different? The appropriate test of significance to answer this question is the *t* test for independent samples. The formula is

$$t = \frac{\overline{X}_1 - \overline{X}_2}{}$$

Does it look bad? Is it? What will it turn into? (The answers are: Yes. No. An arithmetic problem.) If you look at the formula you will see that you are already familiar with each of the pieces. The numerator is simply the difference between the two means $\overline{X}_1$ and $\overline{X}_2$. Each of the *n*s refers to the number of participants in each group; thus, $n_1 = 5$ and $n_2 = 5$. What about the *SS*s? How do we find them? Right! We calculate each *SS* in the same way as we did for the standard deviation. Remember? Okay, let's find each piece. Thus,

$$SS_1 = \Sigma X_1^2 - \frac{(\Sigma X_1)^2}{n_1} \text{ and } SS_2 = \Sigma X_2^2 - \frac{(\Sigma X_2)^2}{n_2}$$

First, let's calculate means, sums, and sums of squares, and let's label the scores for group 1 as X_1 and the scores for group 2 as X_2:

X_1	X_1^2	X_2	X_2^2
3	9	2	4
4	16	3	9
5	25	3	9
6	36	3	9
7	49	4	16
$\Sigma X_1 = 25$	$\Sigma X_1^2 = 135$	$\Sigma X_2 = 15$	$\Sigma X_2^2 = 47$
$\overline{X}_1 = \dfrac{25}{5} = 5$		$\overline{X}_2 = \dfrac{15}{5} = 3$	

Next, we need the *SS*s:

$$SS_1 = \Sigma X_1^2 - \frac{(\Sigma X_1)^2}{n_1}$$
$$= 135 - \frac{(25)^2}{5}$$
$$= 135 - 125$$
$$= 10$$

$$SS_2 = \Sigma X_2^2 - \frac{(\Sigma X_2)^2}{n_2}$$
$$= 47 - \frac{(15)^2}{5}$$
$$= 47 - 45$$
$$= 2$$

Now we have everything we need, and all we have to do is substitute the correct number for each symbol in the formula:

$$t = \frac{\overline{X}_1 - \overline{X}_2}{} = \frac{5 - 3}{\sqrt{\left(\dfrac{10 + 2}{5 + 5 - 2}\right)\left(\dfrac{1}{5} + \dfrac{1}{5}\right)}}$$

Now, if we just do what the formula tells us to do we will have no problem at all. The first thing it says to do is to subtract 3 from 5:

$$= \frac{2}{\sqrt{\left(\frac{10+2}{5+5-2}\right)\left(\frac{1}{5}+\frac{1}{5}\right)}}$$

So far, so good. Now let's add $10 + 2$ and $5 + 5 - 2$, and then add $\frac{1}{5} + \frac{1}{5}$. (Same number on the bottom, so just add the top: $1 + 1$.) What do we have? Right:

$$= \frac{2}{\sqrt{\left(\frac{12}{8}\right)\left(\frac{2}{5}\right)}}$$

Before we go any further, this would be a good time to convert those fractions to decimals. To convert a fraction to a decimal you simply divide the numerator by the denominator. If you are using a calculator, you enter the top number (e.g., 12) first, hit the $\div$ key, and then enter the bottom number (e.g., 8). Thus, $12/8 = 1.5$ and $2/5 = .4$.

Substituting the decimals for the fractions we have

$$t = \frac{2}{\sqrt{\left(\frac{12}{8}\right)\left(\frac{2}{5}\right)}} = \frac{2}{\sqrt{(1.5)(.4)}}$$

Since the parentheses indicate multiplication, we next multiply 1.5 by .4, and get

$$t = \frac{2}{\sqrt{(1.5)(.4)}} = \frac{2}{\sqrt{.60}}$$

Now we have to find the square root of .60 (get your calculator out). It's .774. Substituting .774 for the square root and dividing, gives us

$$t = \frac{2}{\sqrt{.60}} = \frac{2}{.774} = 2.58$$

Therefore, $t = 2.58$.

Assuming we selected $\alpha = .05$, the only thing we need before we go to the t table is the appropriate degrees of freedom. For the t test for independent samples, the formula for degrees of freedom is $n_1 + n_2 - 2$. For our example, $df = n_1 + n_2 - 2 = 5 + 5 - 2 = 8$. Therefore, $t = 2.58$, $\alpha = .05$, $df = 8$.

Now go to Table A.4 in Appendix A. The p values in the table are the probabilities associated with various α levels. In our case, we are really asking the following question: Given $\alpha = .05$, and $df = 8$, what is the probability of getting $t \geq 2.58$ if there really is no difference? Okay, now run the index finger of your right hand across the probability row at the top of the table until you get to .05. Now run the index finger of your left hand down the degrees of freedom column until you get to 8. Now move your right index finger down the column and your left index finger across; they intersect at 2.306. The value 2.306, or 2.31, is the t value required for rejection of the null hypothesis with a $\alpha = .05$ and $df = 8$. Is our t value 2.58 greater than 2.31? Yes, and therefore we reject the null hypothesis. Are the means different? Yes. Are they significantly different? Yes. Was that hard? Of course not. Congratulations! It is useful for beginning researchers to look up p values a few times, but after that, rely on your statistical packages to automatically provide them.

Note that the table value, 2.306 or 2.31, was the value required to reject the null hypothesis given α equal to .05. If, instead of $t = 2.58$, we got $t = 2.31$, then our probability of committing a Type I error would be exactly .05. But, since our value, $t = 2.58$, was greater than the table value, 2.31, our probability of committing a Type I error is less, i.e., $p < .05$. In other words, we got more than we needed so our chances of being wrong are less.

Suppose our t value were 2.29. What would we conclude? We would conclude that there is no significant difference between the groups, because 2.29 is less than 2.31. We could express this conclusion by stating $p > .05$; in other words, because our value is less than required for $\alpha = .05$, our probability of committing a Type I error is greater. Usually, however, if results are not significant, the abbreviation N.S. is used to represent *not* significant. How about if we concluded that our t was almost significant or "approached" significance? Boooo! A t test is not *almost* significant or *really* significant; it is or it is not significant. Period! You will *not* see research reports that say, "The rats almost made it," or "Gosh, that really approached significance!"

What if we selected $\alpha = .01$? Table A.4 indicates that 3.355, or 3.36, is the t value required for rejection of the null hypothesis with $\alpha = .01$ and $df = 8$. Is our value $2.58 > 3.36$? No, and therefore we would not reject the null hypothesis at the .01 level. Are the means different? Yes. Are they significantly different? For $\alpha = .05$, the answer is yes, but for $\alpha = .01$ the answer is no. Thus, we see that the smaller the risk we are willing to take of committing a Type I error, the larger our t value has to be.

What if our t value had been -2.58? (Table A.4 has no negative values.) We would have done exactly what we did; we would have looked up 2.58. The only thing that determines whether the t is positive or negative is the order of the means; the denominator is always positive. In our example we had a mean difference of $5 - 3$, or 2. If we had reversed the means, we would have had $3 - 5$, or -2. As long as we know which mean goes with which group, the order is unimportant. The only thing that matters is the size of the difference. So, if you do not like negative numbers, put the larger mean first. Remember, the table is two-tailed; it is prepared to deal with a difference in favor of either group. Direction does make a difference in one-tailed tests. Are we having fun yet?

We now will carry out an analysis parallel to the one just conducted using SPSS 10.0.

Calculating the t Test for Independent Samples Using SPSS 10.0

The t test for independent samples is used when you want to compare the scores for two groups. Let's suppose that two groups of the students in a class took a test. You would use an independent samples t test to test whether the students in group one did better or worse than the students in group two.

In SPSS you will go to the "Analyze" menu and choose the "Compare Means" option. A submenu will appear as shown in Figure 15.4. From this submenu choose "Independent Samples T Test." In summary, the options are as follows:

> **Analyze**
> > **Compare Means**
> > > **Independent Samples t test . . .**

Once you have done this you will get the "Independent Samples T Test" window, shown in Figure 15.5.

You will move the variable that you are interested in testing into the "Test Variable(s)" section. In the case of our example, we are interested in whether different groups score the same on the posttest, so the variable "posttest" is moved into the "Test Variable(s)" section. Next we need to specify which groups test scores we want compared. We do this by specifying a "Grouping Variable." Since we are interested in comparing the scores for two groups of students, our grouping variable will be the variable "group." Once the grouping variable has been specified, you will need to define the groups. In the case of this example, there are only two groups, but in the future there may be more, so SPSS has a place for you to specify the groups to be compared. To do this click on the "Define Groups" button, shown in Figure 15.6.

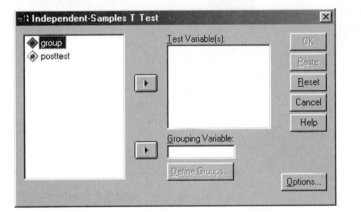

FIGURE 15.4
SPSS menu options for independent samples *t* test.

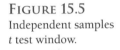

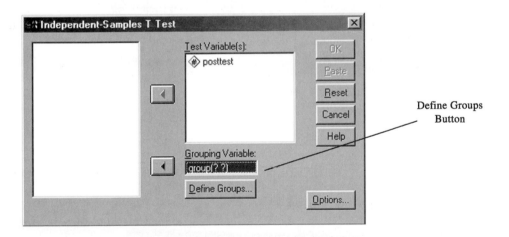

FIGURE 15.5
Independent samples *t* test window.

FIGURE 15.6
Independent samples *t* test window with define groups button.

In the "Define Groups" window, shown in Figure 15.7, you will see a place for two groups to be specified. Since the groups in our data set are specified as group 1 and group 2, you would type the number 1 for "group 1" in the section labeled "Group 1" in the window and type the number 2 in the section labeled "Group 2."

FIGURE 15.7
Define groups window.

FIGURE 15.8
Independent samples
t test window with OK
button.

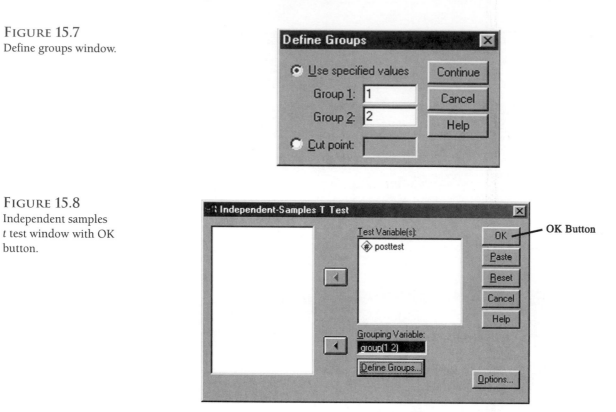

TABLE 15.1

Group Statistics

	GROUP	N	Mean	Std. Deviation	Std. Error Mean
POSTTEST	1.00	5	5.0000	1.5811	.7071
	2.00	5	3.0000	.7071	.3162

Once you have done this you can click "Continue" and you are ready to run your analysis. Once you are back in the "Independent Samples *t* Test" window click on the "OK" button as shown in Figure 15.8.

Once you run your analysis, you will get two tables in your output. The first table is the "Group Statistics" table, shown in Table 15.1. This table shows you the sample size for each group, represented in the "N" column, as well as the mean test score for each group, the standard deviation and the standard error of the mean.

Table 15.2 shows the results of the independent means *t* test. There are many statistics given in the table for which you didn't ask. The first set of statistics comes under the heading of the Levene's test for the equality of variances. This checks to see if the variances of the two groups in the analysis are equal. If they are not, then SPSS makes an adjustment to the remainder of the statistics to account for this difference. If the observed probability value of the Levene's test is greater than 0.05 then you would use the top row of *t* test statistics. If the observed probability value is less than 0.05 for the Levene's test, then you will use the bottom row of *t* test statistics. In Table 15.2 you can see that the observed probability value for the Levene's test is greater than 0.05 (sig. = 0.624) so we will use the top row of *t* test statistics.

TABLE 15.2 Independent Samples *t* Test Statistics

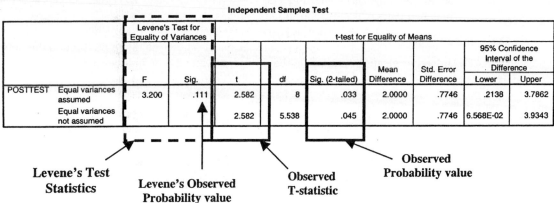

Once you know which set of *t* statistics to use, then you can find the observed *t* statistic value and its corresponding probability value. In Table 15.2, the observed *t* statistic is 2.582 and its observed probability value is 0.033. So there is a statistically significant difference between the average scores of the students in group 1 and group 2.

Calculating the *t* Test for Nonindependent Samples

The ***t* test for nonindependent samples** is used to compare groups that are formed by some type of matching or to compare a single group's performance on a pre- and posttest or on two different treatments. When samples are not independent, the members of one group are systematically related to the members of a second group (especially if it is the same group at two different times). If samples are nonindependent, scores on the dependent variable are expected to be correlated with each other and a special *t* test for correlated, or nonindependent, means is used. When samples are nonindependent, the error term of the *t* test tends to be smaller and there is therefore a higher probability that the null hypothesis will be rejected. Thus, the *t* test for nonindependent samples is used to determine whether there is probably a significant difference between the means of two matched, or nonindependent, samples or between the means for one sample at two different times.

Assume we have the following sets of scores for two matched groups (or pretest and posttest scores for a single group).

X_1	X_2
2	4
3	5
4	4
5	7
6	10

Are these two sets of scores significantly different? They are different, but are they significantly different? The appropriate test of significance to use to answer this question is the *t* test for nonindependent samples. The formula is

$$t = \frac{\overline{D}}{\sqrt{\dfrac{\Sigma D^2 - \dfrac{(\Sigma D)^2}{N}}{N(N-1)}}}$$

Except for the *D*s, the formula should look very familiar. If the *D*s were *X*s, you would know exactly what to do. Whatever *D*s are, we are going to find their mean, $\overline{D}$, add up their squares,

ΣD^2, and square their sum $(\Sigma D)^2$. What do you suppose D could possibly stand for? Right! D stands for *difference*. The difference between what? Yes, D is the difference between the matched pairs of scores. Thus, each D equals $X_2 - X_1$. For our data, the first pair of scores is 2 and 4 and $D = +2$. Okay, find the Ds for each pair of scores. While you're at it, you might as well get the squares, the sums, and the mean. The mean of the Ds is found the same way as any other mean, by adding up the Ds and dividing by the number of Ds:

X_1	X_2	D	D^2
2	4	+2	4
3	5	+2	4
4	4	0	0
5	7	+2	4
6	10	+4	16
		$\Sigma D = 10$	$\Sigma D^2 = 28$

$$\overline{D} = \frac{\Sigma D}{N} = \frac{10}{5} = 2$$

Now we have everything we need, and all we have to do is substitute the numbers for the corresponding symbols in the formula.

$$t = \frac{\overline{D}}{\sqrt{\dfrac{\Sigma D^2 - \dfrac{(\Sigma D)^2}{N}}{N(N-1)}}} = \frac{2}{\sqrt{\dfrac{28 - \dfrac{(10)^2}{5}}{5(5-1)}}}$$

We have another easy arithmetic problem. Now that you are a pro at this, we can solve this arithmetic problem rather quickly.

$$t = \frac{2}{\sqrt{\dfrac{28 - \dfrac{(10)^2}{5}}{5(5-1)}}}$$

$$= \frac{2}{\sqrt{\dfrac{28 - \dfrac{100}{5}}{5(5-1)}}} \qquad \begin{aligned} 10^2 &= 100 \\ 100/5 &= 20 \\ 28 - 20 &= 8 \end{aligned}$$

$$= \frac{2}{\sqrt{\dfrac{8}{5(5-1)}}} \qquad 5(5-1) = 5(4) = 20$$

$$= \frac{5}{\sqrt{\dfrac{8}{20}}}$$

$$= \frac{2}{\sqrt{.4}} \qquad \frac{8}{20} = \frac{4}{10} = .4$$

$$= \frac{2}{.63} \qquad \sqrt{.4} = .63$$

$$t = 3.17$$

Thus, $t = 3.17$. Assuming $\alpha = .05$, the only thing we need before we go to the t table is the appropriate degrees of freedom. For the t test for nonindependent samples, the formula for degrees of freedom is $N - 1$, where N is the number of *pairs* minus 1. For our example, $N - 1 = 5 - 1 = 4$. Therefore, $t = 3.17$, $\alpha = .05$, $df = 4$.

Now go to Table A.4 again. Notice that the t table does not know whether our t is for independent or nonindependent samples. For $\alpha = .05$ and $df = 4$, the table value for t required for rejection of the null hypothesis is 2.776, or 2.78. Is our value 3.17 > 2.78? Yes, and therefore we reject the null hypothesis. Are the groups different? Yes. Are they significantly different? Yes.

Calculating the t Test for Nonindependent Samples Using SPSS 10.0

Once again, you will be using the "Analyze" menu in the SPSS data editor window. To find the nonindependent or dependent samples t test, scroll down the menu until you find the option called "Compare Means . . ." At this point a submenu will appear. Within the submenu you will choose the option called "Paired Samples t Test . . ." This difference in designation may seem a bit confusing. One way to think of it is that you are comparing two sets of scores for the same group of people. So the relationship between the sets of scores is dependent upon the group of people. In this case, you are comparing a "pair" of scores for a particular group. In summary, the options are as follows:

Analyze
    Compare Means
        Paired Samples t Test . . .

The menu options are shown in Figure 15.9.

Notice the paired samples t test window (Figure 15.10) looks similar to the windows of previous analyses. On the left is the list of variables that may be included in the analysis. In the paired samples t test you will be choosing two variables to be compared and moving them to the right section labeled "Paired Variables." Once you have selected the variables to be included in the analysis, the "Current Selections" section of the window shows you which pair of variables are being compared.

Now click on the "OK" button to run the analysis.

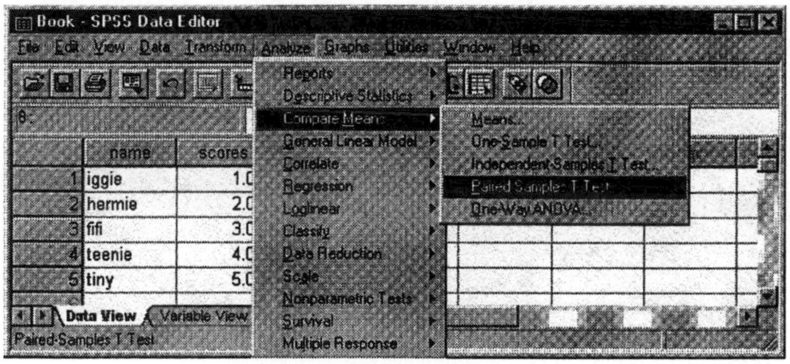

FIGURE 15.9
SPSS menu options for dependent (paired) samples t test.

Variables included in analysis

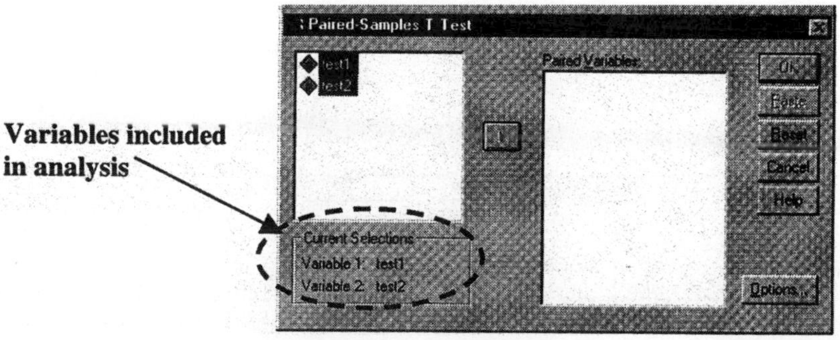

FIGURE 15.10
Dependent (paired) samples t test window.

The first section of the output, displayed in Table 15.3, shows some statistics for each of the variables that are necessary for the *t* test statistic to be computed. First, the average score or the mean for each variable is shown. For TEST1 the mean score is 4 and for TEST2 the mean score is 6. The next number shown is the number of cases or the sample size. Here there are five people who took TEST1 and TEST2. The third statistic shown is the standard deviation for each set of test scores. This is used to compute the final statistic shown in the table, the standard error of the mean scores.

Table 15.4 shows the statistics for your *t* test. Unlike before when you needed to calculate the *t* statistic, find the degrees of freedom and look up the critical value of *t* in a table. SPSS generates the statistic, degrees of freedom, and the *p* value (probability value) for making the decision about the test. The first box in the table shows you which variables are being compared. The next four boxes show you the difference between the mean scores, the standard deviation and standard error of "the difference between the mean scores" and the confidence interval within which you can be 95% confident the real "difference between mean scores" falls. The last three boxes show us the *t* value, the degrees of freedom, and the *p* value. If the *p* value in the box labeled "Sig. (2-tailed)" is less than or equal to $\alpha = 0.05$, then there is a statistically significant difference between how the group scored on TEST1 and how they scored on TEST2.

Why is the *t* value negative instead of positive? This is because SPSS automatically subtracts the second mean score in the list from the first. If the group did better on the second test than the first, then the difference is going to be negative, generating a negative test statistic. This is okay, because the significance level set *a priori,* $\alpha = 0.05$, is specified for a two-tailed test.

Analysis of Gain or Difference Scores

Many researchers think that a viable way to analyze data from two groups who are pretested, treated, and posttested is to (1) subtract each participant's pretest score from his or her posttest score (resulting in a gain, or difference, score), (2) compute the mean gain or difference for each group, and (3) calculate a *t* value for the difference between the two average mean differences. There are two main problems with this approach. First, every

TABLE 15.3   Dependent Samples Output

Paired Samples Statistics

		Mean	N	Std. Deviation	Std. Error Mean
Pair 1	TEST1	4.0000	5	1.5811	.7071
	TEST2	6.0000	5	2.5495	1.1402

TABLE 15.4   Dependent Samples *t* Test Output

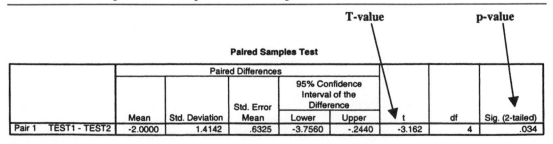

Paired Samples Test

		Paired Differences					t	df	Sig. (2-tailed)
		Mean	Std. Deviation	Std. Error Mean	95% Confidence Interval of the Difference				
					Lower	Upper			
Pair 1	TEST1 - TEST2	-2.0000	1.4142	.6325	-3.7560	-.2440	-3.162	4	.034

participant does not have the same opportunity to gain. A participant who scores very low on a pretest has a large opportunity to gain, but a participant who scores very high has only a small opportunity to improve (referred to as the *ceiling effect*). Who has improved, or gained, more—a participant who goes from 20 to 70 (a gain of 50) or a participant who goes from 85 to 100 (a gain of only 15 but perhaps a perfect score)? Second, gain or difference scores are less reliable than analysis of posttest scores alone.

The appropriate analysis for two pretest-posttest groups depends on the performance of the two groups on the pretest. For example, if both groups are essentially the same on the pretest, neither group has been previously exposed to its treatment, then posttest scores are best compared using a *t* test. If, on the other hand, there is a difference between the groups on the pretest, the preferred approach is the analysis of covariance. Recall that analysis of covariance adjusts posttest scores for initial differences on some variable (in this case the pretest) related to performance on the dependent variable. To determine whether analysis of covariance is necessary, calculate a *t* test on the two pretest means. If there is a significant difference between the two pretest means, use the analysis of covariance. If not, a simple *t* test can be computed on the posttest means.

SIMPLE ANALYSIS OF VARIANCE

Simple, or *one-way,* **analysis of variance (ANOVA)** is used to determine whether there is a significant difference between two or more means at a selected probability level. Thus, for a study involving three groups, ANOVA is the appropriate analysis technique. Like two posttest means in the *t* test, three (or more) posttest means in ANOVA are very unlikely to be identical, so the key question is whether the differences among the means represent true, significant differences or chance differences due to sampling error. To answer this question ANOVA is used and an **F ratio** is computed. You may be wondering why you cannot just compute a bunch of *t* tests, one for each pair of means. Aside from some statistical problems concerning distortion of your probability level, it is more convenient to perform one ANOVA than several *t* tests. For example, to analyze four means, six separate *t* tests would be required $(\overline{X}_1 - \overline{X}_2, \overline{X}_1 - \overline{X}_3, \overline{X}_1 - \overline{X}_4, \overline{X}_2 - \overline{X}_3, \overline{X}_2 - \overline{X}_4, \overline{X}_4 - \overline{X}_3)$. ANOVA is much more efficient and keeps the error rate under control.

The concept underlying ANOVA is that the total variation, or variance, of scores can be divided into two sources—variance between groups (variance caused by the treatment groups) and variance within groups (error variance). A ratio is formed, with group differences as the numerator (variance between groups) and error in the denominator (variance within groups). It is assumed that randomly formed groups of participants are chosen and are essentially the same at the beginning of a study on a measure of the dependent variable. At the end of the study, the researcher determines whether the between groups (or treatment) variance differs from the within groups (or error) variance by more than what would be expected by chance. In other words, if the treatment variance is sufficiently larger than the error variance, a significant *F* ratio results; the null hypothesis is rejected and it is concluded that the treatment had a significant effect on the dependent variable. If, on the other hand, the treatment variance and error variance do not differ by more than what would be expected by chance, the resulting *F* ratio is not significant and the null hypothesis is not rejected. The greater the difference, the larger the *F* ratio. To determine whether the *F* ratio is significant, an *F* table is entered at the place corresponding to the selected probability level and the appropriate degrees of freedom. The degrees of freedom for the *F* ratio are a function of the number of groups and the number of participants.

Calculating Simple Analysis of Variance (ANOVA)

Suppose we have the following set of posttest scores for three randomly selected groups.

X_1	X_2	X_3
1	2	4
2	3	4
2	4	4
2	5	5
3	6	7

We ask the inevitable question: Are these sets of data significantly different? The appropriate test of significance to answer this question is the simple, or one-way, analysis of variance (ANOVA). Recall that the total variation, or variance, is a combination of between (treatment) variance and within (error) variance. In other words:

total sum of squares = between sum of squares + within sum of squares, or

$$SS_{total} = SS_{between} + SS_{within}$$

To compute an ANOVA we need each term, *but,* since C = A + B, or C(SS_{total}) = A($SS_{between}$) + B(SS_{within}), we only have to compute any two terms and we can easily get the third. Since we only have to calculate two we might as well do the two easiest, SS_{total} and $SS_{between}$. Once we have these we can get SS_{within} by subtraction; SS_{within} will equal $SS_{total} - SS_{between}$ (B = C − A). The formula for SS_{total} is as follows:

$$SS_{total} = \Sigma X^2 - \frac{(\Sigma X)^2}{N}$$

How easy can you get? First, we need ΣX^2. You know how to get that; all we have to do is square *every* score in all three groups and add up the squares. For the second term all we have to do is add up *all* the scores ($X_1 + X_2 + X_3$), square the total, and divide by N ($n_1 + n_2 + n_3$). Note that if an X or N refers to a particular group it is subscripted (X_1, X_2, X_3 and n_1, n_2, n_3). If an X or N is not subscripted it refers to the total for all the groups.

Now let's look at the formula for $SS_{between}$:

$$SS_{between} = \frac{(\Sigma X_1)^2}{n_1} + \frac{(\Sigma X_2)^2}{n_2} + \frac{(\Sigma X_3)^2}{n_3} - \frac{(\Sigma X)^2}{N}$$

This formula has more pieces, but each piece is easy. For the first three terms all we have to do is add up all the scores in each group, square the total for each group, and divide by the number of scores in each group. We will have calculated the fourth term, $(\Sigma X)^2/N$, when we figure out SS_{total}. So, what do we need? We need the sum of scores for each group and the total of all the scores, and the sum of all the squares. That should be easy; let's do it:

X_1	X_1^2	X_2	X_2^2	X_3	X_3^2
1	1	2	4	4	16
2	4	3	9	4	16
2	4	4	16	4	16
2	4	5	25	5	25
3	9	6	36	7	49
10	22	20	90	24	122
ΣX_1	ΣX_1^2	ΣX_2	ΣX_2^2	ΣX_3	ΣX_3^2

$$\Sigma X = \Sigma X_1 + \Sigma X_2 + \Sigma X_3 = 10 + 20 + 24 = 54$$
$$\Sigma X^2 = \Sigma X_1^2 + \Sigma X_2^2 + \Sigma X_3^2 = 22 + 90 + 122 = 234$$
$$N = n_1 + n_2 + n_3 = 5 + 5 + 5 = 15$$

Now we are ready. First let us do SS_{total}.

$$SS_{total} = \Sigma X^2 - \frac{(\Sigma X)^2}{N}$$

$$= 234 - \frac{(54)^2}{15}$$

$$= 234 - \frac{2916}{15} \quad (54^2 = 2916)$$

$$= 234 - 194.4 \quad (2916 \div 15 = 194.4)$$

$$= 39.6$$

That was easy. Now let us do $SS_{between}$.[2]

$$SS_{between} = \frac{(\Sigma X_1)^2}{n_1} + \frac{(\Sigma X_2)^2}{n_2} + \frac{(\Sigma X_3)^2}{n_3} - \frac{(\Sigma X)^2}{N}$$

(We already computed the last term, remember?)

$10^2 = 100$
$20^2 = 400$
$24^2 = 576$

$$= \frac{(10)^2}{5} + \frac{(20)^2}{5} + \frac{(24)^2}{5} - 194.4$$

$$= \frac{100}{5} + \frac{400}{5} + \frac{576}{5} - 194.4$$

$\frac{100}{5} = 20$

$$= 20 + 80 + 115.2 - 194.4$$

$\frac{400}{5} = 80$

$$= 215.2 - 194.4$$

$\frac{576}{5} = 115.2$

$$= 20.8$$

$20 + 80 + 115.2 = 215.2$

Now how are we going to get SS_{within}? Right. We subtract $SS_{between}$ from SS_{total}:

$$SS_{within} = SS_{total} - SS_{between}$$

$$= 39.6 - 20.8$$

$$= 18.8$$

Now we have everything we need to begin! Seriously, we have all the pieces but we are not quite there yet. Let us fill in a summary table with what we have and you will see what is missing:

Source of Variation	Sum of Squares	df	Mean Square	F
Between	20.8	$(K - 1)$		
Within	18.8	$(N - K)$		
Total	39.6	$(N - 1)$		

The first thing you probably noticed is that each term has its own formula for degrees of freedom. The formula for the between term is $K - 1$, where K is the number of treatment groups; thus, the degrees of freedom are $K - 1 = 3 - 1 = 2$. The formula for the within term is $N - K$, where N is the total sample size and K is still the number of treatment groups; thus, degrees of freedom for the within term $N - K = 15 - 3 = 12$. We do not need them, but for the total term $df = N - 1 = 15 - 1 = 14$. Now what about mean squares? Mean squares are

---

[2]For more than three groups, the ANOVA procedure is exactly the same except that $SS_{between}$ has one extra term for each additional group. For example, for four groups

$$SS_{between} = \frac{(\Sigma X_1)^2}{n_1} + \frac{(\Sigma X_2)^2}{n_2} + \frac{(\Sigma X_3)^2}{n_3} + \frac{(\Sigma X_4)^2}{n_4} - \frac{(\Sigma X)^2}{N}$$

found by dividing each sum of squares by its appropriate degrees of freedom. Here we represent mean squares as *MS*, using the subscript B for between and W for within. Thus, we have the equation,

$$\text{mean square} = \frac{\text{sum of squares}}{\text{degrees of freedom}}$$

or,

$$MS = \frac{SS}{df}$$

For between, MS_{B}, we get

$$MS_{\text{B}} = \frac{SS_{\text{B}}}{df}$$
$$= \frac{20.8}{2}$$
$$= 10.40$$

For within, MS_{W}, we get

$$MS_{\text{W}} = \frac{SS_{\text{W}}}{df}$$
$$= \frac{18.8}{12}$$
$$= 1.57$$

Now all we need is our *F* ratio. The *F* ratio is a ratio of MS_{B} and MS_{W}:

$$F = \frac{MS_{\text{B}}}{MS_{\text{W}}}$$

Therefore, for our example:

$$F = \frac{MS_{\text{B}}}{MS_{\text{W}}}$$
$$= \frac{10.40}{1.57}$$
$$= 6.62$$

Filling in the rest of our summary table we have

Source of Variation	Sum of Squares	df	Mean Square	F
Between	20.8	$(K - 1) = 2$	10.40	6.62
Within	18.8	$(N - K) = 12$	1.57	
Total	39.6	$(N - 1) = 14$		

Note that we simply divided across ($20.8 \div 2 = 10.40$ and $18.8 \div 12 = 1.57$) and then down ($10.40 \div 1.57 = 6.62$). Thus, $F = 6.62$ with 2 and 12 degrees of freedom.

Assuming $\alpha = .05$, we are now ready to go to our *F* table, Table A.5 in Appendix A. Across the top of Table A.5 the row labeled n_1 refers to the degrees of freedom for the between term, in our case 2. Find it? Down the extreme lefthand side of the table, in the column labeled n_2, are the degrees of freedom for the within term, in our case 12. Find it? Good. Now, where these two values intersect (go down the 2 column and across the 12 row) we find 3.88, the value of *F* required for statistical significance (required in order to reject the null hypothesis) if $\alpha = .05$. The question is whether our *F* value, 6.62, is greater than 3.88. Obviously it is. Therefore we reject the null hypothesis and conclude that there is a significant difference among the group means. Note that because two separate degrees of freedom, 2 and 12, are involved, a separate table is required for each α level. Thus the .05 α table is on one page and the .01 α table is on another.

WHEW!! That was long, but you made it, didn't you?

MULTIPLE COMPARISONS

If the *F* ratio is determined to be nonsignificant, the party is over. But what if it is significant? What do you really know if the *F* ratio is rejected? All you know is that there is at least one significant difference somewhere among the means, but you do not know where that difference is. You do not know which means are significantly different from which other means. It might be, for example, that three of the four means tested are equal but all greater than a fourth mean; $\overline{X}_1 = \overline{X}_2 = \overline{X}_3$ and each is greater than $\overline{X}_4$. Or it might be that $\overline{X}_1 = \overline{X}_2$, and $\overline{X}_3 = \overline{X}_4$, but $\overline{X}_1$ and $\overline{X}_2$ are each greater than $\overline{X}_3$ and $\overline{X}_4$. Or it might be that $\overline{X}_1$ is greater than $\overline{X}_2$, $\overline{X}_3$, and $\overline{X}_4$.

When the *F* ratio is significant and more than two means are involved, **multiple comparison** procedures are used to determine which means are significantly different from which other means. There are a number of different multiple comparison techniques available to the researcher. In essence, they involve calculation of a special form of the *t* test. This special *t* adjusts for the fact that many tests are being executed. When many significant tests are performed, the probability level, α, tends to increase, because doing a large number of significance tests makes it more likely to obtain significant differences. Thus, the chance of finding a significant difference is increased but so is the chance of committing a Type I error. The comparisons of the means to be made should generally be decided on before the study is conducted, not after, and should be based on research hypotheses. Such comparisons, as discussed previously, are called *a priori* (before the fact) or planned comparisons. Often, however, it is not possible to state a priori tests. In these cases we can use *a posteriori* (after the fact) or post hoc comparisons. In either case, multiple comparisons should not be a "fishing expedition" in which the researcher looks for any difference she can find.

Of the many multiple comparison techniques available, the **Scheffé test** is one of the most widely used. It is an *a posteriori* test. The Scheffé test is appropriate for making any and all possible comparisons involving a set of means. The calculations for this approach are quite simple and sample sizes do not have to be equal, as is the case with some multiple comparison techniques. The Scheffé test is very conservative, which is good news and bad news. The good news is that the probability of committing a Type I error for any comparison of means is the least likely. The bad news is that it is entirely possible, given the comparisons selected for investigation, to find no significant differences even though the *F* for the analysis of variance was significant. In general, however, the flexibility of the Scheffé test and its ease of application make it useful for a variety of situations. Other common multiple comparison tests are Tukey's HSD test and Duncan's multiple range test. Here we discuss the Scheffé test.

Calculating Scheffé Multiple Comparisons

We will use the results of the preceding ANOVA example to examine multiple comparisons. In the ANOVA example the only thing the *F* ratio told us was that there was at least one significant difference somewhere among the three means. To find out where, we will apply the Scheffé test. The Scheffé test involves calculation of an *F* ratio for each mean comparison of interest. As you study the following formula, you will notice that we already have almost all of the information we need to apply the Scheffé test:

$$ F = \frac{(\overline{X}_1 - \overline{X}_2)^2}{MS_W\left(\dfrac{1}{n_1} + \dfrac{1}{n_2}\right)(K - 1)} \text{ with } df = (K - 1), (N - K) $$

Where in the world do we get MS_W? Correct! MS_W is the MS_W from the analysis of variance, which is 1.57. The degrees of freedom are also from the ANOVA, 2 and 12. Of course the above formula is for the comparison of $\overline{X}_1$ and $\overline{X}_2$. To compare any other two means we simply change the Xs and the ns. So before we can apply the Scheffé test, we have to calculate the mean for each group.

Looking back at our ANOVA example, the sums for each group were 10, 20, and 24, respectively, and the three $\overline{X}$s are: 2.00, 4.00, and 4.80. Applying the Scheffé test to $\overline{X}_1$ and $\overline{X}_2$ we get

$$F = \frac{(\overline{X}_1 - \overline{X}_2)^2}{MS_W\left(\dfrac{1}{n_1} + \dfrac{1}{n_2}\right)(K-1)} = \frac{(2.00 - 4.00)^2}{1.57\left(\dfrac{1}{5} + \dfrac{1}{5}\right)2}$$

$$= \frac{(-2.00)^2}{1.57\left(\dfrac{2}{5}\right)2}$$

$$= \frac{4}{1.57(.4)2}$$

$$= \frac{4}{1.57(.8)}$$

$$= \frac{4}{1.256}$$

$$= 3.18$$

Since the value of F required for significance is 3.88 if $\alpha = .05$ and $df = 2$ and 12, and since $3.18 < 3.88$, we conclude that there is no significant difference between $\overline{X}_1$ and $\overline{X}_2$. Calculate the Scheffé test for $\overline{X}_1$ and $\overline{X}_3$ and for $\overline{X}_2$ and $\overline{X}_3$ yourself and determine whether there are significant differences between the two sets of means. You should get the following results:

Scheffé Tests

Group 1 vs. Group 2	3.18	fail to reject
Group 1 vs. Group 3	6.24	reject
Group 2 vs. Group 3	0.51	fail to reject

The Scheffé test can also be used to compare combinations of means. Suppose, for example, that group 1 was a control group and we wanted to compare the mean of group 1 to the mean of groups 2 and 3 combined. First we would have to combine the means for groups 2 and 3 as follows:

$$\overline{X}_{2+3} - \frac{n_2\overline{X}_2 + n_3\overline{X}_3}{n_2 + n_3} = \frac{5(4.00) + 5(1.80)}{5 + 5}$$

$$= \frac{20.00 + 24.00}{10}$$

$$= \frac{44.00}{10}$$

$$= 4.40$$

Of course, since $n_2 = n_3$, we could have simply replaced n_3 with n_2 and averaged the means as follows:

$$\overline{X}_{2+3} = \frac{n_2\overline{X}_2 + n_2\overline{X}_3}{n_2 + n_2}$$

$$\overline{X}_{2+3} = \frac{n_2(\overline{X}_2 + \overline{X}_3)}{n_2(1 + 1)}$$

$$\overline{X}_{2+3} = \frac{\overline{X}_2 + \overline{X}_3}{2} = \frac{4.00 + 4.80}{2} = \frac{8.80}{2} = 4.40$$

Next, we calculate the F ratio using $\overline{X}_1 = 2.00$ and the combined mean $\overline{X}_{2+3} = 4.40$:

$$F = \frac{(\overline{X}_1 - \overline{X}_{2+3})^2}{MS_W\left(\dfrac{1}{n_1} + \dfrac{1}{n_2 + n_3}\right)(K - 1)} = \frac{(2.00 - 4.40)^2}{1.57\left(\dfrac{1}{5} + \dfrac{1}{10}\right)2}$$

$$= \frac{(-2.4)^2}{1.57(.2 + .1)2}$$

$$= \frac{5.76}{1.57(.3)2}$$

$$= \frac{5.76}{.94}$$

$$= 6.13$$

Since $6.13 > 3.88$, we would conclude that there is a significant difference between $\overline{X}_1$ and $\overline{X}_{2+3}$. In other words, the experimental groups performed significantly better than the control group.

Calculating Post Hoc Multiple Comparison Tests in SPSS 10.0

We can also use SPSS to run multiple comparison tests to determine which means are significantly different from other means. Click on the "Post Hoc . . ." button in the one-way ANOVA window, shown in Figure 15.11.

The "Post Hoc Multiple Comparison" window is shown in Figure 15.12. To specify the multiple comparison technique, simply click on the box to the left of the named test.

Once you have specified the post hoc tests you wish to have performed, click on the "Continue" button to continue with your analysis.

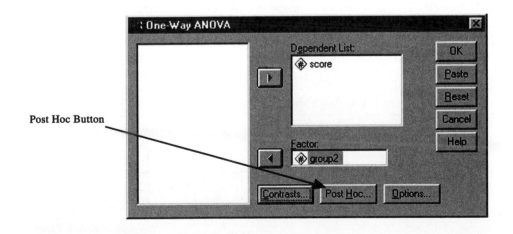

Post Hoc Button

FIGURE 15.11
One-way ANOVA with post hoc button.

FIGURE 15.12   Post
hoc multiple comparison
window.

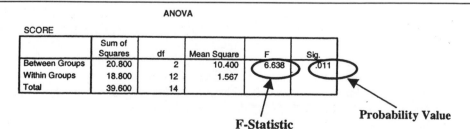

Once you have run your analysis, SPSS produces a series of tables to help you make sense of your analysis. The first table, shown in Table 15.5, is the overall ANOVA solution displaying the observed *F* statistic and the associated probability value. Here one can see that because the probability value associated with the *F* statistic is less than 0.05, there is a statistically significant relationship found. It is important to remember that when SPSS displays the probability value only three decimal places are shown, so in Table 15.5, the probability value is not zero; it is less than 0.000.

If you specified a priori contrasts like in the example above, then the next table SPSS generates is the contrast coefficient table. This table displays the contrast coefficients you specified and the corresponding variable value labels. This table enables you to check to make sure you specified the coefficients properly.

When you specify that you want a multiple comparison post hoc test run as part of your analysis, SPSS provides a summary table for each type of test that you select. Table 15.6 shows a summary table for the Scheffé multiple comparison tests comparing the average test score of each group with all other groups. Each row of the table corresponds to the group of interest being compared to the others. The difference between the average scores is shown along with the standard error of the difference and a probability value for the test. If the probability value is less than 0.05, then a statistically significant difference exists between the scores of the two groups.

Looking at Table 15.6, you can compare the results to that found in the Scheffé test table on page 472. Notice that the first group of interest is group 1. This is the group that will be compared to group 2 and then to group 3. In the calculation on page 472, testing the difference between the average for group 1 and group 2, you can see that the difference between the means is negative 2.00. This is the same value found in the first row of the Mean Difference column in Table 15.6. To tell if the difference is statistically significant, you will need to look in the significance column labeled with the notation "Sig." For the first mean difference, which

TABLE 15.5   Overall ANOVA Solution

ANOVA

SCORE

	Sum of Squares	df	Mean Square	F	Sig.
Between Groups	20.800	2	10.400	6.638	.011
Within Groups	18.800	12	1.567		
Total	39.600	14			

F-Statistic   **Probability Value**

TABLE 15.6 SPSS Summary Table for Scheffé Multiple Comparison Test

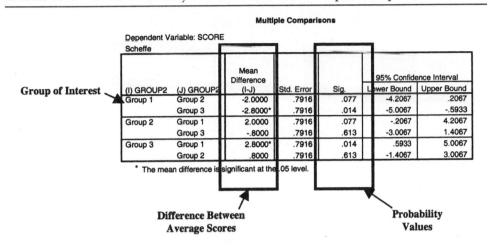

Multiple Comparisons

Dependent Variable: SCORE
Scheffe

(I) GROUP2	(J) GROUP2	Mean Difference (I-J)	Std. Error	Sig.	95% Confidence Interval Lower Bound	Upper Bound
Group 1	Group 2	-2.0000	.7916	.077	-4.2067	.2067
	Group 3	-2.8000*	.7916	.014	-5.0067	-.5933
Group 2	Group 1	2.0000	.7916	.077	-.2067	4.2067
	Group 3	-.8000	.7916	.613	-3.0067	1.4067
Group 3	Group 1	2.8000*	.7916	.014	.5933	5.0067
	Group 2	.8000	.7916	.613	-1.4067	3.0067

* The mean difference is significant at the .05 level.

Group of Interest

Difference Between Average Scores

Probability Values

is the difference between the average of group 1 and the average of group 2, the observed probability value is 0.077, which is larger than 0.05. Hence we fail to reject the null hypothesis. Note in the Scheffé test table on page 472 that the conclusion of the calculated test for the difference between the average scores for group 1 versus group 2 is that you fail to reject the null hypothesis. You can see that the results for the comparison between the average scores for group 1 and group 3 and group 2 and group 3 are consistent as well. The results in SPSS are consistent with the step-by-step calculated test; they are just formatted differently.

SPSS does not print out the F scores as the step-by-step calculation does. Rather, it prints to significance levels (probability values) associated with the test's three groups.

FACTORIAL ANALYSIS OF VARIANCE

If a research study uses a factorial design to investigate two or more independent variables and the interactions between them, the appropriate statistical analysis is a factorial, or multifactor, analysis of variance. The factorial analysis provides a separate F ratio for each independent variable and for each interaction. For example, analysis of the 2×2 factorial presented in Figure 15.13 would yield three F ratios—one for the independent variable (Method), one for the control independent variable (IQ), and one for the interaction between Method and IQ. For the No Interaction example in Figure 15.13 the F for Method would probably be significant since method A appears to be significantly more effective than method B (70 versus 30). The F for IQ would also probably be significant since high IQ participants appear to have performed significantly better than low IQ participants (60 versus 40). The F for the interaction between Method and IQ would not be significant since method A is more effective than method B for both IQ groups (80 > 40 and 60 > 20).

On the other hand, for the Interaction example, the F for Method would not be significant since, overall, method A is equally as effective as method B (50 for A and 50 for B). The F for IQ would probably be significant since high IQ participants have performed significantly better than low IQ subjects (70 versus 30). The F for the interaction between Method and IQ, however, would probably be significant since the methods appear to be differentially effective depending on the IQ level. That is, method A is better for high IQ subjects (80 versus 60) and method B is better for low IQ subjects (20 versus 40). Another way of looking at it is to see that for the No Interaction example (80 + 20) = (60 + 40); for the Interaction example (80 + 40) ≠ (20 + 60).

FIGURE 15.13
Illustration of interaction
and no interaction in a
2 × 2 factorial
experiment.

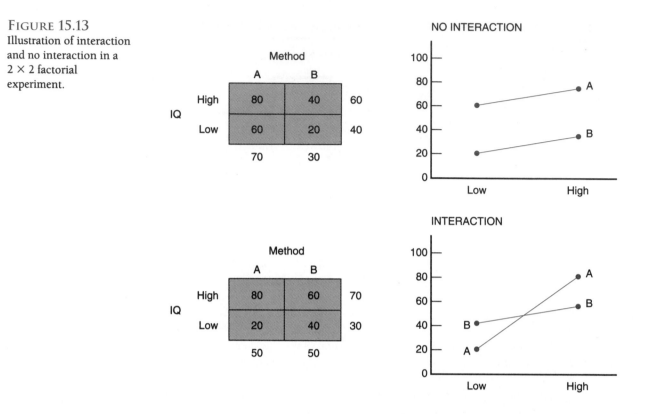

A factorial analysis of variance is not as difficult to calculate as you may think. If no more than two variables are involved, and if you have access to a calculator, it can be performed without too much difficulty. Most statistics texts outline the procedure to be followed. If more than two variables are involved, it is usually better to use a computer if possible.

ANALYSIS OF COVARIANCE

Analysis of covariance (ANCOVA) is used in two major ways, as a technique for controlling extraneous variables and as a means of increasing power. ANCOVA is a form of ANOVA and is a statistical, rather than an experimental, method that can be used to equate groups on one or more variables. Use of ANCOVA is basically equivalent to matching groups on the variable or variables to be controlled. Essentially, ANCOVA adjusts posttest scores for initial differences on a variable and compares the adjusted scores; groups are equalized with respect to the control variable and then compared. It's sort of like handicapping in bowling, in an attempt to equalize teams, high scorers are given little or no handicap, low scorers are given big handicaps, and so forth. Any variable that is correlated with the dependent variable can be controlled for using covariance. Examples of variables commonly controlled using ANCOVA are pretest performance, IQ, readiness, and aptitude. By using covariance we are attempting to reduce variation in posttest scores that is attributable to another variable. Ideally, we would like all posttest variance to be attributable to the treatment conditions.

Analysis of covariance is a control technique used in both causal–comparative studies in which already formed, but not necessarily equal, groups are involved and in experimental studies in which either existing groups or randomly formed groups are involved. Remember, randomization does not guarantee that groups will be equated on all variables. Unfortunately, the situation for which ANCOVA is least appropriate is the situation for which it is most often used. Use of ANCOVA assumes that participants have been randomly assigned to treatment groups. Thus, it is best used in true experimental designs. If existing, or intact, groups are not randomly selected but are assigned to treatment groups randomly, ANCOVA may still be used but results must be interpreted with caution. If covariance is used with existing groups and nonmanipulated independent variables, as in causal–comparative studies, the results are likely to be misleading at best. There are other assumptions associated with the use of analysis of covariance. Violation of these assumptions is not as serious, however, if participants have been randomly assigned to treatment groups.

A second, not previously discussed, function of ANCOVA is that it increases the power of a statistical test by reducing within-group (error) variance. **Power** refers to statistical ability to reject a false null hypothesis, that is, to make a correct decision to reject the null hypothesis. Although increasing sample size also increases power, researchers are often limited to samples of a given size because of financial and practical reasons. Because ANCOVA can reduce random sampling error by "equating" different groups, it increases the power of the significance test. The power-increasing function of ANCOVA is directly related to the degree of randomization involved in formation of the groups. The results of ANCOVA are least likely to be valid when groups have not been randomly selected and assigned. As pointed out before, application of the analysis of covariance technique is quite a complex, lengthy procedure which is hardly ever hand calculated. Almost all researchers use computer programs for reasons of accuracy and sanity!

MULTIPLE REGRESSION

A combination of variables usually results in a more accurate prediction than any single variable. A prediction equation that includes more than one predictor is referred to as a *multiple regression* equation. A multiple regression equation uses variables that are known to individually predict (correlate with) the criterion to make a more accurate prediction. Thus, for example, we might use high school GPA, Scholastic Aptitude Test (SAT) scores, and rank in graduating class to predict college GPA at the end of the first semester of college. Use of multiple regression is increasing, primarily because of its versatility and precision. It can be used with data representing any scale of measurement and can be used to analyze the results of experimental and causal–comparative, as well as correlational, studies. Further, it determines not only whether variables are related, but also the degree to which they are related.

To see how multiple regression works, we will use the stated example concerning college GPA. The first step in multiple regression is to identify the variable that best predicts the criterion, that is, the variable most highly correlated with it. Since past performance is generally the best predictor of future performance, high school GPA would probably be the best predictor. The next step is to identify a second variable that will most improve the prediction. Usually this is a variable that is related to the criterion (college GPA), but uncorrelated with other predictors. In our case, the question would be, "Do we get a more accurate prediction using high school GPA and SAT scores or using high school GPA and rank in graduating class?" The results of multiple regression would give us the answer to that question and would also tell us by how much the prediction was improved. In our case, the answer might be high school GPA and SAT scores. That would leave rank in graduating class as the last variable, and the results of multiple regression would tell us by how much our prediction would be improved if we included it. Since our three predictors would most probably all be correlated with each other to some degree as well as to the criterion, it might be that rank in graduating class adds very little to the accuracy of a prediction based on high school GPA and SAT scores. A study involving more than three variables works exactly the same way; at each step it is determined which variable adds the most to the prediction and how much it adds. (See Chapter 11 for another example of multiple regression.)

The sign, positive or negative, of the relationship between a predictor and the criterion has nothing to do with how good a predictor it is. Recall that $r = -1.00$ represents a relationship just as strong as $r = +1.00$; the only difference indicated is the nature of the relationship. It should also be noted that the number of predictor variables is related to the sample size; the larger the number of variables, the larger the sample size needs to be. Large sample sizes increase the probability that the prediction equation will generalize to groups beyond those involved in creating the initial equation.

With increasing frequency, multiple regression is being used as an alternative to the various analysis of variance techniques. When this is the case, the dependent variable, or posttest scores, becomes the criterion variable, and the predictors include group membership (e.g., experimental versus control) and any other appropriate variables, such as pretest scores. The results indicate not only whether group membership is significantly related to posttest performance, but also the magnitude of the relationship. For analyses such as these, the researcher typically specifies the order in which variables are to be checked. For analysis of covariance, with pretest scores as the covariate, for example, the researcher specifies that pretest scores be entered into the equation first; it can then be determined whether group membership significantly improves the equation.

CHI SQUARE

Chi square, symbolized as χ^2, is a nonparametric test of significance appropriate when the data are in the form of frequency counts or percentages and proportions that can be converted to frequencies. Two or more mutually exclusive categories are required. Thus, chi square is appropriate when the data are a nominal scale and fall into either **true categories** (e.g., male vs. female) or **artificial categories** (e.g., tall vs. short). A chi square test compares the proportions actually observed in a study to the proportions expected, to see if they are significantly different. Expected proportions are usually the frequencies that would be expected if the groups were equal, although occasionally they also may be based on past data. The chi square value increases as the difference between observed and expected frequencies increases. Whether the chi square is significant is determined by consulting a chi square table.

One-Dimensional Chi Square

The chi square can be used to compare frequencies occurring in different categories or groups. As an example, suppose you stopped 90 shoppers in a supermarket and asked them to taste three unlabeled different brands of peanut butter (X, Y, Z) and to tell you which one tasted best. Suppose that 40 of the 90 shoppers chose brand X, 30 chose brand Y, and 20 chose brand Z. If the null hypothesis were true—if there were no difference in taste among the three brands—we would expect an equal number of shoppers to select each brand—30, 30, and 30. We can present our data in what is called a *contingency table,* as shown:

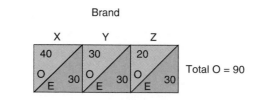

where

  O = observed frequencies
  E = expected frequencies

To determine whether the observed frequencies (40, 30, 20) were significantly different from the expected frequencies (30, 30, 30), a chi square test could be carried out. If the chi square were significant, the null hypothesis would be rejected, and it would be concluded that the brands do taste different.

As another example, you might wish to investigate whether college sophomores prefer to study alone or with others. Tabulation, based on a random sample of 100 sophomores, might reveal that 45 prefer to study alone, and 55 prefer to study with others. The null hypothesis of no preference would suggest a 50–50 split. The corresponding contingency table would look as follows:

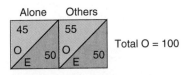

To determine whether the groups were significantly different, you would compare the observed frequencies (45, 55) with the expected frequencies (50, 50) using a chi square test of significance.

Two-Dimensional Chi Square

The chi square may also be used when frequencies are categorized along more than one dimension—sort of a factorial chi square. In the study sequence example, you might select a stratified sample, comprising 50 males and 50 females. Responses could then be classified by study preference and by gender, a two-way classification that would allow you to see whether study preference is related to gender. The corresponding contingency table would be set up as follows:

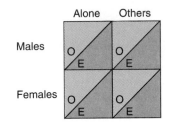

Although 2 × 2 applications are quite common, contingency tables may be based on any number of categories, for example, 2 × 3, 3 × 3, 2 × 4, and so forth. When a two-way classification is used, calculation of expected frequencies is a little more complex, but not difficult.

Calculating Chi Square

A one-dimensional chi square (χ^2) is the easiest statistic of all. In our peanut butter example, we asked 90 people to indicate which brand they thought tasted best; 40 picked brand X, 30 picked brand Y, and 20 picked brand Z. If there were no difference among the brands we would expect the same number of people to choose each brand, 30, 30, 30. Therefore, we have the following table:

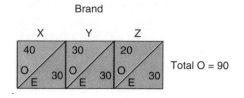

where

O = observed frequencies
E = expected frequencies

To determine whether the observed frequencies are significantly different from the expected frequencies, we apply the following formula:

$$x^2 = \sum \left[\frac{(fo - fe)^2}{fe} \right]$$

Now that is some sum sign! However, all this formula says is that for each cell (X, Y, and Z) we subtract the expected frequency (fe) from the observed frequency (fo), square the difference $(fo - fe)^2$, and then divide by the expected frequency, fe. The big Σ says that after we do the above for each term we add up the resulting values. Thus, substituting our table values into the formula we get the following:

$$
\chi^2 = \underbrace{\frac{(40 - 30)^2}{30}}_{\substack{X \\ fo \quad fe \\ \; \\ fe}} \qquad \underbrace{\frac{(30 - 30)^2}{30}}_{\substack{Y \\ fo \quad fe \\ \; \\ fe}} \qquad \underbrace{\frac{(20 - 30)^2}{30}}_{\substack{Z \\ fo \quad fe \\ \; \\ fe}}
$$

$$
= \frac{(10)^2}{30} \quad + \quad \frac{(0)^2}{30} \quad + \quad \frac{-(10)^2}{30}
$$

$$
= \frac{100}{30} \quad + \quad 0 \quad + \quad \frac{100}{30}
$$

$$
= 3.333 \quad + \quad 0 \quad + \quad 3.333
$$

$$
= 6.67
$$

Thus, $\chi^2 = 6.67$. The degrees of freedom for a one-dimensional chi square are determined by the formula $(C - 1)$, where C equals the number of columns, in our case 3. Thus, $df = 3 - 1 = 2$. Therefore, we have $\chi^2 = 6.67$, $\alpha = .05$, $df = 2$. To determine whether the differences between observed and expected frequencies are significant, we compare our chi square value to the appropriate value in Table A.6 in Appendix A. Run the index finger of your right hand across the top until you find $\alpha = .05$. Now run the index finger of your left hand down the extreme left-hand column and find $df = 2$. Run your left hand across and your right hand down and they will intersect at 5.991, or 5.99. Is our value of 6.67 > 5.99? Yes. Therefore, we reject the null hypothesis. There is a significant difference between observed and expected proportions; the brands of peanut butter compared do taste different! Suppose we selected $\alpha = .01$. The chi square value required for significance would be 9.210, or 9.21. Is our value of 6.67 > 9.21? No. Therefore, we would not reject the null hypothesis and we would conclude that there is no significant difference between observed and expected proportions; the three brands of peanut butter taste the same. Thus, once again you can see that selection of an α level is important; different conclusions may very well be drawn with different α levels.

Now let's look at our study preference example. We asked 100 college sophomores whether they preferred to study alone or with others; 45 said alone and 55 said with others.

Under a null hypothesis of no preference we would expect a 50–50 split. Therefore, we have the following table:

Study Preference

Alone   Others

| 45 | 55 |

O   50   O   50
E   E

Total O = 100

Applying the chi square formula we get:

$$\chi^2 = \frac{(45 - 50)^2}{50} + \frac{(55 - 50)^2}{50}$$

$$= \frac{(-5)^2}{50} \qquad + \qquad \frac{(5)^2}{50}$$

$$= \frac{25}{50} \qquad + \qquad \frac{25}{50}$$

$$= .50 \qquad + \qquad .50$$

$$\chi^2 = 1.00$$

Since degrees of freedom are $C - 1$, we have $2 - 1$, or 1. Thus, $\chi^2 = 1.00$, $\alpha = .05$, $df = 1$. Table A.6 indicates that for $\alpha = .05$ and $df = 1$, the required value is 3.841, or 3.84. Is our value of $1.00 > 3.84$? No. Therefore, we do not reject the null hypothesis. There is not a significant difference between observed and expected proportions; sophomores do not prefer to study alone or with others.

Now suppose we wanted to know if study preference is related to the gender of the students. Our 2 × 2 contingency table might look as follows:

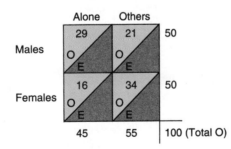

To find the expected frequency for a particular cell, or category, we multiply the corresponding row total by the corresponding column total and divide by the overall total. This isn't as bad as it sounds, honest. So, for males who prefer to study alone, the observed frequency is 29. To find the expected frequency, we multiply the total for the male row (50) by the total for the alone column (45) and divide by the overall total (100):

$$\text{males (alone)} = \frac{50 \times 45}{100} = \frac{2250}{100} = 22.5$$

Similarly, for the other cells, we get

$$\text{males (others)} = \frac{50 \times 55}{100} = \frac{2750}{100} = 27.5$$

$$\text{females (alone)} = \frac{50 \times 45}{100} = \frac{2250}{100} = 22.5$$

$$\text{females (others)} = \frac{50 \times 55}{100} = \frac{2750}{100} = 27.5$$

Now we can fill in the expected frequencies in our table and it looks as follows:

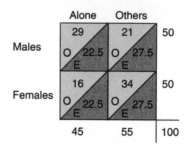

Study Preference

Chi square is calculated in the same way as for the other examples except now we have four terms:

$$\chi^2 = \frac{(29 - 22.5)^2}{22.5} + \frac{(21 - 27.5)^2}{27.5} + \frac{(16 - 22.5)^2}{22.5} + \frac{(34 - 27.5)^2}{27.5}$$

$$= \frac{(6.5)^2}{22.5} + \frac{(-6.5)^2}{27.5} + \frac{(-6.5)^2}{22.5} + \frac{(6.5)^2}{27.5}$$

$$= \frac{42.25}{22.5} + \frac{42.25}{27.5} + \frac{42.25}{22.5} + \frac{42.25}{27.5}$$

$$= 1.88 + 1.54 + 1.88 + 1.54$$

$$\chi^2 = 6.84$$

The degrees of freedom for a two-dimensional chi square are determined by the following formula:

$$df = (R - 1)(C - 1)$$

where

R = the number of rows in the contingency table
C = the number of columns in the contingency table

Since we have two rows and two columns,

$$df = (R - 1)(C - 1) = (2 - 1)(2 - 1) = 1 \times 1 = 1$$

Therefore, we have $\chi^2 = 6.84$, $\alpha = .05$, $df = 1$. The table value for $\alpha = .05$ and $df = 1$ is 3.841, or 3.84. Is our value of 6.84 > 3.84? Yes. Therefore, we conclude that gender is related to study preference. For larger contingency tables (e.g., a 3 × 2), expected frequencies and chi square are calculated in the same way. The only difference is that the number of terms increases; for a 3 × 2, for example, the number of terms is 6 (3 × 2 = 6).

Calculating Chi Square Using SPSS 10.0

To specify the chi square statistic for a given table of data, you must go to the "Descriptive Statistics" submenu in the "Analyze" menu. Within this submenu, you will choose the "Crosstabs" option. (Since a chi square statistic is a nonparametric statistic, it is listed under the descriptive statistics.) Figure 15.14 shows the menu options in SPSS. This is one of the few analysis options in SPSS that does not have a menu option named after the statistic of interest. In summary, the menu options are as follows:

Analyze
  Descriptive Statistics
    Crosstabs . . .

Once in the "Crosstabs" window you need to specify the variable to go in the rows and columns of the table, as shown in Figure 15.15.

This will construct the table used to calculate the chi square statistic, but if you want the statistic computed by SPSS click on the "Statistics" button. Figure 15.156 shows the "Statistics" window where you specify that you want a chi square statistic by clicking on the box to the left of the statistic name. Click on the "Continue" button to return to the Crosstabs window to continue your analysis.

Additionally, you may wish to display the expected frequencies in each cell. To do this click on the "Cells" button, shown in Figure 15.15.

The first table SPSS generates is the cross tabulation table (Table 15.7). This table shows the observed values for each of the cells.

The observed frequency for men preferring to study alone is 29 and the expected frequency is 22.5. Table 15.8 shows the computed chi square statistic generated using the values shown in Table 15.7. The observed chi square is 6.82 with a corresponding probability value equal to 0.009.

Types of Parametric and Nonparametric Statistical Tests

There are many parametric and nonparametric statistical methods, too many to describe in detail here. Table 15.9 provides an overview of some of the more commonly used parametric and nonparametric statistical tests. The table is best used by first identifying the levels of measurement your study is dealing with. Then examine the purpose statements that fit your levels of measurement and select the one that comes closest to the purpose of your significance test. This should narrow your selection. Other information in the table will help in carrying out your significance test. If you have not used or been exposed to the selected test, you should find out more about your test before using it.

Now go to the Companion Website accompanying this text at www.prenhall.com/gay to check your understanding of chapter concepts in the following modules: Objectives, Practice Quiz, and Applying What You Know. Expand your research skills with Evaluating Articles, Analyzing Qualitative Data, Analyzing Quantitative Data, and Research Tools and Tips. Visit Web Links to broaden your knowledge about research.

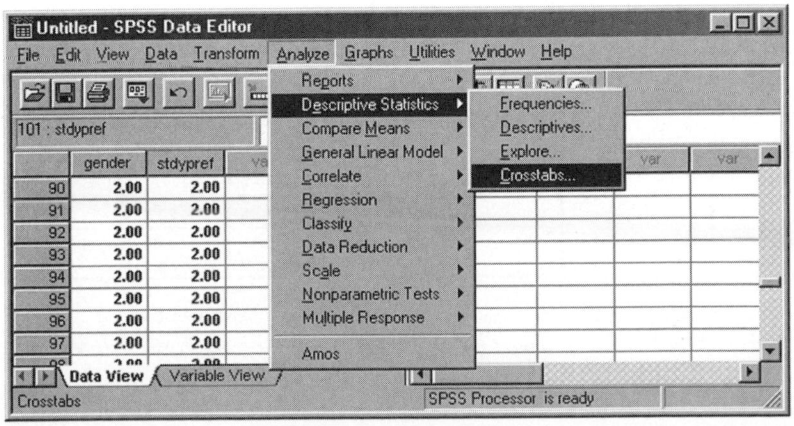

FIGURE 15.14
SPSS menu options for a chi square analysis.

FIGURE 15.15
SPSS crosstabs window
with cells button.

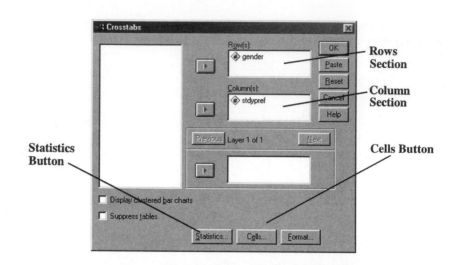

FIGURE 15.16
SPSS crosstabs statistics
window.

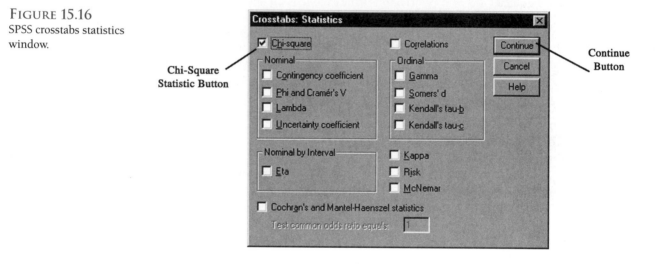

TABLE 15.7   SPSS Cross-Tabulation Table

GENDER * STDYPREF Crosstabulation

			STDYPREF		Total
			Alone	Others	
GENDER	males	Count	29	21	50
		Expected Count	22.5	27.5	50.0
	females	Count	16	34	50
		Expected Count	22.5	27.5	50.0
Total		Count	45	55	100
		Expected Count	45.0	55.0	100.0

Observed and Expected Frequency for males who like to study alone

TABLE 15.8   Chi Square Statistic

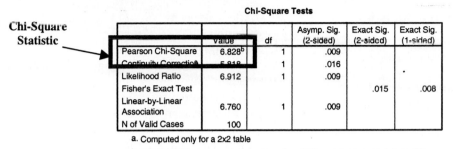

Chi-Square Tests

	Value	df	Asymp. Sig. (2-sided)	Exact Sig. (2-sided)	Exact Sig. (1-sided)
Pearson Chi-Square	6.828[b]	1	.009		
Continuity Correction	5.818	1	.016		
Likelihood Ratio	6.912	1	.009		
Fisher's Exact Test				.015	.008
Linear-by-Linear Association	6.760	1	.009		
N of Valid Cases	100				

a. Computed only for a 2x2 table

b. 0 cells (.0%) have expected count less than 5. The minimum expected count is 22.50.

TABLE 15.9   Commonly Used Parametric and Nonparametric Significance Tests

Name of Test	Test Statistic	df	Parametric (P) Nonparametric (NP)	Purpose	Var 1 Independent	Var 2 Dependent
t test for independent samples	t	$n_1 + n_2 - 2$	P	test difference between means of two independent groups	nominal	interval or ratio
t test for dependent samples	t	$N - 1$	P	test difference between means of two dependent groups	nominal	interval or ratio
analysis of variance	F	SS_B = groups $- 1$; SS_w = participants $-$ groups $- 1$	P	test the difference among three or more independent groups	nominal	interval or ratio
Pearson product correlation	r	$N - 2$	P	test whether a correlation is different from zero (a relationship exists)	interval or ratio	interval or ratio
chi square test	χ^2	rows $- 1$ times column $- 1$	NP	test the difference in proportions in two or more groups	nominal	nominal
median test	χ^2	rows $- 1$ times columns $- 1$	NP	test the difference of the medians of two independent groups	nominal	ordinal
Mann–Whitney U test	U	$N - 1$	NP	test the difference of the medians of two independent groups	nominal	ordinal
Wilcoxon signed rank test	Z	$N - 2$	NP	test the difference in the ranks of two related groups	nominal	ordinal
Kruskal–Wallis test	H	groups $- 1$	NP	test the difference in the ranks of three or more independent groups	nominal	ordinal
Freidman test	χ	groups $- 1$	NP	test the difference in the ranks of three or more dependent groups	nominal	ordinal
Spearman rho	ρ	$N - 2$	NP	test whether a correlation is different from zero	ordinal	ordinal

SUMMARY

Concepts Underlying Inferential Statistics

1. Inferential statistics deal with inferences about populations based on the behavior of samples. Inferential statistics are concerned with determining how likely it is that results based on a sample or samples are the same results that would have been obtained for the entire population.

2. Values calculated from samples, such as the mean, are referred to as *statistics*. The corresponding population values are referred to as *parameters*.

3. The question that guides inferential statistics is whether expected differences are real, significant ones or only the result of sampling errors.

4. Inferences concerning populations provide only probability statements; the researcher is never perfectly certain when making an inference about a population.

Standard Error

5. Expected, chance variation among the means is referred to as *sampling error*. Sampling errors are normally distributed.

6. If a sufficiently large number of equal-sized large samples are randomly selected from a population, all samples will not have the same mean on the variable measured, but the means of those samples will be normally distributed around the population mean. The mean of all the sample means will yield a good estimate of the population mean.

7. A distribution of sample means not only has its own mean but also its own standard deviation. The standard deviation of the sample means (the standard deviation of sampling errors) is usually referred to as the *standard error of the mean* ($SE_{\overline{X}}$).

8. In a normal curve, approximately 68% of the sample means will fall between plus and minus one standard error of the mean, 95% will fall between plus and minus two standard errors, and 99+% will fall between plus and minus three standard errors.

9. In most cases, we do not know the mean or standard deviation of the population, so we estimate the standard error by dividing the standard deviation of the sample by the square root of the sample size minus one.

10. The smaller the standard error of the mean, the less sampling error. As the size of the sample increases, the standard error of the mean decreases. The researcher should make every effort to acquire as large a sample as possible.

11. A standard error can also be calculated for other measures of central tendency as well as measures of variability, relationship, and relative position. Further, a standard error can also be determined for the difference between means.

The Null Hypothesis

12. When we talk about the real or significant difference between two sample means, we mean that the difference was caused by the treatment (the independent variable), and not by chance.

13. The null hypothesis says that there is no true difference or relationship between parameters in the populations and that any differences or relationship found for the samples is the result of sampling error.

14. Rejection of a null hypothesis provides more conclusive support for a positive research hypothesis. The test of significance selected to determine whether a difference between means is a true one provides a test of the null hypothesis. The null hypothesis is either rejected, as being probably false, or not rejected, as being probably true.

15. To test a null hypothesis we need a statistical test of significance, and we need to select a probability level that indicates how much risk we are willing to take that the decision we make is wrong. After we make the decision to reject or not reject the null hypothesis, we make an inference back to our research hypothesis.

Tests of Significance

16. A test of significance helps us to decide whether we can reject the null hypothesis and infer that the difference is a true one, not a chance one resulting from sampling error. A test of significance is made at a preselected probability level that allows us to state that we have rejected the null hypothesis because we would expect to find a difference as large as we have found by chance only 5 times out of every 100 studies, or only 1 time in every 100 studies, or whatever.

17. There are a number of different tests of significance. Factors such as the scale of measurement represented by the data, method of subject selection, the number of groups, and the number of independent variables

determine which test of significance should be selected for a given experiment.

Decision Making: Levels of Significance and Type I and Type II Errors

18. There are four possibilities that can result from testing the null hypothesis. If the null hypothesis is really true, and the researcher agrees that it is true (does not reject it), the researcher makes the correct decision. Similarly, if the null hypothesis is false, and the researcher rejects it (says there is a difference), the researcher also makes the correct decision. But if the null hypothesis is true, there really is no difference, and the researcher rejects it and says there is a difference, the researcher makes an incorrect decision, referred to as a *Type I error.* Similarly, if the null hypothesis is false, there really is a significant difference between the means, but the researcher concludes that the null hypothesis is true and does not reject it, the researcher also makes an incorrect decision, referred to as a *Type II error.*

19. A researcher who makes the decision to reject the null hypothesis does so with a given probability of being incorrect. This probability of being incorrect is referred to as the *significance level,* or *probability level,* of the test of significance.

20. If the decision is made to reject the null hypothesis, the means are concluded to be significantly different, too different to be the result of chance error. If the null hypothesis is not rejected, the means are determined to be not significantly different. The selected level of significance or probability selected determines how large the difference between the means must be to be declared significantly different. The most commonly used probability levels (symbolized as α) are the .05 and the .01 levels.

21. The probability level selected determines the probability of committing a Type I error, that is, of rejecting a null hypothesis that is really true. The smaller the probability level is, the larger the mean difference must be to be a significant difference.

22. As the probability of committing a Type I error decreases, the probability of committing a Type II error, that is, of not rejecting a null hypothesis when you should, increases.

23. The choice of a probability level, α, should be made prior to execution of the study. Rejection of a null hypothesis, or lack of rejection, only supports or does not support a research hypothesis; it does not "prove" it.

Two-Tailed and One-Tailed Tests

24. Tests of significance are usually two-tailed. The null hypothesis states that there is no difference between groups (A = B) and a two-tailed test allows for the possibility that a difference may occur in either direction. That is, either group mean may be higher than the other (A > B or B > A).

25. A one-tailed test assumes that a difference can only occur in one direction; the null hypothesis states that one group is not better than another and the one-tailed test assumes that if a difference occurs it will be in favor of that particular group (A > B). To select a one-tailed test of significance the researcher has to be quite sure that a difference can only occur in one direction.

26. If there is strong evidence for a one-tailed test, the level of the test of significance required for significance is smaller. In other words, it is "easier" to find a significant difference.

Degrees of Freedom

27. Inferential statistics are dependent on degrees of freedom to test hypotheses. Each test of significance has its own formula for determining degrees of freedom. Degrees of freedom are a function of such factors as the number of subjects and the number of groups. The intersection of the probability level and the degrees of freedom, *df,* determine the level needed to reject the null hypothesis.

Tests of Significance: Types

28. Different tests of significance are appropriate for different sets of data. The first decision in selecting an appropriate test of significance is whether a parametric test may be used or whether a nonparametric test must be selected.

29. Parametric tests are more powerful and are generally to be preferred. "More powerful" means more likely to reject a null hypothesis that is false; in other words, the researcher is less likely to commit a Type II error (not rejecting a null hypothesis that should be rejected).

30. Parametric tests require that certain assumptions be met for them to be valid. One of the major assumptions underlying use of parametric tests is that the variable measured is normally distributed in the population. A second major assumption is that the data represent an interval or ratio scale of measurement. A third assumption is that participants are randomly selected for the study. Another assumption is that the variances of the

population comparison groups are equal (or at least that the ratio of the variances is known).

31. With the exception of independence, some violation of one or more of these assumptions usually does not make too much difference in the decision made concerning the statistical significance of the results.

32. If one or more of the parametric assumptions are greatly violated, a nonparametric test should be used. Nonparametric tests make no assumptions about the shape of the distribution. Nonparametric tests are used when the data represent an ordinal or nominal scale, when a parametric assumption has been greatly violated, or when the nature of the distribution is not known. If the data represent an interval or ratio scale, a parametric test should be used unless another of the assumptions is greatly violated.

The *t* Test

33. The *t* test is used to determine whether two means are significantly different at a selected probability level. For a given sample size, the *t* indicates how often a difference as large or larger $(\overline{X}_1 - \overline{X}_2)$ would be found when there is no true population difference.

34. The *t* test makes adjustments for the fact that the distribution of scores for small samples becomes increasingly different from a normal distribution as sample sizes become increasingly smaller.

35. For a given significance level, the values of *t* required to reject a null hypothesis are progressively higher as sample sizes become smaller; as the sample size becomes larger the *t* value required to reject the null hypothesis becomes smaller.

36. The *t* test compares the observed mean difference $(\overline{X}_1 - \overline{X}_2)$ to the difference expected by chance. The *t* test forms a ratio of these two values. The numerator for a *t* test is the difference between the sample means $\overline{X}_1$ and $\overline{X}_2$ and the denominator is the chance difference that would be expected if the null hypothesis were true—the standard error of the difference between the means.

37. The *t* ratio determines whether the observed difference is sufficiently larger than a difference that would be expected by chance. After the numerator is divided by the denominator, the resulting *t* value is compared to the appropriate *t* table value (depending on the probability level and the degrees of freedom); if the calculated *t* value is equal to or greater than the table value, then the null hypothesis is rejected.

38. There are two different types of *t* tests, the *t* test for independent samples and the *t* test for nonindependent

samples. *Independent* samples are samples that are randomly formed. If two groups are randomly formed, the expectation is that they are essentially the same at the beginning of a study with respect to performance on the dependent variable. Therefore, if they are essentially the same at the end of the study, the null hypothesis is probably true; if they are different at the end of the study, the null hypothesis is probably false (that is, the treatment probably makes a difference).

39. *Nonindependent* samples are samples formed by some type of matching, or a single sample being pre- and posttested. When samples are not independent, the members of one group are systematically related to the members of a second group, especially if it is the same group at two different times. If samples are nonindependent, scores on the dependent variable are expected to be correlated and a special *t* for correlated, or nonindependent, means must be used.

Analysis of Gain or Difference Scores

40. There are a number of problems associated with the use of gain or difference scores. The major one is lack of equal opportunity to grow. Every participant does not have the same room to gain. If two groups are essentially the same on a pretest, their posttest scores can be directly compared using a *t* test. If a *t* test between the groups shows a difference on the pretests, the preferred posttest analysis is analysis of covariance.

Simple Analysis of Variance

41. Simple, or one-way, analysis of variance (ANOVA) is used to determine whether there is a significant difference between two or more means at a selected probability level.

42. In ANOVA, the total variation, or variance, of scores is attributed to two sources—variance between groups (variance caused by the treatment) and variance within groups (error variance). As with the *t* test, a ratio is formed (the *F* ratio) with group differences as the numerator (variance between groups) and an error term as the denominator (variance within groups). We determine whether the between groups (treatment) variance differs from the within groups (error) variance by more than what would be expected by chance.

43. The degrees of freedom for the *F* ratio are a function of the number of groups and the number of subjects.

Multiple Comparisons

44. Multiple comparison procedures are used following ANOVA to determine which means are significantly

different from which other means. A special *t* test that adjusts for the fact that many tests are being executed is used because when many tests are performed, the probability level tends to increase, thus increasing the likelihood of finding a spurious significant result.

45. The mean comparisons to be examined should be decided on before, not after, the study is conducted.

46. Of the many multiple comparison techniques available, a commonly used one is the Scheffé test, which is a very conservative test. The calculations for the Scheffé test are quite simple and sample sizes do not have to be equal.

Factorial Analysis of Variance

47. If a research study is based on a factorial design and investigates two or more independent variables and the interactions between them, the appropriate statistical analysis is a factorial, or multifactor, analysis of variance. This analysis yields a separate *F* ratio for each independent variable and one for each interaction.

Analysis of Covariance

48. Analysis of covariance (ANCOVA) is used as a technique for controlling extraneous variables and as a means of increasing power, the statistical ability to reject a false null hypothesis. ANCOVA increases the power of a statistical test by reducing within-group (error) variance.

49. ANCOVA is a form of ANOVA and is a method that can be used to equate groups on one or more variables. Essentially, ANCOVA adjusts posttest scores for initial differences on some variable (such as pretest performance or IQ) and compares adjusted scores.

50. ANCOVA is based on the assumption that participants have been randomly assigned to treatment groups. It is therefore best used in conjunction with true experimental designs. If existing, or intact, groups are involved but treatments are assigned to groups randomly, ANCOVA may still be used but results must be interpreted with due caution.

Multiple Regression

51. A multiple regression equation uses variables that are known to individually predict (correlate with) the criterion to make a more accurate prediction about a criterion variable.

52. Use of multiple regression is increasing, primarily because of its versatility and precision. It can be used with data representing any scale of measurement, and can be used to analyze the results of experimental and causal–comparative, as well as correlational, studies. It determines not only whether variables are related, but also the degree to which they are related.

53. The first step in multiple regression is to identify the variable that best predicts (is most highly correlated with) the criterion. Variables are added to the multiple regression equation based on their likelihood to be correlated with the criterion but not highly correlated with the other predictor variables.

54. With increasing frequency, multiple regression is being used as an alternative to the various analysis of variance techniques. When this is the case, the dependent variable, or posttest scores, becomes the criterion variable, and the predictors include group membership (e.g., experimental versus control) and any other appropriate variables, such as pretest scores.

Chi Square

55. Chi square, symbolized as χ^2, is a nonparametric test of significance appropriate when the data are in the form of frequency counts occurring in two or more mutually exclusive categories. Chi square is appropriate when the data represent a nominal scale, and the categories may be true categories (e.g., male versus female) or artificial categories (e.g., tall versus short).

56. Expected frequencies are usually the frequencies which would be expected if the groups were equal.

57. One-dimensional chi square is used to compare frequencies occurring in different categories so that the chi square is comparing groups with respect to the frequency of occurrence of different events. Data are presented in a contingency table.

58. Two-dimensional chi square is used when frequencies are categorized along more than one dimension, sort of a factorial chi square. Although 2 × 2 applications are quite common, contingency tables may be based on any number of categories, such as 2 × 3, 3 × 3, or 2 × 4.

59. Each inferential statistic described determines significance in the same general way. A significance level is selected (usually .05 or .01). The degrees of freedom are determined. A chart or computer program indicates the value that corresponds to the intersection of the significance level and the degrees of freedom in the appropriate reference table. The value is compared to the results of the study. If the value of the study results exceeds the reference table value, the null hypothesis is rejected. If not, it is not rejected.

"Whether you do your analyses by hand, calculator, or computer, all data should be thoroughly checked and stored in an organized manner." (p. 491)

POSTANALYSIS CONSIDERATIONS

OBJECTIVES

After reading Chapter 16, you should be able to do the following:

1. List guidelines to be followed in verifying and storing quantitative data.
2. Explain how a rejected null hypothesis relates to a research hypothesis.
3. Explain how a null hypothesis that is not rejected relates to a research hypothesis.
4. Identify the major use of significant unhypothesized relationships.
5. Explain the factors that influence the interpretation of research results, including statistical, methodological, and significance.
6. Understand the role of power in significance testing.
7. Describe *replication*.

VERIFYING AND STORING DATA

After you have completed the analyses necessary to describe your data and test your hypothesis, you do not say, "Thank goodness, I'm done!" and happily throw away all your data and your worksheets. Whether you do your analyses by hand, calculator, or computer, all data should be thoroughly checked and stored in an organized manner.

VERIFICATION AND DATA CHECKING

As mentioned in Chapter 8, verification involves double checking the data, organizing it, and evaluating the research conclusion. Original data—as much of it as possible—should be rechecked and the coded data should be compared to the initial uncoded data to make sure coding was done properly. Data kept in a computer should be printed and examined.

When analyses are done by hand or with a calculator, both the accuracy of computations and the reasonableness of the results should be checked. Usually, if the data have been entered correctly into a computer (always check this), the results of the computer analysis will be accurate. This is an advantage of computers. You noticed that in the previous chapters we applied the analysis step by step. This was probably helpful to some readers and annoying to others. Math superstar types seem to derive great satisfaction from doing several steps in a row "in their heads" and listing the results instead of separately recording the result of each step. This may save time in the short run, but not necessarily in the long run. If you end up with a result that just does not look right, it is a lot easier to spot an error if every step is in front of you. Computer analyses rarely show each step, only the final result. This is a disadvantage of computer usage, especially if the researcher is not familiar with the analysis being used.

A very frustrated student once came to one of the authors, quite upset and with a very sad tale about being up all night, rechecking his work over and over and over, and still getting a negative sum of squares in his ANOVA. He was at the point where he could easily have been convinced that the square of a number can be negative! An inspection of his work revealed quickly that the problem was not in his execution of the ANOVA, but in the numbers he was using to do the ANOVA. Early in the game he had added ΣX_1, ΣX_2, and ΣX_3 and obtained a number much, much larger than their actual sum. From that point on, he was doomed. The moral of the story is that if you have checked an analysis or a set of figures several times and they still seem incorrect, do not check them 50 more times. Look elsewhere! For example, make sure you are using the correct formula or make sure you have used the correct numbers. The anecdote also illustrates that the research results should make sense. If your scores range from 20 to 94 and you get a standard deviation of 1.20 you have probably made a mistake somewhere, because 1.20 is not a reasonable value with such a large range. Similarly, if your means are 24.20 and 26.10 and you get a t ratio of 44.82, you had better recheck your data and analysis.

Recall from Chapter 8 again that for analyses done by computer, output must be checked very carefully. Some people are under the mistaken impression that if a result was produced by a computer, it is automatically correct. Remember the human error factor; people make mistakes inputting data and selecting analyses for the computer. Computer analyses are generally accurate *if the data are properly entered* into the computer. However, one way to check for accurate entry of data is to examine the reasonableness of the results. Don't succumb to a "blind faith" view of the computer. Also, don't be one of those persons who uses the computer to perform analyses they do not understand themselves. Computer usage has almost been made too easy. A person with little or no knowledge of analysis of covariance, for example, can, by following directions, have a computer perform the analysis. However, such a person could not possibly know the nuances of interpretation and whether the results make sense. You may now be beginning to understand the wisdom of our prior advice to never use the computer to apply a method that you have not previously done by hand. Also, although you can usually be pretty safe in assuming that the computer will accurately execute each analysis, it is a good idea to spot check. The computer only does what it has been programmed to do and programming errors do occur. Thus, if the computer gives you six F ratios, calculate at least one yourself. If it agrees with the one the computer produced, the rest are most probably also correct.

STORAGE

When you are convinced that your work is accurate, label, organize, and file your data in a safe place. You may need it again. Sometimes an additional analysis is desired either by the original researcher, an advisor, or another researcher who wishes to analyze the data using a different statistical technique. Also, data may be reused from one study in a later study. Therefore, label all data with as many identification labels as possible, labels such as the dates of the study, the nature of each treatment group, and whether data are pretest data, posttest data, or data for a control variable. Store it in a safe place, not in your junk drawer, wet basement, or rental storage unit two states away. If you use a computer, keep one set of data in your computer or hard drive, but also keep a labeled, backup floppy disk or CD-ROM in case your computer or hard drive crashes.

INTERPRETING QUANTITATIVE RESEARCH RESULTS

The product of a test of significance is a number, a value that is or is not statistically significant. What the number actually means requires interpretation by the researcher. The results of statistical analyses need to be interpreted in terms of the purpose of the study, the original research hypothesis, and with respect to other studies that have been conducted in the same area of research.

HYPOTHESIZED RESULTS

You must discuss whether the results support the research hypothesis and why they do or do not. Are the results in agreement with other findings? Why or why not? Minimally, this means that you will state, for example, that hypotheses one and two were supported, and that hypothesis three was not. The supported hypotheses are relatively simple to deal with; unsupported hypotheses require some explanation regarding possible reasons. There may have been validity or reliability problems in your study, for example. Similarly, if your results are not in agreement with other research findings, possible reasons for the discrepancy should be discussed. There may have been validity problems in your study, or you may have discovered a relationship previously not uncovered.

Remember, if you reject a null hypothesis (there is a difference), your research hypothesis may be supported but it is not proven. One study does not prove anything except that in this one instance the research hypothesis was supported (and the null hypothesis was rejected). A supported research hypothesis does not necessarily mean that your treatment would "work" with different populations, different materials, and different dependent variables. As an example, if token reinforcement is found to be effective in improving the behavior of first graders, this does not mean that token reinforcement will necessarily be effective in reducing referrals to the principal at the high school level. In other words, do not overgeneralize your results.

If you do not reject the null hypothesis (there is no difference), so that your research hypothesis (there is a difference) is not supported, do not feel bad and apologize for your results. A common reaction of some researchers in this situation is to be very disappointed; after all, "I didn't find a significant difference." In the first place, failure to reject a null hypothesis does not necessarily mean that your research hypothesis is false. But more importantly, even if significance is not attained, it is just as important to know what does not work as what does. The researcher's task is to carry out a well-designed, well-analyzed study. It is the researcher's responsibility to provide a fair and valid examination of the study hypotheses. It is not the researcher's task to reject the null hypothesis or produce statistically significant results. If researchers knew the results of their study beforehand, there would be no need for research.

Of course if there were some problems with your study, you should describe them in detail. For example, if your study encountered high participant mortality or if intact groups were compared instead of randomly selected ones, this should be reported. There are many problems or threats to validity that can arise in a study that are not the researcher's fault. You should report these when describing your research results. But do not rationalize. If your study was well planned and well conducted, and no unforeseen mishaps occurred, do not try to come up with some reason why your study did not "come out right." It may very well have "come out right"; remember, the null hypothesis might be true for this particular study.

UNHYPOTHESIZED RESULTS

Results that are not hypothesized but appear during a study should be interpreted with great care. Often, during a study, an apparent relationship will be noticed that was not hypothesized. For example, you might notice that the experimental group appears to require fewer examples than the control group to learn new math concepts—an unhypothesized relationship. In such a circumstance, do not go and change your original hypothesis to conform to this new apparent finding, and don't add the unhypothesized finding as a new hypothesis. Hypotheses should be formulated a priori—before the study—based on deductions from theory and/or experience. A true test of a hypothesis comes from its ability to explain and predict what *will* happen, not *what is* happening. You can, however, collect and analyze data on these unforeseen relationships and present your results as such—but don't change or add to your original hypotheses. These unexpected findings may then form the basis for a later study, conducted by yourself or another investigator, specifically designed to test a hypothesis related to your findings. Do not fall into the trap, however, of searching frantically for something that might be significant if your study does not appear to be going as hypothesized. Fishing expeditions in experimental studies are just as bad as fishing expeditions in correlational studies.

STATISTICAL AND METHODOLOGICAL ISSUES

Inferential statistics make inferences about a population based on a sample. To make valid inferences and legitimate conclusions about a target population, two factors must apply: the sample must be representative and the assumptions of the statistical test must be met. When randomization is not possible, as is often the case in educational research, researchers choose their samples by matching or selecting intact groups. The lack of randomized samples can introduce bias into a study and limit its usefulness. Analogously, the statistical procedures used to analyze data have assumptions that underlie the statistics. For example, most parametric statistics assume an underlying normal distribution and that each participant's scores are independent of any other participant's scores. If these assumptions are not met, bias enters into the statistics used, weakening research generalizations.

A number of methodological practices can lead to invalid or inaccurate research results. Three such practices are ignoring measurement error, low statistical power, and performing multiple comparisons. Most statistical models assume error-free measurement, particularly of the independent variables. However, as discussed in Chapter 5, measurements are seldom error free. Large amounts of measurement error hamper the ability to find statistically significant research results. Recall that in parametric significance tests, the denominator is a measure of error. Thus, the larger the denominator, the larger the numerator must be to attain significance.

Statistical power is the probability of avoiding a Type II error; that is, the probability of correctly rejecting the null hypothesis. If an analysis has little statistical power, the researcher is likely to overlook or miss the outcome she desired to discover. The analysis did not have enough power to detect a significant difference that would have been evident if the statistical power had been greater. The power of a significance test depends on three interrelated factors: (1) the sample size, (2) the significance level selected and the directionality of the significance test, and (3) the effect size, which indicates degree of the departure from the null hypothesis. The greater the departure from the null hypothesis, the greater the effect size. As the sample size, significance level, and effect size increase, so does the power of the significance test. For example, power increases automatically with an increase in sample size. Thus, virtually any difference can be made significant if the sample is large enough. However, it is difficult to interpret the practical meaning of small but significant results obtained primarily by using a very large sample.

The higher the level of significance at which the null hypothesis will be rejected, the more powerful the test. Increasing the significance level, say, from .05 to .10, increases power by making it easier to reject the null hypothesis. Further, if a one-tailed test is justified, it will increase the power to reject the null hypothesis (reduce the Type II error). However, although the researcher is likely to know the significance level of the study and its sample size, he is not likely to know the effect size. Without all three pieces of information, the power of the statistical test cannot be determined. Three strategies are used to estimate the effect size.[1] First, the effect sizes of studies of the same phenomenon can be found and used as guidelines for the likely effect size in the proposed study. Second, a cutoff score below which an effect size is judged unimportant may be used to estimate effect size. For example, a researcher might decide that if a new treatment did not have an effect size of .4 or higher, it would not be worth pursuing. Thus, an effect size of .4 would be chosen. Third, conventional, generally agreed-on definitions of small, medium, and large effect sizes can be chosen. For example, for t tests, an effect size of .20 is considered small, .50 is considered medium, and .80 is considered high. Given a desired effect size (say, .50)

---

[1]Cohen, J., and Cohen, P. (1975). *Applied multiple regressions/correlation analysis for the behavioral sciences*. Hillsdale, NJ: Lawrence Erlbaum Associates.

and a significance level (say, .05), one can enter a table that shows that to attain an effect size of .50 for a *t* test at a significance level of .05, a total of 30 participants in each group are needed in the study.

Normally, a researcher would examine the power of a study before beginning it in order to determine whether the power will be sufficient. If the examination shows that the power is insufficient, the researcher can revise the study to increase power, usually by increasing the sample size or significance level.

Another statistical issue is the use of multiple comparison techniques such as the Scheffé to test the significance of a large number of means. This practice can lead to erroneous interpretations. Simply put, the more significance tests one carries out in a study, the more likely that false rejections of the null hypotheses (Type I errors) will occur. Suppose, for example, that a researcher did 100 significance tests at the .05 level. Suppose also that there really were no significance differences among all the 100 tests. However, given the .05 level, how many of the tests are likely to be significant? How about at least 5? Remember, we deal in probabilities, not certainties, and at the .05 level we leave 5% for error. In simple terms, a large number of multiple comparisons enhances the likelihood of Type I errors.

STATISTICAL VERSUS PRACTICAL SIGNIFICANCE

The difference between statistical significance and practical significance is often unclear to those who deal with statistical results. The fact that results are statistically significant does not automatically mean that they are of any educational value, that is, that they have practical significance. **Statistical significance** only means that your results would be likely to occur by chance a certain percentage of the time, say, 5%. This only means that the observed statistical relationship or difference is probably a real one, but not necessarily an important one. Significance in the statistical sense is, as noted in the previous section, largely a function of sample size, significance level, and a valid research design. For example, very large samples can result in statistically significant relationships or differences, but have no real practical use to anybody. As the sample size increases, the error term (denominator) tends to decrease, and thus increases the *r* or *t* ratio so that very large samples with very small correlations or mean differences may become significant. A mean difference of two points might be statistically significant but probably not worth the effort of revising a curriculum.

Thus, in a way, the smaller sample sizes typically used in educational research studies actually have a redeeming feature. Given that smaller sample sizes mean less power, and given that a greater mean difference is probably required for rejection of the null hypothesis, typical education sample sizes are probably more practically significant than if much larger samples were involved. Of course, lack of statistical power due to small sample sizes may keep researchers from finding some important relationships. In any event, you should always take care in interpreting results. The fact that method A is significantly more effective than method B statistically does not mean that the whole world should immediately adopt method A! Always consider the practical significance of statistically significant differences.

Another concern in interpreting the results of research is the difference between research precision and research accuracy. *Precision* refers to how narrowly an estimate is specified. *Accuracy* refers to how close an estimate is to the true value. Estimates can be precise but not accurate. Often, a computer user or a zealous calculator user will report data to the 6th or 10th decimal place; 25.046093 or 7.28403749. This is misused and not useful precision. What is important is the accuracy of the calculated estimates, not the number of digits used to state it. Accuracy is more important in interpreting research outcomes than precision.

In sum, a number of considerations go into interpreting the results of research, including methodological and statistical factors as well as concerns over the difference between statistical and practical significance.

Now go to the Companion Website accompanying this text at www.prenhall.com/gay to check your understanding of chapter concepts in the following modules: Objectives, Practice Quiz, and Applying What You Know. Expand your research skills with Evaluating Articles, Analyzing Qualitative Data, Analyzing Quantitative Data, and Research Tools and Tips. Visit Web Links to broaden your knowledge about research.

REPLICATION OF RESULTS

Perhaps the strongest support for a research hypothesis comes from replication of results. *Replication* means doing the study again. The second (third, etc.) study may be a repetition of the original study, using the same or different subjects, or it may represent an alternative approach to testing the same hypothesis. Repeating the study with the same subjects is feasible only in certain types of research, such as single-subject designs. Repeating the study with different subjects in the same or different settings increases the generalizability of the findings.

The need for replication is especially great when an unusual or new relationship is found, or when the results have practical significance so that the treatment investigated might really make a difference. Interpretation and discussion of a replicated finding will invariably be less tentative than a first-time-ever finding, and rightly so. The significance of a relationship may also be enhanced if it is replicated in a more natural setting. A highly controlled study, for example, might find that method A is more effective than method B in a laboratory-like environment. Interpreting and discussing the results in terms of practical significance and implications for classroom practice would have to be done with due caution. If the same results could then be obtained in a classroom situation, however, the researcher could be less tentative concerning their generalizability.

SUMMARY

Verifying and Storing Data

1. Whether you do your analyses by hand, calculator, or computer, all data should be thoroughly checked and stored in an organized manner.

2. Verification involves double checking the data and evaluating the research results. Coded data should be compared with uncoded data to make sure all data were coded properly.

3. When analyses are done by hand, or with a calculator, both the accuracy of the computations and the reasonableness of the results need to be checked. When analyses are done by computer, the key concern is inputing the data correctly.

4. All of the data should be carefully labeled with as many identification labels as possible, such as the dates of the study, the nature of each treatment group, and whether data are pretest data, posttest data, or data for a control variable. If data are stored in a computer or hard disk, make a backup disk or CD-ROM to protect from computer crashes.

Interpreting Quantitative Research Results

5. The results of statistical analyses need to be interpreted in terms of the purpose of the study and the original research hypothesis, and with respect to other studies that have been conducted in the same area of research.

6. The researcher must discuss both whether the results support the research hypothesis and why or why not, and whether the results are in agreement with other findings and why or why not.

7. A supported research hypothesis does not necessarily mean that your treatment would "work" with different populations, different materials, and different dependent variables.

8. Failure to reject a null hypothesis does not necessarily mean that your research hypothesis is false, but even if it is, it is just as important to know what does not work as what does work.

9. Unhypothesized results should be interpreted with great care and should be kept and analyzed separately from the hypotheses stated before the start of the study.

10. Unhypothesized findings may form the basis for a later study.

11. Statistical and methodological issues influence the interpretation of research results. Statistical requirements such as random selection and normal distributions influence interpretation if not met. Methodological factors such as ignoring measurement error, performing multiple comparisons, and using small samples can lead to inaccurate or invalid research results.

12. Statistical power is the probability of avoiding a Type II error; that is, it is the probability of correctly

rejecting the null hypothesis. Four factors influence power—sample size, significance level, direction of the significance test, and the effect size. Tables exist that indicate how many participants are required to attain a given power level given the significance level and desired effect size.

13. The fact that results are statistically significant does not automatically mean that they are of any educational value. With very large samples a very small mean difference may yield a significant t. A mean difference of two points might be statistically significant but probably not worth the effort of revising a curriculum.

14. *Replication* means that the study is done again. The need for replication is especially great when an unusual or new relationship is found in a study, or when the results have practical significance.

TASK 9   PERFORMANCE CRITERIA

The data that you generate (scores you make up for each subject) should make sense. If your dependent variable is IQ, for example, do not generate scores for your subjects like 2, 11, and 15; generate scores like 84, 110, and 120. Got it? Unlike a real study, you can make your study turn out any way you want!

Depending on the scale of measurement represented by your data, select and compute the appropriate descriptive statistics.

Depending on the scale of measurement represented by your data, your research hypothesis, and your research design, select and compute the appropriate test of significance. Determine the statistical significance of your results for a selected probability level. Present your results in a summary statement and in a summary table, and relate how the significance or nonsignificance of your results supports or does not support your original research hypothesis. For example, you might say the following:

> Computation of a t test for independent samples ($\alpha = .05$) indicated that the group that received weekly reviews retained significantly more than the group that received daily reviews (see Table 1). Therefore, the original hypothesis that "ninth-grade algebra students who receive a weekly review will retain significantly more algebraic concepts than ninth-grade algebra students who receive a daily review" was supported.

Note: Task 9 should look like the results section of a research report. Although your actual calculations should not be part of Task 9, they should be attached to it. We have attached the step-by-step calculations for the Task 9 example. You may also perform your calculations using SPSS 10.0, and attach these computations as well.

On the following pages, an example is presented that illustrates the performance called for by Task 9. (See Task 9 example.) Note that the scores are based on the administration of the test described in Task 5. Note also that the student calculated effect size (ES) as described in Chapter 10.

Additional examples for this and subsequent tasks are included in the *Student Guide* that accompanies this text.

TABLE 1   Means, Standard Deviations, and t for the Daily-Review and Weekly-Review Groups on the Delayed Retention Test

	REVIEW GROUP		
	DAILY	**WEEKLY**	**t**
M	44.82	52.68	2.56*
SD	5.12	6.00	

Note: Maximum score = 65.
*df = 38, $p < .05$.

1

Effect of Interactive Multimedia on the Achievement of 10th-Grade Biology Students

Results

Prior to the beginning of the study, after the 60 students were randomly selected and assigned to experimental and control groups, final science grades from the previous school year were obtained from school records in order to check initial group equivalence. Examination of the means and a t test for independent samples (α = .05) indicated essentially no difference between the groups (see Table 1). A t test for independent samples was used because the groups were randomly formed and the data were interval.

Table 1

Means, Standard Deviation, and t Tests for the Experimental and Control Groups

| | Group | | |
Score	IMM instruction[a]	Traditional instruction[a]	t
Prior			
Grades			
M	87.47	87.63	−0.08*
SD	8.19	8.05	
Posttest			
NPSS:B			
M	32.27	26.70	4.22**
SD	4.45	5.69	

Note. Maximum score for prior grades = 100. Maximum score for posttest = 40.
[a]n = 30.
*p > .05. **p < .05.

At the completion of the eight-month study, during the first week in May, scores on the NPSS:B were compared, also using a t test for independent samples. As Table 1 indicates, scores of the experimental and control groups were significantly different. In fact, the experimental group scored approximately one standard deviation higher than the control group (ES = .98). Therefore, the original hypothesis that "10th-grade biology students whose teachers use IMM as part of their instructional technique will exhibit significantly higher achievement than 10th-grade biology students whose teachers do not use IMM" was supported.

PRIOR GRADES

	EXPERIMENTAL		CONTROL	
S	X_1	X_1^2	X_2	X_2^2
1	72	5184	71	5041
2	74	5476	75	5625
3	76	5776	75	5625
4	76	5776	77	5929
5	77	5929	78	6084
6	78	6084	78	6084
7	78	6084	79	6241
8	79	6241	80	6400
9	80	6400	81	6561
10	84	7056	83	6889
11	85	7225	85	7225
12	87	7569	88	7744
13	87	7569	88	7744
14	88	7744	89	7921
15	89	7921	89	7921
16	89	7921	89	7921
17	90	8100	90	8100
18	91	8281	91	8281
19	92	8464	92	8464
20	93	8649	92	8464
21	93	8649	93	8649
22	93	8649	94	8836
23	94	8836	94	8836
24	95	9025	95	9025
25	95	9025	96	9216
26	97	9409	96	9216
27	97	9409	97	9409
28	98	9604	97	9409
29	98	9604	98	9604
30	99	9801	99	9801
	2624	231,460	2629	232,265
	ΣX_1	ΣX_1^2	ΣX_2	ΣX_2^2

$$\overline{X_1} = \frac{\Sigma X_1}{n_1} = \frac{2624}{30} = 87.47$$

$$\overline{X_2} = \frac{\Sigma X_2}{n_2} = \frac{2629}{30} = 87.63$$

$$SD_1 = \sqrt{\frac{SS_1}{n_1 - 1}} \qquad\qquad SD_2 = \sqrt{\frac{SS_2}{n_2 - 1}}$$

$$SS_1 = \sum X_1^2 - \frac{\left(\sum X_1\right)^2}{n_1} \qquad\qquad SS_2 = \sum X_2^2 - \frac{\left(\sum X_2\right)^2}{n_2}$$

$$= 231{,}460 - \frac{(2624)^2}{30} \qquad\qquad = 232{,}265 - \frac{(2629)^2}{30}$$

$$= 231{,}460 - \frac{6885376}{30} \qquad\qquad = 232{,}265 - \frac{6911641}{30}$$

$$= 231{,}460 - 229{,}512.53 \qquad\qquad = 232{,}265 - 230388.03$$

$$SS_1 = 1947.47 \qquad\qquad SS_2 = 1876.97$$

$$SD_1 = \sqrt{\frac{1947.47}{29}} \qquad\qquad SD_2 = \sqrt{\frac{1876.97}{29}}$$

$$= \sqrt{67.154} \qquad\qquad = \sqrt{64.72}$$

$$SD_1 = 8.19 \qquad\qquad SD_2 = 8.05$$

$$t = \frac{\bar{X}_1 - \bar{X}_2}{\sqrt{\left(\frac{SS_1 + SS_2}{n_1 + n_2 - 2}\right)\left(\frac{1}{n_1} + \frac{1}{n_2}\right)}} \qquad = \frac{87.47 - 87.63}{\sqrt{\left(\frac{1947.47 + 1876.97}{30 + 30 - 2}\right)\left(\frac{1}{30} + \frac{1}{30}\right)}}$$

$$= \frac{-0.16}{\sqrt{\left(\frac{3824.44}{58}\right)\left(\frac{1}{15}\right)}}$$

Note: the t table does not have $df = 58$. To be conservative I used $df = 40$. For $df = 40$ the table value is 2.021

$$= \frac{-0.16}{\sqrt{(65.9386)(.0667)}}$$

$$= \frac{-0.16}{\sqrt{4.398}}$$

$$= \frac{-0.16}{2.097}$$

$$t = -.08 \qquad df = 58 \qquad p < .05$$

POSTTEST   NATIONAL PROFICIENCY SURVEY SERIES: BIOLOGY

EXPERIMENTAL   CONTROL

S	X_1	X_1^2	X_2	X_2^2
1	20	400	15	225
2	24	576	16	256
3	26	676	18	324
4	27	729	20	400
5	28	784	21	441
6	29	841	22	484
7	29	841	22	484
8	29	841	23	529
9	30	900	24	576
10	31	961	24	576
11	31	961	25	625
12	31	961	25	625
13	32	1024	25	625
14	32	1024	26	676
15	33	1089	26	676
16	33	1089	27	729
17	33	1089	27	729
18	34	1156	28	784
19	34	1156	29	841
20	35	1225	29	841
21	35	1225	30	900
22	35	1225	30	900
23	36	1296	31	961
24	36	1296	31	961
25	36	1296	32	1024
26	37	1369	33	1089
27	37	1369	34	1156
28	38	1444	35	1225
29	38	1444	36	1296
30	39	1521	37	1369
	968	31808	801	22327
	ΣX_1	ΣX_1^2	ΣX_2	ΣX_2^2

$$\overline{X_1} = \frac{\Sigma x_1}{n_1} = \frac{968}{30} = 32.27$$

$$\overline{X_2} = \frac{\Sigma x_2}{n_2} = \frac{801}{30} = 26.70$$

$$SD_1 = \sqrt{\frac{SS_1}{n_1 - 1}} \qquad\qquad SD_2 = \sqrt{\frac{SS_2}{n_2 - 1}}$$

$$SS_1 = \sum x_1^2 - \frac{\left(\sum x_1\right)^2}{n_1} \qquad\qquad SS_2 = \sum x_2^2 - \frac{\left(\sum x_2\right)^2}{n_2}$$

$$= 31808 - \frac{(968)^2}{30} \qquad\qquad = 22327 - \frac{(801)^2}{30}$$

$$= 31808 - \frac{937024}{30} \qquad\qquad = 22327 - \frac{641601}{30}$$

$$= 31808 - 31234.13 \qquad\qquad = 22327 - 21386.70$$

$$SS_1 = 573.87 \qquad\qquad SS_2 = 940.30$$

$$SD_1 = \sqrt{\frac{573.87}{29}} \qquad\qquad SD_2 = \sqrt{\frac{940.30}{29}}$$

$$= \sqrt{19.789} \qquad\qquad = \sqrt{32.424}$$

$$SD_1 = 4.45 \qquad\qquad SD_2 = 5.69$$

$$t = \frac{\overline{x}_1 - \overline{x}_2}{\sqrt{\left(\frac{SS_1 + SS_2}{n_1 + n_2 - 2}\right)\left(\frac{1}{n_1} + \frac{1}{n_2}\right)}} = \frac{32.27 - 26.70}{\sqrt{\left(\frac{573.87 + 940.30}{30 + 30 - 2}\right)\left(\frac{1}{30} + \frac{1}{30}\right)}}$$

$$= \frac{5.57}{\sqrt{\left(\frac{1514.17}{58}\right)\left(\frac{1}{15}\right)}}$$

$$= \frac{5.57}{\sqrt{(26.1064)(.0667)}}$$

$$= \frac{5.57}{\sqrt{1.7404}}$$

$$= \frac{5.57}{1.3192}$$

$$t = 4.22 \qquad df = 58 \qquad p < .05$$

PRODUCING AND CONSUMING RESEARCH

In this last part of the book, you will learn to produce a complete research report and learn important criteria for critiquing research reports and articles.

People conduct research for a variety of reasons. The motivation for doing a research project may be no more than that such a project is a degree requirement, or it may come from a strong desire to contribute to educational theory or practice. Whatever the reason for their execution, most research studies culminate with the production of a research report.

A number of elements are common to most reports regardless of the format or style followed. Virtually all research reports, for example, contain a statement of the problem or topic studied, a description of procedures used, and a presentation of results. Unlike a research proposal, which focuses on what will be done, a research report describes what has happened in the study and what results were obtained. All research reports strive to communicate as clearly as possible the purpose, procedures, and findings of the study. Chapter 17 covers the preparation of a research report.

Knowing how to conduct research and produce a research report is a valuable skill, but as a professional, you should also know how to consume and evaluate research. Anyone who reads a newspaper, listens to the radio, or watches television is a consumer of research. Many people uncritically accept and act on medical and health findings, for example, because they are presented by someone in a white lab coat or because they are labeled "research." Very few people question the procedures utilized or the generalizability of the findings from such research. You, on the other hand, as a professional, are required to possess critical evaluation skills. You have a responsibility to be informed concerning the latest findings in your professional area and to be able to differentiate "good" from "poor" research. Normally a researcher critically evaluates each reference and does not consider poorly executed research. Decisions made on the basis of poor research are likely to be bad or ineffective ones. Research results that contain one or more serious flaws are frequently published. Competent evaluation of a research study requires knowledge of each of the components of the research process. Your work in previous chapters has given you that knowledge. Chapter 18 presents criteria necessary to evaluate a research report.

"The research report should . . . reflect scholarship." (p. 508)

PREPARING A RESEARCH REPORT

OBJECTIVES

After reading Chapter 17, you should be able to do the following:

1. Identify and briefly describe the major sections of a research report.
2. List general rules for writing and preparing a research report.

You have already written many of the components of a research report through your work in Tasks 2 through 9. In this chapter, you will integrate all your previous efforts to produce a complete report.

The goal of Chapter 17 is for you, having conducted a study, to be able to produce a complete report. After you have read Chapter 17, you should be able to perform the following task.

TASK 10

Based on Tasks 2, 8, and 9, prepare a research report that follows the general format for a thesis or dissertation. (See Performance Criteria, p. 517)

GENERAL GUIDELINES

If this chapter were written even a few years ago, it would have focused almost exclusively on writing quantitative research reports. However, in recent years the number of qualitative research reports has grown steadily. As noted in prior chapters, there are important differences between the purpose and conduct of these two research approaches. In this chapter we emphasize the general issues and practices associated with writing a research report. It is important that you understand that although qualitative and quantitative research reports require that similar topics be addressed, the contents of the topics may differ given the differences between research emphases. For example, all research reports contain a section describing the topic or problem studied, the review of literature, the description of procedures, and the description of results. However, as seen in earlier chapters, qualitative and quantitative studies address these topics in somewhat different ways and emphases. You are encouraged to examine and compare the research reports excerpted in chapters 6, 7, and 8, and reprinted at the end of chapters 10, 11, 12, and 13 to see their differences. Further, when you are actually writing your report, you should look through journals pertinent to your study to view the sections, level of detail, and types of results commonly reported. This is the best way to determine the appropriate format for your report.

While you are conducting your study, you can profitably use spare time to begin revising or refining the introduction and methods sections of your report. After all the data are analyzed, you are ready to write the report's final sections. The major guideline for all stages of writing is to make an outline. The chances of your report being presented in an organized, logical manner are greatly increased if you think the sequence through before you actually write anything. Formulating an outline greatly facilitates this "thinking through." To review briefly, developing an outline involves identifying and ordering major topics followed by differentiating each major heading into logical subheadings. The time spent in working on an outline is well worth it since it is much easier to reorganize an outline that is not quite right than to reorganize a document written in paragraph form. Of course this does not mean that your first report draft will be your last. Two or three revisions of each section might be needed. Remember, writing inevitably uncovers issues or activities that must be rethought. Each time you read a section you will see ways to improve its organization or clarity. Also, others who review your report for you will see areas in need of rethinking or rewording that you have not noticed.

GENERAL RULES FOR WRITING

Probably the foremost rule of research report writing is that the writer should try to relate aspects of the study in a manner that accurately reflects what was done and what was found. Although the style of reporting may vary between quantitative and qualitative studies, the focus of both should be on providing accurate description for the reader. For example, in quantitative reports personal pronouns such as "I" and "we" are usually avoided; the passive voice should be used. In qualitative reports, the tone is often personal, active, and in the voice of the participants. Such stylistic differences do not alter the need for accurate reporting.

The research report should be written in a clear, simple, straightforward style and reflect scholarship. You do not have to be boring, just concise. In other words, convey what you wish to convey, do it in an efficient way, avoid jargon, and use simple language. For example, instead of saying, "The population comprised all students who matriculated for the fall semester at Egghead University," it would be better to say, "The population was all students enrolled for the fall semester at Egghead University." Obviously the report should contain correct spelling, grammatical construction, and punctuation. Your computer probably has a spelling and grammar checker. Use it. Even if you don't have a computer, you do have access to a dictionary. It is also a good idea to have someone you know, someone who is perhaps stronger in these areas, review your manuscript and indicate errors.

Although different style manuals emphasize different rules of writing, there are several common to most manuals. Use of abbreviations and contractions, for instance, is generally discouraged. For example, do not write "the American Psychological Assn." Write "the American Psychological Association." Also, words like *shouldn't, isn't,* and *won't* should be avoided. Exceptions to the abbreviation rule include commonly used and understood abbreviations (such as IQ and GPA) and abbreviations defined by the researcher to promote clarity, simplify presentation, or reduce repetition. If the same sequence of words is going to be used repeatedly, the researcher will often define an abbreviation in parentheses when first using the sequence and thereafter use only the abbreviation. Authors of cited references are usually referred to in the main body of the report by last name only; first names, initials, and titles are not given. Instead of saying, "Professor Dudley Q. McStrudle (1995) concluded . . .," you normally would say "McStrudle (1995) concluded . . . ." These guidelines hold only for the main body of the report. Tables, figures, footnotes, and references may include abbreviations; footnotes and references usually give at least the author's initials. Another convention followed by most style manuals is with respect to numbers. If the first word of a sentence is a number ("Six schools were contacted . . ."), or if the number is nine or less ("a total of five lists . . ."), numbers are expressed as words. Otherwise, numbers are generally expressed as Arabic numerals ("a total of 500 questionnaires was sent").

The final report should be proofread carefully at least twice. Reading the report silently to yourself will usually be sufficient to identify major errors. If you have a willing listener, however, reading the manuscript out loud often helps you to identify grammatical or constructional errors. Sometimes sentences do not make nearly as much sense when you hear them as when you write them; also, your listener will frequently be helpful in bringing to your attention sections that are unclear. Reading the report backwards, last sentence first, will also help you to identify poorly constructed or unclear sentences. Preparing a research report is greatly facilitated by computer word processing, which commonly provides features such as automatic page numbering and heading centering; the ability to rearrange words, sentences, and paragraphs; and spelling checkers.

FORMAT AND STYLE

Format refers to the general pattern of organization and arrangement of the report. The number and types of headings and subheadings to be included in the report are determined by the format used. *Style* refers to the rules of grammar, spelling, capitalization, punctuation, and word processing followed in preparing the report. Formats may vary in terms of specific headings included, and research reports generally follow a format that parallels the steps involved in conducting a study. For example, while one format may call for a discussion section and another format may require a summary or conclusions and a recommendations section (or both), all formats require a section in which the results of the study are discussed and interpreted. All research reports also include a condensed description of the study, whether it be a summary of a dissertation or an abstract of a journal article.

Most colleges, universities, and professional journals either have developed their own, required style manual or have selected one that must be followed. Check with your advisor about the style used in your institution. Do this before beginning writing, since rearranging a format after the fact is tedious and time consuming. One such manual, which is increasingly being required as a guide for theses and dissertations, is the *Publication Manual of the American Psychological Association,* also called the APA manual (currently in its fifth edition). If you are not bound by any particular format and style system, the APA manual is recommended. In addition to acquiring and studying a copy of the selected manual, it is also very helpful to study several reports that have been written following the same manual. For example, look at existing dissertations (especially those directed by your advisor) to get an idea of format and what is expected. To the degree possible (e.g., with respect to tables, figures, references, and student examples of tasks) this text you are reading reflects APA guidelines, as does the following discussion. Figure 17.1 illustrates some of the basic APA guidelines using a page from the Task 10 example that appears at the end of this chapter.

SECTIONS OF THESES AND DISSERTATIONS

While specifics will vary considerably, most research reports prepared for a degree requirement follow the same general format. Figure 17.2 presents an outline of the typical contents of such a report. As the figure indicates, theses and dissertations include a set of fairly standard preliminary pages, components that directly parallel the research process, and supplementary information, which is included in appendices. The contents of a qualitative study would be similar to a quantitative one except that in the Method section the qualitative report would emphasize the description and selection of the research site, the sampling approach, and the process of data collection.

PRELIMINARY PAGES

The preliminary pages set the stage for the report to follow and indicate where in the report each component, table, and figure can be found. The title page should indicate the major focus of the study. Recall when you reviewed the literature and made initial decisions about the relevance of a source based on its title. A good title should communicate what the study is about. When a title is well constructed it is fairly easy to determine the nature of the topic; when it is vaguely worded it was often difficult to determine the topic without going into the body of the report. After you write your title apply the communication test: Would you know

FIGURE 17.1   Some APA guidelines for preparing your paper.

5

Results

Prior to the beginning of the study, after the 60 students were randomly selected and assigned to experimental and control groups, final science grades from the previous school year were obtained from school records in order to check initial group equivalence. Examination of the means and a *t* test for independent samples ($\alpha = .05$) indicated essentially no difference between the groups (see Table 1). A *t* test for independent samples was used because the groups were randomly formed and the data were interval.

Table 1

Means, Standard Deviation and t Tests for the Experimental and Control Groups

Score	Group		
	IMM instruction[a]	Traditional instruction[a]	*t*
Prior Grades			
M	87.47	87.63	–0.08*
SD	8.19	8.05	
Posttest NPSS:B			
M	32.27	26.70	4.22**
SD	4.45	5.69	

Note. Maximum score for prior grades = 100. Maximum score for posttest = 40.

[a] n = 30.

*$p > .05$. ** $p < .05$.

At the completion of the eight-month study, during the first week in May, scores on the NPSS:B were compared, also using a *t* test for independent samples. As Table 1 indicates, scores of the experimental and control groups were significantly different. In fact, the experimental group scored approximately one standard deviation higher than the control group (ES = .98). Therefore, the original hypothesis that "10th-grade biology students whose teachers use IMM as part of their instructional technique will exhibit significantly higher achievement than 10th-grade biology students whose teachers do not use IMM" was supported.

1. Page numbers go in the top right-hand corner, flush with the right margin and between the top of the page and the first line.

2. First level headings are centered, written in upper- and lowercase, and NOT underlined.

3. All text should be double spaced.

4. All statistical values should be italicized (e.g., *p* < .05).

5. Margins should always be uniform all around (1 inch is the minimum).

Source: Publication Manual of the American Psychological Association, 5/e, pp. 283–320. Copyright by the American Psychological Association. Reprinted with permission.

what the study was about if you read the title in an index? Ask friends or colleagues to describe what they understand from your title.

Most theses and dissertations include an acknowledgments page. This page permits the writer to express appreciation to persons who have contributed significantly to the completion of the report. Notice the word *significant*. You cannot (and should not!) mention everyone who had anything to do with the study or the report. It is acceptable to thank your major professor for her or his guidance and assistance; it is not acceptable to thank your third-grade teacher for giving you confidence in your ability. (Remember the Academy Awards!)

The table of contents is basically an outline of your report that indicates on which page each major section (or chapter) and subsection begins. The list of tables and figures, which

---

PRELIMINARY PAGES

Title page   List of Tables and Figures
Acknowledgments page   Abstract
Table of Contents

MAIN BODY OF THE REPORT

Introduction   Instruments
Statement of the Problem   Design
Review of Related Literature   Procedure
Statement of the Hypothesis   Results
Significance of the Study   Discussion (Conclusions and Recommendations)
Method   References (Bibliography)
Participants

APPENDIXES

FIGURE 17.2
Common components of a research report submitted for a degree requirement.

is presented on a separate page, gives the number and title of each table and figure and the page on which it can be found. Many colleges and universities require an abstract, while others require a summary, but the current trend is in favor of abstracts. The content of abstracts and summaries is identical, only the positioning differs: an abstract precedes the main body of the report and a summary follows the Discussion section. Abstracts are often required to be no more than a given number of words, usually between 100 and 500. Many institutions require abstracts to be no more than 350 words, which is the maximum allowed by Dissertation Abstracts International, a repository of dissertation abstracts. Most APA journals require abstracts that are between 100 and 150 words. Because the abstract of a report is often the only part read, it should briefly describe the most important aspects of the study, including the topic investigated, the type of participants and instruments involved, the data collection procedures, and the major results and conclusions. For example, a 100-word abstract for a study investigating the effect of a writing-oriented curriculum on the reading comprehension of fourth-grade students might read as follows:

> The purpose of this study was to determine the effectiveness of a curriculum that emphasized writing with respect to the reading comprehension of fourth-grade students reading at least one level below grade level. Using a posttest-only control group design and the t test for independent samples, it was found that after 8 months the students ($n = 20$) who participated in a curriculum that emphasized writing achieved significantly higher scores on the reading comprehension subtest of the Stanford Achievement Test, Primary Level 3 (grades 3.5–4.9) than the students ($n = 20$) who did not [t (38) $= 4.83, p < .05$]. It was concluded that the curriculum emphasizing writing was more effective in promoting reading comprehension.

THE MAIN BODY

The body of the report contains information about the topic studied, literature reviewed, hypotheses (if any) posited, participants, instruments, procedures, results, and discussion. The introduction section includes a description of the research problem or topic, a review of related literature, a statement of hypotheses or issues, and a definition of uncommon or important terms. A well-written statement of a problem or topic generally indicates the variables examined in the study. The statement of the problem or topic should be accompanied by a presentation of its background, including a justification for the study in terms of its significance; that is, why should anyone care about this study?

The review of related literature indicates what is known about your problem or topic. Its function is to educate the reader about the area being studied. The review of related literature is not a series of abstracts or annotations but rather an analysis and an integration of the relationships and differences among relevant studies and reports. The review should flow in such a way that the least related references are discussed first and the most related references are discussed last, just prior to the statement of the hypothesis. The review should conclude with a brief summary of the literature and its implications.

A good hypothesis clearly states the expected relationship (or difference) between two variables and defines those variables in operational, measurable terms. The hypothesis (or hypotheses) logically follows the review of related literature and is based on the implications of previous research. A well-developed hypothesis is testable, that is, can be confirmed or disconfirmed. The qualitative researcher is unlikely to state hypotheses as focused as those of a quantitative researcher, but may have and express some hunches about what the study may show. The introduction section also includes operational definition of terms used in the study that do not have a commonly agreed meaning.

METHOD

The method section includes a description of participants, instruments, design, procedure, assumptions, and limitations. A qualitative study may also include a detailed description of the site studied and the nature and length of interactions with the participants. The description of participants includes information about how they were selected and, mainly for quantitative researchers, the population they represent. A description of the sample should indicate its size and major characteristics such as age, grade level, ability level, and socioeconomic status. A good description of the sample enables readers of the report to determine how similar study participants are to participants they are concerned with.

Data collection procedures should be described fully, be they tests, questionnaires, interviews, or observations. The description should indicate the purpose of the procedure, its application, and its validity and reliability. If a procedure has been developed by the researcher, the description needs to be more detailed and should also state the manner in which it was developed, its pretesting, revisions, steps involved in scoring, and guidelines for interpretation. A copy of the instrument, accompanying scoring keys, and other pertinent data related to a newly developed test are generally placed as appendices to the thesis or dissertation proper.

The description of the design is especially important in an experimental study. In other types of research the description of the design may be combined with procedure. In an experimental study, the description of the basic design (or variation of a basic design) applied in the study should include a rationale for selection and a discussion of sources of invalidity associated with the design, and why they may have been minimized in the study being reported.

The procedure section should describe the steps followed in conducting the study, in chronological order, in sufficient detail to permit the study to be replicated by another researcher. It should be clear exactly how participants were assigned to groups, treatments, or the conditions under which qualitative participants were observed or interviewed. In essence, a step-by-step description of what went on during the study should be provided. In many cases, qualitative researchers will have more complex and detailed procedural descriptions than quantitative researchers.

The results section describes the statistical techniques or the inferential interpretations that were applied to the data and the results of these analyses. For each hypothesis, the statistical test of significance selected and applied to the data is described, followed by a statement indicating whether the hypothesis was supported or not supported. Tables present numerical data in rows and columns and usually include descriptive statistics, such as means and standard deviations, and the results of tests of significance, such as t and F ratios. Good tables and figures are uncluttered and self-explanatory; it is better to use two tables (or figures) than one that is crowded. They should stand alone, that is, be interpretable without the aid of related textual material. Tables and figures follow their related textual discussion and are referred to by number, not name or location. In other words, the text should say "see Table 1," not "see the table with the means" or "see the table on the next page." Examine the variety of tables and figures throughout this text to get a perspective on how data can be presented.

Qualitative research reporting tends to be based mainly on descriptions and quotations that support or illustrate the study results. Charts and diagrams showing the relationships among identified topics, categories, and patterns are also useful in presenting the results of a study. The logic and description of the interpretations linked to qualitative charts and diagrams are important aspects of qualitative research reporting.

All research reports have a section that discusses and interprets the results, draws conclusions and implications, and makes recommendations. Interpretation of results may be presented in a separate section titled "Discussion" or it may be included in the same section as the other analysis of results items. What this section (or sections) is called is unimportant; what is important is how well it is constructed. Each result should be discussed in terms of its relation to the topic studied and in terms of its agreement or disagreement with previous results obtained by other researchers. Two common errors are to confuse results and conclusions and to overgeneralize results. A *result* is the outcome of a test of significance or a qualitative analysis. The corresponding *conclusion* is that the original hypothesis or topic was or was not supported by the data. In qualitative reports, the conclusion may simply be a summarizing description of what was observed. *Overgeneralization* refers to stating conclusions that are not warranted by the results. For example, if a group of first graders receiving personalized instruction were found to achieve significantly higher on a test of reading comprehension than a group receiving traditional instruction, it would be an overgeneralization to conclude that personalized instruction is a superior method of instruction for elementary students. Similarly, if a qualitative study about teacher burnout consisted of four interviewees, it would be an overgeneralization to infer that all teachers felt the same about burnout.

The report should also discuss the theoretical and practical implications of the findings and make recommendations for future research or future action. In this portion of the report the researcher is permitted more freedom in expressing opinions that are not necessarily direct outcomes of data analysis. The researcher is free to discuss any possible revisions or additions to existing theory and to encourage studies designed to test hypotheses suggested by the results. The researcher may also discuss implications of the findings for educational practice and suggest studies designed to replicate the study in other settings, with other participants, and in other curricular areas, in order to increase the generalizability of the findings. The researcher may also suggest next-step studies designed to investigate another dimension of the problem investigated. For example, a study finding type of feedback to be a factor in retention might suggest that amount of feedback may also be a factor and recommend further research in that area.

The references, or bibliography, section of the report lists all the sources, alphabetically by authors' last names, that were directly used in writing the report. Every source cited in the paper must be included in the references, and every entry listed in the references must appear in the paper; in other words, the sources in the paper and the sources in the references must correspond exactly. If APA style is being used, secondary sources are not in-

Now go to the Companion Website accompanying this text at www.prenhall.com/gay to check your understanding of chapter concepts in the following modules: Objectives, Practice Quiz, and Applying What You Know. Expand your research skills with Evaluating Articles, Analyzing Qualitative Data, Analyzing Quantitative Data, and Research Tools and Tips. Visit Web Links to broaden your knowledge about research.

cluded in the references. Citations for secondary sources should indicate the primary source from which they were taken; the primary source should be included in the references. For example, you might say: "Nerdfais (cited in Snurd, 1995) found that yellow chalk . . ." The Snurd source would be listed in the references. Note that no year would be given for the Nerdfais study. For thesis and dissertation studies, if sources were consulted that were not directly cited in the main body of the report, these may be included in an appendix. The style manual being followed will determine the form each reference must take. If the style manual to be used is known while the review of related literature is being conducted, the researcher can save time by writing each reference in the proper form initially. Table 17.1 shows APA formats for common references in theses or dissertations.

Appendixes are usually necessary in thesis and dissertation reports to provide information and data pertinent to the study that either are not important enough to be included in the main body of the report or are too lengthy. Appendixes contain such entries as materials especially developed for the study (for example, tests, questionnaires, and cover letters), raw data, and data analysis sheets.

TABLE 17.1   APA Reference Formats

TYPE OF REFERENCE	REFERENCE FORMAT
	The following are examples of many of the types of references you may need to include in your research paper. These examples follow the APA style guidelines set forth in the fifth edition of the *Publication Manual of the American Psychological Association.*
Book	Bandura, A. J. (1977). *Social learning theory.* Englewood Cliffs, NJ: Prentice Hall.
Book, Edited	Gibbs, J. T., & Huang, L. N. (Eds.). (1991). *Children of color: Psychological interventions with minority youth.* San Francisco: Jossey-Bass.
Book, Chapter	O'Neil, J. M., & Egan, J. (1992). Men's and women's gender role journeys: Metaphor for healing, transition, and transformation. In B. R. Wainrib (Ed.), *Gender issues across the life cycle* (pp. 107–123). New York: Springer.
Book Review	Schatz, B. R. (2000). Learning by text or context? [Review of the book *The social life of information.*] *Science, 290,* 1304.
Journal Article	Klimoski, R., & Palmer, S. (1993). The ADA and the hiring process in organizations. *Consulting Psychology Journal: Practice and Research, 45* (2), 10–36.
Electronic Sources, Retrieval Information	Eid, M., & Langeheine, R. (1999). The measurement of consistency and occasion specificity with latent class models: A new model and its application to the measurement of affect. *Psychological Methods, 4,* 100–116. Retrieved November 19, 2000, from the Psyc ARTICLES database.
Abstract	Nakazato, K., Shimonaka, Y., & Homma, A. (1992). Cognitive functions of centenarians: The Tokyo Metropolitan Centenarian Study. *Japanese Journal of Developmental Psychology, 3,* 9–16. (From PsycSCAN: *Neuropsychology,* 1993, 2, Abstract No. 604)
ERIC Reference	Mead, J. V. (1992). *Looking at old photographs: Investigating the teacher tales that novice teachers bring with them* (Report No. NCRTL-RR-92-4). East Lansing, MI: National Center for Research on Teacher Learning. (ERIC Document Reproduction Service No. ED 346 082)
Dissertation (unpublished)	Wilfley, D. E. (1989). *Interpersonal analyses of bulimia: Normal-weight and obese.* Unpublished doctoral dissertation, University of Missouri, Columbia.

Source: All examples from *Publication Manual of the American Psychological Association,* 5th ed., pp. 215–281. Washington, DC: American Psychological Association. Reprinted with permission.

SUMMARY

General Guidelines

1. A major facilitator for writing a research report is making an outline. Developing an outline involves identifying and ordering major topics followed by differentiating each major heading into logical subheadings.
2. A research report is written in the past tense.

General Rules for Writing

3. Probably the foremost rule of research report writing is to relate aspects of the study in a manner that accurately reflects what was done and what was found.
4. Although quantitative and qualitative research approaches differ in many ways, both cover similar topics in their research reports. However, while the general topics are similar, the emphases within them vary depending on which of the two approaches is being reported.
5. The research report should be written in a clear, simple, straightforward style and correct spelling, grammar, and punctuation are expected. Most computers have the capability to check spelling and grammar.
6. Authors of cited references are usually referred to by last name only in the main body of the report.
7. If the first word of a sentence is a number, or if the number is nine or less, numbers are usually expressed as words. Otherwise, numbers are generally expressed as Arabic numerals.
8. Carefully proofread the final report.

Format and Style

9. Most research reports consistently follow a selected system for format and style. *Format* refers to the general pattern of organization and arrangement of the report. *Style* refers to the rules of grammar, spelling, capitalization, punctuation, and word processing followed in preparing the report.
10. Many colleges and universities either have developed their own format or require use of a published style manual. It is also very helpful to study several reports that have been written following the same manual.

Sections of Theses and Dissertations

11. The title page usually includes the title of the report, the author's name, the degree requirement being fulfilled, the name and location of the college or university awarding the degree, the date of submission of the report, and signatures of approving committee members. The title should describe the purpose of the study as clearly as possible.
12. The acknowledgment page allows the writer to express appreciation to persons who have contributed significantly to the completion of the report.
13. The table of contents is basically an outline of the report that indicates on which page each major section (or chapter) and subsection begins. The list of tables and figures, presented on a separate page, gives the number and title of each table and figure and the page on which it can be found.
14. Most colleges and universities require an abstract or summary of the study. The number of pages for each will be specified, and usually range from 100 to 500 words. The abstract should describe the most important aspects of the study, including the problem investigated, the type of participants and instruments, the design, the procedures, and the major results and conclusions.
15. The introduction section is the first section of the main body of the report and includes a well-written description of the problem, a review of related literature, a statement of the hypothesis, and definition of terms.
16. The review of related literature describes and analyzes what has already been done related to your problem.
17. A good hypothesis in a quantitative study states as clearly and concisely as possible the expected relationship (or difference) between two variables, and defines those variables in operational, measurable terms.
18. The introduction also includes operational definitions of terms used in the study that do not have a commonly understood meaning.
19. The method section includes a description of participants, instruments, design, procedure, assumptions, and limitations.
20. The description of participants in a quantitative study includes a definition and description of the population from which the sample was selected and may describe the method used in selecting the participants. The description of participants in a qualitative study will include descriptions of the way participants were selected, why they were selected, and a detailed description of the context in which they function.

21. The description of each instrument should relate the function of the instrument in the study (for example, selection of participants or a measure of the dependent variable), what the instrument is intended to measure, and data related to validity and reliability.

22. The procedure section should describe each step followed in conducting the study, in chronological order, in sufficient detail to permit the study to be replicated by another researcher.

23. The results section describes the statistical techniques or qualitative interpretation that were applied to the data and the results of the analyses. Information about the process applied during data analysis should be provided.

24. Tables and figures are used to present findings in summary or graph form and add clarity to the presentation. Good tables and figures are uncluttered and self-explanatory; it is better to use two tables (or figures) than one that is crowded. Tables and figures follow their related textual discussion and are referred to by number, not name or location.

25. Each research finding or result should be discussed in terms of its agreement or disagreement with previous results obtained by other researchers in other studies or hypotheses stated at the start of the study.

26. *Overgeneralization* refers to stating conclusions that are not warranted by the results, and should be avoided.

27. The researcher should discuss the theoretical and practical implications of the findings and make recommendations for future research or future action.

28. The reference or bibliography section of the report lists all the sources, alphabetically by authors' last names, that were directly used in writing the report. Every source cited in the paper must be included in the references, and every entry listed in the references must appear in the paper.

29. The required style manual will guide the format of various types of references.

30. Appendixes include information and data pertinent to the study that either are not important enough to be included in the main body of the report or are too lengthy—for example, tests, questionnaires, cover letters, raw data, and data analysis sheets.

PERFORMANCE CRITERIA   TASK 10

Your research report should include all the components listed in Figure 17.2, with the possible exceptions of an acknowledgment page and appendixes. Development of Task 10 basically involves combining Tasks 2, 8, and 9, writing a discussion section, and preparing the appropriate preliminary pages (including an abstract) and references. In other words, you have already written most of Task 10.

On the following pages, an example is presented that illustrates the performance called for by Task 10 (see Task 10 example). This example represents the synthesis of the previously presented tasks related to the effects of interactive multimedia on biology achievement. To the degree possible with a student paper, this example follows the guidelines of the *Publication Manual of the American Psychological Association*.

Additional examples for this and other tasks are included in the *Student Guide* that accompanies this text.

Effect of Interactive Multimedia on the Achievement
of 10th-Grade Biology Students
Sara Jane Calderin
Florida International University

Submitted in partial fulfillment of

the requirements for EDF 5481

April, 1994

Table of Contents

List of Tables and Figures

Abstract

The purpose of this study was to investigate the effect of interactive multimedia on the achievement of 10th-grade biology students. Using a posttest-only control group design and a *t* test for independent samples, it was found that after approximately 8 months the students ($n = 30$) who were instructed using interactive multimedia achieved significantly higher scores on the biology test of the National Proficiency Survey Series than did the students ($n = 30$) whose instruction did not include interactive multimedia, $t (58) = 4.22, p < .05$. It was concluded that the interactive multimedia instruction was effective in raising the achievement level of the participating students.

Introduction

One of the major concerns of educators and parents alike is the decline in student achievement. An area of particular concern is science education, where the higher-level thinking skills and problem solving techniques so necessary for success in our technological society need to be developed (Smith & Westhoff, 1992).

Research is constantly providing new proven methods for educators to use, and technology has developed many kinds of tools ideally suited to the classroom. One such tool is interactive multimedia (IMM). IMM provides teachers with an extensive amount of data in a number of different formats including text, sound, and video. This makes it possible to appeal to all the different learning styles of the students and to offer a variety of material for students to analyze (Howson & Davis, 1992).

When teachers use IMM, students become highly motivated, which results in improved class attendance and more completed assignments (O'Connor, 1993). In addition, students also become actively involved in their own learning, encouraging comprehension rather than mere memorization of facts (Kneedler, 1993; Reeves, 1992).

Statement of the Problem

The purpose of this study was to investigate the effect of IMM on the achievement of 10th-grade biology students. IMM was defined as "a computerized database that allows users to access information in multiple forms, including text, graphics, video and audio" (Reeves, 1992, p. 47).

Review of Related Literature

Due to modern technology, such as videotapes and videodiscs, students receive more information from visual sources than they do from the written word (Helms & Helms, 1992), and yet in school the majority of information is still transmitted through textbooks. While textbooks cover a wide range of topics superficially, IMM can provide in-depth information on essential topics in a format that students find interesting (Kneedler, 1993). Smith and Westhoff (1992) note that when student interest is sparked, curiosity levels are increased and students are motivated to ask questions. The interactive nature of multimedia allows students to seek out their own answers, and by so doing they become owners of the concept involved. Ownership translates into comprehension (Howson & Davis, 1992).

Many science concepts are learned through observation of experiments. By using IMM, students can participate in a variety of experiments which are either too expensive, too lengthy, or too dangerous to carry out in the school laboratory (Howson & Davis, 1992; Leonard, 1989; Louie, Sweat, Gresham & Smith, 1991). While observing experiments students can discuss what is happening and ask questions. At the touch of a button teachers are able to replay any part of the proceedings, and they also have random access to related information which can be used to illustrate completely the answer to the question (Howson & Davis, 1992). By answering students' questions in this detailed way, the content becomes more relevant to the needs of the students (Smith & Westhoff, 1992). When knowledge is relevant students are able to use it to solve problems and in so doing develop higher-level thinking skills (Helms & Helms, 1992; Sherwood, Kinzer, Bransford, & Franks, 1987).

A major challenge of science education is to provide students with large amounts of information that will encourage them to be analytical (Howson & Davis, 1992; Sherwood et al., 1987). IMM offers electronic access to extensive information allowing students to organize, evaluate, and use it in the solution of problems (Smith & Wilson, 1993). When information is introduced as an aid to problem solving it becomes a tool with which to solve other problems, rather than a series of solitary, disconnected facts (Sherwood et al., 1987).

Although critics complain that IMM is entertainment and students do not learn from it (Corcoran, 1989), research has shown that student learning does improve when IMM is used in the classroom (Sherwood et al., 1987; Sherwood & Others, 1990). A 1987 study by Sherwood et al., for example, showed that seventh- and eighth-grade science students receiving instruction enhanced with IMM had better retention of that information, and O'Connor (1993) found that the use of IMM in high school mathematics and science increased the focus on students' problem solving and critical thinking skills.

Statement of the Hypothesis

The quality and quantity of software available for science classes has dramatically improved during the past decade. Although some research has been carried out on the effects of IMM on student achievement in science, due to promising updates in the technology involved, further study is warranted. Therefore, it was hypothesized that 10th-grade biology students whose teachers use IMM as part of their instructional technique will exhibit significantly higher achievement than 10th-grade biology students whose teachers do not use IMM.

Method

Participants

The sample for this study was selected from the total population of 213 10th-grade students at an upper middle class all-girls Catholic high school in Miami, Florida. The population was 90% Hispanic, mainly of Cuban-American descent. Sixty students were randomly selected (using a table of random numbers) and randomly assigned to two groups of 30 each.

Instrument

The biology test of the National Proficiency Survey Series (NPSS) was used as the measuring instrument. The test was designed to measure individual student performance in biology at the high school level but the publishers also recommended it as an evaluation of instructional programs. Content validity is good; items were selected from a large item bank provided by classroom teachers and curriculum experts. High school instructional materials and a national curriculum survey were extensively reviewed before objectives were written. The test objectives and those of the biology classes in the study were highly correlated. Although the standard error of measurement is not given for the biology test, the range of KR-20s for the entire battery is from .82 to .91 with a median of .86. This is satisfactory since the purpose of the test was to evaluate instructional programs, not to make decisions concerning individuals. Catholic school students were included in the battery norming procedures, which were carried out in April and May of 1988 using 22,616 students in grades 9–12 from 45 high schools in 20 states.

Experimental Design

The design used in this study was the posttest-only control group design (see Figure 1). This design was selected because it provides control for most sources of invalidity and random assignment to groups was possible. A pretest was not necessary since the final science grades from June 1993 were available to check initial group equivalence and to help control mortality, a potential threat to internal validity with this design. Mortality, however, was not a problem as no students dropped from either group.

Figure 1. Experimental design.

Group	Assignment	*n*	Treatment	Posttest
1	Random	30	IMM instruction	NPSS:B[a]
2	Random	30	Traditional instruction	NPSS:B

[a]National Proficiency Survey Series: Biology

Procedure

Prior to the beginning of the 1993–1994 school year, before classes were scheduled, 60 of the 213 10th-grade students were randomly selected and randomly assigned to two groups of 30 each, the average biology class size; each group became a biology class. One of the classes was randomly chosen to receive IMM instruction. The same teacher taught both classes.

The study was designed to last eight months beginning on the first day of class. The control group was taught using traditional methods of lecturing and open class discussions. The students worked in pairs for laboratory investigations, which included the use of microscopes. The teacher's role was one of information disseminator.

The experimental classroom had 15 workstations for student use, each one consisting of a laserdisc player, a video recorder, a 27-inch monitor, and a Macintosh computer with a 40 MB hard drive, 128 MB RAM, and a CD-ROM drive. The teacher's workstation incorporated a Macintosh computer with CD-ROM drive, a videodisc player, and a 27-inch monitor. The workstations were networked to the school library so students had access to online services such as Prodigy and Infotrac as well as to the card catalogue. Two laser printers were available through the network for the students' use.

In the experimental class the teacher used a videodisc correlated to the textbook. When barcodes provided in the text were scanned, a section of the videodisc was activated and appeared on the monitor. The section might be a motion picture demonstrating a process or a still picture offering more detail than the text. The role of the teacher in the experimental group was that of facilitator and guide. After the teacher had introduced a new topic, the students worked in pairs at the workstations investigating topics connected to the main idea presented in the lesson. Videodiscs, CD-ROMs, and online services were all available as sources of information. The students used HyperStudio to prepare multimedia reports, which they presented to the class.

Throughout the study the same subject matter was covered and the two classes used the same text. Although the students of the experimental group paired up at the workstations, the other group worked in pairs during lab time, thus equalizing any effect from cooperative learning. The classes could not meet at the same time as they were taught by the same teacher, so they met during second and third periods. First period was not chosen as the school sometimes has a special schedule which interferes with first period. Both classes had the same homework reading assignments, which were reviewed in class the following school day. Academic objectives were the same for each class and all tests measuring achievement were identical.

During the first week of May, the biology test of the NPSS was administered to both classes to compare their achievement in biology.

Results

Prior to the beginning of the study, after the 60 students were randomly selected and assigned to experimental and control groups, final science grades from the previous school year were obtained from school records in order to check initial group equivalence. Examination of the means and a *t* test for independent samples ($\alpha = .05$) indicated essentially no difference between the groups (see Table 1). A *t* test for independent samples was used because the groups were randomly formed and the data were interval.

Table 1

Means, Standard Deviation, and *t* Tests for the Experimental and Control Groups

Score	Group		*t*
	IMM instruction[a]	Traditional instruction[a]	
Prior Grades			
M	87.47	87.63	-0.08^{*}
SD	8.19	8.05	
Posttest NPSS:B			
M	32.27	26.70	4.22^{**}
SD	4.45	5.69	

Note. Maximum score for prior grades = 100. Maximum score for posttest = 40.
[a]$n = 30$.
$^{*}p > .05.$ $^{**}p < .05.$

At the completion of the eight-month study, during the first week in May, scores on the NPSS:B were compared, also using a *t* test for independent samples. As Table 1 indicates, scores of the experimental and control groups were significantly different. In fact, the experimental group scored approximately one standard deviation higher than the control group (ES = .98). Therefore, the original hypothesis that "10th-grade biology students whose teachers use IMM as part of their instructional technique will exhibit significantly higher achievement than 10th-grade biology students whose teachers do not use IMM" was supported.

Discussion

The results of this study support the original hypothesis. 10th-grade biology students whose teachers used IMM as part of their instructional technique did exhibit significantly higher achievement than 10th-grade biology students whose teachers did not use IMM. The IMM students' scores were 5.57 points (13.93%) higher than those of the other group. Also, it was informally observed that the IMM instructed students were eager to discover information on their own and to carry on the learning process outside scheduled class hours.

Results cannot be generalized to all classrooms because the study took place in an all-girls Catholic high school with the majority of the students having an Hispanic background. However, the results were consistent with research on IMM in general, and in particular with the findings of Sherwood et al. (1987) and O'Connor (1993) concerning the improvement of student achievement.

IMM appears to be a viable educational tool with applications in a variety of subject areas and with both cognitive and psychological benefits for students. While further research is needed, especially using other software and in other subject areas, the suggested benefits to students' learning offered by IMM warrant that teachers should be cognizant of this instructional method. In this technological age it is important that education take advantage of available tools which increase student motivation and improve academic achievement.

References

Corcoran, E. (1989, July). Show and tell: Hypermedia turns information into a multisensory event. *Scientific American, 261,* 72, 74.

Helms, C. W., & Helms, D. R. (1992, June). *Multimedia in education* (Report No. IR-016-090). Proceedings of the 25th Summer Conference of the Association of Small Computer Users in Education. North Myrtle Beach, SC. (ERIC Document Reproduction Service No. ED 357 732)

Howson, B. A., & Davis, H. (1992). Enhancing comprehension with videodiscs. *Media and Methods, 28*(3), 12–14.

Kneedler, P. E. (1993). California adopts multimedia science program. *Technological Horizons in Education Journal, 20*(7), 73–76.

Lehmann, I. J. (1990). Review of National Proficiency Survey Series. In J. J. Kramer & J. C. Conoley (Eds.), *The eleventh mental measurements yearbook* (pp. 595–599). Lincoln: University of Nebraska, Buros Institute of Mental Measurement.

Leonard, W. H. (1989). A comparison of student reaction to biology instruction by interactive videodisc or conventional laboratory. *Journal of Research in Science Teaching, 26,* 95–104.

Louie, R., Sweat, S., Gresham, R., & Smith, L. (1991). Interactive video: Disseminating vital science and math information. *Media and Methods, 27*(5), 22–23.

O'Connor, J. E. (1993, April). *Evaluating the effects of collaborative efforts to improve mathematics and science curricula* (Report No. TM-019-862). Paper presented at the Annual Meeting of the American Educational Research Association, Atlanta, GA. (ERIC Document Reproduction Service No. ED 357 083)

Reeves, T. C. (1992). Evaluating interactive multimedia. *Educational Technology, 32*(5), 47–52.

Sherwood, R. D., Kinzer, C. K., Bransford, J. D., & Franks, J. J. (1987). Some benefits of creating macro-contexts for science instruction: Initial findings. *Journal of Research in Science Teaching,* 24, 417–435.

Sherwood, R. D., & Others. (1990, April). *An evaluative study of level one videodisc based chemistry program* (Report No. SE-051-513). Paper presented at a Poster Session at the 63rd Annual Meeting of the National Association for Research in Science Teaching, Atlanta, GA. (ERIC Document Reproduction Service No. ED 320 772)

Smith, E. E., & Westhoff, G. M. (1992). The Taliesin project: Multidisciplinary education and multimedia. *Educational Technology, 32,* 15–23.

Smith, M. K., & Wilson, C. (1993, March). *Integration of student learning strategies via technology* (Report No. IR-016-035). Proceedings of the Fourth Annual Conference of Technology and Teacher Education. San Diego, CA. (ERIC Document Reproduction Service No. ED 355 937)

"Were efforts made to overcome observer bias and observer effect?" (p. 535)

EVALUATING A RESEARCH REPORT

OBJECTIVES

After reading Chapter 18, you should be able to do the following:

1. For each of the major sections and subsections of a research report, list at least three questions that should be asked in determining its adequacy.
2. For each of the following types of research, list at least three questions that should be asked in determining the adequacy of a study representing that type:

   Ethnographic research

   Grounded theory research

   Historical research

   Action research

   Survey research

   Correlational research

   Causal–comparative research

   Experimental research

The goal of Chapter 18 is for you to be able to analyze and evaluate research reports. After you have read Chapter 18, you should be able to perform the following task.

TASK 11

Given a reprint of a research report and an evaluation form, evaluate the components of the report. (See Performance Criteria, p. 540.)

GENERAL EVALUATION CRITERIA

As mentioned in the introduction to Part Four, many research studies have flaws of various kinds. Just because a study is published does not necessarily mean that it is a good study or that it is reported adequately. The most common flaw is lack of validity and reliability information about data-gathering procedures such as tests, observations, questionnaires, and interviews. Other common flaws include weaknesses in the research design, inappropriate or biased selection of participants, failure to state limitations in the research, and a general lack of description about the study. These common problems in studies reinforce the importance of being a competent consumer of research reports; they also highlight common pitfalls to avoid in your own research.

At your current level of expertise you may not be able to evaluate every component of every study. For example, you would not be able to determine whether the appropriate degrees of freedom were used in the calculation of an analysis of covariance. There are, however, a number of basic errors or weaknesses you should be able to detect in research studies. You should, for example, be able to identify the sources of invalidity associated with a study based on a one-group pretest-posttest design. You should also be able to detect obvious indications of experimenter bias that may have affected qualitative or quantitative research results. For example, a statement in a research report that "the purpose of this study was to prove . . ." should alert you to a probable bias effect.

As you read a research report, either as a consumer of research keeping up with the latest findings in your professional area or as a producer of research reviewing literature related to a defined problem, there are a number of questions you should ask yourself about the adequacy of a study and its components. The answers to some of these questions are more critical than the answers to others. An inadequate title is not a critical flaw; an inadequate research plan is. Some questions are difficult to answer if the study is not directly in your area of expertise. If your area of specialization is reading, for example, you are probably not in a position to judge the adequacy of a review of literature related to anxiety effects on learning. And, admittedly, the answers to some questions are more subjective than objective. Whether a good design was used is pretty clear and objective; most quantitative researchers would agree that the randomized posttest-only control group design is a good design. Whether the most appropriate design was used, given the problem under study, often involves a degree of subjective judgment. For example, the need for inclusion of a pretest might be a debatable point depending on the study and its design. However, despite the lack of complete agreement in some areas, evaluation of a research report is a worthwhile and important activity. Major problems and shortcomings are usually readily identifiable, and by considering a number of questions you can formulate an overall impression of the quality of the study. In succeeding sections, we list for your consideration evaluative questions about a number of research strategies and areas. This list is by no means exhaustive and, as you read it, you may very well think of additional questions to ask. You will also note that not every criterion below equally applies to both quantitative and qualitative research studies.

INTRODUCTION

Problem

- Is there a statement of the problem or a qualitative topic of study? Does the problem or topic indicate a particular focus of study?
- Is the problem "researchable"; that is, can it be investigated through collecting and analyzing data?
- Is background information on the problem presented?
- Is the educational significance of the problem discussed?
- Does the quantitative problem statement indicate the variables of interest and the specific relationship between those variables that were investigated?
- Does the qualitative problem statement provide a general indication of the research topic or issue?
- When necessary, are variables directly or operationally defined?
- Does the researcher have the knowledge and skill to carry out the proposed research?

Review of Related Literature

- Is the review comprehensive?
- Are all references cited relevant to the problem under investigation?
- Are most of the sources primary (i.e., are there only a few or no secondary sources)?
- Have the references been analyzed and critiqued, and the results of various studies compared and contrasted? That is, is the review more than a series of abstracts or annotations?
- Is the relevancy of each reference explained?
- Is the review well organized? Does it logically flow in such a way that the references least related to the problem are discussed first and the most related references are discussed last? Does it educate the reader about the problem or topic?
- Does the review conclude with a summary and interpretation of the literature and its implications for the problem investigated?

- Do the implications discussed form an empirical or theoretical rationale for the hypotheses that follow?
- Are references cited completely and accurately?

Hypotheses

- Are specific questions to be answered listed or specific hypotheses to be tested stated?
- Does each hypothesis state an expected relationship or difference?
- If necessary, are variables directly or operationally defined?
- Is each hypothesis testable?

METHOD

Participants

- Are the size and major characteristics of the population studied described?
- Are the accessible and target populations described?
- If a sample was selected, is the method of selecting the sample clearly described?
- Does the method of sample selection suggest any limitations or biases in the sample? For example, is stratified sampling used to obtain sample subgroups?
- Are the size and major characteristics of the sample described?
- If the study is quantitative, does the sample size meet the suggested guideline for minimum appropriate sample size?

Instruments

- Do instruments and their administration meet guidelines for protecting human subjects? Have needed permissions been obtained?
- Is the rationale given for the selection of the instruments (or measurements) used?
- Is each instrument described in terms of purpose, content, validity, and reliability?
- Are the instruments appropriate for measuring the intended variables?
- Does the researcher have the needed skills or experience to construct or administer an instrument?
- Is evidence presented to indicate that the instruments are appropriate for the intended sample? For example, is the reading level of an instrument suitable for sample participants?
- If appropriate, are subtest reliabilities given?
- If an instrument was developed specifically for the study, are the procedures involved in its development and validation described?
- If an instrument was developed specifically for the study, are administration, scoring or tabulating, and interpretation procedures fully described?
- Is the correct type of instrument used for data collection (e.g., using a norm-referenced instrument when a criterion-referenced one is more suitable)?

Design and Procedure

- Are the design and procedures appropriate for examining the research question or testing the hypotheses of the study?
- Are the procedures described in sufficient detail to permit them to be replicated by another researcher?
- Do procedures logically relate to each other?
- Are instruments and procedures applied correctly?
- If a pilot study was conducted, are its execution and results described as well as its impact on the subsequent study?

- Are control procedures described?
- Did the researcher discuss or account for any potentially confounding variables that he or she was unable to control?
- Is the application of the qualitative method chosen described in detail?
- Is the context of the qualitative study described in detail?

RESULTS

- Are appropriate descriptive statistics presented?
- Was the probability level at which the results of the tests of significance were evaluated specified in advance of the data analyses? Was every hypothesis tested?
- If parametric tests were used, is there evidence that the researcher avoided violating the required assumptions for parametric tests?
- Are the tests of significance described appropriate, given the hypotheses and design of the study?
- Was the inductive logic used to produce results in a qualitative study made explicit?
- Are the tests of significance interpreted using the appropriate degrees of freedom?
- Are the results clearly described?
- Are the tables and figures (if any) well organized and easy to understand?
- Are the data in each table and figure described in the text?

DISCUSSION (CONCLUSIONS AND RECOMMENDATIONS)

- Is each result discussed in terms of the original hypothesis or topic to which it relates?
- Is each result discussed in terms of its agreement or disagreement with previous results obtained by other researchers in other studies?
- Are generalizations consistent with the results?
- Are the possible effects of uncontrolled variables on the results discussed?
- Are theoretical and practical implications of the findings discussed?
- Are recommendations for future action made?
- Are the suggestions for future action based on practical significance or on statistical significance only (i.e., has the author avoided confusing practical and statistical significance)?

ABSTRACT OR SUMMARY

- Is the problem restated?
- Are the number and type of subjects and instruments described?
- Is the design used identified?
- Are procedures described?
- Are the major results and conclusions restated?

TYPE-SPECIFIC EVALUATION CRITERIA

In addition to general criteria that can be applied to almost any study, there are additional questions you should ask depending on the type of research represented by the study. In other words, there are concerns that are specific to historical studies, and likewise to other qualitative, survey, correlational, causal–comparative, and experimental studies.

QUALITATIVE RESEARCH (IN GENERAL)

- Does the topic to be studied describe a general sense of the study focus?
- Is the purposive sampling procedure described and related to the study focus?
- Is each data collection strategy described?
- Is the role the researcher assumed stated (e.g., observer, participant observer, interviewer, etc.)?
- Is the research site and the researcher's entry into it described?
- Were the data collection strategies used appropriately, given the purpose of the study?
- Were strategies used to strengthen the validity and reliability of the data (e.g., triangulation)?
- Is there a description of how any unexpected ethical issues were handled?
- Were strategies used to minimize observer bias and observer effect described?
- Are the researcher's reactions and notes differentiated from descriptive fieldnotes?
- Are data coding strategies described and examples of coded data given?
- Is the inductive logic applied to the data to produce results stated in detail?
- Are conclusions supported by data (e.g., are direct quotes used to illustrate points made)?

Observation Studies

- Are observational variables defined?
- How were observers trained? Is this training described fully?
- Did different observers work and score independently?
- Were observers required to observe only one behavior at a time?
- Was a coded recording instrument used?
- Are the qualifications and special training of the observers described?
- Was the level of interobserver reliability obtained from at least two independent raters and is the result reported?
- Is the level of interobserver reliability sufficiently high?
- Were efforts made to overcome observer bias and observer effect?
- Was observation of subjects the most appropriate approach for data collection (as opposed to use of some unobtrusive measure)?
- Was a description of how the observational data were analyzed provided?

Interview Studies

- Were the interview procedures pretested?
- Are pilot study procedures and results described?
- Does each item in the interview guide relate to a specific objective of the study?
- When necessary, is a point of reference given in the guide for interview items?
- Are leading questions avoided in the interview guide?
- Is the language and complexity of the questions appropriate for the participants?
- Does the interview guide indicate the type and amount of prompting and probing that was permitted?
- Are the qualifications and special training of the interviewers described?
- Is the method used to record responses described?
- Did the researcher use the most reliable, unbiased method of recording responses that could have been used?
- Did the researcher specify how the responses to semistructured and unstructured items were quantified and analyzed?

EVALUATING VALIDITY AND RELIABILITY IN QUALITATIVE STUDIES[1]

Threats to Internal Validity

- Did the researcher effectively deal with problems of history and maturation by documenting historical changes over time?
- Did the researcher effectively deal with problems of mortality by using a sample large enough to minimize the effects of attrition?
- Was the researcher in the field long enough to effectively minimize observer effects?
- Did the researcher take the time to become familiar and comfortable with participants?
- Were interview questions pretested?
- Were efforts made to ensure intraobserver agreement by training interview teams in coding procedures?
- Were efforts made to cross-check results by conducting interviews with multiple groups?
- Did the researcher interview key informants to verify field observations?
- Were participants demographically screened to ensure that they were representative of the larger population?
- Was data collected using different media (audio- and videotape, etc.) to facilitate cross-validation?
- Were participants allowed to evaluate research results before publication?
- Is sufficient data presented to support findings and conclusions?
- Were dependent and independent variables repeatedly tested to validate results?

Threats to External Validity

- Were construct effects addressed adequately?
- Were both new and adapted instruments pretested to ensure that they were appropriate for the study?
- Did the researcher fully describe participants' relevant characteristics, such as socioeconomic structure, gender makeup, level of urbanization and/or acculturation, and pertinent social and cultural history?
- Does the report address researcher interaction effects by fully documenting the researcher's activities in the setting?
- Were all observations and interviews conducted in a variety of fully described settings and with multiple trained observers?

Reliability

- Is the researcher's relationship with the group and setting fully described?
- Is all field documentation comprehensive, fully cross-referenced and annotated, and rigorously detailed?
- Were observations and interviews documented using multiple means (written notes and recordings, for example)?
- Is interviewers' training documented?
- Is construction, planning, and testing of all instruments documented?
- Are key informants fully described, including information on groups they represent and their community status?
- Are sampling techniques fully documented as being sufficient for the study?

---

[1]The questions in this section are adapted from Schensul, S. L., Schensul, J. J., and LeCompte, M. D. (1999), Essential ethnographic methods: Observations, interviews, and questionnaires. In S. L. Schensul, J. J. Schensul, and M. D. LeCompte (Eds.), *Ethnographer's handbook: Volume 2,* pp. 278–289. Lanham, MD: Alta Mira/Rowman & Littlefield.

HISTORICAL RESEARCH

- Were the sources of data related to the problem mostly primary?
- Was each piece of data subjected to external criticism?
- Was each piece of data subjected to internal criticism?
- Does the researcher examine the possibility of personal bias in the study analysis and conclusions?
- Are causal inferences or conclusions warranted given the data studied?
- Is the report of the study an integrated, synthesized, chronological presentation of the results?

SURVEY (DESCRIPTIVE) RESEARCH

Questionnaire Studies

- Are questionnaire validation procedures described?
- Was the questionnaire pretested?
- Are pilot study procedures and results described?
- Are directions to questionnaire respondents clear?
- Does each item in the questionnaire relate to one of the objectives of the study?
- Does each questionnaire item deal with a single concept?
- When necessary, is a point of reference given for questionnaire items?
- Are leading questions avoided in the questionnaire?
- Are there sufficient alternatives for each questionnaire item?
- Does the cover letter explain the purpose and importance of the study and give the potential responder a good reason for cooperating?
- If appropriate, is confidentiality or anonymity of responses assured in the cover letter?
- What is the percentage of returns and how does it affect the study results?
- Are followup activities to increase returns described?
- If the response rate was low, was any attempt made to determine any major differences between responders and nonresponders?
- Are data analyzed in groups or clusters rather than a series of many single-variable analyses?

CORRELATIONAL RESEARCH

Relationship Studies

- Were variables carefully selected (i.e., was a shotgun approach avoided)?
- Is the rationale for variable selection described?
- Are conclusions and recommendations based on values of correlation coefficients corrected for attenuation or restriction in range?
- Do the conclusions avoid suggesting causal relationships between the variables investigated?

Prediction Studies

- Is a rationale given for selection of predictor variables?
- Is the criterion variable well defined?
- Was the resulting prediction equation validated with at least one other group?

CAUSAL–COMPARATIVE RESEARCH

- Are the characteristics or experiences that differentiate the groups (the independent variable) clearly defined or described?
- Are critical extraneous variables identified?
- Were any control procedures applied to equate the groups on extraneous variables?
- Are causal relationships found discussed with due caution?
- Are plausible alternative hypotheses discussed?

EXPERIMENTAL RESEARCH

- Was an appropriate experimental design selected?
- Is a rationale for design selection given?
- Are sources of invalidity associated with the design identified and discussed?
- Is the method of group formation described?
- Was the experimental group formed in the same way as the control group?
- Were groups randomly formed and the use of existing groups avoided?
- Were treatments randomly assigned to groups?
- Were critical extraneous variables identified?
- Were any control procedures applied to equate groups on extraneous variables?
- Were possible reactive arrangements (e.g., the Hawthorne effect) controlled for?
- Were tables clear and pertinent to the research results?
- Were the results generalized to the appropriate group?

 Now go to the Companion Website accompanying this text at www.prenhall.com/gay to check your understanding of chapter concepts in the following modules: Objectives, Practice Quiz, and Applying What You Know. Expand your research skills with Evaluating Articles, Analyzing Qualitative Data, Analyzing Quantitative Data, and Research Tools and Tips. Visit Web Links to broaden your knowledge about research.

SUMMARY

General Evaluation Criteria

1. There are a number of basic errors or weaknesses that even a beginning researcher should be able to detect in a research study.
2. You should be able to detect obvious indications of experimenter bias that may have affected the results.
3. As you read a research report, either as a consumer of research keeping up with the latest findings in your professional area or as a producer of research reviewing literature related to a defined problem, there are a number of questions you should ask yourself concerning the adequacy of execution of the various components.
4. The answers to some of these questions are more critical than the answers to others.
5. Major problems and shortcomings are usually readily identifiable, and by mentally responding to a number of questions one formulates an overall impression concerning the validity of the study.

Introduction

6. Problem: See page 532.
7. Review of Related Literature: See page 532.
8. Hypotheses: See page 533.

Method

9. Participants: See page 533.
10. Instruments: See page 533.
11. Design and Procedure: See page 533.

Results

12. See page 534.

Discussion (Conclusions and Recommendations)

13. See page 534.

Abstract or Summary

14. See page 534.

Type-Specific Evaluation Criteria

15. In addition to general criteria that can be applied to almost any study, there are additional questions that should be asked depending on the type of research represented by the study.

Qualitative Research (In General)

16. See page 535.
17. Observation Studies: See page 535.
18. Interview Studies: See page 535

Evaluating Validity and Reliability in Qualitative Studies

19. See page 536.

Historical Research

20. See page 537.

Survey (Descriptive) Research

21. Questionnaire Studies: See page 537.

Correlational Research

22. Relationship Studies: See page 537.
23. Prediction Studies: See page 537.

Causal–Comparative Research

24. See page 538.

Experimental Research

25. See page 538.

TASK 11   PERFORMANCE CRITERIA

The evaluation form will list a series of questions about an article to which you must indicate a yes or no response. For example, you might be asked if there is a statement of hypotheses. If the answer is yes, you must indicate where the asked-for component is located in the study. For example, you might indicate a statement of a hypothesis on page 32, paragraph 3, lines 2–6. In addition, if the study is experimental you will be asked to identify and diagram the experimental design that was applied.

On the following pages a research report is reprinted. (See Task 11 example.) Following the report, a form is provided for you to use in evaluating the report. In answering the questions, use the following codes:

> Y = Yes
> N = No
> NA = Question not applicable (e.g., a pilot study was not done)
> ?/X = Cannot tell from information given or, given your current level of expertise, you are not in a position to make a judgment

TASK 11 EXAMPLE

EFFECTS OF USING AN INSTRUCTIONAL GAME ON MOTIVATION AND PERFORMANCE

JAMES D. KLEIN
Arizona State University

ERIC FREITAG
Arizona State University

ABSTRACT   Although many educators theorize that instructional games are effective for providing students with motivating practice, research on instructional gaming is inconclusive. The purpose of this study was to determine the effect on motivation and performance of using an instructional game. The effect of using a supplemental reading on motivation and performance was also examined. We randomly assigned 75 undergraduates to one of two treatments after they had attended a lecture on the information-processing model of learning. The subjects in one treatment group used an instructional board game to practice the material presented in the lecture, while those in the other group practiced using a traditional worksheet. Results indicated that using the instructional game significantly affected the four motivational components of attention, relevance, confidence, and satisfaction. The instructional game did not influence performance. The results also suggested that the subjects who reported completion of a supplemental reading had significantly better performance and confidence than did the subjects who reported that they had not completed the reading. Implications for the design of practice are discussed.

Providing students with an opportunity to practice newly acquired skills and knowledge is an important component in designing an instructional strategy. Although many instructional design theories include recommendations for designing practice activities, Salisbury, Richards, and Klein (1986) have emphasized that most of the theories fail to address how to design practice that is motivational.

Some educators have theorized that instructional games are effective for providing motivating practice of newly acquired skills and information. They have argued that instructional games are motivational because they generate enthusiasm, excitement, and enjoyment, and because they require students to be actively involved in learning (Coleman, 1968; Ernest, 1986; Rakes & Kutzman, 1982; Wesson, Wilson, & Mandlebaum, 1988). Other scholars have theorized that instructional games decrease student motivation. Those authors have suggested that the motivational aspects of instructional games are limited to those who win, and that losing an instructional game produces a failure syndrome and reduces self-esteem (Allington & Strange, 1977; Andrews & Thorpe, 1977).

Whereas theorists have argued about the motivational aspects of instructional games, researchers have investigated the effect of using games on student motivation. Some researchers have reported that the use of instructional gaming increases student interests, satisfaction, and continuing motivation (DeVries & Edwards, 1973; Sleet, 1985; Straus, 1986). In addition, investigators have reported that instructional games influence school attendance. Allen and Main (1976) found that including instructional gaming in a mathematics curriculum helped to reduce the rate of absenteeism of students in inner-city schools. Studies by Raia (1966) and Boseman and Schellenberger (1974) indicated that including games in a college business course has a positive affect on course attendance but not on expressed interest and satisfaction. Others have reported that playing a game does not influence student satisfaction or attitude toward school (DeVries & Slavin, 1978).

In addition to the possible motivational benefits of games, many educators have theorized that games are effective for increasing student performance. They have argued that instructional games make practice more effective because students become active participants in the learning process (Ernest, 1986; Rakes & Kutzman, 1982; Wesson et al., 1988). Others have suggested that games foster incorrect responding and inefficiently use instructional time; also, the rate of practice in a game cannot compare with that of a flashcard drill or reading a connected text (Allington & Strange, 1977; Andrews & Thorpe, 1977).

Researchers have attempted to answer whether instructional games are an effective method for learning. Some investigators have reported that instructional games are effective for assisting students to acquire, practice, and transfer mathematical concepts and problem-solving abilities (Bright, 1980; Bright, Harvey, & Wheeler, 1979; DeVries & Slavin, 1978; Dienes, 1962; Rogers & Miller, 1984). Others have reported that using an instructional game to practice mathematics skills assists slow learners but not more able students (Friedlander, 1977). Research on the use of instructional games in college business courses has produced inconclusive or nonsignificant findings in many studies (Boseman & Schellenberger, 1974; Greenlaw & Wyman, 1973; Raia, 1966), whereas instructional games have positively influenced learning in actual business training settings (Jacobs & Baum, 1987; Pierfy, 1977). Even advocates of instructional gaming are unsure whether games teach intellectual content and skills (Boocock, 1968).

Address correspondence to James D. Klein, Learning and Instruction, College of Education, Arizona State University, Tempe, AZ 85287-0611.

There are several explanations for the inconsistent findings from research concerning the effect of instructional games on motivation and learning. A few authors (Reiser & Gerlach, 1977; Remus, 1981; Stone, 1982) have suggested that much of the research on instructional gaming has been conducted using flawed experimental designs and methods. Another explanation is that many studies on instructional gaming have not investigated the integration of games in an instructional system. Gaming advocates have suggested that games should be used with other instructional methods such as lecture and textbooks (Clayton & Rosenbloom, 1968). A third explanation is that researchers examining the effect of instructional gaming on motivation have not adequately defined and operationalized the variable of motivation. After an extensive review of instructional gaming, Wolfe (1985) indicated, "No rigorous research has examined a game's motivational power, [or] what types of students are motivated by games" (p. 279).

Our purpose in this article is to describe the results of a study conducted to determine the effects on student motivation and performance of using an instructional game as practice. Because the study was designed to integrate the game into an instructional system, we also attempted to determine how using a supplemental reading affects student motivation and performance. Motivation was defined using the ARCS model of motivation (Keller, 1987a). The model suggests that motivation in an instructional setting consists of four conditions: attention, relevance, confidence, and satisfaction. According to Keller (1987a), all four conditions must be met for students to become and remain motivated. We hypothesized that students using an instructional game to practice newly acquired information would indicate that the method enhanced their attention, relevance, confidence, and satisfaction. We also believed that students who reported that they had completed a supplemental reading would perform better on a posttest than would those who reported that they did not complete the reading.

METHOD

Subjects

Our subjects were 75 undergraduate education majors enrolled in a required course in educational psychology at a large southwestern university. Although students in this class were required to participate in one research study during the semester, participation in this particular study was not mandatory.

Materials

Materials used in this study were an instructional game and a worksheet (both designed to provide practice of information and concepts presented in a lecture), the textbook *Essentials of Learning for Instruction* by Gagne & Driscoll (1988), the Instructional Materials Motivation Scale (Keller, 1987b), and a measure of performance.

The term *game* has various meanings, and several characteristics are important to understand the construct of game. In general, most games include a model or representation of reality, a set of rules that describe how to proceed, a specified outcome, and a group of players who act individually or collectively as a team (Atkinson, 1977; Coleman, 1968; Fletcher, 1971; Shubik, 1975,

1989). Games usually require active participation by players and can include elements of competition and cooperation (Orbach, 1979; Shubik, 1989). Games used for instructional purposes should be based on specific educational objectives and provide immediate feedback to participants (Atkinson, 1977; Jacobs & Baum, 1987; Orbach, 1979).

The instructional game used in this study included the elements listed above. We developed the game to provide students with practice on objectives from a unit on the information-processing model of learning. The instructional game consisted of a board that graphically represented the information-processing model, a direction card that explained the rules of the game, and a set of 25 game cards. Each game card had a practice question about the information-processing model of learning on the front and feedback with knowledge of correct results on the back. The rules were developed to encourage cooperation, competition, and active participation. The rules specified that team members should discuss each question among themselves before providing an answer. Teams were also told that they would be playing against another team.

We also developed the worksheet to provide subjects with practice on the information-processing model of learning. The worksheet was four pages in length and included the same 25 questions that appeared on the game cards. After subjects completed a set of five questions, the worksheet instructed subjects to turn to the last page for feedback.

We used the Instructional Materials Motivation Scale (IMMS) developed by Keller (1987b), to measure student perception of the motivational characteristics of the instructional materials. The IMMS includes four subscales to measure the degree to which subjects believe that a set of instructional materials address the motivational components of attention, relevance, confidence, and satisfaction. Keller reported that Cronbach's alpha reliability of the instrument is .89 for attention, .81 for relevance, .90 for confidence, .92 for satisfaction, and .96 for overall motivation.

A 15-item constructed response posttest was used to measure student performance. We developed the items on this posttest to determine subject mastery of the information-processing model. The Kuder-Richardson internal consistency reliability of this measure was .77.

Procedures

All of the subjects attended a 50-min lecture on the information-processing model of learning and were told afterward to read chapter 2 in the textbook, *Essentials of Learning for Instruction,* by Gagne & Driscoll (1988). Two days later, the subjects were randomly assigned to one of two treatment groups. The subjects in both groups were given 30 min to practice the information presented in the lecture and assigned reading by using either the instructional game or the worksheet.

One group of subjects used the instructional game to practice the information-processing model. Those subjects were randomly placed in groups of 8 to 10 and formed into two teams of players. Each group received the game materials described above, and the experimenter read the game rules aloud. Subjects in this group played the game for 30 min. The other group of subjects used the worksheet to practice the same items. The latter group worked individually for 30 min to complete the worksheet. The subjects were told to review incorrect items if time permitted.

Upon completion of the practice activity, all the subjects completed the Instructional Materials Motivation Scale and then took the posttest. The subjects also were asked if they had attended the lecture on the information-processing model and if they had completed the assigned reading from the textbook. Completion of the activities took approximately 15 min.

RESULTS

Motivation

We used a multivariate analysis of variance (MANOVA) to test for an overall difference between groups on the motivation scales. Stevens (1986) indicated that MANOVA should be used when several dependent variables are correlated and share a common conceptual meaning. An alpha level of .05 was set for the MANOVA tests. The analyses were followed by univariate analyses on each of the four IMMS subscales. To account for the possibility of inflated statistical error, we set the alpha at .0125 for the univariate analyses, using the Bonferroni method (Stevens, 1986). To determine the size of the treatment effect for each variable, we calculated effect-size estimates expressed as a function of the overall standard deviation (Cohen, 1969).

Results indicated that using the instructional game to practice information had a significant effect on motivation. A significant MANOVA effect, $F(4, 64) = 6.57$, $p < .001$, was found for the treatment on the motivation measures. Univariate analyses revealed that subjects who played the game rated this method of practice as motivational in the four areas of attention, $F(1, 67) = 21.91$, $p < .001$; relevance, $F(1, 67) = 15.05$, $p < .001$; confidence, $F(1, 67) = 16.80$, $p < .001$; and satisfaction, $F(1, 67) = 24.71$, $p < .001$. Effect-size estimates for each motivation variable were .61 for attention, .91 for relevance, 1.01 for confidence, and 1.23 for satisfaction. Cohen (1969) indicated that an effect size of .80 should be considered large for most statistical tests in psychological research. Table 1 includes a summary of means and standard deviations on each motivation subscale for the game and the nongame groups.

Results also suggested that subject self-report about completion of the reading assignment was significantly related to motivation. A significant MANOVA effect $F(4, 64) = 2.94$, $p < .05$, was found for

this variable on the motivation measures. Follow-up univariate analyses revealed that the motivational area of confidence was significantly related to completion of reading assignment, $F(1, 67) = 6.52$, $p < .0125$. Attention, relevance, and satisfaction were not significantly related to self-reported completion of reading assignment. In addition, a test of the interaction between self-reported completion of reading assignment and the treatment was not statistically significant, $F(4, 64) = 0.97$, $p > .05$.

Performance

We measured performance using a 15-item constructed response posttest. Analysis of variance (ANOVA) was used to test for differences between groups on the performance measure. An alpha level of .05 was set for all statistical tests.

Analysis of the posttest data revealed that self-reported completion of assigned reading was significantly related to performance, $F(2, 71) = 14.87$, $p < .001$. Subjects who indicated that they had read the assigned text ($n = 40$) performed significantly better on the posttest than those who indicated that they did not complete the reading ($n = 35$). The mean performance score of subjects who reported reading the text was 11.25 ($SD = 3.07$), whereas the mean performance score for those who reported that they did not read the text was 8.45 ($SD = 3.22$).

No statistically significant difference was found on the performance measure when the treatment groups were compared. The mean performance score for subjects using the game was 10.49 ($SD = 3.20$), and the mean performance score for those in the nongame group was 9.39 ($SD = 3.61$). In addition, a test of the interaction between the treatment and self-reported completion of reading assignment was not statistically significant, $F(2, 71) = 0.14$, $p > .05$.

DISCUSSION

The major purpose of this study was to determine the effect of using an instructional game on student motivation and performance. The results of the study suggest that using an instructional game as a method of delivering practice did enhance the motivation of students in the four areas of attention, relevance, confidence, and satisfaction. However, the results show that using the instructional game to practice information did not contribute to enhanced performance when compared with a traditional method of practice. There are several possible explanations for the results found in this study.

Table 1.
Means and Standard Deviations on Attention (A), Relevance (R), Confidence (C), Satisfaction (S),
and Performance (P) Measures, by Treatment Group

Group	A	R	C	S	P
Game	4.22	3.71	4.06	3.88	10.49
($n = 37$)	(0.58)	(0.58)	(0.57)	(0.86)	(3.20)
Nongame	3.77	3.13	3.31	2.72	9.39
($n = 38$)	(0.89)	(0.69)	(0.90)	(1.02)	(3.60)

Note. Maximum scores = 5.00 for A, R, C, S and 15.00 for P.

In keeping with established ideas of the characteristics of a game, we used a game board that provided students with a visual representation of the information-processing model of learning and required players to be active participants. Keller (1987a) indicated that visual representations and active participation are two strategies that can increase student attention in an instructional setting. Furthermore, use of the game may have contributed to the results found for attention, because of a novelty effect. Some researchers have reported that student motivation and interest fluctuate and decrease as the novelty effect of a game wears off (Dill, 1961; Greenlaw & Wyman, 1973), whereas others have reported that interest tends to persist over time in gaming settings (Dill & Doppelt, 1963). Although novelty may be a reason for increased attention in this study, instructional designers who are concerned with providing motivating practice to students should consider that explanation as positive. Motivation and attention can be increased when variability and novelty are used in the classroom (Brophy, 1987; Keller, 1983).

The results found in this study for the motivational factor of relevance are consistent with the theories proposed by gaming advocates. Both Abt (1968) and Rogers and Miller (1984) argued that students will not question the relevance of educational content when it is presented via an instructional game. In addition, instruction can be made relevant to students by designing materials that are responsive to their needs (Keller, 1983). Orbach (1979) indicated that games are excellent methods to motivate students with a high need for achievement, because a game can include an element of competition. Orbach (1979) also theorized that games can motivate students with a high need for affiliation when the game requires interaction among individuals and teams. The instructional game used in this study included a moderate level of competition and required students to interact cooperatively through the team approach.

The instructional game used in this study also provided circumstances for student-directed learning. As a motivational strategy, researchers have linked student-centered learning with increased confidence (Keller & Dodge, 1982). The finding that the game increased student confidence is consistent with theorists who have suggested that games can influence student efficacy (Abt, 1968) and with researchers who reported that students rate the task of gaming as less difficult than other instructional techniques (DeVries & Edwards, 1973).

The positive finding for satisfaction is also consistent with theory and research. Some scholars have indicated that instructional games contribute to motivation because they provide intrinsic reward and enjoyment (Coleman, 1968; Ernest, 1986; Rakes & Kutzman, 1982). Researchers have reported that instructional games lead to increases in student satisfaction (DeVries & Edwards, 1973; Strauss, 1986). The results of this study support theorists and researchers who have suggested that students enjoy the gaming approach in instruction.

Although our results did suggest that the instructional game had an effect on student motivation, the game used in this study did not have a significant impact on student performance. However, subjects who reported completing an assigned reading performed significantly better and had more confidence about their performance than those who reported that they did not complete the reading. The results may have occurred because of the nature of the reading.

Even though all the students were provided with necessary concepts and information in a lecture, the textbook, *Essentials of Learning for Instruction* (Gagne & Driscoll, 1988), provided readers with practice and feedback in addition to supplementing the lecture. The additional practice and feedback more than likely influenced both the performance and confidence of those who completed the assigned reading.

The findings of this study have some implications for the design of practice. Although many instructional design theorists have indicated that students should be provided with an opportunity to practice newly acquired skills and knowledge, most fail to address how to design practice that is motivational (Salisbury, Richards, & Klein, 1985). The results of this study suggest that instructional designers can provide students with a motivating practice alternative that is as effective as more traditional methods of practice by including a game into instruction. Although using the game to practice did not have an effect on immediate performance in this short-term study, motivating practice alternatives can possibly influence long-term performance because of increased student contact with materials that they find motivational. Future research should investigate the impact of gaming on long-term performance.

The current study also suggests that instructional designers should include reading assignments that provide additional practice in their instruction. The use of those types of readings will not only increase student performance, but also will lead to increases in student confidence about that performance.

As in our study, future research should integrate instructional games into a system to determine if the method has an impact on educational outcomes. Besides using a game as practice, research could be conducted to examine the effect of using a game to present other instructional events, such as stimulating recall of prior knowledge or as a review of learning. Researchers of instructional gaming should continue to investigate the effect of using a game on student motivation and should be specific in their operational definition of motivation. Implementation of our suggestions will assist us in determining how to design practice that is both effective and motivational.

REFERENCES

Abt, C. C. (1968). Games for learning. In S. S. Boocock & E. O. Schild (Eds.), *Simulation games in learning* (pp. 65–84). Beverly Hills, CA: Sage.

Allen, L. E., & Main, D. B. (1976). The effect of instructional gaming on absenteeism: The first step. *Journal for Research in Mathematics Education, 7*(2), 113–128.

Allington, R. L., & Strange, M. (1977). The problem with reading games. *The Reading Teacher, 31,* 272–274.

Andrews, M., & Thorpe, H. W. (1977). A critical analysis of instructional games. *Reading Improvement, 14,* 74–76.

Atkinson, F. D. (1977). Designing simulation/gaming activities: A systems approach. *Educational Technology, 17*(2), 38–43.

Boocock, S. S. (1968). From luxury item to learning tool: An overview of the theoretical literature on games. In S. S. Boocock and E. O. Schild (Eds.), *Simulation games in learning* (pp. 53–64). Beverly Hills, CA: Sage.

Boseman, F. G., & Schellenberger, R. E. (1974). Business gaming: An empirical appraisal. *Simulation & Games, 5,* 383–401.

Bright, G. W. (1980). Game moves as they relate to strategy and knowledge. *Journal of Experimental Education, 48,* 204–209.

Bright, G. W., Harvey, J. G., & Wheeler, M. M. (1979). Using games to retrain skills with basic multiplication facts. *Journal for Research in Mathematics Education, 10,* 103–110.

Brophy, J. (1987). Synthesis of research on strategies for motivating students to learn. *Educational Leadership, 45*(2), 40–48.

Clayton, M., & Rosenbloom, R. (1968). Goals and designs. In S. S. Boocock & E. O. Schild (Eds.), *Simulation games in learning* (pp. 85–92). Beverly Hills, CA: Sage.

Cohen, J. (1969). *Statistical power analysis for the behavioral sciences.* New York: Academic Press.

Coleman, J. S. (1968). Social processes and social simulation games. In S. S. Boocock & E. O. Schild (Eds.), *Simulation games in learning* (pp. 29–51). Beverly Hills, CA: Sage.

Dienes, Z. P. (1962). *An experimental study of mathematics learning.* New York: Hutchinson.

DeVries, D. L., & Edwards, K. L. (1973). Learning games and student teams: Their effects on classroom process. *American Educational Research Journal, 10,* 307–318.

DeVries, D. L., & Slavin, R. E. (1978). Teams-games-tournaments (TGT): Review of ten classroom experiments. *Journal of Research and Development in Education, 12,* 28–37.

Dill, W. R. (1961). The educational effects of management games. In W. R. Dill (Ed.), *Proceeding of the Conference on Business Games as Teaching Devices* (pp. 61–72). New Orleans, LA: Tulane University.

Dill, W. R., & Doppelt, N. (1963). The acquisition of experience in a complex management game. *Management Science, 10,* 30–46.

Ernest, P. (1986). Games: A rationale for their use in the teaching of mathematics in school. *Mathematics in School,* 2–5.

Fletcher, J. L. (1971). The effectiveness of simulation games as learning environments. *Simulation and Games, 2,* 259–286.

Friedlander, A. (1977). The Steeplechase. *Mathematics Teaching, 80,* 37–39.

Gagne, R. M., & Driscoll, M. P. (1988). *Essentials of learning for instruction* (2nd ed.). Englewood Cliffs, NJ: Prentice Hall.

Greenlaw, P. S., & Wyman, F. P. (1973). The teaching effectiveness of games in collegiate business courses. *Simulation & Games, 4,* 259–294.

Jacobs, R. L., & Baum, M. (1987). Simulation and games in training and development. *Simulation & Games, 18,* 385–394.

Keller, J. M. (1983). Motivational design of instruction. In C. M. Reigeluth (Ed.), *Instructional-design theories and models: An overview of their current status* (pp. 386–434). Hillsdale, NJ: Lawrence-Erlbaum.

Keller, J. M. (1987a). Development and use of the ARCS model of instructional design. *Journal of Instructional Development, 10*(3), 2–10.

Keller, J. M. (1987b). *Instructional materials motivation scale (IMMS).* Unpublished manuscript. Florida State University, Tallahassee, FL.

Keller, J. M., & Dodge, B. (1982). *The ARCS model: Motivational strategies for instruction.* Unpublished manuscript. Syracuse University, Syracuse, NY.

Orbach, E. (1979). Simulation games and motivation for learning: A theoretical framework. *Simulation & Games, 10,* 3–40.

Pierfy, D. (1977). Comparative simulation game research: Stumbling blocks and stepping stones. *Simulation & Games, 8,* 255–269.

Raia, A. P. (1966). A study of the educational value of management games. *Journal of Business, 39,* 339–352.

Rakes, T. A., & Kutzman, S. K. (1982). The selection and use of reading games and activities. *Reading Horizons,* 67–70.

Reiser, R. A., & Gerlach, V. S. (1977). Research on simulation games in education: A critical analysis. *Educational Technology, 17*(12), 13–18.

Remus, W. E. (1981). Experimental designs for analyzing data on games. *Simulation & Games, 12,* 3–14.

Rogers, P. J., & Miller, J. V. (1984). Playway mathematics: Theory, practice, and some results. *Educational Research, 26,* 200–207.

Salisbury, D. F., Richards, B. F., & Klein, J. D. (1986). Prescriptions for the design of practice activities for learning. *Journal of Instructional Development, 8*(4), 9–19.

Shubik, M. (1975). *The uses and methods of gaming.* New York: Elsevier.

Shubik, M. (1989). Gaming: Theory and practice, past and future. *Simulation & Games, 20,* 184–189.

Sleet, D. A. (1985). Application of a gaming strategy to improve nutrition education. *Simulation & Games, 16,* 63–70.

Stevens, J. (1986). *Applied multivariate statistics for the social sciences.* Hillsdale, NJ: Lawrence Erlbaum.

Stone, E. F. (1982). *Research design issues in studies assessing the effects of management education.* Paper presented at the National Academy of Management Conference, New York.

Straus, R. A. (1986). Simple games for teaching sociological perspectives. *Teaching Sociology, 14,* 119–128.

Wesson, C., Wilson, R., & Mandlebaum, L. H. (1988). Learning games for active student responding. *Teaching Exceptional Children,* 12–14.

Wolfe, J. (1985). The teaching effectiveness of games in collegiate business courses. *Simulation & Games, 16,* 251–288.

EFFECTS OF USING AN INSTRUCTIONAL GAME ON MOTIVATION AND PERFORMANCE

SELF-TEST FOR TASK 11

Y = Yes
N = No
NA = Not applicable
?/X = Can't tell/Don't know

GENERAL EVALUATION
INTRODUCTION

CODE

Problem

Is there a statement of the problem?

_____

Is the problem "researchable"? That is, can it be investigated through the collection and analysis of data?

_____

Is background information on the problem presented?

_____

Is the educational significance of the problem discussed?

_____

Does the problem statement indicate the variables of interest and the specific relationship between those variables that was investigated?

_____

When necessary, are variables directly or operationally defined?

_____

Does the researcher have the knowledge and skill to carry out the proposed research?

_____

Review of Related Literature

Is the review comprehensive?

_____

Are all cited references relevant to the problem under investigation?

_____

Are most of the sources primary (i.e., are there only a few or no secondary sources)?

_____

Have the references been critically analyzed and the results of various studies compared and contrasted (i.e., is the review more than a series of abstracts or annotations)?

_____

Is the relevancy of each reference explained?

_____

Is the review well organized? Does it logically flow in such a way that the references least related to the problem are discussed first and the most-related references are discussed last?

_____

Does the review conclude with a brief summary of the literature and its implications for the problem investigated?

_____

Do the implications discussed form an empirical or theoretical rationale for the hypotheses that follow?

_____

Are references cited completely and accurately?

_____

                                                                    CODE

Hypotheses

Are specific questions to be answered listed or specific hypotheses to be
tested stated?   _____

Does each hypothesis state an expected relationship or difference?   _____

If necessary, are variables directly or operationally defined?   _____

Is each hypothesis testable?   _____

METHOD

Participants

Are the size and major characteristics of the population studied described?   _____

Are the accessible and target populations described?   _____

If a sample was selected, is the method of selecting the sample clearly
described?   _____

Does the method of sample selection suggest any limitations or biases
in the sample? For example, is stratified sampling used to obtain sample
subgroups?   _____

Are the size and major characteristics of the sample described?   _____

Does the sample size meet the suggested guidelines for minimum sample
size appropriate for the method of research represented?   _____

Instruments

Do instruments and their administration meet guidelines for protecting
participants? Have needed permissions been obtained?   _____

Is a rationale given for the selection of the instruments (or measurements)
used?   _____

Is each instrument described in terms of purpose, content, validity, and
reliability?   _____

Are the instruments appropriate for measuring the intended variables?   _____

Does the researcher have the needed skills or experience to construct or
administer an instrument?   _____

Is evidence presented that indicates that the instruments are appropriate
for the intended sample? For example, is the reading level of an instrument
suitable for sample participants?   _____

If appropriate, are subtest reliabilities given?   _____

If an instrument was developed specifically for the study, are the procedures
involved in its development and validation described?   _____

If an instrument was developed specifically for the study, are administration,
scoring or tabulating, and interpretation procedures fully described?   _____

Is the correct type of instrument used for data collection (e.g., using a
norm-referenced instrument when a criterion-referenced one is more
suitable)?   _____

Design and Procedure

Is the design appropriate for answering the questions or testing the hypotheses of the study?   _____

Are procedures described in sufficient detail to permit replication by another researcher?   _____

Do procedures logically relate to each other? Are instruments and procedures applied correctly?   _____

If a pilot study was conducted, are its execution and results described, as well as its effect on the subsequent study?   _____

Are control procedures described?

Did the researcher discuss or account for any potentially confounding variables that he or she was unable to control?   _____

Is the application of the qualitative method chosen described in detail?   _____

Is the context of the qualitative study described in detail?   _____

RESULTS

Are appropriate descriptive statistics presented?   _____

Was the probability level, α, at which the results of the tests of significance were evaluated, specified in advance of data analysis?   _____

If parametric tests were used, is there evidence that the researcher avoided violating the required assumptions for parametric tests?   _____

Are the described tests of significance appropriate, given the hypotheses and design of the study?   _____

Was the inductive logic used to produce results in a qualitative study made explicit?   _____

Are the tests of significance interpreted using the appropriate degrees of freedom?   _____

Are the results clearly presented?   _____

Are the tables and figures (if any) well organized and easy to understand? _____

Are the data in each table and figure described in the text?   _____

DISCUSSION (CONCLUSIONS AND RECOMMENDATIONS)

Is each result discussed in terms of the original hypothesis or topic to which it relates?   _____

Is each result discussed in terms of its agreement or disagreement with previous results obtained by other researchers in other studies?   _____

Are generalizations consistent with the results?   _____

Are the possible effects of uncontrolled variables on the results discussed? _____

Are theoretical and practical implications of the findings discussed?   _____

Are recommendations for future action made?   _____

Are the suggestions for future action based on practical significance or on statistical significance only (i.e., has the author avoided confusing practical and statistical significance)?   _____

CODE

ABSTRACT OR SUMMARY

Is the problem restated?   _____

Are the number and type of participants and instruments described?   _____

Is the design used identified?   _____

Are procedures described?   _____

Are the major results and conclusions restated?   _____

Type-Specific Evaluation Criteria

Identify and diagram the experimental design used in this study:

Was an appropriate experimental design selected?   _____

Is a rationale for design selection given?   _____

Are sources of invalidity associated with the design identified and discussed?   _____

Is the method of group formation described?   _____

Was the experimental group formed in the same way as the control group?   _____

Were groups randomly formed and the use of existing groups avoided?   _____

Were treatments randomly assigned to groups?   _____

Were critical extraneous variables identified?   _____

Were any control procedures applied to equate groups on extraneous
variables?   _____

Were possible reactive arrangements (e.g., the Hawthorne effect)
controlled for?   _____

APPENDIX A

REFERENCE TABLES

TABLE A.1　Ten Thousand Random Numbers

	00–04	05–09	10–14	15–19	20–24	25–29	30–34	35–39	40–44	45–49
00	54463	22662	65905	70639	79365	67382	29085	69831	47058	08186
01	15389	85205	18850	39226	42249	90669	96325	23248	60933	26927
02	85941	40756	82414	02015	13858	78030	16269	65978	01385	15345
03	61149	69440	11268	88218	58925	03638	52862	62733	33451	77455
04	05219	81619	81619	10651	67079	92511	59888	72095	83463	75577
05	41417	98326	87719	92294	46614	50948	64886	20002	97365	30976
06	28357	94070	20652	35774	16249	75019	21145	15217	47286	76305
07	17783	00015	10806	83091	91530	36466	39981	62481	49177	75779
08	40950	84820	29881	85966	62800	70326	84740	62660	77379	90279
09	82995	64157	66164	41180	10089	41757	78258	96488	88629	37231
10	96754	17676	55659	44105	47361	34833	86679	23930	53249	27083
11	34357	88040	53364	71726	45690	66334	60332	22554	90600	71113
12	06318	37403	49927	57715	50423	67372	63116	48888	21505	80182
13	62111	52820	07243	79931	89292	84767	85693	73947	22278	11551
14	47534	09243	67879	00544	23410	12740	02540	54440	32949	13491
15	98614	75993	84460	62846	59844	14922	49730	73443	48167	34770
16	24856	03648	44898	09351	98795	18644	39765	71058	90368	44104
17	96887	12479	80621	66223	86085	78285	02432	53342	42846	94771
18	90801	21472	42815	77408	37390	76766	52615	32141	30268	18106
19	55165	77312	83666	36028	28420	70219	81369	41943	47366	41067
20	75884	12952	84318	95108	72305	64620	91318	89872	45375	85436
21	16777	37116	58550	42958	21460	43910	01175	87894	81378	10620
22	46230	43877	80207	88877	89380	32992	91380	03164	98656	59337
23	42902	66892	46134	01432	94710	23474	20523	60137	60609	13119
24	81007	00333	39693	28039	10154	95425	39220	19774	31782	49037
25	68089	01122	51111	72373	06902	74373	96199	97017	41273	21546
26	20411	67081	89950	16944	93054	87687	96693	87236	77054	33848
27	58212	13160	06468	15718	82627	76999	05999	58680	96739	63700
28	70577	42866	24969	61210	76046	67699	42054	12696	93758	03283
29	94522	74358	71659	62038	79643	79169	44741	05437	39038	13163
30	42626	86819	85651	88678	17401	03252	99547	32404	17918	62880
31	16051	33763	57194	16752	54450	19031	58580	47629	54132	60631
32	08244	27647	33851	44705	94211	46716	11738	55784	95374	72655
33	59497	04392	09419	89964	51211	04894	72882	17805	21896	83864
34	97155	13428	40293	09985	58434	01412	69124	82171	59058	82859
35	98409	66162	95763	47420	20792	61527	20441	39435	11859	41567
36	45476	84882	65109	96597	25930	66790	65706	61203	53634	22557
37	89300	69700	50741	30329	11658	23166	05400	66669	48708	03887
38	50051	95137	91631	66315	91428	12275	24816	68091	71710	33258
39	31753	85178	31310	89642	98364	02306	24617	09609	83942	22716
40	79152	53829	77250	20190	56535	18760	69942	77448	33278	48805
41	44560	38750	83635	56540	64900	42912	13953	79149	18710	68618
42	68328	83378	63369	71381	39564	05615	42451	64559	97501	65747
43	46939	38689	58625	08342	30459	85863	20781	09284	26333	91777
44	83544	86141	15707	96256	23068	13782	08467	89469	93842	55349
45	91621	00881	04900	54224	46177	55309	17852	27491	89415	23466
46	91896	67126	04151	03795	59077	11848	12630	98375	53068	60142
47	55751	62515	22108	80830	02263	29303	37204	96926	30506	09808
48	85156	87689	95493	88842	00664	55017	55539	17771	69448	87530
49	07521	56898	12236	60277	39102	62315	12239	07105	11844	01117

Reprinted by permission from *Statistical Methods* by George W. Snedecor and William G. Cochran, sixth edition © 1967 by Iowa State University Press, pp. 543–46.

TABLE A.1   Continued

	50–54	55–59	60–64	65–69	70–74	75–79	80–84	85–89	90–94	95–99
00	59391	58030	52098	82718	87024	82848	04190	96574	90464	29065
01	99567	76364	77204	04615	27062	96621	43918	01896	83991	51141
02	10363	97518	51400	25670	98342	61891	27101	37855	06235	33316
03	96859	19558	64432	16706	99612	59798	32803	67708	15297	28612
04	11258	24591	36863	55368	31721	94335	34936	02566	80972	08188
05	95068	88628	35911	14530	33020	80428	33936	31855	34334	64865
06	54463	47237	73800	91017	36239	71824	83671	39892	60518	37092
07	16874	62677	57412	13215	31389	62233	80827	73917	82802	84420
08	92494	63157	76593	91316	03505	72389	96363	52887	01087	66091
09	15669	56689	35682	40844	53256	81872	35213	09840	34471	74441
10	99116	75486	84989	23476	52967	67104	39495	39100	17217	74073
11	15696	10703	65178	90637	63110	17622	53988	71087	84148	11670
12	97720	15369	51269	69620	03388	13699	33423	67453	43269	56720
13	11666	13841	71681	98000	35979	39719	81899	07449	47985	46967
14	71628	73130	78783	75691	41632	09847	61547	18707	85489	69944
15	40501	51089	99943	91843	41995	88931	73631	69361	05375	15417
16	22518	55576	98215	82068	10798	86211	36584	67466	69373	40054
17	75112	30485	62173	02132	14878	92879	22281	16783	86352	00077
18	80327	02671	98191	84342	90813	49268	94551	15496	20168	09271
19	60251	45548	02146	05597	48228	81366	34598	72856	66762	17002
20	57430	82270	10421	00540	43648	75888	66049	21511	47676	33444
21	73528	39559	34434	88586	54086	71693	43132	14414	79949	85193
22	25991	65959	70769	64721	86413	33475	42740	06175	82758	66248
23	78388	16638	09134	59980	63806	48472	39318	35434	24057	74739
24	12477	09965	96657	57994	59439	76330	24596	77515	09577	91871
25	83266	32883	42451	15579	38155	29793	40914	65990	16255	17777
26	76970	80876	10237	39515	79152	74798	39357	09054	73579	92359
27	37074	65198	44785	68624	98336	84481	97610	78735	46703	98265
28	83712	06514	30101	78295	54656	85417	43189	60048	72781	72606
29	20287	56862	69727	94443	64936	08366	27227	05158	50326	59566
30	74261	32592	86538	27041	65172	85532	07571	80609	39285	65340
31	64081	49863	08478	96001	18888	14810	70545	89755	59064	07210
32	05617	75818	47750	67814	29575	10526	66192	44464	27058	40467
33	26793	74951	95466	74307	13330	42664	85515	20632	05497	33625
34	65988	72850	48737	54719	52056	01596	03845	35067	03134	70322
35	27366	42271	44300	73399	21105	03280	73457	43093	05192	48657
36	56760	10909	98147	34736	33863	95256	12731	66598	50771	83665
37	72880	43338	93643	58904	59543	23943	11231	83268	65938	81581
38	77888	38100	03062	58103	47961	83841	25878	23746	55903	44115
39	28440	07819	21580	51459	47971	29882	13990	29226	23608	15873
40	63525	94441	77033	12147	51054	49955	58312	76923	96071	05813
41	47606	93410	16359	89033	89696	47231	64498	31776	05383	39902
42	52669	45030	96279	14709	52372	87832	02735	50803	72744	88208
43	16738	60159	07425	62369	07515	82721	37875	71153	21315	00132
44	59348	11695	45751	15865	74739	05572	32688	20271	65128	14551
45	12900	71775	29845	60774	94924	21810	38636	33717	67598	82521
46	75086	23537	49939	33595	13484	97588	28617	17979	70749	35234
47	99495	51534	29181	09993	38190	42553	68922	52125	91077	40197
48	26075	31671	45386	36583	93459	48599	52022	41330	60651	91321
49	13636	93596	23377	51133	95126	61496	42474	45141	46660	42338

TABLE A.1   Continued

	00–04	05–09	10–14	15–19	20–24	25–29	30–34	35–39	40–44	45–49
50	64249	63664	39652	40646	97306	31741	07294	84149	46797	82487
51	26538	44249	04050	48174	65570	44072	40192	51153	11397	58212
52	05845	00512	78630	55328	18116	69296	91705	86224	29503	57071
53	74897	68373	67359	51014	33510	83048	17056	72506	82949	54600
54	20872	54570	35017	88132	25730	22626	86723	91691	13191	77212
55	31432	96156	89177	75541	81355	24480	77243	76690	42507	84362
56	66890	61505	01240	00660	05873	13568	76082	79172	57913	93448
57	41894	57790	79970	33106	86904	48119	52503	24130	72824	21627
58	11303	87118	81471	52936	08555	28420	49416	44448	04269	27029
59	54374	57325	16947	45356	78371	10563	97191	53798	12693	27928
60	64852	34421	61046	90849	13966	39810	42699	21753	76192	10508
61	16309	20384	09491	91588	97720	89846	30376	76970	23063	35894
62	42587	37065	24526	72602	57589	98131	37292	05967	26002	51945
63	40177	98590	97161	41682	84533	67588	62036	49967	01990	72308
64	82309	76128	93965	26743	24141	04838	40254	26065	07938	76236
65	79788	68243	59732	04257	27084	14743	17520	94501	55811	76099
66	40538	79000	89559	25026	42274	23489	34502	75508	06059	86682
67	64016	73598	18609	73150	62463	33102	45205	87440	96767	67042
68	49767	12691	17903	93871	99721	79109	09425	26904	07419	76013
69	76974	55108	29795	08404	82684	00497	51126	79935	57450	55671
70	23854	08480	85983	96025	50117	64610	99425	62291	86943	21541
71	68973	70551	25098	78033	98573	79848	31778	29555	61446	23037
72	36444	93600	65350	14971	25325	00427	52073	64280	18847	24768
73	03003	87800	07391	11594	21196	00781	32550	57158	58887	73041
74	17540	26188	36647	78386	04558	61463	57842	90382	77019	24210
75	38916	55809	47982	41968	69760	79422	80154	91486	19180	15100
76	64288	19843	69122	42502	48508	28820	59933	72998	99942	10515
77	86809	51564	38040	39418	49915	19000	58050	16899	79952	57849
78	99800	99566	14742	05028	30033	94889	55381	23656	75787	59223
79	92345	31890	95712	08279	91794	94068	49337	88674	35355	12267
80	90363	65162	32245	82279	79256	80834	06088	99462	56705	06118
81	64437	32242	48431	04835	39070	59702	31508	60935	22390	52246
82	91714	53662	28373	34333	55791	74758	51144	18827	10704	76803
83	20902	17646	31391	31459	33315	03444	55743	74701	58851	27427
84	12217	86007	70371	52281	14510	76094	96579	54853	78339	20839
85	45177	02863	42307	53571	22532	74921	17735	42201	80540	54721
86	28325	90814	08804	52746	47913	54577	47525	77705	95330	21866
87	29019	28776	56116	54791	64604	08815	46049	71186	34650	14994
88	84979	81353	56219	67062	26146	82567	33122	14124	46240	92973
89	50371	26347	48513	63915	11158	25563	91915	18431	92978	11591
90	53422	06825	69711	67950	64716	18003	49581	45378	99878	61130
91	67453	35651	89316	41620	32048	70225	47597	33137	31443	51445
92	07294	85353	74819	23445	68237	07202	99515	62282	53809	26685
93	79544	00302	45338	16015	66613	88968	14595	63836	77716	79596
94	64144	85442	82060	46471	24162	39500	87351	36637	42833	71875
95	90919	11883	58318	00042	52402	28210	34075	33272	00840	73268
96	06670	57353	86275	92276	77591	46924	60839	55437	03183	13191
97	36634	93976	52062	83678	41256	60948	18685	48992	19462	96062
98	75101	72891	85745	67106	26010	62107	60885	37503	55461	71213
99	05112	71222	72654	51583	05228	62056	57390	42746	39272	96659

TABLE A.1 Continued

	50–54	55–59	60–64	65–69	70–74	75–79	80–84	85–89	90–94	95–99
50	32847	31282	03345	89593	69214	70381	78285	20054	91018	16742
51	16916	00041	30236	55023	14253	76582	12092	86533	92426	37655
52	66176	34037	21005	27137	03193	48970	64625	22394	39622	79085
53	46299	13335	12180	16861	38043	59292	62675	63631	37020	78195
54	22847	47839	45385	23289	47526	54098	45683	55849	51575	64689
55	41851	54160	92320	69936	34803	92479	33399	71160	64777	83378
56	28444	59497	91586	95917	68553	28639	06455	34174	11130	91994
57	47520	62378	98855	83174	13088	16561	68559	26679	06238	51254
58	34978	63271	13142	82681	05271	08822	06490	44984	49307	61617
59	37404	80416	69035	92980	49486	74378	75610	74976	70056	15478
60	32400	65482	52099	53676	74648	94148	65095	69597	52771	71551
61	89262	86332	51718	70663	11623	29834	79820	73002	84886	03591
62	86866	09127	98021	03871	27789	58444	44832	36505	40672	30180
63	90814	14833	08759	74645	05046	94056	99094	65091	32663	73040
64	19192	82756	20553	58446	55376	88914	75096	26119	83898	43816
65	77585	52593	56612	95766	10019	29531	73064	20953	53523	58136
66	23757	16364	05096	03192	62386	45389	85332	18877	55710	96459
67	45989	96257	23850	26216	23309	21526	07425	50254	19455	29315
68	92970	94243	07316	41467	64837	52406	25225	51553	31220	14032
69	74346	59596	40088	98176	17896	86900	20249	77753	19099	48885
70	87646	41309	27636	45153	29988	94770	07255	70908	05340	99751
71	50099	71038	45146	06146	55211	99429	43169	66259	99786	59180
72	10127	46900	64984	75348	04115	33624	68774	60013	35515	62556
73	67995	81977	18984	64091	02785	27762	42529	97144	80407	64524
74	26304	80217	84934	82657	69291	35397	98714	35104	08187	48109
75	81994	41070	56642	64091	31229	02595	13513	45148	78722	30144
76	59337	34662	79631	89403	65212	09975	06118	86197	58208	16162
77	51228	10937	62396	81460	47331	91403	95007	06047	16846	64809
78	31089	37995	29577	07828	42272	54016	21950	86192	99046	84864
79	38207	97938	93459	75174	79460	55436	57206	87644	21296	43393
80	88666	31142	09474	89712	63153	62333	42212	06140	42594	43671
81	53365	56134	67582	92557	89520	33452	05134	70628	27612	33738
82	89807	74530	38004	90102	11693	90257	05500	79920	62700	43325
83	18682	81038	85662	90915	91631	22223	91588	80774	07716	12548
84	63571	32579	63942	25371	09234	94592	98475	76884	37635	33608
85	68927	56492	67799	95398	77642	54913	91583	08421	81450	76229
86	56401	63186	39389	88798	31356	89235	97036	32341	33292	73757
87	24333	95603	02359	72942	46287	95382	08452	62862	97869	71775
88	17025	84202	95199	62272	06366	16175	97577	99304	41587	03686
89	02804	08253	52133	20224	68034	50865	57868	22343	55111	03607
90	08298	03879	20995	19850	73090	13191	18963	82244	78479	99121
91	59883	01785	82403	96062	03785	03488	12970	64896	38336	30030
92	46982	06682	62864	91837	74021	89094	39952	64158	79614	78235
93	31121	47266	07661	02051	67599	24471	69843	83696	71402	76287
94	97867	56641	63416	17577	30161	87320	37752	73276	48969	41915
95	57364	86746	08415	14621	49430	22311	15836	72492	49372	44103
96	09559	26263	69511	28064	75999	44540	13337	10918	79846	54809
97	53873	55571	00608	42661	91332	63956	74087	59008	47493	99581
98	35531	19162	86406	05299	77511	24311	57257	22826	77555	05941
99	28229	88629	25695	94932	30721	16197	78742	34974	97528	45447

TABLE A.2   Values of the Correlation Coefficient for Different Levels of Significance

df	.10	.05	.01	.001
			p	
1	.98769	.99692	.99988	.99999
2	.90000	.95000	.99000	.99900
3	.8054	.8783	.95873	.99116
4	.7293	.8114	.91720	.97406
5	.6694	.7545	.8745	.95074
6	.6215	.7067	.8343	.92493
7	.5822	.6664	.7977	.8982
8	.5494	.6319	.7646	.8721
9	.5214	.6021	.7348	.8471
10	.4973	.5760	.7079	.8233
11	.4762	.5529	.6835	.8010
12	.4575	.5324	.6614	.7800
13	.4409	.5139	.6411	.7603
14	.4259	.4973	.6226	.7420
15	.4124	.4821	.6055	.7246
16	.4000	.4683	.5897	.7084
17	.3887	.4555	.5751	.6932
18	.3783	.4438	.5614	.6787
19	.3687	.4329	.5487	.6652
20	.3598	.4227	.5368	.6524
25	.3233	.3809	.4869	.5974
30	.2960	.3494	.4487	.5541
35	.2746	.3246	.4182	.5189
40	.2573	.3044	.3932	.4896
45	.2428	.2875	.3721	.4648
50	.2306	.2732	.3541	.4433
60	.2108	.2500	.3248	.4078
70	.1954	.2319	.3017	.3799
80	.1829	.2172	.2830	.3568
90	.1726	.2050	.2673	.3375
100	.1638	.1946	.2540	.3211

Table A.2 is taken from Table VII of Fisher and Yates: *Statistical Tables for Biological, Agricultural and Medical Research,* published by Longman Group Ltd., London (previously published by Oliver and Boyd, Edinburgh), and by permission of the authors and publishers.

TABLE A.3 Standard Normal Curve Areas

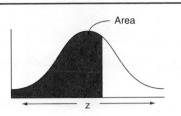

Area

z

z	Area	z	Area	z	Area	z	Area
−3.00	.0013						
−2.99	.0014	−2.64	.0041	−2.29	.0110	−1.94	.0262
−2.98	.0014	−2.63	.0043	−2.28	.0113	−1.93	.0268
−2.97	.0015	−2.62	.0044	−2.27	.0116	−1.92	.0274
−2.96	.0015	−2.61	.0045	−2.26	.0119	−1.91	.0281
−2.95	.0016	−2.60	.0047	−2.25	.0122	−1.90	.0287
−2.94	.0016	−2.59	.0048	−2.24	.0125	−1.89	.0294
−2.93	.0017	−2.58	.0049	−2.23	.0129	−1.88	.0301
−2.92	.0018	−2.57	.0051	−2.22	.0132	−1.87	.0307
−2.91	.0018	−2.56	.0052	−2.21	.0136	−1.86	.0314
−2.90	.0019	−2.55	.0054	−2.20	.0139	−1.85	.0322
−2.89	.0019	−2.54	.0055	−2.19	.0143	−1.84	.0329
−2.88	.0020	−2.53	.0057	−2.18	.0146	−1.83	.0336
−2.87	.0021	−2.52	.0059	−2.17	.0150	−1.82	.0344
−2.86	.0021	−2.51	.0060	−2.16	.0154	−1.81	.0351
−2.85	.0022	−2.50	.0062	−2.15	.0158	−1.80	.0359
−2.84	.0023	−2.49	.0064	−2.14	.0162	−1.79	.0367
−2.83	.0023	−2.48	.0066	−2.13	.0166	−1.78	.0375
−2.82	.0024	−2.47	.0068	−2.12	.0170	−1.77	.0384
−2.81	.0025	−2.46	.0069	−2.11	.0174	−1.76	.0392
−2.80	.0026	−2.45	.0071	−2.10	.0179	−1.75	.0401
−2.79	.0026	−2.44	.0073	−2.09	.0183	−1.74	.0409
−2.78	.0027	−2.43	.0075	−2.08	.0188	−1.73	.0418
−2.77	.0028	−2.42	.0078	−2.07	.0192	−1.72	.0427
−2.76	.0029	−2.41	.0080	−2.06	.0197	−1.71	.0436
−2.75	.0030	−2.40	.0082	−2.05	.0202	−1.70	.0446
−2.74	.0031	−2.39	.0084	−2.04	.0207	−1.69	.0455
−2.73	.0032	−2.38	.0087	−2.03	.0212	−1.68	.0465
−2.72	.0033	−2.37	.0089	−2.02	.0217	−1.67	.0475
−2.71	.0034	−2.36	.0091	−2.01	.0222	−1.66	.0485
−2.70	.0035	−2.35	.0094	−2.00	.0228	−1.65	.0495
−2.69	.0036	−2.34	.0096	−1.99	.0233	−1.64	.0505
−2.68	.0037	−2.33	.0099	−1.98	.0239	−1.63	.0516
−2.67	.0038	−2.32	.0102	−1.97	.0244	−1.62	.0526
−2.66	.0039	−2.31	.0104	−1.96	.0250	−1.61	.0537
−2.65	.0040	−2.30	.0107	−1.95	.0256	−1.60	.0548

TABLE A.3   Continued

z	Area	z	Area	z	Area	z	Area
−1.59	.0559	−1.19	.1170	−0.79	.2148	−0.39	.3483
−1.58	.0571	−1.18	.1190	−0.78	.2177	−0.38	.3520
−1.57	.0582	−1.17	.1210	−0.77	.2206	−0.37	.3557
−1.56	.0594	−1.16	.1230	−0.76	.2236	−0.36	.3594
−1.55	.0606	−1.15	.1251	−0.75	.2266	−0.35	.3632
−1.54	.0618	−1.14	.1271	−0.74	.2296	−0.34	.3669
−1.53	.0630	−1.13	.1292	−0.73	.2327	−0.33	.3707
−1.52	.0643	−1.12	.1314	−0.72	.2358	−0.32	.3745
−1.51	.0655	−1.11	.1335	−0.71	.2389	−0.31	.3783
−1.50	.0668	−1.10	.1357	−0.70	.2420	−0.30	.3821
−1.49	.0681	−1.09	.1379	−0.69	.2451	−0.29	.3859
−1.48	.0694	−1.08	.1401	−0.68	.2483	−0.28	.3897
−1.47	.0708	−1.07	.1423	−0.67	.2514	−0.27	.3936
−1.46	.0721	−1.06	.1446	−0.66	.2546	−0.26	.3974
−1.45	.0735	−1.05	.1469	−0.65	.2578	−0.25	.4013
−1.44	.0749	−1.04	.1492	−0.64	.2611	−0.24	.4052
−1.43	.0764	−1.03	.1515	−0.63	.2643	−0.23	.4090
−1.42	.0778	−1.02	.1539	−0.62	.2676	−0.22	.4129
−1.41	.0793	−1.01	.1562	−0.61	.2709	−0.21	.4168
−1.40	.0808	−1.00	.1587	−0.60	.2743	−0.20	.4207
−1.39	.0823	−0.99	.1611	−0.59	.2776	−0.19	.4247
−1.38	.0838	−0.98	.1635	−0.58	.2810	−0.18	.4286
−1.37	.0853	−0.97	.1660	−0.57	.2843	−0.17	.4325
−1.36	.0869	−0.96	.1685	−0.56	.2877	−0.16	.4364
−1.35	.0885	−0.95	.1711	−0.55	.2912	−0.15	.4404
−1.34	.0901	−0.94	.1736	−0.54	.2946	−0.14	.4443
−1.33	.0918	−0.93	.1762	−0.53	.2981	−0.13	.4483
−1.32	.0934	−0.92	.1788	−0.52	.3015	−0.12	.4522
−1.31	.0951	−0.91	.1814	−0.51	.3050	−0.11	.4562
−1.30	.0968	−0.90	.1841	−0.50	.3085	−0.10	.4602
−1.29	.0985	−0.89	.1867	−0.49	.3121	−0.09	.4641
−1.28	.1003	−0.88	.1894	−0.48	.3156	−0.08	.4681
−1.27	.1020	−0.87	.1922	−0.47	.3192	−0.07	.4721
−1.26	.1038	−0.86	.1949	−0.46	.3228	−0.06	.4761
−1.25	.1056	−0.85	.1977	−0.45	.3264	−0.05	.4801
−1.24	.1075	−0.84	.2005	−0.44	.3300	−0.04	.4840
−1.23	.1093	−0.83	.2033	−0.43	.3336	−0.03	.4880
−1.22	.1112	−0.82	.2061	−0.42	.3372	−0.02	.4920
−1.21	.1131	−0.81	.2090	−0.41	.3409	−0.01	.4960
−1.20	.1151	−0.80	.2119	−0.40	.3446	0.00	.5000

TABLE A.3 Continued

z	Area	z	Area	z	Area	z	Area
0.01	.5040	0.41	.6591	0.81	.7910	1.21	.8869
0.02	.5080	0.42	.6628	0.82	.7939	1.22	.8888
0.03	.5120	0.43	.6664	0.83	.7967	1.23	.8907
0.04	.5160	0.44	.6700	0.84	.7995	1.24	.8925
0.05	.5199	0.45	.6736	0.85	.8023	1.25	.8944
0.06	.5239	0.46	.6772	0.86	.8051	1.26	.8962
0.07	.5279	0.47	.6808	0.87	.8078	1.27	.8980
0.08	.5319	0.48	.6844	0.88	.8106	1.28	.8997
0.09	.5359	0.49	.6879	0.89	.8133	1.29	.9015
0.10	.5398	0.50	.6915	0.90	.8159	1.30	.9032
0.11	.5438	0.51	.6950	0.91	.8186	1.31	.9049
0.12	.5478	0.52	.6985	0.92	.8212	1.32	.9066
0.13	.5517	0.53	.7019	0.93	.8238	1.33	.9082
0.14	.5557	0.54	.7054	0.94	.8264	1.34	.9099
0.15	.5596	0.55	.7088	0.95	.8289	1.35	.9115
0.16	.5636	0.56	.7123	0.96	.8315	1.36	.9131
0.17	.5675	0.57	.7157	0.97	.8340	1.37	.9147
0.18	.5714	0.58	.7190	0.98	.8365	1.38	.9162
0.19	.5753	0.59	.7224	0.99	.8389	1.39	.9177
0.20	.5793	0.60	.7257	1.00	.8413	1.40	.9192
0.21	.5832	0.61	.7291	1.01	.8438	1.41	.9207
0.22	.5871	0.62	.7324	1.02	.8461	1.42	.9222
0.23	.5910	0.63	.7357	1.03	.8485	1.43	.9236
0.24	.5948	0.64	.7389	1.04	.8508	1.44	.9251
0.25	.5987	0.65	.7422	1.05	.8531	1.45	.9265
0.26	.6026	0.66	.7454	1.06	.8554	1.46	.9279
0.27	.6064	0.67	.7486	1.07	.8577	1.47	.9292
0.28	.6103	0.68	.7517	1.08	.8599	1.48	.9306
0.29	.6141	0.69	.7549	1.09	.8621	1.49	.9319
0.30	.6179	0.70	.7580	1.10	.8643	1.50	.9332
0.31	.6217	0.71	.7611	1.11	.8665	1.51	.9345
0.32	.6255	0.72	.7642	1.12	.8686	1.52	.9357
0.33	.6293	0.73	.7673	1.13	.8708	1.53	.9370
0.34	.6331	0.74	.7704	1.14	.8729	1.54	.9382
0.35	.6368	0.75	.7734	1.15	.8749	1.55	.9394
0.36	.6406	0.76	.7764	1.16	.8770	1.56	.9406
0.37	.6443	0.77	.7794	1.17	.8790	1.57	.9418
0.38	.6480	0.78	.7823	1.18	.8810	1.58	.9429
0.39	.6517	0.79	.7852	1.19	.8830	1.59	.9441
0.40	.6554	0.80	.7881	1.20	.8849	1.60	.9452

TABLE A.3   Continued

z	Area	z	Area	z	Area	z	Area
1.61	.9463	1.96	.9750	2.31	.9896	2.66	.9961
1.62	.9474	1.97	.9756	2.32	.9898	2.67	.9962
1.63	.9484	1.98	.9761	2.33	.9901	2.68	.9963
1.64	.9495	1.99	.9767	2.34	.9904	2.69	.9964
1.65	.9505	2.00	.9772	2.35	.9906	2.70	.9965
1.66	.9515	2.01	.9778	2.36	.9909	2.71	.9966
1.67	.9525	2.02	.9783	2.37	.9911	2.72	.9967
1.68	.9535	2.03	.9788	2.38	.9913	2.73	.9968
1.69	.9545	2.04	.9793	2.39	.9916	2.74	.9969
1.70	.9554	2.05	.9798	2.40	.9918	2.75	.9970
1.71	.9564	2.06	.9803	2.41	.9920	2.76	.9971
1.72	.9573	2.07	.9808	2.42	.9922	2.77	.9972
1.73	.9582	2.08	.9812	2.43	.9925	2.78	.9973
1.74	.9591	2.09	.9817	2.44	.9927	2.79	.9974
1.75	.9599	2.10	.9821	2.45	.9929	2.80	.9974
1.76	.9608	2.11	.9826	2.46	.9931	2.81	.9975
1.77	.9616	2.12	.9830	2.47	.9932	2.82	.9976
1.78	.9625	2.13	.9834	2.48	.9934	2.83	.9977
1.79	.9633	2.14	.9838	2.49	.9936	2.84	.9977
1.80	.9641	2.15	.9842	2.50	.9938	2.85	.9978
1.81	.9649	2.16	.9846	2.51	.9940	2.86	.9979
1.82	.9656	2.17	.9850	2.52	.9941	2.87	.9979
1.83	.9664	2.18	.9854	2.53	.9943	2.88	.9980
1.84	.9671	2.19	.9857	2.54	.9945	2.89	.9981
1.85	.9678	2.20	.9861	2.55	.9946	2.90	.9981
1.86	.9686	2.21	.9864	2.56	.9948	2.91	.9982
1.87	.9693	2.22	.9868	2.57	.9949	2.92	.9982
1.88	.9699	2.23	.9871	2.58	.9951	2.93	.9983
1.89	.9706	2.24	.9875	2.59	.9952	2.94	.9984
1.90	.9713	2.25	.9878	2.60	.9953	2.95	.9984
1.91	.9719	2.26	.9881	2.61	.9955	2.96	.9985
1.92	.9726	2.27	.9884	2.62	.9956	2.97	.9985
1.93	.9732	2.28	.9887	2.63	.9957	2.98	.9986
1.94	.9738	2.29	.9890	2.64	.9959	2.99	.9986
1.95	.9744	2.30	.9893	2.65	.9960	3.00	.9987

TABLE A.4   Distribution of t

df	.20	.10	.05	.02	.01	.001
			PROBABILITY			
1	3.078	6.314	12.706	31.821	63.657	636.619
2	1.886	2.920	4.303	6.965	9.925	31.598
3	1.638	2.353	3.182	4.541	5.841	12.941
4	1.533	2.132	2.776	3.747	4.604	8.610
5	1.476	2.015	2.571	3.365	4.032	6.859
6	1.440	1.943	2.447	3.143	3.707	5.959
7	1.415	1.895	2.365	2.998	3.499	5.405
8	1.397	1.860	2.306	2.896	3.355	5.041
9	1.383	1.833	2.262	2.821	3.250	4.781
10	1.372	1.812	2.228	2.764	3.169	4.587
11	1.363	1.796	2.201	2.718	3.106	4.437
12	1.356	1.782	2.179	2.681	3.055	4.318
13	1.350	1.771	2.160	2.650	3.012	4.221
14	1.345	1.761	2.145	2.624	2.977	4.140
15	1.341	1.753	2.131	2.602	2.947	4.073
16	1.337	1.746	2.120	2.583	2.921	4.015
17	1.333	1.740	2.110	2.567	2.898	3.965
18	1.330	1.734	2.101	2.552	2.878	3.922
19	1.328	1.729	2.093	2.539	2.861	3.883
20	1.325	1.725	2.086	2.528	2.845	3.850
21	1.323	1.721	2.080	2.518	2.831	3.819
22	1.321	1.717	2.074	2.508	2.819	3.792
23	1.319	1.714	2.069	2.500	2.807	3.767
24	1.318	1.711	2.064	2.492	2.797	3.745
25	1.316	1.708	2.060	2.485	2.787	3.725
26	1.315	1.706	2.056	2.479	2.779	3.707
27	1.314	1.703	2.052	2.473	2.771	3.690
28	1.313	1.701	2.048	2.467	2.763	3.674
29	1.311	1.699	2.045	2.462	2.756	3.659
30	1.310	1.697	2.042	2.457	2.750	3.646
40	1.303	1.684	2.021	2.423	2.704	3.551
60	1.296	1.671	2.000	2.390	2.660	3.460
120	1.289	1.658	1.980	2.358	2.617	3.373
∞	1.282	1.645	1.960	2.326	2.576	3.291

Source: R. A. Fisher and F. Yates, *Statistical Tables for Biological, Agricultural, and Medical Research,* published by Longman Group Ltd., London (previously published by Oliver and Boyd, Edinburgh), and by permission of the authors and publishers.

TABLE A.5   Distribution of F

$p = .10$

n_2**	n_1*					
	1	2	3	4	5	6
4	4.54	4.32	4.19	4.11	4.05	4.01
5	4.06	3.78	3.62	3.52	3.45	3.40
6	3.78	3.46	3.29	3.18	3.11	3.05
7	3.59	3.26	3.07	2.96	2.88	2.83
8	3.46	3.11	2.92	2.81	2.73	2.67
9	3.36	3.01	2.81	2.69	2.61	2.55
10	3.28	2.92	2.73	2.61	2.52	2.46
11	3.23	2.86	2.66	2.54	2.45	2.39
12	3.18	2.81	2.61	2.48	2.39	2.33
13	3.14	2.76	2.56	2.43	2.35	2.28
14	3.10	2.73	2.52	2.39	2.31	2.24
15	3.07	2.70	2.49	2.36	2.27	2.21
16	3.05	2.67	2.46	2.33	2.24	2.18
17	3.03	2.64	2.44	2.31	2.22	2.15
18	3.01	2.62	2.42	2.29	2.20	2.13
19	2.99	2.61	2.40	2.27	2.18	2.11
20	2.97	2.59	2.38	2.25	2.16	2.09
21	2.96	2.57	2.36	2.23	2.14	2.08
22	2.95	2.56	2.35	2.22	2.13	2.06
23	2.94	2.55	2.34	2.21	2.11	2.05
24	2.93	2.54	2.33	2.19	2.10	2.04
25	2.92	2.53	2.32	2.18	2.09	2.02
26	2.91	2.52	2.31	2.17	2.08	2.01
27	2.90	2.51	2.30	2.17	2.07	2.00
28	2.89	2.50	2.29	2.16	2.06	2.00
29	2.89	2.50	2.28	2.15	2.06	1.99
30	2.88	2.49	2.28	2.14	2.05	1.98
40	2.84	2.44	2.23	2.09	2.00	1.93
60	2.79	2.39	2.18	2.04	1.95	1.87
120	2.75	2.35	2.13	1.99	1.90	1.82
∞	2.71	2.30	2.08	1.94	1.85	1.77

*n_1 = degrees of freedom for the mean square between
**n_2 = degrees of freedom for the mean square within

Source: From Table V of Fisher and Yates: *Statistical Tables for Biological, Agricultural and Medical Research,* published by Longman Group Ltd., London (previously published by Oliver and Boyd, Edinburgh), and by permission of the authors and publishers.

TABLE A.5 Continued

$p = .05$

n_2^{**}	n_1^*					
	1	2	3	4	5	6
4	7.71	6.94	6.59	6.39	6.26	6.16
5	6.61	5.79	5.41	5.19	5.05	4.95
6	5.99	5.14	4.76	4.53	4.39	4.28
7	5.59	4.74	4.35	4.12	3.97	3.87
8	5.32	4.46	4.07	3.84	3.69	3.58
9	5.12	4.26	3.86	3.63	3.48	3.37
10	4.96	4.10	3.71	3.48	3.33	3.22
11	4.84	3.98	3.59	3.36	3.20	3.09
12	4.75	3.88	3.49	3.26	3.11	3.00
13	4.67	3.80	3.41	3.18	3.02	2.92
14	4.60	3.74	3.34	3.11	2.96	2.85
15	4.54	3.68	3.29	3.06	2.90	2.79
16	4.49	3.63	3.24	3.01	2.85	2.74
17	4.45	3.59	3.20	2.96	2.81	2.70
18	4.41	3.55	3.16	2.93	2.77	2.66
19	4.38	3.52	3.13	2.90	2.74	2.63
20	4.35	3.49	3.10	2.87	2.71	2.60
21	4.32	3.47	3.07	2.84	2.68	2.57
22	4.30	3.44	3.05	2.82	2.66	2.55
23	4.28	3.42	3.03	2.80	2.64	2.53
24	4.26	3.40	3.01	2.78	2.62	2.51
25	4.24	3.38	2.99	2.76	2.60	2.49
26	4.22	3.37	2.98	2.74	2.59	2.47
27	4.21	3.35	2.96	2.73	2.57	2.46
28	4.20	3.34	2.95	2.71	2.56	2.44
29	4.18	3.33	2.93	2.70	2.54	2.43
30	4.17	3.32	2.92	2.69	2.53	2.42
40	4.08	3.23	2.84	2.61	2.45	2.34
60	4.00	3.15	2.76	2.52	2.37	2.25
120	3.92	3.07	2.68	2.45	2.29	2.17
∞	3.84	2.99	2.60	2.37	2.21	2.10

$^*n_1$ = degrees of freedom for the mean square between
$^{**}n_2$ = degrees of freedom for the mean square within

TABLE A.5   Continued

$p = .01$

n_2**	n_1*					
	1	2	3	4	5	6
4	21.20	18.00	16.69	15.98	15.52	15.21
5	16.26	13.27	12.06	11.39	10.97	10.67
6	13.74	10.92	9.78	9.15	8.75	8.47
7	12.25	9.55	8.45	7.85	7.46	7.19
8	11.26	8.65	7.59	7.01	6.63	6.37
9	10.56	8.02	6.99	6.42	6.06	5.80
10	10.04	7.56	6.55	5.99	5.64	5.39
11	9.65	7.20	6.22	5.67	5.32	5.07
12	9.33	6.93	5.95	5.41	5.06	4.82
13	9.07	6.70	5.74	5.20	4.86	4.62
14	8.86	6.51	5.56	5.03	4.69	4.46
15	8.68	6.36	5.42	4.89	4.56	4.32
16	8.53	6.23	5.29	4.77	4.44	4.20
17	8.40	6.11	5.18	4.67	4.34	4.10
18	8.28	6.01	5.09	4.58	4.25	4.01
19	8.18	5.93	5.01	4.50	4.17	3.94
20	8.10	5.85	4.94	4.43	4.10	3.87
21	8.02	5.78	4.87	4.37	4.04	3.81
22	7.94	5.72	4.82	4.31	3.99	3.76
23	7.88	5.66	4.76	4.26	3.94	3.71
24	7.82	5.61	4.72	4.22	3.90	3.67
25	7.77	5.57	4.68	4.18	3.86	3.63
26	7.72	5.53	4.64	4.14	3.82	3.59
27	7.68	5.49	4.60	4.11	3.78	3.56
28	7.64	5.45	4.57	4.07	3.75	3.53
29	7.60	5.42	4.54	4.04	3.73	3.50
30	7.56	5.39	4.51	4.02	3.70	3.47
40	7.31	5.18	4.31	3.83	3.51	3.29
60	7.08	4.98	4.13	3.65	3.34	3.12
120	6.85	4.79	3.95	3.48	3.17	2.96
∞	6.64	4.60	3.78	3.32	3.02	2.80

*n_1 = degrees of freedom for the mean square between
**n_2 = degrees of freedom for the mean square within

TABLE A.5 Continued

$p = .001$

n_2^{**}	n_1^*					
	1	2	3	4	5	6
4	74.14	61.25	56.18	53.44	51.71	50.53
5	47.18	37.12	33.20	31.09	29.75	28.84
6	35.51	27.00	23.70	21.92	20.81	20.03
7	29.25	21.69	18.77	17.19	16.21	15.52
8	25.42	18.49	15.83	14.39	13.49	12.86
9	22.86	16.39	13.90	12.56	11.71	11.13
10	21.04	14.91	12.55	11.28	10.48	9.92
11	19.69	13.81	11.56	10.35	9.58	9.05
12	18.64	12.97	10.80	9.63	8.89	8.38
13	17.81	12.31	10.21	9.07	8.35	7.86
14	17.14	11.78	9.73	8.62	7.92	7.43
15	16.59	11.34	9.34	8.25	7.57	7.09
16	16.12	10.97	9.00	7.94	7.27	6.81
17	15.72	10.66	8.73	7.68	7.02	6.56
18	15.38	10.39	8.49	7.46	6.81	6.35
19	15.08	10.16	8.28	7.26	6.62	6.18
20	14.82	9.95	8.10	7.10	6.46	6.02
21	14.59	9.77	7.94	6.95	6.32	5.88
22	14.38	9.61	7.80	6.81	6.19	5.76
23	14.19	9.47	7.67	6.69	6.08	5.65
24	14.03	9.34	7.55	6.59	5.98	5.55
25	13.88	9.22	7.45	6.49	5.88	5.46
26	13.74	9.12	7.36	6.41	5.80	5.38
27	13.61	9.02	7.27	6.33	5.73	5.31
28	13.50	8.93	7.19	6.25	5.66	5.24
29	13.39	8.85	7.12	6.19	5.59	5.18
30	13.29	8.77	7.05	6.12	5.53	5.12
40	12.61	8.25	6.60	5.70	5.13	4.73
60	11.97	7.76	6.17	5.31	4.76	4.37
120	11.38	7.32	5.79	4.95	4.42	4.04
∞	10.83	6.91	5.42	4.62	4.10	3.74

*n_1 = degrees of freedom for the mean square between
**n_2 = degrees of freedom for the mean square within

TABLE A.6   Distribution of χ^2

df	.10	.05	.01	.001
1	2.706	3.841	6.635	10.827
2	4.605	5.991	9.210	13.815
3	6.251	7.815	11.345	16.266
4	7.779	9.488	13.277	18.467
5	9.236	11.070	15.086	20.515
6	10.645	12.592	16.812	22.457
7	12.017	14.067	18.475	24.322
8	13.362	15.507	20.090	26.125
9	14.684	16.919	21.666	27.877
10	15.987	18.307	23.209	29.588
11	17.275	19.675	24.725	31.264
12	18.549	21.026	26.217	32.909
13	19.812	22.362	27.688	34.528
14	21.064	23.685	29.141	36.123
15	22.307	24.996	30.578	37.697
16	23.542	26.296	32.000	39.252
17	24.769	27.587	33.409	40.790
18	25.989	28.869	34.805	42.312
19	27.204	30.144	36.191	43.820
20	28.412	31.410	37.566	45.315
21	29.615	32.671	38.932	46.797
22	30.813	33.924	40.289	48.268
23	32.007	35.172	41.638	49.728
24	33.196	36.415	42.980	51.179
25	34.382	37.652	44.314	52.620
26	35.563	38.885	45.642	54.052
27	36.741	40.113	46.963	55.476
28	37.916	41.337	48.278	56.893
29	39.087	42.557	49.588	58.302
30	40.256	43.773	50.892	59.703
32	42.585	46.194	53.486	62.487
34	44.903	48.602	56.061	65.247
36	47.212	50.999	58.619	67.985
38	49.513	53.384	61.162	70.703
40	51.805	55.759	63.691	73.402
42	54.090	58.124	66.206	76.084
44	56.369	60.481	68.710	78.750
46	58.641	62.830	71.201	81.400
48	60.907	65.171	73.683	84.037
50	63.167	67.505	76.154	86.661

Source: From Table IV of Fisher and Yates: *Statistical Tables for Biological, Agricultural and Medical Research,* published by Longman Group Ltd., London (previously published by Oliver and Boyd, Edinburgh), and by permission of the authors and publishers.

MATH REVIEW

Name: _____ Date: _____

Worksheet 1: MATH REVIEW: ORDER OF OPERATIONS

RIDDLE: Why did the bored man cut a hole in the carpet?

Directions: To find the answer to the riddle, write the answers to the problems on the lines. The letter in the solution section beside the answer to the first problem is the first letter in the answer to the riddle, the letter beside the answer to the second problem is the second letter, and so on.

1. 5 x 10 + 6 x 2 = _____

2. 3 + 4 x 9 = _____

3. (9 + 28) x 6 = _____

4. 159 − 66 x 2 = _____

5. 15 x 14 − 8 x 20 = _____

6. 19 − 5 + 2 x 3 = _____

7. 70 − 5 x 3 x 4 = _____

8. 6 + 8 x 1 x 5 = _____

9. 33/1 + 1 x 3 = _____

10. 8/4 + (6)(0) = _____

11. 169/(12 + 1) = _____

12. (2 + 3 + 4)/3 = _____

13. (2 + 18)/(9 − 5) = _____

14. (1 + 5)(3) + (7)(2) = _____

15. (9 + 9)(10 − 9)(2) = _____

16. (15 − 4)(21/7)(63 − 59) = ____

17. (3)(1)(1) + (6/2)(9) = _____

SOLUTION SECTION:

112(B)	62(T)	39(O)	10(H)	780(Y)	222(S)	3(O)
2(L)	63(A)	27(E)	177(Z)	186(X)	13(O)	5(R)
32(S)	50(E)	4,040(D)	20(T)	46(E)	30(W)	70(F)
132(O)	102(K)	36(F)	324(H)	187(B)	1(J)	48(I)

Write the answer to the riddle here, putting one letter on each line:

___ ___   ___ ___ ___   ___ ___ ___

___ ___ ___ ___ ___   ___ ___ ___

Name: _____   Date: _____

Worksheet 2: MATH REVIEW: NEGATIVES

RIDDLE: What did the owner of the wreck of a car say about the noise it makes?

Directions: To find the answer to the riddle, write the answers to the problems on the lines. The word in the solution section beside the answer to the first problem is the first word in the answer to the riddle, the word beside the answer to the second problem is the second word, and so on.

1. $(-10)(-2)$ = _____   7. $19 + -3$ = _____   13. $(-15)(-33)$ = _____

2. $(-5)(47)$ = _____   8. $-28 + -28$ = _____   14. $(-11)(44)$ = _____

3. $(6)(-16)$ = _____   9. $-88 + 18$ = _____   15. $-2178/33$ = _____

4. $15/-3$ = _____   10. $15 - -15$ = _____   16. $188 + -99$ = _____

5. $-144/12$ = _____   11. $-29 - 14$ = _____   17. $-279 + -188$ = _____

6. $-169/-13$ = _____   12. $-30 - -29$ = _____   18. $-399 - 59$ = _____

SOLUTION SECTION:

−20(GARAGE)	235(TWO)	340(SKY)	20(THERE'S)	−96(ONE)
−235(ONLY)	96(ROAD)	−56(THAT)	−70(DOESN'T)	−1(SORT)
−458(HORN)	−467(THE)	5(IS)	−12(ON)	−5(THING) 13(MY)
−13(USE)	16(CAR)	12(BE)	30(MAKE)	0(FIX) 22(BUS)
495(OF)	−484(NOISE)	56(AN)	−66(AND)	70(TRANSPORTATION)
89(THAT'S)	−43(SOME)		−15(ALWAYS)	−59(HIGHWAY)
−495(MECHANIC)	66(BROKEN)		484(STRANDED)	467(FREEWAY)

Write the answer to the riddle here, putting one word on each line:

_____ _____ _____ _____ _____ _____

_____ _____ _____ _____ _____ _____

_____ _____ _____ _____ _____ _____

Name: _____ Date: _____

Worksheet 3: MATH REVIEW: ROUNDING

RIDDLE: What did the psychologist put on a sign in her office to make her patients pay?

Directions: To find the answer to the riddle, write the answers to the problems on the lines. The word in the solution beside the answer to the first problem is the first word in the answer to the riddle, the word beside the answer to the second problem is the second word, and so on.

Round as usual except when rounding off a number ending in a five (5). If the number immediately preceding a five is odd, round up. If the number immediately preceding a five is even, round down. Another way to state this principle is: "round to the nearest even number all numbers ending in 5." For example, 4.85 rounds to 4.8; 4.75 rounds to 4.8. Notice, however, that 4.851, which ends in a value greater than "5," rounds to 4.9.

1. Round 10.543 to the nearest hundredth: _____

2. Round 8.67 to the nearest tenth: _____

3. Round 8.4 to the nearest whole number: _____

4. Round 9.8452 to the nearest thousandth: _____

5. Round 15.839 to the nearest tenth: _____

6. Round 29.5 to the nearest whole number: _____

7. Round 15.86 to the nearest tenth: _____

8. Round 3.945 to the nearest hundredth: _____

9. Round 8.45 to the nearest tenth: _____

10. Round 10.555555 to the nearest hundredth: _____

SOLUTION SECTION:

29(CRAZY)   15.9(THE)   8.7(THE)   30(PAY)   3.95(AM)   8(AMNESIA)

10.56(ADVANCE) 8.4(IN) 8.5(ONLY) 3.94(PSYCHOLOGIST) 15.8(MUST)

9845(IS)   15.4(BILL)   9.85(HELPS)   9.846(NEVER)   10(LOVING)

9.845(PATIENTS) 9(LIFE) 10.54(ALL) 10.5(COUNSELING) 4(DISTURBED)

Write the answer to the riddle here, putting one word on each line:

_____   _____   _____   _____   _____   _____

_____   _____   _____   _____

Name: _____   Date: _____

Worksheet 4: MATH REVIEW: DECIMALS

RIDDLE: What did the bore do to help the party?

Directions: To find the answer to the riddle, write the answers to the problems on the lines. The letter in the solution section beside the answer to the first problem is the first letter in the answer to the riddle, the letter beside the answer to the second problem is the second letter, and so on.

   If an answer has more than two decimal places, round to two.

1. 0.02 multiplied by 1 = _____

2. 1.1 multiplied by 1.11 = _____

3. 5.999 multiplied by 0 = _____

4. 3.77 multiplied by 4.69 = _____

5. 12.4 divided into 169.38 = _____

6. 15.9 divided by 1 = _____

7. 12.1 plus 99.98 = _____

8. 3.11 plus 8.99 = _____

9. 18.3 subtracted from 25.46 = _____

10. 10.01 minus 8.873 = _____

SOLUTION SECTION:

1.22(E)	0.2(C)	0.14(X)	7.16(M)	71.6(D)	0(W)
6.00(K)	2.11(F)	0.02(H)	112.08(H)	101.19(P)	
15.9(T)	1.59(B)	13.66(N)	1.21(J)	17.68(E)	
1.366(G)	12.10(O)	0.177(R)	1.14(E)	1.111(S)	

Write the answer to the riddle here, putting one letter on each line:

___ ___   ___ ___ ___ ___   ___ ___ ___ ___

Name: _____   Date: _____

Worksheet 5: MATH REVIEW: FRACTIONS AND DECIMALS

RIDDLE: Why should you respect the lily?

Directions: To find the answer to the riddle, write the answers to the problems on the lines. The word in the solution section beside the answer to the first problem is the first word in the answer to the riddle, the word beside the answer to the second problem is the second word, and so on. Express fractions in lowest terms.

1. $1/5 + 3/5$ = _____   5. $2/3 \times 2/3$ = _____

2. $1/5 + 1/10$ = _____   6. $2/5 \times 4/7$ = _____

3. $3/9 - 1/9$ = _____   7. $2/9$ divided by $1/9$ = _____

4. $1 - 7/8$ = _____   8. 5 divided into $2/3$ = _____

9. What is the decimal equivalent of $1/2$? = _____

10. What is the decimal equivalent of $3/4$? = _____

11. What is the decimal equivalent of 2 and $2/3$? = _____

12. What is the decimal equivalent of 2 and $3/4$? = _____

13. What is the decimal equivalent of 2 and $1/10$? = _____

14. What fraction corresponds to 0.2? = _____

15. What fraction corresponds to 0.11? = _____

16. What fraction corresponds to 0.555? = _____

SOLUTION SECTION:

4/5(NEVER)   2/5(SEE)   3/10(LOOK)   11/20(IS)   0.5(DAY)

0.55(FLOWERS)   2/3(FLORIST)   4/9(A)   2/9(DOWN)   2.1(LOOK)

1/5(DOWN)   11/100(ON)   2/35(CLEAN)   8/35(LILY)   1/8(ON)

2/81(HOPE)   2(BECAUSE)   2/15(ONE)   0.75(A)   2.67(LILY)

2.75(WILL)   111/200(YOU)   8/8(EASTER)   3 1/3(BEAUTIFUL)

Write the answer to the riddle here, putting one word on each line:

_____ _____ _____ _____ _____ _____ _____ _____

_____ _____ _____ _____ _____ _____ _____ _____

Name: _____   Date: _____

Worksheet 6: MATH REVIEW: ALGEBRAIC MANIPULATIONS

RIDDLE: When do actors and actresses get stage fright?

Directions: To find the answer to the riddle, write "T" for "true" or "F" for "false" on the line to the left of each statement. The word at the end of the first true statement is the first word in the answer to the riddle, the word at the end of the second true statement is the second word, and so on.

All variables are distinct from one another; that is, no variable equals any other variable.

_____ 1. If $A = C/D$, then $C = (A)(D)$ (WHEN)

_____ 2. If $A = C/D$, then $D = C/A$ (THEY)

_____ 3. If $P/B = F$, then $P = F/B$ (GET)

_____ 4. If $X + Y = 10$, then $X = 10 - Y$ (SEE)

_____ 5. If $25 = A + B$, then $A = 25 - B$ (AN)

_____ 6. If $X + 25 = W$, then $X = W + 25$ (CURTAIN)

_____ 7. If $A = C - D$, then $D = C + A$ (APPLAUSE)

_____ 8. If $A - D = F$, then $A = F + D$ (EGG)

_____ 9. If $A = F - G - H$, then $F = A - G - H$ (STAGE)

_____ 10. If $(B)(C) = P$, then $B = P/C$ (OR)

_____ 11. If $Y = (B)(F)$, then $B = F/Y$ (SCRIPT)

_____ 12. If $X = (N)(B)(C)$, then $B = X/(N)(C)$ (A)

_____ 13. If $X + Y = B - C$, then $B = X + (Y)(C)$ (VOICE)

_____ 14 If $(B)(Y) = (X)(C)$, then $C = (B)(Y)/X$ (TOMATO)

Write in the answer to the riddle here, putting one word on each line:

_____   _____   _____   _____   _____   _____

_____   _____

CONCISE KEY

Worksheet 1: 1. 62, 2. 39, 3. 222, 4. 27, 5. 50, 6. 20, 7. 10, 8. 46, 9. 36, 10. 2, 11. 13, 12. 3, 13. 5, 14. 32, 15. 324, 16. 132, 17. 30   The answer to the riddle is: "To see the floor show."

Worksheet 2: 1. 20, 2. –235, 3. –96, 4. –5, 5. –12, 6. 13, 7. 16, 8. –56, 9. –70, 10. 30, 11. –43, 12. –1, 13. 495, 14. –484, 15. –66, 16. 89, 17. –467, 18. –458   The answer to the riddle is: "There's only one thing on my car that doesn't make some sort of noise and that's the horn."

Worksheet 3: 1. 10.54, 2. 8.7, 3. 8, 4. 9.845, 5. 15.8, 6. 30, 7. 15.9, 8. 3.94, 9. 8.4, 10. 10.56   The answer to the riddle is: "All the amnesia patients must pay the psychologist in advance."

Worksheet 4: 1. 0.02, 2. 1.22, 3. 0, 4. 17.68, 5. 13.66, 6. 15.9, 7. 112.08, 8. 12.10, 9. 7.16, 10. 1.14   The answer to the riddle is: "He went home."

Worksheet 5: 1. 4/5, 2. 3/10, 3. 2/9, 4. 1/8, 5. 4/9, 6. 8/35, 7. 2, 8. 2/15, 9. 0.5, 10. 0.75, 11. 2.67, 12. 2.75, 13. 2.1, 14. 1/5, 15. 11/100, 16. 111/200   The answer to the riddle is: "Never look down on a lily because one day a lily will look down on you."

Worksheet 6: 1. T, 2. T, 3. F, 4. T, 5. T, 6. F, 7. F, 8. T, 9. F, 10. T, 11. F, 12. T, 13. F, 14. T   The answer to the riddle is: "When they see an egg or a tomato."

STEP-BY-STEP KEY

WORKSHEET 1:

Order of operations: Do all work inside parentheses first. Perform multiplication and division before performing addition and subtraction.

1. $5 \times 10 + 6 \times 2$
   $= 50 + 12$
   $= 62$

2. $3 + 4 \times 9$
   $= 3 + 36$
   $= 39$

3. $(9 + 28) \times 6$
   $= 37 \times 6$
   $= 222$

4. $159 - 66 \times 2$
   $= 159 - 132$
   $= 27$

5. $15 \times 14 - 8 \times 20$
   $= 210 - 160$
   $= 50$

6. $19 - 5 + 2 \times 3$
   $= 19 - 5 + 6$
   $= 14 + 6$
   $= 20$

7. $70 - 5 \times 3 \times 4$
   $= 70 - 15 \times 4$
   $= 70 - 60$
   $= 10$

8. $6 + 8 \times 1 \times 5$
   $= 6 + 8 \times 5$
   $= 6 + 40$
   $= 46$

9. $33/1 + 1 \times 3$
   $= 33 + 3$
   $= 36$

10. $8/4 + (6)(0)$
    $= 8/4 + 0$
    $= 2 + 0$
    $= 2$

11. $169/(12 + 1)$
    $= 169/13$
    $= 13$

12. $(2 + 3 + 4)/3$
    $= 9/3$
    $= 3$

13. $(2 + 18)/(9 - 5)$
    $= 20/4$
    $= 5$

14. $(1 + 5)(3) + (7)(2)$
    $= (6)(3) + (7)(2)$
    $= 18 + 14$
    $= 32$

15. $(9 + 9)(10 - 1)(2)$
    $- (18)(9)(2)$
    $= (162)(2)$
    $= 324$

16. $(15 - 4)(21/7)(63 - 59)$
    $- (11)(3)(4)$
    $= (33)(4)$
    $= 132$

17. $(3)(1)(1) + (6/2)(9)$
    $= 3 + (3)(9)$
    $= 3 + 27$
    $= 30$

WORKSHEET 2:

Rules for working with positive and negative numbers:

Multiplication:

When a negative number is multiplied by a positive number, the result is negative. When two negative numbers are multiplied, the result is positive.

1. $(-10)(-2) = 20$,   **2.** $(-5)(47) = -235$,   **3.** $(6)(-16) = -96$

Division:

When two numbers with the same sign are divided, the result is positive. When two numbers with opposite signs are divided, the result is negative.

4. $15/-3 = -5$,   **5.** $-144/12 = -12$,   **6.** $-169/-13 = 13$

Addition:

When numbers all have the same sign, add as usual. When numbers have different signs, first add all positive numbers together, then add all negative numbers together, and then subtract the negative sum from the positive sum.

7. $19 + -3 = 16$,   **8.** $-28 + -28 = -56$,   **9.** $-88 + 18 = -70$

Subtraction:

When subtracting negative numbers, change the sign of the number being subtracted and then add:

10. $15--15 = 30$,   **11.** $-29 - 14 = -43$,   **12.** $-30--29 = -1$

For items 13 through 18, follow the rules given above.

13. 495,   **14.** −484,   **15.** −66,   **16.** 89,   **17.** −467,   **18.** −458

WORKSHEET 3:

See the directions on Worksheet 3 for rules on rounding numbers that end in five (5).

1. Read 10.543 as 10.5(tenth's)4(hundredth's)3(thousandth's); therefore, to the nearest hundredth, 10.543 rounds to 10.54.
2. Read 8.67 as 8.6(tenth's)7(hundredth's); therefore, to the nearest tenth, 8.67 rounds to 8.7.
3. Read 8.4 as 8(whole number, one's place).4(tenth's); therefore, to the nearest whole number, 8.4 rounds to 8.
4. Read 9.8452 as 9.8(tenth's)4(hundredth's)5(thousandth's)2(ten thousandth's); therefore, to the nearest thousandth, 9.8452 rounds to 9.845.
5. 15.839, to the nearest tenth, rounds to 15.8.
6. Because 29.5 ends in 5, round to the nearest even number, which is 30.
7. 15.86 rounds to 15.9.
8. Because 3.945 ends in 5, round to the nearest even number, which is 3.94. (Notice that the "4" in the hundredth's place is even.)
9. Because 8.45 ends in 5, round to the nearest even number, which is 8.4. (Notice that the "4" in the tenth's place is even.)
10. Beyond the hundredth's place are four 5's. Therefore, at the point at which you are rounding, the number does not end in "5"; it ends in "5555," which is greater than 5. Therefore, 10.555555, to the nearest hundredth, rounds to 10.56.

WORKSHEET 4:

1. When multiplying, the answer has the total number of decimal places as the total number in the two multipliers. Since 0.02×1 has a total of two digits to the right of the decimal place, the answer is 0.02, which also has two digits to the right.
2. 1.1×1.11 has three digits to the right; therefore, the answer is 1.221, which rounds to 1.22.
3. Any number multiplied by zero equals zero.
4. (See explanation for item 1.) $3.77 \times 4.69 = 17.6813$ (four decimal places), which rounds to 17.68.
5. When dividing with a calculator, enter the numbers as shown. When dividing by hand, first move the decimal place in the divisor to the far right. (In this case, change 12.4 to 124.) Then, move the decimal place in 169.38 the same number of places to the right, changing 169.38 to 1693.8. Then divide as usual. The answer is $13.660 = 13.66$.
6. (See explanation for item 5. Notice the difference between "divided into" and "divided by." This wording usually is not used in textbooks, but your instructor may use it in lectures.) The answer is 15.9. (Notice that division by one has no effect.)
7. Before adding, line up the decimal places one above the other and then add.

$$\begin{array}{r} 12.1 \\ +99.98 \\ \hline 112.08 \end{array}$$

8. (See explanation for item 7.) The answer is 12.10.
9. Before subtracting, line up the decimal places one above the other and then subtract.

$$\begin{array}{r} 25.46 \\ -18.3 \\ \hline 7.16 \end{array}$$

10. (See explanation for number 9. Notice the difference between "subtracted from" and "minus.")

$$\begin{array}{r} 10.01 \\ -8.873 \\ \hline 1.137 \end{array}, \text{ which rounds to } 1.14$$

WORKSHEET 5:

(General note: For most beginning students, it is best to convert fractions to their decimal equivalents as soon as permitted under the rules of mathematics. For example, to convert $\frac{1}{5}$, divide 1 by 5, which yields 0.2. This is desirable since most calculators will not allow you to operate directly on fractions. In addition, it is conventional to report statistics with their decimal equivalents for fractional parts.

Knowledge of fractions is important for understanding the meaning of certain statistics and for understanding their derivations, however.)

1. When adding fractions with a common denominator (same denominator), add the numerators and retain the common denominator. Thus, $\frac{1}{5} + \frac{3}{5} = \frac{4}{5}$.

2. When adding fractions with unlike denominators, first convert so that they both have the same denominator. In this case, by multiplying both the numerator and denominator of $\frac{1}{5}$ by 2, the equivalent fraction of $\frac{2}{10}$ is obtained. Then follow the instructions for item 1. Thus, $\frac{2}{10} + \frac{1}{10} = \frac{3}{10}$.

3. When subtracting fractions with a common denominator, subtract the numerators and retain the common denominator. Thus, $\frac{3}{9} - \frac{1}{9} = \frac{2}{9}$.

4. When subtracting a fraction from a whole number, first convert the whole number to a fractional equivalent with the same denominator. In this case, $1 = \frac{8}{8}$. Thus, $\frac{8}{8} - \frac{7}{8} = \frac{1}{8}$.

5. When multiplying fractions, multiply the numerators, then multiply the denominators. For example, $\frac{2}{3} \times \frac{2}{3} = \frac{4}{9}$.

6. (See the explanation for item number 5.) The answer is $\frac{8}{35}$.

7. To divide one fraction by another, invert the divisor (i.e., $\frac{1}{9}$ becomes $\frac{9}{1}$). Then multiply: $\frac{2}{9} \times \frac{9}{1} = \frac{18}{9}$. To simplify when the numerator is evenly divisible by the denominator, divide the denominator into the numerator: 18 divided by 9 = 2, which is the answer.

8. (See the explanation for item 7.) Note the difference in wording of items 7 and 8. In this case, 5 is the divisor; when inverted, it becomes $\frac{1}{5}$. Thus, $\frac{2}{3} \times \frac{1}{5} = \frac{2}{15}$.

9. To find the decimal equivalent of a fraction, divide the numerator by the denominator. In this case, divide 1 by 2, which yields an answer of 0.5.

10. (See the explanation for item 9.) The answer is 0.75.

11. To find the decimal equivalent of a mixed number (i.e., a whole number plus a fractional part), retain the whole number and convert the fractional part as described in the explanation for item 9. In this case, 2 and $\frac{2}{3}$ becomes 2 and .666, which rounds to 2.67.

12. (See the explanation for item 11.) The answer is 2.75.

13. (See the explanation for item 11.) The answer is 2.1.

14. Note that 0.2 is read as "two tenths." Therefore, it is equivalent to $\frac{2}{10}$. Since both the numerator and denominator are evenly divisible by 2, divide both by 2, which yields $\frac{1}{5}$, which is the answer expressed in lowest terms.

15. Note that 0.11 is read as "eleven one hundredths." Therefore, the answer is expressed as $\frac{11}{100}$.

16. Note that 0.555 is read as "five hundred fifty-five one thousandths." Therefore, it is equivalent to $\frac{555}{1000}$. Since 5 will divide evenly into both the numerator and denominator, simplify by division. This gives an answer of $\frac{111}{200}$.

WORKSHEET 6:

1. If $A = \frac{C}{D}$, then $C = (A)(D)$
$A = \frac{C}{D}$
$\frac{C}{D} = A$
$(\frac{C}{D})(D) = (A)(D)$
$C = (A)(D)$
Therefore, the statement is true.

2. If $A = \frac{C}{D}$, then $D = \frac{C}{A}$
$A = \frac{C}{D}$
$(A)(D) = (\frac{C}{D})(D)$
$(A)(D) = C$
$\frac{(A)(D)}{A} = \frac{C}{A}$
$D = \frac{C}{A}$
Therefore, the statement is true.

3. If $\frac{P}{B} = F$, then $P = \frac{F}{B}$
$\frac{P}{B} = F$
$(\frac{P}{B})(B) = (F)(B)$
$P = (F)(B)$
Therefore, the statement is false.

4. If $X + Y = 10$, then $X = 10 - Y$
$X + Y = 10$
$X + Y - Y = 10 - Y$
$X = 10 - Y$
Therefore, the statement is true.

5. If $25 = A + B$, then $A = 25 - B$
$25 = A + B$
$A + B = 25$
$A + B - B = 25 - B$
$A = 25 - B$
Therefore, the statement is true.

6. If $X + 25 = W$, then $X = W + 25$
$X + 25 = W$
$X + 25 - 25 = W - 25$
$X = W - 25$
Therefore, the statement is false.

7. If $A = C - D$, then $D = C + A$
$A = C - D$
$A + D = C - D + D$
$A + D = C$
$A + D - A = C - A$
$D = C - A$
Therefore, the statement is false.

8. If $A - D = F$, then $A = F + D$
$A - D = F$
$A - D + D = F + D$
$A = F + D$
Therefore, the statement is true.

9. If $A = F - G - H$, then
$F = A - G - H$
$A = F - G - H$
$F - G - H = A$
$F - G - H + G = A + G$
$F - H = A + G$
$F - H + H = A + G + H$
$F = A + G + H$
Therefore, the statement is false.

10. If $(B)(C) = P$, then $B = \frac{P}{C}$
$(B)(C) = P$
$\frac{(B)(C)}{C} = \frac{P}{C}$
$B = \frac{P}{C}$
Therefore, the statement is true.

11. If $Y = (B)(F)$, then $B = \frac{F}{Y}$
$Y = (B)(F)$
$(B)(F) = Y$
$\frac{(B)(F)}{F} = \frac{Y}{F}$
$B = \frac{Y}{F}$
Therefore, the statement is false.

12. If $X = (N)(B)(C)$, then $B = \frac{X}{(N)(C)}$
$X = (N)(B)(C)$
$(N)(B)(C) = X$
$\frac{(N)(B)(C)}{(N)(C)} = \frac{X}{(N)(C)}$
$B = \frac{X}{(N)(C)}$
Therefore, the statement is true.

13. If $X + Y = B - C$, then $B = X + (Y)(C)$
$X + Y = B - C$
$B - C = X + Y$
$B - C + C = X + Y + C$
$B = X + Y + C$
Therefore, the statement is false.

14. If $(B)(Y) = (X)(C)$, then $C = \frac{(B)(Y)}{X}$
$(B)(Y) = (X)(C)$
$(X)(C) = (B)(Y)$
$\frac{(X)(C)}{X} = \frac{(B)(Y)}{X}$
$C = \frac{(B)(Y)}{X}$
Therefore, the statement is true.

SUGGESTED RESPONSES

SELF-TEST FOR TASK 1-A (PAGE 27)

Motivational Effects on Test Scores of Elementary Students

The Problem. The purpose of this study was to determine the effect of experimentally manipulated motivational conditions on elementary students' mathematical scores.

The Procedures. Pairs of normal, heterogeneous classes at each grade level (3, 4, 6, 7 and 8) from each of three public schools were randomly chosen to participate; classes were selected for experimental and control conditions by a flip of a coin (i.e., one class of each pair became an experimental group and the other a control group). Form 7 of the Mathematics Concepts subtest of the Iowa Tests of Basic Skills (ITBS) was the measuring instrument. Prior to taking the test, all students were given the instructions from the ITBS test manual. Experimental students were also read a brief motivational script on the importance of doing well. All participating teachers were trained to administer the test, and experimental teachers were given additional training regarding the script (e.g., read it exactly as it is written).

The Method of Analysis. An analysis of variance was run (on test scores) to test the effects of the experimental and normal (control) conditions (as well as several other variables).

The Major Conclusion. Students asked to try especially hard did considerably better than those who were given the usual standardized test instructions only.

SELF-TEST FOR TASK 1-B (PAGE 35)

A Really Good Art Teacher Would Be Like You, Mrs. C.: A Qualitative Study of a Teacher and Her Artistically Gifted Middle School Students

The Problem. The purpose of this study is to expand comprehension of *teacher effectiveness* through the in-depth study of a teacher and her artistically gifted students.

The Procedures. The participants studied included one teacher and 26 artistically gifted sixth, seventh, and eighth graders in a middle school, members of an existing gifted art program; students had previously been formally screened. The researcher was a participant observer, interacting with students and the teacher weekly during two semesters and several summer school class sessions. Primary data collection included informal interviews, photographing and recording class interactions on audio and video tape, and gathering slides, photos, and videos of art work as well as class artifacts that served as secondary sources. The researcher focused on social interactions among participants and studying the teacher's curriculum and effectiveness as a translator of the art world to her students.

The Method of Analysis.   Transcripts from audio and video tapes and field notes were analyzed using constant comparison method of analysis, producing codes and patterns. In addition, 7 graduate and undergraduate art education students rated interaction behaviors in 5 selected video clips, producing codes that were compared with the researcher's codes for the same clips, which reflected an inter-rater reliability of .91. Theoretical memos were written during analysis and linkages were found between patterns. The codes, patterns, and linkages were triangulated with interview and secondary data information, and scanned for disconfirming data.

The Major Conclusion.   The study described how students learned about art processes and identified themselves as real artists through substantive, effective teaching.

SELF-TEST FOR TASK 1-C (PAGE 36)

1. Research Approach: Historical. Historical research involves studying, understanding, and interpreting past events; in this study, changes in public schools' legal responsibilities over the past 50 years are studied.
2. Research Approach: Action research. Action research studies focus on ways teachers can improve their practice.
3. Research Approach: Survey research. Survey research involves collecting data to answer questions about the current status of issues or topics; a questionnaire was administered to find out how teachers feel about an issue.
4. Research Approach: Correlational research. Correlational research seeks to determine whether, and to what degree, a statistical relationship exists between two or more variables. Here, the researchers are interested in the similarity of the two tests.
5. Research Approach: Causal–comparative research. In causal–comparative research, at least two groups (fifth graders from single-parent families and those from two-parent families) are compared on a dependent variable or effect (in this case, achievement of reading).
6. Research Approach: Experimental research. Experimental research allows researchers to make cause–effect statements about a study. In addition, researchers have a great deal of control over the study; here the researchers determined the two groups (at random) and applied different treatments (the two methods of conflict resolution) to the two groups.
7. Research Approach: Ethnography. Ethnographic research studies participants in their natural culture or setting; the culture of recent Armenian emigrants is examined in their new setting.

SELF-TEST FOR TASK 11 (PAGES 546–549)

Effects of Using an Instructional Game on Motivation and Performance

GENERAL EVALUATION CRITERIA

Introduction

Problem	CODE
A statement?	Y
Paragraph (//)7, sentence (S)1[1]	
Researchable?	Y
Background information?	Y
e.g., //2	
Significance discussed?	Y
e.g., //1	
Variables and relationships discussed?	Y
Definitions?	Y
e.g., //7, S3	

Review of Related Literature	
Comprehensive?	?/X
Appears to be	
References relevant?	Y
Sources primary?	Y
Critical analysis?	Y
e.g., //6	
Well organized?	Y
Summary?	N
Rationale for hypotheses?	N

Hypotheses	
Questions or hypotheses?	Y
//7, S6 & 7	
Expected differences stated?	Y
Variables defined?	Y
Testable?	Y

Method

Participants	CODE
Population described?	Y&N
Very briefly	
Sample selection method described?	NA
Selection method "good"?	NA
Avoidance of volunteers?	?/X
Hard to say; see //1, S2	
Sample described?	Y&N
Size, yes; characteristics, no	
Minimum sizes?	Y
$n^1 = 37$; $n^2 = 38$	

---

[1] //7 refers to paragraph 7 of the introduction section of the article. The introduction section ends where Method begins.

CODE

Instruments

Rationale for selection?	N
Instrument described?	Y
//6 & 7	
Appropriate?	Y
Evidence that it is appropriate for sample?	N
Validity discussed?	N
Reliability discussed?	Y
//6 & 7	
Subtest reliabilities?	Y
//6	
Procedures for development described?	N
Performance posttest not described	
Administration, scoring, and interpretation procedures described?	N

Design and Procedure

Design appropriate?	Y
Procedures sufficiently detailed?	Y
Pilot study described?	NA
Control procedures described?	Y
e.g., //9	
Confounding variables discussed?	Y
e.g., //10, S2	

Results

Appropriate descriptive statistics?	Y
Table 1	
Probability level specified in advance?	Y
e.g., //1	
Parametric assumptions not violated?	Y
Tests of significance appropriate?	Y or ?/X
Every hypothesis tested?	Y
Appropriate degrees of freedom?	Y or ?/X
Results clearly presented?	Y
Tables and figures well organized?	Y
Data in each table and figure described?	Y

Discussion (Conclusions and Recommendations)

Results discussed in terms of hypothesis?	Y
Results discussed in terms of previous research?	Y
e.g., //3	
Generalizations consistent with results?	Y
e.g., //1	
Effects of uncontrolled variables discussed?	Y
e.g., //2	
Implications discussed?	Y
e.g., //7	
Recommendations for action?	Y
e.g., //8	

	CODE
Suggestions based on practical significance?	Y
Effect sizes were presented under Results, //2, S4 & 5	
Recommendations for research?	Y
e.g., //9	

Abstract (or Summary)

	CODE
Problem restated?	Y
Subjects and instruments described?	Y&N
Subjects briefly; instruments indirectly	
Design identified?	Y
Not named, but described	
Procedures?	Y
Results and conclusions?	Y

TYPE-SPECIFIC EVALUATION CRITERIA

Design used:

Basically a posttest-only control group design. The independent variable was type of practice.

$$
\begin{array}{lll}
R & X_1 0 & X_1 = \text{game} \\
R & X_2 0 & X_2 = \text{worksheet} \\
      &   & 0 = \text{Motivation scale performance posttest}
\end{array}
$$

Because of the inclusion of a second, unmanipulated independent variable, completion versus noncompletion of reading assignment, the design was a 2 × 2 factorial design, based on a posttest-only control group design.

	CODE
Design appropriate?	Y
Design selection rationale?	N
Invalidity discussed?	N
But mortality was not a problem	
Group formation described?	Y
Random assignment	
Groups formed in same way?	Y
Groups randomly formed?	Y
Treatments randomly assigned?	?/X
Extraneous variables described?	Y
e.g., //6, S3–5	
Groups equated?	N
Reactive arrangements controlled for?	N
But discussed, under Discussion, //2, S3–6	

A-B design A single-subject design in which baseline measurements are repeatedly made until stability is presumably established, treatment is introduced, and an appropriate number of measurements are made during treatment.

A-B-A design A single-subject design in which baseline measurements are repeatedly made until stability is presumably established, treatment is introduced, and an appropriate number of measurements are made. The treatment phase is followed by a second baseline phase.

A-B-A-B design A single-subject design in which baseline measurements are repeatedly made until stability is presumably established, treatment is introduced, and an appropriate number of measurements are made. The treatment phase is followed by a second baseline phase, which is followed by a second treatment phase.

abstract A summary of a study, which appears at the beginning of the report and describes the most important aspects of the study, including major results and conclusions.

accessible population Refers to the population from which the researcher can realistically select participants.

accidental sampling *See* convenience sampling.

achievement test An instrument that measures the current status of individuals with respect to proficiency in given areas of knowledge or skill.

action research An approach in which teachers study their own problems or concerns in their own classrooms.

additive designs Refers to variations of the A-B design that involve the addition of another phase or phases in which the experimental treatment is supplemented with another treatment.

affective Mental characteristic relating to emotion, such as attitude, interest, and value.

affective test Assessment designed to measure affective characteristics.

alternating treatments design A variation of a multiple-baseline design that involves the relatively rapid alternation of treatments for a single participant.

alternative assessment *See* performance assessment.

analysis of covariance A statistical method of equating groups on one or more variables and for increasing the power of a statistical test; adjusts scores on a dependent variable for initial differences on some variable such as pretest performance or IQ.

analysis of variance Inferential statistics technique used to determine if there exists a significant difference among the means of three or more data groups.

analytic induction A method of identifying regularities in qualitative data, determining their explanation, and finding other contexts to determine whether the explanations hold up.

anonymity In research, this means that the researcher does not know the identities of participants in a study.

applied research Research conducted for the purpose of applying, or testing, theory and evaluating its usefulness in solving problems.

aptitude test A measure of potential used to predict how well someone is likely to perform in a future situation.

artificial categories Categories that are operationally defined by the researcher.

assessment The general term for the process of collecting, synthesizing, and interpreting information. A *test* is a type of assessment.

assumption Any important fact presumed to be true but not actually verified; assumptions should be described in the procedures section of a research plan or report.

attenuation Refers to the principle that correlation coefficients tend to be lowered because less-than-perfectly reliable measures are used.

attitude scale Measurement instrument used to determine what respondents believe, perceive, or feel about self, others, activities, institutions, or situations.

attrition *See* mortality.

authentic assessment *See* performance assessment.

baseline measure Multiple measures of pretest peformance conducted in single-subject research designs to control for sources of invalidity.

basic research Research conducted for the purpose of theory development or refinement.

bias Distortion of research data that renders the data suspect or invalid. May occur due to characteristics of the researcher, the respondent, or the research design itself.

case study The in-depth investigation of one unit, e.g., individual, group, institution, organization, program, or document.

category A classification of ideas and concepts in qualitative data analysis.

causal–comparative research Research that attempts to determine the cause, or reason, for existing differences in the behavior or status of groups of individuals; also referred to as *ex post facto research*.

census survey Survey research that attempts to acquire data from each and every member of a population.

changing criterion design   A variation of the A-B-A design in which the baseline phase is followed by successive treatment phases, each of which has a more stringent criterion for acceptable (improved) behavior.

chi square   A nonparametric test of significance appropriate when the data are in the form of frequency counts; it compares proportions actually observed in a study with proportions expected to see if they are significantly different.

clinical replication   Refers to the development and application of a treatment package, composed of two or more interventions that have been found to be effective individually, designed for persons with complex behavior disorders.

cluster sampling   Sampling in which intact groups, not individuals, are randomly selected.

coefficient alpha (α)   *See* Cronbach's alpha.

cognitive   Mental characteristic relating to intellect, such as mathematics achievement, literacy, reasoning, or problem solving.

cognitive test   Assessment designed to measure cognitive processes.

common variance   The variation in one variable that is attributable to its tendency to vary with another variable. Also called *shared variance.*

compensatory rivalry   *See* John Henry effect.

concurrent validity   The degree to which the scores on a test are related to the scores on another, already established test administered at the same time, or to some other valid criterion available at the same time.

confidentiality   In research, this means that the researcher knows the identities of participants in a study but promises to not reveal the information to others.

consequential validity   Examination of test instruments to locate and identify known and unknown potentially harmful effects of instrument use.

constant comparison   A qualitative method for identifying similarities and differences by comparing new evidence to prior evidence.

construct   An abstraction that connot be observed directly; a concept invented to explain behavior.

construct validity   The degree to which a test measures an intended hypothetical construct, or nonobservable trait, that explains behavior.

contamination   The situation that exists when the researcher's familiarity with the participants affects the outcome of the study.

content analysis   The systematic, quantitative description of the composition of the object of the study.

content validity   The degree to which a test measures an intended content area; it is determined by expert judgment and requires both item validity and sampling validity.

context   The temporal, geographical, and cultural specifics of a qualitative research setting.

control   Efforts on the part of the researcher to remove the influence of any variable other than the independent variable that might affect performance on a dependent variable.

control group   The group in a research study that either receives a different treatment than the experimental group or is treated as usual.

control variable   A nonmanipulated variable, usually a physical or mental characteristic of the participants (such as IQ).

convenience sampling   The process of using as the sample whoever happens to be available, e.g., volunteers. Also referred to as *accidental* sampling and *haphazard* sampling.

correlation   A quantitative measure of the degree of correspondence between two or more variables.

correlational research   Research that involves collecting data to determine whether, and to what degree, a relationship exists between two or more quantifiable variables.

correlation coefficient   A decimal number between .00 and ±1.00 that indicates the degree to which two variables are related.

counterbalanced design   A quasi-experimental design in which all groups receive all treatments, each group receives the treatments in a different order, the number of groups equals the number of treatments, and all groups posttested after each treatment.

credibility   A term used in qualitative research to indicate that the topic was accurately identified and described.

criterion   In a prediction study, the variable that is predicted.

criterion referenced   Comparing an individual's performance on an assessment to a predetermined, external standard.

criterion-related validity   Validity determined by relating performance on a test to performance on another criterion; includes concurrent and predictive validity.

Cronbach's alpha (α)   The general formula for estimating internal consistency based on a determination of how all items on a test relate to all other items and to the total test. Kuder-Richardson (KR-20) is a special case of the Cronbach's alpha general formula. Also referred to as *coefficient alpha* and *Cronbach's coefficient alpha.*

cross-validation   Validation of a prediction equation with at least one group other than the group it was based on; variables found to no longer relate to the criterion measure are removed from the equation.

curvilinear relationship   A relationship in which increase in one variable is associated with a corresponding increase in another variable to a point, at which point further increase in the first variable is associated with a corresponding decrease in the other variable (or vice versa).

data   Pieces of information (singular, *datum*).

data analysis   A process of simplifying quantitative or qualitative data for better understanding, involving application of statistical techniques to numerical data or coding and finding patterns or themes in narrative data.

database A sortable, analyzable collection of units of information maintained on a computer.

data saturation A point in qualitative research when so much data are collected that it is very unlikely that additional data will add to what is already collected.

deductive hypothesis A hypothesis derived from theory that provides evidence that supports, expands, or contradicts the theory.

deductive reasoning Reasoning based on developing specific predictions from general principles, observations, or experiences.

demographic In research, a statistically significant characteristic of a study population.

dependent variable The change or difference in behavior that occurs as a result of the independent variable; also referred to as the *criterion variable,* the *effect,* the *outcome,* or the *posttest.*

descriptive statistics Data analysis techniques enabling the researcher to meaningfully describe many scores with a small number of numerical indices.

design A general strategy or plan for conducting a research study written to describe the study's basic structure and goals.

developmental survey Studies concerned with behavior variables that differentiate children at different levels of age, growth, or maturation.

diagnostic test A type of achievement test yielding multiple scores for each area of achievement measured that facilitate identification of specific areas of deficiency.

differential selection of participants Refers to the fact that groups may be different before a study even begins, and this initial difference may at least partially account for posttest differences.

direct replication Refers to the replication of a study by the same investigator, with the same participants or with different participants, in a specific setting.

ecological validity *See* external validity.

educational research The formal, systematic application of the scientific and disciplined inquiry approach to the study of educational problems.

emic Qualitative approach to the way members (participants) of a given context perceive their world.

environmental variable A variable in the setting in which a study is conducted that might cause unwanted differences between groups (e.g., learning materials).

equivalence Exists when two tests are identical in every way except for the actual items included.

equivalent-forms reliability Indicates score variation that occurs from form to form of a test; also referred to as *alternate-forms reliability.*

ethnography A qualitative approach that studies the cultural patterns and perspectives of participants in their natural setting.

ethnomethodology A qualitative approach that studies how participants make sense of their everyday activities to act in a social way.

etic Qualitative approach to the way nonmembers (outsiders) perceive and interpret a context.

evaluation The systematic process of collecting and analyzing data in order to make decisions.

evaluation research Research concerned with the quality, effectiveness, merit, or value of educational programs, products, or practices.

experimental group The group in a research study that typically receives a new, or novel, treatment, a treatment under investigation.

experimental research Research in which at least one independent variable is manipulated, other relevant variables are controlled, and the effect on one or more dependent variables is observed.

experimenter bias A situation in which the researcher's expectations concerning the outcomes of the study actually contribute to producing various outcomes.

experimenter effects Threats to an experiment's external validity from the researcher's unintentional or intentional influences on participants or on study procedures.

ex post facto research *See* causal–comparative research.

external criticism The analysis of data to determine their authenticity.

external observation *See* nonparticipant observation.

external validity The degree to which results are generalizable, or applicable, to groups and environments outside the experimental setting. Also called *ecological validity.*

F ratio A computation used in analyses of variance to determine whether variances among sample means are significant.

factorial analysis of variance The appropriate statistical analysis if a study is based on a factorial design. Investigates two or more independent variables and the interactions between them; yields a separate F ratio for each independent variable and one for each interaction.

factorial design An experimental design that involves two or more dependent variables (at least one of which is manipulated) in order to study the effects of the variables individually and in interaction with each other.

field notes Qualitiative research material gathered, recorded, and compiled onsite during the course of a study.

fieldwork A qualitative research strategy that involves spending considerable time in the setting under study, immersing oneself in this setting, and collecting as much relevant information as possible as unobtrusively as possible.

followup study A study conducted to determine the status of a group of interest after some period of time.

gatekeeper   Person in a research setting who is responsible for authorizing or disallowing a study.

generosity error   The tendency to give an individual the benefit of the doubt whenever there is insufficient knowledge to make an objective judgment.

grounded theory   Theory based on data collected in real-world settings that reflect what naturally occurred over an extended period of time.

halo effect   The phenomenon whereby initial impressions concerning an individual (positive or negative) affect subsequent measurements.

haphazard sampling   *See* convenience sampling.

hardcopy   Refers to computer output that is printed out on paper.

hardware   Refers to the actual equipment, the computer itself and related accessories such as printers.

Hawthorne effect   A type of reactive arrangement resulting from the participants' knowledge that they are involved in an experiment, or their feeling that they are in some way receiving special attention.

historical research   The systematic collection and evaluation of data related to past occurrences in order to describe causes, effects, or trends of those events that may help to explain present events and anticipate future events.

history   Any event that is not part of the experimental treatment but that may affect performance on the dependent variable.

hypothesis   A tentative, reasonable, testable explanation for the occurrence of certain behaviors, phenomena, or events.

independent variable   An activity or characteristic believed to make a difference with respect to some behavior; also referred to as the *experimental variable,* the *cause,* and the *treatment.*

inductive hypothesis   A generalization based on observation.

inductive reasoning   Reasoning based on developing generalizations from a limited number of related observations or experiences.

inferential statistics   Data analysis techniques for determining how likely it is that results based on a sample or samples are the same results that would have been obtained for an entire population.

instrument   In educational research, a test or other tool used to collect data.

instrumentation   Unreliability in measuring instruments that may result in invalid assessment of participants' performance.

interaction   Refers to the situation in which different values of the independent variable are differentially effective depending on the level of the control variable.

interjudge reliability   The consistency of two (or more) independent scorers, raters, or observers.

internal criticism   The analysis of data to determine their accuracy, which takes into consideration the knowledge and competence of the author, the time delay between the occurrence and recording of events, biased motives of the author, and consistency of the data.

internal validity   The degree to which observed differences on the dependent variable are a direct result of manipulation of the independent variable, not some other variable.

interpretive research   Collective, generic term for qualitiative researsh approaches.

interval scale   *See* interval variable.

interval variable   A measurement scale that classifies and ranks participants. It is based on predetermined equal intervals, but does not have a true zero point.

intervening variable   A variable that intervenes between, or alters the relationship between, an independent variable and a dependent variable, which cannot be directly observed or controlled (e.g., anxiety) but that can be controlled for.

interview   An oral, in-person question-and-answer session with individual respondents used to collect research data. It is a purposive interaction between two or more persons, with one trying to obtain information from the other.

intrajudge reliability   The consistency of the scoring, rating, or observing of an individual.

item validity   The degree to which test items represent measurement in the intended content area.

John Henry effect   The phenomenon whereby if for any reason members of a control group feel threatened or challenged by being in competition with an experimental group, they may outdo themselves and perform way beyond what would normally be expected. Also called *compensatory rivalry.*

judgment sampling   *See* purposive sampling.

keyword   A topic-specific term used in computer and library searches to locate information related to the research problem being investigated.

Likert scale   An instrument that asks individuals to respond to a series of statements by indicating whether they strongly agree (SA), agree (A), are undecided (U), disagree (D), or strongly disagree (SD) with each statement.

limitation   An aspect of a study that the researcher knows may negatively affect the results or generalizability of the results, but over which the researcher has no control.

linear relationship   The situation in which an increase (or decrease) in one variable is associated with a corresponding increase (or decrease) in another variable.

logical validity   Validity determined primarily through judgment; includes content validity.

matching   A technique for equating groups on one or more variables, resulting in each member of one group having a direct counterpart in another group.

maturation   Physical or mental changes that occur within participants over a period of time and that may affect their performance on a measure of the dependent variable.

mean   The arithmetic average of a set of scores.

measurement   The process of quantifying or scoring respondents' performance on an assessment instrument.

measurement scale   A group of several related statements that vary by differing degrees that research participants select from to indicate their agreement or lack of agreement.

measures of central tendency   Indices representing the average or typical score attained by a group of participants.

measures of variability   Indices indicating how spread out the scores are in a distribution.

median   That point in a distribution above and below which are 50% of the scores.

memo   A form of thinking briefly on paper used in qualitiative research to complement field notes and aid in evolving data analysis.

menu driven   Refers to computer programs that allow the user to select desired analyses from a list, or menu, of options.

meta-analysis   A statistical approach to summarizing the results of many studies that have investigated basically the same problem.

mode   The score that is attained by more participants in a group than any other score.

modem   A device that permits telephone communication between two computers by converting computer language to audiotones.

mortality   Refers to the fact that participants who drop out of a study may share a characteristic such that their absence has a significant effect on the results of the study.

multiple-baseline design   A single-subject design in which baseline data are collected on several behaviors for one participant or one behavior for several participants and treatment is applied systematically over a period of time to each behavior (or each participant) one at a time until all behaviors (or participants) are under treatment.

multiple comparisons   Procedures used following application of analysis of variance to determine which means are significantly different from which other means. Also called *post hoc* comparisons.

multiple regression equation   A prediction equation using two or more variables that individually predict a criterion to make a more accurate prediction.

multiple time-series design   A variation of the time-series design that involves the addition of a control group to the basic design.

multiple-treatment interference   Refers to the carryover effects from an earlier treatment that make it difficult to assess the effectiveness of a later treatment.

naturalistic observation   Observation in which the observer purposely controls or manipulates nothing, and in fact works very hard at not affecting the observed situation in any way.

negative case   One that contradicts an emerging category or pattern; provides an alternative perspective.

negatively skewed distribution   A distribution in which there are more extreme scores at the lower end than at the upper, or higher, end.

nominal scale   *See* nominal variable.

nominal variable   The lowest level of measurement that classifies persons or objects into two or more categories; a person can only be in one category, and members of a category have a common set of characteristics.

nonequivalent control group design   A quasi-experimental design involving at least two groups, both of which are pretested; one group receives the experimental treatment, and both groups are posttested.

nonparametric test   A test of significance appropriate when the data represent an ordinal or nominal scale, when a parametric assumption has been greatly violated, or when the nature of the distribution is not known.

nonparticipant observation   Observation in which the observer is not directly involved in the situation to be observed, i.e., the observer does not intentionally interact with or affect the object of the observation. Also called *external observation*.

nonprobability sampling   The process of selecting a sample using a technique that *does not* permit the researcher to specify the probability, or chance, that each member of a population has of being selected for the sample.

norm referenced   Comparing an individual's performance on an assessment to the performance of others.

novelty effect   A type of reactive arrangement resulting from increased interest, motivation, or participation on the part of participants simply because they are doing something different.

null hypothesis   States that there is no relationship (or difference) between variables and that any relationship found will be a chance relationship, the result of sampling error, not a true one.

observational research   Descriptive research in which the desired data is obtained not by asking individuals for it but through such means as direct observation.

observer bias   The phenomenon whereby an observer does not observe objectively and accurately, thus producing invalid observations.

observer effects   The phenomenon whereby persons being observed behave atypically simply because they are being observed, thus producing invalid observations.

one-group pretest-posttest design   A pre-experimental design involving one group that is pretested, exposed to a treatment, and posttested.

one-shot case study   A pre-experimental design involving one group that is exposed to a treatment and then posttested.

one-way analysis of variance   A modification of the *t* test that compares all possible pairs of means under analysis. The resulting procedures are commonly called *post hoc comparisons* or *multiple comparisons*.

operational definition   One that defines concepts in terms of processes, or operations.

ordinal scale   *See* ordinal variable.

ordinal variable   A measurement scale that classifies participants and ranks them in terms of the degree to which they possess a characteristic of interest.

organismic variable   A characteristic of a participant, or organism (e.g., gender) that cannot be directly controlled but that can be controlled for.

parameter   A numerical index describing the behavior of a population.

parametric test   A test of significance appropriate when the data represent an interval or ratio scale of measurement and other assumptions have been met.

participant   A person who provided data for a research study.

participant effects   *See* reactive arrangements.

participant observation   Observation in which the observer actually becomes a part of, a participant in, the situation to be observed.

participant variable   A variable on which participants in different groups in a study might differ (e.g., intelligence).

pattern   In qualitative analysis, links between and among categories that further organize study data.

Pearson *r*   A measure of correlation appropriate when the data represent either interval or ratio scales; it takes into account each and every score and produces a coefficient between .00 and ±1.00.

percentile rank   A measure of relative position indicating the percentage of scores that fall at or below a given score.

performance assessment   Assessment types emphasizing the respondent's performing a process or creating a product. Also called *authentic* and *alternative* assessment.

phenomenology   The experience of an activity or concept from participants' perspectives.

pilot study   A small-scale study conducted prior to the conducting of the actual study; the entire study is conducted, every procedure is followed, and the resulting data are analyzed according to the research plan.

placebo effect   Refers to the discovery in medical research that any medication could make participants feel better, even sugar and water.

population   The group to which the researcher would like the results of a study to be generalizable.

positively skewed distribution   A distribution in which there are more extreme scores at the upper, or higher, end than at the lower end.

post hoc comparisons   *See* multiple comparisons.

posttest-only control group design   A true experimental design involving at least two randomly formed groups; one group receives a new, or unusual, treatment and both groups are posttested.

power   The ability of a significance test to avoid making a Type II error.

prediction study   An attempt to determine which of a number of variables are most highly related to a criterion variable, a complex variable to be predicted.

predictive validity   The degree to which a test is able to predict how well an individual will do in a future situation.

predictor   In a prediction study, the variable the prediction is based on.

pretest-posttest control group design   A true experimental design that involves at least two randomly formed groups; both groups are pretested, one group receives a new, or unusual treatment, and both groups are posttested.

pretest sensitization   *See* testing.

pretest–treatment interaction   Refers to the fact that participants may respond or react differently to a treatment because they have been pretested.

primary source   Firsthand information such as the testimony of an eyewitness, an original document, a relic, or a description of a study written by the person who conducted it.

probability sampling   The process of selecting a sample using a sampling technique that permits the researcher to specify the probability, or chance, that each member of a defined population has of being selected for the sample.

problem statement   A statement that indicates the variables of interest to the researcher and the specific relationship between those variables that is to be, or was, investigated.

prospective causal–comparative research   A variation of the basic approach to causal–comparative research that involves starting with the causes and investigating effects.

purposive sampling   The process of selecting a sample that is *believed* to be representative of a given population. Also referred to as *judgment* sampling.

qualitative approach   The collection of extensive narrative data to gain insights into phenomena of interest.

qualitative research   The collection of extensive narrative data on many variables over an extended period of time, in a naturalistic setting, to gain insights not possible using other types of research.

quantitative research   The collection of numerical data to explain, predict, and/or control phenomena of interest.

quartile deviation   One-half of the difference between the upper quartile (the 75th percentile) and the lower quartile (the 25th percentile) in a distribution.

questionnaire   A written collection of self-report questions to be answered by a selected group of research participants.

quota sampling   The process of selecting a sample based on required, exact numbers, or quotas, of persons of varying characteristics.

random sampling   The process of selecting a sample in such a way that all individuals in the defined population have an equal and independent chance of being selected for the sample.

range   The difference between the highest and lowest score in a distribution.

rating scale   Measurement instrument used to determine respondent's attitude toward self, others, activities, institutions, or situations.

rational equivalence reliability   An estimate of internal consistency based on a determination of how all items on a test relate to all other items and to the total test.

ratio scale   *See* ratio variable.

ratio variable   The highest level of measurement that classifies participants, ranks participants, is based upon predetermined equal intervals, and has a true zero point.

raw score   The numerical calculation of the number of items scored correctly on an assessment.

reactive arrangements   Threats to the external validity of a study associated with the way in which a study is conducted and the feelings and attitudes of the participants involved. Also called *participant effects.*

readiness test   A test administered prior to instruction or training in a specific area to determine whether and to what degree a student is ready for, or will profit from, instruction.

refereed journal   Journal in which articles are reviewed by a panel of experts in the field and are thus seen as more "scholarly" and "trustworthy."

relationship study   An attempt to gain insight into the variables, or factors, that are related to a complex variable such as academic achievement, motivation, and self-concept.

reliability   The degree to which a test consistently measures whatever it measures.

replication   Refers to when a study is done again; the second study may be a repetition of the original study using different participants, or it may represent an alternative approach to testing the same hypothesis.

research   The formal, systematic application of the scientific and disciplined inquiry approach to the study of problems.

research hypothesis   A statement of the expected relationship (or difference) between two variables.

research plan   A detailed description of a proposed study designed to investigate a given problem.

response set   The tendency of an assessed individual to continually respond in a particular way to a variety of instruments, such as when a respondent repeatedly answers as she or he believes the researcher desires even when such answers do not reflect the respondent's true feelings. Also used to refer to the tendency of an observer to rate the majority of observees the same regardless of the observees' actual behavior.

retrospective causal–comparative research   The basic approach to causal–comparative research that involves starting with effects and investigating causes.

review of literature   The systematic identification, location, and analysis of documents containing information related to a research problem.

sample   A number of individuals selected from a population for a study, preferably in such a way that they represent the larger group from which they were selected.

sample survey   Research in which information about a population is inferred based on the responses of a sample selected from that population.

sampling   The process of selecting a number of individuals (a sample) from a population, preferably in such a way that the individuals selected represent the larger group from which they were selected.

sampling bias   Systematic sampling error; two major sources of sampling bias are the use of volunteers and the use of available groups.

sampling error   Expected, chance variation in variables that occurs when a sample is selected from a population.

sampling validity   The degree to which a test samples the total intended content area.

Scheffé test   A conservative multiple comparison technique appropriate for making any and all possible comparisons involving a set of means.

search engine   World Wide Web tool that allows users to search large portions of the Internet for specific information.

secondary source   Secondhand information, such as a brief description of a study written by someone other than the person who conducted it.

selection–maturation interaction   Refers to the fact that if already formed groups are used in a study, one group may profit more (or less) from treatment or have an initial advantage (or disadvantage) because of maturation factors; selection may also interact with factors such as history and testing.

selection–treatment interaction   Refers to the fact that if nonrepresentative groups are used in a study, the results of the study may hold only for the groups involved and may not be representative of the treatment effect in the population.

self-referenced   Comparing an individual's repeated performances over time on a single assessment.

self-report research   Descriptive research in which information is solicited from individuals using, for example, questionnaires or interviews.

semantic differential scale   An instrument that asks an individual to give a quantitative rating to the participant of the attitude scale on a number of bipolar adjectives such as good–bad, friendly–unfriendly, positive–negative.

shrinkage   Refers to the tendency of a prediction equation to become less accurate when used with a different group, a group other than the one on which the equation was originally formulated.

simple analysis of variance (ANOVA)   A parametric test of significance used to determine whether there is significant difference between or among two or more means at a selected probability level.

simulation observation   Observation in which the researcher creates the situation to be observed and tells the participant what activities they are to engage in.

simultaneous replication   Refers to when replication is done on a number of participants with the same problem, at the same location, at the same time.

single-subject experimental designs Designs applied when the sample size is one; used to study the behavior change which an individual exhibits as a result of some intervention, or treatment.

single-variable designs A class of experimental designs involving only one independent variable (which is manipulated).

single variable rule An important principle of single-subject research, which states that only one variable should be manipulated at a time.

skewed distribution A nonsymmetrical distribution in which there are more extreme scores at one end of the distribution than the other.

sociometric study A study that assesses and analyzes the interpersonal relationships within a group of individuals.

software Refers to the programs that give instructions to a computer concerning desired operations.

Solomon four-group design A true experimental design that involves random assignment of participants to one of four groups; two groups are pretested, two are not; one of the pretested groups and one of the unpretested groups receive the experimental treatment, and all four groups are posttested.

Spearman rho A measure of correlation appropriate when the data for at least one of the variables are expressed as ranks; it produces a coefficient between .00 and ± 1.00.

specificity of variables Refers to the fact that a given study is conducted with a specific kind of participant, using specific measuring instruments, at a specific time, under a specific set of circumstances; factors that affect the generalizability of the results.

split-half reliability A type of reliability based on the internal consistency of a test that is estimated by dividing a test into two equivalent halves and correlating the scores on the two halves.

stability The degree to which scores on a test are consistent, or stable, over time.

standard deviation The most stable measure of variability that takes into account each and every score in a distribution. Calculated as the square root of the *variance,* or amount of spread among test scores, it is the most frequently used statistical index of variability.

standard error of the mean The standard deviation of sample means that indicates by how much the sample means can be expected to differ if other samples from the same population are used.

standard error of measurement An estimate of how often one can expect errors of a given size in an individual's test score.

standard score A derived score that expresses how far a given raw score is from some reference point, typically the mean, in terms of standard deviation units.

standardized test A test that is administered, scored, and interpreted the same every time and place it is used,

stanines Standard scores that divide a distribution into nine parts.

static-group comparison A pre-experimental design that involves at least two nonrandomly formed groups; one receives a new, or unusual, treatment and both are posttested.

statistic A numerical index describing the behavior of a sample or samples.

statistical regression The tendency of participants who score highest on a pretest to score lower on a posttest, and of participants who score lowest on a pretest to score higher on a posttest.

statistical significance The conclusion that results are unlikely to have occurred by chance; the observed relationship or difference is probably a real one.

statistics A set of procedures for describing, synthesizing, analyzing, and interpreting quantitative data.

strata A subgroup derived from a sample; a variable that can be divided into groups.

stratified sampling The process of selecting a sample in such a way that identified subgroups in the population are represented in the sample in the same proportion that they exist in the population or in equal proportion.

structured interview Interview questions that provide options for participants to select from.

structured item A question and a list of alternative responses from which the responder selects; also referred to as a *closed-ended* item.

survey An attempt to collect data from members of a population to determine the current status of that population with respect to one or more variables.

systematic replication Refers to replication that follows direct replication and that involves different investigators, behaviors, or settings.

systematic sampling Sampling in which individuals are selected from a list by taking every Kth name, where K equals the number of individuals on the list divided by the number of participants desired for the sample.

target population Refers to the population to which the researcher would ideally like to generalize results.

terminal A device for communicating with a computer that consists of a display screen and a keyboard.

test A means of measuring the knowledge, skill, feelings, intelligence, or aptitude of an individual or group.

testing A threat to experimental validity that refers to improved scores on a posttest that are a result of participants having taken a pretest. Also referred to as *pretest sensitization.*

test objectivity Refers to a situation in which an individual's score is the same, or essentially the same, regardless of who is doing the scoring.

test of significance A statistical test used to determine whether there is a significant difference between or among two or more means at a selected probability level.

test–retest reliability   *See* stability.

theory   A tentative, abstract statement of supposed relationship, testable by formulating and testing one or more hypotheses.

time-series design   A quasi-experimental design involving one group that is repeatedly pretested, exposed to an experimental treatment, and repeatedly posttested.

topic   A research question, issue, or problem that can be examined or answered by collecting and analyzing data.

treatment diffusion   A threat to an experiment's external validity that occurs when different treatment groups communicate with and learn from each other.

triangulation   The use of multiple methods, data collection strategies, and/or data sources to get a more complete picture and to cross-check information.

true categories   Categories into which persons or objects naturally fall, independently of the research study.

T score   A standard score derived from a z score by multiplying the z score by 10 and adding 50.

t test   Inferential statistics technique used to determine whether the means of two data groups are significantly different from one another.

t test for independent samples   A parametric test of significance used to determine whether there is a significant difference between the means of two independent samples at a selected probability level.

t test for nonindependent samples   A parametric test of significance used to determine whether there is a significant difference between the means of two matched, or nonindependent, samples at a selected probability level.

Type I error   The rejection by the researcher of a null hypothesis that is actually true.

Type II error   The failure of a researcher to reject a null hypothesis that is actually false.

unobtrusive measures   Inanimate objects (such as school suspension lists) that can be observed to obtain desired information.

unstructured interview   Interview questions prompted by the flow of the interview itself.

unstructured item   A question giving the responder complete freedom of response.

validity   The degree to which a test measures what it is intended to measure; a test is valid for a particular purpose for a particular group.

variable   A concept that can assume any one of a range of values (e.g., intelligence, height, aptitude).

variance   The amount of spread among test scores.

z score   The most basic standard score that expresses how far a score is from a mean in terms of standard deviation.

Z score   *See T* score.

AUTHOR INDEX

SUBJECT INDEX

A-B-A-B design, 387–388
A-B-A design, 386–387
A-B-A withdrawal designs, 386–388
A-B design, 386
Abstract
 criteria for evaluating, 534
 defining, 48
 example of, 521
 of mixed-method study, 188
Abstracting, 58–59
Accessible (or available) population, 102–103
Accidental sampling, 115
Achievement tests, 130
Action research
 action planning/reporting on, 270 271
 comparison of traditional and, 262
 conducting, 265–271
 data analysis in, 270
 data collection, 267–270
 described, 14–15, 168–169
 interacting spiral of data collection in, 269, 270
 purpose of, 271
 school-based, 261–265
 selecting topic in, 174
AERA-K Division Teaching and Teacher Education listserve, 41
Affective characteristics, 128
Affective tests, 131
Alternating treatments design, 390–391
American Educational Research Association List, 41
American Psychological Association, 79
American Psychologist, 172
Analysis of covariance (ANCOVA), 343, 370–371, 476–477
Analysis of gain or difference scores, 466–467
Analysis of variance, 343
Analytic induction, 233
Annual Review of Psychology, 53
Anonymity, 84
ANOVA (simple analysis of variance), 467–470
APA (Publication Manual of the American Psychological Association), 509, 514
Appendixes, 514
Application for Approval of a Research Project Involving Human Subject, 83

Applied research, 7
Aptitude tests, 130–131
Aristotle, 4
Artificial categories, 478
Assessment, 128
Assumption statement, 91
Attenuation, 320
Attitude scales
 action research, 268
 described, 131–133
Attrition (or morality), 361–362

Baseline measures, 384–385
Baseline stability, 385
Basic research, 7
Bias
 experimenter, 366
 instrument, 134–135
 of observers, 213–215
 sampling, 114
Bibliography/references, 513–514, 528
Bill Huitt's Home Page, 55
Buckley Amendment (Family Educational Rights and Privacy Act), 79–80, 81
Budget, 93
Buros Institute of Mental Measurements, 129
Buros Institute Web site, 129

California Achievement Test, 130
Canonical correlation, 323
Case study, 386
Categories
 defining, 232
 diagram of organization/levels of, 237
 patterns between, 236
 qualitative analytic strategies and, 233–236
 true and artificial, 478
Causal-comparative research
 control procedures used in, 341–343
 criteria for evaluating, 538
 data analysis/interpretation in, 343–344
 definition/purpose of, 11–12, 337–340
 design and procedure of, 340–341
 example of, 345–350
 retrospective and prospective, 338
 variables frequently used in, 339
Census survey, 281
Changing criterion design, 386

Chi square
 calculating, 479–482
 calculating using SPSS, 482–483, 484
 function of, 343, 478
 one-dimensional, 478–479
 two-dimensional, 479
CIJE (Current Index to Journals in Education), 51
Clinical replication, 392
Cluster, 108
CMMS (Columbia Mental Maturity Scale), 130
Coding procedures, 410–412
Coefficient of stability, 142
Cognitive characteristics, 128
Cognitive tests, 130–131
Cohort survey, 281
Collaborators. *See* Participants
Common (or shared) variance, 315
Compensatory rivalry, 367
Computers. *See also* SPSS
 checking accuracy/storage of data on, 254
 data prepared for analysis using, 412
 used in qualitative data analysis, 237–238
Concurrent validity, 137–138
Confidentiality, 84
Confounding, 368
Consequential validity, 140–141
Constant comparison analysis, 17, 233. *See also* Grounded theory
Constructs. *See also* Variables
 defining, 124
 validity of, 139–140
Consulting computer databases, 50–53
Content validity, 136–137
Context, 166
Control, 358
Control group, 356–357
Control techniques
 analysis of covariance, 343
 used in causal-comparative research, 341–342
 comparing homogeneous groups/subgroups, 342–343, 370
 group experimental design, 368–371
 matching, 343